Life in the Kitchens of Southern Living

All recipes that appear in Southern Living *are tested, tasted, and reviewed in our test kitchens. Three kitchens—country, gourmet, and garden—open off a dining area where staff members often meet for lunch. Here they are introduced (left to right in each photograph).*

Above: *Becky Brennan, Editorial Assistant; Linda Welch, Assistant Foods Editor; Beverly Morrow, Editorial Assistant*

Above Right: *Peggy Smith, Foods Assistant; Susan Payne, Assistant Foods Editor; Jean Wickstrom Liles, Foods Editor, in the Country Kitchen*

Right: *Foods Assistants Karen Parker and Diane Hogan in the Gourmet Kitchen*

Above, Page iii: *Susan Payne, Martha Hinrichs, Margaret Chason, Donna Taylor, Jane Elliott,* Southern Living *Editor Gary McCalla, Jean Wickstrom Liles, Karen Parker, Diane Hogan, Peggy Smith, and Becky Brennan*

Left, Page iii: *Assistant Foods Editors Jane Elliott and Margaret Chason*

Right, Page iii: *Donna Taylor, Foods Assistant, and Martha Hinrichs, Test Kitchen Director, in the Garden Kitchen*

Southern Living
1980 ANNUAL RECIPES

Oxmoor House, Inc., Birmingham

Copyright © 1980 by Oxmoor House, Inc.
Book Division of Southern Progress Corporation
P.O. Box 2463, Birmingham, Alabama 35201

Eugene Butler   Chairman of the Board
Emory Cunningham   President and Publisher
Vernon Owens, Jr.   Executive Vice President

Conceived, edited and published by Oxmoor House, Inc., under the
direction of:

Don Logan   Vice President and General Manager
Gary McCalla   Editor, *Southern Living*
John Logue   Editor-in-Chief
Jean Wickstrom Liles   Foods Editor, *Southern Living*
Ann H. Harvey   Managing Editor
Jerry Higdon   Production Manager

Southern Living® 1980 Annual Recipes

Associate Production Manager: Joan Denman

Assistant Editors: Susan Payne, Annette Thompson

Designer: Carol Middleton
Illustrator: Susan Waldrip
Photographers: Jerome Drown: cover, pages i, 28, 61, 62, 95, 96, 168
    and 169, 170, 204 (above), 205, 206, 239, 274, 291, 292 and 293, 294;
    John O'Hagan: pages iv, 97 (below), 131, 133, 167; Charles Walton:
    pages ii and iii, 203, 204 (below), 273; Van Chaplin: page 97 (above)

Southern Living Advisers
Production Manager: Clay Nordan
Editorial Assistants: Rebecca Brennan, Beverly Morrow
Assistant Foods Editors: Margaret Chason, Jane Elliott, Susan Payne,
    Linda Welch
Foods Assistants: Martha Hinrichs, Diane Hogan, Karen Parker,
    Peggy Smith, Donna Taylor

Library of Congress Catalog Number: 79-88364
ISBN: 0-8487-0516-5

Manufactured in the United States of America
Fourth Printing 1982

Cover: *Sample the best of home-style baking
with these traditional holiday specialties.
Clockwise from top: Cream Cheese Cookies
(page 282), Chocolate Fudge Cake (page
279), Apricot Cookie Rolls (page 282),
Cranberry-Banana Bread (page 281), Fluffy
Pumpkin Pie (page 283), and Holiday
Savarin (page 280).*

Page i: *After simmering in an orange-
flavored sauce, Orange-Avocado Chicken
(page 38) is colorfully garnished with fruit.*

Page iv: *Fresh peaches flavor an assortment
of summer treats: Peaches and Cream Cake
(page 142), Rosy Peach-Banana Jam (page
142), Peach Dumplings (page 143), and
Brandy Spiced Peaches (page 142).*

Table of Contents

Brownie Baked Alaska (page 66)

Ham (page 110)

Refreshing Macaroni Salad (page 177)

Our Year at Southern Living

Last year *Southern Living* introduced a new annual cookbook, *1979 Annual Recipes,* and it has proved to be one of your favorites and one of our best-sellers.

When we decided to publish a cookbook containing all the recipes published during a year in *Southern Living,* we were convinced that it would be a popular addition to many kitchen libraries. The letters we received during the years told us that many readers clipped and saved each month's recipes. We also noted that those recipes when shared with family and friends were often misplaced. We viewed *Southern Living 1979 Annual Recipes* as a solution for the misplaced recipes and as a handy, convenient collection of the best recipes prepared by some of the South's best cooks.

There was never a doubt that *1979 Annual Recipes* would be followed by *1980 Annual Recipes.* Reader response to the 1979 volume mandated that we continue what we believe will be a long tradition. Similar in format to the 1979 version, this year's *Annual Recipes* contains every recipe published in *Southern Living* during 1980. Since virtually all the recipes published in *Southern Living* are contributed by our readers, this cookbook presents the best of eating for 1980.

But *1980 Annual Recipes* is more than a collection of this year's recipes. It includes every food article, 32 full-color pages, cooking tips and hints, and extensive cooking and kitchen guides in the Appendices. Because a major goal is to make it easy for you to locate this wealth of material, the Table of Contents lists the month and name of every

Southern Living food article in the order in which it appears in the cookbook. This broad overview of the 1980 food features also includes the bonus articles, those food articles which are featured in different state issues in different months. By referring to the Table of Contents, you can easily determine where in the book a specific article appears.

This volume also contains three detailed indexes to assist you in finding specific recipes. First, the Recipe Title Index includes every recipe alphabetized according to the first word of the title. Second, the Month-by-Month Index lists every article and the recipes contained in that article. Third, the General Recipe Index cross-references every recipe in this cookbook by food category and/or major ingredient.

It would not be an understatement to say that this book and each month's issue of *Southern Living* would not be possible without the tremendous response and cooperation of our readers. Every month we receive one to four thousand recipes from readers throughout the South who have already taste-tested these recipes in their own kitchens.

Because we have a quantity of time-tested recipes from which to choose, our staff of home economists re-test these to present to you the best recipes the South has to offer. In 1980, we published 1,200 recipes but tested over 1,800 in our three test kitchens. In so doing, we utilized 1/5 ton of all-purpose flour, 1/4 ton of sugar, and over 1/2 mile of aluminum foil. *1980 Annual Recipes* represents both a busy year at *Southern Living* and the best recipes of 1980.

Since Southerners still take time to enjoy cooking and entertaining in their homes, we feature in *Southern Living* special entertaining sections in addition to our regular monthly food sections. In March we offered fresh new ways to entertain family and friends with *Breakfasts & Brunches.* Our July *Summer Suppers* suggested ways for you to relax and still have fun in the summer heat. To help you celebrate the merry holiday season, our November *Holiday Dinners* shared warm hospitality and good food. For Texas readers September offered *Mexican Food Fest* which we include as a bonus in this cookbook for all our readers. We think you'll agree that the Tex-Mex and true Mexican cuisines offer a wealth of colorful and tantalizing dishes.

In presenting *1980 Annual Recipes* we would be remiss not to call to your attention our dedicated and competent staff of home economists who test, taste, and evaluate each recipe. In addition, a number of talented editors, photographers, and artists have contributed their skills to this book.

1980 Annual Recipes presents to you the best of *Southern Living* for the past year, and we sincerely believe you will find it a welcome and helpful addition to your kitchen library. If you'd like to share with us one of your favorite recipes, do write us. In the meantime, we hope this 1980 cookbook will make cooking and eating in your home a little easier and a lot more fun.

Jean Wickstrom Liles

January

Southern custom promises good luck to all who eat black-eyed peas on New Year's Day. Whether you eat them because you're superstitious or just because you like them, you'll surely enjoy traditional Hopping John and Hopping Good Peas.

January also marks the peak of the season for stone crabs and rock shrimp. A few of our staff members took a fishing boat out in Southern waters and helped fishermen harvest these seafood delicacies. They brought back a freezer-full of shellfish and perfected the recipes you will find in this chapter.

If you think winter is not the time for fresh fruits and vegetables, take a look at our salads chock full of in-season produce. These colorful salads will brighten any wintertime meal.

Unexpected Delicacies From The Sea

Rock shrimp and stone crab claws may not be as familiar as other shellfish yielded by Southern waters, but they are every bit as delicious.

Besides offering flavor and tenderness equal to regular shrimp, rock shrimp are more economical. And even though stone crab claws are more expensive than blue crab, these giant claws are so thick with rich meat that it takes only three per person for a meal.

Rock shrimp are not new on the seafood market. In fact, they've been harvested for years. But according to Sally Patrenos, merchandising manager for the Florida Department of Natural Resources, "Rock shrimp were not popular because people didn't know how to prepare them. Handled properly, they're one of the best items on the market."

Rock shrimp are purchased according to size, and a pound of the largest generally available contains about 21 to 25 shrimp. It's helpful to know that when properly cleaned and cooked, rock shrimp yield about half the weight of the raw product. For example, from 2 pounds of raw, unpeeled shrimp, you will get 1 pound of peeled, deveined, cooked shrimp—enough for about six people.

Easily mistaken for a miniature lobster tail, the hard shell of the rock shrimp encloses a meat that tastes like a cross between lobster and shrimp. However, it is much more perishable than either of these, and that's the reason most rock shrimp must be marketed in the raw, frozen state, as either whole or split tails. Although the split tails cost slightly more, they are the easier to prepare. With either type, thaw the frozen shrimp under cold, running water; be prepared to cook immediately. Remove the shell before simmering or frying; when broiling, leave the meat in the split shell. To split whole tails, follow the procedure illustrated in the sketch.

Since rock shrimp cook much more quickly (in 30 to 45 seconds) than regular shrimp, be sure to watch them carefully to avoid overcooking.

If stored in the refrigerator, cooked rock shrimp will maintain their quality for two to three days. Thawed and uncooked, they will deteriorate rapidly, even in the refrigerator.

Even at first glance, **stone crabs** are easily distinguished from other species of crabs because of their large, black-tipped claws. They are found along the coast from North Carolina to Mexico, but "They are commercially landed only in Florida," explains Mrs. Patrenos.

Stone crabs have the ability to regenerate their claws up to three or four times during their life. Because of this, Florida law allows commercial harvesting of only the claws, not the whole stone crab. To further help ensure a continuing supply of stone crab, regulations have limited the harvesting season to October through May of each year.

Since freezing or icing raw stone crab claws causes the meat to stick to the inside of the shell, the claws are cooked immediately when brought ashore. Then the cooked claws are sold either frozen or just refrigerated.

Thaw frozen claws by placing them in the refrigerator for 12 to 18 hours. Before serving, crack and remove the shell, leaving black-tipped portion of claw intact. Most people prefer stone crab claws cold, but they may be heated. To heat, place the claws on a rack over a small amount of boiling water; cover and steam just until thoroughly heated.

Rock Shrimp And Stone Crab: The Basics

The recipes are here—the Sweet-and-Sour Rock Shrimp Tails, plus recipes for frying or broiling the rock shrimp and recipes for sauces to serve with the stone crab claws.

ROCK SHRIMP CONGA

½ pound peeled and deveined split rock shrimp tails
2 tablespoons lime juice
½ teaspoon salt
¼ teaspoon pepper
¼ cup butter or margarine, softened
½ (3-ounce) package cream cheese, softened
½ ounce blue cheese (about 2 tablespoons crumbled)

Place shrimp in a 1½-quart shallow baking dish. Sprinkle with lime juice, salt, and pepper.

Combine butter, cream cheese, and blue cheese, creaming until smooth; spread over shrimp. Cover tightly with foil; bake at 400° for 8 to 10 minutes. Yield: 25 to 30 appetizer servings.

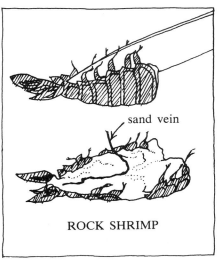

sand vein

ROCK SHRIMP

To clean whole, unsplit rock shrimp tails, follow this procedure: Thaw shrimp under cold, running water. Place shrimp on cutting board with swimmerets facing upward. With a sharp knife, make a cut between swimmerets, through meat, to the hard shell (commercially split tails are already in this form). Rinse well to remove sand vein. Remove meat from shell for simmering or frying, or leave in shell for broiling.

BATTER-FRIED ROCK SHRIMP TAILS

½ cup vegetable oil
1 egg
1 cup all-purpose flour
½ cup milk
¼ cup water
¾ teaspoon seasoned salt
¼ teaspoon salt
1½ pounds peeled and deveined split rock shrimp tails
Vegetable oil

Combine ½ cup vegetable oil and egg, beating well. Add next 5 ingredients, stirring until well blended. Dip shrimp into batter, and fry in 1 inch vegetable oil heated to 350°; cook about 30 seconds on each side or until lightly browned (watch shrimp carefully to avoid overcooking). Yield: 6 servings.

BROILED ROCK SHRIMP TAILS

2½ pounds deveined split rock shrimp
    tails (unpeeled)
½ cup melted butter or margarine
¾ teaspoon salt
¼ teaspoon white pepper
Dash of paprika
Lemon Butter (optional)

Place shrimp tails in a shallow baking pan, meat side up. Combine melted butter and seasonings, mixing well. Baste shrimp with butter mixture.

Broil 4 inches from source of heat 2 minutes (avoid overcooking) or until tails turn upward. Serve immediately with Lemon Butter, if desired. Yield: about 6 servings.

Lemon Butter:

½ cup melted butter
2 to 4 tablespoons lemon juice

Combine ingredients, stirring until blended. Yield: ½ cup.

SWEET-AND-SOUR ROCK SHRIMP TAILS

2½ tablespoons salt
6 cups water
1 pound peeled and deveined split rock
    shrimp tails
2 (8¼-ounce) cans pineapple chunks,
    undrained
1 medium onion, thinly sliced
1 small green pepper, cut into 1-inch
    squares
¼ cup melted margarine or vegetable oil
½ cup vinegar
½ teaspoon dry mustard
2 tablespoons cornstarch
1 tablespoon soy sauce
¼ cup sugar
¼ teaspoon salt
⅔ cup cherry tomato halves or thin
    tomato wedges
3 cups hot cooked rice
½ cup toasted slivered almonds
3 to 4 tablespoons dried parsley flakes

Combine 2½ tablespoons salt and water in a medium saucepan; bring to a boil. (Rock shrimp cook faster than regular shrimp and require close attention to avoid overcooking.) Place shrimp in boiling water, and simmer 30 to 45 seconds; drain. Rinse in cold water 2 minutes. Cut large shrimp in half; set aside.

Drain pineapple chunks, reserving syrup; set aside.

Sauté onion and green pepper in margarine until crisp-tender. Add vinegar, dry mustard, and cornstarch, blending until smooth. Stir in pineapple syrup, soy sauce, sugar, and ¼ teaspoon salt; cook over low heat, stirring constantly, until smooth and thickened.

Gently stir cooked shrimp, pineapple chunks, and cherry tomatoes into sauce; heat thoroughly.

Combine rice, almonds, and parsley flakes; toss lightly. Serve shrimp mixture over rice. Yield: 6 servings.

STONE CRAB MUSTARD SAUCE

½ cup commercial sour cream
1½ tablespoons prepared mustard
2 teaspoons melted butter or margarine
½ teaspoon dried parsley flakes
⅛ teaspoon salt

Combine all ingredients in a small saucepan. Cook over low heat just until sauce is warm, stirring constantly. Yield: about ⅔ cup.

TANGY STONE CRAB SAUCE

1 cup mayonnaise
1 teaspoon dry mustard
1½ teaspoons lime juice
⅛ teaspoon salt
⅛ teaspoon hot sauce
6 drops tarragon vinegar
Dash of fresh ground pepper

Combine all ingredients in a small bowl, mixing well. Yield: about 1 cup.

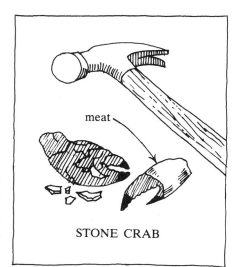

meat

STONE CRAB

Stone crab claws are cooked when purchased. To serve, crack all sections of shell with a hammer or nutcracker. Do not crack black-tipped claw portion. Remove the cracked shell, leaving meat attached to the intact claw.

Keep Canned Seafood On Hand

Canned seafood is an excellent staple to keep on hand. Just reach for a can when guests arrive unexpectedly or when you've forgotten to take something out of the freezer.

Easy Salmon Loaf, made with canned red or pink salmon, can be prepared in a jiffy and bakes in just 35 minutes. Or layer canned crabmeat and frozen spinach with a cheesy sauce for a delicious and filling casserole.

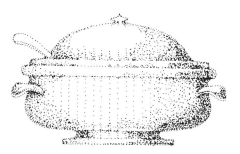

CREAMY CRAB AND SPINACH CASSEROLE

2 (10-ounce) packages frozen spinach
1 (10¾-ounce) can cream of mushroom
    soup
¼ cup sherry
¼ cup half-and-half
3 to 4 teaspoons Worcestershire sauce
2 cups (8 ounces) shredded sharp
    Cheddar cheese, divided
Dash of pepper
1 (6½-ounce) can crabmeat, drained and
    flaked
½ cup soft breadcrumbs
2 teaspoons melted butter or margarine
Paprika

Cook spinach according to package directions, omitting salt; drain well.

Combine soup, sherry, half-and-half, Worcestershire sauce, 1 cup cheese, and pepper in a medium saucepan. Cook over medium heat, stirring constantly, until cheese melts.

Combine spinach and ⅓ cup soup mixture, mixing well; spread half in a buttered 10- x 6- x 2-inch baking dish. Spread with half of crabmeat. Repeat layers; pour remaining soup mixture over top.

Combine breadcrumbs and butter, mixing well; sprinkle over soup mixture. Top with 1 cup cheese, and sprinkle with paprika. Bake at 350° for 30 minutes. Yield: 6 servings.

Fran McKinney,
Shreveport, Louisiana.

EASY SALMON LOAF

⅓ cup milk
1 cup soft breadcrumbs
1 (15½-ounce) can red or pink salmon
2 eggs, separated
Juice of 1 lemon
½ teaspoon salt
¼ teaspoon onion salt
⅛ teaspoon pepper
Medium white sauce (recipe follows)

Stir milk into breadcrumbs, and set aside. Drain salmon; remove skin and bones. Flake salmon with a fork.

Beat egg yolks until thick and lemon colored. Stir breadcrumb mixture, egg yolks, lemon juice, and seasonings into salmon. Beat egg whites until stiff but not dry; fold into salmon mixture.

Spoon into a greased 7½- x 3- x 2-inch loafpan. Bake at 400° for 35 minutes. Serve with white sauce. Yield: 6 servings.

Medium White Sauce:

2 tablespoons butter or margarine
2 tablespoons all-purpose flour
1 cup milk
Salt and pepper to taste

Melt butter in a heavy saucepan over low heat; add flour, stirring until smooth. Cook 1 minute, stirring constantly. Gradually add milk; cook over medium heat, stirring constantly, until thickened and bubbly. Stir in salt and pepper. Yield: about 1 cup.
Mrs. Harris Skettel,
Damascus, Maryland.

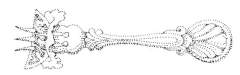

CONFETTI SALAD

1 cup elbow macaroni
1½ cups chopped celery
1 (12½-ounce) can tuna, drained and flaked
¼ cup sliced green olives
2 tablespoons chopped green or red pepper
1 tablespoon chopped onion
1 cup mayonnaise
¼ teaspoon pepper

Cook macaroni according to package directions; drain. Rinse macaroni with cold water; drain.

Combine macaroni and next 5 ingredients, mixing well. Combine mayonnaise and pepper; pour over macaroni mixture, stirring well. Chill. Yield: about 8 servings. *Mrs. John Taylor, Jonesboro, Tennessee.*

Salads Especially For Winter

A colorful salad may be exactly what's needed to add a lift to your winter menus. Even now, there are plenty of fresh ingredients available to make a salad that's large and luscious, whether your choice is fruit or vegetables. Start with a base of in-season produce, such as potatoes, citrus, salad greens, or apples; then add extra flavor and color by piling on the onions, hard-cooked eggs, or cheese. And don't forget what crisp, crumbled bacon can do for a vegetable salad.

Should you want to serve a salad as a main dish, we offer two choices: Tossed Shrimp-Egg Salad and Tossed Chicken-Avocado Salad.

TOSSED SHRIMP-EGG SALAD

8 cups torn mixed salad greens
6 hard-cooked eggs, quartered
1 pound peeled and deveined cooked shrimp
10 to 12 cherry tomatoes
1 cup sliced celery
¼ cup minced parsley
1½ cups mayonnaise
½ cup chili sauce

Combine salad greens, eggs, shrimp, tomatoes, and celery; toss gently, and sprinkle with parsley. Combine mayonnaise and chili sauce, mixing well; serve over salad. Yield: 6 servings.
Mrs. Margaret L. Hunter,
Princeton, Kentucky.

TOSSED CHICKEN-AVOCADO SALAD

2 cups torn fresh spinach
2 cups torn romaine
2 cups torn leaf lettuce
4 tomatoes, cut into wedges
1 avocado, sliced
3 cups chopped cooked chicken, chilled
6 slices bacon, cooked and crumbled
2 hard-cooked eggs, chopped
2 tablespoons minced fresh parsley
Russian dressing (recipe follows)

Combine all ingredients except dressing in a large salad bowl. Just before serving, toss gently. Top with Russian dressing. Yield: 6 to 8 servings.

Russian Dressing:

½ cup mayonnaise
2 tablespoons lemon juice
1 tablespoon chili sauce
2 tablespoons milk
2 tablespoons chopped stuffed olives
1 tablespoon minced onion
1 tablespoon minced green pepper
1 tablespoon prepared horseradish
¼ teaspoon salt

Combine all ingredients in container of electric blender; blend well. Chill. Yield: about 1 cup. *Mrs. J. A. Tuthill, Virginia Beach, Virginia.*

CRUNCHY CAULIFLOWER SALAD

2 cups diced raw cauliflower
¼ cup chopped celery
3 hard-cooked eggs, chopped
½ cup diced Cheddar cheese
¼ cup chopped green pepper
¼ cup chopped sweet pickle
½ teaspoon salt
¼ teaspoon white pepper
½ cup mayonnaise
½ medium head lettuce, torn into bite-size pieces

Combine all ingredients in a large salad bowl; toss lightly. Chill well. Yield: 6 to 8 servings.
Charlotte J. Frolick,
Birmingham, Alabama.

CHINESE SALAD

1 (15½-ounce) can French-style green beans, drained
1 (16-ounce) can mixed Chinese vegetables, drained
1 (8½-ounce) can English peas, drained
1 cup diced celery
1 medium onion, thinly sliced and separated into rings
1 cup sugar
¾ cup vinegar
½ teaspoon salt
⅛ teaspoon pepper

Combine first 5 ingredients in a medium bowl. Combine sugar, vinegar, salt, and pepper; mix well. Pour over vegetable mixture, tossing lightly to coat. Cover and chill at least 24 hours. Salad may be stored in refrigerator up to one week. Yield: 6 to 8 servings.
Rosemarie Blaedon,
Reidsville, North Carolina.

OVERNIGHT GREEN VEGETABLE SALAD

9 cups shredded iceberg lettuce
Salt and pepper to taste
½ to 1 teaspoon sugar
9 hard-cooked eggs, sliced
1½ (10-ounce) packages frozen English peas, thawed
1½ pounds bacon, cooked and crumbled
3 cups (¾ pound) shredded Swiss cheese
1½ cups mayonnaise or salad dressing
½ cup sliced green onions with tops
Paprika

Place half of lettuce in a 3-quart bowl; sprinkle with salt, pepper, and sugar. Arrange hard-cooked eggs over lettuce, and sprinkle with salt.

Over eggs, layer peas, remaining lettuce, bacon, and cheese (in that order). Spread mayonnaise over top, sealing to edge of bowl. Cover tightly, and chill 24 to 48 hours.

At serving time, arrange green onion around edge of bowl, and sprinkle salad with paprika. Yield: 10 to 12 servings.

Mrs. John Lile,
Pine Bluff, Arkansas.

CONFETTI POTATO SALAD

12 medium potatoes
1 tablespoon lemon juice
1 tablespoon salt
1 bunch green onions, thinly sliced
1 medium-size green pepper, finely chopped
2 stalks celery, thinly sliced
1 tablespoon minced parsley
1 medium carrot, shredded
4 to 6 large stuffed olives, thinly sliced
6 hard-cooked eggs, chopped
1 (12-ounce) bottle commercial slaw dressing
⅓ cup commercial sour cream
2 tablespoons lemon juice or vinegar
Leaf lettuce (optional)

Combine potatoes, 1 tablespoon lemon juice, and salt in a Dutch oven; add enough water to cover potatoes. Cook potatoes until tender; peel and dice. Combine potatoes, onion, green pepper, celery, parsley, carrot, olives, and eggs in a large salad bowl.

Combine slaw dressing, sour cream, and 2 tablespoons lemon juice; stir well. Add dressing to potato salad, tossing gently. Serve on lettuce, if desired. Yield: 10 to 12 servings.

Mrs. H. Mark Webber,
New Port Richey, Florida.

LAYERED SPINACH SALAD

1 pound fresh spinach, torn
Salt and pepper to taste
Sugar to taste (about ½ to 1 teaspoon)
1 pound bacon, cooked and crumbled
6 hard-cooked eggs, chopped
1 (10-ounce) package frozen English peas, thawed
1 medium onion, minced
2 stalks celery, chopped
½ cup mayonnaise
½ cup salad dressing
½ cup shredded Cheddar cheese

Place spinach in a 3-quart bowl; sprinkle with salt, pepper, sugar, and bacon. Arrange eggs over spinach, and sprinkle with salt, pepper, and sugar.

Over eggs, layer peas, onion, and celery (in that order). Spread mayonnaise and salad dressing over top, sealing to edge of bowl. Sprinkle with shredded cheese. Cover and chill overnight. Yield: 10 to 12 servings.

Betty Jane Morrison,
Lakewood, Colorado.

PEANUT-APPLE SALAD

3 cups diced unpeeled apple
1 cup chopped celery
1 teaspoon lemon juice
1 tablespoon sugar
2 tablespoons mayonnaise
½ cup plain yogurt
½ cup coarsely chopped peanuts
Lettuce (optional)

Combine apple and celery; sprinkle with lemon juice, and toss well. Combine sugar, mayonnaise, and yogurt; mix well, and fold into apple mixture. Chill well. Add peanuts, tossing lightly. Serve on lettuce, if desired. Yield: 4 servings.

Mrs. Elizabeth Moore,
Huntsville, Alabama.

OLD-FASHIONED AMBROSIA

9 oranges, peeled, seeded, and sectioned
2 (20-ounce) cans crushed pineapple, drained
1 cup honey
1 to 2 teaspoons almond extract
1 cup flaked coconut

Combine all ingredients in a bowl, and refrigerate overnight. Yield: about 6 to 8 servings. *Mrs. Karl Koenig,*
Dallas, Texas.

CARROT-MARSHMALLOW AMBROSIA

4 cups shredded carrots
¼ cup lemon juice
1 (3½-ounce) can flaked coconut
1½ cups miniature marshmallows
1 cup chopped orange sections
¼ cup mayonnaise
½ cup commercial sour cream
3 tablespoons honey
Lettuce (optional)

Combine first 5 ingredients, tossing gently. Combine mayonnaise, sour cream, and honey; mix well. Add to carrot mixture, stirring gently until well coated. Serve on lettuce, if desired. Yield: 6 to 8 servings.

Mrs. Gladys C. Milton,
Brandon, Florida.

Special Desserts Make Smooth Endings

The just-right dessert can turn a meal into something special. If your menu calls for a light, informal dessert, select simple Date Nut Cake. For an extra-rich treat, try Crunchy Peanut Butter Parfaits or Tropical Sour Cream Pie. For an impressive finale, serve refreshing Peppermint Wafer Dessert or pretty Daffodil Sponge Cake.

DATE NUT CAKE

1 cup sugar
½ cup vegetable oil
4 eggs
1 cup all-purpose flour
1 teaspoon salt
1 (1-pound) package pitted dates
4 cups pecan halves

Combine sugar, oil, and eggs, mixing well. Stir in flour and salt; add dates and nuts. Spoon mixture into a greased and floured 9- x 5- x 3-inch loafpan. Place in a cold oven; set oven at 300°, and bake 2 hours. Remove cake from pan immediately, and cool on a wire rack. Yield: one 9-inch loaf.

Mrs. Pete Beckham,
Philadelphia, Mississippi.

Layers of an oats and peanut mixture alternate with peanut butter-flavored pudding to make attractive Crunchy Peanut Butter Parfaits.

CRUNCHY PEANUT BUTTER PARFAITS

¾ cup quick-cooking oats, uncooked
⅓ cup firmly packed brown sugar
¼ cup chopped peanuts
3 tablespoons butter or margarine, melted
½ cup firmly packed brown sugar
¼ cup all-purpose flour
2 cups milk
2 egg yolks, beaten
⅔ cup peanut butter
½ teaspoon vanilla extract

Combine oats, ⅓ cup brown sugar, peanuts, and butter, stirring well. Spread oat mixture in an ungreased 13- x 9- x 2-inch baking pan; bake at 350° for 15 minutes, stirring occasionally. Let cool; then crumble.

Combine ½ cup brown sugar, flour, milk, and egg yolks in a saucepan; cook, stirring constantly, over low heat until thickened and bubbly. Cook 1 additional minute, stirring constantly. Stir in peanut butter and vanilla. Cover the surface with waxed paper; chill.

Spoon alternate layers of peanut butter pudding and oat mixture into 4 parfait glasses. Yield: 4 servings.

Mrs. William T. Hunter,
Princeton, Kentucky.

TROPICAL SOUR CREAM PIE

1 (8-ounce) can crushed pineapple, undrained
1 tablespoon sugar
1 cup milk
1 (4¾-ounce) package vanilla-flavored pudding and pie filling mix
1 (8-ounce) carton commercial sour cream
1½ cups flaked coconut, divided
1 medium banana, sliced
1 baked 9-inch pastry shell
1 (4½-ounce) carton frozen whipped topping, thawed

Combine pineapple, sugar, milk, and pudding mix in a medium saucepan; cook over medium heat, stirring constantly, until mixture comes to a boil. Remove from heat. Add a small amount of hot mixture to sour cream, mixing well; add sour cream mixture to remaining hot mixture, mixing well. Stir in 1 cup coconut; allow to cool.

Place banana slices in pastry shell. Spoon custard over bananas; spread with whipped topping, and sprinkle with remaining ½ cup coconut. Chill at least 3 hours. Yield: one 9-inch pie.

Gailya Godfrey,
Charlotte, North Carolina.

DAFFODIL SPONGE CAKE

1 cup sifted cake flour
½ cup sugar, divided
4 egg yolks
½ teaspoon lemon extract
10 egg whites, at room temperature
1 teaspoon cream of tartar
½ teaspoon salt
¾ cup sugar
½ teaspoon vanilla extract

Sift flour and ½ cup sugar together 3 times; set aside.

Beat egg yolks at high speed of electric mixer 4 minutes or until thick and lemon colored. Add lemon extract; beat at medium speed 5 more minutes or until thick. Set aside.

Beat egg whites until foamy. Add cream of tartar and salt; beat until soft peaks form. Add ¾ cup sugar, 2 tablespoons at a time; continue beating 5 minutes or until stiff peaks form.

Sprinkle one-fourth of flour mixture over egg whites; gently fold in with a rubber spatula. Repeat procedure with remaining flour, adding one-fourth of the mixture at a time. Divide egg white mixture in half.

Fold vanilla extract into half of the egg white mixture. Gently fold the beaten egg yolks into remaining egg white mixture.

Pour half of the yellow mixture into an ungreased 10-inch tube pan; then gently add half of the white mixture. Repeat procedure with the remaining mixture.

Bake at 350° for 55 to 60 minutes or until cake springs back when touched lightly with fingers. Invert cake; cool (about 40 minutes). Loosen cake from sides of pan, using a small metal spatula. Remove cake from pan; place on a serving platter. Yield: one 10-inch cake.

Mrs. Mabel B. Couch,
Chelsea, Oklahoma.

PEPPERMINT WAFER DESSERT

1½ teaspoons unflavored gelatin
2 tablespoons cold water
1 (8-ounce) package soft-type peppermint
  sticks
½ cup whipping cream
1½ cups whipping cream, whipped
1 (8½-ounce) package chocolate wafers

Soften gelatin in water; set aside.

Combine candy and ½ cup whipping cream in top of a double boiler; cook, stirring often, until candy melts. Add gelatin, stirring until dissolved. Chill mixture until slightly thickened; fold in whipped cream.

Line bottom of a 9-inch square pan with wafers; break additional wafers in half, and stand around the sides of pan. Spoon half the peppermint mixture into pan; cover with a layer of wafers. Spoon remaining peppermint mixture over top. Chill dessert for at least 8 hours. Yield: 9 servings.

Mrs. Mildred Sherrer,
Bay City, Texas.

Bring On The Black-Eyed Peas

If black-eyed peas are a New Year's Day tradition at your house, chances are you might think immediately of serving hopping John. But as good as that dish is, other black-eyed pea concoctions are just as tasty.

In this selection of recipes, we've included a traditional version of hopping John as well as a variation of it that has onion, celery, tomatoes, and chili powder. For something really different, try Pea Flips, a pea-and-ground beef mixture wrapped in pastry and deep fried.

HOPPING GOOD PEAS

1 (16-ounce) can tomatoes
4 cups frozen black-eyed peas
1 ham hock
1 cup chopped onion
1 cup chopped celery
2 to 3 teaspoons salt
2 teaspoons chili powder
¼ teaspoon dried basil leaves
1 bay leaf
1 cup uncooked regular rice

Drain tomatoes, reserving juice. Cut tomatoes into small pieces.

Combine all ingredients except rice in a Dutch oven. Cook, uncovered, over medium heat, stirring occasionally, 25 minutes. Stir in rice; cover and cook 20 minutes. Yield: 8 to 10 servings.

Mrs. Margot Foster,
Hubbard, Texas.

HOPPING JOHN

2 pounds dried black-eyed peas
2 ham hocks
2 to 3 teaspoons salt
4½ cups cooked rice

Sort and wash peas well. Place in a large, heavy Dutch oven; cover with water. Bring to a boil, and boil 2 minutes. Cover and let soak 1 hour.

Add ham hocks and salt to peas. Boil gently, not completely covered with lid, until tender (about 1 to 1½ hours).

Remove ham hocks from saucepan. Remove meat from bones, and return to peas. Stir in rice. Yield: 10 to 12 servings.

Note: Peas may be covered with 2½ times as much water and soaked overnight; then cook as directed.

Mrs. Ansel L. Todd,
Royston, Georgia.

PEA FLIPS

½ pound ground beef
1 cup cooked black-eyed peas
¼ teaspoon salt
¼ teaspoon chili powder
¼ teaspoon garlic powder
Pastry (recipe follows)
½ cup (2 ounces) shredded American
  cheese, divided

Cook ground beef until brown, stirring to crumble; drain. Add peas, salt, chili powder, and garlic powder; stir well. Spoon about ¼ cup of pea mixture into center of each pastry circle; sprinkle each with one-sixth of the cheese. Moisten edges of circles; fold pastry in half, making sure edges are even. Press edges together with fork or finger to seal.

Fry in deep hot oil (375°) for 3 minutes or until golden brown. Drain on paper towels. Yield: 6 servings.

Pastry:

2 cups all-purpose flour
½ teaspoon salt
½ teaspoon soda
½ cup shortening
1 tablespoon vinegar
¼ cup water

Combine flour, salt, and soda in mixing bowl. Cut in shortening until mixture resembles coarse crumbs; stir in vinegar and water. Cover bowl with a damp cloth; let stand for 20 minutes. Roll dough to about ⅛-inch thickness; cut into 6-inch circles. Yield: enough pastry for 6 Pea Flips.

Mrs. J. C. Graham,
Athens, Texas.

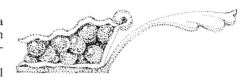

Little Pastry Treats

These delicious little turnovers are made with a rich cream cheese pastry and filling of preserves. We used apricot or pineapple preserves, but you could use any flavor preserves you wish.

Try these little pastries as a special addition to breakfast or as a simple dessert or snack.

PRESERVE-FILLED FOLDOVERS

2 cups all-purpose flour
1 (8-ounce) package cream cheese,
  softened
1 cup butter or margarine, softened
1 tablespoon commercial sour cream
½ cup apricot or pineapple preserves

Combine first 4 ingredients, mixing well. Chill dough 2 to 3 hours.

Roll dough out on a floured board to ¼-inch thickness; cut into 3-inch squares.

Spoon ½ teaspoon preserves onto the center of each square. Moisten edges of squares; fold pastry in half diagonally, making sure edges are even. Press edges together with fork or finger to seal.

Place foldovers on ungreased baking sheets, and bake at 325° for 30 to 35 minutes or until golden brown. Yield: about 2 dozen.

Joyce Johnson,
Reeds Spring, Missouri.

Chicken In Wine Sauce For Two

Chicken is a basic when it comes to cooking for two; besides the endless ways in which chicken can be prepared, it's especially easy to buy and prepare in small quantities.

These elegant entrées for two all call for chicken breasts. Chicken in Wine Sauce is a tender breast of chicken topped with a wine sauce full of mushrooms and cashews. Herb-Seasoned Fried Chicken is a nice version of fried chicken. And in Cashew Chicken, crunchy bits of fried chicken are served over rice.

HERB-SEASONED FRIED CHICKEN

½ cup all-purpose flour
¾ teaspoon salt
¼ teaspoon paprika
¼ teaspoon ground thyme
¼ teaspoon ground marjoram
Pinch of pepper
1 whole chicken breast, halved
¼ cup buttermilk
Vegetable oil

Combine first 6 ingredients; stir well. Dip each piece of chicken in buttermilk; dredge in flour mixture, coating well. Heat 1 inch of oil in a skillet; add chicken, and cook over medium heat 20 minutes or until golden brown, turning occasionally. Drain on paper towels. Yield: 2 servings. *Mrs. Paul T. Cain, Hopkinsville, Kentucky.*

CASHEW CHICKEN

1 pound boned, skinned chicken breasts
1 cup all-purpose flour
2 eggs
½ cup milk
¼ teaspoon salt
Pinch of pepper
Vegetable or peanut oil
Hot cooked rice
Bouillon Sauce
Cashews
Sliced green onion
Soy sauce (optional)

Cut chicken into 1- x 1½-inch pieces. Dredge in flour; let stand 15 minutes.

Combine eggs, milk, salt, and pepper. Place chicken in egg mixture, and let stand 10 minutes. Dredge chicken in flour. Fry in deep hot oil (375°) 3 to 5 minutes or until golden brown.

Serve chicken over rice. Spoon Bouillon Sauce over chicken; top with cashews and onion. Sprinkle with soy sauce, if desired. Yield: 2 servings.

Bouillon Sauce:

2 chicken bouillon cubes
1 cup hot water
2 tablespoons cornstarch
1 teaspoon sugar
2 teaspoons oyster flavor sauce

Dissolve bouillon cubes in water; pour ¾ cup broth into a small saucepan. Stir cornstarch into remaining broth.

Add cornstarch mixture, sugar, and oyster sauce to broth; cook, stirring constantly, over low heat until thickened and bubbly. Yield: about ¾ cup.
Sharlande Sledge, Springfield, Missouri.

CHICKEN IN WINE SAUCE

1 whole chicken breast, split, boned, and skinned
Salt
Ground nutmeg
2 tablespoons melted butter or margarine
2 tablespoons minced onion
¼ pound fresh mushrooms, quartered
⅔ cup dry white wine
¼ cup cashews (optional)
1 teaspoon cornstarch
2 teaspoons dry white wine
Hot cooked rice

Sprinkle chicken with salt and nutmeg; brown each side in butter in a heavy skillet. Add onion, mushrooms, and ⅔ cup wine; add cashews, if desired. Bring to a boil; reduce heat, cover, and simmer 15 minutes. Remove chicken.

Combine cornstarch and 2 teaspoons wine; mix well and stir into skillet. Cook, stirring constantly, until sauce is thickened.

Serve chicken and sauce over hot cooked rice. Yield: 2 servings.
Martha B. Sabin, Knoxville, Tennessee.

Homemade Puddings—An Oldtime Favorite

It could be the nutritional value or use of economical ingredients that have made puddings a longtime favorite dessert throughout the South, but then there's also the unbeatable variety of flavors.

From North Carolina and Kentucky come recipes for old-fashioned bread puddings: Chocolate Bread Pudding is not too sweet and is best served warm with a dollop of whipped cream. Raisins and nutmeg add special flavor to an Amish Bread Pudding. Hansel Pudding is filled with nuts and cherries. And what Southerner can think of pudding without conjuring up banana pudding? This delightful version is best described by its title—delicious.

CHOCOLATE BREAD PUDDING

3 cups soft breadcrumbs
4 tablespoons cocoa
½ cup chopped nuts
2 eggs
½ cup sugar
3 cups milk
1 teaspoon vanilla extract
¼ teaspoon salt
Whipped cream (optional)

Stir together breadcrumbs, cocoa, and chopped nuts; set mixture aside.

Beat eggs until foamy; add sugar, beating well for 1 minute. Stir in milk, vanilla, salt, and breadcrumb mixture. Pour into a lightly greased 1¾-quart casserole. Bake at 350° for 45 to 50 minutes or until set. Serve warm with whipped cream, if desired. Yield: 6 to 8 servings. *Mrs. Donald C. Vanhoy, Salisbury, North Carolina.*

AMISH BREAD PUDDING

2 cups milk, scalded
¼ cup butter or margarine
2 eggs
½ cup sugar
¼ teaspoon salt
1 teaspoon ground nutmeg
3 cups soft breadcrumbs
½ cup raisins

Combine milk and butter; stir until butter is melted. Cool to lukewarm.

Combine eggs, sugar, salt, and nutmeg; beat at medium speed of electric mixer for 1 minute. Slowly stir in milk mixture.

Place breadcrumbs in a lightly greased 1½-quart casserole; sprinkle with raisins. Add milk mixture. Bake at 350° for 50 minutes or until set. Serve warm. Yield: 6 to 8 servings.

Mrs. J. W. R. Miller,
Liberty, Kentucky.

DELICIOUS BANANA PUDDING

¼ cup butter or margarine
1½ cups firmly packed brown sugar
2 tablespoons all-purpose flour
Dash of salt
1 (13-ounce) can evaporated milk
¾ cup water
3 eggs, separated
1 teaspoon vanilla extract
Vanilla wafers
3 to 4 bananas
2 tablespoons sugar

Melt butter in top of a double boiler; stir in brown sugar, flour, and salt. Gradually stir in milk and water; cook until thickened, stirring constantly (about 15 to 20 minutes).

Beat egg yolks until thick and lemon colored. Stir some of hot mixture into yolks; add to remaining hot mixture, stirring constantly. Cook 2 minutes longer or until thickened. Remove from heat, and stir in vanilla. Cool.

Line bottom and sides of a lightly greased 1¾-quart casserole with vanilla wafers. Slice enough bananas to cover bottom layer; top with half of pudding. Layer with vanilla wafers, remaining banana slices, and remaining pudding.

Beat egg whites (at room temperature) until soft peaks form; gradually add 2 tablespoons sugar, and continue beating until stiff peaks form. Spread over pudding. Bake at 350° for 10 minutes or until top is brown. Serve warm or chilled. Yield: 8 servings.

Eddie W. Taylor,
Kingsport, Tennessee.

Tip: Whenever a recipe calls for a reheating process, the dish can be made in advance up to that point.

HANSEL PUDDING

1 envelope unflavored gelatin
½ cup cold water
5 eggs, separated
1 cup sugar
1 cup milk
1 cup vanilla wafer crumbs
1 cup chopped nuts
1 cup chopped maraschino cherries
Whipped cream (optional)
Maraschino cherries (optional)

Combine gelatin and cold water; let stand 5 minutes.

Beat egg yolks until thick and lemon colored. Combine egg yolks, sugar, and milk in top of a double boiler; cook, stirring constantly, until thickened (about 20 minutes). Stir in gelatin mixture and vanilla wafer crumbs; cook 2 minutes longer, stirring constantly. Cool. Stir in nuts and chopped maraschino cherries.

Beat egg whites (at room temperature) until stiff; fold into pudding mixture. Spoon into a lightly greased 9-inch square glass pan; chill until set (about 2 hours).

Spoon into individual serving dishes; garnish with whipped cream and a cherry, if desired. Yield: 10 to 12 servings.

Mrs. Paula Anderson,
McAlester, Oklahoma.

Microwave These Casseroles

Casseroles are easier than ever with the speed and convenience of a microwave oven. And these recipes have all been kitchen-tested especially for cooking in a microwave oven.

Almost any of your favorite casserole recipes will convert to microwave cooking. Before adapting a recipe, however, compare it with a similar microwave recipe for amounts of ingredients, cooking times, and power settings. Here are some other pointers.

—Because there is less evaporation when microwaving than during conventional cooking, the amount of liquid should be reduced. The amount needed varies with casseroles, but a good rule of thumb is to reduce the liquid by half. Seasonings also need to be reduced since there is less liquid to dilute them.

Most herbs and spices should be reduced by half.

—Casseroles will cook more evenly when they use ingredients of similar size and shape. Occasional stirring or turning of the dish will also help promote even cooking, as will covering. When covering with clear plastic wrap, turn back one corner to allow excess steam to escape.

—The high fat content of cheese attracts microwave energy and will cook more rapidly than foods with a lower fat content. Since overcooking will cause cheese to be tough or stringy, always sprinkle it over the top of a casserole toward the end of the cooking period.

—Casseroles that contain a cheese or sour cream sauce should be cooked on less than full power. Medium or 50% of full power is usually the best setting to achieve fast cooking without overcooking or curdling.

—Pasta takes as long to cook in the microwave oven as it does conventionally. It also tends to hydrate unevenly when microwaved, causing hard spots. We recommend cooking it conventionally. However, some microwave manufacturers give instructions for cooking pasta. So if you'd like to try it, follow their directions for best results.

BEEFY SAUSAGE DINNER

½ pound ground beef
½ pound bulk pork sausage
½ cup chopped onion
¼ cup chopped green pepper
1 cup macaroni, cooked and drained
1 (12-ounce) can whole kernel corn, drained
2 (8-ounce) cans tomato sauce
½ teaspoon ground oregano
¼ teaspoon salt
⅛ teaspoon pepper
1 cup (4 ounces) shredded American cheese

Crumble beef and sausage into a 2-quart casserole; stir in onion and green pepper. Cover with clear plastic wrap; microwave at HIGH for 5 to 7 minutes or until meat is done, stirring twice. Drain off excess drippings.

Add macaroni, corn, tomato sauce, and seasonings to meat mixture; mix well. Cover and microwave at MEDIUM HIGH for 9 to 11 minutes or until thoroughly heated. Sprinkle with cheese; cover and microwave at MEDIUM for 2 to 3 minutes or until cheese melts. Yield: 6 to 8 servings.

CHICKEN DIVAN

2 whole chicken breasts, boned
1 cup water
⅛ teaspoon dried rosemary leaves
¼ teaspoon salt
⅛ teaspoon pepper
2 (10-ounce) packages frozen chopped broccoli
2 (10¾-ounce) cans cream of chicken soup, undiluted
¼ cup dry white wine
½ cup (2 ounces) shredded process Swiss cheese
¼ cup grated Parmesan cheese
Paprika

Cut chicken into ¼-inch cubes. Combine chicken, water, rosemary, salt, and pepper in a 1½-quart casserole. Cover with clear plastic wrap; microwave at MEDIUM HIGH for 5 to 7 minutes or until done. Drain chicken, reserving ¼ cup broth; set aside.

Pierce broccoli packages with a fork; place packages in a flat baking dish. Microwave at HIGH for 7 to 9 minutes or until done, rearranging packages once. Drain broccoli.

Combine soup, wine, Swiss cheese, and reserved broth, mixing well. Place chicken in a 12- x 8- x 2-inch baking dish; pour half of soup mixture over chicken. Top with broccoli. Pour remaining soup mixture over broccoli. Cover with waxed paper; microwave at MEDIUM for 9 to 11 minutes or until thoroughly heated. Sprinkle with Parmesan cheese and paprika. Cover and microwave at MEDIUM for 1½ to 2½ minutes. Yield: 6 to 8 servings.

HAM-ASPARAGUS DINNER

2 (10-ounce) packages frozen cut asparagus
1 (10¾-ounce) can cream of celery soup, undiluted
¼ cup milk
¼ cup finely chopped onion
⅛ teaspoon dried rosemary leaves
⅛ teaspoon dried marjoram leaves
½ cup (2 ounces) shredded American cheese
3 cups diced cooked ham
¼ cup round buttery cracker crumbs

Pierce asparagus packages with a fork; place packages in a flat baking dish. Microwave at HIGH for 7 to 9 minutes or until done, rearranging packages once. Drain asparagus, and set aside.

Combine soup, milk, onion, and herbs in a 4-cup glass measure. Microwave at HIGH for 3½ to 5½ minutes or until hot and bubbly, stirring once. Add cheese; stir until cheese melts.

Layer half of ham, half of asparagus, and half of cheese sauce in a 2-quart casserole. Repeat layers. Cover with waxed paper; microwave at MEDIUM for 9 to 11 minutes or until thoroughly heated. Sprinkle with cracker crumbs. Yield: 6 to 8 servings.

QUICK 'N EASY LASAGNA

1 pound ground beef
½ cup sliced fresh mushrooms
½ cup chopped onion
¼ cup chopped green pepper
1 clove garlic, minced
1 (15½-ounce) jar spaghetti sauce
½ teaspoon dried whole oregano
¼ teaspoon dried basil leaves
¼ teaspoon salt
⅛ teaspoon pepper
4 ounces lasagna noodles, cooked and drained
1 cup cottage cheese
1 (8-ounce) package sliced mozzarella cheese

Crumble beef into a 2-quart casserole; add mushrooms, onion, green pepper, and garlic. Cover with waxed paper; microwave at HIGH for 5 to 6 minutes or until done, stirring twice. Drain off excess drippings.

Add spaghetti sauce and seasonings to meat mixture, stirring well. Cover and microwave at HIGH for 2 to 3 minutes or until thoroughly heated, stirring once.

Layer half each of the noodles, cottage cheese, mozzarella cheese, and meat mixture in a 12- x 8- x 2-inch baking dish; repeat layers. Cover and microwave at MEDIUM HIGH for 6 to 8 minutes or until thoroughly heated, giving dish a half-turn after 5 minutes. Let lasagna stand 10 minutes before serving. Yield: 6 to 8 servings.

Get The Most From Liver

Sliced thin and smothered with tomatoes and onions or coated with French dressing and fried until crispy brown, liver could easily become a popular addition to your family menus. Liver, a well-known source of iron, is also a delicious way to lighten your meat budget.

Upon purchase, liver may be kept in the freezer for up to six months. Do not store fresh liver at refrigerator temperature for more than one or two days.

FRENCH-STYLE LIVER

⅔ cup all-purpose flour
¼ teaspoon garlic salt
½ teaspoon salt
¼ teaspoon pepper
1 pound thinly sliced beef liver
½ cup commercial French dressing
3 tablespoons bacon drippings

Combine flour, salt, and pepper. Dip liver in French dressing; dredge in flour mixture. Heat bacon drippings in a medium skillet. Cook liver in hot drippings until golden brown, turning once. Serve immediately. Yield: 4 servings.

Anna May Simmons,
Gainesville, Florida.

LIVER AND GRAVY

¼ cup all-purpose flour
¼ teaspoon salt
⅛ teaspoon pepper
1 pound thinly sliced beef liver
2 tablespoons bacon drippings
2 cloves garlic, minced
2 medium onions, chopped
3 tablespoons bacon drippings
1 tablespoon all-purpose flour
1½ cups water
1 teaspoon salt
½ teaspoon whole basil
½ teaspoon whole thyme
¼ teaspoon pepper

Combine ¼ cup flour, ¼ teaspoon salt, and ⅛ teaspoon pepper. Coat liver in seasoned flour mixture, and brown in 2 tablespoons bacon drippings. Remove liver, and place in a shallow 1½-quart baking dish. Sprinkle with garlic.

Sauté onion in 3 tablespoons bacon drippings. Add 1 tablespoon flour, stirring occasionally until brown. Gradually add water, stirring until smooth. Stir in seasonings; pour over liver. Bake at 350° for 40 minutes or until gravy is thickened and liver is tender. Yield: 4 servings. *Mrs. Parke LaGourgue Cory, Neosho, Missouri.*

SPANISH-STYLE LIVER

1 small onion, thinly sliced
2 tablespoons chopped green pepper
3 tablespoons melted butter or margarine
1 tablespoon chopped pimiento
½ cup chopped mushrooms
1 clove garlic
2 cups canned whole tomatoes, chopped
1 teaspoon salt
⅛ teaspoon pepper
½ cup all-purpose flour
½ teaspoon salt
¼ teaspoon pepper
6 slices (about 1¾ pounds) beef liver
¼ cup olive oil or vegetable oil

Sauté onion and green pepper in butter 10 minutes. Add pimiento, mushrooms, garlic, tomatoes, 1 teaspoon salt, and ⅛ teaspoon pepper; simmer 50 to 60 minutes over low heat or until thickened. Remove garlic and discard. Set sauce aside, and keep warm.

Combine flour and remaining salt and pepper. Coat liver in seasoned flour mixture, and brown in hot oil. Place liver on a heated platter, and serve sauce over top. Yield: 6 servings.
Mrs. J. A. Satterfield, Fort Worth, Texas.

SKILLET LIVER LOAF

1 pound pork liver, ground
1 pound bulk pork sausage
¾ to 1 pound ground beef
1 cup milk
1 cup breadcrumbs or cracker crumbs
2 eggs
1 teaspoon salt
½ cup tomato sauce

Combine all ingredients except tomato sauce; mix well. Spoon into a lightly greased 10-inch cast-iron skillet. Bake at 350° for 1 hour. Remove from oven, and drain off pan drippings. Spoon tomato sauce over loaf, and return to oven. Bake loaf an additional 10 minutes. Yield: 8 to 10 servings.
Mrs. Sara McCullough, Broaddus, Texas.

CREAMY LIVER AND NOODLE DINNER

6 slices bacon
6 thin slices (about 2½ pounds) beef liver
1 medium onion, chopped
1 cup commercial sour cream
2 tablespoons chopped parsley
Hot cooked noodles

Cook bacon in a large skillet until crisp; drain, reserving drippings. Crumble bacon, and set aside.

Sauté liver in 1 tablespoon reserved bacon drippings. Remove to heated platter and keep warm.

Sauté onion in 1 tablespoon reserved bacon drippings until tender. Add sour cream; cook over low heat, stirring, until heated through (do not boil). Spoon mixture over liver; sprinkle with crumbled bacon and parsley. Serve with noodles. Yield: 6 servings.
Jay Amonette, Tulsa, Oklahoma.

Spice Up Meals With Chili

A steaming bowl of chili is perfect for serving on a cold winter day, and it makes an ideal dish for casual entertaining. Everyone likes chili with a different degree of spiciness, different kinds of beans, and sometimes different combinations of meat, as these recipes prove.

OLD-FASHIONED SPICY CHILI

2 pounds ground beef
1 medium onion, chopped
4 cloves garlic, minced
2 tablespoons ground cumin
2 teaspoons salt
4 to 6 tablespoons chili powder
2 tablespoons all-purpose flour
1½ tablespoons sugar
2 (16-ounce) cans kidney beans, undrained
1 (16-ounce) can whole tomatoes, undrained and chopped
1 (6-ounce) can tomato paste

Combine first 5 ingredients in a large Dutch oven; cook over medium heat, stirring to crumble meat, until meat is browned and onion is tender. Drain off

pan drippings. Stir in chili powder, flour, and sugar. Add remaining ingredients; stir well (mixture will be very thick). Cover and simmer 30 minutes over low heat. Yield: 8 servings.
Cathy Huddleston, Charlotte, North Carolina.

RANCH CHILI AND BEANS

3 pounds ground beef
6 cups water
2 bay leaves
8 cloves garlic, crushed
4 to 6 tablespoons chili powder
2 teaspoons salt
1 teaspoon ground cumin
1 teaspoon oregano leaves
¼ teaspoon pepper
¼ to ½ teaspoon cayenne pepper
2 to 3 tablespoons paprika
1 tablespoon sugar
2 (15-ounce) cans ranch-style beans

Cook ground beef in a large Dutch oven until browned, stirring to crumble; drain off pan drippings. Add water and bay leaves; cover and simmer over low heat 1½ hours. Add next 9 ingredients; simmer 30 minutes. Stir in beans; simmer an additional 15 to 20 minutes. Yield: 6 to 8 servings.
Mrs. Diana McConnell, Denton, Texas.

SIMPLE CHILI

1 clove garlic, crushed
2 large onions, chopped
2 tablespoons vegetable oil
2 pounds lean ground beef
2 (16-ounce) cans whole tomatoes, undrained and chopped
1 (6-ounce) can tomato paste
2 tablespoons chili powder
½ teaspoon vinegar
⅛ teaspoon ground red pepper
1 teaspoon salt
2 (16-ounce) cans kidney beans, undrained and mashed
2 whole cloves
1 small bay leaf

Sauté garlic and onion in oil. Add ground beef; cook over low heat until browned, stirring to crumble. Add remaining ingredients; simmer, uncovered, 1 hour. Yield: 10 servings.
Mrs. S. D. Thomas, Dothan, Alabama.

DOUBLE-MEAT CHILI

½ pound dried pinto beans
2 (28-ounce) cans whole tomatoes,
 undrained and chopped
1½ pounds (about 5 large) onions,
 chopped
1 pound (about 4 large) green peppers,
 chopped
2 cloves garlic, crushed
½ cup chopped parsley
2½ pounds ground beef or venison
1 pound lean ground pork
½ cup melted butter or margarine
1½ tablespoons vegetable oil
½ cup chili powder
2 tablespoons salt
1½ teaspoons pepper
1½ teaspoons cumin seeds
1½ teaspoons monosodium glutamate

Sort and wash pinto beans. Place in a 6-quart Dutch oven, and cover with water until it is 2 inches above beans. Let beans soak overnight.

Cook beans in water over medium heat about 1 hour or until tender. Reduce heat; add tomatoes and simmer 5 minutes. Add onion and green pepper; cook about 10 minutes or until tender, stirring often. Stir in garlic and parsley.

Cook meat in butter and oil until browned, stirring to crumble; add to bean mixture. Stir in remaining ingredients; cover and simmer 1 hour. Uncover and simmer an additional 30 minutes. Yield: 12 to 15 servings.
DeLea Lonadier,
Montgomery, Louisiana.

ROUNDUP CHILI

1 to 1½ pounds ground beef
1 (28-ounce) can tomatoes, undrained
3½ cups water
2 (16-ounce) cans kidney beans, undrained
1 (6-ounce) can tomato paste
2 to 3 stalks celery, chopped
1 green pepper, chopped
1 large onion, chopped
1 tablespoon chili powder
Salt and pepper to taste

Cook ground beef in a Dutch oven until browned, stirring frequently to crumble. Drain off pan drippings. Stir in remaining ingredients; simmer 2 to 2½ hours, stirring occasionally. Yield: 5 to 6 servings.
Mrs. Barbara Bodensick,
Newport News, Virginia.

Tip: Recipes often call for small amounts of tomato paste. Spoon the rest into a freezer container and freeze.

Enjoy Broccoli When It's Fresh

When the menu calls for a green vegetable, you can't go wrong with fresh broccoli. Available all year, broccoli shows its versatility in these special side dishes.

Water chestnuts, soy sauce, and garlic add an Oriental touch to stir-fried Broccoli With Sesame. Sherry and chicken stock flavor Jade-Green Broccoli, and Cheddar cheese tops sherry-laced Glazed Broccoli With Almonds.

BROCCOLI WITH WHITE WINE

¼ cup olive oil
1 teaspoon minced garlic
5 to 6 cups chopped fresh broccoli
1½ cups dry white wine
½ teaspoon salt
Freshly ground black pepper

Heat olive oil in a heavy skillet; sauté garlic briefly. Add broccoli, stirring until coated well. Stir in wine, salt, and pepper to taste; simmer, uncovered, for 2 minutes, stirring occasionally. Cover and simmer 10 minutes.

Drain broccoli, reserving liquid; place broccoli in serving dish and keep warm. Boil reserved liquid until reduced to ½ cup; pour liquid over broccoli. Yield: 5 to 6 servings.
Mrs. M. E. Natto,
Locust Grove, Virginia.

GLAZED BROCCOLI WITH ALMONDS

2 pounds fresh broccoli
½ teaspoon salt
1 beef bouillon cube
¾ cup hot water
1 cup half-and-half
¼ cup butter or margarine
¼ cup all-purpose flour
2 tablespoons sherry
2 tablespoons lemon juice
⅛ teaspoon pepper
2 teaspoons monosodium glutamate
½ cup (2 ounces) shredded Cheddar cheese
¼ cup slivered almonds

Trim off large leaves of broccoli. Remove tough ends of lower stalks, and wash broccoli thoroughly; separate into spears. Cook broccoli, covered, in a small amount of boiling salted water for 10 minutes or until crisp-tender. Drain well and place in a 12- x 8- x 2-inch baking dish.

Dissolve bouillon cube in ¾ cup water; stir in half-and-half, and set aside.

Melt butter in a heavy saucepan over low heat; blend in flour, stirring until smooth. Cook 1 minute, stirring constantly. Gradually stir in bouillon mixture; cook over medium heat, stirring constantly, until thickened and bubbly. Stir in sherry, lemon juice, pepper, and monosodium glutamate.

Pour sauce over broccoli; sprinkle with cheese and almonds. Bake at 375° for 25 to 30 minutes. Yield: 6 servings.
Mrs. E. A. Kraus,
Louisville, Kentucky.

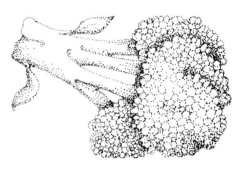

JADE-GREEN BROCCOLI

1 tablespoon sugar
1 tablespoon cornstarch
2 tablespoons soy sauce
½ cup chicken stock or water
1 bunch fresh broccoli
¼ cup vegetable oil
¼ teaspoon salt
1 clove garlic, minced
2 tablespoons sherry

Combine sugar, cornstarch, soy sauce, and chicken stock; mix well and set aside.

Trim off large leaves of broccoli. Remove tough ends of lower stalks, and wash broccoli thoroughly. Cut away tops; cut stems into ¼-inch slices and set aside.

Heat wok or skillet over medium-high heat (325°) for 3 minutes; pour oil around top of wok, coating sides. Add salt and garlic, and stir-fry briefly. Add broccoli tops and slices; stir-fry 2 minutes. Add sherry; cover and cook 2 minutes. Stir in cornstarch mixture; cook, stirring constantly, until sauce is thickened. Yield: 4 to 6 servings.
Connie Carpenter,
Tallahassee, Florida.

BROCCOLI WITH SESAME

1 bunch fresh broccoli
2 tablespoons sesame seeds
3 tablespoons vegetable oil
2 teaspoons minced garlic
½ cup sliced water chestnuts
3 tablespoons white wine
3 tablespoons soy sauce
½ teaspoon salt
½ teaspoon sugar

Trim off large leaves of broccoli. Remove tough ends of lower stalks, and wash broccoli thoroughly. Cut away tops, and set aside. Cut stems into ¼-inch slices; set aside.

Toast sesame seeds in wok or skillet; remove and set aside. Pour oil into wok; heat at 325° for 3 minutes. Add garlic; stir-fry briefly. Add broccoli stalks, and stir-fry 5 minutes. Add water chestnuts, wine, soy sauce, salt, sugar, and broccoli tops; mix well. Cover and cook 5 minutes; sprinkle sesame seeds over top. Yield: 5 to 6 servings.
Roxanne Gaudin,
Evansville, Indiana.

Citrus Freshens Winter Meals

Winter meals get a lift when citrus is on the menu. Enjoy the fresh flavor of oranges in a sauce for chicken or combined with plump grapefruit sections in Sweet-and-Sour Fruit Salad. And you'll have to taste Fresh Lemon Charlotte Russe to believe its delectable flavor.

FRESH LEMON CHARLOTTE RUSSE

4 eggs, separated
½ cup lemon juice
⅛ teaspoon salt
1 envelope unflavored gelatin
1½ cups sugar, divided
3 tablespoons butter or margarine
1½ teaspoons grated lemon rind
1 teaspoon vanilla extract
12 ladyfingers, split in half lengthwise
1 cup whipping cream, whipped
Sweetened whipped cream (optional)

Combine egg yolks, lemon juice, and salt in top of a double boiler; mix well. Stir in gelatin and 1 cup sugar. Cook

over simmering water about 10 minutes or until thickened, stirring constantly. Add butter, lemon rind, and vanilla, stirring until butter melts. Chill mixture until partially thickened.

Arrange ladyfingers around bottom and sides of a 9½-inch springform pan; set aside.

Beat egg whites until soft peaks form. Gradually add remaining sugar, and continue beating until stiff peaks form. Fold whipped cream and gelatin mixture into egg whites. Spoon into prepared pan. Cover and chill 4 to 5 hours or until firm. Garnish with sweetened whipped cream, if desired. Yield: 8 servings. *Mrs. Edward A. Smith, Jr.,*
Charlottesville, Virginia.

SWEET-AND-SOUR FRUIT SALAD

2 grapefruit, peeled, seeded, and sectioned
2 oranges, peeled, seeded, and sectioned
1 (15¼-ounce) can unsweetened pineapple chunks, undrained
½ cup chopped dates
½ cup chopped pecans
2 tablespoons sugar
2 tablespoons orange juice or orange-flavored liqueur

Combine all ingredients, stirring gently. Chill salad well before serving. Yield: 6 servings. *Mrs. Earl Schwartz,*
Pfafftown, North Carolina.

CHICKEN IN ORANGE-ALMOND SAUCE

1 (2- to 3-pound) chicken, cut up and skinned
Salt
3 tablespoons melted butter or margarine
2 tablespoons all-purpose flour
⅛ teaspoon ground ginger
⅛ teaspoon ground cinnamon
1½ cups orange juice
½ cup slivered almonds
½ cup raisins
1 cup orange sections
Hot cooked rice

Sprinkle chicken with ¼ teaspoon salt, and brown in butter in a large skillet. Remove chicken from skillet, reserving drippings. Cool chicken, and remove meat from bones.

Add flour, spices, and ¼ teaspoon salt to reserved drippings; stir until smooth. Cook 1 minute, stirring constantly. Gradually add orange juice;

cook over low heat, stirring constantly, until thickened and bubbly.

Stir chicken, almonds, and raisins into sauce. Cover and cook over low heat 45 minutes or until chicken is tender. Add orange sections, and heat thoroughly. Serve over hot cooked rice. Yield: about 6 servings. *Mrs. Charles Simms,*
Palestine, Illinois.

BAKED ORANGE ELEGANCE

6 medium oranges
2 cups sugar
2 cups water
6 tablespoons butter

Cook oranges in boiling water 30 minutes; drain and set aside to cool.

Combine sugar and 2 cups water in a medium saucepan. Bring to a boil; reduce heat, and simmer 10 minutes.

Cut oranges in half crosswise; arrange orange halves, cut side up, in a 13- x 9- x 2-inch baking dish. Dot each with 1½ teaspoons butter. Pour syrup evenly over oranges. Bake at 325° for 1½ hours, basting occasionally.

Remove oranges from baking dish. Pour syrup into a small saucepan. Bring to a boil; boil 30 minutes or until syrup thickens. Return orange halves to baking dish. Pour syrup over oranges; let stand about 15 minutes before serving. Yield: 12 servings.
Mrs. W. Harold Groce,
Arden, North Carolina.

Garlic Can Be Subtle Or Pungent

Pungent or subtle, garlic adds the right accent to these entrées and side dishes. Garlic tastes sharpest when finely minced or crushed, and uncooked. Garlic Dressing is a pungent example.

Garlic becomes milder and more subtle in Mixed Vegetable Stir-Fry. Here, cooking large pieces of garlic tames its potency and imparts a sweet, nutlike flavor.

When buying garlic, select firm, plump bulbs that have dry, unbroken skins. Store in a cool, dry place that is well ventilated. The flavor will remain sharp for up to four months.

GARLIC SHRIMP

2 tablespoons vegetable oil
2 tablespoons butter or margarine
8 cloves garlic, chopped
1 pound shrimp, peeled and deveined
Salt and pepper to taste
Lemon or lime wedges

Heat oil and butter in a large skillet. Add garlic and shrimp; sprinkle with salt and pepper. Sauté 2 to 3 minutes or until shrimp turn pink. Turn shrimp with spatula; cook 2 minutes longer on the other side. Remove shrimp to serving platter; garnish with lemon wedges. Yield: 2 to 3 servings.

Mrs. James W. Bachus,
Austin, Texas.

MIXED VEGETABLE STIR-FRY

2 tablespoons vegetable oil
1 medium clove garlic, cut in half
2 carrots, diagonally sliced ¼-inch thick
2 stalks celery, diagonally sliced ¼-inch thick
3 to 4 green onions, cut into 1-inch pieces
2 medium-size yellow squash, diagonally sliced ¼-inch thick
1 green or red pepper, cut into ½-inch strips
1 tablespoon soy sauce
Salt and pepper to taste
1 tablespoon sliced almonds (optional)

Heat vegetable oil in a wok or a heavy skillet. Add the garlic, and sauté over medium heat until garlic is golden brown. Discard garlic.

Add carrots and celery; stir-fry 3 to 4 minutes or until partially cooked. Add onion, squash, and green pepper; stir-fry 2 to 4 minutes or until vegetables are crisp-tender. Add soy sauce, salt, and pepper; mix lightly. Sprinkle with almonds, if desired. Yield: 4 servings.

Mrs. Nancy Reel,
Kirbyville, Texas.

SAVORY BROCCOLI

1 pound fresh broccoli, cut into spears
¼ cup olive oil
2 cloves garlic
2 red or green peppers, cut into strips
2 tablespoons vinegar
¼ cup beef broth
Salt and white pepper to taste

Cook broccoli in boiling salted water 10 minutes or until tender; drain.

Heat oil in large skillet; add garlic and sauté until golden brown. Remove garlic and set aside. Add red pepper to skillet; sauté 2 to 3 minutes. Crush garlic; add garlic, vinegar, broth, salt, and pepper to red pepper; stir well. Simmer 10 minutes. Add broccoli, and cook until heated. Arrange broccoli and red pepper on serving platter; pour pan juices over vegetables. Yield: 4 to 6 servings.

Mrs. Maruja Hatheway,
Austin, Texas.

COMPANY HASH BROWNS

4 large baking potatoes, peeled and cut into 1-inch cubes
½ pound fresh mushrooms, thinly sliced
4 tablespoons melted butter or margarine, divided
¼ cup olive or vegetable oil
¾ teaspoon salt
⅛ teaspoon pepper
¾ cup cooked English peas
2 tablespoons chopped parsley
2 cloves garlic, minced

Cook potatoes in boiling salted water, uncovered, for 4 minutes; drain.

Sauté mushrooms in 2 tablespoons butter until tender; set aside.

Heat oil in large skillet; add potato cubes. Cook until tender and golden brown, turning as necessary. Sprinkle with salt and pepper. Add mushrooms and butter mixture, peas, and remaining butter; cook over low heat until hot. Add parsley and garlic; stir gently, mixing well. Yield: about 6 servings.

Lilly S. Bradley,
Salem, Virginia.

GARLIC SPOONBREAD

¾ cup cornmeal
1½ cups water
2 cups (½ pound) shredded sharp Cheddar cheese
¼ cup butter or margarine, softened
2 cloves garlic, crushed
½ teaspoon salt
1 cup milk
5 egg yolks, beaten
½ pound bacon, cooked and crumbled
4 egg whites

Combine cornmeal and water in a large saucepan; cook over medium heat until thickened. Remove from heat. Add cheese, butter, garlic, and salt; stir until cheese melts. Gradually stir in milk; add egg yolks, stirring well. Add crumbled bacon, reserving a small amount for garnish; mix well.

Beat egg whites until stiff but not dry. Gently fold egg whites into cornmeal mixture. Pour into a lightly greased 2½-quart soufflé dish. Bake at 325° for 65 minutes. Sprinkle reserved bacon on top. Serve spoonbread immediately. Yield: 6 to 8 servings.

Mrs. John Rucker,
Louisville, Kentucky.

GARLIC DRESSING

1 cup vegetable oil
½ cup sugar
¼ cup red wine vinegar
⅔ cup catsup
½ cup chili sauce
1 large onion, finely chopped
4 cloves garlic, crushed
1 teaspoon salt
1 teaspoon paprika
Juice of 1 lemon

Combine oil, sugar, and vinegar; beat with wire whisk until blended. Add remaining ingredients, mixing well. Yield: 3½ cups.

Note: Three-fourths cup of mayonnaise may be added to make Thousand Island Dressing, if desired.

Judy Eveloff,
Springfield, Illinois.

Avocados—The Wintertime Fruit

While many fruits are unavailable or of lower quality during the winter months, avocados are at their peak. Here they garnish a hearty ground beef-lettuce-cheese salad and provide the creamy dressing for a guacamole salad.

GUACAMOLE SALAD

4 cups torn lettuce
2 tomatoes, cut into wedges
½ cup sliced pitted ripe olives
¼ cup chopped green onion
Crumbled cooked bacon
Avocado Dressing

Combine lettuce, tomatoes, olives, and green onion in a large salad bowl; toss. Sprinkle with bacon; serve with Avocado Dressing. Yield: 6 servings.

Avocado Dressing:
½ cup mashed ripe avocado
1 tablespoon lemon juice
½ cup commercial sour cream
⅓ cup vegetable oil
½ teaspoon sugar
½ teaspoon chili powder
¼ teaspoon salt
¼ teaspoon hot sauce
1 clove garlic, crushed

Combine all ingredients in container of an electric blender; blend well. Yield: about 1 cup.

Mrs. Sue-Sue Hartstern,
Louisville, Kentucky.

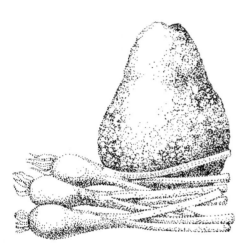

DUDE RANCH SALAD

1 pound lean ground beef
1 (15½-ounce) can kidney beans
1 head iceberg lettuce, shredded
1 large onion, chopped
4 tomatoes, diced
¼ pound Cheddar cheese, cubed
1 (8-ounce) bottle commercial French dressing
1 large avocado, peeled and sliced
1 (7-ounce) package tortilla chips, crumbled

Cook ground beef and beans in a medium skillet until meat is browned; cool. Combine beef mixture and next 5 ingredients in a large salad bowl; mix well. Garnish with avocado slices and chips. Yield: about 12 servings.

Mrs. Charles Simms,
Palestine, Illinois.

Pick A Date For Natural Goodness

Often called "nature's own candy," dates provide an excellent way to satisfy a sweet tooth with little or no refined sugar. The natural sweetness of dates adds to the richness of Festive Fruit Salad—there's no sugar added.

Where additional sweetness is desired, the less refined nature of brown sugar brings out the full flavor of dates. One taste of our Blue Ribbon Date-Walnut Loaf or Rolled Fruit Cookies will prove this a flavorful combination.

DATE-PECAN PIE

1 (8-ounce) package chopped dates
1 cup pecans, coarsely chopped
¼ cup all-purpose flour
2 cups sugar
¾ cup butter or margarine, softened
1½ teaspoons vanilla extract
Pinch of salt
4 eggs, separated
¾ cup milk
2 unbaked 9-inch pastry shells

Combine dates, pecans, and flour; stir well and set aside.

Combine sugar, butter, vanilla, and salt in a large mixing bowl; mix well. Add egg yolks and milk, mixing well. Stir in pecans and dates.

Beat egg whites until stiff but not dry. Fold egg whites into creamed mixture. Pour batter evenly into pastry shells. Bake at 300° for 45 minutes. Increase temperature to 325°, and bake 30 additional minutes or until firm. Yield: two 9-inch pies.

Mrs. Leslie Villeneuve,
Neptune Beach, Florida.

ROLLED FRUIT COOKIES

½ cup shortening
1 cup firmly packed dark brown sugar
1 egg
2 cups all-purpose flour
½ teaspoon soda
½ teaspoon salt
1 teaspoon ground cinnamon
Date Filling

Cream shortening and sugar until light and fluffy. Add egg and beat well. Combine flour, soda, salt, and cinnamon; gradually add to creamed mixture, stirring well. Shape dough into a ball. (Dough will be stiff.)

Place dough on a lightly floured surface; roll into a 16- x 8-inch rectangle. Spread Date Filling over dough, leaving a ½-inch margin on all sides. Starting at long end, carefully roll dough crosswise, jellyroll fashion; pinch lengthwise seam and ends of roll to seal. Cover and refrigerate 1 hour or until firm.

Slice dough into ⅓-inch-thick slices. Arrange on greased cookie sheet, 1 inch apart. Bake at 350° for 15 minutes. Yield: about 4 dozen.

Date Filling:
1 (8-ounce) package pitted dates
½ cup sugar
¼ cup water
1 cup finely chopped pecans

Combine dates, sugar, and water in a medium saucepan; mix well. Cook over medium heat 3 to 5 minutes or until thickened, stirring constantly. Remove from heat; stir in pecans. Let cool. Yield: about 1¾ cups.

Mrs. C. C. Kerns,
Exmore, Virginia.

BLUE RIBBON DATE-WALNUT LOAF

2 cups chopped dates
1 cup chopped walnuts
⅓ cup shortening
1 cup boiling water
⅓ cup cold water
¾ cup firmly packed brown sugar
1 egg, well beaten
1 teaspoon vanilla extract
2 cups all-purpose flour
1 teaspoon baking powder
1 teaspoon soda
1½ teaspoons salt

Combine dates, walnuts, and shortening in a large mixing bowl. Add boiling water, stirring just until shortening melts. Stir in cold water. Add sugar, egg, and vanilla, mixing well.

Combine dry ingredients, and add gradually to date mixture, beating well. Pour mixture into a greased 9- x 5- x 3-inch loafpan. Bake at 350° for 1 hour and 15 minutes or until loaf tests done. Cool in pan 10 minutes; remove from pan and cool on a wire rack. Yield: 1 loaf.

Mrs. Roderick W. McGrath,
Orlando, Florida.

Tip: Bread made with fruit or nuts should be tested with a straw or wire cake tester in the center. The tester should come out perfectly clean if the bread is done.

FESTIVE FRUIT SALAD

½ cup diced dates
1 tablespoon grated orange rind
⅛ teaspoon almond extract
½ cup whipping cream, whipped
6 pear halves
6 lettuce cups
3 maraschino cherries, halved
¼ cup finely chopped walnuts

Combine dates, orange rind, and almond extract; gently fold date mixture into whipped cream.

Place each pear half on a lettuce cup. Spoon whipped cream mixture onto each pear half; top with a cherry half. Sprinkle walnuts over top. Yield: 6 servings. *Jo Gwyn Baldwin, Abilene, Texas.*

Perfect Muffins Every Time

The crust is thin and golden, the top is symmetrical but rough, the texture is light and tender—a perfect muffin. The secret: Don't overmix the batter.

When making muffins, add liquid ingredients to dry ingredients all at once and stir only until the batter is barely moistened. If the batter is overmixed, the muffins will have a peaked or flat top and a tough texture.

And for attractive, nicely browned muffins, use pans made of dull metal, anodized aluminum, or glass. If only part of a muffin pan is needed, fill unused cups with water to keep the pan from scorching during baking.

BLUEBERRY BUTTERMILK MUFFINS

2 cups all-purpose flour
½ cup sugar
2¼ teaspoons baking powder
1 teaspoon salt
¼ teaspoon soda
1 egg, slightly beaten
1 cup buttermilk
¼ cup melted butter or margarine
1 cup blueberries

Combine dry ingredients in a mixing bowl; set aside. Combine egg, buttermilk, and butter; mix well. Make a well in center of dry ingredients; pour in liq-

When making muffins, make a well in the center of the dry ingredients; then pour the liquid ingredients into the well, all at once.

uid ingredients. Stir just until moistened. Fold in blueberries.

Fill greased muffin pans two-thirds full. Bake at 425° for 20 to 25 minutes. Remove from pan immediately. Yield: 1½ dozen muffins. *Mrs. Donald Terry, Decatur, Alabama.*

JELLY-FILLED MUFFINS

2 cups all-purpose flour
¼ cup sugar
1 tablespoon baking powder
½ teaspoon salt
1 egg, slightly beaten
1 cup milk
¼ cup melted butter or margarine
Jelly, jam, or preserves of your choice

Combine dry ingredients in a large mixing bowl. Combine egg, milk, and butter; mix well. Make a well in center of dry ingredients; pour in liquid ingredients, and stir just until moistened.

Fill greased muffin pans one-fourth full. Spoon 1 teaspoon jelly in center of each muffin cup; spoon remaining batter over jelly, filling each cup half full. Bake at 400° for 20 to 25 minutes. Remove from pan immediately. Yield: 8 to 10 muffins. *Carolyn Willis Williams, North Augusta, South Carolina.*

Stir dry and liquid ingredients together just until barely moistened; do not overmix. In fact, the batter should still be lumpy.

PECAN MUFFINS

1½ cups all-purpose flour
½ cup sugar
½ cup chopped pecans
2 teaspoons baking powder
½ teaspoon salt
1 egg, slightly beaten
½ cup milk
¼ cup vegetable oil

Combine first 5 ingredients in a large bowl; stir well. Combine egg, milk, and oil. Make a well in center of dry ingredients; pour in liquid ingredients, and stir just until moistened.

Fill greased muffin pans two-thirds full. Bake muffins at 400° for 20 to 25 minutes. Remove from pan immediately. Yield: 10 muffins.
Mrs. J. B. Davis, Asheboro, North Carolina.

Tip: To keep raisins, currants, and other dried fruit from falling to the bottom of the cake, use a small amount of flour used in the recipe to coat them before adding to the batter.

February

Start those nippy February mornings with sweet yeast breads and a piping hot cup of coffee. We tastetested these recipes first thing in the morning so we could do just that. Our tempting array of breakfast breads offers fruit, nut, and spice fillings topped with a sugar coating or glaze.

Another cool weather favorite is homemade vegetable soup. A bowlful of Hearty Vegetable Soup or Cheesy Vegetable Chowder is guaranteed to take the chill away.

Splurge for dessert with a luscious cheesecake. We tasted two or three cheesecakes every afternoon for a week before we found the four recipes included in this chapter. And we warn you, they're rich and filling!

The Wok Stirs A Southern Following

The Chinese may have invented the wok, but more and more Southerners are adopting it and enjoying some delightful bonuses in the process. Just consider the party possibilities of a wok. With an electric model or a conventional wok set on a portable burner, you can do the cooking right at the table. That way, the cooking becomes part of the entertainment, especially if guests are encouraged to help.

But perhaps the biggest bonus of wok cookery is the way the food tastes and looks, as well as knowing that its nutrients have been retained. And that's due to the rapid cooking over high heat. Vegetables cook only until crisp-tender, which preserves their natural flavor, color, and food value—often lost due to overcooking. Meats are thinly sliced so they brown quickly but remain juicy.

Stir-frying is the most common method used in wok cookery. The food is cooked rapidly in a small amount of oil and stirred almost constantly to ensure even cooking. Since there's no time to prepare ingredients once stir-frying begins, be sure to chop, measure, and assemble everything before heating the wok. Stir-frying offers another bonus for wok cookery: It requires less oil than pan frying, so there are fewer calories and less fat.

Here are some pointers to ensure your success.

—Peanut oil is an excellent choice for use in the wok because it can be heated to high temperature without smoking. Vegetable oil also works satisfactorily in most recipes, but never use solid shortening, butter, or margarine.

—Oil should be added to a preheated wok, then allowed to heat before adding other ingredients. Pour oil around the top of the wok so the sides are coated. If a recipe does not specify the amount of oil to use, remember that very little is required. Use only enough to cover the cooking surface.

—Be sure to carefully slice and chop all ingredients. Proper cutting can bring food close to tenderness even before it is cooked and also improves its appearance.

Meat should be cut across the grain into thin slices (partial freezing of meat before cutting will make this easier).

Cut fibrous vegetables, such as celery and broccoli, diagonally to expose the largest possible area to the heat; this also applies to less-tender vegetables such as carrots. Hold the knife at a 45-degree angle to the food, and make thin slices across.

—When cooking a delicate vegetable, such as mushrooms, with a fibrous vegetable, cut the delicate vegetable into larger pieces or add it later to prevent overcooking.

—If some ingredients are cooking faster than others, push them up the sides of the wok. The sides are known as the warming area and do not cook as rapidly as the bottom.

The Wok and Its Accessories

There are a number of woks on the market, but all have the classic cone shape. The conventional style with the slightly rounded bottom comes with a collar that adapts it to a portable burner or kitchen range. More recent introductions are the electric wok and the type that sits directly on the range. Most styles are available in sets, which include some accessories.

The classic wok is made of iron, but steel is the most common material used today. Some models feature nonstick or nonrust finishes. Prices vary with material, style, and number of accessories included.

Accessories are available for wok cookery, but you may have everything you need on hand. In fact, if you don't want to buy a wok, you can use a heavy skillet.

A Chinese spatula and stirring spoon are useful for stir-frying, but a long-handled spoon can be substituted. For proper chopping and slicing of meats and vegetables, a Chinese slicing knife or other sharp knife is essential. You'll also find you'll need a special Chinese strainer or slotted spoon when deep frying in the wok in order to easily remove the food from the hot oil.

A steamer tray or rack designed to fit inside the wok increases its versatility, as it can be used for reheating any food and preparing many vegetables, as well as rice. The traditional Chinese steaming utensils are made of bamboo because it is inexpensive and seldom cracks.

A bamboo wok brush is good for removing food particles from the wok without scratching a well-seasoned surface. Nylon pot scrubbers will not harm the surface either, but do not use steel wool or strong detergents. To clean, fill the wok with hot water, and soak to loosen food particles. Wipe and dry thoroughly to prevent rust.

Adventure Into Wok Cookery

With dishes like Chicken-in-a-Garden for inspiration, you'll want to try your hand at wok cookery. Besides chicken and beef entrées, you have a choice of flavorful side dishes, such as Egg Fried Rice and spinach stir-fried with mushrooms. Each recipe gives heat settings for both electric and conventional woks.

CHICKEN-IN-A-GARDEN

3 whole chicken breasts, skinned and boned
½ teaspoon garlic powder
3 tablespoons peanut oil, divided
2 tablespoons soy sauce, divided
3 tablespoons cornstarch, divided
½ teaspoon salt
¼ teaspoon pepper
3 green peppers, cut into 1-inch pieces
1 cup diagonally sliced celery (1-inch pieces)
8 scallions, cut into ½-inch slices
1 (6-ounce) package frozen Chinese pea pods, thawed and drained
¼ teaspoon sugar
⅛ teaspoon ground ginger
¾ cup chicken bouillon, cooled
3 medium tomatoes, peeled and cut into eighths
Hot cooked rice

Cut chicken breasts into 1-inch pieces, and set aside.

Combine garlic powder, 1 tablespoon oil, 1 tablespoon soy sauce, 1 teaspoon cornstarch, salt, pepper, and chicken; mix well, and let stand 20 minutes.

Pour remaining oil around top of preheated wok, coating sides; allow to heat at medium high (325°) for 2 minutes. Add green pepper, and stir-fry 4 minutes. Add celery, scallions, and pea pods; stir-fry 2 minutes. Remove vegetables from wok, and set aside.

Combine remaining soy sauce and cornstarch; stir in sugar, ginger, and chicken bouillon. Set mixture aside.

Add chicken to wok, and stir-fry 3 minutes; add stir-fried vegetables, tomatoes, and bouillon mixture. Stir-fry over low heat (225°) for 3 minutes or until thickened and bubbly. Serve over hot cooked rice. Yield: 6 servings.

Tip: To hasten any meal preparation, assemble all ingredients before starting. This eliminates trips to pantry.

STIR-FRY BEEF AND PEA PODS

¾ pound boneless sirloin steak
½ cup water
1 tablespoon cornstarch
1½ teaspoons sugar
¼ cup plus 1 tablespoon soy sauce
1½ to 2 tablespoons oyster-flavored sauce
3 tablespoons peanut oil
¼ teaspoon salt
1 large onion, thinly sliced and separated into rings
3 stalks celery, diagonally sliced
4 ounces fresh mushrooms, sliced
½ cup coarsely chopped water chestnuts
1 (6-ounce) package frozen Chinese pea pods, thawed and drained
Hot cooked rice

Partially freeze steak; slice across grain into 2- x ¼-inch strips. Set aside.

Combine water, cornstarch, sugar, soy sauce, and oyster sauce; set aside.

Pour oil around top of preheated wok, coating sides; allow to heat at medium high (325°) for 2 minutes. Add steak and salt; stir-fry about 3 minutes.

Push meat up sides of wok, forming a well in center. Place onion, celery, mushrooms, and water chestnuts in well; stir-fry 2 to 3 minutes. Add pea pods; cover and reduce heat to medium (275°). Simmer 2 to 3 minutes.

Stir in soy sauce mixture. Cook on medium-high heat (325°), stirring constantly, until thickened and bubbly. Serve over rice. Yield: 4 to 6 servings.
Mrs. Michael Champagne,
Covington, Louisiana.

SPINACH WITH MUSHROOMS

1 tablespoon lemon juice
1 teaspoon salt
1 teaspoon sugar
Dash of nutmeg
3 tablespoons peanut oil
1 cup sliced fresh mushrooms
1 onion, chopped
1 clove garlic, chopped
1 pound fresh spinach, washed and drained

Combine lemon juice, salt, sugar, and nutmeg; set aside.

Pour oil around top of preheated wok, coating sides; allow to heat at high (375°) for 2 minutes. Add mushrooms, onion, and garlic; stir-fry 3 minutes. Add spinach, and stir-fry 3 minutes or until spinach wilts. Add lemon juice mixture, tossing lightly. Yield: 4 servings.
Roxanne Gaudin,
Evansville, Indiana.

EGG FRIED RICE

2 tablespoons peanut oil
⅓ cup chopped onion
3 cups cooked rice, cooled
1 egg, slightly beaten
2 tablespoons soy sauce

Pour oil around top of preheated wok, coating sides; allow to heat at medium high (325°) for 2 minutes. Add onion, and stir-fry 2 minutes. Add rice, and stir-fry until thoroughly heated.

Push rice-onion mixture up sides of wok, forming a well in center. Pour egg into well, and stir-fry until set. Stir rice mixture into egg; add soy sauce, stirring well. Yield: 6 servings.
John N. Riggins,
Nashville, Tennessee.

STIR-FRY BROCCOLI

¼ cup boiling water
2 tablespoons soy sauce
1 tablespoon dry sherry
1 teaspoon sugar
¼ teaspoon salt
1 bunch fresh broccoli
¼ cup peanut oil
1 small onion, chopped

Combine first 5 ingredients; stir well, and set aside.

Trim off large outer leaves of broccoli, and remove tough ends of stalks. Wash broccoli thoroughly in cold water. Cut stalks diagonally into 1-inch-thick slices; if stalks are more than 1 inch in diameter, cut in half lengthwise. Cut flowerets into 1-inch pieces.

Pour oil around top of preheated wok, coating sides; allow to heat at medium high (325°) for 2 minutes. Add broccoli, and stir-fry 2 minutes; add onion, and stir-fry 3 minutes. Add soy sauce mixture; cover and reduce heat to low (225°). Cook 5 minutes or until broccoli is crisp-tender. Yield: 6 servings.
Cathy Huddleston,
Charlotte, North Carolina.

Make It Egg Foo Yong

Canned chop suey vegetables, shrimp, and soy sauce are combined to give this dish its distinctive Oriental flair. For each serving, portions of rice are topped with two light egg patties and a generous amount of sauce.

EGG FOO YONG

4 eggs, beaten
1 (16-ounce) can chop suey vegetables, drained
1 (10-ounce) package frozen cooked shrimp
½ cup chopped green onion
2 teaspoons chicken-flavored instant bouillon
Vegetable oil
Hot cooked rice
Sauce (recipe follows)

Combine eggs, vegetables, shrimp, onion, and bouillon. Let stand 10 minutes; mix well.

Heat small amount of vegetable oil in a large skillet. Spoon ¼ cup egg mixture into hot oil, shaping into a 3-inch circle with a spatula. Cook until brown on one side; turn and brown other side. Repeat until all egg mixture is used; add oil to skillet as necessary. Serve egg patties over rice; top with sauce. Yield: 6 servings.

Sauce:

1½ cups water
1 tablespoon soy sauce
2 teaspoons chicken-flavored instant bouillon
2 tablespoons cornstarch
½ cup water

Combine 1½ cups water, soy sauce, and bouillon in a medium saucepan. Cook over low heat until bouillon dissolves. Combine cornstarch and ½ cup water, stirring well; stir into bouillon mixture. Cook over low heat until thickened, stirring constantly. Yield: 2 cups.
Mrs. Anna Maidhof,
Lehigh Acres, Florida.

Tip: Add raw cucumber and carrot strips, green beans, and cauliflowerets to liquid left in dill pickle jar. Refrigerate for several days to make delicious dill-flavored cocktail snacks.

Wonton wrappers are folded over a creamy crabmeat mixture for golden Crab Puffs. They're served with a sweet-and-sour sauce.

Crab With An Oriental Flair

These crispy little puffs, served with their own Sweet-and-Sour Sauce, make an ideal party appetizer.

CRAB PUFFS

1 (8-ounce) package cream cheese, softened
Dash of Worcestershire sauce
2 tablespoons soft breadcrumbs
1 (6-ounce) can crabmeat, drained and flaked
2½ dozen wonton wrappers
Vegetable oil
Sweet-and-Sour Sauce

Combine cream cheese and Worcestershire sauce in a medium mixing bowl; mix well. Stir in breadcrumbs and crabmeat.

Place 1 heaping teaspoon of crabmeat mixture on center of each wonton wrapper. Moisten edges of wrapper, and fold in half diagonally. Using a fork, press edges firmly together.

Place crab puffs in deep oil heated to 375°. Cook until golden brown on both sides; drain well. Keep warm in oven. Serve with Sweet-and-Sour Sauce. Yield: 2½ dozen.

Sweet-and-Sour Sauce:

½ cup firmly packed brown sugar
2 tablespoons cornstarch
¼ cup vinegar
3 tablespoons soy sauce
½ cup pineapple juice
Salt to taste

Combine sugar and cornstarch in a small saucepan, stirring well. Gradually add vinegar, soy sauce, and pineapple juice; cook over low heat, stirring constantly, until thick and smooth. Add salt. Yield: about 1 cup.

Note: If preferred, Crab Puffs may be prepared by placing 1 heaping teaspoon of crabmeat mixture off-center (towards you) on each wonton wrapper. Fold two sides of wrapper over filling; roll edge of wrapper nearest you over filling. Brush exposed edge of wrapper with water. Finish rolling and seal end.
Carole Garner,
Little Rock, Arkansas.

Fresh Breads Warm The Morning

What better way to start your day than with fresh yeast bread and a piping hot cup of coffee. This inviting breakfast is welcome any time of the year, but is especially treasured on a cold winter morning.

Filled with fruits, nuts, and spices, topped with a sugar coating or glaze, these morning breads are diverse in flavor and in shape. Whether you prefer making the dough into loaves, buns, or coffee cakes, you'll find some of each offered here.

For a fruit-filled bread, try Cherry Blossom Coffee Cake. The dough is wrapped around cherry pie filling, shaped into a coil, then sprinkled with sugar before baking. Rum-Raisin Buns are dressed up with a powdered sugar glaze, while a fresh-orange butter adds refreshing flavor to Orange Rolls.

DANISH COFFEE RING

1 package dry yeast
¼ cup warm water (105° to 115°)
½ cup milk, scalded
¼ cup shortening
¼ cup sugar
½ teaspoon salt
1 egg, slightly beaten
½ teaspoon vanilla extract
1 teaspoon grated lemon rind
2½ to 3 cups all-purpose flour
2 tablespoons melted butter or margarine
½ cup raisins
½ cup toasted slivered almonds
⅓ cup sugar
1½ teaspoons ground cinnamon
Glaze (recipe follows)

Dissolve the yeast in warm water, and set aside.

Combine milk, shortening, ¼ cup sugar, and salt; stir well. Cool mixture to 105° to 115°.

Combine milk mixture, egg, vanilla, lemon rind, and 1 cup flour; beat until smooth. Stir in yeast mixture; add remaining flour to make a soft dough.

Turn dough out onto a floured surface; knead 8 to 10 minutes or until dough is smooth and elastic. Place dough in a well-greased bowl, turning once to grease top. Cover; let rise in a warm place (85°), free from drafts, until doubled in bulk (about 1½ hours).

Punch dough down; turn out onto a floured surface. Cover dough, and let rest 10 minutes. Roll out dough into a 21- x 7-inch rectangle.

Brush butter evenly over dough, leaving a 1-inch margin. Combine raisins, almonds, ⅓ cup sugar, and cinnamon; sprinkle mixture evenly over dough, leaving a 1-inch margin.

Roll up dough, jellyroll fashion, beginning at long side; pinch edges to seal. Place roll on large, greased cookie sheet, seam side down; shape into a ring, and pinch ends together to seal.

Using kitchen shears, make cuts in dough every inch around ring, cutting two-thirds of the way through roll at each cut. Gently turn each piece of dough on its side, slightly overlapping slices.

Cover; let rise in a warm place (85°), free from drafts, for 45 to 55 minutes or until doubled in bulk. Bake at 375° for 15 to 20 minutes or until golden brown. Transfer from cookie sheet to a wire rack; drizzle with glaze while hot. Yield: 16 to 20 servings.

Glaze:

1 cup powdered sugar
1 tablespoon plus 1 teaspoon milk
½ teaspoon vanilla extract
Dash of salt

Combine all ingredients; stir until smooth. Yield: about ½ cup.

Rosanne Petton,
Farmers Branch, Texas.

CHERRY BLOSSOM COFFEE CAKE

½ cup milk, scalded
⅓ cup sugar
⅓ cup butter
2 teaspoons salt
1 package dry yeast
¼ cup warm water (105° to 115°)
2 eggs
4 cups all-purpose flour
¼ cup softened butter, divided
1 (21-ounce) can cherry pie filling, divided
¾ cup sugar

Combine milk, ⅓ cup sugar, ⅓ cup butter, and salt; stir until butter melts. Cool to 105° to 115°.

Combine yeast and water; let stand 5 minutes. Stir in milk mixture, eggs, and flour; beat until mixture is smooth and leaves sides of bowl.

Turn dough out onto a floured surface; knead until dough is smooth and elastic (about 5 minutes).

Place dough in a greased bowl, turning to grease top. Cover and let rise in a warm place (85°), free from drafts, 2 to 2½ hours or until doubled in bulk.

Punch dough down, and divide in half. Roll out half the dough into a 24- x 6-inch rectangle. Spread 2 tablespoons softened butter down the center of dough, leaving a 2½-inch margin on each side. Spoon half of cherry pie filling over butter, leaving a 1-inch margin at both ends; sprinkle ¼ cup sugar over cherries. Fold one long side of dough over filling; fold opposite side of dough to overlap. Seal edges.

Place one end of pastry, seam side down, in the center of a well-greased 9-inch round baking pan. Wrap pastry to form a coil. Flatten dough slightly with your hand.

Starting at the center of coil, make deep slashes 1 inch apart along top of dough. Sprinkle 2 tablespoons sugar over dough. Repeat procedure with remaining half of dough. Cover and let rise in a warm place (85°), free from drafts, 1 hour or until doubled in bulk.

Bake at 350° for 35 to 40 minutes or until golden brown. Let cool 15 to 20 minutes before removing from pan. Yield: two 9-inch coffee cakes.

Georgia W. Kimmel,
Tulsa, Oklahoma.

HONEY-WALNUT SWIRL

6½ to 7 cups all-purpose flour
1 cup sugar
2 packages dry yeast
½ cup water
½ cup milk
1 cup butter, softened
3 eggs, slightly beaten
Honey-Walnut Filling
Glaze (recipe follows)
¼ cup coarsely chopped walnuts, divided

Combine 6½ cups flour, sugar, and yeast; stir well to distribute yeast.

Combine water, milk, and butter in a small saucepan; place over low heat until very warm (120° to 130°). Gradually add milk mixture to dry ingredients, stirring well. Add eggs, and beat dough 2 minutes (dough will be soft). Cover and let rise in a warm place (85°), free from drafts, until doubled in bulk.

Punch dough down, and divide in half. Turn half of dough out onto a heavily floured surface; knead lightly 6 to 8 times to form a smooth ball. Cover and let rest 15 minutes.

Place stockinette cover on rolling pin; flour well. Roll out dough into a 10- x 18-inch rectangle. Spread 1 cup Honey-Walnut Filling evenly over rectangle, leaving a 1-inch margin. Roll up dough lengthwise; pinch edge and ends to seal. Place roll, seam side down, on a greased cookie sheet.

Cover and let rise in a warm place (85°), free from drafts, until doubled in bulk. Bake at 350° for 40 to 50 minutes or until loaf sounds hollow when tapped. Transfer loaf to wire rack to cool.

Repeat procedure with the remaining half of dough. Spread half of the glaze on top of each loaf; then sprinkle each with 2 tablespoons chopped walnuts. Yield: 2 loaves.

Honey-Walnut Filling:

¾ pound walnuts, ground
¾ cup honey
¼ cup milk
¾ teaspoon ground cinnamon
½ teaspoon almond extract
½ teaspoon vanilla extract

Combine all ingredients in a small bowl; stir well. Yield: about 2 cups.

Glaze:

2 cups powdered sugar
3 to 4 tablespoons milk

Combine sugar and milk; stir until smooth. Yield: about 1 cup.

Billie Tollstam,
Fairhope, Alabama.

Tip: Non-fat dry milk costs about half as much as fluid whole milk. Keep a supply of reconstituted dry milk in the refrigerator and use it for cooking. Serve it very cold for drinking—or combine it half-and-half with whole milk if you prefer the taste.

RUM-RAISIN BUNS

1 cup milk, scalded
¼ cup sugar
¼ cup shortening
1¼ teaspoons salt
1 package dry yeast
1 egg
1½ teaspoons rum extract
3½ cups all-purpose flour, divided
2 tablespoons butter or margarine, melted
¼ cup sugar, divided
¼ cup raisins, chopped
1½ cups powdered sugar
3 tablespoons hot water
1½ teaspoons rum extract

Combine milk, ¼ cup sugar, shortening, and salt; stir until shortening melts. Cool to 105° to 115°. Add yeast, egg, 1½ teaspoons rum extract, and 1¾ cups flour; beat until smooth. Add remaining flour, and beat until mixture leaves sides of bowl.

Turn dough out onto a floured surface; knead until dough is smooth and elastic (about 5 minutes).

Place dough in a greased bowl, turning to grease top. Cover and let rise in a warm place (85°), free from drafts, 2 hours or until doubled in bulk.

Punch dough down, and divide in half. Roll each half into a 12- x 4-inch rectangle; brush with melted butter. Sprinkle 2 tablespoons sugar on each dough strip; top each with half of the raisins.

Starting at widest end, roll up each strip in jellyroll fashion; seal edges. Cut each roll into 1½-inch slices. Place slices, cut side down, in greased muffin tins. Cover and let rise in a warm place (85°), free from drafts, 1 hour and 40 minutes or until doubled in bulk.

Bake at 400° for 10 to 12 minutes or until golden brown. Remove from pan to cooling racks. Combine remaining ingredients in a small bowl; drizzle glaze over hot rolls. Yield: about 1½ dozen.
Mrs. Elizabeth Moore,
Huntsville, Alabama.

ORANGE ROLLS

1 package dry yeast
¼ cup warm water (105° to 115°)
1 cup milk, scalded
¼ cup sugar
1 teaspoon salt
¼ cup vegetable oil
1 egg, beaten
About 3½ cups all-purpose flour
Orange butter (recipe follows)

Dissolve yeast in warm water; set mixture aside.

Combine milk, sugar, and salt; stir well. Cool to 105° to 115°.

Combine yeast mixture, milk mixture, oil, and egg; stir well. Add 1¾ cups flour, and beat well. Stir in remaining flour; beat well. Cover and let rise in a warm place (85°), free from drafts, until doubled in bulk.

Punch dough down, and divide in half. Turn dough out onto a heavily floured surface (dough will be very soft). Knead each dough half lightly 6 to 8 times to form a smooth ball.

Place stockinette cover on rolling pin; flour well. Roll out each dough ball to a 14- x 9-inch rectangle. Spread ¾ cup orange butter evenly over each rectangle, leaving a 1-inch margin.

Roll up rectangles lengthwise; pinch long edges to seal (do not seal ends). Cut into 1½-inch slices. Place rolls, cut side down, in 2 well-greased 9-inch cakepans, leaving about ½ inch space between rolls. Cover and let rise in a warm place (85°), free from drafts, for 30 minutes or until doubled in bulk.

Bake at 375° for 25 to 30 minutes or until golden brown. Remove rolls from pan while hot. Yield: about 2 dozen.

Orange Butter:

½ cup butter or margarine, softened
1 cup sugar
Grated rind of 2 oranges

Combine all ingredients; beat at medium speed of electric mixer until fluffy. Yield: about 1½ cups. *Nancy Sloan,*
Lake Village, Arkansas.

CINNAMON RAISIN BREAD

2 cups milk, scalded
¼ cup butter
2 cups all-purpose flour
½ cup plus 1 tablespoon sugar
½ teaspoon salt
1 package dry yeast
3¼ to 3¾ cups all-purpose flour
1½ cups raisins
2 tablespoons plus 2 teaspoons sugar
2 teaspoons ground cinnamon
¼ cup melted butter, divided
Additional melted butter (optional)

Combine milk and ¼ cup butter, stirring until butter melts. Cool mixture to 105° to 115°.

Combine 2 cups flour, ½ cup plus 1 tablespoon sugar, salt, and yeast. Gradually add milk mixture to dry ingredients, mixing at low speed of electric mixer. Beat 2 minutes on medium speed, scraping bowl occasionally. Add ¾ cup flour; beat at medium-high speed 2 minutes. Stir in enough remaining flour to make a soft dough (2½ to 3 cups); stir in raisins.

Turn dough out onto a lightly floured surface; knead until smooth and elastic (about 7 minutes).

Place dough in a greased bowl, turning to grease top. Cover and let rise in a warm place (85°), free from drafts, 1 hour and 20 minutes or until doubled in bulk.

Punch dough down; turn out on a lightly floured surface. Cover and let dough rest 15 minutes.

Combine 2 tablespoons plus 2 teaspoons sugar and cinnamon; divide in half. Set aside.

Divide dough in half, and place on a lightly floured surface. Roll each half into an 18- x 8-inch rectangle; brush each rectangle with 2 tablespoons melted butter. Sprinkle each with half of sugar mixture. Roll up rectangles in jellyroll fashion, beginning at narrow edge. Pinch seams and ends together to seal. Place rolls, seam side down, in 2 well-greased 9- x 5- x 3-inch loafpans.

Cover and let rise 55 minutes or until doubled in bulk. Bake at 350° for 25 to 30 minutes or until loaves sound hollow when tapped. Brush with melted butter, if desired. Remove from pans; cool on wire racks. Yield: 2 loaves.
Mrs. Carolee Followill,
Tuscaloosa, Alabama.

CINNAMON-NUT BUBBLE BREAD

1 cup commercial sour cream
½ cup sugar
2 packages dry yeast
1 teaspoon salt
3 eggs
½ cup butter or margarine, softened
4½ cups all-purpose flour, divided
1 cup sugar
1 cup chopped walnuts
¾ teaspoon ground cinnamon
½ cup melted butter or margarine
1 cup powdered sugar
2 tablespoons milk

Combine sour cream, ½ cup sugar, yeast, and salt; mix well. Add eggs, ½ cup butter, and 2¼ cups flour; beat until mixture is smooth. Add remaining flour; mix well.

Turn dough out onto a floured surface; knead until dough is smooth and elastic (5 to 8 minutes).

Place dough in a greased bowl, turning to grease top. Cover and let rise in a warm place (85°), free from drafts, 1½ to 2 hours or until doubled in bulk.

Punch dough down; turn dough over and cover. Let rise 45 minutes.

Combine 1 cup sugar, walnuts, and cinnamon; stir well. Punch dough down; shape into 1½-inch balls. Dip each in butter; roll in sugar mixture. Layer dough balls in a well-greased 10-inch tube pan (one piece). Cover and let rise in a warm place (85°), free from drafts, 45 minutes or until doubled in bulk.

Bake at 375° for 40 to 50 minutes. Cool bread 10 minutes in pan; invert onto serving platter.

Combine powdered sugar and milk; drizzle over warm bread. Yield: one 10-inch coffee cake.
Claudette McLeod,
McLean, Virginia.

STICKY BUNS

¾ cup milk, scalded
¼ cup sugar
¼ cup shortening
1 teaspoon salt
¼ cup warm water (105° to 115°)
1 package dry yeast
1 egg, slightly beaten
3½ to 3¾ cups all-purpose flour
⅔ cup firmly packed brown sugar
⅔ cup light corn syrup
1 tablespoon melted butter or margarine
Dash of ground cinnamon
2 tablespoons softened butter or margarine
1 tablespoon plus 1 teaspoon sugar
1 teaspoon ground cinnamon
¼ to ½ cup raisins

Combine milk, ¼ cup sugar, shortening, and salt; stir until shortening melts. Cool to 105° to 115°.

Combine water and yeast; let mixture stand 5 minutes.

Add yeast mixture, egg, and 2 cups flour to milk mixture; beat until smooth. Add enough remaining flour to make a soft dough (about 1½ to 1¾ cups).

Turn dough out on a lightly floured surface; knead until dough is smooth and elastic (5 to 8 minutes). Place in a well-greased bowl, turning to grease top. Cover and let rise in a warm place (85°), free from drafts, 1½ hours or until doubled in bulk.

Combine brown sugar, corn syrup, melted butter, and a dash of cinnamon; stir well. Spread mixture in a lightly greased 9-inch square pan; set aside.

Punch dough down; turn out on a lightly floured surface. Roll out dough to a 20- x 10-inch rectangle (about ¼ inch thick); spread butter over dough, leaving a narrow margin on all sides. Combine 1 tablespoon plus 1 teaspoon sugar and 1 teaspoon cinnamon; sprinkle over butter. Sprinkle dough with raisins.

Roll up dough, jellyroll fashion, beginning at long side. Pinch edges and ends to seal. Cut roll into 1½-inch slices. Place slices, cut side down, over syrup mixture in pan. Bake at 400° for 15 to 20 minutes or until golden brown. Invert immediately onto serving platter. Serve warm. Yield: about 16 rolls.
Mrs. Gracie Moore,
Winchester, Tennessee.

Cheesecakes To Rave About

Tempting is the only way to describe these cheesecakes. Their golden graham cracker crusts and firm, rich fillings are hard to resist. Each recipe offers a slight variation to this all-time favorite, but the basic theme remains the same—delicious.

Sweet toppings complete Fruit-Glazed Cheesecake and the Cherry-Topped Cheesecake. Deluxe Cheesecake is exactly as its name implies. And although cream cheese is usually the basis for cheesecake, we've included one recipe that also calls for cottage cheese.

CHERRY-TOPPED CHEESECAKE

1 cup graham cracker crumbs
3 tablespoons sugar
3 tablespoons butter or margarine, melted
¼ teaspoon ground cinnamon
3 (8-ounce) packages cream cheese, softened
2 teaspoons lemon juice
1 cup sugar
5 eggs
¼ teaspoon salt
1½ cups commercial sour cream
2 tablespoons sugar
½ teaspoon vanilla extract
1 (21-ounce) can cherry pie filling

Combine graham cracker crumbs, 3 tablespoons sugar, butter, and cinnamon in a medium bowl; mix well. Press into a 10-inch springform pan; set aside.

Beat cream cheese and lemon juice in a large mixing bowl until soft and creamy. Add 1 cup sugar, eggs, and salt; beat on medium speed of electric mixer for 10 minutes. Pour mixture into crust. Bake at 350° for 45 minutes. Remove to wire rack and let stand 20 minutes.

Combine sour cream, 2 tablespoons sugar, and vanilla in a small bowl; stir well. Spread over cheesecake. Bake at 350° for 10 minutes; cool. Chill before removing from pan; top with cherry pie filling. Yield: 10 to 12 servings.
Mrs. George Sellers,
Newport News, Virginia.

DELUXE CHEESECAKE

1½ cups graham cracker crumbs
2 tablespoons sugar
¼ cup plus 2 tablespoons butter or margarine, melted
1½ teaspoons ground cinnamon
3 (8-ounce) packages cream cheese, softened
1 cup sugar
3 eggs
1 teaspoon vanilla extract, divided
1 (16-ounce) carton commercial sour cream
3 tablespoons sugar

Combine crumbs, 2 tablespoons sugar, butter, and cinnamon in a medium bowl; mix well. Press into a 10-inch springform pan; set aside.

Beat cream cheese in a large mixing bowl until soft and creamy. Gradually add 1 cup sugar, beating until fluffy. Add eggs, one at a time, beating well after each addition. Stir in ½ teaspoon vanilla. Pour cream cheese mixture into crust; bake at 375° for 25 to 35 minutes or until cheesecake is set.

Beat sour cream on medium speed of electric mixer for 2 minutes. Add 3 tablespoons sugar and remaining ½ teaspoon vanilla; beat 1 minute longer. Spread over cheesecake.

Bake at 500° for 5 to 8 minutes or until bubbly. Cool; chill 8 hours or overnight. Remove from pan before serving. Yield: 10 to 12 servings.
Mrs. Hugh Ellis,
Gadsden, Alabama.

Tip: Press plastic wrap directly on surface of custards, puddings or white sauce right after cooking, to prevent a skin from forming.

COTTAGE CHEESE CHEESECAKE

1¼ cups graham cracker crumbs
⅓ cup butter or margarine, melted
1 tablespoon sugar
2 cups small-curd cottage cheese
2 (8-ounce) packages cream cheese, softened
1 (16-ounce) carton commercial sour cream
1½ cups sugar
4 eggs, beaten
½ cup butter or margarine, melted
3 tablespoons all-purpose flour
3 tablespoons cornstarch
1 tablespoon plus 1 teaspoon lemon juice
1 teaspoon vanilla extract

Combine crumbs, ⅓ cup butter, and 1 tablespoon sugar; mix well. Press into a 10-inch springform pan; set aside.

Place cottage cheese in container of electric blender; blend until smooth, turning blender off every 15 seconds to scrape down sides.

Combine cottage cheese and remaining ingredients in a large mixing bowl; beat until fluffy. Pour mixture into crust.

Bake at 325° for 1 hour and 20 minutes. Turn off oven; allow cheesecake to remain in oven 2 hours. Chill overnight; remove from pan before serving. Yield: 10 to 12 servings.

Billie Soncrant,
Tarpon Springs, Florida.

FRUIT-GLAZED CHEESECAKE

1½ cups graham cracker crumbs
⅓ cup powdered sugar
½ cup butter or margarine, melted
3 (8-ounce) packages cream cheese, softened
1 cup sugar
4 eggs
1 teaspoon vanilla extract
1 (16-ounce) carton commercial sour cream
1 (21-ounce) can fruit pie filling

Combine crumbs, powdered sugar, and butter in a medium bowl; mix well. Press into a 10-inch springform pan; set aside.

Beat cream cheese in a large mixing bowl until soft and creamy. Gradually add sugar, beating until fluffy. Add eggs, one at a time, beating well after each addition. Stir in vanilla.

Pour cream cheese mixture into crust. Bake at 350° for 50 minutes. Spread sour cream over top; bake 5 additional minutes. Cool; top with fruit pie filling. Chill overnight; remove from pan before serving. Yield: 10 to 12 servings.

Mrs. Elizabeth Moore,
Huntsville, Alabama.

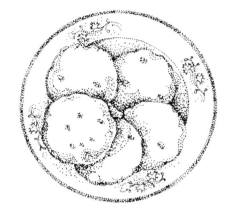

A Sweet Touch Of Raisins

With many fresh fruits in short supply, you'll find raisins a bountiful and flavorful complement to many types of foods. We think you'll like the tasty combinations presented here.

CURRIED APPLE-RAISIN SALAD

2 apples, cored and cubed
1 cup chopped celery
½ cup raisins
½ cup coarsely chopped walnuts
¼ cup mayonnaise
¼ cup commercial sour cream
1 tablespoon lemon juice
1 teaspoon salt
¼ to ½ teaspoon curry powder
Lettuce leaves
Apple wedges (optional)

Combine apple, celery, raisins, and walnuts; toss lightly to mix. Combine mayonnaise, sour cream, lemon juice, salt, and curry powder, mixing well.

Pour the sauce mixture over apple mixture; stir gently, coating apples thoroughly. Serve in a lettuce-lined bowl; garnish with apple wedges, if desired. Yield: 6 servings.

Mrs. Janis Moyer,
Farmersville, Texas.

ALLTIME FAVORITE RAISIN COOKIES

2 cups raisins
1 cup water
1¾ cups sugar
1 cup shortening
2 eggs, slightly beaten
1 teaspoon vanilla extract
3½ cups all-purpose flour
1 teaspoon baking powder
1 teaspoon soda
1 teaspoon salt
½ teaspoon ground cinnamon
½ teaspoon ground nutmeg
1 cup chopped pecans or walnuts

Combine raisins and water in a medium saucepan; bring to a boil, and boil about 3 minutes. Cool. (Do not drain.)

Gradually add sugar to shortening, beating well after each addition. Add eggs; beat well. Stir in raisins with liquid and vanilla.

Combine dry ingredients; gradually add to raisin mixture, stirring after each addition. Stir in pecans.

Drop by tablespoonfuls 2 inches apart onto well-greased cookie sheets. Bake at 375° for 10 to 12 minutes or until browned. Yield: 6 dozen.

Mrs. Elmer Underwood,
Knoxville, Tennessee.

ORANGE-RAISIN CARROTS

1 pound carrots, peeled and sliced
¾ cup water
½ teaspoon salt
2 tablespoons cornstarch
1 cup orange juice
½ cup raisins
1 tablespoon sugar

Combine carrots, water, and salt in a medium saucepan; bring to a boil. Cover, reduce heat, and simmer 6 to 8 minutes or until carrots are crisp-tender.

Dissolve cornstarch in orange juice; stir into carrot mixture. Stir in raisins and sugar. Cook over medium heat, stirring constantly, until smooth and thickened. Yield: 4 servings.

C. Breithaupt,
Boerne, Texas.

Tip: If only drained fruit is called for in a recipe, use quarters and halves rather than the more costly whole fruit.

Soups Brimming With Vegetables

Soups are a welcome addition to any meal during the chilly winter months. In this selection of recipes you'll find a variety of soups and chowders that call for vegetables as a base. Served with a sandwich or with cheese and crackers, they make a satisfying lunch or supper.

Cheesy Vegetable Chowder is chock full of bacon, onion, carrots, potatoes, and corn, while seven vegetables are simmered together for flavorful Hearty Vegetable Soup. We've also included soups filled with fresh mushrooms, dried beans, and cabbage.

QUICK BEEFY VEGETABLE SOUP

1 pound ground beef
1 (16-ounce) package frozen mixed
    vegetables
2 cups tomato juice
2 cups beef broth
2 cups cubed potatoes
½ teaspoon salt
¼ teaspoon pepper

Brown beef in a 3-quart saucepan, stirring to crumble; drain off drippings. Return beef to saucepan. Add remaining ingredients; bring to a boil. Reduce heat, and simmer 20 to 25 minutes or until potatoes are tender. Yield: 4 servings.
Mrs. LeRoy Miller,
Hydro, Oklahoma.

CHEESY VEGETABLE CHOWDER

10 slices bacon, chopped
1 cup chopped onion
1 cup chopped carrot
1 cup water
2½ cups diced potatoes
2 chicken bouillon cubes
3 cups milk
1 (17-ounce) can whole kernel corn,
    drained
3 cups (12 ounces) shredded Cheddar
    cheese
3 tablespoons all-purpose flour
Pepper to taste

Cook bacon in a 4-quart Dutch oven until browned. Remove bacon, reserving drippings in Dutch oven; set bacon aside.

Sauté onion in drippings until tender. Add bacon, carrot, water, potatoes, and bouillon cubes; bring to a boil. Reduce heat; cover and simmer 20 to 25 minutes or until potatoes are tender. Stir in milk and corn; heat thoroughly.

Combine cheese and flour, tossing until cheese is well coated. Add to soup; stir until cheese melts. Season to taste with pepper. Yield: 6 to 8 servings.
Mrs. W. J. Scherffius,
Mountain Home, Arkansas.

SAUSAGE-POTATO SOUP

1 pound bulk pork sausage
5 cups sliced uncooked potatoes
2 medium onions, sliced
1½ cups water
1½ teaspoons salt
¼ teaspoon celery seeds
3 tablespoons finely chopped parsley
2½ to 3 cups milk

Brown sausage, stirring to crumble; drain and set aside.

Combine potatoes, onion, water, salt, and celery seeds in a large Dutch oven; cover and bring to a boil. Reduce heat, and simmer about 20 to 25 minutes or until potatoes are tender. Slightly mash potatoes. Add sausage, parsley, and milk; heat well. Yield: 6 to 8 servings.
Mrs. Rich Hendrick,
Russellville, Kentucky.

HEARTY CABBAGE CHOWDER

3 tablespoons melted butter or margarine
2½ cups (½ pound) finely chopped
    cabbage
1 large potato, finely chopped
1½ cups water, divided
1 chicken bouillon cube
2 cups milk
Salt and pepper to taste
1 cup (4 ounces) shredded Swiss cheese

Combine butter, cabbage, potato, and ½ cup water in a 3-quart saucepan; cover and cook over low heat about 20 to 25 minutes or until potatoes are tender. Slightly mash potatoes. Add remaining water, bouillon cube, and milk; cover and simmer over low heat 15 minutes. Add salt, pepper, and cheese; stir until cheese melts. Yield: 6 servings.
Mrs. Everett Peck,
Isle of Palms, South Carolina.

MUSHROOM-ONION SOUP

2 pounds fresh mushrooms, sliced
1 large onion, thinly sliced
1 clove garlic, minced
¼ cup melted butter or margarine
2 tablespoons tomato paste
6 (10¾-ounce) cans chicken broth,
    undiluted
¼ cup grated Parmesan cheese
1 cup dry white wine
2 teaspoons salt
¼ teaspoon pepper
Croutons (optional)
Grated Parmesan cheese (optional)

Sauté mushrooms, onion, and garlic in butter in a heavy 4-quart saucepan until onion is tender. Stir in tomato paste; simmer about 1 minute. Add broth, ¼ cup Parmesan cheese, wine, salt, and pepper; simmer 1 hour. Serve with croutons and additional cheese, if desired. Yield: 10 to 12 servings.
Diane E. France,
Charlottesville, Virginia.

BEAN SOUP

3 cups (1½ pounds) dried navy beans
1 (16-ounce) can tomatoes, undrained
1 large onion, finely chopped
1 meaty ham hock (about 1 pound)
2 cups chicken broth
½ cup white wine
Salt and pepper to taste

Wash beans thoroughly; cover with water, and soak overnight.

Drain beans, and place in a large, heavy Dutch oven. Drain tomatoes, reserving juice. Chop tomatoes coarsely. Add tomatoes, reserved juice, onion, ham hock, chicken broth, and wine to beans. Add enough water to cover the beans; bring to a boil. Reduce heat; cover and simmer about 1 to 1½ hours or until beans are tender, adding more water during cooking, if necessary.

Remove ham hock and half the beans; remove meat from ham hock. Shred meat with a fork, and set aside. Place beans in container of electric blender or food processor; puree. Return meat and pureed beans to Dutch oven; heat thoroughly, stirring occasionally. Season to taste with salt and pepper. Yield: 12 to 15 servings.
Mrs. William J. Morris,
Titusville, Florida.

Tip: If soups, stews, or other foods are too salty, add a teaspoon of vinegar and a teaspoon of sugar and reheat.

HEARTY VEGETABLE SOUP

7 cups water
1 (28-ounce) can whole tomatoes, chopped
1 cup chopped onion
1 cup diced potatoes
1 cup sliced carrots
1 (10-ounce) package frozen peas
1 (10-ounce) package frozen baby lima beans
1 (10-ounce) package frozen whole kernel corn
4 chicken bouillon cubes
2 teaspoons salt
1 bay leaf
¼ teaspoon pepper

Combine all ingredients in a 4-quart Dutch oven; bring to a boil. Reduce heat, and simmer 1 hour or until vegetables are tender. Yield: 12 to 14 servings.
Mrs. Rose Naquin,
Melville, Louisiana.

Perk Up
Plain Vegetables

This collection of vegetable recipes boasts a variety of simple additions that make a good vegetable even better. Most include ingredients you will probably have on hand and can be mixed up in minutes.

A luscious pimiento-and-cheese sauce highlights the flavor in Lima Beans Deluxe. For a really sweet vegetable, try the Sweet Potato Casserole with a crunchy, nutty topping.

ITALIAN-STYLE EGGPLANT AND ZUCCHINI

⅔ cup all-purpose flour
Salt
1 medium eggplant, peeled and cut into ¼-inch slices
⅓ cup milk
Hot vegetable oil
2 medium zucchini, thinly sliced
1 medium onion, chopped
⅛ teaspoon red pepper
2 cups cottage cheese
2 eggs
½ cup dry breadcrumbs
1 (8-ounce) package mozzarella cheese, diced
1 (15½-ounce) jar spaghetti sauce with mushrooms

Combine flour and 1 teaspoon salt, mixing well. Dip eggplant slices in milk; dredge in flour mixture, and fry in hot oil until golden brown. Drain on paper towels, and set aside. Reserve drippings in skillet.

Add zucchini and onion to skillet; sauté vegetables until barely tender. Stir in red pepper.

Combine cottage cheese, eggs, and ½ teaspoon salt in a small bowl; mix well, and set aside.

Arrange half of eggplant slices in a lightly greased 13- x 9- x 2-inch baking dish. Spoon half of zucchini and onion mixture over eggplant. Top with half of breadcrumbs, half of cottage cheese mixture, half of mozzarella cheese, and half of spaghetti sauce. Repeat layers. Bake at 350° for 1 hour or until bubbly. Yield: 6 to 8 servings.
Mrs. James Tuthill,
Virginia Beach, Virginia.

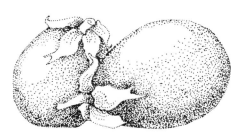

LIMA BEANS DELUXE

2 tablespoons butter or margarine
2 tablespoons all-purpose flour
1 cup milk
1 teaspoon salt
⅛ teaspoon pepper
2 cups cooked and drained lima beans
½ cup chopped pimiento
1 cup (¼ pound) shredded Cheddar cheese
2 tablespoons catsup
2 tablespoons melted butter or margarine
½ cup soft breadcrumbs

Melt 2 tablespoons butter in a heavy saucepan over low heat; blend in flour and cook 1 minute, stirring constantly. Gradually add milk; cook over medium heat, stirring constantly, until thickened and bubbly. Stir in salt and pepper.

Add beans, pimiento, cheese, and catsup to sauce; mix well, and pour into a greased 1½-quart casserole. Combine melted butter and breadcrumbs; mix well, and sprinkle over top. Bake at 375° for 30 minutes. Yield: 6 servings.
Mrs. Mae McClaugherty,
Marble Falls, Texas.

BRUSSELS SPROUTS AND RICE

1 (10¾-ounce) can cream of celery soup, undiluted
1 cup milk
1 cup water
1 tablespoon butter or margarine
1 teaspoon salt
⅔ cup uncooked regular rice
2 (10-ounce) packages frozen brussels sprouts

Combine soup, milk, 1 cup water, butter, and salt in a medium saucepan; bring to a boil. Stir in rice and cover; reduce heat and simmer mixture 15 minutes, stirring occasionally. Stir in brussels sprouts; cover and cook 15 minutes or until brussels sprouts are tender. Yield: 6 to 8 servings.
Mrs. Kenneth George,
Dickson, Tennessee.

SWEET POTATO CASSEROLE

3 cups cooked, mashed sweet potatoes
1 cup sugar
2 eggs
1 teaspoon vanilla extract
⅓ cup milk
½ cup butter or margarine
1 cup firmly packed brown sugar
⅓ cup all-purpose flour
⅓ cup butter or margarine
1 cup finely chopped pecans

Combine sweet potatoes, sugar, eggs, vanilla, milk, and ½ cup butter; beat with electric mixer until smooth. Spoon into a greased 2-quart shallow casserole. Combine brown sugar, flour, ⅓ cup butter, and pecans; sprinkle over top of casserole. Bake at 350° for 30 minutes. Yield: 8 to 10 servings. *Nancy Sturup,*
Columbus, Georgia.

Right: *Enjoy rock shrimp like you would regular shrimp, as appetizer or main dish. This is Sweet-and-Sour Rock Shrimp Tails (page 3) served over almond-topped rice. Complete the meal with a fruit-vegetable salad and hot rolls.*

Page 28: *This tempting array of hot yeast breads includes Cherry Blossom Coffee Cake (page 21), Honey-Walnut Swirl (page 21), and Rum-Raisin Buns (page 22).*

Fabulous Meat Entrées Are His Specialty

John Condon of Tulsa, Oklahoma, doesn't do much cooking for his family on an everyday basis; but when it's time to entertain, he takes over in the kitchen with a capable hand. John and his wife, Rosemary, are known for their sit-down dinner parties for up to 60 people, and that's when John shows his cooking expertise.

When he's cooking for such a large group, John likes to prepare large meat entrées, such as Buffet Turkey and Prune-Stuffed Pork Loin Roast. He might accompany them with an authentic Southern side dish, like Grits Soufflé, and a Polish bread. Since John has a keen eye for garnishing, his entrées always have an elegant look to match their outstanding flavor.

Along with John's specialties are recipes from other men who like to cook.

BUFFET TURKEY

1 (16- to 18-pound) turkey
2 tablespoons salt
1 tablespoon grated fresh gingerroot
1 teaspoon cumin seeds
½ cup butter or margarine, softened
1 bay leaf, crumbled
1½ teaspoons fresh tarragon leaves or ½ teaspoon dried tarragon leaves
1½ teaspoons fresh rosemary leaves or ½ teaspoon dried rosemary leaves
1½ teaspoons fresh dillweed or ½ teaspoon dried dillweed
1 tablespoon honey
1 tablespoon good gravy base
3 to 6 drops hot sauce
About ¼ cup dry sherry
Cranberry glaze (recipe follows)
Fresh parsley sprigs (optional)

Remove giblets, and cut excess fat from turkey. Rinse turkey thoroughly with cold water; pat dry.

Rub cavity and skin of turkey with salt, gingerroot, and cumin seeds. Wrap turkey securely in plastic wrap or place in a large plastic bag; refrigerate overnight.

Let turkey sit at room temperature for 1 hour. Rub cavity and skin of turkey with butter; sprinkle the remaining herbs except the parsley into cavity of turkey.

Tie ends of legs to tail with cord or twine, or tuck them under flap of skin around tail. Lift wingtips up and over back so they are tucked under bird. Place turkey on a roasting rack, breast side up.

Combine honey, gravy base, and hot sauce; stir well. Brush turkey with honey mixture and some of the sherry. Insert meat thermometer in breast or meaty part of thigh, making sure end of thermometer does not touch bone. Bake at 325° for 1 hour or until turkey begins to brown. Reduce heat to 300°, and bake 20 minutes per pound (about 5½ to 6 hours), or until thermometer reaches 185°. (Turkey will be very brown.) During entire baking time, rotate pan one-half turn every 20 minutes; brush turkey with sherry, and baste with drippings.

When turkey is two-thirds done, cut the cord or band of skin holding the drumstick ends to the tail; this will ensure that the inside of the thighs is cooked. Turkey is done when drumsticks are easy to move up and down.

Place turkey on platter; brush cooled Cranberry Glaze over turkey, using all of glaze. Garnish with parsley, if desired. Yield: 30 to 40 servings.

Cranberry Glaze:

1½ cups cranberry juice cocktail
½ cup sugar
1½ tablespoons cornstarch

Combine all ingredients in a small saucepan. Cook over low heat, stirring constantly, 2 minutes; cook an additional 8 minutes or until thickened and bubbly, stirring frequently. Let glaze cool. Yield: about 1¼ cups.

PRUNE-STUFFED PORK LOIN ROAST

1 (15-ounce) package pitted prunes
2 cups hard cider
¾ cup dry sherry, divided
1 (8¼-ounce) can pineapple slices, drained
1 tablespoon seasoned salt
1 tablespoon lemon pepper
1 tablespoon grated fresh gingerroot
1 (6- to 8-pound) boneless double pork loin roast, cut for rolling

Combine prunes and cider in a medium saucepan. Bring to a boil; lower heat and simmer 20 minutes. Remove from heat; stir in ½ cup sherry.

Pour remaining ¼ cup sherry over pineapple; set aside.

Combine seasonings; rub on roast. Place one roast on a roasting rack, fat side down. Reserve 4 prunes in liquid; remove remaining prunes with a slotted spoon and place on roast. Place remaining roast, fat side up, atop prunes. Tie roast at 2- to 3-inch intervals with cord.

Insert meat thermometer into thickest part of roast, making sure end of thermometer does not touch prunes or fat. Bake at 325° for 35 to 40 minutes per pound or until thermometer reaches 170°, basting often with reserved prune liquid.

Remove pineapple from sherry. Garnish roast with pineapple slices and reserved prunes; serve with pan drippings. Yield: 14 to 16 servings.

KOLECZ (POLISH BREAD)

2 cups milk, scalded
½ cup butter or margarine, melted
1 package dry yeast
¼ cup warm water (105° to 115°)
3 eggs, beaten
1 teaspoon vanilla extract
About 7 cups all-purpose flour
1 teaspoon ground cinnamon
¼ teaspoon ground nutmeg
2 teaspoons salt
½ cup sugar
1 (15-ounce) package golden seedless raisins
1 cup cottage cheese
2 eggs, beaten

Combine milk and butter in a small saucepan; cool to 105° to 115°. Dissolve yeast in warm water. Add the yeast mixture, 3 eggs, and vanilla to the milk mixture.

Combine dry ingredients and raisins. Pour milk mixture into a large bowl; gradually stir in flour mixture, mixing well. Cover and let rise in a warm place (85°), free from drafts, about 1½ hours or until doubled. Punch dough down.

Cover a large baking sheet with aluminum foil; lightly grease foil. Divide dough into 3 equal parts; shape into round loaves and place on foil. Let rise 1 hour in a warm place (85°).

Combine cottage cheese and 2 eggs in a small bowl, mixing well; spread over top of loaves. Bake at 350° for 45 to 50 minutes or until done. Yield: 3 loaves.

Tip: Bread stays fresher, longer, at room temperature or frozen. Do NOT store in refrigerator.

GRITS SOUFFLE

1½ cups regular grits
6 cups boiling water
2 teaspoons seasoned salt
1 teaspoon onion salt
1 teaspoon garlic salt
¾ teaspoon Worcestershire sauce
½ cup butter or margarine
3 eggs, slightly beaten
½ to 1 pound Longhorn cheese, cubed
Paprika

Cook grits in boiling water 5 minutes. Stir in salt, Worcestershire sauce, and butter.

Stir 2 to 3 tablespoons grits into eggs; stir egg mixture into grits. Add cheese; stir until cheese melts. Pour into a buttered 2-quart soufflé dish; sprinkle heavily with paprika. Cover and refrigerate overnight. Bake at 350° for 1½ hours. Yield: 12 to 16 servings.

SPAGHETTI WITH PARSLEY AND WALNUT SAUCE

3 cups fresh parsley sprigs
1 cup walnut halves or pieces
3 cloves garlic
3 tablespoons grated Parmesan cheese
1 teaspoon basil leaves
1 cup olive oil
Salt to taste
1 (16-ounce) package spaghetti
Additional walnut halves (optional)
Additional Parmesan cheese (optional)

Combine parsley, 1 cup walnuts, garlic, 3 tablespoons Parmesan cheese, basil, and olive oil in container of electric blender; process until smooth. Add salt, and set aside.

Cook spaghetti according to package directions; drain well. Pour parsley mixture over hot spaghetti, tossing lightly. If desired, garnish with additional walnut halves and serve with additional Parmesan cheese. Yield: 6 servings.
Gene Leyden,
Bluemont, Virginia.

SAVORY POTATO SALAD

6 medium potatoes, peeled and cut into
    1-inch cubes
1 medium onion, chopped
2 hard-cooked eggs, chopped
1 cup mayonnaise
1 tablespoon olive oil
1 tablespoon vinegar
½ teaspoon dried dillweed
Salt and pepper

Cook potatoes in a small amount of boiling salted water for 10 to 15 minutes or until just tender; drain well.

Combine potatoes, onion, and eggs; set aside. Combine mayonnaise, oil, vinegar, and dillweed; gently stir into potato mixture. Season potato salad with salt and pepper to taste. Serve warm, or cover and chill. Yield: 6 to 8 servings.
Randall De Trinis,
Brevard, North Carolina.

SPECIAL BLUE CHEESE DRESSING

1 cup mayonnaise
¾ cup buttermilk
1 (6-ounce) package blue cheese, crumbled
1 teaspoon steak sauce
7 drops hot sauce
1 tablespoon Italian seasoning
1 tablespoon parsley flakes
1 clove garlic, pressed

Combine all ingredients in a medium bowl; stir well. Chill thoroughly in a covered container. Serve on tossed salad or with assorted raw vegetables. Yield: about 2½ cups. *Jack Different,*
Pass Christian, Mississippi.

Chicken In A Biscuit

Here's a new idea for leftover chicken using convenient, refrigerated crescent dinner rolls as the basis for golden-brown Chicken in a Biscuit.

Chopped chicken is combined with cream cheese, pimientos, and onion. The mixture is then wrapped in the dough, topped with breadcrumbs, and baked. The result is a pastry so plump that two or three will make a filling meal.

CHICKEN IN A BISCUIT

1 (3-ounce) package cream cheese,
    softened
2 tablespoons milk
2 cups finely chopped cooked chicken
2 tablespoons drained, chopped pimiento
2 tablespoons minced onion or chives
Salt and pepper to taste
1 (8-ounce) can refrigerated crescent
    dinner rolls
¼ cup melted butter or margarine
¼ cup Italian-style breadcrumbs

Flaky pastry surrounds a moist chicken mixture in this recipe for Chicken in a Biscuit.

Combine cream cheese and milk; beat until smooth. Add chicken, pimiento, onion, salt, and pepper; stir well.

Separate dinner roll dough into 2 rectangles, firmly pressing perforations to seal; cut each rectangle into four 4- x 5-inch rectangles. Place a heaping tablespoonful of chicken mixture on each rectangle. Fold sides and ends of dough toward center, moisten edges with water, and pinch to seal. Shape into biscuits. Place seam side down on cookie sheet; brush with butter, and sprinkle with breadcrumbs. Bake at 350° for 25 minutes or until golden brown. Yield: 8 biscuits. *Mrs. Sarah Phelps, Baltimore, Maryland.*

CUCUMBER SPREAD

2 cucumbers, unpeeled and grated
1 small onion, grated
1 (8-ounce) package cream cheese, softened
2 tablespoons salad dressing or mayonnaise
½ teaspoon seasoned salt
¼ teaspoon lemon juice (optional)

Place cucumber and onion on paper towels, and squeeze out moisture.

Beat cream cheese until smooth, and stir in vegetables, salad dressing, and salt; add lemon juice, if desired. Serve spread with fresh vegetables or crackers. Yield: about 2 cups.
Varniece Warren, Hermitage, Arkansas.

CHEESE BISCUITS

2 cups (½ pound) shredded sharp Cheddar cheese
2¼ cups all-purpose flour
1 cup butter or margarine, softened
1 cup chopped pecans
1 teaspoon Worcestershire sauce
½ teaspoon salt
½ teaspoon red pepper

Combine all ingredients, mixing well. Drop by heaping teaspoonfuls onto ungreased baking sheets. Bake at 425° for 12 to 15 minutes. Yield: 6 dozen.
Clara McWillie, Tulsa, Oklahoma.

You're Prepared With These Appetizers

Be prepared for guests with appetizers that can be served in minutes. A handful of Spiced Pecans will keep your guests satisfied while you have time to slice and bake Asparagus Rolls. Cucumber Spread is also handy to keep in the refrigerator, ready to be served with assorted fresh vegetables or crackers.

ASPARAGUS ROLLS

20 slices white bread, crusts removed
3 ounces blue cheese
1 (8-ounce) package cream cheese, softened
1 egg, beaten
1 (14½-ounce) can asparagus spears, drained
1 cup melted butter or margarine

Use a rolling pin to flatten each slice of bread. Combine blue cheese, cream cheese, and egg in a small mixing bowl, mixing well. Spread evenly on bread, covering to edges.

Place 1 asparagus spear on each slice of bread; roll up, and secure with 3 toothpicks. Dip in melted butter. Place on a baking sheet and freeze.

Partially thaw the asparagus rolls, and slice each roll into 3 equal pieces. Bake the rolls at 375° for 15 minutes. Yield: 60 appetizer servings.
Mrs. James Petty, Columbia, South Carolina.

SPICED PECANS

1 cup sugar
1 to 2 teaspoons ground cinnamon
1 teaspoon salt
½ teaspoon ground nutmeg
¼ teaspoon ground cloves
¼ cup water
2 cups pecan halves

Combine first 6 ingredients in a large saucepan; stir well. Place over medium heat, stirring constantly until sugar dissolves; then cook to soft ball stage (about 232°). Remove from heat; add pecans, stirring until well coated.

Spread pecans on waxed paper, and separate nuts with a fork. Let cool. Yield: 2 cups. *Mrs. Ed Lee Niles, Marshall, North Carolina.*

SURPRISE CHEESE PUFFS

1 cup (¼ pound) shredded Cheddar cheese
½ cup all-purpose flour
¼ cup butter or margarine, softened
½ teaspoon paprika
¼ teaspoon salt
About 3 dozen pimiento-stuffed olives

Combine first 5 ingredients; mix well with a fork.

Drain olives well on paper towels. Shape a thin layer of cheese mixture around each olive; place on an ungreased cookie sheet. Bake at 425° for 8 to 10 minutes or until lightly browned. Yield: about 3 dozen.
Note: Cocktail onions may be substituted for olives. *Lilly S. Bradley, Salem, Virginia.*

Make A Wintertime Jam

Jam making doesn't have to be a summertime activity. Dried and canned fruits are available year-round and provide a delicious start for jam.

Before beginning jam making, prepare jelly glasses or canning jars. Be sure all jars are in perfect condition and use only new lids. Jars should be washed in warm suds and boiled 10 minutes to sterilize. The jars should be kept hot until used to prevent cracking.

Let sealed jars stand overnight before storing to be sure the seal has been made. Label with name of product and date. Store in a cool, dark, dry place.

GOLDEN APRICOT JAM

3 cups chopped dried apricots
1 (20-ounce) can crushed pineapple, undrained
½ cup lemon juice
4 cups water
8 cups sugar

Combine all ingredients in a large saucepan; bring to a boil, stirring often. Reduce heat, and simmer for 1 hour to 1 hour and 15 minutes or until temperature registers 221° on a candy thermometer; stir almost constantly during cooking to prevent scorching.

Ladle hot mixture into hot sterilized jars; leaving ½-inch headspace; cover at once with metal lids, and screw metal bands tight. Yield: about 8 cups.
Ruth Sellers, Abilene, Texas.

These Cornish Hens Are Brandied

These Cornish hens are stuffed with a cornbread dressing enhanced with brandy and pecans. Brandy also flavors the butter sauce used to baste the hens during baking.

BRANDY-BUTTERED CORNISH HENS

6 (1- to 1½-pound) Cornish hens
Salt and pepper
Pecan Stuffing
½ cup melted butter or margarine
¼ cup apricot-, peach-, or plum-flavored brandy

Remove giblets from hens; reserve for another use. Rinse hens with cold water, and pat dry. Sprinkle cavity of each with salt and pepper. Secure neck skin to back with toothpick; lift wingtips up and over back so they are tucked under hen.

Lightly stuff cavity of hens with Pecan Stuffing; close cavity, and secure with toothpicks. Tie leg ends to tail with cord or string. Brush hens with butter, and sprinkle generously with pepper. Combine remaining butter with brandy.

Place hens, breast side up, in a large shallow baking pan. Bake at 350° for 1 to 1½ hours, depending on size of hens; baste every 10 minutes with brandy mixture. Yield: 6 servings.

Pecan Stuffing:

1 cup unsweetened apple juice
¼ cup apricot-, peach-, or plum-flavored brandy
¼ cup butter or margarine
1 (8-ounce) package cornbread stuffing mix
¾ cup chopped pecans

Combine apple juice, brandy, and butter in a large saucepan; cook over medium heat, stirring occasionally, until butter melts. Add stuffing mix and pecans, stirring lightly. Yield: enough stuffing for 6 Cornish hens.

Mrs. James Bright,
Anniston, Alabama.

Tip: Freeze small portions of leftover meat or fowl until you have enough for a pot pie, curry, or rice casserole.

Try A One-Dish Dinner

When you find yourself short on time and out of ideas for what to fix for dinner, try one of our one-dish dinners. From Cheesy Spinach Lasagna to Taco Casserole, you'll find a variety of flavors to suit every taste.

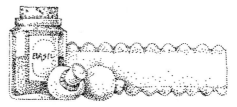

CHEESY SPINACH LASAGNA

1 pound lean ground beef
1 large onion, minced
½ pound fresh mushrooms, sliced
1 teaspoon whole oregano
½ teaspoon basil leaves
1½ teaspoons salt, divided
¼ teaspoon pepper
1 (12-ounce) can cocktail vegetable juice
1 cup milk
½ cup all-purpose flour
1 cup cream-style cottage cheese
2 eggs
2 (10-ounce) packages frozen chopped spinach, thawed
1 (8-ounce) package lasagna noodles
1 (8-ounce) package mozzarella cheese, thinly sliced
2 tablespoons grated Parmesan cheese
Chopped fresh parsley

Cook ground beef until brown, stirring to crumble meat. Add onion, mushrooms, oregano, basil, 1 teaspoon salt, and pepper; cook until vegetables are tender. Stir in vegetable juice.

Combine milk and flour; mix well, and stir into skillet mixture. Cook, stirring constantly, until thick and bubbly.

Combine cottage cheese and 1 egg; mix well, and set aside.

Drain spinach well. Combine spinach, 1 egg, and remaining ½ teaspoon salt; mix well, and spread evenly in a greased 13- x 9- x 2-inch baking dish. Layer half of noodles, half of cottage cheese mixture, half of cheese slices, and half of meat mixture over spinach; repeat layers. Sprinkle with Parmesan cheese; bake at 375° for 30 minutes. Sprinkle lightly with parsley. Yield: 6 to 8 servings.

Lilly S. Bradley,
Salem, Virginia.

HOT SEAFOOD PIE

2½ cups crushed potato chips, divided
½ cup melted margarine
2 (6½-ounce) cans crabmeat, drained and flaked
2 (4½-ounce) cans medium shrimp, drained
1 cup chopped celery
½ cup chopped green pepper
1 tablespoon grated onion
2 tablespoons lemon juice
¼ cup chopped pimiento
1 cup mayonnaise
½ cup shredded Cheddar cheese

Combine 1½ cups crushed potato chips and margarine; press into a 9-inch pieplate. Bake at 375° for 5 minutes. Cool.

Combine crabmeat, shrimp, celery, green pepper, onion, lemon juice, pimiento, and mayonnaise in a large bowl; stir well. Spoon mixture into potato chip crust. Combine remaining crushed potato chips and cheese; sprinkle over top. Bake at 375° for 10 minutes or until cheese melts. Yield: 6 to 8 servings.

Mrs. Warren D. Davis,
Yulee, Florida.

CHICKEN AND GREEN NOODLE CASSEROLE

3 whole chicken breasts, split
2 (5-ounce) packages green noodles
1 cup chopped green pepper
1 cup chopped onion
1 cup chopped celery
½ cup melted butter or margarine, divided
1 (8-ounce) package process cheese spread, cubed
1 (10¾-ounce) can cream of mushroom soup, undiluted
1 (3-ounce) jar pimiento-stuffed olives, sliced
1 (4½-ounce) jar sliced mushrooms, drained
1 cup crushed bite-size Cheddar cheese crackers

Cook chicken in salted water for 25 to 30 minutes or until tender; drain, reserving stock. Bone chicken, and cut meat into bite-size pieces; set aside.

Cook noodles in stock until tender; drain and set aside.

Sauté green pepper, onion, and celery in ¼ cup butter until tender; add cheese. Cook, stirring constantly, until the cheese melts. Stir in soup, olives, and mushrooms; cook until bubbly. Add chicken and noodles, mixing well;

spoon into a greased 13- x 9- x 2-inch baking dish. Combine remaining ¼ cup butter and cracker crumbs, stirring well; sprinkle over the chicken mixture. Bake at 325° for 40 to 45 minutes. Yield: about 8 to 10 servings.

Mrs. Henry DeBlieux, Sr.
Natchitoches, Louisiana.

TACO CASSEROLE

1 pound ground beef
1 cup chopped onion
1 clove garlic, minced
1 (8-ounce) can tomato sauce
¼ cup water
1 tablespoon chili powder
¼ teaspoon whole oregano, crushed
1 (15½-ounce) can kidney beans, undrained
2 cups corn chips, crushed
1¾ cups shredded lettuce

Combine ground beef, onion, and garlic in a large skillet; cook until meat is browned. Drain.

Combine meat mixture, tomato sauce, water, and seasonings in a medium bowl; stir well. Place half of meat mixture in a lightly greased 2-quart casserole; top with half of kidney beans. Sprinkle with half of crushed corn chips. Repeat layers.

Cover and bake at 350° for 30 minutes. Uncover and bake an additional 5 minutes. To serve, top casserole with shredded lettuce. Yield: 4 to 5 servings.

Karen O'Kelley,
Burkburnett, Texas.

SAUSAGE AND BROCCOLI CASSEROLE

1 pound sausage links, cut into small pieces
1 (10-ounce) package frozen chopped broccoli
¼ cup shredded mild Cheddar cheese
3 tablespoons chopped green pepper
2 tablespoons grated onion
3 tablespoons minced fresh parsley
2 tablespoons all-purpose flour
3 hard-cooked eggs, sliced
1 (10¾-ounce) can cream of mushroom soup, undiluted
⅓ cup milk
½ cup dry breadcrumbs
3 tablespoons melted butter or margarine
Hot cooked rice

Cook sausage until browned; drain. Cook broccoli according to package directions; drain well. Place broccoli in a lightly greased 1½-quart casserole.

Combine sausage, cheese, green pepper, onion, parsley, and flour in a medium bowl; spoon half of sausage mixture over broccoli in casserole. Top sausage mixture with egg slices; spoon remaining sausage mixture over eggs.

Combine soup and milk; pour over casserole. Combine breadcrumbs and butter; sprinkle over casserole. Bake at 375° for 30 minutes. Serve over hot cooked rice. Yield: 6 servings.

Martha Ann Edminster,
East Freetown, Massachusetts.

Marinate A Vegetable Salad

Marinated salads are the key to serving fresh vegetable salads when there isn't much time for last-minute preparation. The real advantage to these salads, however, is the outstanding flavor that results from marinating the vegetables in a savory dressing.

From Favorite Carrot Salad and Marinated Zucchini to Fresh Vegetable Marinate, made with a medley of vegetables, there's one for every menu and every taste. Be sure to try our Coleslaw With Tomatoes—a delicious layered salad that you can prepare the night before serving.

MARINATED ZUCCHINI

3 to 4 medium zucchini, thinly sliced
½ cup chopped onion
½ cup chopped green pepper
1 (10¾-ounce) can tomato soup, undiluted
¾ cup sugar
¾ cup vinegar
½ cup vegetable oil
½ teaspoon salt
1 teaspoon Worcestershire sauce

Combine zucchini, onion, and green pepper; toss lightly. Combine remaining ingredients; mix well, and pour over vegetables. Cover and refrigerate overnight. Yield: 8 servings.

Mrs. Frank Tetrault,
Southlake, Texas.

FRESH VEGETABLE MARINATE

4 stalks fresh broccoli
8 large fresh mushrooms, sliced
1 medium-size green pepper, chopped
3 stalks celery, chopped
1 small head cauliflower, broken into flowerets
1 cup sugar
2 teaspoons dry mustard
1 teaspoon salt
½ cup vinegar
1½ cups vegetable oil
1 small onion, grated
2 tablespoons poppy seeds

Remove flowerets from broccoli; cut into bite-size pieces. Reserve stalks for other use. Combine flowerets, mushrooms, pepper, celery, and cauliflower; toss lightly.

Combine remaining ingredients; mix well, and pour over vegetables. Chill at least 3 hours. Yield: 10 to 12 servings.

Gail Hatter,
McGregor, Texas.

FAVORITE CARROT SALAD

1 pound carrots, sliced diagonally
1 cup chopped celery
½ cup chopped green pepper
1 medium onion, thinly sliced
1 teaspoon celery seeds
1 cup sugar
½ cup vinegar
½ cup water
⅓ cup vegetable oil

Cook carrots in boiling salted water about 10 minutes or until crisp-tender; drain well.

Place carrots, celery, green pepper, onion, and celery seeds in a large shallow dish; toss lightly, and set aside.

Combine remaining ingredients in a small saucepan, mixing well; bring to a boil, stirring often. Pour over vegetables; cover and chill 8 to 10 hours or overnight. Yield: 6 servings.

Mrs. Brenda W. Arehart,
Fairfield, Virginia.

Tip: Leftover vegetables go nicely in salad. Or make a chef's salad with leftover meats, cheese, and cold cuts cut in strips and tossed with leftover vegetables, greens, and salad dressing.

COLESLAW WITH TOMATOES

1 large head cabbage, shredded
1 large green pepper, cut into rings
2 medium onions, sliced and separated
   into rings
½ cup sugar
1 cup vinegar
¾ cup vegetable oil
2 teaspoons sugar
1 teaspoon celery seeds
1 teaspoon dry mustard
2 teaspoons salt
1 cup cherry tomatoes, halved

Alternate layers of cabbage, green pepper, and onion in a large bowl. Sprinkle with ½ cup sugar.

Combine next 6 ingredients in a small saucepan; bring to a boil. Pour over layered ingredients. Cover and chill at least 4 hours.

To serve, add tomatoes and toss gently. Yield: 8 servings.

Note: If sweeter coleslaw is desired, an additional ½ cup sugar may be added.   *Mrs. J. M. Hamilton,*
                   Fort Mill, South Carolina.

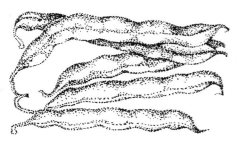

Speed Up Dinner With Frozen Foods

Rather than spending hours in the kitchen after a busy day, let frozen foods help you prepare gourmet dishes that are as easy as opening a package. These recipes use a wide range of frozen foods—juices, vegetables, fish, and fruits—in everything from beverages to dessert.

Processed at their nutritional peak, many frozen fruits and vegetables are cheaper than their fresh or canned counterparts and feature shorter cooking times in most cases. There is no waste to worry about with frozen foods, since they are conveniently packaged in a variety of sizes to suit the needs of each family.

SEAFOOD GUMBO

3 tablespoons vegetable oil
3 tablespoons all-purpose flour
2 tablespoons butter or margarine
1 medium onion, chopped
1 clove garlic, minced
1 quart plus 2 cups water
2 tablespoons Worcestershire sauce
4 to 5 dashes hot sauce
3 to 4 bay leaves
1½ teaspoons salt
½ teaspoon pepper
1 (10-ounce) package frozen cut okra
1 (6-ounce) package frozen crabmeat,
   thawed and undrained
2 (6-ounce) packages frozen cooked
   shrimp
1 pint fresh oysters, drained
Cooked rice

Heat oil in a 3-quart Dutch oven; add flour, stirring constantly. Cook on medium heat, stirring constantly, 10 to 15 minutes or until roux is the color of a copper penny.

Melt butter in a small skillet; add onion and garlic, and cook until tender. Stir into roux mixture. Gradually add water, Worcestershire sauce, hot sauce, bay leaves, salt, and pepper; simmer 1 hour.

Add okra; cook 15 minutes, stirring occasionally to separate okra. Stir in seafood; cook over medium heat 5 minutes or until oysters curl at edges. Serve gumbo hot over cooked rice. Yield: about 4 to 6 servings.

Winifred K. Crow,
Baton Rouge, Louisiana.

HERBED FISH AND POTATO BAKE

1 (10-ounce) package frozen chopped
   spinach
1 (3-ounce) package instant mashed
   potatoes
½ cup commercial sour cream
Dash of pepper
1 (16-ounce) package frozen perch fillets,
   thawed
¼ cup milk
½ cup herb-flavored stuffing mix, crushed
2 tablespoons butter or margarine, melted
Lemon wedges

Prepare spinach according to package directions; drain well.

Prepare instant potatoes according to package directions, reducing water by ¼ cup. Stir in drained spinach, sour cream, and pepper. Spoon mixture into a lightly greased 10- x 6- x 2-inch baking dish.

Remove skin from fish fillets. Dip one side of each fillet in milk, then in stuffing mix. Fold fillets in half, coating side out; place fish on potato mixture. Drizzle butter over fish.

Bake at 350° for 30 to 35 minutes or until fish flakes when tested with a fork. Serve warm with lemon wedges. Yield: 4 to 5 servings.   *Barbara L. Williams,*
                Lawrenceville, Georgia.

GREEN VEGETABLE MEDLEY

1 (10-ounce) package frozen peas
1 (10-ounce) package frozen lima beans
1 (9-ounce) package frozen French-style
   green beans
1 cup water
Salt
¼ cup finely chopped onion
2 tablespoons butter or margarine, melted
1 tablespoon all-purpose flour
½ cup commercial sour cream
½ cup mayonnaise
½ teaspoon basil leaves, crushed
¼ teaspoon salt
⅛ teaspoon pepper
¾ cup shredded sharp Cheddar cheese

Place frozen peas in a colander; pour hot water over peas to remove frost. Set peas aside.

Combine lima beans, green beans, and 1 cup salted water in a saucepan. Bring to a boil; reduce heat and simmer 3 minutes. Drain; set aside.

Sauté onion in butter in a large skillet until tender. Stir in flour; remove from heat. Add vegetables, sour cream, mayonnaise, and seasonings; spoon mixture into a lightly greased 1½-quart casserole dish.

Bake at 325° for 15 minutes; sprinkle cheese on top, and bake 5 minutes longer. Yield: 6 to 8 servings.

Mrs. Don Heun,
Louisville, Kentucky.

Tip: Here's an easy way to tell if the casserole you're reheating is heated throughout. Insert the blade of a table knife into the center for a few seconds, then draw it out and touch it with the tip of your finger. It should be really hot.

CAULIFLOWER AND ASPARAGUS SUPREME

1 (10-ounce) package frozen cut asparagus
1 (10-ounce) package frozen cauliflower
1 (10¾-ounce) can cream of celery soup, undiluted
½ cup milk
1 cup (¼ pound) shredded process American cheese
1 teaspoon prepared mustard
1 teaspoon Worcestershire sauce
⅓ cup wheat germ
2 tablespoons melted butter or margarine

Prepare vegetables according to package directions; drain.

Combine soup, milk, cheese, mustard, and Worcestershire sauce in a 2-quart saucepan; cook over medium heat, stirring frequently, until cheese is melted. Remove from heat; stir in the vegetables.

Place vegetable mixture in a lightly greased 1½-quart shallow casserole. Combine wheat germ and butter; sprinkle over casserole. Bake at 375° for 20 to 25 minutes. Yield: 6 servings.

Susie Beckes,
Franklin, Tennessee.

FROZEN RASPBERRY SALAD

1½ cups miniature marshmallows
⅓ cup orange juice
1 (3-ounce) package cream cheese, softened
¼ cup mayonnaise
1 (10-ounce) package frozen raspberries, thawed
½ cup whipping cream, whipped
¾ cup chopped pecans
Lettuce (optional)

Combine marshmallows and orange juice in top of a double boiler; cook over boiling water, stirring frequently, until marshmallows are melted. Let cool.

Add cream cheese and mayonnaise to cooled juice mixture; beat until smooth. Stir in next 3 ingredients. Pour mixture into a lightly oiled 7½- x 3- x 2-inch loafpan; freeze overnight.

Remove loafpan from freezer 10 to 15 minutes before serving; invert salad onto a lettuce-lined serving platter, if desired. Yield: 8 servings.

Mrs. H. J. Sherrer,
Bay City, Texas.

Combine brown sugar, pecans, and cinnamon; set aside for topping.

Pour half of batter into a lightly greased 13- x 9- x 2-inch baking pan. Spoon strawberries over batter; sprinkle with half of topping mixture. Top with remaining batter, and sprinkle with remaining topping.

Bake at 350° for 30 to 35 minutes or until cake tests done. Let cool; cut into 15 squares. Top each square with Strawberry Glaze and whipped cream. Yield: 15 servings.

Strawberry Glaze:

Reserved strawberry juice
1 tablespoon plus 1 teaspoon cornstarch
2 teaspoons lemon juice

Combine strawberry juice and cornstarch in a small saucepan; cook over medium heat, stirring constantly, until thickened. Remove from heat; stir in lemon juice. Serve warm over cake. Yield: 1¼ cups.

Mrs. Donald C. Vanhoy,
Salisbury, North Carolina.

EASY RUM ROLLS

1 (1-pound) loaf frozen bread dough, thawed
2 tablespoons melted butter or margarine
1 cup sugar
½ cup water
⅓ cup rum or 2 teaspoons rum extract
Powdered sugar
Maraschino cherries (optional)

Cut dough into 12 pieces; place each dough piece in a greased muffin cup. Brush tops of dough with melted butter. Cover; let rise in a warm place (85°), free from drafts, until dough rises ½ inch above muffin cups (about 2 to 2½ hours). Bake at 375° for 12 to 15 minutes or until golden brown.

Combine sugar, water, and rum in a small saucepan; place over medium heat, and bring to a rapid boil. Reduce heat, and simmer 2 minutes.

Remove rolls from pan onto a wire rack; prick tops of rolls with a fork. Spoon rum syrup over hot rolls to coat. Sift powdered sugar on each roll, and top with a cherry, if desired. Allow the rolls to cool thoroughly.

Wrap rolls tightly in foil to store. To serve, place foil package in 350° oven; heat about 15 minutes. Serve hot. Yield: 1 dozen. *Mrs. W. P. Chambers,*
Louisville, Kentucky.

STRAWBERRY CRUNCH CAKE

2 (10-ounce) packages frozen sliced strawberries, thawed
2 cups all-purpose flour
1 teaspoon baking powder
½ teaspoon soda
½ teaspoon salt
1¼ cups sugar
1 cup butter or margarine, softened
2 eggs
1 cup commercial sour cream
⅓ cup firmly packed light brown sugar
½ cup chopped pecans
1 teaspoon ground cinnamon
Strawberry Glaze
Whipped cream

Drain strawberries, reserving juice for glaze. Combine flour, baking powder, soda, and salt; set aside.

Combine 1¼ cups sugar and butter in a large mixing bowl, creaming well. Add eggs, beating until smooth. Slowly mix in sour cream. Add flour mixture, and stir well.

ORANGE-LEMON MIST

1 (6-ounce) can frozen orange juice concentrate, thawed
1½ to 1¾ cups water
¼ cup lemon juice
2 tablespoons Triple Sec or other orange-flavored liqueur
1 pint orange sherbet
Fresh mint leaves (optional)

Combine orange juice concentrate, water, and lemon juice in container of electric blender; cover and blend until frothy. Add Triple Sec and sherbet; blend until combined. Serve immediately; garnish with fresh mint leaves, if desired. Yield: 4 to 5 servings.

Mrs. J. John Stearman,
Louisville, Kentucky.

Tip: Use odd pieces of candy to make a topping for ice cream. Plain chocolate, mints, or cream candies may be placed in top of a double boiler with a little cream and heated until well blended. Serve hot over ice cream or cake, or store in refrigerator and use later cold.

As an alternative to plain baked potatoes, serve Creamy Shrimp-Stuffed Potatoes. They are made with cream of shrimp soup.

LEMON AND NUTMEG POTATOES

8 large potatoes
½ cup melted butter or margarine
1 teaspoon grated lemon rind
⅓ cup lemon juice
3 teaspoons salt
½ teaspoon ground nutmeg
½ teaspoon pepper
2 green onions with tops, chopped
½ cup whipping cream, whipped
½ cup shredded Cheddar cheese
Paprika

Peel and cube potatoes. Cook in boiling water to cover 15 to 20 minutes or until tender. Drain and set aside.

Combine next 7 ingredients, stirring well; add potatoes and toss gently. Spoon mixture into a lightly greased 2-quart casserole. Top with whipped cream; sprinkle with cheese and paprika. Bake at 350° for 15 to 20 minutes or until lightly browned. Yield: 6 to 8 servings.
Martha Ann Rabon,
Stapleton, Alabama.

Potatoes Get A Perk-Me-Up

The reliable potato goes from plain vegetable to fancy accompaniment with a number of special treatments. Cream of shrimp soup is whipped into stuffed baked potatoes. Cubed potatoes are turned into a casserole with a lemon-and nutmeg-flavored dressing. Mashed potatoes are transformed into golden deep-fried puffs. And grated cooked potatoes are baked into pancakes so light and moist that they melt in your mouth.

CREAMY SHRIMP-STUFFED POTATOES

4 large baking potatoes
Vegetable oil
¼ cup butter or margarine, softened
1 (10¾-ounce) can cream of shrimp soup, undiluted
¼ teaspoon salt
⅛ teaspoon pepper
Shredded Cheddar cheese

Wash potatoes, and rub skins with oil. Bake at 425° for 1 hour or until done.

Allow potatoes to cool to touch; cut in half lengthwise. Carefully scoop out pulp, leaving shells intact; mash pulp. Combine potato pulp, butter, soup, salt, and pepper; mix well. Stuff shells with potato mixture; sprinkle with cheese. Place on baking sheet, and bake 8 to 10 minutes or until cheese melts. Yield: 8 servings.

Note: Stuffed potato shells may be wrapped in foil and frozen before adding cheese. Before baking, bring to room temperature. Remove foil and place potatoes on baking sheet; bake at 425° for 15 to 20 minutes. Sprinkle tops with cheese; return to oven, and bake an additional 8 to 10 minutes or until the cheese is melted.
Mrs. Sherri Johnston,
Columbus, Georgia.

POTATO PUFFS

2 cups mashed potatoes (about 5 to 6 medium potatoes)
1 cup all-purpose flour
2 teaspoons baking powder
2 eggs, slightly beaten
1 teaspoon salt
¼ teaspoon pepper
Hot vegetable oil

Combine first 6 ingredients, stirring well. Chill 1 hour.

Drop by heaping teaspoonfuls into deep hot oil (375° to 390°); cook until golden brown. Yield: 4 servings.
Helen G. C. Walker,
Towson, Maryland.

MOIST POTATO PANCAKES

4 medium potatoes, cooked, peeled, and shredded
2 eggs, beaten
¾ to 1 cup milk
¼ cup chopped onion
2 tablespoons all-purpose flour
2 tablespoons melted butter or margarine
1 teaspoon salt
1 teaspoon baking powder

Combine potatoes and eggs, mixing well. Gradually add milk, using enough to obtain desired consistency. Add remaining ingredients, mixing well; let stand 10 minutes.

Drop batter by heaping tablespoonfuls onto a hot, lightly greased skillet; shape into 2½-inch circles with the back of a spoon. Cook until brown on one side; turn and brown other side. Yield: about 3½ dozen.
Mrs. J. John Stearman,
Louisville, Kentucky.

Tip: When a recipe says "greased pan," grease the pan with solid shortening or an oil, unless butter is specified. Do not use commercial whipped margarine in place of butter unless the recipe calls for melting the butter.

March

The fresh spring winds of March spark Southerners to look for new entertaining ideas. In honor of the season we present *Breakfasts & Brunches,* a special section filled with eye-opening recipes and entertainment suggestions. Features range from an elegant brunch to old family favorites and include many recipes to give you a headstart on breakfast.

Southerners know this season as the time to enjoy the parties, parades, and food of Mardi Gras. We celebrated with the New Orleanians and brought back recipes from favorite restaurants that you can enjoy in your own home. Skinning the turtle was a "first" for our test kitchen, but Turtle Soup Au Gratin from Delmonico was definitely worth the effort!

Let The Chicken Be Special

Fine dining doesn't have to be expensive, not when your menu is centered around one of these exceptional chicken entrées. Each is special, each different—proof of the wonderful versatility of chicken.

On the light side, we suggest crabmeat-stuffed chicken breasts served with a white grape sauce, Orange-Avocado Chicken, or bits of chicken combined with Monterey Jack cheese in a filling for crêpes. Of course, the classics are always good choices, and we've included two: Chicken Kiev and a sherried version of Chicken Divan.

Or you might prefer to emphasize the savory side of chicken with Chicken Cacciatore or serve it in the Oriental manner with pineapple chunks and crisp-tender vegetables.

ORANGE-AVOCADO CHICKEN

4 whole chicken breasts, split
4 whole chicken leg quarters
¼ cup melted butter or margarine
1 teaspoon grated orange rind
1 cup orange juice, divided
½ cup chopped onion
1 teaspoon salt
1 teaspoon paprika
½ teaspoon ground ginger
½ teaspoon tarragon leaves, crushed
2 tablespoons cornstarch
2 oranges, peeled and sliced crosswise
1 avocado, peeled and sliced
Fresh parsley sprigs

Rinse chicken, and pat dry. Brown on both sides in butter over medium heat; add orange rind, ½ cup orange juice, onion, and seasonings. Reduce heat to low; cover and cook 30 minutes or until chicken is tender. Remove chicken to serving dish, and keep warm.

Combine remaining ½ cup orange juice and cornstarch, stirring until smooth; add to pan drippings. Cook over low heat, stirring constantly, until thickened.

Arrange orange and avocado slices around chicken; pour orange sauce over top before serving. Garnish with parsley sprigs. Yield: 8 to 12 servings.
Lilly S. Bradley,
Salem, Virginia.

SHERRIED CHICKEN DIVAN

3 whole chicken breasts
1½ pounds fresh broccoli or 2 (10-ounce) packages frozen broccoli
¼ cup butter or margarine
¼ cup all-purpose flour
½ cup whipping cream
3 tablespoons cooking sherry
½ teaspoon salt
Dash of pepper
¼ cup plus 2 tablespoons grated Parmesan cheese

Cook chicken breasts in boiling salted water until tender. Drain, reserving 2 cups broth. Let chicken breasts cool to touch; discard skin. Thinly slice chicken breasts to yield 18 slices; set aside.

Cook broccoli in a small amount of boiling salted water just until crisp-tender; drain well, and set aside.

Melt butter in a heavy saucepan over low heat; add flour, stirring until smooth. Cook 1 minute, stirring constantly. Gradually stir in reserved broth, whipping cream, and sherry; cook over medium heat, stirring constantly, until thickened and bubbly. Stir in salt and pepper; remove from heat.

Arrange broccoli in a lightly greased 13- x 9- x 2-inch glass baking dish; top with half of sauce. Arrange chicken slices over broccoli. Stir ¼ cup Parmesan cheese into the remaining sauce; spoon over chicken. Sprinkle with 2 tablespoons Parmesan cheese.

Bake at 350° for 20 to 25 minutes or until bubbly; then broil 2 minutes or until top of casserole is delicately browned. Yield: 6 to 8 servings.
Mrs. S. Bruce Jones,
Nashville, Tennessee.

STUFFED CHICKEN BREASTS WITH WHITE GRAPE SAUCE

12 whole chicken breasts, skinned and boned
12 slices white bread, cut into ¼-inch cubes
½ cup minced onion
½ cup finely chopped celery
¼ cup melted butter or margarine
½ teaspoon salt
¼ teaspoon pepper
¼ teaspoon rubbed sage
1 (6-ounce) package frozen crabmeat, thawed, undrained, and flaked
1 cup all-purpose flour
½ cup melted butter or margarine
White Grape Sauce

Place each chicken breast on a sheet of waxed paper; flatten to ¼-inch thickness, using a meat mallet or rolling pin.

Combine next 8 ingredients, stirring well. Spoon stuffing into center of each chicken breast. Fold long sides of chicken over stuffing; fold ends over, and secure with toothpicks.

Dredge each chicken breast in flour. Brown chicken on all sides in ½ cup melted butter. Transfer chicken to a 15- x 10- x 1-inch jellyroll pan. Bake at 375° for 25 minutes or until tender. Serve with White Grape Sauce. Yield: 12 servings.

White Grape Sauce:

3 tablespoons butter or margarine
3 tablespoons all-purpose flour
1½ cups chicken broth
2 tablespoons sugar
½ teaspoon salt
2 teaspoons lemon juice
1 (16-ounce) can white grapes, drained

Melt butter in a heavy saucepan over low heat; add flour, stirring until smooth. Cook 1 minute, stirring constantly. Gradually add broth; cook over medium heat, stirring constantly, until thickened and bubbly. Stir in sugar, salt, and lemon juice. Add grapes just before serving. Yield: about 2½ cups.
Mrs. R. M. Lancaster,
Brentwood, Tennessee.

SCARBOROUGH CHICKEN

2 whole chicken breasts, halved
1 envelope seasoned coating mix for chicken
1 teaspoon parsley flakes
½ teaspoon whole rosemary, crushed
½ teaspoon leaf sage
½ teaspoon whole thyme leaves
1 (10¾-ounce) can golden mushroom soup, undiluted
½ cup chicken broth
½ cup dry sherry
1 (8-ounce) can mushroom stems and pieces, drained (optional)
Hot buttered rice (optional)

Dredge chicken with coating mix, and place in a lightly greased 13- x 9- x 2-inch baking dish. Sprinkle chicken with herbs; bake at 400° for 30 minutes.

Combine soup, broth, and sherry in a small bowl; add mushrooms, if desired. Stir well, and pour over chicken. Bake 30 minutes longer or until chicken is done. Serve over rice, if desired. Yield: 4 servings.
L. Marilyn Frailey,
Sparta, New Jersey.

CHICKEN KIEV

¾ cup butter, softened
1 tablespoon chopped parsley
1 tablespoon finely chopped fresh chives
1 tablespoon finely chopped green onion
½ teaspoon salt
⅛ teaspoon pepper
6 whole chicken breasts, skinned and boned
Salt and pepper
1 egg
1 tablespoon water
1 cup all-purpose flour
⅔ cup soft breadcrumbs
¼ cup melted butter

Combine first 6 ingredients; mix well, and shape into a stick (like butter). Cover and chill or freeze about 45 minutes or until firm.

Place each chicken breast on a sheet of waxed paper; flatten to ¼-inch thickness, using a meat mallet or rolling pin.

Cut stick of butter mixture into 6 portions; place a piece in center of each chicken breast. Fold long sides of chicken over butter; fold ends over, and secure with toothpicks. Lightly sprinkle chicken with salt and pepper.

Combine egg and water, beating well. Dredge each chicken breast in flour, dip in egg, and coat with breadcrumbs.

Sauté chicken in ¼ cup melted butter over medium heat until golden brown on all sides, turning gently. Transfer to a 13- x 9- x 2-inch baking dish. Bake at 400° for 15 to 20 minutes or until tender. Yield: 6 servings.

*Linda Radomski,
Birmingham, Alabama.*

CHICKEN CACCIATORE

1 (2½- to 3-pound) broiler-fryer, cut up
¼ cup olive oil
2 medium onions, cut into ¼-inch slices
2 cloves garlic, minced
1 (16-ounce) can whole tomatoes
1 (15-ounce) can tomato-herb sauce
1 teaspoon salt
1 teaspoon dried oregano or basil leaves, crushed
½ teaspoon celery seeds
¼ teaspoon pepper
1 to 2 bay leaves
¼ cup Sauterne cooking wine
Hot cooked spaghetti
Grated Parmesan cheese

Brown chicken in olive oil in a large skillet; remove chicken, and set aside. Add onion and garlic to pan drippings; sauté until tender.

Combine next 7 ingredients, stirring well. Return chicken to skillet, and add sauce. Cover and simmer 30 to 45 minutes; stir in cooking wine. Cook, uncovered, 15 to 20 minutes over very low heat or until chicken is tender; turn chicken occasionally. Skim off excess fat. Serve chicken and sauce over spaghetti; sprinkle with Parmesan cheese. Yield: 6 servings.   *Doris Garton,
Shenandoah, Virginia.*

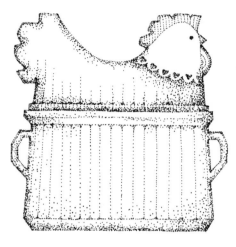

CHICKEN CREPES

2 cups chopped cooked chicken
1 (10¾-ounce) can cream of mushroom soup, undiluted and divided
1½ cups (6 ounces) shredded Monterey Jack cheese, divided
Pepper
1 teaspoon instant minced onion
½ teaspoon dried parsley flakes
¼ teaspoon paprika
¼ teaspoon salt
Garlic powder to taste (optional)
Crêpes (recipe follows)
1 teaspoon instant minced onion
½ teaspoon dried parsley flakes
¼ teaspoon paprika

Combine chicken, ½ cup soup, ¾ cup cheese, pinch of pepper, and next 5 ingredients; mix well.

Spread 2 tablespoons filling in center of each crêpe; roll up, and place seam side down in a 13- x 9- x 2-inch baking dish.

Combine remaining soup, pinch of pepper, remaining seasonings, and ¾ cup cheese; stir well. Spoon over crêpes. Bake at 375° for 15 to 20 minutes or until bubbly. Yield: 5 servings.

Crêpes:

1 cup all-purpose flour
1¼ cups milk
2 eggs, beaten
3 tablespoons melted butter or margarine
Vegetable oil

Combine flour and milk, beating until smooth. Add eggs, and beat well; stir in butter. Refrigerate batter 1 hour. (This allows flour particles to swell and soften so the crêpes are light in texture.)

Brush the bottom of a 6½- or 7-inch crêpe pan with vegetable oil; place pan over medium heat until just hot, not smoking.

Pour 2 tablespoons batter into pan; quickly tilt pan in all directions so batter covers the pan in a thin film. Cook 1 minute.

Lift edge of crêpe to test for doneness. Crêpe is ready for flipping when it can be shaken loose from pan. Flip the crêpe, and cook about 30 seconds on other side. (This side is rarely more than spotty brown.)

When the crêpes are done, place on a towel and allow to cool. Stack between layers of waxed paper to prevent sticking. Yield: 10 crêpes.

*Barbara Bartolomeo,
Houston, Texas.*

COMPANY CHICKEN

1 (2½- to 3-pound) broiler-fryer, cut up
Salt
Cayenne pepper
2 tablespoons bacon drippings
¼ cup slivered almonds
⅓ cup raisins
1 (20-ounce) can pineapple chunks, drained
1½ cups orange juice
⅛ teaspoon ground cinnamon
⅛ teaspoon ground cloves
2 tablespoons all-purpose flour
¼ cup water

Sprinkle chicken with salt and cayenne; brown in hot bacon drippings in a large skillet. Combine next 6 ingredients, and pour over chicken. Cover and simmer 30 to 45 minutes or until tender. Remove chicken pieces to serving platter.

Combine flour and water, stirring until smooth; stir into pan drippings. Cook over low heat, stirring constantly, until thickened. Serve gravy with chicken. Yield: 4 to 6 servings.

*Mrs. Harland Stone,
Ocala, Florida.*

ORIENTAL CHICKEN

1 (2- to 2½-pound) broiler-fryer
2 large green peppers, cut into strips
1 large onion, diced
1 (6-ounce) package frozen Chinese pea pods
1 (8½-ounce) can water chestnuts, drained and sliced
1 (4-ounce) can mushroom stems and pieces
3 tablespoons soy sauce
1 tablespoon sugar
½ teaspoon curry powder
1 (8-ounce) can pineapple chunks, drained

Cook chicken in boiling salted water until tender. Drain, reserving ⅓ cup broth. When cool, bone and skin chicken; cut meat into small pieces.

Cook green pepper, onion, and pea pods in reserved broth until crisp-tender. Add remaining ingredients except pineapple, and cook about 2 minutes. Stir in pineapple, and heat thoroughly. Yield: 4 servings.
Patsy W. Ezzell,
Rocky Mount, North Carolina.

Turn Vegetables Into Dessert

You're in for a real surprise when you find that vegetables are the main ingredient in these desserts. Chocolate Beet Cake, with a deep, rich color, has a flavor similar to a devil's food cake. Carrots, too, find a place for dessert in Golden Carrot-Lemon Squares. These cakelike squares are topped with a lemon glaze.

Even pinto beans make an exceptionally flavorful pie when combined with sugar and spices. The few simple ingredients make it a surprisingly easy-to-prepare dessert.

PINTO BEAN PIE

1½ cups sugar
1 teaspoon ground allspice
1 teaspoon ground cinnamon
1 teaspoon ground nutmeg
1½ cups cooked, mashed pinto beans
1 egg, beaten
2 egg yolks, beaten
1 teaspoon vanilla extract
1 unbaked 9-inch pastry shell

Combine sugar and spices in a medium mixing bowl; mix well. Add beans, egg, egg yolks, and vanilla; mix until smooth. Pour into pastry shell; bake at 350° for 15 minutes. Reduce heat to 300°, and bake 45 minutes or until set; let cool before serving. Yield: one 9-inch pie.
Mrs. C. J. Hueske,
Waco, Texas.

CHOCOLATE BEET CAKE

2 cups all-purpose flour
2 teaspoons baking powder
½ teaspoon salt
⅓ cup cocoa
3 eggs
1 cup sugar
1 cup cooked grated beets
½ cup corn oil
¼ cup orange juice
2 teaspoons grated orange rind
1 teaspoon vanilla extract
1 (6-ounce) package semisweet chocolate morsels
Powdered sugar (optional)

Combine flour, baking powder, salt, and cocoa; set aside. Combine eggs and sugar in a large mixing bowl; mix well. Add beets, oil, orange juice, and orange rind to sugar mixture; beat well. Stir in flour mixture and vanilla, mixing well. Stir in chocolate morsels.

Pour into a greased 9-inch square baking pan. Bake at 350° for 40 minutes or until cake tests done. Let cool 10 minutes in pan. Remove from pan, and cool completely on wire rack. Sprinkle with powdered sugar, if desired. Yield: 16 servings.
Mrs. J. Lee Stringfield,
Cottageville, South Carolina.

PUMPKIN BARS

1 (3½-ounce) can flaked coconut
1 cup graham cracker crumbs
1 cup chopped walnuts
¼ cup butter or margarine, melted
2 cups cooked, mashed pumpkin
1 (14-ounce) can sweetened condensed milk
2 eggs
2 teaspoons pumpkin pie spice
½ teaspoon salt

Combine coconut, graham cracker crumbs, walnuts, and butter; mix well. Pat two-thirds of mixture into an ungreased 13- x 9- x 2-inch baking pan.

Combine remaining ingredients, stirring well. Spoon evenly over coconut mixture in pan; sprinkle with remaining coconut mixture. Bake at 375° for 30 to 35 minutes or until knife inserted in center comes out clean. Cool in pan; then chill. Cut into 2- x 3-inch bars. Yield: about 2 dozen.
Mrs. Harvey Kidd,
Hernando, Mississippi.

BUTTERNUT SQUASH PIE

2 cups cooked, mashed butternut squash
1 cup sugar
2 eggs
¼ cup milk
¼ cup melted butter or margarine
1 teaspoon ground nutmeg
1 unbaked 9-inch pastry shell

Combine first 6 ingredients in a medium mixing bowl; mix well. Pour into pastry shell. Bake at 400° for 40 to 50 minutes or until knife inserted halfway between center and edge of pie comes out clean; cool before serving. Yield: one 9-inch pie.
Gwen Love,
Albany, Georgia.

GOLDEN CARROT-LEMON SQUARES

1 cup melted margarine
1¼ cups sugar
4 eggs
1 cup cooked, mashed carrots
2 cups all-purpose flour
1 teaspoon baking powder
1½ teaspoons vanilla extract
¾ teaspoon lemon extract
2¼ cups powdered sugar
¼ cup water
1½ teaspoons lemon extract

Combine margarine and sugar in a large mixing bowl; mix well. Add eggs, one at a time, beating well after each addition. Add carrots, flour, and baking powder; beat 1 minute. Stir in vanilla and ¾ teaspoon lemon extract. Spoon into a greased 15- x 10- x 1-inch jellyroll pan, spreading to edges. Bake at 350° for 25 minutes. Cool.

Combine powdered sugar, water, and 1½ teaspoons lemon extract; stir until smooth. Pour glaze over cooled cake. Let stand until glaze is firm. Cut into squares. Yield: about 5 dozen (1½-inch) squares.
Doris Amonette,
Tulsa, Oklahoma.

The South Serves It Sunny Side Up

There's nothing really wrong with ham and eggs, but breakfast can get to be predictable. And any brunch plans should include something different—an ideal time, really, to try a surprise or two.

In this *Breakfasts & Brunches* section, you will find a wide range of recipes suitable for a special occasion or for becoming a new morning favorite for your family. A suggested hearty breakfast menu, for example, includes Hot Brandied Fruit, Quail With Red Plum Sauce, Cottage-Scrambled Eggs, Pork Sausage Ring, and Baked Cheese Grits. How's that for a tempting starter?

We take a standard breakfast item—the grapefruit—and present several of our readers' favorite ways to make it special. Grapefruit Supreme is topped with a sauce made with fresh strawberries and orange juice; Sherried Broiled Grapefruit is just what it sounds like, and delicious; there is even a homemade Combination Citrus Marmalade that includes grapefruit.

Breakfast breads that either accompany or stand alone range from sweet to cheesy: Caramel-Orange Coffee Ring, Blueberry Streusel Muffins, Butter Cheese Dips, Cinnamon-Buttermilk Coffee Cake. The aroma alone will get you going. And for quick but tantalizing breakfast or brunch dishes, we offer several make-ahead recipes, including Overnight Coffee Cake and Scrambled Egg Casserole.

Since even one special item can make the difference between a memorable or ho-hum morning meal, there is a selection of side dishes, ranging from Banana-Orange Slush to Sausage-Stuffed Tomatoes; we found them particularly good and quite easy to do.

Our round-the-clock breakfast ideas—Breakfast Tacos, Spicy Wheat Germ Squares, Ham Waffles, Nutritious Brunch Crêpes, Sour Cream Soufflé—recognize the fact that there are many occasions when something breakfasty sounds right other than for morningtime.

Put Guests At Ease With Brunch

Temple Heights stands tall in Columbus, Mississippi, a fine four-story Greek Revival house that was built by early settler Richard T. Brownrigg in 1837, not long after the town was settled. It's easy to imagine grand rooms and the open gallery alive with entertaining over the decades.

It's even easier when sixth and present owners of the house, Mr. and Mrs. Carl Butler III, keep up the tradition with special parties, and Saturday brunches are a favorite. When the weather is nice, Dixie Butler encourages guests to spill out onto the gallery and across the lawn where Temple Heights shows its full height.

Why is brunch a favorite? "Well, it's often easier to catch people that time of day," observes Mrs. Butler. "And guests like a midmorning party because it is different. The menu usually lends itself to serving more people, and because we use the whole house there's plenty of room to mix and mingle."

And for anyone who's been there, seeing the house on a sun-dappled spring day is a treat in itself.

Guests are welcomed with Lemon Balm Punch, made with fresh lemon and mint leaves, which they can sip in the garden. Depending upon the weather and the season, the buffet is set up either in the house or on the large, columned gallery that wraps three sides of the house.

So she can be a part of the party, Dixie Butler selects a menu that can be prepared in advance. She prefers to serve "fork food" whenever possible because it's easy to manage and guests can relax more. The buffet recipes chosen for the brunch tend to be the kind "just as easy to fix a lot of as a little," so the invitation list can be quite expansive.

Fresh fruits and vegetables fit the brunch mood and taste, so this menu includes colorful fruit with Celery-Honey Dressing. Romano Broiled Tomatoes and Jeweled Asparagus make bright vegetable accompaniments.

Venison Sausage Balls is the highlight of the brunch menu. Many of the Butlers' friends hunt, so venison is shared and, in this case, turned into spicy meatballs. Scrambled Eggs With Wild Rice, which Dixie invented with leftover rice one day, seems just right with the sausage balls.

A spoonbread recipe, which was discovered in a scrapbook recording previous Temple Heights parties and menus, is served at most gatherings, this brunch included, with fluffy Sweetened Biscuits also offered.

For dessert, guests are served coffee and President Tyler's Puddin' Pies, which were reportedly served at the White House during his administration. The tiny pies are very tasty, easy to serve, and quite simple to prepare.

Perhaps the Butlers' menu will give you ideas for a brunch. Flavors are complementary, and as mentioned, most dishes can be prepared in advance.

Lemon Balm Punch
Fresh Fruit Salad
With Celery-Honey Dressing
Venison Sausage Balls
Scrambled Eggs With Wild Rice
Jeweled Asparagus
Romano Broiled Tomatoes
Sweetened Biscuits   Spoonbread
President Tyler's Puddin' Pies
Coffee

LEMON BALM PUNCH

¼ cup sugar
¼ cup boiling water
½ cup fresh lemon balm leaves, finely chopped
½ cup fresh mint leaves, finely chopped
½ cup lemon juice
4 quarts ginger ale, chilled
Orange slices (optional)
Fresh lemon balm leaves (optional)

Combine sugar and water, stirring until sugar dissolves. Combine sugar mixture, ½ cup lemon balm leaves, mint leaves, and lemon juice in a small bowl; cover and let stand overnight.

To serve, strain syrup mixture into a large pitcher or punch bowl; pour in ginger ale, stirring gently. Garnish with orange slices and additional lemon balm leaves, if desired. Yield: about 4 quarts.

FRESH FRUIT SALAD WITH CELERY-HONEY DRESSING

2 cups fresh pineapple chunks
2 cups fresh cantaloupe balls
1 cup seedless green grapes
2 cups fresh strawberries
1 cup fresh blackberries
Celery-Honey Dressing

Combine fruit in a large bowl, tossing gently but well. Refrigerate until thoroughly chilled. Serve with Celery-Honey Dressing. Yield: about 16 servings.

Celery-Honey Dressing:
½ cup sugar
1 teaspoon dry mustard
1 teaspoon paprika
¼ teaspoon salt
⅓ cup honey
1 tablespoon lemon juice
¼ cup vinegar
1 cup vegetable oil
1 teaspoon grated onion
1 teaspoon celery seeds

Combine first 7 ingredients in container of electric blender; blend well. Slowly add oil, continuing to blend until thick; stir in onion and celery seeds. Cover and store in refrigerator. Yield: about 1¾ cups.

VENISON SAUSAGE BALLS

1½ pounds ground venison
½ cup dry breadcrumbs
1 egg, beaten
1 teaspoon salt
½ cup mashed potatoes
½ teaspoon brown sugar
¼ teaspoon pepper
¼ teaspoon ground allspice
¼ teaspoon ground nutmeg
⅛ teaspoon ground cloves
⅛ teaspoon ground ginger
¼ cup melted butter or margarine
Orange and lemon slices (optional)
Parsley sprigs (optional)

Combine first 11 ingredients, mixing well. Shape into 1-inch balls. Brown well in butter, stirring occasionally. Cover and cook over low heat 15 minutes. Arrange on serving platter; garnish with fruit and parsley, if desired. Yield: about 5 dozen.

SCRAMBLED EGGS WITH WILD RICE

8 eggs
1 cup cooked wild rice
½ cup milk
1 teaspoon salt
¼ teaspoon pepper
1 tablespoon bacon drippings

Beat eggs with a fork until blended; stir in rice, milk, salt, and pepper. Heat bacon drippings in a 10-inch skillet until warm; add egg mixture.

As eggs begin to set, lift cooked portion to allow uncooked portion to flow underneath. Cook until eggs are thickened but still moist (3 to 5 minutes). Yield: 6 servings.

JEWELED ASPARAGUS

½ cup butter or margarine
1 green pepper, thinly sliced
1 cup sliced celery
Juice of 1 lemon
1 (2-ounce) jar diced pimiento, drained
1 (8-ounce) can water chestnuts, drained and sliced
2 pounds fresh asparagus, cooked

Melt butter in a large skillet; add green pepper, celery, and lemon juice. Sauté until vegetables are tender. Stir in pimiento and water chestnuts; remove from heat. Serve over hot asparagus. Yield: 10 to 12 servings.

ROMANO BROILED TOMATOES

6 tomatoes, halved
Salt and pepper
¼ cup butter or margarine
¼ cup chopped fresh parsley
¼ cup grated Romano cheese

Sprinkle cut side of tomato halves with salt and pepper. Broil 5 minutes, about 4 inches from heat. Place 1 teaspoon butter, 1 teaspoon parsley, and 1 teaspoon cheese on each; broil until cheese melts. Yield: 12 servings.

SWEETENED BISCUITS

2½ cups all-purpose flour
½ teaspoon salt
1½ tablespoons baking powder
3 tablespoons sugar
¾ cup shortening
⅔ cup milk

Combine flour, salt, baking powder, and sugar; cut in shortening until mixture resembles coarse meal. Add milk, stirring until well blended. Turn dough out onto floured surface, and knead lightly about 3 to 4 times.

Roll dough to ½-inch thickness, and cut into rounds with a 2½-inch cutter. Place on an ungreased baking sheet; bake at 450° for 15 minutes or until golden. Yield: about 1½ dozen.

SPOONBREAD

1 cup cornmeal
1½ teaspoons salt
1 cup water
2 cups hot milk
2 eggs, beaten
3 tablespoons melted shortening
Parsley sprigs (optional)

Combine cornmeal and salt in a medium saucepan; stir in water. Gradually add milk, stirring until smooth. Place over low heat; cook, stirring constantly, until thickened.

Spoon a small amount of hot mixture into eggs, and mix well. Add egg mixture to remaining hot mixture, stirring constantly. Add shortening, stirring well. Pour into a well-greased 1½-quart baking dish, and bake at 375° for 40 to 50 minutes. Garnish with parsley, if desired. Yield: 6 to 8 servings.

PRESIDENT TYLER'S PUDDIN' PIES

16 (2-inch) individual pastry shells
½ cup butter, softened
¾ cup sugar
¾ cup firmly packed dark brown sugar
2 eggs
½ cup half-and-half
½ teaspoon vanilla extract
Ground nutmeg
Whipped cream

Bake pastry shells at 350° for 4 to 5 minutes; set aside.

Combine butter and sugar, creaming until light and fluffy. Add eggs, half-and-half, and vanilla; beat well. Spoon filling into pastry shells, and sprinkle lightly with nutmeg.

Bake at 350° for 15 to 20 minutes or until set (filling will settle while pies are cooling).

At serving time, top with whipped cream and sprinkle lightly with nutmeg. Yield: 16 (2-inch) pies.

Serve Breakfast Round The Clock

Eggs and sausage, pancakes and waffles are generally thought of as morning fare but are just as welcome for a casual family supper or a midnight gathering after a party.

Serve the eggs and sausage as a filling for Breakfast Tacos; they can be prepared on last-minute notice. Pancakes and waffles? Stir bits of ground ham into the waffle batter for extra flavor. (Ham Waffles are great topped with a fried, poached, or scrambled egg.) And the old breakfast standby, oats, is the basis for Oatmeal Pancakes.

Spicy Wheat Germ Squares, great for breakfast on the run, also pack well for school lunches or snacks.

BREAKFAST TACOS

1 cup hash brown potato mix with onions
2 cups hot water
¾ teaspoon salt
8 flour tortillas
6 eggs, well beaten
½ pound bulk pork sausage, cooked, crumbled, and drained
½ teaspoon salt
Freshly ground pepper to taste
2 tablespoons butter or margarine
Picante sauce (optional)

Combine hash browns, water, and ¾ teaspoon salt; mix well. Let stand 15 minutes, uncovered. Drain hash browns.

Wrap tortillas securely in aluminum foil; bake at 350° for 10 minutes or until thoroughly heated.

Combine hash browns, eggs, sausage, ½ teaspoon salt, and pepper; mix well. Melt butter in a large skillet. Add egg mixture to skillet; cook over low heat, stirring gently, until eggs are done. Spoon egg mixture evenly into tortillas; fold tortillas in half. Spoon picante sauce over tortillas, if desired. Yield: 8 servings.

*Phyllis Patterson,
San Antonio, Texas.*

SOUR CREAM SOUFFLE

3 eggs, separated
¼ cup plus 2 tablespoons sugar
½ teaspoon salt
⅓ cup all-purpose flour
1½ cups commercial sour cream
2 teaspoons grated orange rind

Lightly butter and sugar a 1½-quart soufflé dish. Cut a piece of aluminum foil long enough to circle the dish, allowing a 1-inch overlap. Fold foil lengthwise into thirds, and lightly butter and sugar one side. Wrap foil, buttered side against dish, so it extends 3 inches above rim. Secure foil with string.

Beat egg whites until stiff; add sugar, 1 tablespoon at a time, continuing to beat to a stiff meringue. Combine egg yolks and salt, beating well; stir in flour and ½ cup sour cream. Fold in remaining sour cream, orange rind, and egg whites. Spoon into prepared soufflé dish.

Bake at 350° for 40 minutes or until firm. Remove collar before serving. Yield: 6 to 8 servings.

*Mary Lou Vaughn,
Dallas, Texas.*

Tip: Use a preheated griddle for evenly browned pancakes. The griddle is the right temperature when it reaches 390° or when a few drops of water sprinkled on the surface dance around violently before evaporating.

NUTRITIOUS BRUNCH CREPES

1 cup small-curd cottage cheese
1 cup vanilla yogurt
¼ cup powdered sugar
3 cups fresh strawberries, halved
⅓ cup sugar
Whole Wheat Crêpes

Put cottage cheese through a sieve or food mill. Combine cottage cheese, yogurt, and powdered sugar; set aside.

Combine strawberries and sugar. Spread the center of each crêpe with 1 tablespoon cheese filling and a few strawberries; roll up crêpes and place on a serving platter.

Spoon the remaining cheese filling and strawberries on top of crêpes. Yield: 8 servings.

Whole Wheat Crêpes:

1 cup whole wheat flour
2 eggs
½ cup milk
½ cup water
¼ teaspoon salt
2 tablespoons melted butter or margarine

Combine all ingredients in container of electric blender; blend 30 seconds. Scrape down sides of container with a rubber spatula; blend 30 additional seconds or until smooth.

Refrigerate batter at least 1 hour. (This allows flour particles to swell and soften so that the crêpes will be light in texture.)

Brush the bottom of a 6- or 7-inch crêpe pan or heavy skillet with salad oil; place over medium heat until just hot, not smoking.

Pour 2 tablespoons batter into pan; quickly tilt pan in all directions so batter covers the pan in a thin film. Cook about 1 minute.

Lift edge of crêpe to test for doneness. Crêpe is ready for flipping when it can be shaken loose from pan. Flip crêpe, and cook about 30 seconds on the other side. (This is rarely more than spotty brown and is used as the side on which the filling is placed.)

Remove crêpe from pan, and repeat procedure until all batter is used. Stack crêpes between layers of waxed paper to prevent sticking. Yield: 16 crêpes.
Mrs. R. K. Edwards,
Greenville, South Carolina.

OATMEAL PANCAKES

¾ cup regular or quick-cooking oats, uncooked
1½ cups milk
2 eggs, beaten
¼ cup melted shortening
1¼ cups all-purpose flour
2 tablespoons sugar
1 tablespoon baking powder
1 teaspoon salt

Combine oats and milk; set aside 5 minutes. Add eggs and shortening to oat mixture, mixing well.

Combine dry ingredients; add oat mixture, and stir just until blended. Pour about ¼ cup batter on hot griddle for each pancake. When pancakes have a bubbly surface and slightly dry edges, turn to cook the other side. Yield: 4 to 5 servings. *Mrs. E. L. Hackman,*
Hagerstown, Maryland.

HAM WAFFLES

2 cups all-purpose flour
1 teaspoon soda
½ teaspoon salt
1 tablespoon sugar
2 eggs, separated
2 cups buttermilk
¼ cup melted margarine
1½ cups cooked ground ham

Combine flour, soda, salt, and sugar; set aside. Combine egg yolks, buttermilk, and margarine; beat well, and add to flour mixture. Add ham, and stir well.

Beat egg whites until stiff peaks form; carefully fold into batter. Bake in preheated waffle iron. Yield: about 6 (8-inch) waffles. *Mary B. Quesenberry,*
Dugspur, Virginia.

Tip: Reheat frozen pancakes for a quick breakfast by popping them into the toaster. Or thaw and heat them in sauce, butter, or margarine in a frypan or chafing dish over moderate heat.

SPICY WHEAT GERM SQUARES

½ cup butter or margarine, softened
½ cup firmly packed brown sugar
½ cup molasses
2 eggs
½ cup water
1½ cups all-purpose flour
1½ teaspoons baking powder
¼ teaspoon soda
½ teaspoon salt
½ cup wheat germ
1 teaspoon ground ginger
½ teaspoon ground cinnamon
¼ teaspoon ground cloves
½ cup chopped almonds

Combine butter and sugar, creaming until light and fluffy. Add molasses and eggs, beating until smooth. Add water, and mix well.

Combine next 8 ingredients; add to molasses mixture, mixing well. Stir in almonds. Spread evenly in a greased 13- x 9- x 2-inch baking pan. Bake at 350° for 25 to 30 minutes. Cool in pan. Cut into 2-inch squares. Yield: about 2 dozen. *Linda Clark,*
Charlottesville, Virginia.

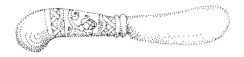

Give Breakfast Breads A New Twist

One whiff of any of these oven-fresh breakfast breads will convince you that they're well worth the time spent in preparation. Even if you can't spare the time in the morning, you can still enjoy them for breakfast, for all can be prepared ahead and reheated just before serving.

Although each bread is delicious, one that deserves special mention is the Caramel-Orange Coffee Ring—yeast rolls flavored with orange rind and cinnamon, then shaped into a ring and baked in Nutty Orange Glaze.

Also worthy of acclaim are Blueberry Streusel Muffins and the crescent-shaped Austrian Twists, which are filled with a mixture of sugar, pecans, and cinnamon.

CINNAMON-BUTTERMILK COFFEE CAKE

2 cups all-purpose flour
2 cups firmly packed brown sugar
½ cup butter, softened
⅓ cup all-purpose flour
1 egg
1 cup buttermilk
1 teaspoon soda
1 teaspoon ground cinnamon
½ cup chopped nuts

Combine 2 cups flour and sugar in a large mixing bowl. Cut in butter until mixture resembles coarse meal. Set aside ¾ cup crumb mixture.

Combine remaining crumb mixture and ⅓ cup flour. Add egg, buttermilk, soda, and cinnamon; stir until mixture is moistened.

Pour batter into a greased 9-inch square pan. Combine reserved crumb mixture with nuts; sprinkle over batter. Bake at 325° for 1 hour or until coffee cake tests done. Cut into squares. Yield: 9 servings.

Mrs. Robert Crisman,
Cleveland, Mississippi.

CARAMEL-ORANGE COFFEE RING

1 (13¾-ounce) package hot roll mix
⅔ cup warm milk (105° to 115°)
2 eggs, slightly beaten
2 tablespoons plus 2 teaspoons grated orange rind, divided
2 tablespoons plus 2 teaspoons butter or margarine, softened
⅓ cup firmly packed brown sugar
1 teaspoon ground cinnamon
Nutty Orange Glaze

Remove yeast package from roll mix. Sprinkle yeast over warm milk in a large mixing bowl, stirring until dissolved (about 5 minutes). Stir in eggs and 2 teaspoons orange rind. Add roll mix; blend with dough hook of electric mixer until combined. Shape dough into a ball in mixing bowl (dough will be very soft).

Cover and let rise until doubled in bulk (about 1 hour). Turn dough out onto a floured surface; pat top with a small amount of flour. Roll into a 16- x 12-inch rectangle, and spread with butter. Combine sugar, 2 tablespoons orange rind, and cinnamon; sprinkle over butter.

Starting at long edge, roll up dough jellyroll fashion; press seam to seal. Cut into 16 (1-inch) slices.

Grease a 10-inch tube pan; spoon Nutty Orange Glaze into pan, spreading evenly. Stand 10 dough slices along edge of pan, cut side against side of pan. Stand remaining 6 slices up, cut side against center tube of pan.

Cover and let rise until doubled in bulk (about 1 hour). Bake at 375° for 30 to 35 minutes. Cool 2 minutes, and turn out onto a serving platter. Yield: one 10-inch coffee cake.

Nutty Orange Glaze:

½ cup firmly packed brown sugar
¼ cup butter or margarine, softened
2 tablespoons light corn syrup
3 tablespoons chopped nuts
1 tablespoon grated orange rind

Combine sugar, butter, and corn syrup in a small mixing bowl; beat until fluffy. Stir in remaining ingredients. Yield: about ¾ cup.

Mrs. Elizabeth Moore,
Huntsville, Alabama.

AUSTRIAN TWISTS

1 package dry yeast
3 cups all-purpose flour
1 cup butter, softened
3 egg yolks
1 (8-ounce) carton commercial sour cream
½ cup sugar
½ cup chopped pecans
¾ teaspoon ground cinnamon
Powdered sugar glaze (recipe follows)

Combine yeast and flour; add butter, mixing well. Stir in egg yolks and sour cream. Shape dough into 4 balls; wrap in waxed paper, and refrigerate overnight.

Combine sugar, pecans, and cinnamon; set aside.

Work with 1 portion of dough at a time; place on a lightly floured surface, and roll into a ¼-inch-thick circle. Spread ¼ cup sugar mixture evenly over each circle, and cut into 16 equal wedges. Roll up each wedge, beginning at wide end and rolling to point; seal points firmly. Place on greased baking sheets, point side down.

Bake at 350° for 18 minutes or until lightly browned. Transfer to wire racks; drizzle with glaze while still warm. Yield: 64 twists.

Powdered Sugar Glaze:

2 cups powdered sugar
3 tablespoons milk

Combine sugar and milk, stirring until smooth. Yield: about 1 cup.

Mrs. Doug Hail,
Moody, Texas.

CHEESY POPOVER RING

1 cup water
½ cup butter or margarine
1 teaspoon salt
⅛ teaspoon pepper
1 cup all-purpose flour
4 eggs
1 cup (4 ounces) finely diced sharp Cheddar cheese

Bring water, butter, salt, and pepper to a boil in a saucepan. Add flour quickly, all at once, beating with a wooden spoon until mixture forms a ball that leaves sides of pan. Remove from heat.

Add eggs to flour mixture, one at a time, beating well after each addition. (Mixture will separate as each egg is added to it.)

Set aside 2 tablespoons diced Cheddar cheese; stir remaining cheese into flour mixture.

Drop dough by rounded tablespoonfuls (about 11) onto a greased baking sheet to form an 8-inch ring, leaving a 2½- to 3-inch-diameter hole in center. Sprinkle reserved cheese over top.

Bake at 425° for 50 to 55 minutes or until puffy and golden brown. Serve hot. Yield: 8 to 10 servings.

Ruth Woodin,
Darlington, Maryland.

BLUEBERRY STREUSEL MUFFINS

⅓ cup sugar
¼ cup butter or margarine, softened
1 egg
2⅓ cups all-purpose flour
1 tablespoon plus 1 teaspoon baking powder
½ teaspoon salt
1 cup milk
1 teaspoon vanilla extract
1½ cups fresh or frozen blueberries, thawed
½ cup sugar
⅓ cup all-purpose flour
½ teaspoon ground cinnamon
¼ cup butter or margarine, softened

Combine ⅓ cup sugar and ¼ cup butter in a small mixing bowl, creaming until light and fluffy. Add egg, beating well.

Combine 2⅓ cups flour, baking powder, and salt; add to creamed mixture alternately with milk, stirring well after each addition. Stir in vanilla extract, and fold in blueberries.

Spoon batter into greased muffin cups, filling two-thirds full. Combine ½ cup sugar, ⅓ cup flour, and cinnamon; cut in ¼ cup butter until mixture resembles crumbs. Sprinkle on top of muffin batter. Bake at 375° for 25 to 30 minutes or until golden brown. Yield: 1½ dozen.

Note: If using frozen blueberries, rinse and drain thawed berries; pat dry with paper towels. This will prevent discoloration of batter.

Mrs. Barrett F. Rosen,
Nashville, Tennessee.

BUTTER CHEESE DIPS

½ cup butter or margarine
2 tablespoons shortening
2 cups sifted self-rising flour
1 cup (4 ounces) shredded sharp Cheddar cheese
⅔ cup plus 1 tablespoon milk

Melt butter in a 15- x 10- x 1-inch jellyroll pan.

Cut shortening into flour until mixture resembles coarse crumbs. Stir in cheese and milk.

Turn dough out onto floured surface, and knead 2 to 3 times. Roll to about ¼-inch thickness, and cut with a small biscuit cutter. Dip both sides of biscuits in melted butter, placing them side by side in remaining melted butter for baking. Bake at 450° for 12 to 15 minutes. Yield: about 5 dozen.   *Jane Beverly, Fayetteville, Tennessee.*

FOUR-GRAIN MUFFINS

½ cup cornmeal
¼ cup regular oats, uncooked
¼ cup all-purpose flour
1½ teaspoons wheat germ
2 tablespoons sugar
1¼ teaspoons baking powder
½ teaspoon salt
½ cup buttermilk
¼ cup vegetable oil
1 egg, beaten

Combine first 4 ingredients in a medium bowl; stir in sugar, baking powder, and salt. Add buttermilk, oil, and egg, stirring just until moistened (batter will be lumpy).

Fill well-greased muffin cups two-thirds full. Bake at 375° for 20 to 25 minutes. Yield: about 10 muffins.
Phyllis Elaine Winfrey, Athens, Georgia.

Tip: Bake leftover pancake batter or make extra pancakes when convenient and freeze for later use. Fold, roll, or stack with two sheets of waxed paper between each; then place in foil or sealable bag for freezer storage. Plan to use within 3 weeks.

When You're Cooking With Eggs

From omelets and quiches to cakes and soufflés, eggs are an important ingredient no cook can do without. In addition to the important ways eggs function in recipes, they are also one of the most economical and nutritious foods available. To make the most of cooking with eggs, follow these tips.

—To avoid waste when a recipe calls for only egg yolks, freeze the whites. Freeze each white in an ice cube tray; then transfer to a freezer-proof bag or plastic container, and seal tightly. Thaw frozen egg whites overnight in the refrigerator, or place the container under cold, running water. Use thawed whites as you would fresh ones. Each egg white from a large egg measures about 1½ tablespoons.

—When a recipe indicates that egg yolks are to be beaten until thick and lemon colored or until they form a ribbon, you can stop beating when the mixture is a pastel yellow and falls from the beater in a long, flat string that folds upon itself.

—The chalaza, that thick, white coil next to the egg yolk, is a natural component of the egg and anchors the yolk in the thick white. It is the same material as the white, only more concentrated; there is no reason to remove it before cooking. In fact, the presence of prominent chalazae indicates fresh, high-quality eggs. As eggs lose freshness, the chalaza tends to disappear.

—Neither the cooking performance of the egg nor its flavor or nutritive value is affected by the color of the shell. Shell color is determined by the breed of hen, and the only difference in the eggs is the color of the shell.

—Air incorporated into egg whites when they are beaten acts as the leavening agent in many recipes. Beaten egg whites should be gently folded into a mixture, using a rubber spatula; never stir, as this will force air out of the whites. To fold, cut through whites and mixture you are folding into with a downward, across, up, and over motion until no streaks remain in the mixture.

Freeze leftover egg whites in an ice cube tray. When frozen, transfer to a freezer-proof bag or plastic container; seal tightly. Thaw the frozen whites when needed, and use just as you would fresh ones.

When egg yolks are added to a hot mixture, first stir a small amount of the hot mixture into the yolks; then stir the warmed yolk mixture into the remaining hot mixture.

—Eggs are sold by sizes, and egg size is determined by the minimum weight per dozen. Although the eggs within a carton may vary slightly, the minimum weight per dozen must be met.

Here's how to determine which size egg will give you the most for your money: If there is less than a 7-cent price spread per dozen between one size and the next smaller size of the same grade, you will get more for your money when you buy the larger size.

—When making meringues and in making some cakes, sugar is slowly added to beaten egg whites. This serves to increase the stability of the foam. If the sugar is added too fast, however, it can retard the foaming of the whites and thus decrease the volume.

—For stirred custard mixtures, recipes instruct to cook until mixture coats a metal spoon. This point of coating a metal spoon is 20 to 30 degrees below boiling. The eggs are cooked to the proper doneness when a thin film adheres to a metal spoon dipped into the custard. Stirred custard should never boil, as the finished product should be soft and thickened but not set. Stirred custard will thicken slightly after being refrigerated.

—Egg yolks will cook instantly, forming lumps, if added directly to a hot mixture. To prevent this, first stir a small amount of the hot mixture into the yolks to warm them; then stir the warmed yolk mixture into the remaining hot mixture.

Side Dishes From Light To Lively

These special side dishes are what you're looking for to round out your brunch or breakfast menu. For a lively touch, serve Garlic Cheese Grits or Sausage-Stuffed Tomatoes. For a beverage with the light touch of fruit, the Banana-Orange Slush is made to order. In fact, you can prepare it the night before.

SAUSAGE-STUFFED TOMATOES

4 large firm tomatoes
½ cup soft breadcrumbs
3 tablespoons finely chopped celery
3 tablespoons finely chopped green pepper
½ pound mild bulk pork sausage, cooked, crumbled, and drained
Salt and pepper
½ cup (2 ounces) shredded Cheddar cheese
Fresh parsley sprigs

Cut tops from tomatoes; scoop out pulp, leaving shells intact. Chop pulp; combine tomato pulp, breadcrumbs, celery, green pepper, and cooked sausage, mixing well.

Sprinkle inside of tomato shells with salt and pepper; spoon sausage mixture into shells. Arrange tomatoes in an 8-inch square baking pan; bake at 350° for 15 minutes or until tomatoes are thoroughly heated. Sprinkle tomatoes with cheese. Bake 1 additional minute or until cheese melts. Garnish with parsley, if desired. Yield: 4 servings.

Mrs. Jerryl Adams,
Chattanooga, Tennessee.

GARLIC CHEESE GRITS

4 cups water
½ teaspoon salt
1 cup regular uncooked grits
½ cup butter or margarine
1 (6-ounce) roll process cheese food with garlic
2 cups (8 ounces) shredded Cheddar cheese
2 tablespoons Worcestershire sauce
½ teaspoon garlic salt
Paprika (optional)

Combine water and salt in a medium saucepan; bring to a boil. Add grits; cover and reduce heat to low. Cook about 10 minutes or until thickened, stirring occasionally; remove from heat. Add next 5 ingredients; stir until cheese melts. Pour mixture into a greased 1½-quart casserole; sprinkle with paprika, if desired. Bake at 350° for 15 to 20 minutes. Yield: 6 servings.

Mrs. Herman Moore,
Dunwoody, Georgia.

Banana-Orange Slush, Garlic Cheese Grits, and Sausage-Stuffed Tomatoes are three special additions to the morning menu.

BANANA-ORANGE SLUSH

1 cup sugar
2 cups boiling water
1 (6-ounce) can frozen orange juice
   concentrate, undiluted
1 (15¼-ounce) can crushed pineapple,
   undrained
1 (10-ounce) jar maraschino cherries,
   drained
3 bananas, peeled and sliced
2½ tablespoons lemon juice
Fresh mint sprigs (optional)

Combine all ingredients except mint; mix well. Refrigerate for 24 hours, stirring occasionally.

Freeze overnight or until firm. Remove from freezer 15 to 20 minutes before serving (mixture should be slushy). Garnish with fresh mint sprigs, if desired. Yield: about 2 quarts.
Mrs. R. H. McCoin,
Greenville, Missouri.

SCRAMBLED GRITS

2½ cups cold, cooked grits
2 eggs, beaten
Bacon drippings

Place grits in medium bowl; break into pieces with a fork. Gently stir in eggs. Melt enough bacon drippings to cover bottom of heavy skillet. Spread grits evenly in skillet; cook until browned on bottom. Stir through mixture; spread evenly, and cook until consistency of scrambled eggs. Yield: 4 servings.
Jean Grebing,
Fort Worth, Texas.

Quail Makes This Breakfast Special

Everything about this breakfast says it's special, from the Hot Brandied Fruit that begins the feast to tender quail served with plum sauce.

The menu also offers scrambled eggs for those who prefer something more traditional than wild game. But even the eggs aren't everyday fare. They're cooked with cottage cheese in a white sauce and spooned into a sausage ring flavored with tart apple.

Hot Brandied Fruit
Quail With Red Plum Sauce
Pork Sausage Ring
Cottage-Scrambled Eggs
Baked Cheese Grits   Angel Biscuits
Orange Juice   Coffee

HOT BRANDIED FRUIT

1 (30-ounce) can apricot halves
1 (29-ounce) can pear halves
1 (29-ounce) can peach halves
1 (20-ounce) can pineapple slices
1 (10-ounce) jar maraschino cherries
½ cup butter or margarine
¾ cup firmly packed brown sugar
½ cup brandy
10 whole cloves
4 sticks cinnamon

Drain fruit, and combine juices; stir well, and set aside 1 cup of the fruit juice mixture.

Melt butter; add sugar, stirring until smooth. Add reserved juice, brandy, and spices; stir until well blended.

Combine fruit in a 2½-quart casserole, and pour in brandy mixture. Bake at 350° for 30 minutes or until bubbly. Yield: 8 to 10 servings.
Mrs. Robert Crisman,
Cleveland, Mississippi.

QUAIL WITH RED PLUM SAUCE

6 quail, cleaned and split down back
¾ cup all-purpose flour
Salt
Pepper
½ cup plus 1 tablespoon butter or
   margarine, divided
½ cup chopped onion
3 quail giblets or 3 chicken livers
½ cup dry white wine
¼ cup dry sherry
6 (1-inch-thick) slices Italian or French
   bread, toasted
Red Plum Sauce
Spiced crabapples (optional)
Parsley sprigs (optional)

Spread quail open, and pat dry with paper towels. Combine flour, 1 teaspoon salt, and ½ teaspoon pepper;

dredge quail in flour mixture, and set aside.

Melt 2 tablespoons butter in a skillet; add onion and giblets, and sauté 4 minutes. Remove onion and giblets from skillet, and set aside.

Place quail in drippings in skillet, and brown on both sides. Remove to a 13- x 9- x 2-inch baking pan. Add white wine to drippings in skillet; bring to a boil, scraping sides and bottom of skillet. Pour over quail. Bake at 350° for 30 minutes.

Mash giblets and onion; add remaining butter, sherry, dash of salt, and dash of pepper. Mix well, and spread on toasted bread; broil 5 to 6 inches away from heat until bubbly.

Place a quail on each toast slice; serve with Red Plum Sauce. Yield: 6 servings.

Red Plum Sauce:

1 cup red plum jelly
Grated rind and juice of 1 lemon
Grated rind and juice of 1 orange
½ teaspoon dry mustard

Combine all ingredients, mixing well; place over medium heat. Cook, stirring constantly, until jelly melts and the mixture boils. Serve hot. Yield: about 1½ cups.
*Edna Chadsey,
Corpus Christi, Texas.*

PORK SAUSAGE RING

2 eggs, slightly beaten
½ cup milk
1½ cups cracker crumbs
¼ cup minced onion
1 cup peeled, chopped cooking apple
2 pounds bulk pork sausage
Parsley sprigs (optional)

Combine all ingredients except parsley, mixing well. Press into a greased 6½-cup mold; unmold onto a 15- x 10- x 1-inch jellyroll pan. Bake at 350° for 1 hour. Immediately remove to serving platter. Spoon Cottage-Scrambled Eggs into center and around edges. Garnish with parsley sprigs, if desired. Yield: 8 to 10 servings. *Mrs. Jim Caughman,
Charlotte, North Carolina.*

COTTAGE-SCRAMBLED EGGS

3 tablespoons butter or margarine
3 tablespoons all-purpose flour
1 cup milk
10 eggs
1 cup cream-style cottage cheese
½ teaspoon salt
Dash of pepper

Melt butter in a heavy saucepan over low heat; add flour, stirring until smooth. Cook 1 minute, stirring constantly. Gradually add milk; cook over medium heat, stirring constantly, until thickened and bubbly.

Combine eggs, cottage cheese, salt, and pepper; beat well, and stir into white sauce. Cook, stirring often, until eggs are firm but still moist. Spoon into center and around edges of Pork Sausage Ring. Yield: 8 to 10 servings.
*Kathleen Cramer,
Crowley, Louisiana.*

BAKED CHEESE GRITS

2½ cups milk
¾ cup uncooked regular grits
½ cup margarine
½ teaspoon salt
⅓ cup grated Parmesan cheese
1 (5-ounce) jar sharp process cheese
  spread

Bring milk to a boil; add grits and cook until thickened (about 10 minutes), stirring often. Stir in margarine, salt, and cheese; spoon into a lightly greased 1-quart casserole. Bake at 325° for 20 minutes. Yield: 6 to 8 servings.
*Mrs. S. J. Flowers,
Louisville, Kentucky.*

ANGEL BISCUITS

1 package dry yeast
2 tablespoons warm water (105° to 115°)
2 cups buttermilk
5 cups all-purpose flour
¼ cup sugar
1 tablespoon baking powder
1 teaspoon soda
1 teaspoon salt
1 cup shortening

Combine yeast and warm water; let stand 5 minutes or until bubbly. Add buttermilk to yeast mixture, and set aside.

Combine dry ingredients in a large bowl; cut in shortening until mixture resembles coarse crumbs. Add buttermilk mixture, mixing with a fork until dry ingredients are moistened. Turn dough out on a floured surface, and knead lightly about 3 or 4 times.

Roll dough to ½-inch thickness; cut into rounds with a 2-inch cutter, and place on lightly greased baking sheets. Bake at 400° for 10 to 12 minutes. Yield: about 3 dozen.
*Mrs. John G. Lile,
Pine Bluff, Arkansas.*

Take A Fresh Look At Grapefruit

One of the best ways to add sunshine to your breakfast or brunch is to serve grapefruit. Whether sliced and broiled, sectioned for a salad, or ground for a marmalade, the tart flavor of grapefruit is the perfect way to begin or end a morning meal. And while grapefruit juice is delicious by itself, it combines well with other beverages for a refreshing drink.

When purchasing, select firm, well-rounded grapefruit that are heavy for their size. If stored at room temperature, grapefruit will keep for a day or two; when refrigerated, they will keep up to four months.

THREE-FRUIT DRINK

1 banana, peeled and broken into chunks
1 cup grapefruit juice
1 cup orange juice
1 cup milk
2 tablespoons honey

Combine all ingredients in container of electric blender; process until frothy. Chill until serving time. Yield: about 4 to 5 servings. *Regyna Day, Westminster, Colorado.*

SHERRIED BROILED GRAPEFRUIT

2 large grapefruit, halved
4 tablespoons brown sugar
Cocktail sherry

Remove seeds, and loosen sections of grapefruit halves; sprinkle 1 tablespoon sugar over top of each.
Broil grapefruit 4 inches from heat for 2 minutes; sprinkle 2 to 3 teaspoons sherry over top of each half. Broil 1 to 2 minutes longer or until bubbly and lightly browned. Yield: 4 servings.
Mrs. J. W. Elliott, Jr., Roanoke, Virginia.

GRAPEFRUIT SUPREME

½ cup sugar
¼ cup orange juice
1 pint fresh strawberries, washed and capped
3 large grapefruit, halved

Combine sugar and orange juice in a medium saucepan; mix well. Bring to a boil; let boil 1 minute or until sugar dissolves, stirring constantly. Remove from heat, and stir in strawberries. Refrigerate until thoroughly chilled.
Remove seeds, and loosen sections of each grapefruit half. Spoon strawberry mixture evenly over grapefruit halves. Yield: 6 servings.
Mrs. J. M. Hamilton, Fort Mill, South Carolina.

GRAPEFRUIT COMBO SALAD

3 large grapefruit, peeled and sectioned
3 large oranges, peeled and sectioned
2 cucumbers, peeled and thinly sliced
1 medium onion, thinly sliced and separated into rings
1 apple, cored and diced
1 cup miniature marshmallows (optional)
¾ cup sugar
1 cup orange juice
¾ cup red wine vinegar
1½ teaspoons salt
¼ teaspoon pepper
Lettuce leaves (optional)

Combine first 6 ingredients; set aside. Combine sugar, orange juice, vinegar, salt, and pepper; mix lightly with a wire whisk. Pour juice mixture over fruit, tossing gently. Cover; chill 2 to 3 hours.
To serve, drain salad. Place in a lettuce-lined bowl, if desired. Serve immediately. Yield: 12 to 14 servings.
Note: For best flavor, salad should not be stored overnight.
Mrs. Shelia Melton, Tallahassee, Florida.

COMBINATION CITRUS MARMALADE

1 large grapefruit
1 large orange
1 lemon
7½ cups water
8 cups sugar

Wash fruit; cut in half crosswise. Remove seeds and membrane in center of each. Cut fruit in quarters; grind unpeeled fruit in meat grinder or food processor using steel chopping blade.
Combine fruit and water in a large Dutch oven; heat to boiling. Reduce heat, and boil 10 minutes. Remove from heat; cool. Cover; let stand overnight.
Add sugar to fruit mixture; cook over medium heat until mixture reaches 220° on candy thermometer (about 1 hour). Remove from heat, and let cool to 190°. Pour into hot sterilized jars, leaving ⅛-inch headspace. Cover with metal lids, and process in boiling-water bath for 10 minutes. Yield: 4½ pints.
Charlotte B. Taylor, Ringgold, Virginia.

Beverages To Brighten The Morning

These eye-opening beverages will get your brunch or breakfast off to a good start. Hot or cold, made with coffee, milk, or fruit juices, they're great to wake up to.
There's Orange Blush, a blend of orange and cranberry juices sparkling with club soda, and Spiced Hot Chocolate, flavored with bits of chocolate and ground cinnamon. For a late-morning brunch, we suggest serving an assortment of Tropical Fruit Punch, Bloody Marys, and Coffee Punch.

SPICED HOT CHOCOLATE

6 cups milk
½ cup sugar
3 (1-ounce) squares unsweetened chocolate, cut into small pieces
1 teaspoon ground cinnamon
¼ teaspoon salt
2 eggs, beaten
2 teaspoons vanilla extract

Combine first 5 ingredients in a saucepan, mixing well; cook over medium heat, stirring constantly, until chocolate melts. Gradually stir a small amount of hot mixture into eggs. Add eggs to remaining hot mixture; cook over low heat 2 to 3 minutes, stirring constantly. Remove from heat; add vanilla, and beat on medium speed of an electric mixer until frothy. Yield: about 6 cups.
Martha T. Leoni, New Bern, North Carolina.

COFFEE PUNCH

2 quarts strong coffee
2 cups milk
½ cup sugar
1 teaspoon vanilla extract
1 cup whipping cream
1 cup dark rum
1 quart chocolate or vanilla ice cream
Miniature marshmallows (optional)

Combine coffee, milk, sugar, and vanilla; stir until sugar dissolves. Chill until ready to serve.

Just before serving, stir whipping cream and rum into coffee mixture. Scoop ice cream into a punch bowl; gradually pour coffee mixture over ice cream. Float marshmallows on top, if desired. Yield: about 1 gallon.

Mrs. C. E. McWilliams,
Montgomery, Alabama.

BLOODY MARYS

1½ cups tomato juice
¼ cup vodka
2 teaspoons Worcestershire sauce
2 teaspoons lemon juice
2 dashes hot sauce
2 dashes celery salt
Coarsely ground pepper to taste
Celery stalks

Combine first 7 ingredients, mixing well. Pour over ice cubes; garnish each serving with a stalk of celery. Yield: about 2 cups. *Margie Humphrey,*
Front Royal, Virginia.

ORANGE BLOSSOM FLIPS

1 (6-ounce) can frozen orange juice
    concentrate, undiluted
1 cup half-and-half
¾ cup cream sherry
1 egg
Dash of salt
2 ice cubes

Combine all ingredients in container of electric blender; process until smooth and frothy. Yield: about 2½ cups.

Mrs. Barry D. Goss,
Atlanta, Georgia.

ORANGE BLUSH

1 (6-ounce) can frozen orange juice
    concentrate, thawed and undiluted
1 cup cranberry juice
¼ cup sugar
2 cups club soda

Combine orange juice, cranberry juice, and sugar; stir until sugar dissolves. Chill.

Just before serving, add club soda to fruit juice mixture. Serve over crushed ice. Yield: about 4 cups.

Mrs. W. E. Sivley, Jr.,
Decatur, Alabama.

TROPICAL FRUIT PUNCH

3 cups pineapple juice
2 cups grapefruit carbonated beverage
2 cups rum
½ cup lime juice
Orange slices
Pineapple chunks
Maraschino cherries

Combine pineapple juice, grapefruit carbonated beverage, rum, and lime juice; mix well. Serve over ice cubes or crushed ice. Garnish with orange slices, pineapple chunks, and cherries skewered on toothpicks. Yield: 7½ cups.

Dr. Arthur Bradsher,
Windsor, North Carolina.

Get A Headstart On Breakfast

Breakfast is a breeze when you prepare it the day before. Select a make-ahead entrée or coffee cake or both, prepare them the day before serving, and store them in the refrigerator. The next morning you're ready to pop them in the oven and serve a very special breakfast in no time at all.

That's what you do with all the recipes given here. In fact, our rich Overnight Coffee Cake, with a crumbly topping of brown sugar, walnuts, and cinnamon, must be refrigerated overnight before it is baked.

SCRAMBLED EGG CASSEROLE

1 cup cubed ham or Canadian bacon
¼ cup chopped green onion
3 tablespoons melted butter or margarine
1 dozen eggs, beaten
1 (4-ounce) can sliced mushrooms,
    drained
Cheese sauce (recipe follows)
¼ cup melted butter or margarine
2¼ cups soft breadcrumbs
⅛ teaspoon paprika

Sauté ham and green onion in 3 tablespoons butter in a large skillet until onion is tender. Add eggs and cook over medium-high heat, stirring to form large, soft curds; when eggs are set, stir in mushrooms and cheese sauce. Spoon eggs into a greased 13- x 9- x 2-inch baking pan. Combine ¼ cup melted butter and crumbs, mixing well; spread evenly over egg mixture. Sprinkle with paprika. Cover and chill casserole overnight.

Uncover and bake at 350° for 30 minutes or until heated thoroughly. Yield: 12 to 15 servings.

Cheese Sauce:

2 tablespoons butter or margarine
2½ tablespoons all-purpose flour
2 cups milk
½ teaspoon salt
⅛ teaspoon pepper
1 cup (4 ounces) shredded process
    American cheese

Melt butter in a heavy saucepan over low heat; blend in flour, and cook 1 minute. Gradually add milk; cook over medium heat until thickened, stirring constantly. Add salt, pepper, and cheese, stirring until cheese melts and mixture is smooth. Yield: about 2½ cups. *Kay Viergever,*
Denison, Texas.

BREAKFAST SANDWICHES

Softened butter
8 slices bread
1 pound bulk pork sausage, cooked,
    crumbled, and drained
1 cup (4 ounces) shredded Cheddar cheese
2 eggs, beaten
2 cups milk
1½ teaspoons prepared mustard

Spread butter on bread slices. Place 4 slices, buttered side down, in a single layer in a greased shallow baking dish. Top each bread slice with sausage and remaining bread slices, buttered side up. Sprinkle with cheese. Combine remaining ingredients; pour over sandwiches. Cover and refrigerate overnight.

Remove dish from refrigerator, and allow to reach room temperature. Uncover and bake at 350° for 45 minutes. Reduce oven temperature to 300°, and bake an additional 10 minutes or until set. Yield: 4 servings.
Mrs. William E. Wilson,
Versailles, Kentucky.

OVERNIGHT COFFEE CAKE

¾ cup butter or margarine, softened
1 cup sugar
2 eggs
1 (8-ounce) carton commercial sour cream
2 cups all-purpose flour
1 teaspoon baking powder
1 teaspoon soda
½ teaspoon salt
1 teaspoon ground nutmeg
¾ cup firmly packed brown sugar
½ cup chopped walnuts
1 teaspoon ground cinnamon

Combine butter and sugar; cream until light and fluffy. Add eggs and sour cream, mixing well. Combine next 5 ingredients; add to batter, and mix well. Pour batter into a greased and floured 13- x 9- x 2-inch baking pan.

Combine brown sugar, walnuts, and cinnamon; mix well, and sprinkle evenly over batter. Cover and chill overnight; uncover and bake at 350° for 35 to 40 minutes or until cake tests done. Yield: 15 servings. *Mrs. Frank J. Kolar,*
Oak Brook, Illinois.

POTATO BREAKFAST CASSEROLE

1 (6-ounce) package hash brown potato
    mix with onions
1 quart hot water
5 eggs
½ cup cottage cheese
1 cup (4 ounces) shredded Swiss cheese
1 green onion, chopped
1 teaspoon salt
⅛ teaspoon pepper
4 drops hot sauce
6 slices bacon, cooked, drained, and
    crumbled
Paprika

Cover hash browns with hot water; let stand 10 minutes. Drain well.

Beat eggs; add potatoes and remaining ingredients except bacon and paprika. Pour mixture into a buttered 10-inch piepan. Sprinkle with bacon and paprika. Cover dish, and refrigerate overnight.

Place cold piepan, uncovered, in cold oven. Bake at 350° for 35 minutes or until potatoes are tender and eggs done. Yield: 6 to 8 servings. *Barbara Payne,*
Shawnee, Oklahoma.

REFRIGERATOR GINGERBREAD

1 cup shortening
1 cup sugar
1 cup dark molasses
4 eggs
2 teaspoons soda
1 cup buttermilk
4 cups all-purpose flour
2 teaspoons ground ginger
½ teaspoon ground allspice
½ teaspoon ground cloves
½ teaspoon ground cinnamon
1 cup chopped pecans
1 cup seedless raisins

Combine shortening and sugar, creaming until light and fluffy. Stir in molasses; add eggs, one at a time, beating well after each addition. Dissolve the soda in the buttermilk.

Combine flour and spices; add to creamed mixture alternately with buttermilk, beating well after each addition. Stir in pecans and raisins. Store batter in an airtight container in refrigerator.

When ready to bake, fill greased 1½-inch muffin cups two-thirds full. Bake at 350° about 20 minutes or until muffins test done.

Batter may be stored for several weeks in refrigerator. Yield: about 6 dozen.

Note: To bake without chilling batter, reduce baking time to 15 minutes.
Mrs. James A. Mallow,
Brady, Texas.

INDIVIDUAL FROZEN SOUFFLES

2 tablespoons butter or margarine
¼ cup all-purpose flour
½ teaspoon salt
¼ teaspoon pepper
¼ teaspoon dry mustard
1 cup milk
1½ cups (6 ounces) shredded sharp
    Cheddar cheese
6 eggs, separated

Melt butter in a heavy saucepan over low heat. Blend in flour, salt, pepper, and mustard; cook 1 minute. Gradually add milk; cook over medium heat, stirring constantly, until thickened. Add cheese, stirring until melted; remove from heat, and cool slightly.

Beat egg yolks until thick and lemon colored. Add a small amount of cheese sauce to yolks, and mix well; stir yolk mixture into remaining cheese mixture.

Beat egg whites until stiff but not dry; fold into cheese mixture. Pour into 6 buttered 1-cup soufflé dishes; cover with plastic wrap and freeze. To bake, place frozen soufflés on baking dish. Bake at 350° for 40 minutes or until lightly browned. Yield: 6 servings.
Mrs. H. E. McElhaney,
Auburn, Alabama.

Frozen Fish Takes To Microwaves

Microwave cooking can do wonders for frozen fish fillets. What are the advantages? Minimal handling is required when microwaving, preventing the fragile fillets from breaking apart, and the rapid cooking special to the microwave preserves the moist texture and delicate flavor of the fish.

Because microwave energy cooks rapidly, cooking will continue after the microwave cycle is complete. Therefore, care must be taken to avoid overcooking fish; if overcooked, it will be dry and tough. Fish is done when it is opaque and flakes easily when tested with a fork. When microwaving, cook fish for the minimum time, and allow to stand about 2 minutes. If it does not test done after standing, continue cooking briefly.

The recipes included here will acquaint you with the ease of preparing frozen fish fillets in the microwave oven. Since the wattage of microwave ovens varies, the cooking times will vary. A time range is given in our recipes to allow for the difference. To prevent overcooking, always check for doneness at the lower end of the range.

You'll also find the following guidelines on power settings, covering, and defrosting helpful when microwaving those frozen fillets.

Power settings: Most fillets cook well on HIGH power; however, if cooked in a sauce with high sugar content or in a delicate cream sauce, the setting should be lowered. Sugar attracts microwave energy and can cause uneven or overcooking; cream sauces can curdle if cooked too rapidly. Thicker cuts of fish, such as steaks and whole fish, also require a lower setting for even cooking.

Covering: Fish should be covered to seal in juices and promote even cooking. Some manufacturers say that crumb-coated fish need not be covered because the coating seals in juices. However, we recommend covering all fillets.

Clear plastic wrap is a good covering for fish cooked in delicate sauces, as they require extra shielding. When using plastic wrap, turn back one corner to allow some steam to escape. Excessive steam makes sauces watery and increases the possibility of burning yourself when removing the covering from the fish.

Waxed paper is a good covering for fillets cooked in a sturdy sauce or with a crumb coating. Since the fish is shielded by the sauce or crumbs, the waxed paper simply promotes even heating and prevents spattering.

Defrosting: Fillets can be left in their original package for defrosting in the microwave. Since fish defrosts rapidly, care must be taken not to toughen it by over-defrosting in the microwave oven. Remove the fish from the package while still slightly icy; hold under cold, running water to complete defrosting.

Weight and shape of the package affects defrosting time; thick packages take longer than flatter ones of the same weight. Use LOW or DEFROST setting, and allow about 6 to 9 minutes per pound if fillets are solidly frozen. The package should be turned over and given a quarter-turn after half the defrosting time has elapsed. Check fillets after minimum time has elapsed. If necessary, continue to microwave, checking every 30 seconds.

POACHED FISH IN CREAMY SWISS SAUCE

3 tablespoons water
2 tablespoons dry white wine
1 medium carrot, cut into ½-inch pieces (about ½ cup)
1 stalk celery, cut into 1-inch pieces (about ½ cup)
1 medium onion, sliced and separated into rings
½ lemon, sliced
3 peppercorns
1 bay leaf
2 tablespoons chopped fresh parsley
⅛ teaspoon salt
1 (16-ounce) package frozen fish fillets, thawed
Creamy Swiss Sauce
Seasoned dry breadcrumbs
Paprika

Combine first 10 ingredients in a 12- x 8- x 2-inch baking dish; stir well, being sure vegetables are evenly distributed in dish. Cover with clear plastic wrap; microwave at HIGH for 4 to 6 minutes or until vegetables are crisp-tender.

Arrange fish fillets over vegetables with thicker portions to outside of dish (thinner portions may overlap, if necessary). Cover and microwave at HIGH for 3 to 5 minutes or until fish flakes easily when tested with a fork, giving dish one half-turn during cooking. Remove fish fillets, and keep warm. Strain fish stock, and discard vegetables. Add enough water to fish stock to measure ½ cup; use to prepare Creamy Swiss Sauce.

Return fish fillets to baking dish; spoon sauce over fillets. Sprinkle with breadcrumbs and paprika. Cover and microwave at MEDIUM for 2 to 3 minutes or until bubbly. Yield: 4 servings.

Creamy Swiss Sauce:

3 tablespoons butter or margarine
3 tablespoons all-purpose flour
¼ teaspoon salt
⅛ teaspoon white pepper
1 cup half-and-half
½ cup reserved fish stock
¾ cup (3 ounces) shredded process Swiss cheese

Place butter in a 1-quart glass measure or casserole dish. Microwave at HIGH for 30 seconds or until butter melts; blend in flour, salt, and pepper. Gradually add half-and-half and fish stock, stirring well.

Microwave at HIGH for 2½ minutes; stir well. Microwave at HIGH for 1½ to 2½ minutes or until thickened and bubbly, stirring at 1-minute intervals. Add cheese, stirring until melted. Yield: about 2 cups.

LEMON-COATED FILLETS

¼ cup butter or margarine
2 teaspoons lemon juice
1 (16-ounce) package frozen fish fillets, thawed
Salt and pepper to taste
¾ cup seasoned dry breadcrumbs
Paprika
Lemon slices (optional)
Fresh parsley sprigs (optional)

Place butter in a 1-cup glass measure. Microwave at HIGH for 30 seconds or until butter is melted. Stir in lemon juice.

Sprinkle fillets with salt and pepper; brush both sides of each with butter mixture. Gently dredge fillets in breadcrumbs, and sprinkle with paprika. Arrange fillets in a 12- x 8- x 2-inch baking dish with thicker portions to outside (thinner portions may overlap, if necessary). Cover with waxed paper.

Microwave at HIGH for 3 to 5 minutes or until fish flakes easily when tested with a fork, giving dish one half-turn during cooking. Garnish with lemon slices and parsley, if desired. Yield: 4 servings.

Fillet of Fish Amandine takes only minutes to prepare in a microwave oven, and the quick cooking preserves the moist texture and delicate flavor of the fish.

Combine cornstarch and cold water in a 2-quart glass measure or deep casserole dish, stirring well to dissolve cornstarch. Add the tomato sauce, pineapple chunks, brown sugar, vinegar, onion, and green pepper; stir well to dissolve the sugar.

Microwave at HIGH for 4 minutes, stirring once; then stir well at end of cooking period. Microwave at HIGH for 4 to 6 minutes or until sauce is thickened and bubbly, stirring at 1-minute intervals.

Arrange fillets in a 12- x 8- x 2-inch baking dish with thicker portions to outside of dish (thinner portions may overlap, if necessary). Pour sauce evenly over fillets. Cover with waxed paper; microwave at MEDIUM HIGH for 7 to 9 minutes or until fish flakes easily when tested with a fork, giving dish one half-turn during cooking. Yield: 4 servings.

Tossed-Up Salad Greens

Crisp fresh salad greens are the first step to a good salad. But as good as greens are alone, just consider all the possibilities of added ingredients.

Fresh Greens and Tuna Salad combines endive, romaine, Bibb, iceberg, and Boston lettuce with tuna and hard-cooked eggs. This salad is substantial enough to be served as a main dish.

We toss spinach with lots of good things. Try Fresh Spinach With Spicy Dressing or Southern Spinach Salad, made with fresh fruit and spinach.

FILLET OF FISH AMANDINE

¼ cup butter or margarine
¼ cup sliced almonds
1½ teaspoons lemon juice
1 (16-ounce) package frozen fish fillets, thawed
Salt to taste
Lemon slices (optional)
Parsley sprigs (optional)

Place butter, almonds, and lemon juice in a 12- x 8- x 2-inch baking dish. Microwave at HIGH for 6 to 8 minutes or until almonds are golden, stirring twice. Remove almonds with a slotted spoon, reserving butter mixture in baking dish; set almonds aside.

Sprinkle fillets with salt, and coat with butter mixture. Arrange in dish with thickest portion to outside (thinner portions may overlap, if necessary). Cover with clear plastic wrap.

Microwave at HIGH for 2 to 4 minutes or until fish flakes easily when tested with a fork, giving dish one half-turn during cooking. Carefully remove fish to a serving platter; spoon almonds over top. Yield: 4 servings.

SWEET-AND-SOUR FISH

3 tablespoons cornstarch
¼ cup cold water
1 (8-ounce) can tomato sauce
1 (8-ounce) can pineapple chunks, undrained
½ cup firmly packed brown sugar
⅓ cup red wine vinegar
¼ cup chopped onion
1 small green pepper, cut into ½-inch strips
1 (16-ounce) package frozen fish fillets, thawed

MIXED GREEN SALAD WITH CHICKEN

1 cup mayonnaise
¼ cup tarragon vinegar
1 (1-ounce) package anchovy fillets, chopped
¼ cup chopped fresh parsley
2 tablespoons chopped green onion
2 tablespoons chopped chives
½ teaspoon dry mustard
¼ teaspoon salt
½ small head iceberg lettuce, torn
4 to 5 endive leaves, torn
1 head Bibb lettuce, torn
½ head romaine, torn
3 cups chopped cooked chicken
2 medium tomatoes, sliced

Combine first 8 ingredients, mixing well. Refrigerate several hours.

Combine salad greens and chicken; toss with dressing. Line a large salad bowl with the tomato slices; fill with salad. Serve immediately. Yield: about 6 to 8 servings. *Mrs. Cindy Murphy, Knoxville, Tennessee.*

FRESH GREENS AND TUNA SALAD

½ head romaine, torn
½ head Bibb lettuce, torn
4 endive leaves, torn
½ head iceberg lettuce, torn
1 head Boston lettuce, torn
1 cup chopped cucumber
1 small onion, thinly sliced
2 (7-ounce) cans tuna, drained and flaked
4 hard-cooked eggs
¼ cup lemon juice
½ cup olive oil
3 tablespoons chopped fresh parsley
1 teaspoon mayonnaise
½ teaspoon dry mustard
¾ teaspoon salt
Dash of pepper

Combine first 8 ingredients in a large salad bowl. Cut 3 hard-cooked eggs into wedges; add the wedges to the salad greens and tuna.

Press remaining egg through a sieve; add remaining ingredients, mixing well. Pour dressing over salad; toss gently. Yield: 6 to 8 servings.
Florence L. Costello, Chattanooga, Tennessee.

SOUTHERN SPINACH SALAD

6 cups torn fresh spinach
2 cups shredded iceberg lettuce
2 oranges, sectioned
2 grapefruit, sectioned
3 tablespoons vegetable oil
2 tablespoons tarragon vinegar
1 teaspoon sugar
½ teaspoon salt
½ teaspoon ground ginger
Paprika

Combine spinach, lettuce, orange sections, and grapefruit sections in a large salad bowl.

Combine next 5 ingredients; mix well. Toss spinach mixture with dressing. Sprinkle with paprika. Yield: about 6 to 8 servings. *Eva G. Key, Isle of Palms, South Carolina.*

FRESH SPINACH WITH SPICY DRESSING

½ pound fresh spinach, torn
1 (16-ounce) can bean sprouts, drained
½ head iceberg lettuce, torn
½ cup cooked, crumbled bacon
3 hard-cooked eggs, chopped
Spicy Dressing

Combine all ingredients except Spicy Dressing in a large salad bowl. Serve with dressing. Yield: 6 servings.

Spicy Dressing:

1 cup vegetable oil
¼ cup vinegar
½ cup sugar
⅓ cup catsup
1 small onion, chopped
1 tablespoon Worcestershire sauce
1 teaspoon salt

Combine oil and vinegar; beat with electric mixer 3 to 5 minutes. Add remaining ingredients; beat well. Yield: about 2 cups. *Mrs. E. W. Hanley, Elberton, Georgia.*

Everything Is Rosy In His Kitchen

On pretty, sunny days, you'll find Arthur Cottingham of Greenville, South Carolina, outside tending his 500 roses. But on rainy days, look in the kitchen, because that's where he'll be, working on one of his newest culinary creations.

Arthur says he has been cooking for 30 years, "But just for fun," he says. "Someone gave me a copy of one of Julia Child's cookbooks, and that got me started."

After performing a cooking demonstration on a local television program, Arthur's cooking skills became well known in the Greenville area. "But," he proudly adds, "I'm most noted for being an accredited rose judge. I've judged rose shows from Knoxville to Savannah."

One of Arthur's favorite recipes is a vegetable-filled fried rice that he prepares in a wok. "The beauty of Chinese food is in the crispness of the vegetables," Arthur points out. "It takes a while to chop all of the ingredients and get them together, but the cooking is quick."

In addition to the Fried Rice Special, we've also included his recipe for Vacherin Moka.

VACHERIN MOKA

4 egg whites (at room temperature)
1 cup sugar
½ teaspoon ground cinnamon
Mocha Filling
Powdered sugar
½ cup whipping cream, whipped
Sliced almonds

Draw two 8-inch circles on brown paper. Cut circles out and place each in the center of a baking sheet.

Beat egg whites in a small mixing bowl until soft peaks form; gradually add 1 tablespoon sugar, beating until glossy and stiff peaks form. Fold in remaining sugar and cinnamon.

Spoon half of meringue mixture onto paper circle on baking sheet. Using back of spoon, shape meringue into a circle about 8 inches in diameter; then shape circle into a shell (sides should be about 1 inch high). Repeat procedure with remaining meringue.

Bake at 275° for 1 hour. Let meringues cool to touch; remove from paper, and allow the layers to cool completely on wire racks.

Place one meringue on a serving platter; fill with Mocha Filling. Top with remaining meringue shell. Sift powdered sugar lightly over top. Top with whipped cream (a decorating bag may be used to make rosettes, if desired). Stand sliced almonds in whipped cream or in the center of each rosette. Chill thoroughly. Yield: 8 to 10 servings.

Mocha Filling:

1 tablespoon brown sugar
½ teaspoon instant coffee granules
1 tablespoon hot water
1½ cups whipping cream

Combine sugar and instant coffee; add hot water, stirring until sugar dissolves. Let cool to room temperature.

Beat whipping cream in a small mixing bowl until slightly thickened; add coffee mixture, and continue beating until mixture is stiff. Store in refrigerator. Yield: about 3 cups.

Note: Handle cooled meringue shells carefully to avoid cracking.

Tip: Perfect hard-cooked eggs: Place eggs in a saucepan and cover with water; bring to boiling, lower heat to simmer, and cook 14 minutes. Pour off hot water and add cold water; shells will come off easily.

FRIED RICE SPECIAL

3 tablespoons vegetable oil, divided
2 eggs, beaten
¼ cup thinly sliced carrots
¼ cup sliced green onion
1 (8-ounce) can bamboo shoots, drained
1¼ cups sliced fresh mushrooms
2 cups cooked rice
2 tablespoons soy sauce
2 tablespoons dry sherry
¾ cup cooked diced ham
1 cup cooked diced chicken

Heat 1 tablespoon oil to 350° in a wok or electric skillet. Add eggs, and stir-fry until firm but still moist; set aside.

Heat remaining oil. Stir-fry carrots 1 minute; add onion, bamboo shoots, and mushrooms. Continue to stir-fry 1 minute. Add rice, soy sauce, sherry, ham, and chicken; cook, stirring constantly, 1 minute longer. Stir in eggs. Serve immediately. Yield: 8 to 10 servings.

CORN SOUP

½ cup chopped onion
2 tablespoons bacon drippings
1 (17-ounce) can whole kernel corn, drained
1 (28-ounce) can tomatoes, drained
4 medium potatoes, peeled and cubed
1 tablespoon salt
½ teaspoon pepper
½ cup chopped celery
2 quarts water
1 pound peeled raw shrimp
½ cup chopped parsley

Sauté onion in bacon drippings in a Dutch oven until tender. Add next 6 ingredients; simmer 15 minutes, stirring occasionally. Add water, and bring mixture to a boil. Stir in shrimp, and continue to cook 10 additional minutes. Sprinkle parsley over soup; reduce heat, and cook 25 minutes. Yield: 8 to 10 servings.

G. K. Lasseigne,
Houma, Louisiana.

PISTACHIO PIE

1 (3¾-ounce) package instant pistachio pudding and pie filling mix
1 pint vanilla ice cream, softened
¾ cup milk
1 (9-inch) graham cracker crust, baked
1 (4-ounce) carton frozen whipped topping, thawed
1 (1 3/16-ounce) English toffee candy bar

Combine pudding mix, ice cream, and milk; beat with an electric mixer until smooth and blended. Pour into pie crust; freeze 1 hour or until firm.

Spread whipped topping evenly over pie. Crumble candy bar; sprinkle over whipped topping. Store in freezer.

Before serving, allow pie to sit at room temperature 5 to 10 minutes. Yield: one 9-inch pie.

David Berolzheimer,
Largo, Florida.

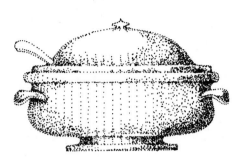

Try Your Hand At Some New Orleans Favorites

Perhaps more than any other city, New Orleans is known for good food. Here we present favorite recipes from some of the city's most popular restaurants. Because some chefs are hesitant to divulge all their secrets, and because their skill is difficult to match, we can't promise you'll get an exact duplicate of their specialties. But each has been thoroughly tested, so your results should be very close to theirs.

■ **Felix's Restaurant and Bar** laces oysters with bacon to create this delicious hot sandwich.

OYSTERS BROCHETTE

1 dozen fresh oysters
All-purpose flour
6 bacon slices, cut into 1-inch pieces
Vegetable oil
1 slice bread, toasted and cut in half lengthwise
Shredded lettuce
Tomato slices
Dill pickle slices
French fries (optional)
Fresh parsley sprigs (optional)

Dredge oysters in flour; alternate with bacon on 2 wooden skewers. Deep fry in hot oil until golden brown. Drain well. Place on toast to serve. Arrange lettuce, tomato, and pickles on plate. Serve with French fries and garnish with parsley, if desired. Yield: 2 servings.

■ Seafood is the specialty at **Delmonico**. There's turtle soup; Fillet of Snapper Rome, topped with a creamy crabmeat mixture; and Trout Delmonico, topped with oysters and shrimp. Catfish Meunière is garnished deliciously with shrimp stuffed with crabmeat.

TURTLE SOUP AU SHERRY

1½ to 2 pounds turtle meat, finely diced
2 quarts water
2 stalks celery, sliced
1 onion, chopped
1 clove garlic, minced
¼ teaspoon salt
¼ cup olive oil
¼ cup vegetable oil
¼ cup all-purpose flour
1½ cups chopped leeks or green onions
1 cup chopped tomato
Salt to taste
Dry sherry
4 hard-cooked eggs, chopped

Combine turtle meat, water, celery, onion, garlic, and ¼ teaspoon salt in a 4-quart Dutch oven; heat to boiling. Reduce heat; simmer 30 minutes, skimming top if necessary.

Heat oil in a medium skillet until warm. Stir in flour; cook over low heat, stirring constantly, until flour is browned. Add leeks and tomato; cook, stirring frequently, until leeks are lightly browned. Stir flour mixture into hot broth; cook until thickened and bubbly. Add salt to taste; stir in additional water if soup is too thick.

Ladle soup into serving bowls; stir about 1 teaspoon sherry into each, and top with chopped egg. Yield: about 8 servings.

Tip: Use fish as an economical dish. It has very little waste. A pound of fish, dressed or filleted, will often yield four full servings at a cost less than that of lean meat.

TROUT DELMONICO

6 large trout fillets
18 large shrimp
¼ cup butter, melted
1 tablespoon lemon juice
18 oysters
Chopped fresh parsley
Fresh parsley sprigs (optional)
Lemon wedges (optional)
Tomato wedges (optional)

Arrange trout fillets and shrimp in a 15- x 10- x 1-inch jellyroll pan. Combine butter and lemon juice; baste fillets and shrimp lightly with some of butter mixture. Bake at 350° for 10 minutes, basting occasionally with butter mixture.

Arrange oysters over fillets. Baste with remaining butter mixture; sprinkle with chopped parsley. Broil for 3 to 4 minutes or until edges of oysters begin to curl. Garnish with parsley sprigs, lemon wedges, and tomato wedges, if desired. Yield: 6 servings.

CATFISH MEUNIERE

12 jumbo shrimp, peeled and deveined
1 small onion, chopped
2 green onions, sliced
6 tablespoons butter
½ cup crabmeat
1 cup soft breadcrumbs
½ medium-size green pepper, cut into strips
1½ cups milk
2 eggs
1 teaspoon salt
¼ teaspoon pepper
6 catfish fillets
1 cup all-purpose flour
Vegetable oil
½ cup butter
½ cup lemon juice
Tomato wedges (optional)
Lemon wedges (optional)
Fresh parsley sprigs (optional)

Slit each shrimp down the front, starting at large end and continuing to where tail begins to curl; slice deeply to make shrimp lie flat.

Sauté onion in 6 tablespoons butter until tender. Stir in crabmeat, and sauté about 3 minutes. Add breadcrumbs; mix well. Stuff each shrimp with crabmeat mixture. Arrange shrimp and green pepper strips in a 13- x 9- x 2-inch baking pan; set aside.

Combine milk, eggs, salt, and pepper; mix well. Dredge fillets in flour; then dip in egg mixture. Dredge in flour again. Fry fillets in deep hot oil until golden brown. Drain well.

Combine remaining ½ cup butter and lemon juice in a small saucepan; cook over medium heat, stirring often, until heated thoroughly. Place fish on serving platter; spoon lemon butter over fish.

Broil shrimp and green pepper 3 to 5 minutes. Arrange shrimp and green pepper on serving platter with catfish. Garnish with tomato wedges, lemon wedges, and parsley, if desired. Yield: 6 servings.

FILLET OF SNAPPER ROME

½ cup butter
¼ cup lemon juice
Dash of Worcestershire sauce
4 red snapper fillets
1 cup crabmeat
¼ cup melted butter
1½ teaspoons butter
1½ teaspoons all-purpose flour
½ cup half-and-half
½ teaspoon salt
Dash of white pepper
½ cup dry breadcrumbs
8 green pepper strips

Combine ½ cup butter, lemon juice, and Worcestershire sauce in a small saucepan; cook over medium heat, stirring often, until heated thoroughly. Place fillets in a 13- x 9- x 2-inch baking pan; broil 10 to 15 minutes, basting often with lemon butter.

Sauté crabmeat in ¼ cup butter about 3 minutes; set aside.

Melt remaining 1½ teaspoons butter in a heavy saucepan over low heat; add flour, stirring until smooth. Cook 1 minute, stirring constantly. Gradually stir in half-and-half; cook over medium heat, stirring constantly, until thickened and bubbly. Stir in salt and pepper; add crabmeat, stirring well.

Spoon crabmeat mixture on top of each fillet. Sprinkle breadcrumbs over crabmeat mixture; garnish each fillet with 2 strips of green pepper. Bake at 350° for 10 minutes. Broil fillets just until breadcrumbs are browned. Yield: 4 servings.

■ Use fresh or frozen soft-shell crabs to prepare Soft-Shell Crab Meunière, a specialty at **Pascal's Manale**.

SOFT-SHELL CRAB MEUNIERE

2 large or 4 small fresh or thawed frozen
    soft-shell crabs
½ cup melted margarine
Meunière Sauce
Lemon halves (optional)
Fresh parsley sprigs (optional)
Paprika (optional)

To clean fresh crabs: Remove spongy substance (gills) that lies under the tapering points on either side of back shell. Place crabs on back, and remove the small piece at lower part of shell which terminates in a point (called the apron). Wash crabs thoroughly.

Sauté crabs in margarine 5 minutes or until lightly browned, turning once. Remove from heat; drain off margarine. Pour Meunière Sauce over crabs; return to heat, and bring to a boil. Reduce heat and simmer 5 minutes. Garnish with lemon halves, parsley, and paprika, if desired. Yield: 2 servings.

Meunière Sauce:

¼ cup melted butter
¼ cup lemon juice
¼ cup Worcestershire sauce

Combine all ingredients; mix well. Yield: ¾ cup.

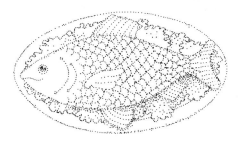

■ The pecan pie from the **Camellia Grill** is so delicious they often get requests to mail pies across the country.

PECAN PIE

4 eggs
¼ teaspoon salt
¼ cup melted butter
1¼ cups light corn syrup
1¼ cups firmly packed brown sugar
1 teaspoon vanilla extract
1 unbaked 9-inch pastry shell
1 cup chopped pecans

Beat eggs with a wire whisk or fork. Add salt, butter, syrup, sugar, and vanilla; mix well. Pour into pastry shell; sprinkle with pecans. Bake at 350° for 45 to 50 minutes. Yield: one 9-inch pie.

■ Cannoli from **Angelo Brocato's Ice Cream Co.** features a rich ricotta and chocolate filling.

CANNOLI

½ cup plus 1 tablespoon shortening
2 cups all-purpose flour
1 egg, beaten
¼ cup dry red wine
1 egg white, slightly beaten
Vegetable oil
Ricotta Filling
Powdered sugar
Grated sweet chocolate

Cut shortening into flour until mixture resembles coarse crumbs; stir in beaten egg. Gradually stir in red wine, mixing well. Shape the dough into a ball; then cover and let stand for 15 minutes.

Turn dough out onto a lightly floured surface; roll dough to 1/16-inch thickness. Cut into 3½-inch circles; roll circles into 5-inch ovals with a rolling pin. Place a cannoli form down the lengthwise center of the oval. Roll dough around the form; seal edge with beaten egg white.

Fry in deep hot oil (350°) about 1 minute or until golden brown. Drain on paper towels; let cool about 5 seconds, then carefully remove cannoli form. Cool shells completely before filling. Spoon Ricotta Filling carefully into cannoli shells; sprinkle with powdered sugar and garnish with grated chocolate as desired. Yield: 15 cannoli.

Ricotta Filling:

1 (15-ounce) carton ricotta cheese
1 cup plus 2 tablespoons powdered sugar
⅔ cup finely diced citron
1 cup grated sweet chocolate

Let ricotta drain in a large strainer to remove excess liquid. Remove ricotta to a small bowl; fold in powdered sugar. Press ricotta mixture through a wire strainer to remove excess lumps. Gently fold in citron and chocolate. Chill several hours before filling cannoli shells. Yield: about 2½ cups.

Note: Consistency of ricotta cheese varies among brands. If filling is not thick enough to mound when dropped from a spoon before chilling, additional powdered sugar may be added.

Tip: Keep cut cheese from drying out by dipping the cut surface in melted paraffin then storing, wrapped in foil or plastic wrap, in the refrigerator.

■ Bouilli, or boiled beef, is a favorite with regular customers at **Maylie's.** Also popular is their version of remoulade sauce, which they serve over deviled eggs or boiled shrimp.

BOUILLI

1 (3- to 4-pound) beef brisket
6 quarts water

Place brisket and water in a large kettle. Bring water to a boil; reduce heat to low, and cook, uncovered, for 4 hours. Serve brisket with Creole mustard, prepared horseradish, or catsup. Yield: 12 to 16 servings.

REMOULADE SAUCE

2 (5¼-ounce) jars Creole mustard
¼ cup plus 2 tablespoons olive oil
3 tablespoons catsup
1 tablespoon vinegar
1 tablespoon lemon juice
3 green onions, chopped
1 stalk celery with leaves, minced
1 heart of celery, minced
Salt and pepper to taste

Combine all ingredients in a medium mixing bowl; stir well. Cover and chill thoroughly. Store sauce in refrigerator. Yield: about 2 cups.

■ At **Bon Ton**, specialties include the traditional Creole red beans and rice. For dessert, there's bread pudding, made with French bread and topped with a strong whiskey-flavored sauce.

RED BEANS AND RICE

1 pound dried red beans
2 large onions, chopped
2 stalks celery, chopped
1 medium-size green pepper, chopped
1 clove garlic, minced
2 teaspoons salt
½ teaspoon pepper
¼ cup chopped parsley
Hot cooked rice
2 pounds smoked sausage

Sort and wash beans. Combine red beans, onion, celery, green pepper, and garlic in a Dutch oven; cover with water, and bring to a boil. Reduce heat; cover and simmer 2 to 2½ hours or until beans are tender and a thick gravy

is formed. If necessary, add more water to prevent beans from sticking. Stir in salt, pepper, and parsley.

Cook sausage according to package directions; cut into serving pieces.

Mound rice in the middle of serving plates. Spoon beans around rice, and place sausage on plate with beans. Yield: 8 to 10 servings.

BREAD PUDDING WITH WHISKEY SAUCE

1 (1-pound) loaf French bread
1 quart milk
3 eggs, slightly beaten
2 cups sugar
2 tablespoons vanilla extract
1 cup raisins
3 tablespoons margarine
Whiskey Sauce

Break bread into small chunks and place in a large, shallow bowl. Add milk, and let soak about 10 minutes; crush with hands until well mixed. Add eggs, sugar, vanilla, and raisins.

Melt margarine in a 13- x 9- x 2-inch baking pan. Spoon pudding mixture into pan; bake at 325° for 40 to 45 minutes or until very firm. Let cool; cut into squares. Place each square in an ovenproof dessert dish. When ready to serve, pour Whiskey Sauce over squares, and broil until bubbly. Yield: 15 servings.

Whiskey Sauce:

1 cup butter or margarine, softened
2 cups sugar
2 eggs, beaten
¼ to ½ cup whiskey

Cream butter and sugar until light and fluffy; place in top of a double boiler. Place over boiling water and cook about 30 minutes, stirring often, until very hot. Stir a small amount of hot mixture into eggs; stir eggs into hot mixture.

Cook an additional 3 minutes, stirring constantly; let cool. Stir in whiskey to taste. Yield: 2 cups.

Tip: Dried fruits such as raisins, dates, prunes, peaches, and apricots are good sources of iron. In addition to being healthful, they are great for snacking— sweet and delicious.

Flavorful, Affordable Roasts

As meat prices continue to soar, it makes good sense to take a look at the more economical cuts of roasts. Chuck, arm, and blade roasts are usually less expensive than the higher quality cuts, such as sirloin tip and rib. And with proper preparation, the results are the same—a tender and flavorful roast.

The secret to tenderness is cooking the less expensive roasts in liquid. These recipes call for simmering the roast in wine, beef bouillon, tomato sauce, and even pineapple juice.

POT ROAST WITH VEGETABLES

1 (4-pound) boneless pot roast
3 tablespoons vegetable oil
Salt and pepper to taste
1½ cups dry white wine
1 cup water
1 bay leaf
5 large sprigs fresh parsley
1½ teaspoons dried thyme leaves
12 small carrots, peeled
12 small potatoes, peeled around middle
12 small onions, peeled
1 (10-ounce) package frozen whole green beans
¼ cup plus 2 tablespoons all-purpose flour
½ cup water

Brown roast on all sides in hot oil in a large Dutch oven; sprinkle with salt and pepper. Add wine and 1 cup water; bring to a boil. Remove from heat.

Tie bay leaf, parsley, and thyme in a cheesecloth bag; place in Dutch oven with beef. Cover and bake at 325° for 1½ hours. Add carrots; cover and bake an additional 30 minutes. Add potatoes and onions; cover and continue to bake an additional hour or until all vegetables are tender. Remove from oven; set aside and keep warm.

Cook green beans according to package directions; drain and set aside.

Remove roast and vegetables to large serving platter, reserving 2¾ cups drippings in Dutch oven. Arrange green beans on platter with roast.

Combine flour and ½ cup water, mixing well to form a paste. Gradually stir flour mixture into reserved pan drippings; cook, stirring constantly, until thickened and bubbly. Serve gravy with roast. Yield: 8 to 10 servings.
Phyllis Ehlers,
Dallas, Texas.

MARINATED CHUCK ROAST

1 tablespoon meat tenderizer
1 (3- to 4-pound) boneless chuck roast
1 (5-ounce) bottle soy sauce
1½ cups water
½ cup bourbon (optional)
½ cup firmly packed brown sugar
1 tablespoon lemon juice
1 teaspoon Worcestershire sauce

Sprinkle tenderizer on all sides of roast; pierce with a fork.

Place roast in a 13- x 9- x 2-inch baking pan. Combine remaining ingredients in a small bowl, stirring well; pour over roast. Cover and chill 12 hours or overnight.

Bake, covered, at 325° for 2½ hours or until meat is tender. Serve with marinade. Yield: 4 to 6 servings.
Mrs. Patricia Britton,
Chattanooga, Tennessee.

SWEDISH POT ROAST

2 teaspoons salt
1 teaspoon ground allspice
½ teaspoon pepper
1 (3½- to 4-pound) chuck or arm pot roast
3 tablespoons melted butter or margarine
3 tablespoons brandy
2 medium onions, sliced
⅓ cup hot beef bouillon
2 tablespoons vinegar
2 tablespoons molasses
3 anchovy fillets, minced
2 bay leaves
¼ cup all-purpose flour
½ cup water

Combine salt, allspice, and pepper; rub over surface of roast.

Brown roast on all sides in butter in a Dutch oven. Remove pan from heat; let stand 3 to 4 minutes or until pan drippings stop sizzling. Pour brandy over roast, and carefully ignite. Allow flames to die down.

Place onion on top of roast. Combine remaining ingredients except flour and water; pour over roast. Return pan to heat; cover and simmer 2 hours or until roast is tender.

Remove roast to platter; reserve pan drippings. Combine flour and water; stir until smooth. Pour flour mixture into pan drippings; cook, stirring constantly, until thickened and bubbly. Serve gravy with roast. Yield: 6 to 8 servings.
Arlene Granberg,
Knoxville, Tennessee.

POLYNESIAN POT ROAST

1 (3- to 4-pound) boneless pot roast
1 cup sliced mushrooms
1 cup unsweetened pineapple juice
¼ cup soy sauce
1½ teaspoons ground ginger
½ teaspoon salt
1 large onion, sliced
1 tablespoon cornstarch
2 tablespoons water

Place roast and mushrooms in a large Dutch oven. Combine pineapple juice, soy sauce, ginger, and salt; mix well, and pour over roast. Let stand 1 hour at room temperature, turning once. Add onion; place over high heat, and bring to a boil. Reduce heat; cover and simmer 2½ to 3 hours or until the roast is tender.

Remove roast and vegetables to warm serving dish. Combine cornstarch and water, mixing well; stir into pan drippings. Cook mixture over medium-high heat, stirring constantly, until thickened and bubbly. Ladle sauce over roast. Yield: 8 servings.
Charlotte Elms,
Satsuma, Alabama.

POT ROAST WITH SPAGHETTI

1 (2½- to 3-pound) boneless pot roast
8 cloves garlic
Salt and pepper to taste
2 tablespoons vegetable oil
3 (8-ounce) cans tomato sauce
2 tablespoons vinegar
1 teaspoon ground nutmeg
6 to 8 whole cloves
½ teaspoon ground allspice
Hot cooked spaghetti

Make 8 slits in roast, and insert 1 clove garlic in each slit; sprinkle roast with salt and pepper. Brown roast on all sides in hot oil in a Dutch oven.

Combine next 5 ingredients; mix well. Pour tomato sauce mixture over roast. Cover and cook 1 hour and 45 minutes or until tender. Remove and discard garlic cloves. Remove roast to serving platter; keep warm. Cook sauce over medium-high heat 3 to 5 minutes or until reduced to 3 cups. Cut roast into serving pieces, and serve with spaghetti and sauce. Yield: 4 to 6 servings.
Betty Collier,
Fern Creek, Kentucky.

Oats Give It A Different Twist

Treat your family to the flavor and nutritional benefit of oats, not just as a breakfast cereal, but in some of the following great ways. Served hot with butter, Honey Oatmeal Bread is wonderful for a light breakfast. Orange-Glazed Oatmeal Cookies are a nice variation of the standard oatmeal cookie. Oats also serve as a nutritious meat extender in Barbecued Meat Loaf.

When buying oats, select the type that is the most convenient for your use; regular-cooking oats may be less expensive but take longer to prepare, while quick-cooking oats are ready in minutes.

ORANGE-GLAZED OATMEAL COOKIES

1½ cups all-purpose flour
2 teaspoons baking powder
1 teaspoon ground cinnamon
½ teaspoon salt
½ cup firmly packed brown sugar
½ cup shortening
1 egg
⅔ cup evaporated milk
⅔ cup orange juice, divided
2 cups quick-cooking oats, uncooked
1 cup raisins
½ cup chopped pecans
3 cups powdered sugar
1 teaspoon grated orange rind

Combine first 4 ingredients; set aside.
Combine brown sugar and shortening, creaming well. Add egg; beat on medium speed of electric mixer until smooth. Gradually add milk and ⅓ cup orange juice, beating constantly on low speed. Add flour mixture to batter; mix on low speed until blended. Stir in oats, raisins, and pecans.

Drop by rounded teaspoonfuls onto lightly greased cookie sheets. Bake at 350° for 10 to 12 minutes. Let cool on wire rack.

Combine powdered sugar, remaining ⅓ cup orange juice, and orange rind; mix well. Dip tops of cookies in glaze. Yield: about 7½ dozen.   *Pat Davis,*
Durham, North Carolina.

Tip: To shape cookies without rolling and cutting: Roll dough into 1-inch balls and place on cookie sheet 2 inches apart; flatten each ball with bottom of glass dipped in sugar.

HONEY OATMEAL BREAD

2¼ cups milk
¼ cup shortening
⅓ cup honey
2½ teaspoons salt
2 packages dry yeast
½ cup warm water (105° to 115°)
2 cups regular oats, uncooked
6 to 6½ cups all-purpose flour
Melted butter or margarine (optional)

Scald milk; add shortening, honey, and salt, stirring until the shortening melts. Let mixture cool to 105° to 115°.
Combine yeast and water in a large bowl; let stand 5 minutes. Add milk mixture, oats, and 2 cups flour; mix well. Stir in enough remaining flour to make a soft dough (about 4 to 4½ cups).
Turn dough out onto a lightly floured surface; knead until smooth and elastic (about 8 to 10 minutes).
Place dough in a greased bowl, turning to grease top. Cover and let rise in a warm place (85°), free of drafts, 1 hour or until doubled in bulk.
Punch dough down; cover and let dough stand 10 minutes.
Divide dough in half, and place on a lightly floured surface. Roll each half into a 15- x 9-inch rectangle. Roll up in jellyroll fashion, beginning at narrow edge. Pinch seams and ends together to seal; place rolls, seam side down, in 2 well-greased 9- x 5- x 3-inch loafpans. Brush with melted butter, if desired.
Cover and let rise 50 minutes or until doubled in bulk. Bake at 375° for 45 minutes or until loaves sound hollow when tapped. Remove from pans; cool on wire racks. Yield: 2 loaves.
Miss Elizabeth Downing,
Tampa, Florida.

BARBECUED MEAT LOAF

1 pound ground beef
1 cup regular oats, uncooked
1 medium onion, finely chopped
1 egg, beaten
1½ teaspoons salt
½ teaspoon pepper
1 (8-ounce) can tomato sauce
½ cup water
2 tablespoons brown sugar
2 tablespoons prepared mustard
2 tablespoons vinegar

Combine beef, oats, onion, egg, salt, pepper, and ½ cup tomato sauce; mix well, and pack into a lightly greased 9- x 5- x 3-inch loafpan. Bake loaf at 350° for 15 minutes.

Combine remaining ½ cup tomato sauce with remaining ingredients; stir well. Pour over meat loaf, and bake 45 minutes longer. Yield: 6 to 8 servings.
Edna Bailiff,
Elizabethton, Tennessee.

There's A Surprise In The Cookies

Here's a cookie with a surprise in every bite. You begin with a peanut butter- and cinnamon-flavored dough, then wrap it around milk chocolate stars. Finally, each cookie is rolled in powdered sugar. The cookies take time to make, but they're worth the effort.

CHOCO SURPRISE COOKIES

1 cup all-purpose flour
1 teaspoon baking powder
¾ to 1 teaspoon ground cinnamon
1 cup peanut butter
½ cup butter or margarine, softened
1 cup firmly packed brown sugar
2 eggs
1 (16-ounce) package milk chocolate stars
Powdered sugar

Combine flour, baking powder, and cinnamon; set aside.
Combine peanut butter, butter, and brown sugar in a large mixing bowl; cream until fluffy. Add eggs; beat well. Gradually add dry ingredients, mixing well. Cover dough and chill at least 30 minutes (dough may be chilled in the refrigerator overnight).
Shape 1 teaspoon dough around each chocolate star; place on lightly greased baking sheets. Bake at 350° for 9 to 11 minutes or until lightly browned. Cool slightly on wire racks; then roll cookies in powdered sugar. Cool completely before storing. Yield: 8 dozen.
Mrs. Hobert Howell,
Waco, Texas.

Right: Assemble Scrambled Egg Casserole (page 51) the night before baking for a delicious headstart on breakfast.

Above: *Blueberry Streusel Muffins (page 46), Caramel-Orange Coffee Ring (page 45), and Austrian Twists (page 45) are three of the nicest things that can happen to breakfast.*

Left: *Grapefruit halves are topped with a delightful combination of orange juice and strawberries in Grapefruit Supreme (page 50).*

Stuff Eggplant With Cheese

If eggplant is a favorite at your house, you'll want to try this casserole. The homemade Italian Sauce complements the hearty cheese filling.

ROLLED STUFFED EGGPLANT

1 medium eggplant
Salt
1 egg, slightly beaten
½ cup milk
2 teaspoons vegetable oil
½ cup all-purpose flour
Hot vegetable oil
½ cup grated Romano cheese
½ cup shredded farmer cheese
2 tablespoons chopped fresh parsley
Dash of pepper
Italian Sauce

Peel eggplant, and cut lengthwise into ⅛-inch slices; sprinkle generously with salt. Stack slices between paper towels; let stand 40 minutes. Press each slice between paper towels to remove excess moisture.

Combine egg, milk, and 2 teaspoons oil; mix well. Add flour and ⅛ teaspoon salt, beating until smooth. Dip eggplant slices in batter; brown on both sides in hot oil. Drain on paper towels.

Combine cheese, parsley, and pepper; mix well. Place about 1 tablespoon cheese mixture lengthwise down center of each eggplant slice. Roll each slice crosswise, jellyroll fashion.

Pour ½ cup hot Italian Sauce in a lightly greased 12- x 8- x 2-inch baking dish. Arrange eggplant rolls in sauce, seam side down; top with 1 cup Italian Sauce. Cover and bake at 375° for 30 minutes. Yield: 6 to 8 servings.

Italian Sauce:

¾ cup chopped onion
2 small cloves garlic, minced
3 tablespoons chopped fresh parsley
2 tablespoons vegetable oil
1 (28-ounce) can whole tomatoes, undrained
1 (6-ounce) can tomato paste
2 teaspoons sugar
1½ teaspoons whole oregano
½ teaspoon salt

Sauté onion, garlic, and parsley in oil until tender; set aside.

Place tomatoes in container of electric blender, and process until smooth; add to onion mixture. Stir in remaining ingredients. Bring to a boil; reduce heat, and simmer 1 hour or until sauce is reduced to about 3½ cups. Set aside 1½ cups for Rolled Stuffed Eggplant; use remainder as pizza sauce or in other Italian dishes. Yield: about 3½ cups.
Norma Patelunas,
St. Petersburg, Florida.

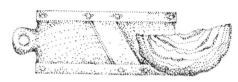

Try Something Different With Cabbage

Tex-Mex Cabbage, Cottage Coleslaw, Beef-and-Cabbage Rollups—side dish, salad, main dish—all testify to the versatility of cabbage. And to further prove that point, these recipes also offer some delicious and unusual ways to vary the flavor of cabbage.

CREAMY CABBAGE CASSEROLE

1 medium cabbage, coarsely chopped
3 tablespoons butter or margarine
¼ cup all-purpose flour
½ cup milk
1 cup whipping cream
½ teaspoon salt
¼ teaspoon pepper
⅛ teaspoon ground nutmeg
¼ cup grated Parmesan cheese
⅓ cup toasted breadcrumbs
2 tablespoons melted butter or margarine

Cook cabbage, covered, 10 minutes in a small amount of boiling salted water. Drain well, and set aside.

Melt 3 tablespoons butter in a heavy saucepan over low heat; add flour, stirring until smooth. Cook 1 minute, stirring constantly. Gradually add milk and whipping cream; cook over medium heat, stirring constantly, until thickened and bubbly. Stir in salt, pepper, and nutmeg.

Add cabbage to white sauce, mixing well; spoon into a buttered 1½-quart casserole. Sprinkle with cheese, and top with breadcrumbs; drizzle with 2 tablespoons melted butter. Bake at 375° for 20 minutes. Yield: 8 servings.
Mrs. Mary Pappas,
Richmond, Virginia.

BEEF-AND-CABBAGE ROLLUPS

1 cup water
8 large cabbage leaves
1 pound ground chuck
1 onion, chopped
¾ cup cooked rice
1 (15-ounce) can tomato sauce
1 teaspoon salt
½ teaspoon pepper
1 tablespoon honey
¼ cup vinegar

Bring water to a boil in a Dutch oven; add cabbage leaves, and steam 5 minutes. Drain well, and set aside.

Combine meat, onion, rice, ¾ cup tomato sauce, salt, and pepper; mix well. Spoon equal amounts of meat mixture onto cabbage leaves; roll up, turning edges in. Place cabbage rolls, seam side down, in a large skillet.

Combine remaining tomato sauce, honey, and vinegar; mix well, and pour the sauce over cabbage rolls. Cover and simmer 1 hour. Yield: 8 servings.
Gayle Wallace,
Memphis, Tennessee.

TEX-MEX CABBAGE

1 medium cabbage
2 tablespoons butter or margarine
1 tablespoon sugar
1 medium onion, thinly sliced
1 green pepper, thinly sliced into rings
1 (28-ounce) can tomatoes, drained and quartered
½ teaspoon salt
¼ teaspoon pepper
¾ cup (3 ounces) shredded Cheddar cheese

Cut cabbage into 6 wedges, removing core; cover and cook 10 minutes in a small amount of lightly salted boiling water. Drain well, and carefully place wedges in a greased 2-quart shallow baking dish.

Melt butter in a medium saucepan; add sugar, onion, and green pepper; cook over medium heat, stirring constantly, until vegetables are tender. Stir in tomatoes, salt, and pepper; pour vegetable mixture over cabbage.

Sprinkle cheese over vegetables, and bake at 350° for 20 to 30 minutes or until thoroughly heated. Yield: 6 to 8 servings.
Mrs. R. E. Bunker,
Bartlett, Texas.

Tip: Shred Cheddar or Swiss cheese and freeze; whenever you need some for cooking, just measure.

COTTAGE COLESLAW

½ cup cottage cheese
½ cup mayonnaise or salad dressing
3 tablespoons vinegar or lemon juice
1½ teaspoons onion juice
¾ teaspoon salt
½ teaspoon pepper
1 teaspoon caraway seeds (optional)
6 cups finely shredded cabbage
2 cups diced apple
½ cup chopped green pepper (optional)

Combine cottage cheese and mayonnaise, mixing well; stir in vinegar, onion juice, salt, and pepper. Add caraway seeds, if desired.

Combine cabbage and apple; add green pepper, if desired. Pour cheese mixture over cabbage mixture, tossing lightly. Chill coleslaw several hours. Yield: 8 servings. *Margaret W. Cotton, Franklin, Virginia.*

WILTED CABBAGE

4 slices bacon
½ cup chopped green pepper
2 tablespoons vinegar
2 tablespoons water
1 tablespoon sugar
½ teaspoon salt
4 cups shredded cabbage
1½ cups peeled, finely chopped cooking apple

Cook bacon until crisp in a large skillet; drain on paper towels, reserving drippings in skillet.

Sauté green pepper in drippings until tender; stir in vinegar, water, sugar, and salt. Bring to a boil; add cabbage and apple, tossing gently. Cover and cook over medium heat 5 minutes. Spoon into serving dish; crumble bacon, and sprinkle over top. Yield: 6 servings. *Marge Bourke, Chesapeake, Virginia.*

CABBAGE MEDLEY

1 tablespoon vegetable oil
3 cups coarsely shredded cabbage
½ medium eggplant, cut into 2- x ¼-inch strips
1 medium onion, thinly sliced
1 cup canned bean sprouts, drained
1 small green pepper, thinly sliced into strips
2 tomatoes, diced
½ cup thinly sliced carrots
1 teaspoon salt
¼ teaspoon pepper

Heat oil in a large skillet; add vegetables, salt, and pepper. Cook over medium heat 5 minutes, stirring constantly. Yield: 6 servings. *Eileen Martin, Myrtle Beach, South Carolina.*

Explore Clay Cookery

Have you ever made beef stew in a clay cooker? Or stuffed pork chops? While clay cookers are widely acclaimed for baking poultry, they give that same natural moistness to a wide selection of other dishes.

Explore these entrée ideas, and don't be afraid to experiment with some of your favorite recipes. Because manufacturers' directions vary for soaking cookers, be sure to check your instructions before using.

CORNISH HENS WITH WILD RICE STUFFING

1 (6-ounce) package long grain and wild rice mix
1 medium onion, minced
3 tablespoons melted butter or margarine, divided
1 large Delicious apple, peeled, cored, and coarsely shredded
1 egg, beaten
1 tablespoon minced fresh parsley
⅛ teaspoon ground thyme
2 (1-pound 6-ounce) Cornish hens
Salt and pepper

Soak clay cooker in water according to manufacturer's directions. Prepare rice according to package directions.

Sauté onion in 2 tablespoons butter until onion is tender, but not brown.

Combine rice, onion, apple, egg, parsley, and thyme; stir lightly.

Sprinkle inside of hens with salt and pepper. Stuff hens lightly with some of the rice mixture; set remaining rice aside. Close cavity, and secure with toothpicks; truss. Brush hens with 1 tablespoon butter, and place breast side up in cooker. Sprinkle hens with salt

and pepper. Cover cooker, and place in a cold oven. Turn oven to 400°, and bake for 2 hours. Remove cooker from oven, and place on a heat-resistant pad. (Do not uncover so hens will remain hot.)

Reduce oven temperature to 350°. Spoon extra rice into a lightly greased 1-quart casserole. Bake at 350° for 30 minutes. Serve rice with Cornish hens. Yield: 2 to 4 servings.
Kathleen A. Wilson, Port Arthur, Texas.

STUFFED BAKED PORK CHOPS

2 cups soft breadcrumbs
1 small onion, minced
¼ cup melted butter or margarine
½ teaspoon Worcestershire sauce
¼ teaspoon salt
Dash of pepper
6 (1¼-inch-thick) pork chops, cut with pockets
1½ cups water
3 tablespoons catsup

Soak clay cooker in water according to manufacturer's directions.

Combine breadcrumbs, onion, butter, Worcestershire sauce, salt, and pepper.

Stuff pockets of pork chops with breadcrumb mixture, and secure with toothpicks. Place chops in cooker. Combine water and catsup, stirring well; pour over pork chops.

Cover cooker, and place in a cold oven. Bake at 400° for 45 minutes to 1 hour. Yield: 6 servings.
Mrs. J. W. Hopkins, Abilene, Texas.

OVEN BEEF STEW

1½ pounds lean boneless beef, cut into 1-inch cubes
3 tablespoons vegetable oil
1 (16-ounce) can whole tomatoes
2 large onions, quartered
1 medium rutabaga, peeled and cut into 8 wedges
1 teaspoon salt
1 teaspoon pepper
1 teaspoon sugar
½ teaspoon thyme leaves
1 (9-ounce) package frozen cut green beans
¼ cup all-purpose flour
¼ cup water

Soak clay cooker in water according to manufacturer's directions.

Sauté meat in oil in a skillet until brown; transfer to cooker. Add tomatoes, onion, and rutabaga; sprinkle with salt, pepper, sugar, and thyme.

Cover cooker, and place in a cold oven. Bake at 400° for 1 hour and 30 minutes. Add beans; cover and bake an additional 30 minutes. Remove meat and vegetables from cooker, using a slotted spoon; place in a serving dish.

Transfer meat drippings to a saucepan. Combine flour and water in a jar; tighten lid, and shake well. Stir flour mixture into meat drippings; cook over medium heat, stirring constantly, until thickened and bubbly. Serve gravy over meat and vegetables. Yield: 6 servings.
Mrs. Mildred Sherrer,
Bay City, Texas.

Stuffing Peps Up Peppers

Green peppers stuffed with your choice of fillings make an attractive entrée for any day of the week. They're easy on your food budget and a great way to use up leftovers.

Mexican Green Peppers stretches a pound of ground beef into dinner for six; the chili-flavored stuffing also features rice, onion, and fresh tomatoes. Some leftover ham added to corn, pimiento, and onion makes a colorful stuffing for Ham-Stuffed Green Peppers. And if your family likes macaroni and cheese, try serving it baked in pepper shells.

HAM-STUFFED GREEN PEPPERS

4 large green peppers
1½ cups chopped cooked ham
1 (12-ounce) can whole kernel corn, drained
2 tablespoons chopped pimiento
1 tablespoon chopped onion
¼ teaspoon salt
⅛ teaspoon pepper
Dash of hot sauce
4 slices process American cheese

Cut off tops of green peppers; remove seeds. Cook peppers 5 minutes in boiling salted water to cover; drain. Set aside.

Combine next 7 ingredients; mix well. Fill peppers with ham mixture; place in an 8-inch square baking dish. Bake at 375° for 30 minutes.

Place a slice of cheese on each pepper; bake 15 minutes. Yield: 4 servings.
Florence L. Costello,
Chattanooga, Tennessee.

MEXICAN GREEN PEPPERS

6 medium-size green peppers
1 pound ground beef
1 large onion, chopped
1⅓ cups chopped fresh tomatoes
1 cup cooked rice
1½ teaspoons salt
1 teaspoon chili powder
½ teaspoon pepper
1 (8-ounce) can tomato sauce

Cut off tops of green peppers; remove seeds. Cook peppers 5 minutes in boiling salted water to cover; drain. Set aside.

Combine next 7 ingredients; mix well. Fill peppers with meat mixture; place in a 2-quart shallow casserole. Pour tomato sauce over and around the peppers. Bake at 375° for 45 to 50 minutes. Yield: 6 servings.
Myra Brinkley,
Elk Park, North Carolina.

DEVILISH CHICKEN PEPPERS

4 large green peppers
4 whole chicken breasts, skinned and boned
¼ cup finely chopped green pepper
¼ cup finely chopped onion
¼ cup melted butter or margarine
1½ cups crushed barbecue-flavored potato chips
1 (3-ounce) can smoke-flavored deviled ham
1 egg, slightly beaten
1 (15-ounce) can tomato sauce
½ cup (2 ounces) shredded Cheddar cheese

Cut off tops of green peppers; remove seeds. Cook peppers 5 minutes in boiling salted water to cover; drain. Set aside.

Cut chicken into bite-size pieces. Cook chicken, chopped green pepper, and onion in butter over medium heat 5 to 7 minutes, stirring frequently. Drain well.

Combine chicken mixture, potato chips, ham, and egg; mix well. Fill peppers with mixture; place in a 1¾-quart shallow baking dish. Pour tomato sauce over and around peppers. Bake at 375° for 25 minutes. Sprinkle cheese over peppers; bake 5 additional minutes. Yield: 4 servings.
Mrs. John W. Stevens,
Lexington, Kentucky.

MACARONI-AND-CHEESE-STUFFED PEPPERS

6 small green peppers
2 cups (8 ounces) shredded Cheddar cheese, divided
1 cup cooked elbow macaroni
1 cup canned tomatoes, chopped
1 cup soft breadcrumbs
¼ teaspoon Worcestershire sauce
¼ teaspoon salt
Dash of pepper

Cut off tops of green peppers; remove seeds. Cook peppers 5 minutes in boiling salted water to cover; drain. Set aside.

Combine 1⅓ cups cheese with next 6 ingredients; mix well. Fill peppers with macaroni mixture; place in a lightly greased 9-inch square baking pan. Bake at 350° for 25 minutes. Sprinkle remaining cheese over peppers; bake an additional 5 minutes. Yield: 6 servings.
Mrs. Dennis Wear,
Bells, Tennessee.

RICE-STUFFED PEPPERS

6 medium-size green peppers
1 cup cooked rice
1 (14½-ounce) can stewed tomatoes, drained
¼ cup butter or margarine
1 (1.375-ounce) package onion soup mix
½ cup (2 ounces) shredded Cheddar cheese

Cut off tops of green peppers; remove seeds. Cook peppers 5 minutes in boiling salted water to cover; drain. Set aside.

Combine rice, tomatoes, butter, and onion soup mix; mix well. Fill peppers with rice mixture; place in a 9-inch square baking dish. Pour ½ inch hot water into dish. Bake at 350° for 25 minutes. Sprinkle cheese over peppers; bake an additional 5 minutes. Yield: 6 servings.
Mrs. Frances Huffstetler,
Van Buren, Arkansas.

Baked Alaska Is Easier Than You Think

The secret to this dessert is baking and serving before the ice cream center has a chance to melt. It really isn't magical, only a matter of technique. With this recipe and step-by-step instructions, you'll find that dazzling doesn't always mean difficult.

BROWNIE BAKED ALASKA

1 quart vanilla ice cream
½ cup margarine, softened
2 cups sugar, divided
2 eggs
1 cup all-purpose flour
½ teaspoon baking powder
2 tablespoons cocoa
¼ teaspoon salt
1 teaspoon vanilla extract
5 egg whites

Line a 1-quart mixing bowl (about 7 inches in diameter) with waxed paper, leaving an overhang around the edges. Pack ice cream into bowl, and freeze until very firm.

Combine margarine and 1 cup sugar, creaming until light and fluffy. Add

eggs, one at a time, beating well after each addition. Combine flour, baking powder, cocoa, and salt; add to creamed mixture, mixing well. Stir in vanilla.

Spoon batter into a greased and floured 8-inch round cakepan. Bake at 350° for 25 to 30 minutes. Let cool in pan 10 minutes; remove to wire rack, and allow to cool completely.

Place cake on an ovenproof wooden board or serving dish. Invert bowl of ice cream onto brownie layer, leaving waxed paper intact; remove bowl. Place ice cream-topped cake in freezer.

Beat egg whites until frothy; gradually beat in 1 cup sugar. Continue beating until stiff peaks form. Remove ice cream-topped cake from freezer, and peel off waxed paper. Quickly spread meringue over entire surface, making sure edges are sealed.

Bake at 500° for 2 minutes or until meringue peaks are browned. Serve immediately. Yield: 10 to 12 servings.

Note: After meringue is sealed, the dessert can be returned to the freezer for up to 1 week and baked just before serving.
Mrs. Fay M. Russell,
Doraville, Georgia.

Step 1—*Line a 1-quart mixing bowl with waxed paper, leaving a generous overhang around edges. Pack ice cream into bowl, and freeze until firm. Prepare cake, and let cool completely.*

Step 3—*Prepare meringue. Remove ice cream-topped cake layer from freezer, and peel off waxed paper.*

Beneath the lightly browned peaks of meringue, Brownie Baked Alaska reveals a center of vanilla ice cream and a layer of rich chocolate cake.

Step 2—*Place cake layer on an ovenproof wooden board or serving dish. (Be sure to use a natural wooden surface, as the finish on some often burns.) Invert bowl of ice cream onto cake layer; remove bowl, leaving waxed paper intact. Freeze assembled cake and ice cream.*

Step 4—*Quickly spread meringue over entire surface, being sure to seal edges. Bake at 500° for 2 to 3 minutes or until meringue peaks are browned. Serve immediately.*

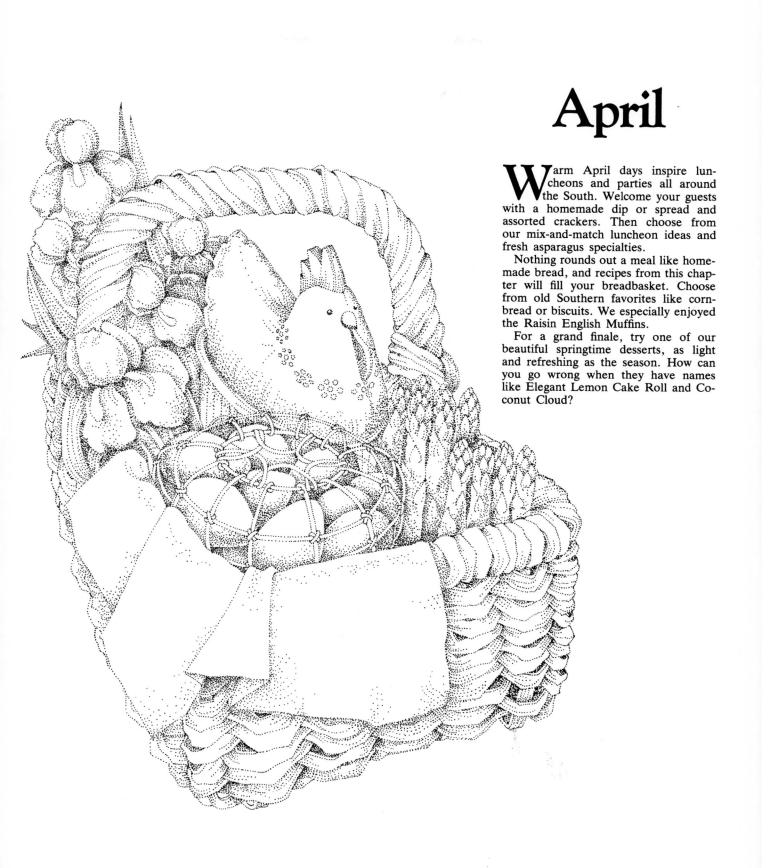

April

Warm April days inspire luncheons and parties all around the South. Welcome your guests with a homemade dip or spread and assorted crackers. Then choose from our mix-and-match luncheon ideas and fresh asparagus specialties.

Nothing rounds out a meal like homemade bread, and recipes from this chapter will fill your breadbasket. Choose from old Southern favorites like cornbread or biscuits. We especially enjoyed the Raisin English Muffins.

For a grand finale, try one of our beautiful springtime desserts, as light and refreshing as the season. How can you go wrong when they have names like Elegant Lemon Cake Roll and Coconut Cloud?

Turn Omelets Into A Party

George Seminoff has quite a reputation for cooking omelets. The reason? When George cooks omelets it's not for a quiet family breakfast, but for a party that may include anywhere from 10 to 80 guests. The preparation is just as showy as the finished omelet, with George preparing each one in front of the waiting recipient.

Just before the omelet is done, the guest chooses his fillings and George generously piles them on. After folding the omelet, he tops it with a spoonful of sautéed mushrooms. Then he quickly moves on to the next guest and happily repeats his performance.

Because a single-burner portable stove and a 10-inch omelet pan are the only equipment needed, the Seminoffs can move their entertaining to various locations. The pool area of their Oklahoma City home is a favorite. But not to be restricted, George once took his equipment on the road to a friend's summer home in Michigan where he cooked omelets for 80 guests.

Regardless of the location, everyone is impressed with George's omelet preparation. The technique is so perfected that he doesn't need a fork or spatula for preparing his specialties.

"I never use anything to stir," he explains. "I shake the pan vigorously and never turn it over. Each omelet takes only about 30 to 45 seconds."

There are secrets to this technique, George admits. He uses only clarified butter, which won't stick; and his omelet pan, which is reserved just for omelet cooking, has a non-stick finish. His final hint for the perfect omelet is adding only water to the egg mixture. "Never add milk; it makes them stick," he advises.

While the omelet cooking is strictly a one-man show, George gets assistance on the remaining dishes from his wife, Sharon, and his two daughters, Mia and Emily. And on occasion, a friend, Gene Binning, brings along his renowned whole wheat bread.

Dessert at the Seminoff parties is a show stopper almost equal to the omelet preparation. The tart Daiquiri Soufflé is elegantly garnished with pistachio nuts, crystallized violets, and a twist of lime. It can be served frozen or simply chilled until set. Either way, George likes to make the soufflé a day in advance so the flavors can blend.

The Makings For An Omelet Party

George shares his party recipes, along with the recipe for his friend's special whole wheat bread.

Tossed Green Salad
George's Omelets
Binning Bread   Butter
Elegant Daiquiri Soufflé
Chablis   Coffee

GEORGE'S OMELETS

2½ cups butter
¼ cup butter or margarine
4 cups sliced mushrooms
36 eggs
1½ cups water
Cubed ham
Shredded Cheddar cheese
Greek Omelet Filling
Spanish Omelet Filling

Melt 2½ cups butter over medium heat in a 1-quart saucepan; heat to boiling. Remove from heat; skim white foam off top with a metal spoon. Set aside to cool 5 to 10 minutes. Pour butter into a heavy glass liquid measuring cup; allow to sit about 10 minutes or until solids settle to the bottom. Carefully spoon off the clear portion and set aside for omelets.

Melt ¼ cup butter in a large skillet; add mushrooms, and sauté about 3 minutes. Set aside, and keep warm. Combine eggs and water; mix well.

Heat a 10-inch omelet pan or heavy skillet until it is hot enough to sizzle a drop of water. Add 2 tablespoons clarified butter; rotate pan to coat bottom.

Pour ¾ cup of egg mixture into pan all at once. Shake pan vigorously (or use a spatula to lift cooked portion) so uncooked portion flows underneath. Slide pan back and forth over heat to keep mixture in motion.

When eggs are set and top is still moist and creamy, spoon either cubed ham, cheese, or one of special fillings over half of omelet. Fold unfilled side over filling; spoon about ¼ cup sautéed mushrooms over omelet. Slide omelet onto plate, and serve immediately.

Repeat procedure with remaining ingredients. Yield: 1 dozen omelets.

GREEK OMELET FILLING

4 medium onions
¼ cup olive oil
1 pound Greek olives, coarsely chopped
2 tablespoons dry white wine
2 teaspoons rosemary leaves, crushed
¼ teaspoon salt
¼ teaspoon pepper

Starting at top, cut onions in half lengthwise; cut each half crosswise into ¼-inch slices. Sauté onion in oil until translucent. Stir in remaining ingredients; simmer 20 to 30 minutes. Yield: 3 cups.

Note: Filling may be made a day in advance and stored in refrigerator. Before serving, place mixture in a saucepan and heat thoroughly.

SPANISH OMELET FILLING

3 medium onions, chopped
3 tablespoons olive oil
1 (15-ounce) can tomato sauce
2 medium-size green peppers, chopped
2 bay leaves
½ teaspoon dried oregano, crushed
¼ teaspoon ground marjoram
¼ teaspoon ground thyme
¼ to ½ teaspoon chili powder
⅛ teaspoon hot sauce
⅛ teaspoon pepper
Dash of salt

Sauté onion in oil until translucent. Stir in remaining ingredients, and simmer 20 to 30 minutes. Yield: 3½ cups.

Note: Filling may be made a day in advance and stored in refrigerator. Before serving, place filling in a saucepan and heat thoroughly.

BINNING BREAD

¼ cup warm water (105° to 115°)
1 teaspoon sugar
2 packages dry yeast
2 cups milk, scalded
1 cup water
2 tablespoons butter or margarine
1 tablespoon salt
2 teaspoons brewer's yeast
1 tablespoon honey
1 tablespoon blackstrap molasses
1 egg
1 cup all-purpose flour
2 tablespoons gluten flour
7¼ cups whole wheat flour

Combine ¼ cup warm water, sugar, and dry yeast; let stand 5 minutes.

Combine milk, 1 cup water, and butter; cool to lukewarm (105° to 115°). Add salt, brewer's yeast, honey, molasses, and egg; mix well. Stir in yeast mixture. Add all-purpose flour and gluten flour; beat until smooth. Gradually add 6 cups whole wheat flour, mixing well. Add remaining flour, kneading constantly with dough hooks or by hand until mixture leaves the sides of bowl.

Lightly grease hands; place dough in a well-greased bowl. Cover; let rise in a warm place (85°), free from drafts, until doubled (about 40 minutes). Punch dough down; turn out on a lightly greased surface and knead 3 to 5 minutes. Divide dough; place in 2 well-greased 9- x 5- x 3-inch loafpans. Cover loafpans; let rise in a warm place (85°), free from drafts, until doubled in bulk (about 45 minutes).

Bake at 350° for 30 to 35 minutes or until loaves sound hollow when tapped. Remove from pans; cool on wire racks. Yield: 2 loaves.

ELEGANT DAIQUIRI SOUFFLE

½ cup light rum
2 envelopes unflavored gelatin
10 eggs, separated
2 cups sugar, divided
½ cup lime juice
½ cup lemon juice
Grated rind of 2 limes
Grated rind of 2 lemons
Dash of salt
3 cups whipping cream, divided
1 (2-ounce) package pistachio nuts, shelled
    and finely chopped
Crystallized violets (optional)
Slice of lime

Cut a piece of waxed paper or aluminum foil long enough to fit around a 1½-quart soufflé dish, allowing a 1-inch overlap. Fold paper in half; wrap around dish, allowing paper to extend 5 inches above rim of dish to form a collar. Secure with tape. Lightly grease or oil soufflé dish and collar; set aside.

Combine light rum and gelatin; let stand 5 minutes.

Beat egg yolks until light and fluffy; gradually add 1 cup sugar, beating constantly until thick and lemon colored.

Combine yolk mixture, fruit juices, grated rind, and salt in a 2½-quart saucepan; stir well. Cook over low heat, stirring constantly, until thickened (about 12 minutes). Remove from heat;

add gelatin mixture, stirring until dissolved. Allow to cool.

Beat egg whites (at room temperature) until soft peaks form; gradually add ½ cup sugar and continue to beat until stiff peaks form.

Combine remaining ½ cup sugar and 2 cups whipping cream in a large chilled mixing bowl; beat until stiff peaks form.

Pour cooled yolk mixture into a very large bowl (about 6 quarts); fold in beaten egg whites, then whipped cream. Pour into soufflé dish. Chill until firm.

Remove collar; gently pat crushed pistachio nuts onto exposed sides of soufflé.

Whip remaining 1 cup cream until stiff peaks form; spoon in mounds on top of soufflé, or fill a pastry bag and decorate top with rosettes and petals. Garnish with crystallized violets and a twisted slice of lime, if desired. Yield: 20 to 24 servings.

Note: This soufflé may be made ahead and served frozen.

Spring Comes Up Desserts

Bring all the liveliness of spring to the table with desserts as light and refreshing as the season. Coconut Cloud, Elegant Lemon Cake Roll—even the names are enticing.

Speaking of lemon, you'll also want to try that tart, fresh taste in Lemon Ice Cream Pie, vanilla ice cream shaped into a pie shell and filled with lemon custard.

Strawberries are also a favorite springtime flavor. In Strawberry Tarts, the plump, juicy berries are nestled atop a smooth vanilla filling.

ICE CREAM DELIGHT

1 cup saltine cracker crumbs
1 cup graham cracker crumbs
½ cup melted butter or margarine
1 quart butter-pecan ice cream, softened
2 (3¾-ounce) packages instant vanilla
    pudding and pie filling mix
2 cups milk
1 (12-ounce) carton frozen whipped
    topping, thawed
3 (1 3/16-ounce) chocolate-covered toffee
    bars, chopped

Combine cracker crumbs and butter, stirring well; press into a 13- x 9- x 2-inch baking pan. Bake at 350° for 5 to 8 minutes. Allow to cool.

Combine ice cream, pudding mix, and milk; beat at low speed of electric mixer 2 minutes. Pour ice cream mixture over crust, and chill until set.

Spread whipped topping over ice cream, and sprinkle with candy. Yield: 12 to 15 servings.

Mrs. Harry B. Dawson,
Jacksonville, Florida.

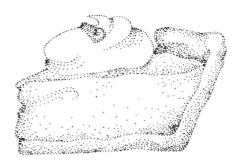

CHOCOLATE-CREAM CHEESE PIE

1½ cups finely crushed chocolate wafers
⅓ cup margarine, melted
1 (8-ounce) package cream cheese,
    softened
¼ cup sugar
1 teaspoon vanilla extract
2 egg yolks
1 (6-ounce) package semisweet chocolate
    morsels, melted
2 egg whites (at room temperature)
¼ cup sugar
1 cup thawed frozen whipped topping
¾ cup chopped pecans
Whipped topping (optional)
Chocolate curls (optional)

Combine crushed wafers and margarine, stirring well. Press mixture into a 9-inch piepan, and bake at 325° for 10 minutes. Cool completely.

Combine cream cheese, ¼ cup sugar, and vanilla; beat until smooth and creamy. Add egg yolks, beating until smooth. Stir in melted chocolate.

Beat egg whites until foamy; gradually add ¼ cup sugar, beating until stiff peaks form. Fold gently into chocolate mixture.

Gently fold 1 cup whipped topping and pecans into chocolate mixture; pour into prepared crust. Freeze pie at least 3 hours. Serve with a dollop of whipped topping, and garnish with chocolate curls, if desired. Yield: one 9-inch pie.

Janet M. Filer,
Arlington, Virginia.

COCONUT CLOUD

1 cup graham cracker crumbs
3 tablespoons sugar
3 tablespoons butter or margarine, melted
2 (1.5-ounce) envelopes whipped topping mix
¾ cup milk
1 (3¾-ounce) package vanilla instant pudding and pie filling mix
½ teaspoon vanilla extract
1 cup commercial sour cream
1 cup flaked coconut, divided

Combine graham cracker crumbs, sugar, and butter; mix well, and press onto bottom of an 8-inch springform pan. Bake at 350° for 8 minutes; cool completely.

Prepare whipped topping mix according to package directions. Set aside.

Combine milk, pudding mix, and vanilla; beat at medium speed of electric mixer 1 minute. Add sour cream, mixing well. Fold in half of prepared whipped topping and ¾ cup coconut.

Spoon filling over prepared crust. Top with remaining whipped topping, and sprinkle with ¼ cup coconut. Chill overnight. Yield: 6 to 8 servings.
Penny Owen,
Raleigh, North Carolina.

STRAWBERRY TARTS

¼ cup sugar
1 tablespoon all-purpose flour
Dash of salt
½ cup milk
1 egg, well beaten
¼ teaspoon vanilla extract
⅓ cup whipping cream, whipped
8 (3-inch) baked tart shells
1 pint fresh strawberries, washed and hulled
Currant jelly

Combine sugar, flour, and salt in top of a double boiler; stir in milk. Cook mixture over boiling water, stirring constantly, until thickened.

Stir some of hot mixture into egg. Stir egg mixture into remaining hot mixture. Cook over boiling water, stirring constantly, until thickened. Remove from heat, and add vanilla. Set aside to cool.

Fold cooled custard into whipped cream. Spoon into tart shells, filling half full. Arrange 4 to 5 strawberries over filling. Spread 1 teaspoon jelly on each tart, filling in between strawberries. Chill well before serving. Yield: 8 servings.
Rita Horman,
Satellite Beach, Florida.

ORANGE NUT CAKE

½ cup butter or margarine, softened
¼ cup shortening
1½ cups sugar
3 eggs
2½ cups all-purpose flour
1½ teaspoons soda
¾ teaspoon salt
1½ cups buttermilk
1½ teaspoons vanilla extract
1 cup golden raisins, chopped
1 cup finely chopped pecans or walnuts
1 tablespoon grated orange rind
Orange Buttercream Frosting

Combine butter, shortening, and sugar; cream until light and fluffy. Add eggs, one at a time, beating well after each addition. Add flour, soda, salt, buttermilk, and vanilla; mix just until blended. Beat at high speed of electric mixer 3 minutes.

Stir raisins, pecans, and orange rind into batter; spoon into 3 greased and floured 8-inch cakepans. Bake at 350° for 30 to 35 minutes or until cake tests done. Cool 5 to 10 minutes in pans; remove from pans, and cool completely.

Spread Orange Buttercream Frosting between layers and on top and sides of cake. Yield: one 8-inch layer cake.

Orange Buttercream Frosting:

1½ cups butter or margarine, softened
4½ cups powdered sugar
2 tablespoons orange juice
1 tablespoon grated orange rind

Combine butter and sugar, creaming until light and fluffy. Add orange juice; beat until spreading consistency. Stir in orange rind. Yield: enough for one 3-layer cake.
Mrs. Sue-Sue Hartstern,
Louisville, Kentucky.

ELEGANT LEMON CAKE ROLL

4 eggs, separated
¼ cup sugar
1 teaspoon lemon extract
1 tablespoon vegetable oil
½ cup sugar
⅔ cup sifted cake flour
1 teaspoon baking powder
¼ teaspoon salt
Powdered sugar
Creamy Lemon Filling
½ cup flaked coconut
½ teaspoon water
1 to 2 drops yellow food coloring

Beat egg yolks until light and lemon colored; gradually add ¼ cup sugar,

beating constantly. Stir in lemon extract and vegetable oil; set aside.

Beat egg whites until foamy; gradually add ½ cup sugar, beating until stiff but not dry. Fold yolk mixture into whites. Combine flour, baking powder, and salt; fold into egg mixture.

Grease a 15- x 10- x 1-inch jellyroll pan, and line with waxed paper; grease and flour waxed paper. Spread batter evenly in pan. Bake at 375° for 10 to 12 minutes.

Sift powdered sugar in a 15- x 10-inch rectangle on a linen towel. When cake is done, immediately loosen from sides of pan and turn out on sugar. Peel off waxed paper. Starting at narrow end, roll up cake and towel together; cool on a wire rack, seam side down.

Unroll cake; spread with half of Creamy Lemon Filling, and reroll. Place on serving plate, seam side down; spread remaining filling on all sides.

Combine coconut, water, and food coloring in a plastic bag; close securely, and shake well. Sprinkle colored coconut over cake roll. Refrigerate for 1 to 2 hours before serving. Yield: 8 to 10 servings.

Creamy Lemon Filling:

1 (14-ounce) can sweetened condensed milk
⅓ cup lemon juice
1 to 2 teaspoons grated lemon rind
5 drops yellow food coloring
1 (4-ounce) carton frozen whipped topping, thawed

Combine sweetened condensed milk, lemon juice, lemon rind, and food coloring; mix well. Fold in whipped topping. Yield: about 3 cups.
Margaret Cotton,
Franklin, Virginia.

LEMON ICE CREAM PIE

1½ pints vanilla ice cream
3 eggs
½ cup sugar
½ teaspoon salt
¼ cup lemon juice
1 cup whipping cream, whipped
Grated lemon rind (optional)
Mint leaves (optional)

Cut ice cream into ½-inch slices, and arrange on bottom and sides of a lightly greased 9-inch piepan. Let ice cream soften slightly; then smooth slices together with a spoon, forming a pie shell. Freeze 2½ hours or until firm.

Combine 1 egg and 2 egg yolks in a small, heavy saucepan; beat well. Stir in sugar, salt, and lemon juice. Cook over low heat, stirring constantly, until thickened. Set aside to cool. Fold mixture into whipped cream.

Beat 2 egg whites until stiff; fold into lemon mixture. Spoon filling into ice cream shell. Freeze until firm (about 5 hours). Let stand at room temperature 5 minutes before slicing. Garnish with grated lemon rind and mint leaves, if desired. Yield: one 9-inch pie.

Mrs. C. R. Simms,
Palestine, Illinois.

CHOCOLATE-MINT CUPS

2 (1-ounce) squares unsweetened chocolate, melted
1 cup butter, softened
2 cups powdered sugar
4 eggs
2 teaspoons vanilla extract
1 teaspoon peppermint extract
12 vanilla wafers, finely crushed
¼ cup finely chopped pecans

Melt chocolate over low heat, stirring constantly. Set chocolate aside to cool.

Combine butter and sugar, creaming until light and fluffy. Add eggs, one at a time, beating well after each addition. Add chocolate and flavorings; mix well.

Combine vanilla wafer crumbs and pecans; stir well. Sprinkle half of crumb mixture into 12 ungreased muffin cups.

Spoon chocolate mixture over crumb mixture, and top with remaining crumb mixture. Cover and freeze until firm.

To serve, run a knife around edge of each muffin cup; gently lift out dessert with knife. Yield: 12 servings.

Mrs. Michael Champagne,
Covington, Louisiana.

CHARLOTTE RUSSE

1 envelope unflavored gelatin
¼ cup milk
2 eggs
1 cup sugar
¼ teaspoon salt
2 cups milk
3 tablespoons cream sherry
1 teaspoon vanilla extract
2 cups whipping cream, whipped
About 10 ladyfingers, split lengthwise

Soften gelatin in ¼ cup milk; set aside.

Combine eggs and sugar, beating until thick and lemon colored; stir in salt and 2 cups milk. Cook in top of double boiler, stirring constantly, until thickened. Remove from heat, and stir in gelatin mixture; cool.

Stir sherry and vanilla into custard; fold in whipped cream. Line sides of a 2-quart bowl with about 7 ladyfingers. Pour in filling; chill until set. Garnish with remaining ladyfingers. Yield: 8 to 10 servings.   *Mary Frances Thomson,*
Daphne, Alabama.

Sour Cream In These Rolls

There is nothing quite like fresh homemade rolls to make a meal complete. Sour Cream Rolls, a yeast bread with a light, delicate texture, can be shaped into crescents, but for variety you can shape the dough into Parker House, cloverleaf, fan tan, or pan rolls.

SOUR CREAM ROLLS

½ cup butter or margarine
1 (8-ounce) carton commercial sour cream
½ cup sugar
2 packages dry yeast
½ cup warm water (105° to 115°)
2 eggs, beaten
4 cups all-purpose flour
1 teaspoon salt
Melted butter or margarine

Place butter in a small saucepan, and bring to a boil. Remove from heat; stir in sour cream and sugar. Cool mixture to lukewarm.

Dissolve yeast in warm water in a large mixing bowl. Stir in sour cream mixture and eggs. Combine flour and salt; gradually add to yeast mixture, mixing well. Cover dough and refrigerate overnight.

Punch dough down, and divide into 4 equal parts. Roll each into a 10-inch circle on a floured surface; brush with butter. Cut each circle into 12 wedges; roll up each wedge, beginning at wide end. Place on greased baking sheets.

Cover and let rise in a warm place (85°), free from drafts, until doubled in bulk (about 1 hour). Bake at 375° for 10 to 12 minutes or until golden brown. Yield: 4 dozen. *Mrs. R. M. Lancaster,*
Brentwood, Tennessee.

Are You Ready For Marinated Pork Roast?

Mention pork to any Southerner, and barbecue almost always comes to mind. Barbecued pork is delicious, particularly in the two recipes included here—one for Boston butt, the other for spareribs.

But you'll miss some real treats if you don't try pork in combination with other flavors: herbs, for example. For Marinated Pork Roast, the rolled loin is marinated in a thyme-flavored sauce before being roasted. The slices are served with a sherried apricot sauce. Pork steaks also feature the flavor of herbs in a dish called Herbed Pork Steaks.

MARINATED PORK ROAST

2 tablespoons dry mustard
2 teaspoons whole thyme leaves
½ cup dry sherry
½ cup soy sauce
2 cloves garlic, minced
1 teaspoon ground ginger
1 (4- to 5-pound) pork loin roast, boned, rolled, and tied
1 (10-ounce) jar apricot preserves or jelly
1 tablespoon soy sauce
2 tablespoons dry sherry

Combine first 6 ingredients in a shallow dish, stirring well. Place roast in dish; cover and marinate 3 to 4 hours in refrigerator, turning occasionally.

Remove roast from marinade, and place on a rack in a shallow roasting pan. Insert meat thermometer at an angle into thickest part of roast. Bake, uncovered, at 325° until thermometer registers 170° (2½ to 3 hours total cooking time).

Combine preserves, 1 tablespoon soy sauce, and 2 tablespoons sherry in a small saucepan; cook over low heat, stirring occasionally, until preserves melt. Serve with sliced roast. Garnish as desired. Yield: 12 to 14 servings.
Jeanne Owens Glasscock,
Celeste, Texas.

Tip: Reheat leftover food briefly. If it is overcooked, it will lose color, texture, nutritive value, and taste.

Boston butt is the basis for our version of Barbecued Pork. Slices are baked in a tangy sauce, just right for piling on a toasted bun.

If desired, prepare mushroom gravy according to package directions. Serve with steaks. Yield: 4 servings.

Mrs. Mildred Keing,
Blackwell, Oklahoma.

PORK CHOPS ITALIANO

4 (1-inch-thick) loin pork chops
Salt and pepper to taste
1 tablespoon vegetable oil
½ pound fresh mushrooms, sliced
1 medium onion, chopped
1 small clove garlic, crushed
2 medium-size green peppers, cut into thin strips
2 (8-ounce) cans tomato sauce
¼ teaspoon whole oregano or basil
1 tablespoon lemon juice
¼ cup dry sherry

Sprinkle pork chops with salt and pepper; brown on both sides in hot oil. Place chops in a shallow 2-quart baking dish; cover with mushrooms, and set aside.

Add onion, garlic, and green pepper to skillet; cook until tender. Add remaining ingredients, and simmer 5 minutes; pour over chops. Bake at 350° for 1 hour or until chops are done. Yield: 4 servings.

Cindy Marks,
Gainesville, Florida.

SWEET-AND-SOUR PORK

1 egg, beaten
¼ cup all-purpose flour
1 teaspoon salt
¼ cup cornstarch
¾ cup chicken broth, divided
1 to 1½ pounds boneless pork, trimmed of fat and cut into ¾-inch cubes
Vegetable oil
1 (15¼-ounce) can pineapple chunks
1 medium-size green pepper, cut into thin strips
1 clove garlic, minced
2 to 3 medium carrots, cut into 2-inch strips
¼ cup sugar
¼ cup red wine vinegar
1 teaspoon soy sauce
2 tablespoons cold water
1 tablespoon cornstarch
Hot cooked rice

Combine egg, flour, salt, ¼ cup cornstarch, and ¼ cup chicken broth; beat until smooth. Dip pork cubes in batter, coating well; deep fry in hot oil (375°) for 5 to 6 minutes or until golden brown. Drain and set aside.

BARBECUED PORK

1 (5- to 6-pound) Boston butt
Salt
1 teaspoon chili sauce
1 teaspoon celery seeds
1 cup catsup
¼ cup Worcestershire sauce
¼ cup vinegar
1 teaspoon brown sugar
1 cup water

Cook pork in lightly salted water over low heat 2 to 2½ hours; drain, reserving 1 cup broth. Cut pork into thin slices, and place in a large shallow baking pan.

Combine 1 teaspoon salt, reserved broth, and remaining ingredients; mix well, and pour over pork slices. Bake at 325° for 30 to 45 minutes. Yield: about 10 to 12 servings. *Mrs. Perry Forsyth,*
Guys, Tennessee.

HERBED PORK STEAKS

1 egg
3 tablespoons milk
⅓ cup grated Parmesan cheese
1¼ cups herb-seasoned stuffing mix, finely crushed
4 (½- to ¾-inch-thick) pork steaks
2 to 4 tablespoons shortening
1 (1-ounce) package mushroom gravy mix (optional)

Combine egg and milk in a shallow dish, beating with a fork until well blended. Combine cheese and stuffing mix in a shallow dish. Dip steaks into egg mixture; then dredge in stuffing mixture, coating well.

Heat shortening to 350° in an electric skillet; cook steaks until browned on both sides. Cover and reduce heat to 250°; cook 30 minutes or until steaks are done.

Drain pineapple, reserving juice. Heat 2 tablespoons oil in a large skillet; add green pepper, garlic, carrots, and pineapple. Cook 2 to 3 minutes, stirring occasionally. Stir in pineapple juice, remaining chicken broth, sugar, vinegar, and soy sauce; boil 1 minute.

Slowly add 2 tablespoons cold water to 1 tablespoon cornstarch, stirring until smooth; stir into vegetable mixture, and cook until thickened. Stir in pork, and serve over rice. Yield: 4 to 6 servings.
Mrs. Steve Toney,
Helena, Arkansas.

LEMONY SWEET SPARERIBS

3 pounds spareribs, cut into serving-size pieces
1 (6-ounce) can frozen lemonade concentrate, thawed and undiluted
1½ cups water
3 tablespoons soy sauce
½ teaspoon salt
3 tablespoons catsup
3 tablespoons brown sugar
2 tablespoons water
2 tablespoons cornstarch

Place spareribs in a large Dutch oven; cover with salted water, and cook over low heat 1 hour. Drain.

Combine next 6 ingredients, and pour over ribs. Cover and cook over low heat 1 hour. Remove ribs to serving platter.

Combine 2 tablespoons water and cornstarch, stirring until smooth; add to pan drippings. Cook until thickened and bubbly, stirring constantly. Serve sauce with ribs. Yield: 6 servings.
Mrs. Russell Rehkemper,
Tampa, Florida.

BARBECUED COUNTRY-STYLE SPARERIBS

2 medium onions, thinly sliced
2 tablespoons melted butter or margarine
1 large clove garlic, minced
½ cup chopped celery
1 cup catsup
¾ cup water
1 teaspoon dry mustard
1 teaspoon salt
¼ teaspoon pepper
2 tablespoons brown sugar
2 tablespoons vinegar
2 tablespoons lemon juice
2 tablespoons Worcestershire sauce
3½ pounds country-style spareribs

Sauté onion in butter until golden brown; stir in next 11 ingredients. Bring sauce to a boil; reduce heat, and simmer 20 minutes.

Place ribs, meaty side up, on a rack in a shallow baking dish. Bake at 325° for about 2 hours or until well done, basting with sauce and turning every 30 minutes. Yield: 4 servings.
Mrs. J. R. Salisbury,
St. Petersburg, Florida.

The Cheese Goes In The Soup

Cheese lovers will especially enjoy these soups, as each contains either Cheddar cheese, Swiss cheese, process cheese spread, or American cheese. Teamed up with vegetables and just the right spices, they make a delightful main dish or appetizer.

GOLDEN CHEESE CHOWDER

½ cup butter or margarine
½ cup all-purpose flour
4 cups milk
4 cups (1 pound) shredded sharp Cheddar cheese
3 cups water
4 medium potatoes, peeled and diced
1 cup sliced celery
1 cup sliced carrot
½ cup diced onion
¾ teaspoon salt
¼ teaspoon pepper
2 cups diced cooked ham
Hot sauce

Melt butter in a heavy 2-quart saucepan over low heat; add flour, stirring until smooth. Cook 1 minute, stirring constantly. Gradually stir in milk; cook over medium heat, stirring constantly, until thickened and bubbly. Add cheese, stirring until cheese is melted. Remove from heat, and set aside.

Combine water, vegetables, salt, and pepper in a 5-quart Dutch oven; heat to boiling. Reduce heat and cover; simmer 10 minutes or until vegetables are tender. Stir in cheese sauce, ham, and hot sauce to taste. Cook over low heat until thoroughly heated (do not boil). Yield: 12 to 14 servings.
Doris Amonette,
Tulsa, Oklahoma.

CHEESY VEGETABLE SOUP

2 tablespoons butter or margarine
¼ cup chopped celery
¼ cup chopped carrot
¼ cup chopped onion
¼ cup diced potato
3 tablespoons all-purpose flour
3 cups chicken broth
⅛ teaspoon pepper
1 (8-ounce) jar pasteurized process cheese spread
2 tablespoons diced pimiento (optional)

Melt butter in a 2-quart saucepan over low heat; add celery, carrot, onion, and potato. Cook over low heat, stirring occasionally, until vegetables are crisp-tender (about 5 to 7 minutes).

Blend in flour, stirring constantly. Gradually stir in broth; cook over medium heat, stirring constantly, until thickened and bubbly. Add pepper; reduce heat, and simmer 10 minutes.

Add cheese and pimiento, if desired, stirring until cheese is melted. Serve warm. Yield: 4 servings. *Nancy Polk,*
Nashville, Tennessee.

SWISS-BROCCOLI CHOWDER

1 pound ham hocks or meaty ham bone
1 (10-ounce) package frozen chopped broccoli
¼ cup water
2 tablespoons all-purpose flour
1 cup milk
1 cup half-and-half
1 cup (4 ounces) shredded process Swiss cheese
Dash of pepper

Cook ham hocks in water for 1½ hours or until meat falls off bone. Drain, reserving 1½ cups broth. Let ham cool; dice and set aside.

Combine broccoli and reserved ham broth in a 3-quart Dutch oven; heat to boiling. Cover and reduce heat; simmer 5 minutes or until the broccoli is tender.

Combine ¼ cup water and flour, stirring well. Gradually stir flour mixture, milk, half-and-half, and cheese into broccoli. Cook over medium heat, stirring constantly, until thickened. Add diced ham and pepper; heat thoroughly (do not boil). Yield: about 6 servings.
Jo Ann Beam,
Anderson, South Carolina.

CHEESE VELVET SOUP

¼ cup butter or margarine
¼ cup minced onion
¼ cup all-purpose flour
1 teaspoon salt
4 cups milk
1 cup (4 ounces) shredded process
   American cheese
½ cup frozen green peas, cooked
¼ cup diced pimiento

Melt butter in a 3-quart Dutch oven over low heat. Sauté onion until tender. Blend in flour and salt; cook 1 minute, stirring constantly. Gradually stir in milk; cook over medium heat, stirring constantly, until thickened and bubbly.

Reduce heat; add cheese, stirring until melted. Stir in peas and pimiento; heat soup thoroughly (do not boil). Yield: 6 to 8 servings.
Mrs. Pete Beckham,
Philadelphia, Mississippi.

Fresh Ideas For Salad Dressings

There's nothing quite like the flavor of a fresh, homemade dressing to top off a crisp green salad. These recipes offer some new combinations as well as versions of the classic Thousand Island dressing and Roquefort dressing.

Cucumber Dressing is a tasty blend of cucumber and onion in a mayonnaise base. Dilly Dressing is just as its name implies: It is flavored with dillweed. And our version of guacamole can be served as a dressing or as a dip for corn chips.

For a fresh dressing that's really quick and easy, Barbecue Salad Dressing is made in just a matter of minutes from six basic ingredients.

THOUSAND ISLAND DRESSING

1 cup cottage cheese
¼ cup chili sauce
¼ cup milk
2 tablespoons vegetable oil
1 teaspoon paprika
½ teaspoon salt
2 hard-cooked eggs, chopped
2 tablespoons finely chopped celery
2 tablespoons finely chopped green pepper
1 to 2 tablespoons sweet pickle relish
1 tablespoon finely chopped onion

Combine first 6 ingredients in container of electric blender; blend until smooth. Stir in remaining ingredients. Chill before serving. Yield: about 2¼ cups.
Mrs. James L. Twilley,
Macon, Georgia.

DILLY DRESSING

1 medium onion, finely chopped
¾ cup vegetable oil
½ cup catsup
½ cup sugar
¼ cup vinegar
¼ cup water
1 teaspoon dillweed
½ teaspoon salt
¼ teaspoon paprika

Combine all ingredients in container of electric blender; blend well. Chill. Serve dressing over salad greens. Yield: about 2½ cups.
Mrs. Clarence L. Goldsmith,
Crewe, Virginia.

GUACAMOLE

2 small avocados, peeled and mashed
1 tablespoon lemon juice
1 medium onion, minced
1 small clove garlic, crushed
1 large tomato, peeled and finely chopped
½ teaspoon salt
½ teaspoon seasoned salt
½ teaspoon seasoned pepper
½ teaspoon chili powder
Dash of hot sauce

Combine all ingredients; mix well. Cover and chill thoroughly. Serve over salad greens. Yield: about 2 cups.
Note: May be served as a dip with corn chips.
Ramona Hook,
Hazelwood, Missouri.

ROQUEFORT DRESSING

1 (3-ounce) package Roquefort cheese,
   crumbled
1 tablespoon minced onion
1 small clove garlic, minced
½ cup mayonnaise or salad dressing
½ cup commercial sour cream
1 tablespoon vinegar
1 tablespoon lemon juice
Dash of pepper

Combine cheese, onion, and garlic in a small mixing bowl; mix on low speed of electric mixer 3 minutes. Add remaining ingredients; beat mixture 2 minutes or until smooth. Chill. Yield: 1½ cups.
Mrs. Mary Dishon,
Stanford, Kentucky.

BARBECUE SALAD DRESSING

½ cup mayonnaise
¼ cup barbecue sauce
1 tablespoon minced onion
1 tablespoon lemon juice
½ teaspoon salt
¼ teaspoon pepper

Combine all ingredients in a small mixing bowl; mix well. Cover and chill. Serve over salad greens. Yield: about ¾ cup.
Mrs. Bobby W. Zeagler,
Baytown, Texas.

CUCUMBER DRESSING

1 medium cucumber
1 small onion
2 tablespoons sugar
1 tablespoon plus 1 teaspoon lemon juice
2 teaspoons Worcestershire sauce
Dash of garlic powder
1⅓ cups mayonnaise or salad dressing

Grate cucumber and onion; then drain well. Pat dry with paper towels.

Combine remaining ingredients; stir until blended. Add cucumber and onion, stirring well. Yield: about 2⅔ cups.
Susan Erickson,
State University, Arkansas.

Tip: Freshen wilted lettuce by letting it stand about 10 minutes in cold water to which a few drops of lemon juice have been added; store in plastic bag in refrigerator until needed.

English Muffins To Split And Toast

For a special breakfast surprise, try some homemade English muffins. These raisin-filled treats are every bit as attractive and tasty as those from the bakery.

To ease the morning breakfast rush, the muffins can be prepared ahead and stored in an airtight container; just split and toast before serving.

RAISIN ENGLISH MUFFINS

1 package dry yeast
1 cup warm water (105° to 115°)
1 cup milk
2 tablespoons sugar
1 teaspoon salt
3 tablespoons butter or margarine, softened
1 cup raisins
5½ to 6 cups all-purpose flour, divided
Cornmeal

Dissolve yeast in water in a large mixing bowl; let stand 5 minutes.

Combine milk, sugar, salt, and butter in a small saucepan. Cook over medium-low heat, stirring until butter melts. Cool to lukewarm (105° to 115°).

Stir milk mixture, raisins, and 3 cups flour into yeast mixture; beat until smooth. Add 2½ to 3 cups flour to form a stiff dough.

Turn dough out onto a floured surface, and knead 2 minutes or until dough can be shaped into a ball (dough will be slightly sticky). Place in a well-greased bowl, turning to grease top. Cover and let rise in a warm place (85°), free of drafts, about 1 hour or until doubled in bulk.

Punch dough down, and divide in half. Turn each half out onto a smooth surface heavily sprinkled with cornmeal. Pat one half of dough into a circle, ½ inch thick, using palms of hands; cut dough into rounds with a 2¾-inch cutter. (Cut carefully, as any leftover dough should not be reused.)

Sprinkle 2 baking sheets with cornmeal. Transfer cut dough rounds to baking sheets, placing 2 inches apart with cornmeal side down (one side of dough should remain free of cornmeal). Repeat process with remaining half of dough. Cover and let rise in a warm place (85°), free of drafts, for 30 minutes or until doubled in bulk.

Using a wide spatula, transfer rounds to a preheated 360°, lightly greased electric skillet. Place cornmeal side down; cook for 6 minutes. Turn and cook 6 additional minutes. Cool on wire racks. To serve, split muffins and toast until lightly browned. Store muffins in an airtight container. Yield: 1½ dozen muffins.

Note: Muffins may be cooked over direct medium-high heat in a skillet.

Diane Lang,
Joppa, Maryland.

Chicken Meant For The Microwave

The natural tenderness of chicken makes it an excellent choice for microwave cooking. In addition to being ready to serve in a fraction of the time required with conventional preparation, the chicken remains moist and tender.

To prove how easy it is to achieve outstanding results when microwaving chicken, we present a variety of entrées developed in our test kitchens.

Each recipe gives a time range for microwaving. This allows for the variation in wattage of microwave ovens, as well as for different weights of chickens. The times given are based on chickens weighing between 2½ and 3 pounds. Remember that the larger the chicken, the more time it takes to cook. Also, a microwave oven with lower wattage requires more time to complete cooking than one with higher wattage.

Tips for Microwaving Chicken

—To take full advantage of the speed of a microwave oven, select a broiler-fryer chicken rather than a stewing hen. Because stewing hens are larger and have a tougher skin, they must be microwaved at MEDIUM (50% power). This means that the cooking time will be almost as long as conventional preparation; in addition, the skin will not tenderize well during microwaving.

—Rearranging the chicken pieces about halfway through microwaving will promote even cooking; so will turning them. However, crumb-coated chicken should not be turned because the coating will not be as crisp.

—Plain chicken will neither brown nor become crisp when microwaved like it does when cooked conventionally. However, a browned appearance can be achieved by brushing the chicken with a mixture of melted butter and a brown sauce, such as soy sauce, teriyaki sauce, or brown bouquet sauce.

—Since microwave energy first enters food at the edge of the dish, arrange chicken pieces so the meatier portions are around the outside of the dish.

—Check for doneness by cutting into chicken pieces next to the bone. Test several pieces in different areas of the baking dish. If some require additional cooking, remove those that are done and briefly microwave the remainder.

CHICKEN TETRAZZINI

1 (7-ounce) package spaghetti
1 (2½- to 3-pound) broiler-fryer, cut up and skinned
1½ cups water
¼ cup butter or margarine
1 cup sliced fresh mushrooms
1 medium onion, chopped
2 teaspoons lemon juice
⅓ cup all-purpose flour
2 teaspoons salt
¼ teaspoon paprika
⅛ teaspoon ground nutmeg
1 cup half-and-half
½ cup grated Parmesan cheese
Paprika

Cook spaghetti according to package directions; drain and set aside.

Arrange chicken in a 12- x 8- x 2-inch baking dish, placing meatier portions to outside of dish; pour water over chicken. Cover with heavy-duty plastic wrap; microwave at HIGH for 6 to 9 minutes.

Turn chicken and rearrange so uncooked portions are to outside of dish. Cover and microwave at HIGH for 5 to 8 minutes. Remove chicken from dish, and set aside; reserve 1½ cups broth.

Combine butter, mushrooms, onion, and lemon juice in a 1½-quart casserole. Cover with waxed paper; microwave at HIGH for 2 to 4 minutes or until onion is tender. Blend in flour, salt, ¼ teaspoon paprika, and nutmeg. Gradually add reserved broth and half-and-half, stirring well. Microwave at HIGH for 2½ minutes; stir well. Microwave at HIGH for 3 to 5 minutes or until thickened and bubbly, stirring at 1-minute intervals.

Place spaghetti in a 12- x 8- x 2-inch baking dish, and arrange chicken on top. Pour sauce over chicken, and sprinkle with Parmesan cheese and paprika. Cover with waxed paper; microwave at HIGH for 4 to 6 minutes or until chicken is done. Yield: 4 servings.

CHICKEN TERIYAKI

½ cup dry white wine
⅓ cup soy sauce
3 tablespoons honey
1 (2½- to 3-pound) broiler-fryer, cut up and skinned
1 (8-ounce) can sliced water chestnuts, drained
2 tablespoons water
1 tablespoon cornstarch
Hot cooked rice

Combine wine, soy sauce, and honey. Place chicken in a heavy-duty plastic bag, and add soy sauce mixture; tie bag securely, and place in a 12- x 8- x 2-inch baking dish. Marinate 1 hour at room temperature or 8 hours in refrigerator.

Drain marinade into baking dish. Arrange chicken in baking dish, placing meatier portions to outside of dish. Sprinkle with water chestnuts. Cover with waxed paper, and microwave at HIGH for 7 to 12 minutes.

Turn chicken and rearrange so uncooked portions are to outside of dish. Cover and microwave at HIGH for 8 to 13 minutes or until done.

Remove chicken, reserving liquid. Set chicken aside, and keep warm. Combine water and cornstarch in a 4-cup glass measure, stirring well. Gradually stir in reserved liquid. Microwave at HIGH for 2 minutes; stir well. Microwave at HIGH for 1 to 2 minutes or until thickened and bubbly; stir once. Arrange chicken over rice, and spoon sauce over top. Yield: 4 servings.

ZESTY BARBECUED CHICKEN

½ cup minced onion
¼ cup minced green pepper
¾ cup chili sauce
2 tablespoons brown sugar
1 tablespoon red wine vinegar
1½ teaspoons prepared mustard
1 (2½- to 3-pound) broiler-fryer, cut up and skinned

Combine first 6 ingredients, mixing well. Arrange chicken in a 12- x 8- x 2-inch baking dish, placing meatier portions to outside of dish. Brush about half of sauce over chicken. Cover with waxed paper, and microwave at HIGH for 7 to 10 minutes. Drain off excess fat.

Turn chicken and rearrange so uncooked portions are to outside of dish; brush with remaining sauce. Cover and microwave at HIGH for 8 to 13 minutes or until done. Yield: 4 servings.

CRISPY PARMESAN CHICKEN

1 cup fine dry breadcrumbs
½ cup grated Parmesan cheese
¼ cup chopped fresh parsley
½ cup butter or margarine
⅛ teaspoon garlic powder
1 (2½- to 3-pound) broiler-fryer, cut up and skinned
Salt and pepper
Paprika
Fresh parsley sprigs (optional)

Combine breadcrumbs, cheese, and chopped parsley in a piepan; mix well, and set aside. Place butter in a small glass bowl; microwave at HIGH for 1 minute or until melted. Stir in garlic powder.

Sprinkle chicken with salt and pepper; dip in butter. Roll each piece in crumb mixture; sprinkle with paprika.

Arrange chicken in a 12- x 8- x 2-inch baking dish, placing meatier portions to outside of dish. Cover with waxed paper, and microwave at HIGH for 8 to 10 minutes. Rearrange chicken (do not turn) so uncooked portions are to outside of dish. Cover and microwave at HIGH for 9 to 12 minutes or until done. Garnish with parsley, if desired. Yield: 4 servings.

ELEGANT CHICKEN WITH WILD RICE

3 tablespoons olive oil
1 medium onion, sliced and separated into rings
1 cup sliced fresh mushrooms
1 clove garlic, minced
Salt
2 tablespoons olive oil
1 tablespoon bottled brown bouquet sauce
1 (2½- to 3-pound) broiler-fryer, cut up
½ cup dry white wine
Cooked long-grain and wild rice
Fresh parsley sprigs (optional)

Combine 3 tablespoons olive oil, onion rings, sliced mushrooms, and garlic in a shallow baking dish; sprinkle mixture with salt. Cover with waxed paper; microwave at HIGH for 3 to 6 minutes or until onion is crisp-tender. Set aside.

Combine 2 tablespoons olive oil and brown bouquet sauce in a custard cup; brush on chicken. Arrange chicken, skin side down, in a 12- x 8- x 2-inch baking dish, placing meatier portions to outside of dish. Cover with waxed paper, and microwave at HIGH for 10 minutes.

Turn chicken and rearrange so uncooked portions are to outside of dish. Spoon onion mixture over chicken, and add wine. Cover and microwave at HIGH for 5 to 8 minutes or until done. Serve with rice; garnish with parsley, if desired. Yield: 4 servings.

Who Can Resist Fresh Asparagus?

Spring signals the season for fresh asparagus to be enjoyed in a variety of dishes. It's hard to resist those bright-green spears, which go equally well served hot or cold, as a salad or side dish. Asparagus Vinaigrette is just one delicious example: Fresh asparagus is dressed with vinegar, oil, herbs, and hard-cooked eggs. Serve it as a first course or to accompany a springtime luncheon.

When buying fresh asparagus, always select stalks that are green and tender; tips should be well formed and tightly closed. To help retain freshness, cut a thin slice from the base of each stalk; wrap a moist paper towel around the bottom of stalks before refrigerating.

CREAMY ASPARAGUS CASSEROLE

2 pounds fresh asparagus spears
2 tablespoons butter or margarine
2 tablespoons all-purpose flour
2 cups milk
½ teaspoon salt
Dash of pepper
4 hard-cooked eggs, sliced
¼ cup cracker crumbs
2 tablespoons butter or margarine, melted

Snap off tough ends of asparagus. Remove the scales with a knife or a vegetable peeler. Cut asparagus into 1½-inch pieces.

Cook asparagus, covered, in a small amount of boiling water about 6 to 8 minutes or until crisp-tender; drain, and set aside.

Melt 2 tablespoons butter in a heavy saucepan over low heat; blend in flour and cook 1 minute, stirring constantly. Gradually add milk; cook over medium heat, stirring constantly, until smooth and thickened. Stir in salt and pepper.

Arrange half the asparagus in a lightly greased 8-inch square baking dish. Top with egg slices and half the white sauce. Repeat with remaining asparagus and white sauce.

Combine cracker crumbs and 2 tablespoons melted butter; sprinkle over sauce. Bake at 350° for 30 to 35 minutes or until bubbly. Yield: 6 servings.

Mrs. C. D. Marshall,
Culpeper, Virginia.

ASPARAGUS VINAIGRETTE

1 to 1½ pounds fresh asparagus spears
2 hard-cooked eggs, chopped
¾ cup olive oil
¼ cup vinegar
2 tablespoons Dijon mustard
2 tablespoons minced shallots
2 tablespoons chopped fresh parsley
1 tablespoon chopped fresh chives
1½ teaspoons chopped fresh tarragon or
   ½ teaspoon dried tarragon leaves

Snap off tough ends of asparagus. Remove the scales with either a knife or a vegetable peeler.

Cook asparagus in boiling salted water about 8 minutes or until crisp-tender; drain. Arrange asparagus in a serving dish; chill.

Combine remaining ingredients; mix well, and pour over asparagus. Yield: 4 to 6 servings.

Margaret Cotton,
Franklin, Virginia.

ASPARAGUS SUPREME

4 pounds fresh asparagus spears
2 tablespoons butter or margarine
2 tablespoons all-purpose flour
2 cups half-and-half
1 cup diced cooked ham
2 teaspoons lemon juice
¼ teaspoon salt
⅛ teaspoon ground nutmeg
¼ cup shredded Swiss cheese

Snap off tough ends of asparagus. Remove the scales with either a knife or a vegetable peeler.

Cook asparagus, covered, in small amount of boiling water about 8 minutes or until crisp-tender. Drain, and arrange on a serving platter; keep warm.

Melt butter in a heavy saucepan over low heat; blend in flour and cook 1 minute, stirring constantly. Gradually add half-and-half; cook over medium heat,

stirring constantly, until thickened and bubbly. Add ham, lemon juice, salt, nutmeg, and cheese; stir until cheese melts. Serve sauce with asparagus. Yield: about 12 servings.

Mrs. Rose Naquin,
Melville, Louisiana.

ASPARAGUS-SPAGHETTI CASSEROLE

1 (7-ounce) package spaghetti
2½ to 3 cups fresh asparagus pieces
   (1-inch lengths)
1 teaspoon butter or margarine
1 (10¾-ounce) can cream of mushroom
   soup, undiluted
1 cup (4 ounces) shredded American or
   Cheddar cheese
½ cup milk

Cook spaghetti according to package directions; drain. Cook asparagus with butter in a small amount of boiling water until asparagus is tender; drain.

Place half of spaghetti in a lightly greased 2-quart casserole. Top with half of asparagus, half of soup, and half of cheese. Repeat layers. Pour milk over casserole. Bake at 400° for 3 to 5 minutes or until thoroughly heated. Yield: 6 to 8 servings.

Mrs. Benjamin N. Thompson,
Buies Creek, North Carolina.

Biscuits Can Be Quick And Easy

Don't let a busy schedule keep you from serving freshly baked biscuits with any meal. With these recipes, biscuits were never so quick and easy—and good. You'll find that our Whipping Cream Biscuits not only stir up in minutes, but they're also one of the richest and lightest biscuits you'll ever taste.

Prepare Feather Biscuits just as quickly. Store the dough in the refrigerator, and roll and cut biscuits as needed. Cheesy Sausage Biscuits, however, eliminate the rolling and cutting step altogether. Stir up a few simple ingredients, and drop dough by tablespoonfuls onto a baking sheet.

Biscuits are at their best when freshly baked, but leftovers can be just as tasty when properly handled. Cool leftovers

completely, wrap tightly in foil, and freeze for up to three months. To serve, thaw in the wrapper at room temperature. Bake at 375° for 10 minutes or until piping hot.

WHIPPING CREAM BISCUITS

2 cups self-rising flour
1 teaspoon sugar
1 cup whipping cream

Combine all ingredients; mix well. (Dough will be stiff.) Turn dough out on a lightly floured surface, and knead 10 or 12 times.

Roll dough to ⅜-inch thickness; cut with a 2-inch biscuit cutter. Place biscuits on a lightly greased baking sheet; bake at 450° for 10 to 12 minutes. Yield: about 1½ dozen.

Mrs. Martha Giles,
Augusta, Georgia.

OLD-FASHIONED BUTTERMILK BISCUITS

4 cups all-purpose flour
2 tablespoons baking powder
1 teaspoon soda
¾ teaspoon salt
1 tablespoon sugar
⅔ cup margarine, softened
1½ cups buttermilk
¼ cup melted margarine

Combine flour, baking powder, soda, salt, and sugar; cut in ⅔ cup margarine until mixture resembles coarse meal. Add buttermilk, stirring until dry ingredients are moistened. Turn dough out on a lightly floured surface; knead lightly 4 or 5 times.

Roll dough to ¾-inch thickness; cut with a 2¾-inch biscuit cutter. Place biscuits on a lightly greased baking sheet; brush tops with melted margarine. Bake at 450° for 15 minutes or until golden brown. Yield: 15 biscuits.

Pam Snellgrove,
LaGrange, Georgia.

FEATHER BISCUITS

1 package dry yeast
2 tablespoons warm water (105° to 115°)
2 cups buttermilk
5 cups self-rising flour
¼ cup sugar
1 cup shortening

Dissolve yeast in warm water. Stir yeast mixture into buttermilk; mix well, and set aside.

Combine flour and sugar; cut in shortening until mixture resembles coarse meal. Add buttermilk mixture; stir until dry ingredients are moistened. Cover and let rise in a warm place until doubled. Or cover bowl tightly, and store in refrigerator until needed. (Dough may be stored up to 3 days.)

Punch dough down; turn dough out on a lightly floured surface. Knead lightly 3 or 4 times.

Roll dough to ½-inch thickness; cut with a 2-inch biscuit cutter. Place biscuits on lightly greased baking sheets; bake at 450° for 10 to 12 minutes or until lightly browned. Yield: about 3 dozen.   *Mrs. Carol Noble,*
Maple Hill, North Carolina.

CHEESY SAUSAGE BISCUITS

1 pound mild bulk pork sausage
1 small onion, finely chopped
1 (11-ounce) can Cheddar cheese soup, undiluted
½ cup water
3 cups biscuit mix

Crumble sausage into a large skillet; add onion and cook over medium heat until sausage is browned. Drain well on paper towels.

Combine all ingredients, stirring until dry ingredients are moistened. Drop batter by heaping tablespoonfuls about 2 inches apart on lightly greased baking sheets. Bake at 425° for 15 minutes or until lightly browned. Yield: 4 dozen.
Mrs. A. R. Welch, Jr.,
Duke, Oklahoma.

Tip: The next time a recipe calls for a cup of buttermilk and you don't have any, try this handy substitute: put 1 tablespoon vinegar or lemon juice in measuring cup; add enough whole milk to make 1 cup. Let stand 5 minutes to thicken slightly.

Mix-And-Match Luncheon Favorites

Warm spring days call for lunches that are light, refreshing, and easy to prepare. Here we offer a collection of ideas designed to give your lunches a lift. You'll find salads, soups, sandwiches, and a delicious pecan-stuffed egg recipe. Pick your favorites; then mix and match them to suit whatever the occasion may be.

SUBTLE POTATO POTAGE

2¼ cups diced potatoes
1 pound leeks, sliced, or 1½ to 2 cups sliced green onion
2 quarts water
1 tablespoon salt
2 tablespoons parsley flakes
1 cup whipping cream
1 (10¾-ounce) can chicken broth, undiluted

Combine potatoes, leeks, water, and salt in a Dutch oven; bring to a boil. Reduce heat, and simmer 1 hour. Remove from heat; mash vegetables in liquid, and allow to cool. Stir in parsley flakes, whipping cream, and chicken broth; chill. Yield: 6 to 8 servings.

Note: Soup may be served hot. Omit whipping cream and broth; stir 2 tablespoons butter into hot soup.
Anna Hoosack,
Knob Noster, Missouri.

PECAN-STUFFED EGGS

6 hard-cooked eggs
¼ cup mayonnaise
½ cup chopped pecans
1 teaspoon grated onion
1 teaspoon vinegar
½ teaspoon dry mustard
½ teaspoon salt
½ teaspoon minced parsley
Fresh parsley sprigs (optional)

Slice eggs in half lengthwise, and carefully remove yolks. Mash yolks with a fork; add next 7 ingredients, mixing well. Spoon pecan mixture into egg whites. Garnish with parsley sprigs, if desired. Yield: 6 servings.
Vivian Carter,
Pisgah, Alabama.

SPECIAL SPINACH SALAD

1 pound fresh spinach, torn
3 or 4 hard-cooked eggs, chopped
1 (8-ounce) can water chestnuts, drained and sliced
3 cups fresh bean sprouts
12 to 14 slices bacon, cooked and crumbled (about ¾ pound)
Blender Dressing

Combine all ingredients except dressing in a large bowl; toss. Serve with Blender Dressing. Yield: 6 servings.

Blender Dressing:

1 cup vegetable oil
½ cup vinegar
1 medium onion, chopped
⅓ cup catsup
¼ cup sugar
2 teaspoons salt
1 teaspoon Worcestershire sauce

Combine all ingredients in container of electric blender; process well. Yield: about 2 cups.   *Linda Radomski,*
Birmingham, Alabama.

AVOCADO-BANANA-YOGURT SOUP

4 (8-ounce) cartons plain yogurt
2 ripe avocados, peeled, seeded, and cut into ½-inch slices
3 bananas, cut into 2-inch slices
1 cup sugar
1 cup milk
3 tablespoons lemon juice
1 teaspoon ground cinnamon

Combine all ingredients in a large bowl. Pour about one-third of mixture in container of electric blender; process until smooth. Pour into a bowl or pitcher; repeat procedure with remaining mixture. Cover and chill several hours. Yield: 9 cups.
Jane Mollenkamp,
Atlanta, Georgia.

OPEN-FACED CHEESY BACON SANDWICHES

2 eggs, well beaten
2 cups (8 ounces) shredded sharp Cheddar cheese
1 teaspoon Worcestershire sauce
½ teaspoon salt
¼ teaspoon paprika
6 slices sandwich bread
6 slices bacon, cut in half crosswise

For a delicious spring luncheon, serve Open-Faced Cheesy Bacon Sandwiches, Pecan-Stuffed Eggs, and Sour Cream Potato Salad.

Combine first 5 ingredients in a small mixing bowl; mix well. Lightly toast 1 side of bread. Spread the cheese mixture on untoasted side of bread; then place bread slices on a large baking sheet.

Fry bacon until partially cooked; place 2 pieces on each cheese toast. Broil until cheese melts and bacon is crisp. Yield: 6 servings.

Lynda Schraub,
Hurst, Texas.

LETTUCE AND GREEN BEAN SALAD

⅓ cup chopped onion
1 teaspoon salt
Dash of pepper
¼ cup plus 2 tablespoons cider vinegar
½ teaspoon sugar
1 medium head lettuce, torn into bite-size pieces
4 cups cooked green beans, drained
3 slices bacon, diced
2 hard-cooked eggs, chopped

Combine first 5 ingredients, and set aside. Place lettuce in a large salad bowl, and pour hot green beans on top. Pour onion mixture over beans. Cook bacon until crisp; pour bacon and drippings over green beans. Toss lightly, and sprinkle eggs over top. Yield: 6 to 8 servings.

Lily Jo Drake,
Satellite Beach, Florida.

MARINATED BROCCOLI

3 bunches fresh broccoli
1 cup cider vinegar
1 tablespoon dillweed
1 tablespoon sugar
1 tablespoon monosodium glutamate
1 teaspoon salt
1 teaspoon pepper
1 teaspoon garlic salt
1½ cups vegetable oil

Trim off large leaves of broccoli. Remove tough ends of lower stalks, and wash broccoli thoroughly; cut flowerets from stems, reserving stems for use in other recipes.

Combine remaining ingredients; mix well and pour over broccoli flowerets. Cover and chill 8 hours or overnight. Drain marinade before serving. Yield: 8 to 10 servings.

Judy Bonorato,
Huntsville, Alabama.

SOUR CREAM POTATO SALAD

1½ cups mayonnaise
1 (8-ounce) carton commercial sour cream
1½ teaspoons prepared horseradish
1 teaspoon celery seeds
8 medium potatoes, cooked, peeled, and sliced
1 cup fresh minced parsley, divided
¾ cup chopped green onion, divided

Combine first 4 ingredients; set aside.

Place half of sliced potatoes in a medium bowl; sprinkle with ⅓ cup parsley and ¼ cup onion. Top with half of mayonnaise mixture. Repeat layers. Use remaining parsley and onion to garnish top. Cover and chill. Yield: 8 to 10 servings.

Mrs. Gary Witschy,
Marietta, Georgia.

Ground Beef Gets All Dressed Up

How do you serve your company something special for dinner and still keep costs within bounds? Simple. Make ground beef the center of your menu, and discover how easy it is to dress up plain ground beef for special occasions.

Choose the right type of ground beef to suit your needs. The kinds of ground beef differ in the amount of fat they contain, the value of the cut of meat, and, of course, in price. The type labeled simply ground beef will contain 70% to 75% lean meat; ground chuck or lean ground beef, 75% to 80% lean meat; ground round or extra-lean ground beef is 80% to 85% lean meat; and ground sirloin or chopped sirloin has very little fat.

ROLLED STUFFED MEAT LOAF

2 cups herb-seasoned stuffing mix, crushed
½ cup shredded carrot
2 tablespoons parsley
¼ cup water
2 pounds ground chuck
2 (10¾-ounce) cans cream of mushroom soup, undiluted and divided
1 egg, beaten
⅓ cup finely chopped onion
1 teaspoon salt
½ cup milk

Combine 1½ cups stuffing mix, carrot, parsley, and water; stir well and set mixture aside.

Combine beef, ½ cup soup, egg, onion, salt, and remaining ½ cup stuffing mix. Shape into a 12- x 9-inch rectangle on a sheet of waxed paper. Spread reserved stuffing mixture on top, leaving a 1-inch margin around edges. Begin at long end and roll jellyroll fashion, lifting waxed paper to help roll. Press edges and ends to seal.

Place roll, seam side down, in a lightly greased shallow baking dish. Bake at 350° for 45 minutes to 1 hour or until done. Remove 3 tablespoons pan drippings for sauce, if any has collected. Let loaf stand 10 minutes before serving.

Combine remaining soup, milk, and reserved drippings in a saucepan; cook over low heat, stirring occasionally, until hot. Serve sauce over meat loaf. Yield: about 8 servings.
Mrs. Harvey Kidd,
Hernando, Mississippi.

SPANISH STEAK

2 pounds ground chuck
½ cup finely chopped onion
4 slices bacon, cooked and crumbled
1 egg
1 teaspoon salt
1 teaspoon paprika
⅛ teaspoon pepper
Dash of hot sauce
1 (16-ounce) can tomato wedges, drained
12 pimiento-stuffed olives, sliced
½ cup shredded Cheddar cheese
1 green pepper, cut into rings
1 medium onion, sliced and separated into rings

Combine first 8 ingredients; mix lightly. Place meat mixture on a lightly greased sheet of aluminum foil, and shape into an oval loaf, 2 inches thick. Top with remaining ingredients; seal foil and place in a 13- x 9- x 2-inch baking pan. Bake at 400° for 35 to 40 minutes or until done. Yield: 6 servings.
Mrs. Carl Ramay,
Englewood, Colorado.

SWEDISH MEATBALLS

1½ pounds ground beef
1 (3-ounce) can fried onion rings, finely crushed
1½ cups dry breadcrumbs
1½ teaspoons salt
1 teaspoon ground nutmeg
1 teaspoon paprika
¼ teaspoon pepper
2 eggs, beaten
½ cup milk
¼ cup melted butter or margarine
¼ cup all-purpose flour
1 (10½-ounce) can beef consommé, undiluted
½ cup water
1 cup commercial sour cream
Hot cooked rice (optional)

Combine first 9 ingredients; mix well, and shape into 1-inch balls. Sauté in butter in a 3-quart Dutch oven until browned; drain meat well, and set aside.

Blend flour into hot pan drippings, stirring until smooth. Cook over medium heat 1 minute, stirring constantly. Gradually add consommé and water; cook, stirring constantly, until thickened. Stir in sour cream; reduce heat, and heat gently. Add meatballs; heat thoroughly. Serve over hot cooked rice, if desired. Yield: 6 to 8 servings.
Debbie Yates,
Louisville, Kentucky.

CRESCENT TACO PIE

1 (8-ounce) can crescent dinner rolls
1 pound ground beef
½ cup hot taco sauce
⅓ cup sliced pimiento-stuffed olives
1½ cups crushed corn chips
1 cup commercial sour cream
1 cup (4 ounces) shredded Cheddar cheese
Shredded lettuce (optional)
Avocado slices (optional)

Separate rolls into triangles. Arrange triangles in a 9-inch piepan with the points meeting in the center. Press dough until edges mesh together; trim excess dough and flute edges.

Cook ground beef over medium heat in a 10-inch skillet until browned, stirring to crumble; drain well. Add taco sauce and olives; simmer 5 minutes.

Sprinkle half of corn chips into pie shell. Spoon meat mixture evenly over corn chips. Spread sour cream over meat mixture, and top with cheese; sprinkle with remaining corn chips. Bake at 350° for 25 minutes. Garnish with lettuce and avocado slices, if desired. Yield: about 8 servings.
Mrs. Frank Wheelies,
Copperas Cove, Texas.

BEEF ROULADES

1 cup all-purpose flour
1 tablespoon sugar
Dash of salt
3 eggs, beaten
1 cup milk
Melted butter
Beef Filling
¼ cup dry sherry
½ cup grated Parmesan cheese
1 (6-ounce) package sliced mozzarella cheese
Paprika
¼ cup melted butter

Combine flour, sugar, and salt; add eggs, mixing well. Add milk and 2 tablespoons melted butter, mixing until smooth. Let batter stand 2 hours, or refrigerate overnight.

Brush the bottom of a 7-inch crêpe pan with melted butter; place pan over medium heat until butter is just hot, but not smoking.

Pour a scant ¼ cup batter into pan; quickly tilt pan in all directions so batter covers the pan in a thin film. Cook about 1 minute.

Lift the edge of crêpe to test for doneness. Crêpe is ready for flipping when it can be shaken loose from pan. Flip the crêpe, and cook about 30 seconds on the other side. (This side is rarely more than spotty brown.)

When crêpes are done, place on a towel to cool. Stack between layers of waxed paper to prevent sticking.

Spoon about ½ cup Beef Filling in the center of each crêpe; roll up, and place seam side down in a lightly greased 13- x 9- x 2-inch glass baking dish. Pour sherry over crêpes, then sprinkle Parmesan cheese on top.

Cut each slice of mozzarella cheese in half lengthwise; place a cheese slice over each crêpe. Sprinkle with paprika; drizzle with ¼ cup melted butter. Bake at 400° for 5 to 8 minutes or until cheese is melted. Yield: 6 to 8 servings.

Beef Filling:

¾ pound ground beef
1 cup fresh minced mushrooms
1 medium onion, chopped
2 cloves garlic, minced
½ cup catsup
1 tablespoon steak sauce
½ teaspoon salt
1 teaspoon dry mustard
Dash of pepper
1 teaspoon fresh minced parsley
¼ teaspoon whole oregano
¼ teaspoon rosemary leaves
1 bay leaf, crumbled
½ cup grated Parmesan cheese
2 cups (½ pound) shredded sharp
  Cheddar cheese

Combine beef, mushrooms, onion, and garlic in a 10-inch skillet; cook over medium heat until meat is browned, stirring to crumble. Drain off drippings.

Add catsup, steak sauce, salt, dry mustard, and pepper to skillet; cook over low heat about 5 minutes. Add herbs and cheese, stirring until cheese is slightly melted; remove from heat. Yield: about 4½ cups filling.

Mrs. Dean Piercy,
Memphis, Tennessee.

MOCK FILET MIGNON

1½ pounds ground chuck
1 (2-ounce) can mushroom stems and
  pieces, drained and finely chopped
1 tablespoon minced onion
1 tablespoon soy sauce
¼ teaspoon pepper
6 slices bacon

Combine first 5 ingredients; mix lightly. Shape mixture into 6 patties 1½ inches thick.

Wrap 1 slice bacon around each patty; secure with a wooden pick. Place on a broiler rack; broil 3 to 6 minutes on each side, depending on desired degree of doneness. Yield: 6 servings.

M. L. Schroeder,
Sigourney, Iowa.

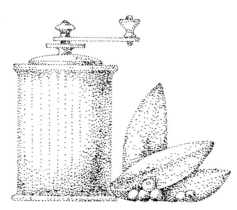

BEEFY LASAGNA

1 pound ground beef
4 slices bacon, finely diced
¾ cup chopped onion
2 large cloves garlic, minced
2 stalks celery, chopped
1 carrot, peeled and chopped
2 tablespoons fresh minced parsley
1 (8-ounce) can tomato sauce
1 cup tomato puree
3 tablespoons tomato paste
½ cup dry red wine
1 teaspoon salt
½ teaspoon pepper
1 cup ricotta cheese
6 lasagna noodles, cooked and drained
2 (8-ounce) packages mozzarella cheese,
  shredded

Combine beef, bacon, onion, and garlic in a 10-inch skillet; brown meat well over medium heat. Drain.

Combine beef mixture, celery, carrot, parsley, tomato sauce, tomato puree, tomato paste, wine, salt, and pepper in skillet; heat to boiling. Cover; reduce heat and simmer 40 to 50 minutes, stirring occasionally.

Layer half of meat sauce, ricotta cheese, noodles, and mozzarella in a lightly greased 12- x 8- x 2-inch glass baking dish. Repeat layers. Bake at 375° for 25 to 30 minutes. Yield: about 6 to 8 servings.

Mrs. Jo Gwyn Baldwin,
Abilene, Texas.

Look At What Basil Can Do

Hearty beef and sausage casseroles with tomato-base sauces just seem to call for the sweet accent of basil. This lively herb is also a natural for eggplant dishes and marinated mushrooms.

While these recipes call for dried basil, you can substitute fresh basil. Just remember that it takes 1 tablespoon of fresh basil to equal 1 teaspoon of the dried herb.

ITALIAN CASSEROLE

1½ pounds ground chuck
1½ cups chopped onion
2 cloves garlic, minced
1 (32-ounce) jar spaghetti sauce
⅓ cup water
1½ teaspoons salt
1 teaspoon dried basil leaves
1 teaspoon dried oregano leaves
1 teaspoon sugar
¼ teaspoon pepper
5 medium potatoes, peeled and thinly
  sliced
1 (8-ounce) package mozzarella cheese,
  shredded

Combine ground chuck, onion, and garlic in a large skillet; cook over medium heat until meat is browned and onion is tender. Drain; stir in spaghetti sauce, water, salt, basil, oregano, sugar, and pepper, mixing well. Cook over medium heat for 2 minutes.

Spoon one-third of meat mixture into a lightly greased 13- x 9- x 2-inch baking dish. Top with half of potato slices; cover with one-third of meat mixture. Add remaining potato slices and remaining meat mixture. Cover tightly with foil. Bake at 375° for 1 hour or until potatoes are tender. Remove foil; sprinkle cheese over casserole. Bake an additional 5 minutes or until cheese melts. Let casserole stand 10 minutes before serving. Yield: 10 to 12 servings.

Nancy Sturup,
Columbus, Georgia.

Tip: When cutting thin slices of raw meat, place meat in freezer for half an hour to make slicing easier.

SPICY VEGETABLES AND SAUSAGE

2 tablespoons vegetable oil
2 medium onions, sliced and separated into rings
3 green peppers, cut into strips
2 cloves garlic, crushed
1 (28-ounce) can whole tomatoes, drained and chopped, or 3 large fresh tomatoes, peeled and cubed
3 medium zucchini, thinly sliced
1 medium eggplant, peeled and diced
2 tablespoons chopped fresh parsley
1 teaspoon salt
¼ teaspoon pepper
1 (6-ounce) can tomato paste
½ cup dry white wine
½ teaspoon sugar
½ teaspoon dried basil leaves
¼ teaspoon dried marjoram leaves
¼ teaspoon seasoned pepper
1 pound Polish sausage, cut into 1-inch slices

Heat oil to 375° in an electric skillet. Add onion, green pepper, garlic, tomatoes, zucchini, eggplant, parsley, salt, and pepper; sauté for 10 minutes. Stir in tomato paste, wine, sugar, basil, marjoram, and seasoned pepper. Add sausage; cover and cook until sausage is hot and vegetables are crisp-tender (about 5 minutes). Yield: 8 servings.
Mrs. David R. Gallrein,
Anchorage, Kentucky.

EGGPLANT BAKE

1½ cups cooked brown rice
1 large eggplant, peeled and thinly sliced
1 (6-ounce) can tomato paste
1 cup cottage cheese
1 (8-ounce) carton plain yogurt
3 tablespoons water
¾ teaspoon dried basil leaves
½ teaspoon dried oregano leaves
½ teaspoon onion powder
½ teaspoon garlic salt
1 cup shredded Cheddar cheese
1 cup whole-grain breadcrumbs
1 tablespoon butter or margarine

Spread rice evenly in a lightly greased 12- x 8- x 2-inch baking dish. Arrange eggplant slices over rice.
Combine tomato paste, cottage cheese, yogurt, water, basil, oregano, onion powder, and garlic salt, mixing well. Pour sauce evenly over eggplant. Sprinkle cheese and breadcrumbs over casserole. Dot with butter. Bake at 350° for 30 minutes or until eggplant is done. Yield: 10 servings. *Connie Carpenter,*
Tallahassee, Florida.

MARINATED MUSHROOMS

¾ cup vegetable oil
½ cup vinegar
¼ cup water
1 teaspoon salt
2 teaspoons garlic powder
¼ teaspoon pepper
2 tablespoons dried basil leaves
½ cup sliced onion, separated into rings
1 pound fresh mushrooms

Combine first 6 ingredients in a medium saucepan; bring to a boil. Add remaining ingredients; reduce heat, and simmer 15 minutes. Drain; cover and refrigerate overnight. Yield: 4 to 6 servings. *Elizabeth S. Woodruff,*
Abingdon, Virginia.

ITALIAN SALAD DRESSING

½ cup olive oil
2 tablespoons minced onion
1 tablespoon grated Parmesan cheese
2 teaspoons salt
¾ teaspoon Worcestershire sauce
¾ teaspoon dried basil leaves
¾ teaspoon dry mustard
¾ teaspoon dried oregano leaves
¾ teaspoon sugar
¾ teaspoon pepper
¼ cup red wine vinegar
1 tablespoon lemon juice

Combine first 10 ingredients in container of electric blender; process for 30 seconds. Add vinegar and lemon juice; process 30 seconds. Yield: 1 cup.
Mrs. Bernie Benigno,
Gulfport, Mississippi.

Call For Cauliflower

Cauliflower makes a versatile accompaniment to meals when French fried, baked with English peas for a two-vegetable side dish, or tossed in a salad. In Main-Dish Cauliflower, the flowerets are topped with chunks of ham and baked in a cheese sauce.

When selecting cauliflower, look for a head that is firm, compact, and creamy white. Size of the head is not an indication of quality.

FRENCH-FRIED CAULIFLOWER AU GRATIN

1 small head cauliflower
1 egg
1 tablespoon water
Fine cracker crumbs
Salad oil
Cheese sauce (recipe follows)

Wash cauliflower, and break into flowerets. Cook, covered, in a small amount of boiling salted water about 10 minutes or until crisp-tender; drain.
Combine egg and water; beat well. Dredge flowerets in cracker crumbs; then dip in egg. Dredge again in cracker crumbs. Deep fry in hot salad oil (375°) until golden brown. Serve with cheese sauce. Yield: 6 servings.

Cheese Sauce:

2 tablespoons butter or margarine
2 tablespoons all-purpose flour
1 cup milk
¼ teaspoon salt
Dash of pepper
1 cup (¼ pound) shredded Cheddar cheese

Melt butter in a heavy saucepan over low heat; add flour, stirring until smooth. Cook 1 minute, stirring constantly. Gradually add milk; cook over medium heat, stirring constantly, until thickened and bubbly. Add salt, pepper, and cheese, stirring until cheese melts. Serve with fried cauliflower. Yield: about 1 cup.
Mrs. William O. Warren,
Hermitage, Arkansas.

CAULIFLOWER AND PEAS WITH CURRIED ALMONDS

1 large head cauliflower or 2 (10-ounce) packages frozen cauliflower
1 (10-ounce) package frozen English peas
2 tablespoons butter or margarine, divided
2 tablespoons all-purpose flour
1½ cups commercial sour cream
1 teaspoon onion salt
1 teaspoon curry powder
½ cup slivered almonds

Wash cauliflower, and break into flowerets. Cook, covered, in a small amount of boiling salted water 10 minutes; drain well. Cook peas according to package directions; drain.
Melt 1 tablespoon butter in a heavy saucepan over low heat; add flour, and

stir until smooth. Cook 1 minute, stirring constantly. Add sour cream; cook over low heat, stirring constantly, just until well heated.

Combine cauliflower, peas, sour cream mixture, and onion salt; mix well. Spoon mixture into a lightly greased 1½-quart casserole dish.

Melt remaining butter in saucepan; stir in curry powder and almonds. Cook over medium heat, stirring frequently, until almonds are golden (3 to 5 minutes). Spoon over cauliflower. Bake at 325° for 25 minutes. Yield: 6 servings.
Mrs. Ledlie Wilson,
Georgetown, Kentucky.

MAIN-DISH CAULIFLOWER

1 large head cauliflower
1 cup chopped cooked ham
¼ cup butter or margarine
¼ cup all-purpose flour
1½ cups milk
½ pound sharp Cheddar cheese, diced
1 cup soft breadcrumbs
2 tablespoons melted butter or margarine

Remove large outer leaves, and break cauliflower into flowerets; wash thoroughly. Place in a small amount of boiling salted water; cover and cook about 20 minutes or until tender. Drain well. Place cauliflower in a lightly greased 2-quart casserole dish, and sprinkle with chopped ham.

Melt ¼ cup butter in a heavy saucepan; blend in flour, and cook until bubbly. Gradually add milk; cook over medium heat, stirring constantly, until thickened and bubbly. Add cheese, stirring until melted. Spoon sauce over the cauliflower and ham.

Combine breadcrumbs and remaining butter; spoon over sauce. Bake at 350° for 30 minutes. Yield: 6 servings.
Mrs. R. E. Bunker,
Bartlett, Texas.

CAULIFLOWER SALAD

1 large head cauliflower
½ pound bacon, cooked and crumbled
2 medium tomatoes, diced
1 bunch green onions, chopped
1 cup diced Cheddar cheese
½ cup pimiento-stuffed olives, sliced
½ cup mayonnaise

Remove outer green leaves, and break cauliflower into flowerets; wash them thoroughly. Toss cauliflower with the remaining ingredients. Yield: about 10 to 12 servings. *Margaret Connelly, Fort Worth, Texas.*

Curry Blends In Nicely With Shrimp, Lamb

Curry, a blend of as many as 16 different spices, is one of the world's oldest seasonings. Essential to the blend are ginger, turmeric, red pepper, and coriander, while a wide range of other spices may be added to give each curry its distinctive flavor.

Whether you select a mild or a hot curry powder is a matter of individual taste, but you will want to use your choice in the following recipes. Our selections range from a shrimp curry and a lamb curry served with traditional condiments to a tangy curry dip delicious served with fresh vegetables.

CURRIED CHICKEN DIVAN

3 whole chicken breasts
2 (10-ounce) packages frozen broccoli spears
1 (10¾-ounce) can cream of chicken soup, undiluted
½ cup mayonnaise
⅓ cup evaporated milk
½ cup shredded process American cheese
1 teaspoon lemon juice
½ teaspoon curry powder
1 tablespoon melted butter or margarine
½ cup breadcrumbs

Cook chicken until tender in salted water. Remove from water; cool. Bone chicken and cut into quarters.

Cook broccoli according to package directions; drain. Arrange in a lightly greased 2-quart casserole; then top with cooked chicken.

Combine soup, mayonnaise, milk, cheese, lemon juice, and curry powder; stir well, and pour over chicken. Combine butter and breadcrumbs; sprinkle over casserole.

Bake at 350° for 25 to 30 minutes or until bubbly. Yield: about 6 servings.
Mrs. Ted Beckwith,
Lebanon, Tennessee.

SOUR CREAM SHRIMP CURRY

⅓ cup chopped onion
¼ cup chopped green pepper
1 clove garlic, minced
2 tablespoons melted butter or margarine
1 cup commercial sour cream
1¼ pounds medium shrimp, peeled, deveined, and cooked
1 teaspoon curry powder
¼ teaspoon salt
Pepper to taste
Hot cooked rice

Sauté onion, green pepper, and garlic in butter until tender. Add remaining ingredients except rice; cook over low heat until thoroughly heated, stirring often. Serve over rice. Yield: about 4 servings. *Mrs. R. M. Lancaster, Brentwood, Tennessee.*

■ An important part of this curried dish is the accompanying condiments, which guests sprinkle over the rice and curried lamb.

LAMB CURRY WITH RICE

¾ pound boneless lamb, cut into 1½-inch cubes
3 tablespoons vegetable oil
1 medium onion, minced
1 cooking apple, peeled and chopped
¼ cup melted butter or margarine
3 tablespoons all-purpose flour
1 cup milk
1 tablespoon curry powder
1 tablespoon lemon juice
1½ teaspoons salt
¼ teaspoon ground ginger
Dash of pepper
Hot cooked rice

Cook lamb in oil until brown; drain and set aside.

Sauté onion and apple in butter until tender. Add flour and cook 1 minute, stirring constantly. Gradually add milk; cook over medium heat, stirring constantly until thickened and bubbly. Stir in next 5 ingredients. Add lamb to sauce mixture; serve over rice.

Serve with several of the following condiments: currants, raisins, peanuts, onion, green pepper, or orange sections. Yield: 4 servings.
Regina Campbell,
Universal City, Texas.

CURRIED RICE SALAD

2 cups cooked brown rice, chilled
½ cup finely chopped celery
¼ cup grated carrot
¼ cup canned green peas, drained
½ cup mayonnaise
¼ cup yogurt
1 teaspoon lemon juice
¼ teaspoon curry powder
Lettuce leaves

Combine first 8 ingredients; mix well. Serve salad on lettuce leaves. Yield: 4 to 6 servings.

Kathie Koerwer,
Augusta, Georgia.

CURRY DIP

1 cup mayonnaise
1 tablespoon finely grated onion
1 teaspoon garlic salt
1 teaspoon curry powder
1 teaspoon prepared horseradish
1 teaspoon tarragon vinegar

Combine all ingredients, mixing well. Chill at least 3 hours; serve with fresh vegetables. Yield: about 1 cup.

Patricia Pashby,
Memphis, Tennessee.

Ice Cream Is In The Cake

Ice cream isn't served only to the side; it's stirred into the batter of this Praline Ice Cream Cake, giving it extra flavor and moistness. After baking, a praline topping is spread over the hot cake.

PRALINE ICE CREAM CAKE

1½ cups all-purpose flour
⅔ cup sugar
1 cup graham cracker crumbs
1 tablespoon baking powder
½ teaspoon salt
½ cup butter or margarine
1 pint vanilla ice cream, softened
2 eggs, beaten
Topping (recipe follows)
½ cup chopped pecans

Combine first 5 ingredients in a medium bowl, and set aside.

Melt butter in a 2-quart saucepan over low heat; remove from heat. Add ice cream, flour mixture, and eggs; stir until batter is smooth.

Pour batter into a lightly greased 13- x 9- x 2-inch baking pan; spoon ⅓ cup topping over batter. Bake at 350° for 30 minutes or until cake tests done.

Stir pecans into remaining ⅔ cup topping; spread over hot cake. Cool on wire rack. Yield: about 15 servings.

Topping:

1 cup firmly packed brown sugar
½ cup commercial sour cream
2 tablespoons butter or margarine
2 teaspoons cornstarch
½ teaspoon vanilla extract

Combine first 4 ingredients in a small saucepan over low heat; cook over medium heat until thickened and bubbly, stirring constantly. Remove from heat, and stir in vanilla. Yield: about 1 cup.

Mrs. P. A. Carraway,
Amarillo, Texas.

Entrées To Serve Two

Pork Chop Dinner and Spaghetti With Pizzazz are just two delightful ways to meet the challenge of preparing a nutritious, appetizing main dish for two. Besides the spaghetti, you'll also want to take advantage of pennywise ground beef in a savory stuffing for green peppers.

For those occasions when something a little extra special is in order, we offer either French Shrimp or Apricot-Glazed Cornish Hens.

STUFFED PEPPERS FOR TWO

2 medium-size green peppers
½ pound ground beef
¼ cup uncooked instant rice
1 (8-ounce) can tomato sauce with cheese, divided
1 tablespoon chopped onion
½ teaspoon salt
Dash of pepper
½ teaspoon Worcestershire sauce
1 egg, beaten

Cut off top of each green pepper; remove seeds. Cook 5 minutes in boiling salted water to cover. Drain; set aside.

Combine ground beef, rice, ¼ cup tomato sauce, and remaining ingredients. Stuff peppers with mixture, and place in a small baking pan.

Pour remaining tomato sauce over stuffed peppers. Cover and bake at 350° for 50 to 60 minutes or until meat is done, basting peppers twice with drippings. Yield: 2 servings.

Mrs. Charles Orr,
Higgins, Texas.

APRICOT-GLAZED CORNISH HENS

1 cup herb-seasoned stuffing
¼ cup water
2 tablespoons melted butter
2 (1-pound) Cornish hens
½ cup apricot preserves
½ cup water
1 (¾-ounce) envelope brown gravy mix
Dash of ground cloves

Combine stuffing, ¼ cup water, and butter; mix well. Stuff hens with dressing, and truss securely. Place hens breast side up in a 9-inch square baking pan.

Combine preserves, ½ cup water, gravy mix, and cloves in a small saucepan; cook over medium heat, stirring constantly, just until sauce reaches a boil. Spoon half of sauce over hens; use remainder for basting.

Bake at 350° for 1 hour or until juice runs clear when thigh is pierced with a fork; baste hens occasionally with sauce during baking. Yield: 2 servings.

Evelynn B. Walker,
Shreveport, Louisiana.

PORK CHOP DINNER

2 (½-inch-thick) loin pork chops
Salt and pepper to taste
1 tablespoon vegetable oil
¼ cup diced onion
¼ cup diced green pepper
½ cup uncooked regular rice
1½ cups canned tomatoes
1 teaspoon salt
½ teaspoon sugar
½ teaspoon prepared mustard

Sprinkle pork chops with salt and pepper; brown on both sides in hot oil. Remove chops, and drain on paper towels. Reserve drippings in skillet.

Add onion and green pepper to skillet; sauté until tender. Stir in rice, tomatoes, salt, sugar, and mustard; add pork chops. Bring to a boil. Reduce heat; cover and simmer about 30 minutes or until rice is tender and pork chops are done. Yield: 2 servings.

Mrs. Geneva P. Tobias,
Albemarle, North Carolina.

FRENCH SHRIMP

2 tablespoons butter or margarine
1 tablespoon plus 1½ teaspoons
    all-purpose flour
¾ cup milk
¼ teaspoon salt
Dash of pepper
Dash of paprika
2 tablespoons dry sherry
½ pound cooked, peeled, and deveined
    small shrimp
Grated Parmesan cheese

Melt butter in a heavy saucepan over low heat; add flour, stirring until smooth. Cook 1 minute, stirring constantly. Gradually add milk; cook over medium heat, stirring constantly, until thickened and bubbly. Stir in salt, pepper, paprika, sherry, and shrimp.

Spoon into 2 (10-ounce) ramekins; sprinkle each with Parmesan cheese. Broil 3 to 4 inches from heat until cheese is lightly browned. Yield: 2 servings.

Mrs. Ursula Bambrey,
Springfield, Virginia.

SPAGHETTI WITH PIZZAZZ

½ pound ground beef
1 (4-ounce) can tomato paste
1 cup water
¼ cup diced green pepper
¼ cup minced onion
1 bay leaf
½ teaspoon garlic salt
¼ teaspoon salt
¼ teaspoon pepper
¼ teaspoon chili powder
¼ teaspoon hot sauce
1 (2-ounce) can sliced mushrooms,
    drained
Hot cooked spaghetti

Cook ground beef until browned, and drain well; stir in tomato paste and water. Bring to a boil, and stir in next 8

Hot Cheesy Beef Dip, covered with pecans, is made with dried beef and cream cheese.

ingredients. Reduce heat; cover and simmer 40 minutes, adding water as needed.

Stir in mushrooms, and simmer 5 additional minutes; remove bay leaf. Serve over spaghetti. Yield: 2 servings.

Janet Gibson,
Prattville, Alabama.

A Dip Or Spread For Your Party

When it's time for a party, you'll naturally want to serve a tempting dip or spread. These recipes, all easy to prepare, offer you an assortment of hot and cold appetizers.

For a hot appetizer, offer Hot Cheesy Beef Dip, Hot Chicken Dip, or Baked Crab Spread. For something cold, there's Spinach Dip and Water Chestnut Dip. And for a really elegant touch, we suggest Sherried Liver Spread.

HOT CHEESY BEEF DIP

⅓ cup chopped pecans
1½ tablespoons melted butter or
    margarine
1 (2½-ounce) jar dried beef
1 (8-ounce) package cream cheese,
    softened
2 tablespoons milk
¼ cup finely chopped green pepper
¼ cup finely chopped green onion
1 clove garlic, pressed
½ teaspoon white pepper
½ cup commercial sour cream

Sauté pecans in butter 3 to 5 minutes; drain on paper towels, and set aside.

Place dried beef in container of electric blender or food processor; chop finely and set aside.

Combine cream cheese and milk in a medium mixing bowl; beat on medium speed of electric mixer until smooth. Stir in beef, green pepper, onion, garlic, and white pepper, mixing well. Stir in sour cream; spoon into a greased 1-quart casserole. Sprinkle pecans on top; bake at 350° for 25 minutes. Serve dip hot with assorted crackers. Yield: about 2 cups.

Mrs. Harry A. Smith,
Corbin, Kentucky.

HOT CHICKEN DIP

1 (10¾-ounce) can cream of mushroom
   soup, undiluted
1 (8-ounce) package cream cheese
1 (5-ounce) can chunk white chicken
1 (2¾-ounce) package slivered almonds
1 (2-ounce) can sliced mushrooms,
   drained
½ teaspoon Worcestershire sauce
⅛ teaspoon garlic powder
⅛ teaspoon pepper

Combine all ingredients in a 1-quart
saucepan or fondue pot. Cook over medium heat, stirring often, until blended
and heated thoroughly. Serve dip hot
with chips. Yield: about 3½ cups.
Susan Erickson,
State University, Arkansas.

SHERRIED LIVER SPREAD

1½ pounds chicken livers
⅓ cup minced blanched almonds
3 tablespoons butter or margarine, melted
3 tablespoons dry sherry
2 tablespoons finely chopped parsley
1 tablespoon grated onion
1½ teaspoons anchovy paste
¾ teaspoon dried basil leaves
½ teaspoon dried oregano leaves
¼ teaspoon pepper
6 slices bacon, cooked and crumbled

Cook chicken livers in a small amount
of boiling salted water about 5 minutes;
drain well.

Place livers in container of food processor; process with metal blade until
smooth. Add next 9 ingredients; process
until smooth. Stir in crumbled bacon.
Spread dip on crackers or party rye
bread. Yield: about 2½ cups.
Mrs. Opal Moffitt,
Springfield, Missouri.

BAKED CRAB SPREAD

1¾ cups crabmeat
1 (8-ounce) package cream cheese,
   softened
¼ cup slivered almonds
2 tablespoons milk
2 tablespoons minced onion
1 teaspoon prepared horseradish
½ teaspoon salt
½ teaspoon pepper

Combine all ingredients in a medium
bowl; mix well. Spoon mixture into a
1-quart casserole dish. Bake at 375° for
20 minutes. Serve dip hot with assorted
crackers. Yield: about 3 cups.
Mrs. George A. Michie,
Fort Madison, Iowa.

WATER CHESTNUT DIP

1 (8-ounce) carton commercial sour cream
1 cup mayonnaise
2 (8-ounce) cans water chestnuts, drained
   and finely chopped
¼ cup chopped onion
¼ cup chopped fresh parsley
¾ teaspoon soy sauce
½ teaspoon salt

Combine all ingredients in a medium
bowl; stir well. Chill. Serve dip with
potato chips or crackers. Yield: 3
cups.
Ron Barker,
Mesquite, Texas.

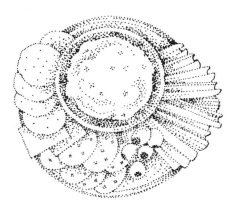

SPINACH DIP

1 (10-ounce) package frozen chopped
   spinach
1 cup mayonnaise
1 cup commercial sour cream
1 medium onion, chopped
1 (8-ounce) can water chestnuts, chopped
1 (1⅜-ounce) package vegetable soup mix

Thaw spinach; place on paper towels,
and press until barely moist.

Combine spinach, mayonnaise, sour
cream, onion, water chestnuts, and vegetable soup mix; stir well. Cover and
chill mixture several hours. Serve dip
with crackers or raw vegetables. Yield:
about 3 cups.
Mrs. Gary Witschy,
Marietta, Georgia.

Peanut-Flavored Treats

If you have peanut fans in your family (and whose family doesn't?) then
you'll want to try these dessert and
snack treats that are sure to please.

Rich and delicious, Peanut-Chocolate
Dessert features layers of creamy peanut butter filling and whipped topping
over a crunchy peanut crust. Our moist
Peanut-Butter Banana Cake starts with
a convenient cake mix. And if you like
to serve muffins, try Peanut Butter Muffins; crunchy peanut butter gives them
flavor and crunch.

PEANUT BUTTER MUFFINS

2 cups self-rising flour
¼ cup sugar
⅓ cup chunky peanut butter
1 cup milk
2 eggs, beaten
2 tablespoons vegetable oil or melted
   shortening

Combine flour and sugar in a large
bowl; cut in chunky peanut butter until
mixture resembles coarse meal. Set
flour mixture aside.

Combine remaining ingredients, beating well. Add milk mixture to dry ingredients; stir just until mixture is
moistened. Spoon batter into greased 3-
inch muffin pans, filling two-thirds full.
Bake at 400° for 20 to 25 minutes.
Yield: 1 dozen muffins. *Teri Isenhour,*
Charlotte, North Carolina.

PEANUT-CHOCOLATE DESSERT

½ cup butter or margarine, softened
1 cup all-purpose flour
⅔ cup finely chopped dry roasted peanuts
1 (8-ounce) package cream cheese,
   softened
⅓ cup peanut butter
1 cup powdered sugar
1 (12-ounce) carton frozen whipped
   topping, thawed and divided
1 (3¾-ounce) package vanilla instant
   pudding and pie filling mix
1 (4½-ounce) package chocolate instant
   pudding and pie filling mix
2¾ cups milk
1 (1.2-ounce) milk chocolate candy bar,
   shaved
⅓ cup chopped dry roasted peanuts

Cut butter into flour until mixture resembles coarse meal; stir ⅔ cup peanuts into flour mixture. Press peanut mixture into a 13- x 9- x 2-inch baking pan. Bake at 350° for 20 minutes; cool crust completely.

Combine cream cheese, peanut butter, and powdered sugar; beat until fluffy. Stir 1 cup whipped topping into cream cheese mixture. Spread over crust; chill.

Combine pudding mix and milk; beat 2 minutes at medium speed of electric mixer. Spread pudding over cream cheese layer. Spread remaining whipped topping over pudding layer. Sprinkle the top with shaved chocolate and ⅓ cup chopped peanuts. Store in refrigerator. Yield: about 15 servings.

Anne Ringer,
Warner Robins, Georgia.

PEANUT BRITTLE

2 cups sugar
1 cup light corn syrup
2½ cups raw peanuts
½ teaspoon soda
1 teaspoon water
1 teaspoon vanilla extract

Combine sugar and syrup in a Dutch oven; cook over low heat until candy thermometer reaches 240°. Add peanuts; cook, stirring constantly, until candy thermometer registers 300°. Remove from heat; stir in soda, water, and vanilla. Spread mixture onto a warm buttered 15- x 10- x 1-inch jellyroll pan. Allow peanut brittle to cool; break into pieces. Yield: about 2 pounds.

Mrs. J. L. Hurst,
Yorktown, Texas.

CHOCOLATE-PEANUT BUTTER BALLS

½ cup melted margarine
2 cups peanut butter
1 (16-ounce) package powdered sugar
4 cups crisp rice cereal
1 (12-ounce) package semisweet chocolate morsels
2 tablespoons melted paraffin

Combine margarine, peanut butter, and powdered sugar; mix well. Add rice cereal, and mix well. Roll mixture into 1-inch balls; set aside.

Combine chocolate morsels and paraffin in top of a double boiler; place over hot water, stirring until chocolate is melted. Place several peanut butter balls in chocolate mixture; roll with spoon to coat evenly. Remove from mixture with spoons, and place on waxed paper to cool. Continue process until all peanut butter balls are covered. Yield: about 7 dozen peanut butter balls.

Note: If desired, 2 tablespoons melted shortening may be substituted for paraffin in chocolate mixture. Refrigerate candy to prevent stickiness.

Mrs. Elizabeth Moore,
Huntsville, Alabama.

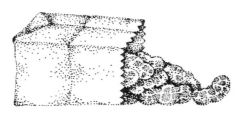

PEANUT BUTTER-BANANA CAKE

1 (18.5-ounce) package banana cake mix with pudding
½ cup peanut butter
Creamy Peanut Frosting

Prepare cake mix according to package directions, adding ½ cup peanut butter before beating.

Grease two 9-inch round cakepans; line with greased waxed paper, and dust with flour. Pour batter into prepared pans, and bake at 350° for 25 to 30 minutes or until cake tests done. Cool thoroughly on wire racks.

Spread 1 cup Creamy Peanut Frosting between layers; spread remaining frosting on top and sides of cake. Store cake in refrigerator. Yield: one 9-inch cake.

Creamy Peanut Frosting:

1 (8-ounce) package cream cheese, softened
1 cup peanut butter
¼ to ⅓ cup milk
½ cup honey
¼ cup powdered sugar
2 teaspoons vanilla extract
1 teaspoon imitation banana flavor
½ teaspoon ground nutmeg
1 cup ground roasted peanuts

Beat cream cheese until fluffy; add remaining ingredients except peanuts, and beat until well blended. Stir peanuts into frosting. Yield: enough for one 9-inch two-layer cake.

Mrs. M. L. Shannon,
Fairfield, Alabama.

Dip In With An Artichoke

Looking for an elegant appetizer? If so, we recommend freshly cooked artichokes served with a savory dip. For the dip, we offer two delicious choices. Seasoned Mayonnaise Artichoke Dip is easily made with ingredients you probably have on hand. If you prefer a hot dip, serve Deluxe Artichoke Dip, flavored with anchovy fillets.

To cook artichokes, wash thoroughly and trim stem even with base. Slice about ¾ inch off top of artichoke, and remove discolored leaves at base. Trim off thorny leaf tips. Spread leaves apart; pull out center leaves, and scrape off the fuzzy thistle center (choke) with a spoon. Place artichokes in a Dutch oven with about 4 cups of water and ½ teaspoon salt. Cover tightly, and bring to a boil; reduce heat, and simmer 35 to 55 minutes or until leaves pull out easily.

SEASONED MAYONNAISE ARTICHOKE DIP

½ cup mayonnaise
1 tablespoon lemon juice
¼ teaspoon salt
Dash of pepper

Combine all ingredients in a small bowl; stir well. Serve with cooked artichokes. Store dip in refrigerator. Yield: ½ cup.

Barbara Morris,
Birmingham, Alabama.

DELUXE ARTICHOKE DIP

1 cup butter or margarine
½ cup peanut oil
2 (2-ounce) cans anchovy fillets, drained and chopped

Combine all ingredients in a small saucepan; cook over low heat until butter melts. Transfer to a chafing dish set over low heat; serve with cooked artichokes. Yield: about 1½ cups.

Maryse H. Rose,
Mary Esther, Florida.

Tip: A whole lemon heated in hot water for 5 minutes will yield about 1 tablespoon more juice than an unheated lemon.

A Bunch Of Banana Treats

From the alltime favorite banana bread to a refreshing Banana Crush, bananas add flavor and nutritional value to a variety of foods. Banana Muffins, served hot from the oven, make a great breakfast bread. And you'll find Whole Wheat Banana Bread to be moist and flavorful.

WHOLE WHEAT BANANA BREAD

1 cup whole wheat flour
½ cup all-purpose flour
1 teaspoon soda
¾ teaspoon salt
½ cup butter or margarine, softened
¾ cup sugar
1 egg
1¼ cups mashed bananas or 3 small
    bananas, mashed
¼ cup buttermilk

Combine flour, soda, and salt; stir well, and set aside.

Combine butter and sugar; cream mixture until light and fluffy. Add egg, and mix well.

Combine bananas and buttermilk; add to creamed mixture alternately with dry ingredients, stirring only until just combined.

Pour batter into a greased and floured 9- x 5- x 3-inch loafpan. Bake at 350° for 50 minutes or until bread tests done. Cool 10 minutes in pan; remove to wire rack, and cool completely. Yield: 1 loaf.   *Terri Burke,*
Belington, West Virginia.

BANANA MUFFINS

½ cup margarine, softened
1 cup sugar
2 eggs, beaten
3 ripe bananas, mashed
1¼ cups all-purpose flour
½ teaspoon soda

Combine margarine and sugar; beat until light and fluffy. Add eggs, and beat well. Stir in bananas. Combine flour and soda; add to creamed mixture, stirring just enough to moisten the dry ingredients.

Fill muffin pans two-thirds full. Bake at 350° for 25 minutes or until done. Serve hot. Yield: about 1¼ dozen.
Mrs. Paul Ritter,
Lake Charles, Louisiana.

BANANA CRUSH

4 cups sugar
6 cups water
2½ cups orange juice
½ cup lemon juice
4 cups pineapple juice
5 bananas, mashed
1 (64-ounce) bottle lemon-lime carbonated
    beverage

Combine sugar and water in a medium saucepan; cook over medium heat until sugar dissolves, stirring constantly. Add juices and bananas, mixing well. Pour into a plastic container; cover and freeze.

To serve, thaw slightly. Place in punch bowl, and stir with a fork to break into chunks. Add carbonated beverage. Yield: about 5½ quarts.
Diana Curtis,
Albuquerque, New Mexico.

Currants In The Teacakes

The tart taste of dried currants is what gives these teacakes their special flavor. They're prepared and shaped like biscuits but have a sweet taste and texture all their own. Serve them for breakfast or enjoy them as a snack.

CURRANT TEACAKES

4 cups all-purpose flour
4 teaspoons baking powder
1 teaspoon salt
¼ cup sugar
1½ cups margarine, softened
3 cups currants
¾ to 1 cup milk

Combine flour, baking powder, salt, and sugar in a large mixing bowl; cut in margarine until mixture resembles coarse crumbs. Stir in currants. Gradually add enough milk to form a soft dough, mixing well. Turn dough out on a floured surface; knead lightly 4 or 5 times.

Roll dough to ½-inch thickness; cut with a 2-inch biscuit cutter. Place on lightly greased baking sheets; bake at 450° for 10 to 12 minutes or until lightly browned. Yield: about 4 dozen.
Mrs. Harland Stone,
Ocala, Florida.

The Many Ways With Carrots

As long as you have carrots, you have the beginnings of an assortment of dishes, from soup to salad to side dish. These recipes offer some imaginative choices.

The carrots are sliced for Carrot Soup, sautéed with onion and celery, simmered in chicken broth, and lightly flavored with cheese. In Orange-Carrot Salad, a molded delight, shredded carrots get a sweet touch with crushed pineapple and mandarin oranges.

And instead of serving cooked carrots with just melted butter, try tossing them with an apricot sauce. Or mash the cooked carrots, stir in mashed potatoes and seasonings, shape into patties, and fry until golden brown.

CARROT SOUP

3 tablespoons margarine
6 carrots, peeled and sliced
2 medium onions, finely chopped
1 cup chopped celery
¼ cup all-purpose flour
2 tablespoons cornstarch
2 quarts chicken broth
¼ teaspoon salt
¼ teaspoon pepper
½ cup diced process cheese spread

Melt margarine in a large Dutch oven; add carrots, onion, and celery. Sauté until onion is tender.

Stir flour and cornstarch into vegetable mixture; cook over low heat 1 minute, stirring constantly. Gradually stir in chicken broth, salt, and pepper. Simmer over medium heat about 8 minutes or until the carrots are crisp-tender, stirring occasionally.

Reduce heat to low; add cheese to soup, stirring until melted. Yield: 10 to 12 servings.   *Mrs. Kenneth D. Epps,*
Birmingham, Alabama.

CARROTS IN WINE SAUCE

8 medium carrots, peeled and sliced
¼ cup minced onion
½ clove garlic
1 tablespoon melted butter or margarine
1 tablespoon all-purpose flour
½ cup consommé, undiluted
¼ cup dry white wine
¼ teaspoon salt
⅛ teaspoon pepper

Cook carrots in small amount of boiling salted water until crisp-tender; drain and set aside.

Sauté onion and garlic in butter until onion is tender; discard garlic. Stir flour into onion mixture; cook over low heat 1 minute, stirring constantly. Gradually add consommé and wine; cook over low heat, stirring constantly, until thickened. Stir in carrots, salt, and pepper; heat thoroughly. Yield: 4 servings.

Mrs. George Hardy,
Berlin, Maryland.

ORANGE-CARROT SALAD

1 (6-ounce) package orange-flavored gelatin
2 cups boiling water
1½ cups cold water
2 large carrots, shredded
1 (11-ounce) can mandarin oranges, drained
1 (15½-ounce) can crushed pineapple, undrained
½ cup chopped pecans
Lettuce
Carrot curls
Pecan halves

Dissolve gelatin in boiling water, and stir in cold water. Chill until partially set.

Fold carrots, oranges, pineapple, and chopped pecans into thickened gelatin. Spoon into an oiled 2-quart mold; chill until set. Unmold on lettuce, and garnish with carrot curls and pecan halves. Yield: 12 to 15 servings.

Mrs. Roy Carlisle,
Columbus, Georgia.

CARROT PATTIES

1½ cups mashed cooked carrots
1 cup mashed cooked potatoes
2 tablespoons melted butter or margarine
¼ cup grated Parmesan cheese
¼ cup chopped fresh parsley
2 tablespoons dry breadcrumbs
1 egg yolk
½ teaspoon salt
⅛ teaspoon pepper
All-purpose flour
Hot vegetable oil

Combine first 9 ingredients, mixing well. Shape into 8 patties, and dust each lightly with flour. Fry in hot oil until browned on both sides. Drain on absorbent towels. Yield: 8 servings.

Mrs. Sandy Wallace,
Pompano Beach, Florida.

Carrots, pecans, mandarin oranges, and pineapple create a flavorful combination in Orange-Carrot Salad.

APRICOT GLAZED CARROTS

4 cups sliced carrots
3 tablespoons melted butter or margarine
⅓ cup apricot preserves
¼ teaspoon salt
¼ teaspoon grated orange rind
¼ teaspoon ground nutmeg
2 teaspoons lemon juice

Cook carrots until tender in enough salted water to cover (about 20 minutes); drain. Combine remaining ingredients, stirring until well blended. Spoon over carrots, and toss well. Serve at once. Yield: 6 to 8 servings.

Kathleen D. Stone,
Houston, Texas.

Help Yourself To Cornbread

Just the aroma of oven-fresh cornbread is enough to entice most Southerners to the table. Served hot and smothered with butter, this traditional bread is delightful, especially when it is accompanied by heaping bowls of vegetables.

Several of our readers have shared their best recipes for this old favorite. Sour cream, shredded carrots, and cottage cheese are just a few of the extra ingredients they add to make their cornbread something special.

CARROT CORNBREAD

1 cup all-purpose flour
1 cup cornmeal
¼ cup sugar
3 teaspoons baking powder
1 teaspoon salt
¼ cup butter or margarine, softened
1 egg, beaten
2 medium carrots, peeled and shredded
1 cup buttermilk

Sift first 5 ingredients; cut in butter until mixture is blended. Set aside.

Combine egg, carrots, and buttermilk; add to cornmeal mixture, stirring well.

Spoon batter into a lightly greased 9-inch square baking pan. Bake at 425° for 20 minutes or until lightly browned. Cool slightly; cut into squares for serving. Yield: 9 servings.

Mrs. Judy Cunningham,
Roanoke, Virginia.

ULTIMATE CORNBREAD

2 cups chopped onion
¼ cup melted butter or margarine
1 (8-ounce) carton commercial sour cream
1 cup (4 ounces) shredded Cheddar cheese, divided
1½ cups self-rising cornmeal
2 tablespoons sugar (optional)
¼ teaspoon dillweed
2 eggs, beaten
1 (8¾-ounce) can cream-style corn
¼ cup milk
¼ cup vegetable oil
Dash of hot sauce

Sauté onion in butter until tender; remove from heat. Stir in sour cream and ½ cup cheese; set aside.

Combine cornmeal, sugar, and dillweed; set aside.

Stir together eggs, corn, milk, oil, and hot sauce; add to cornmeal mixture, stirring well. Spoon into a lightly greased 9-inch square pan. Spread sour cream mixture over batter; sprinkle with remaining ½ cup cheese.

Bake at 375° for 30 to 35 minutes. Cool slightly, then cut into 3-inch squares. Yield: 9 servings.
Alice Garcia,
South Daytona, Florida.

COTTAGE CHEESE CORNBREAD

2 cups self-rising cornmeal mix
¼ cup sugar
1 egg, beaten
1 cup buttermilk
¾ cup cottage cheese

Combine cornmeal mix, sugar, egg, and buttermilk; mix well. Stir in the cottage cheese.

Pour batter into a hot, lightly greased 10-inch skillet. Bake at 450° for 20 to 25 minutes or until golden brown. Serve warm. Yield: 8 to 10 servings.
Frances S. Parker,
Louisville, Kentucky.

CORNMEAL MUFFINS

1 cup yellow cornmeal
1 cup all-purpose flour
⅓ cup sugar
2 teaspoons baking powder
1 teaspoon soda
¾ teaspoon salt
1 egg, beaten
1¼ cups commercial sour cream
¼ cup shortening, melted

Combine first 6 ingredients. Stir together egg, sour cream, and shortening; add to dry ingredients, mixing well.

Fill lightly greased muffin tins two-thirds full. Bake at 425° for 15 minutes or until golden brown. Yield: 1½ dozen.
Mrs. Albert Carr,
Palm Harbor, Florida.

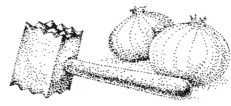

Chicken Rollups With A Surprise

Here is an original way to prepare stuffed chicken breasts. To the boned and flattened breast add a slice of dried beef and a spinach-filled stuffing. Roll up the layers, secure with a slice of bacon, then bake in sour cream and cream of celery soup.

CHICKEN AND SPINACH ROLLUPS

1 (10-ounce) package frozen chopped spinach, thawed and drained
1 cup herb-seasoned stuffing
1 medium onion, finely chopped
3 eggs, beaten
¼ cup grated Parmesan cheese
¼ cup butter or margarine, melted
½ teaspoon whole thyme leaves
½ teaspoon garlic powder
½ teaspoon pepper
6 whole chicken breasts, split, boned, and skinned
1 (2½-ounce) jar sliced dried beef
12 slices bacon
1 (10¾-ounce) can cream of celery soup, undiluted
1 (8-ounce) carton commercial sour cream

Combine first 9 ingredients, mixing well; shape into 12 balls, and set aside.

Place each half of chicken breast on waxed paper. Flatten to ¼-inch thickness, using a meat mallet or rolling pin.

Place 1 slice of dried beef on each flattened chicken breast. Place 1 ball of spinach on top of beef. Roll up each breast, and secure with a wooden pick.

Cook bacon briefly on both sides until partly done but still pliable. Wrap 1 slice of bacon around each roll; place rolls in a greased 13- x 9- x 2-inch baking dish.

Combine soup and sour cream; mix well. Spoon soup mixture over chicken breasts; cover and bake at 350° for 45 minutes. Remove cover; bake an additional 30 minutes. Yield: 12 servings.
Vivian Billingsley,
Fairfax, Virginia.

Taste This Dream Of A Pie

In this delicious recipe for Dream Pie, sliced bananas and a strawberry gelatin mixture full of red tart cherries and crushed pineapple are topped with whipped topping and a sprinkling of chopped nuts. As a bonus, the recipe yields two pies.

DREAM PIE

1½ cups sugar
¼ cup all-purpose flour
1 teaspoon salt
1 (20-ounce) can crushed pineapple, undrained
1 (16-ounce) can red tart pitted cherries, undrained
1 (3-ounce) package strawberry-flavored gelatin
4 bananas
2 baked 9-inch pastry shells
1 (1½-ounce) package whipped topping mix
1 cup chopped nuts (optional)

Combine sugar, flour, salt, pineapple, and cherries in a large saucepan; stir well. Cook over medium heat until thickened and bubbly. Remove from heat; add gelatin, stirring well. Allow mixture to cool.

Thinly slice bananas; arrange an equal amount of slices in each pastry shell. Pour fruit mixture evenly into pastry shells.

Prepare whipped topping mix according to package directions; spread over pies. Refrigerate at least 3 hours before serving. Sprinkle with nuts, if desired. Yield: two 9-inch pies. *Stelle Ennis,*
South Shore, Kentucky.

May

The longer days and busy schedules of May bring the need for more relaxed meals. Sandwiches are the obvious choice, but our selection is anything but ordinary. One Giant Pizza Sandwich or Oyster Submarine Sandwich will provide ample servings for an entire family.

Take advantage of the delicate sweet flavor and crunch of fresh English peas now in season. Complement them with one of our cool congealed salads that range from fruit or vegetable to main dish selections.

And if you thought you could only get crispy fried onion rings from a restaurant, try one of our easy versions. But we warn you—they're habit-forming! We tried them all in the same day and ate every one!

Make The Sandwich, Make The Meal

Plump oysters nestled in a loaf of French bread, ground beef filling spooned into pocket bread or over toasted buns, a ham-vegetable combination served in hard rolls—that's just a sampling of what you can put undercover for a sandwich that's a meal in itself.

OYSTER SUBMARINE SANDWICH

1 (1-pound) loaf French or Vienna bread
1 cup unsalted butter, divided
⅛ teaspoon garlic salt
8 slices bacon
1 egg, beaten
2 tablespoons water
2 large tomatoes, sliced ¼ inch thick
½ cup dry breadcrumbs
1 pint oysters, undrained
2 tablespoons all-purpose flour
½ teaspoon salt
⅛ teaspoon freshly ground pepper
1 teaspoon Worcestershire sauce
Pinch of garlic salt
Pinch of ground mace
1 medium onion, thinly sliced
1 green pepper, cut into strips
2 tablespoons melted butter or margarine
¼ cup mayonnaise
½ teaspoon mustard with horseradish
1 lemon, cut into 8 wedges
Parsley sprigs

Slice off top third of loaf; hollow out bottom section, reserving crumbs for use in other recipes.

Allow ½ cup unsalted butter to soften; add ⅛ teaspoon garlic salt, mixing well. Spread on inside surfaces of loaf. Place on baking sheet, and broil until lightly browned; set aside.

Fry bacon until crisp, and drain well on paper towels. Reserve drippings in the skillet.

Combine egg and water, beating well. Dip tomato slices into egg mixture, and dredge in breadcrumbs; place on a wire rack, and let stand 30 minutes. Fry tomato slices in reserved bacon drippings until browned. Drain on paper towels.

Cook oysters over medium heat about 3 minutes or until edges begin to curl. Drain oysters, reserving 1 cup liquid.

Melt ½ cup unsalted butter in a heavy saucepan over low heat; add flour, stirring until smooth. Cook 1 minute, stirring constantly. Gradually stir in reserved oyster liquid; cook over medium heat, stirring constantly, until thickened and bubbly. Stir in oysters, salt, pepper, Worcestershire sauce, garlic salt, and mace. Cook 1 minute, stirring constantly.

Pour oyster mixture into cavity of toasted bread. Arrange tomato slices over oyster mixture. Top with onion, green pepper, and bacon. Place top of loaf over filling. Brush loaf with melted butter, and wrap in aluminum foil. Bake at 400° for 15 or 20 minutes or until loaf is thoroughly heated.

Combine mayonnaise and mustard. Slice loaf into serving-size portions, and spread each with mayonnaise mixture. Garnish with lemon wedges and parsley. Yield: 8 to 10 servings.

Fred T. Marshall,
Hollywood, Maryland.

ITALIAN SAUSAGE SANDWICH

6 large French rolls
1 pound Italian sausage, sliced ¼ inch thick
½ Spanish onion, sliced and separated into rings
¾ cup thinly sliced green pepper strips
2 tomatoes, peeled and cut into wedges
2 tablespoons water
¼ teaspoon salt
¼ teaspoon whole oregano
½ cup shredded mozzarella cheese
1 cup shredded lettuce

Bake rolls according to package directions; split in half, and set aside.

Brown sausage over medium heat, and drain well; add onion, green pepper, tomato, and water. Cook over low heat, stirring constantly, until vegetables are tender (about 7 minutes). Remove from heat, and stir in seasonings.

Spoon meat mixture on bottom half of each roll; sprinkle with cheese. Bake at 400° for 2 minutes or until cheese melts. Top each with lettuce and roll top. Yield: 6 servings. *Mary Mostoller,*
Tallahassee, Florida.

BUNWICHES

6 hard-cooked eggs, chopped
⅓ cup chopped green pepper
2 tablespoons minced onion
½ teaspoon minced garlic
¼ cup melted butter or margarine
2 tablespoons chopped pimiento
¼ cup chili sauce
¼ teaspoon salt
Pinch of pepper
¼ cup shredded process American cheese
4 submarine sandwich buns, split

Combine first 10 ingredients, mixing well; set aside.

Hollow out bottom half of each bun, reserving crumbs for use in other recipes; fill each shell with egg mixture, and cover with bun top.

Wrap each sandwich in aluminum foil; chill at least 1 hour. Bake foil-wrapped sandwiches at 400° for 8 minutes. Yield: 4 servings.

Mrs. James L. Twilley,
Macon, Georgia.

SAUCY BEEF POCKET SANDWICH

1 medium head cabbage, shredded
1 (3-pound) boneless chuck or rump roast
1 (10¾-ounce) can tomato soup
1 cup chopped onion
2 tablespoons sugar
2 tablespoons vinegar
2 tablespoons Worcestershire sauce
½ cup catsup
¼ teaspoon ground oregano
2 teaspoons chili powder
1 teaspoon salt
¼ teaspoon pepper
¼ cup water
¼ cup all-purpose flour
9 (6-inch) pocket bread rounds

Place cabbage in a large Dutch oven; place roast on top of cabbage.

Combine next 10 ingredients; mix well, and pour over roast. Cover and simmer over low heat 3½ to 4 hours or until roast is very tender. Remove roast to a chopping board; trim off fat and discard. Cut meat into bite-size pieces.

Combine water and flour, stirring until smooth. Gradually stir into sauce; cook over medium heat until sauce is thickened, stirring constantly. Add the meat; reduce heat and simmer 10 minutes, stirring occasionally.

Cut pocket bread rounds in half; fill each half with the meat sauce. Yield: 18 sandwiches. *Linda Radomski,*
Birmingham, Alabama.

TANGY CLUB SANDWICHES

1 (2-ounce) package blue cheese, crumbled
1 (3-ounce) package cream cheese, softened
1 teaspoon instant minced onion
Dash of Worcestershire sauce
Mayonnaise
12 slices white sandwich bread, toasted
8 slices tomato
8 slices cooked turkey or chicken
4 slices Swiss cheese
Salt and pepper
8 slices bacon, cooked and drained
Lettuce leaves

Combine blue cheese, cream cheese, onion, Worcestershire sauce, and 1 tablespoon mayonnaise; mix well. Spread cheese mixture on each of 4 slices of toast. Top each with 2 slices tomato, 2 slices turkey, and 1 slice Swiss cheese; sprinkle with salt and pepper. Add second slice of toast; top with 2 slices bacon and lettuce.

Spread remaining toast with mayonnaise, and place over lettuce. Secure sandwiches with toothpicks; cut into triangles to serve. Yield: 4 servings.

Mrs. Peggy Fowler Revels,
Woodruff, South Carolina.

SALAD BOATS

3 cups coarsely chopped cabbage
1 (8¾-ounce) can whole kernel corn, drained
1 cup diced cooked ham
½ cup diced Cheddar cheese
¼ cup sliced pitted ripe olives
1 small green pepper, coarsely chopped
1 (2-ounce) jar diced pimiento, drained
½ teaspoon salt
½ cup commercial Italian dressing
6 to 8 large hard rolls
¼ cup commercial Italian dressing
Lettuce
Raw vegetables

Combine first 9 ingredients; mix well, and let stand about 30 minutes.

Cut a slice from top of each roll; hollow out rolls, leaving a ⅛-inch shell. Break bread removed from rolls into small pieces; toss in ¼ cup Italian dressing. Spread on a lightly greased baking sheet; bake at 350° for 12 minutes or until golden brown, turning or stirring occasionally.

Fill shells with ham mixture; top with toasted bread. Serve on lettuce; garnish with raw vegetables. Yield: 6 to 8 servings. *Mrs. Earl L. Faulkenberry,*
Lancaster, South Carolina.

HEARTY POCKET SANDWICHES

1 package dry yeast
1¼ cups warm water (105° to 115°)
2¾ to 3 cups whole wheat flour
½ cup bran
1½ teaspoons salt
Meat filling (recipe follows)
Shredded lettuce
Chopped tomato

Dissolve yeast in warm water in a large mixing bowl. Add 1 cup flour, bran, and salt; mix well. Add the remaining flour, ½ cup at a time, beating well after each addition.

Turn dough out on a lightly floured surface, and knead 10 minutes or until smooth and elastic. Divide dough into 10 equal portions; form into balls. Roll each ball into a 5-inch round on a lightly floured surface.

Place dough rounds on lightly greased baking sheets; cover and let rise in a warm place, free from drafts, 45 minutes or until slightly puffy.

Carefully turn rounds over; bake at 500° for 8 minutes. Cut a 7-inch slit around edge of each bread round; stuff with meat filling, lettuce, and tomato. Yield: 10 servings.

Meat Filling:

1 pound ground beef
¼ cup chopped onion
5 mild cherry peppers, seeded and diced
1 clove garlic, diced
2 tablespoons Worcestershire sauce
⅓ cup chili sauce or tomato sauce
1 (15-ounce) can pinto beans, drained and mashed
½ teaspoon salt

Combine ground beef, onion, peppers, and garlic in a large skillet; cook until meat is browned. Drain. Add Worcestershire sauce, chili sauce, beans, and salt; stir well. Cook over medium heat, stirring occasionally, until thoroughly heated. Yield: filling for 10 sandwiches.

Jeri Holcomb,
Boaz, Alabama.

SAUCY BURGERS

1 pound lean ground beef
½ cup chopped onion
1 tablespoon hot vegetable oil
1 (10¾-ounce) can chicken gumbo soup, undiluted
1 tablespoon prepared mustard
3 tablespoons catsup
Salt and pepper to taste
8 hamburger buns, split and toasted
Sliced onion (optional)

Combine ground beef and chopped onion; sauté in oil until meat is browned, stirring to crumble meat. Drain on paper towels. Return meat mixture to skillet, and add next 4 ingredients; simmer 5 to 10 minutes, stirring occasionally.

Spoon beef mixture on bottom half of buns; top with sliced onion, if desired. Cover with bun tops. Yield: 8 servings.

Mrs. H. E. Mertens,
Kingsville, Texas.

GIANT PIZZA SANDWICH

½ pound Italian sausage
¼ cup chopped onion
¼ cup chopped green pepper
1 (4-ounce) can sliced mushrooms, drained
2 tablespoons sliced pimiento-stuffed olives
½ teaspoon whole oregano
1 cup (4 ounces) shredded mozzarella cheese, divided
2 (13-ounce) frozen cheese pizzas
Sliced pimiento-stuffed olives

Remove casings from sausage, and crumble sausage into a large skillet; add onion, green pepper, mushrooms, 2 tablespoons sliced olives, and oregano. Cook over medium heat until meat is browned; stir in ½ cup cheese.

Place 1 pizza on a lightly greased baking sheet, cheese side up. Spoon sausage mixture over pizza; top with second pizza, cheese side down. Wrap sandwich securely in aluminum foil. Bake at 375° for 15 minutes. Remove foil, and bake an additional 10 minutes.

Sprinkle remaining cheese on top of sandwich; bake an additional 5 minutes. Garnish with olives. Yield: 6 servings.

Mrs. Margaret L. Hunter,
Princeton, Kentucky.

Capture The Flavor
Of Florida's Frontier

Mention Florida and most people think of long, sandy coastlines and busy resorts. But head toward the state's interior and you find that the land takes on another look and the food a special flavor.

About halfway between the cities of Gainesville and Ocala, turn off U.S. 441 and proceed inland, toward the Florida backwoods. The narrow scenic roads, lined with scrub palmettos and huge moss-draped trees, lead you to the sleepy, serene villages of McIntosh, Evinston, and Cross Creek. All three communities lie on the banks of beautiful Orange Lake.

Marjorie Kinnan Rawlings, author of the Pulitzer Prize-winning novel *The Yearling,* selected Cross Creek as the location for her home. In numerous books, she discussed her love for the land, often referred to as the home of true Florida "Crackers."

After spending much of her time working and living with the natives, Mrs. Rawlings found herself especially captivated with the details of Cracker cooking. In fact, she was so interested in this aspect of the territory that she compiled a cookbook, *Cross Creek Cookery,* in order to preserve what she believed to be the best Cracker recipes. In her book, Mrs. Rawlings describes techniques for obtaining and preparing freshwater turtle, frog legs, alligator steak, and swamp cabbage salad—all of which are still familiar favorites for most residents.

Then, as now, the lay of the land surrounding Orange Lake made it possible for the people to draw from a variety of natural resources for their income, as well as their food. Three completely different types of land can be found within a few miles of the lake.

A Citrus Tradition

The flat, southern side of Orange Lake lends itself to the production of small citrus groves, some vegetable farming, and cattle grazing. At one time, citrus was big business; but after the freeze of 1895, many of the citrus growers turned to vegetable farming. The groves that remain today were replanted and, for the most part, are fairly small. According to Ollie Huff, owner of Orange Lake Citrus Shop, "We are a little too far north to be considered in the Citrus Belt. The Orange Lake area is 10 to 20 degrees cooler than the central citrus-production area."

Remaining groves and groups of individually owned trees still provide ample fruit. Some citrus is shipped to other areas, but much is used right at home by the growers. It's no wonder that over the years some luscious citrus recipes have been handed down. Mouth-watering treats like Tart Lemon-Apple Pie, Citrus Marmalade, and Fresh Orange Shortcake are just a few.

As vegetable farms replaced some citrus groves, more interest grew in preserving and enjoying the farm products. Today, Cracker kitchens still produce an abundance of colorful vegetable dishes. Sadie Alston, Anice Johnson, and Dot Cake, three Orange Lake residents, demonstrate their fondness for fresh vegetables by often preparing Cold Stuffed Tomatoes and Old-Fashioned Pole Beans filled with thick pieces of ham hock.

Ride Through Horse Country

It's hard to believe the drastic difference in the land when you move up the western side of Orange Lake. Characterized by gently sloping hills, this land has been found to be ideal for raising thoroughbreds and Arabian horses.

The green pastureland, lying on the Ocala Limerock Formation, is choice horse country. "The unique relationship of soils and pasture grasses is extremely important to the growth of new foals and the proper conditioning of mares in foal," explains Bud Kernell, who is the farm manager for Town and Country Farms.

A haven for horse raisers and trainers, this side of Orange Lake specializes in producing a blend of citrus groves, vegetable farms, and cattle ranches. A mealtime visit to most any of the homes dotting the rolling hills will reveal tables laden with a variety of the best fruits and vegetables this area has to offer.

Down by the Lake

The grassy hills are left behind as the northern and eastern portions of Orange Lake are approached. Except for a few areas where the banks are infested with scrub palmettos, cypress trees, or marshland, the water is accessible and several landings can be found where boats are launched. Since this is one of the largest bass-fishing lakes in Florida, it is easy to see why fishing, along with frog gigging, is a prime industry and pastime.

After a successful day on the lake, it has become a tradition for fishermen to get together for a fish fry—cooking large batches of fresh frog legs, bass, and cooter. Golden hush puppies and cheese grits are often served with them.

A Visit to Evinston and McIntosh

In contrast to the varied terrain surrounding Orange Lake, the residents of the area are all the same—down home, warm, and sincere. They are proud of their community and love to share it with visitors. One of the first stops they suggest is in Evinston, to meet Fred Woods and see his country store.

The town of Evinston was named after Fred's grandfather, who came into the area in 1879. Fred is now about the closest you can come to meeting a real Florida Cracker. "I've been here most of my life. It's a very close-knit area," Fred explained with pride.

Until his recent retirement, Fred was one of Florida's oldest postmasters. He still rents out about 50 post office boxes in the old store, which boasts one gas pump, a deep freeze, and a drink cooler. Fred says that he used to sell a lot of groceries, but most people come in now for cold drinks and conversation. "Sometimes I sell fresh collards right out of my garden, and I wonder how many miles I've walked in here selling bubble gum. It's been one of my big sellers."

The cypress-shaded town of McIntosh can be considered the real metropolis of the area. Mrs. Margie Karow likes to show off the beauty of this town and encourages visitors to stop, especially during the yearly 1890 festival which is held during the fall. The citizens gather at the festival mostly for fun, but are seriously concerned about donating all proceeds to help preserve the unspoiled beauty of their area.

Right: Anything but ordinary, these sandwiches are great for supper, as well as for informal special occasions. Take your pick of Oyster Submarine Sandwich (page 92), Giant Pizza Sandwich (page 93), and Salad Boats (page 93).

Page 98: Florida Cracker cooks often use bass fillets, fresh from the lake, for making Orange Lake Amandine (page 99).

Above: *Health-Kick Punch (page 174) is a refreshing cooler on a summer afternoon.*

Left: *Elegant Daiquiri Soufflé (page 69) is garnished with pistachio nuts, crystallized violets, and a twist of lime.*

Far left: *Elegant Lemon Cake Roll (page 70) is a delicate sponge-type cake filled and frosted with a light, creamy lemon filling.*

Try Regional Specialties From Orange Lake

We know you'll enjoy the following recipes, which came from some of the best cooks in the Orange Lake area.

■ Florida Crackers prefer frog legs fried crispy brown. Allow six small pairs of legs or three jumbo pairs per person.

CRISPY FROG LEGS

5 pounds small frog legs
¾ cup lemon juice or vinegar
Crushed ice
1 cup milk
6 eggs, separated
2 tablespoons olive or vegetable oil
¼ teaspoon salt
Salt and pepper
1½ cups all-purpose flour
Vegetable oil

Wash frog legs thoroughly. Place in a large Dutch oven; sprinkle with lemon juice, and cover with crushed ice. Refrigerate 1 to 3 hours.

Combine milk, egg yolks, olive oil, and ¼ teaspoon salt; mix well. Beat egg whites until stiff; fold into batter.

Sprinkle frog legs with salt and pepper; dip each in batter, and dredge in flour. Fry until golden brown in deep oil heated to 375°. Drain on paper towels. Yield: about 6 servings.

■ An Orange Lake fish dinner isn't complete without Orange Lake Amandine, fried catfish, hush puppies—and a heaping bowl of cheese grits.

ORANGE LAKE AMANDINE

½ cup slivered blanched almonds
¼ cup butter or margarine, melted
12 large bass or trout fillets
Salt and pepper to taste
Thyme leaves to taste
Milk
All-purpose flour
½ cup vegetable oil
2 teaspoons chopped parsley
Lemon wedges (optional)

Sauté almonds in butter until golden brown; set aside.

Sprinkle fillets with salt, pepper, and thyme; dip in milk, and dredge in flour. Fry fillets in hot oil over medium heat until golden brown on both sides. Drain on paper towels. Remove to serving dish; sprinkle with almonds and parsley. Garnish with lemon wedges, if desired. Yield: 6 to 8 servings.

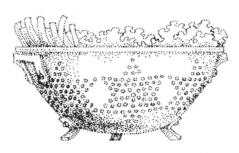

CRACKER HUSH PUPPIES

1¼ cups commercial hush puppy mix
1 (8-ounce) can whole tomatoes, drained and chopped
1 small onion, chopped
¼ cup chopped green pepper
1 egg, beaten
⅓ cup beer
¼ teaspoon salt
¼ teaspoon pepper
¼ teaspoon crushed red pepper
⅛ teaspoon garlic powder
Pinch of baking powder
Vegetable oil

Combine all ingredients; stir well. Drop batter by tablespoonfuls into deep hot oil (375°); fry only a few at a time, turning once. Cook until hush puppies are golden brown (3 to 5 minutes). Drain on paper towels. Yield: about 1½ dozen.

GOLDEN FRIED CATFISH

6 small catfish, cleaned and dressed
1 teaspoon salt
¼ teaspoon pepper
2 cups self-rising cornmeal
Vegetable oil

Sprinkle catfish with salt and pepper. Place cornmeal in a paper bag; drop in catfish, one at a time, and shake until coated. Fry in deep hot oil (375°) until golden brown; drain well. Serve hot. Yield: 4 to 6 servings.

BAKED CHEESE GRITS

6 cups water
2½ teaspoons salt
1½ cups uncooked regular grits
½ cup butter or margarine
4 cups (1 pound) shredded medium-sharp Cheddar cheese, divided
3 eggs, beaten

Combine water and salt; bring to a boil. Stir in grits; cook until done, following package directions. Remove from heat. Add butter and 3¾ cups cheese; stir until completely melted. Add a small amount of hot grits to eggs, stirring well; stir egg mixture into remaining grits. Pour grits into a lightly greased 2½-quart baking dish; sprinkle with remaining ¼ cup cheese. Bake at 350° for 1 hour and 15 minutes. Yield: 6 to 8 servings.

■ The flavor of battered and fried cooter (soft-shell turtle) is similar to that of pork or veal.

FRIED COOTER (SOFT-SHELL TURTLE)

2 pounds turtle, cut into 2- to 4-inch pieces
½ cup vinegar
1 teaspoon salt
½ cup all-purpose flour
¼ cup plus 1 tablespoon milk
2 eggs, separated
2 teaspoons olive or vegetable oil
⅛ teaspoon salt
Vegetable oil

Combine turtle, vinegar, and 1 teaspoon salt. Cover with water; simmer 1 hour or until tender. Drain and set aside.

Combine flour, milk, egg yolks, olive oil, and ⅛ teaspoon salt; mix well. Beat egg whites until stiff; fold into batter.

Dip turtle pieces into batter; fry until golden brown in deep oil heated to 375°. Drain well on paper towels. Yield: 4 to 6 servings.

Tip: To help soften the greasy coating on bottom of pans and skillets, cover area with paper towel soaked in ammonia to loosen coating; tie pan in plastic bag overnight and rub off grease with steel wool the next day.

■ Orange Lake area residents have a way with preparing vegetable dishes.

COLD STUFFED TOMATOES

6 large tomatoes
Salt
⅓ cup finely diced cucumber
⅓ cup grated onion
⅓ cup chopped green pepper
⅓ cup chopped celery
⅓ cup finely shredded cabbage
½ teaspoon salt
Dash of pepper
⅓ cup mayonnaise
Dash of hot sauce
Dash of curry powder
Lettuce leaves

Wash tomatoes; place in boiling water 1 minute. Drain and immediately plunge into cold water. Gently remove skins.

With stem end up, cut each tomato into 4 wedges, cutting to, but not through, base of tomato. Spread wedges slightly apart. Sprinkle inside of shells with salt. Cover and chill 1½ hours.

Combine next 7 ingredients; cover and chill.

To serve, spoon vegetable filling into shells. Combine mayonnaise with hot sauce and curry powder. Top each tomato with a dollop of mayonnaise mixture. Serve on lettuce leaves. Yield: 6 servings.

OLD-FASHIONED POLE BEANS

3 pounds fresh pole beans
5 cups water
1 (½-pound) ham hock
2 teaspoons salt
¼ teaspoon pepper

Remove strings from beans, cutting beans into 2-inch pieces. Wash beans.

Place water and ham hock in a Dutch oven; bring to a boil. Reduce heat; cover and simmer 1 hour. Add beans, salt, and pepper; cook 30 minutes or until tender. Yield: 10 to 12 servings.

Tip: For the best baked sweet potatoes, select potatoes of the same size; place on rack in the middle of oven. Do not wrap; bake at 400° for 15 minutes. Reduce heat to 375°; bake medium-size potatoes for 45 minutes and large ones for 1 hour. Turn off heat, and let potatoes remain in oven about 30 minutes.

■ Baked beans are a must when serving fish, frog legs, or cooter.

BAKED BEAN MEDLEY

1½ pounds ground beef
1 small onion, chopped
1 teaspoon salt
1 (15½-ounce) can kidney beans
1 (16-ounce) can lima beans
1 (16-ounce) can pork and beans
½ cup catsup
¼ cup firmly packed brown sugar
2 tablespoons vinegar

Combine ground beef, onion, and salt in a 10-inch skillet. Cook over medium heat until browned; drain.

Combine beef mixture with remaining ingredients; stir well. Place mixture in a lightly greased 2½-quart casserole. Bake at 350° for 30 to 35 minutes or until bubbly. Yield: 10 to 12 servings.

■ Many Orange Lake residents raid their own trees to make citrus marmalades, salads, salad dressing, and desserts.

TART LEMON-APPLE PIE

2 medium lemons
2 medium cooking apples, peeled, cored, and grated
3 cups sugar
4 eggs, slightly beaten
Pastry for two double-crust 8-inch pies

Cut lemons in half, and remove seeds; grind pulp and rind. Add apples, sugar, and eggs; mix well. Spoon half of mixture into each pastry-lined piepan. Top with pastry, and crimp edges to seal. Cut slits in each to act as steam vents. Bake at 425° for 40 to 50 minutes or until golden brown. Yield: two 8-inch pies.

FRESH ORANGE SHORTCAKE

12 to 16 medium oranges
¾ cup sugar
⅓ cup butter or margarine
1 tablespoon cornstarch
¾ cup water
1½ teaspoons lemon juice
½ teaspoon grated orange rind
Shortcake Pastry
Whipped cream or whipped topping

Peel and section enough oranges to make 5 cups of orange sections; drain, reserving ¾ cup juice. Set aside 1 cup of sections for topping.

Combine sugar, butter, orange juice, cornstarch, water, lemon juice, and orange rind in a medium saucepan. Cook over low heat, stirring constantly, until slightly thickened and bubbly. Remove from heat; stir in 4 cups of orange sections.

Place 1 pastry round on each serving dish; cover each with ⅓ cup orange sauce. Top with remaining pastry rounds. Spoon remaining orange sauce over each. Garnish with a dollop of whipped cream and an orange section. Yield: 10 servings.

Shortcake Pastry:

3 cups all-purpose flour
1 tablespoon sugar
2 teaspoons salt
1 cup vegetable oil
¼ cup milk

Combine dry ingredients; add oil and milk, stirring until mixture forms a ball.

Roll dough out on a lightly floured surface to ⅛-inch thickness; cut into rounds with a 2½-inch biscuit cutter. Using a metal spatula, lift rounds and place on a lightly greased baking sheet. Bake at 350° for 18 to 20 minutes or until lightly browned. (Pastry will be very fragile.) Cool on wire racks. Store in an airtight container, or freeze until needed. Yield: 20 pastry rounds.

GRAPEFRUIT-CUCUMBER SALAD

Grapefruit Layer:

1½ cups fresh grapefruit sections
¼ cup sugar
1 teaspoon unflavored gelatin
¼ cup cold water
1 (3-ounce) package lime-flavored gelatin
1 cup boiling water
1 tablespoon lemon juice

Combine grapefruit sections and sugar, stirring gently; let stand 15 minutes. Drain, reserving juice, and set grapefruit aside. Add enough water to juice to make 1 cup, and set aside.

Soften unflavored gelatin in ¼ cup cold water; combine with lime-flavored gelatin and 1 cup boiling water, stirring until dissolved. Add lemon juice and grapefruit sections and liquid; pour into lightly oiled 2-quart ring mold. Chill until set.

Cucumber Layer:
1 teaspoon unflavored gelatin
¼ cup cold water
1 (3-ounce) package lime-flavored gelatin
1 cup boiling water
1 teaspoon salt
1 tablespoon vinegar
1 teaspoon onion juice
1 teaspoon Worcestershire sauce
1 cup commercial sour cream
1 cup finely chopped cucumber
Lettuce leaves

Soften unflavored gelatin in ¼ cup cold water; combine with lime-flavored gelatin and 1 cup boiling water, stirring until dissolved. Add salt, vinegar, onion juice, and Worcestershire sauce. Chill until partially set. Stir sour cream and cucumber into thickened gelatin; spoon over grapefruit layer. Chill until firm; unmold on lettuce leaves. Yield: 8 to 10 servings.

GRAPEFRUIT FRENCH DRESSING

⅔ cup vegetable oil
¼ cup vinegar
¼ cup fresh grapefruit juice
1 teaspoon salt
1 teaspoon sugar
1 teaspoon paprika
1 teaspoon dried tarragon leaves or dried parsley flakes

Combine all ingredients, mixing well; cover and refrigerate 1 to 2 hours. Yield: about 1¼ cups.

CITRUS MARMALADE

1 large orange
1 large grapefruit
1 large tangerine
⅛ teaspoon soda
1½ cups water
3 tablespoons lime or lemon juice
5 cups sugar
1 (3-ounce) package liquid fruit pectin

Remove rind in quarters from fruit, leaving half the inner white portion of rind on fruit. Cut rind into thin strips, 1 to 1½ inches long; set aside. Section, seed, and dice fruit over a bowl, squeezing juice from membrane; set aside.

Combine rind, soda, and water in an 8-quart Dutch oven; bring to a boil. Reduce heat; cover and simmer 20 minutes, stirring often. Add fruit and juice. Cover; simmer 10 minutes. Stir in lime juice and sugar; bring to full rolling boil over high heat. Boil 1 minute, stirring constantly.

Remove from heat; immediately stir in pectin. Skim off foam with a metal spoon. Alternate stirring and skimming 7 minutes. Pour into hot sterilized jars, leaving ¼-inch headspace; cover at once with metal lids, screwing bands tight. Process in boiling-water bath for 10 minutes. Yield: 6 cups.

Green Peas Fresh From The Pod

Enjoy the delicate, sugar-sweet flavor of fresh green peas by combining them with a few simple ingredients, like scallions, mushrooms, sherry—or even carrots and cabbage. These recipes are quick to prepare since the peas, once shelled, cook in only 8 to 12 minutes.

COUNTRY-STYLE PEAS

2 pounds fresh green peas
1 cup boiling water
1 chicken bouillon cube
3 small carrots, peeled and diced
½ cup shredded cabbage
2 tablespoons melted butter or margarine
1 teaspoon salt
¼ teaspoon pepper
¼ teaspoon Worcestershire sauce
¼ head lettuce, shredded

Shell and wash peas; drain.
Combine water and bouillon cube; stir until bouillon is dissolved.

Sauté carrots and cabbage in butter 2 minutes; stir in peas, bouillon, salt, pepper, and Worcestershire sauce. Cover; simmer 5 minutes. Add lettuce; cook an additional 3 to 7 minutes. Yield: 4 to 6 servings.

Note: 2 cups frozen peas may be substituted for fresh peas. *Linda Clark, Elizabethton, Tennessee.*

PEAS AND SCALLIONS

2 pounds fresh green peas
12 to 14 scallions, cut into 1-inch pieces
2 tablespoons melted butter or margarine
2 teaspoons all-purpose flour
1 teaspoon sugar
½ teaspoon salt
¼ teaspoon ground nutmeg
⅛ teaspoon pepper

Shell and wash peas; add enough boiling salted water to cover. Reduce heat; cover and cook 8 to 12 minutes or until tender. Drain, reserving ¾ cup liquid.

Sauté scallions in butter 3 to 5 minutes. Combine flour, sugar, salt, nutmeg, and pepper; stir into scallions. Add reserved liquid; cook over medium heat, stirring constantly, until thickened. Stir in peas; cook 1 minute. Yield: 4 to 6 servings.

Note: 2 cups frozen peas may be substituted for fresh peas.
Patricia Chapman, Huntsville, Alabama.

GREEN PEAS WITH MUSHROOMS

3 pounds fresh green peas
¼ pound fresh mushrooms, sliced
3 tablespoons melted butter or margarine
¼ cup water
1 whole pimiento, diced
1 teaspoon salt
¼ teaspoon sugar
Dash of pepper
¼ cup whipping cream

Shell and wash peas; drain.
Sauté mushrooms in butter 3 minutes; stir in peas, water, pimiento, salt, sugar, and pepper. Cover and simmer 8 to 12 minutes or until peas are tender. Stir in whipping cream; cook 1 minute. Yield: 6 servings.

Note: 3 cups frozen peas may be substituted for fresh peas.

Thelma Wofford, New Castle, Delaware.

PEAS WITH SHERRY

2 pounds fresh green peas
1 (4-ounce) can sliced mushrooms
¼ cup minced onion
2 tablespoons melted butter or margarine
2 tablespoons dry sherry
¼ teaspoon salt
⅛ teaspoon marjoram
Dash of pepper

Shell and wash peas; add enough boiling salted water to cover. Reduce heat; cover and cook 8 to 12 minutes or until tender. Drain.

Sauté mushrooms and onion in butter 5 minutes; stir in remaining ingredients. Cook 1 minute. Yield: 4 servings.

Note: 2 cups frozen peas may be substituted for fresh peas.

Mrs. Margaret J. Richter,
Bristol, Tennessee.

GREEN PEAS AND DUMPLINGS

3 pounds fresh green peas
3 cups water
2 teaspoons salt
Dash of pepper
½ cup butter or margarine
¼ cup all-purpose flour
½ cup evaporated milk
1 (8-ounce) package refrigerated biscuits
Onion salt

Shell and wash peas; drain.

Combine water, salt, and pepper; bring to a boil. Add peas; simmer 5 minutes.

Melt butter in a heavy saucepan over low heat; add flour and cook 1 minute, stirring constantly. Gradually add milk; cook over medium heat, stirring constantly, until thickened and bubbly. Stir sauce into peas. Top with biscuits. Sprinkle lightly with onion salt. Cover; cook 15 minutes or until biscuits are done. Yield: 6 servings.

Note: 3 cups frozen peas may be substituted for fresh peas. A recipe for 10 to 12 drop dumplings may be substituted for refrigerated biscuits.

Mrs. Walter Perdue,
Collinsville, Virginia.

Tip: Fresh pineapple does not ripen further after it's picked. Choose one that is firm and fresh looking and use within 3 to 5 days.

Feature The Inviting Pineapple

What could be better for dessert than Pineapple Pudding, a nut-filled layered custard ringed with vanilla wafers, or Pineapple Upside-Down Cake, always a favorite. While both of these call for canned pineapple, our Pineapple Boat Aloha uses a scooped-out fresh pineapple as a container for a mixture of fresh fruit. Fresh or canned, pineapple brings a tangy sweetness to these recipes.

PINEAPPLE PUDDING

2 tablespoons butter or margarine
1½ cups sugar
3 tablespoons all-purpose flour
Pinch of salt
3 eggs, beaten
2 cups milk
¼ cup evaporated milk
1 (8¼-ounce) can crushed pineapple, undrained
1 teaspoon vanilla extract
1 cup chopped pecans or walnuts
Vanilla wafers (about 4 dozen)
1 cup whipping cream, whipped

Melt butter in a heavy saucepan. Stir in sugar, flour, and salt. Add eggs and milk, stirring until blended. Cook over medium heat, stirring, until thickened. Remove from heat; stir in pineapple, vanilla, and pecans. Cool.

Line bottom and sides of a lightly greased 1½-quart casserole with vanilla wafers. Spoon in half of pudding. Top with a layer of vanilla wafers and remaining pudding. Arrange additional vanilla wafers around outside edge of pudding, and top with whipped cream. Yield: 6 to 8 servings.

Mrs. W. W. Wright,
Charlotte, North Carolina.

PINEAPPLE BOAT ALOHA

2 fresh pineapples
2 cups sliced strawberries
2 cups sliced bananas
Dressing (recipe follows)

Cut pineapples in half lengthwise. Scoop out pulp, leaving shells ½ inch thick; set shells aside.

Cut pineapple pulp into bite-size pieces, discarding core. Add strawberries and bananas; toss gently. Spoon into pineapple shells; spoon dressing over fruit. Yield: 10 to 12 servings.

Dressing:

¾ cup firmly packed brown sugar
1 teaspoon dry mustard
1 teaspoon salt
⅓ cup lime juice
1½ tablespoons light rum
1 cup vegetable oil

Combine first 5 ingredients in container of electric blender; process on high speed 1 minute. Gradually add oil, and continue to blend. Yield: 1½ cups.

Mrs. S. M. Phillips,
Candler, North Carolina.

PINEAPPLE UPSIDE-DOWN CAKE

3 tablespoons butter or margarine, melted
1 cup firmly packed brown sugar
1 (15½-ounce) can sliced pineapple, drained
½ cup shortening
1 cup sugar
2 eggs
1½ cups all-purpose flour
2 teaspoons baking powder
½ teaspoon salt
⅔ cup milk
1 teaspoon vanilla extract

Melt butter in a 10-inch cast-iron skillet. Spread brown sugar evenly over butter. Arrange pineapple on sugar.

Combine shortening and sugar, creaming until light and fluffy. Add eggs, and mix well.

Stir in remaining ingredients; beat 2 minutes or until batter is smooth and fluffy. Spoon batter evenly over pineapple slices. Bake at 350° for 50 to 55 minutes or until cake tests done. Cool 5 minutes, and invert cake onto plate. Yield: one 10-inch cake.

Mrs. V. O. Walker,
Pennington, Texas.

SPICED PINEAPPLE

1 (20-ounce) can pineapple chunks
¾ cup vinegar
1¼ cups sugar
Dash of salt
6 to 8 whole cloves
1 (3½-inch) stick cinnamon

Drain pineapple, reserving juice. Combine pineapple juice, vinegar, sugar, salt, cloves, and cinnamon in a medium saucepan; simmer over low heat 10 minutes. Add pineapple, and bring to a boil. Cover and chill overnight. Serve with a slotted spoon. Yield: about 2 cups. *Regina Cooper, Huntsville, Alabama.*

Meet A Food Processor Fan

Southern cooks are using the food processor more and more to save time and effort. This means that many time-consuming recipes once reserved for special occasions can be quickly prepared and served more often.

To give you some practical suggestions on getting the most from your food processor, we introduce you to Mary Len Costa of New Orleans.

Mary Len decided to purchase a food processor when she was faced with a 60-pound pear crop. "I had intended to get one, but decided it was time when I saw all those pears. I usually put up about 300 jars of jams, jellies, marmalades, and relishes," Mary Len continued, "and I use the processor to chop everything."

But Mary Len's expertise with the processor doesn't end with food preservation. She uses it every day. For one of her favorite dishes, she grinds pecans to a fine flour in the processor and uses it for a trout batter. She also likes to use her processor for chopping leftovers, such as carrots and radishes, for use in dressings.

According to Mary Len, "The more I use it, the more I learn just what a processor can do. I've learned to use the slicing blade for chopping when I need bigger pieces. For example, I just cut a green pepper into eighths, and then run it through the slicing blade to get nice, large pieces of pepper."

Here Mary Len shares her own version of a popular New Orleans recipe, Oysters St. Jacques.

OYSTERS ST. JACQUES

8 slices bread
½ bunch fresh parsley
2 to 4 small cloves garlic, peeled
5 to 6 green onions
2 pints Select oysters, undrained
2 eggs, beaten
¾ teaspoon salt
⅛ teaspoon dried thyme leaves
⅛ teaspoon cayenne pepper
⅛ teaspoon pepper
Grated Parmesan cheese
Butter
Fresh parsley sprigs (optional)
Lemon slices (optional)

Position knife blade in processor bowl. Tear bread slices into quarters; add about 4 slices at a time to bowl, and process until crumbs are formed. (This should yield 2 cups soft breadcrumbs.) Remove breadcrumbs, and set aside.

Wash ½ bunch parsley, and dry thoroughly (wet parsley will not process well). Cut leaves from stems. Position dry knife blade in dry bowl; add parsley leaves. Process until parsley is evenly chopped, pulsing 4 to 5 times. Remove parsley to mixing bowl, and set aside.

Position knife blade in dry bowl. Drop garlic cloves through food chute with processor running; process 3 to 5 seconds or until garlic is minced. Add garlic to parsley, mixing well.

Wash green onions, and remove all but 3 inches of tops. Cut onions into 1-inch pieces. Position knife blade in bowl; add onion. Pulse 3 to 4 times until onions are evenly chopped, scraping bowl as needed. Add onion to parsley mixture.

Check oysters carefully, and remove any pieces of shell. Place oysters and oyster liquid in a saucepan; cook over low heat about 3 to 5 minutes or until edges of oysters curl. Drain oysters, reserving ¼ cup plus 1 tablespoon oyster liquid. Pat oysters dry with paper towels, and set aside to cool.

Combine 1⅔ cups breadcrumbs and reserved oyster liquid; mix well with a fork, and set aside.

Position knife blade in processor bowl; add oysters. Pulse 2 to 3 times until oysters are chopped (do not overprocess).

Combine parsley mixture, breadcrumb mixture, oysters, eggs, salt, thyme, cayenne, and pepper; mix well. Spoon into 8 small, buttered ramekins or individual baking shells.

Place ramekins in a 15- x 10- x 1-inch baking pan. Sprinkle with remaining ⅓ cup breadcrumbs and Parmesan cheese; dot each with butter. Bake at 375° for 20 minutes or until bubbly and lightly browned. Garnish with fresh parsley sprigs and lemon slices, if desired. Yield: 8 servings. *Mary Len Costa, New Orleans, Louisiana.*

Congealed Salads Bring A Light Touch

If you're having friends over for a casual lunch, round out your menu with one of these congealed salads. Asparagus Mold, Sunshine Aspic, and Pickled Peach Salad are all refreshingly light. If you'd like a salad as the main course, you can't go wrong with Corned Beef Salad or Chilly Salmon Salad.

Whatever your choice, the good news is that all can be prepared a day ahead.

SUNSHINE ASPIC

3 cups tomato juice, divided
1 bay leaf
½ teaspoon celery salt
½ teaspoon onion salt
2 (3-ounce) packages lemon-flavored gelatin
¾ cup water
¼ cup vinegar
3 hard-cooked eggs, sliced
Mayonnaise

Combine 2 cups tomato juice, bay leaf, celery salt, and onion salt in a medium saucepan; bring to a boil. Add gelatin, and stir until dissolved. Discard bay leaf. Add remaining tomato juice, water, and vinegar; chill until slightly thickened.

Pour gelatin mixture into a lightly oiled 6-cup ring mold. Chill until thick but not set. Arrange egg slices along outer edge of thickened mixture; gently push egg slices into mixture. Chill until firm. Serve with mayonnaise. Yield: 8 to 10 servings. *Marsha Berman, Dover, Delaware.*

Tip: Quick-chill gelatin mixtures for aspics or molds by pouring in metal pan and placing in freezer about 15 minutes.

CHILLY SALMON SALAD

1 envelope unflavored gelatin
½ cup cold water
½ cup boiling water
2 tablespoons lemon juice
1 (7¾-ounce) can salmon, drained and flaked
1 teaspoon salt
Pepper to taste
1½ cups small-curd cottage cheese
½ cup mayonnaise
¾ cup chopped celery
¼ teaspoon celery salt
2 tablespoons chopped chives
2 tablespoons pickle relish
Lettuce leaves

Soften gelatin in cold water; stir in boiling water and lemon juice. Add remaining ingredients except lettuce leaves, mixing well. Pour into a lightly oiled 8-inch square pan; chill until firm. Cut into squares; serve on lettuce leaves. Yield: 6 to 9 servings.

Jeannine Allen,
McAllen, Texas.

CORNED BEEF SALAD

1 (3-ounce) package lemon-flavored gelatin
1 cup boiling water
¾ cup cold water
1 cup mayonnaise or salad dressing
1 (12-ounce) can corned beef, shredded
1 cup diced celery
3 hard-cooked eggs, finely chopped
1 small onion, finely chopped
1 (2-ounce) jar chopped pimiento, drained
Lettuce leaves (optional)
Egg slices (optional)

Dissolve gelatin in boiling water. Add ¾ cup cold water, and chill until slightly thickened. Add remaining ingredients except lettuce and egg, stirring well. Pour into a lightly oiled 8-inch square pan; chill until firm. Cut into rectangles; serve on lettuce leaves and garnish with egg slices, if desired. Yield: 6 servings. *Mrs. Bert E. Uebele, Jr.,*
Boca Raton, Florida.

LIME SHERBET SALAD

1 (8-ounce) can crushed pineapple
1 (3-ounce) package lime-flavored gelatin
1 cup lime sherbet
1 fresh pear, peeled and diced
1 cup chopped pecans

Drain pineapple, reserving juice; add enough water to juice to make 1 cup liquid. Bring juice to a boil; add gelatin, stirring to dissolve. Stir in sherbet. Add pineapple, pear, and pecans; mix well, and pour into a lightly oiled 6-cup mold. Chill until set. Yield: 6 to 8 servings. *Mrs. William S. Bell,*
Chattanooga, Tennessee.

ASPARAGUS MOLD

1 teaspoon unflavored gelatin
½ cup cold water
1 (3-ounce) package lemon-flavored gelatin
2 chicken bouillon cubes
1 cup boiling water
½ cup commercial green goddess dressing
1 tablespoon lemon juice
1 (14½-ounce) can cut asparagus, drained
½ cup diced celery
2 tablespoons finely chopped green pepper
Lettuce leaves (optional)
Mayonnaise (optional)

Soften unflavored gelatin in cold water; set aside.

Dissolve lemon-flavored gelatin and bouillon in boiling water; add softened gelatin, stirring until dissolved. Add green goddess dressing and lemon juice, stirring with a wire whisk until smooth. Chill until slightly thickened.

Stir asparagus, celery, and green pepper into gelatin mixture. Pour into a lightly oiled 1-quart mold, and chill salad until firm.

Unmold on lettuce leaves, and garnish with a dollop of mayonnaise, if desired. Yield: 6 servings.

Mrs. Loren Martin,
Knoxville, Tennessee.

CHERRY COLA SALAD

1 (16½-ounce) can pitted dark sweet cherries
1 (20-ounce) can crushed pineapple
1 (3-ounce) package black cherry-flavored gelatin
1 (3-ounce) package raspberry-flavored gelatin
1 (12-ounce) can cola-type beverage, chilled
1 cup finely chopped celery
1 cup pecans, chopped
½ cup flaked coconut (optional)
2 (3-ounce) packages cream cheese, softened

Drain cherries and pineapple, reserving juice; add enough water to juice to make 2 cups liquid. Bring liquid to a boil; add gelatin, stirring to dissolve. Stir in cola beverage. Chill until slightly thickened.

Combine celery, pecans, cherries, pineapple, and coconut, if desired. Beat cream cheese until smooth and fluffy; add to fruit mixture, stirring well. Fold cream cheese mixture into gelatin; pour into a 13- x 9- x 2-inch pan. Chill until firm. Cut into squares to serve. Yield: 15 servings. *Mrs. Jack Corzine,*
St. Louis, Missouri.

PICKLED PEACH SALAD

1 (29-ounce) jar pickled peaches
1 (6-ounce) package orange-flavored gelatin
1 cup boiling water
1 (8-ounce) package cream cheese, softened
1 (8-ounce) can crushed pineapple, drained
Lettuce leaves

Drain peaches, reserving 1 cup juice. Mash peaches with a fork; set aside.

Dissolve gelatin in boiling water; add cream cheese, stirring until blended. Stir in reserved peach juice; chill salad until slightly thickened.

Combine peaches and pineapple; add to gelatin mixture, stirring well. Pour into a lightly oiled 13- x 9- x 2-inch pan; chill until firm. Cut into rectangles; serve on lettuce leaves. Yield: 12 servings. *Vivian Carter,*
Pisgah, Alabama.

Cookies With Oats And More

A fresh batch of oatmeal cookies is always a treat, and these recipes offer something more. Like salted peanuts and coconut stirred into Peanutty Oatmeal Cookies. Or chocolate morsels and nuts baked into Chocolate-Oatmeal Cookies. And our Giant Oatmeal-Spice Cookies are big on flavor as well as in size, with cinnamon, cloves, allspice, and ginger giving them their special taste.

CHOCOLATE-OATMEAL COOKIES

2 cups all-purpose flour
1 teaspoon soda
½ teaspoon baking powder
½ teaspoon salt
1 cup sugar
1 cup firmly packed brown sugar
1 cup shortening
2 eggs
1 teaspoon vanilla extract
2 cups quick-cooking oats, uncooked
1 (6-ounce) package semisweet chocolate morsels
1 cup chopped nuts (optional)

Combine flour, soda, baking powder, and salt; set aside.

Combine sugar and shortening, creaming well; beat in eggs and vanilla. Add flour mixture; mix well. Stir in oats and chocolate morsels; add chopped nuts, if desired.

Drop dough by heaping teaspoonfuls onto lightly greased cookie sheets. Bake at 350° for 12 to 14 minutes. Cool slightly on cookie sheets; remove to wire racks to cool completely. Yield: about 6½ dozen.
Mrs. Russell Rehkemper,
Tampa, Florida.

There's no such thing as a plain oatmeal cookie in this assortment: Slice-and-Bake Oatmeal Cookies, Giant Oatmeal-Spice Cookies, and Chocolate-Oatmeal Cookies.

GIANT OATMEAL-SPICE COOKIES

1½ cups all-purpose flour
½ teaspoon soda
½ teaspoon salt
2 teaspoons ground cinnamon
2 teaspoons ground cloves
2 teaspoons ground allspice
1 teaspoon ground ginger
1 cup butter or margarine, softened
1 cup sugar
1 cup firmly packed brown sugar
2 eggs
1 teaspoon vanilla extract
3 cups quick-cooking oats, uncooked
1 cup chopped nuts (optional)

Combine flour, soda, salt, and spices; set aside.

Combine butter and sugar, creaming well; beat in eggs and vanilla. Add flour mixture, mixing well. Stir in oats; add nuts, if desired.

Drop dough by a ¼-cup measure 5 inches apart onto lightly greased cookie sheets. Bake at 375° for 12 to 14 minutes or until lightly browned. Cool slightly on cookie sheets; remove to wire racks to cool completely. Yield: about 2 dozen.
Mrs. C. C. Cabaniss,
Shelby, North Carolina.

SLICE-AND-BAKE OATMEAL COOKIES

1½ cups all-purpose flour
1 teaspoon soda
1 teaspoon salt
1 cup sugar
1 cup firmly packed brown sugar
1 cup shortening
2 eggs
1 teaspoon vanilla extract
3 cups quick-cooking oats, uncooked
½ cup chopped pecans

Combine flour, soda, and salt; stir well, and set aside.

Combine sugar and shortening, creaming well; beat in eggs and vanilla. Add flour mixture, mixing well. Stir in oats and pecans.

Divide dough in half; shape each half into a 12- x 2-inch roll. Wrap in waxed paper, and chill overnight.

Slice dough into ¼-inch-thick slices; place slices on ungreased cookie sheets. Bake at 375° for 8 to 10 minutes or until lightly browned. Remove to wire racks to cool. Yield: about 6 dozen.
Note: Dough may be shaped into rolls and frozen. Slice as directed while frozen, and bake at 375° for 12 minutes.
Mrs. Bill Anthony,
North Little Rock, Arkansas.

EASY OATMEAL COOKIES

1¼ cups all-purpose flour
1 teaspoon soda
½ teaspoon salt
½ teaspoon ground cinnamon
1 cup shortening
1 cup firmly packed brown sugar
1 cup sugar
2 eggs
½ teaspoon vanilla extract
3 cups quick-cooking or regular oats, uncooked
½ cup chopped pecans

Combine flour, soda, salt, and cinnamon; set aside.

Cream shortening and sugar; beat in eggs and vanilla. Add flour mixture, mixing well. Stir in oats and pecans.

Shape dough into 1-inch balls, and place 1 inch apart on lightly greased cookie sheets. Bake at 350° for 12 to 15 minutes or until lightly browned. Yield: about 8 dozen.
Mrs. Earl E. Crimm,
Gordo, Alabama.

Tip: Keep herbs and spices in alphabetical order for convenience.

OLD-FASHIONED OATMEAL COOKIES

1 cup all-purpose flour
½ teaspoon soda
½ teaspoon salt
1 teaspoon ground cinnamon
¼ teaspoon ground nutmeg
½ cup firmly packed brown sugar
¼ cup sugar
½ cup shortening
1 egg
2 tablespoons milk
2 cups quick-cooking oats, uncooked
1 cup raisins

Combine flour, soda, salt, and spices; set aside.

Combine sugar and shortening, creaming well; beat in egg and milk. Add flour mixture, mixing well. Stir in the oats and raisins.

Drop dough by heaping teaspoonfuls onto lightly greased cookie sheets. Bake at 375° for 10 to 12 minutes or until lightly browned. Cool slightly on cookie sheets; remove to wire racks to cool completely. Yield: about 3½ dozen.
Mrs. Cheryl B. Hagler,
Huntsville, Alabama.

PEANUTTY OATMEAL COOKIES

2 cups all-purpose flour
½ teaspoon soda
½ teaspoon salt
1 cup sugar
1 cup firmly packed brown sugar
⅓ cup butter or margarine, softened
½ cup shortening
2 eggs
¼ cup milk
1 teaspoon vanilla extract
3 cups quick-cooking oats, uncooked
½ cup shredded coconut
½ cup finely chopped salted peanuts

Combine flour, soda, and salt; stir well, and set aside. Combine sugar, butter, and shortening; cream well. Beat in eggs, milk, and vanilla. Add the flour mixture, mixing well. Stir in oats, shredded coconut, and the peanuts.

Drop dough by heaping teaspoonfuls onto lightly greased cookie sheets. Bake at 350° for 10 to 13 minutes or until lightly browned. Yield: about 7 dozen.
Mrs. Donald C. Vanhoy,
Salisbury, North Carolina.

Round Steak Gets A Royal Treatment

Round steak is a versatile and flavorful cut that is also a good choice when watching the meat budget. This collection of recipes offers some welcome variations on favorite dishes.

For instance, Royal Beef Bourguignon is flavored with sherry as well as the traditional Burgundy. Swiss steak is given a taste of mustard in Deviled Swiss Steak and takes on a new flavor in Swiss Steak Cheese Skillet, where it's topped with mozzarella cheese.

SWISS STEAK CHEESE SKILLET

2 pounds boneless round steak
¼ cup all-purpose flour
¼ cup butter or margarine, melted
1 (16-ounce) can tomatoes
½ teaspoon salt
¼ teaspoon whole basil leaves
⅛ teaspoon pepper
½ cup chopped onion
⅓ cup chopped green pepper
1½ cups (6 ounces) shredded mozzarella cheese

Trim excess fat from steak; cut into serving-size pieces.

Dredge steak in flour; sauté in butter until browned. Add tomatoes, salt, basil, and pepper to steak; cover and simmer 1 hour. Stir in onion and green pepper; cook an additional 30 minutes. Sprinkle cheese over meat, and heat just until melted. Yield: 4 to 6 servings.
Mrs. Ted Beckwith,
Lebanon, Tennessee.

PARMESAN ROUND STEAK

1 (1½-pound) boneless round steak,
　¾ inch thick
1 egg, beaten
⅓ cup milk
½ cup fine dry breadcrumbs
1 teaspoon salt
⅛ teaspoon pepper
1 tablespoon Ac'cent
3 tablespoons bacon drippings
½ cup water
¼ teaspoon dried whole oregano
¼ cup grated Parmesan cheese
6 small onions, peeled
¼ teaspoon salt
¼ teaspoon paprika

Trim excess fat from steak, and pound to ½-inch thickness. Cut steak into serving-size pieces.

Combine egg and milk; beat well. Combine breadcrumbs, 1 teaspoon salt, pepper, and Ac'cent. Dip steak in egg mixture, dredge in breadcrumb mixture, and brown in bacon drippings. Place steak in a lightly greased 2-quart baking dish. Add water and sprinkle with oregano and cheese.

Add onions to steak; sprinkle with ¼ teaspoon salt and paprika. Cover tightly and bake at 325° for 1 hour and 15 minutes or until tender. Yield: 6 servings.
Florence Costello,
Chattanooga, Tennessee.

ROYAL BEEF BOURGUIGNON

2 pounds top round steak, cut into 2-inch cubes
2 tablespoons butter or margarine, melted
3 tablespoons all-purpose flour
½ cup dry sherry
5 slices bacon
24 (about 1 pound) small onions, peeled
1 pound small fresh mushrooms
¾ cup commercial consommé, undiluted
¼ cup water
1 cup Burgundy
2 tablespoons tomato paste
2 bay leaves
Pinch of frozen chopped chives
Pinch of dried thyme leaves
Pinch of dried tarragon leaves
Pinch of chopped parsley

Brown steak in butter in a heavy Dutch oven. Combine flour and sherry, stirring until well blended; stir into Dutch oven.

Cook bacon until crisp; drain, reserving drippings. Crumble bacon, and add to steak.

Sauté onions in bacon drippings until tender; remove with a slotted spoon, and add to steak. Sauté mushrooms in remaining bacon drippings; drain well, and set aside.

Add remaining ingredients, except mushrooms, to steak; cover and simmer over low heat 1½ hours. Add mushrooms; cover and simmer an additional 30 minutes. Yield: 6 servings.
Eunice H. Tinsley,
Huntington, West Virginia.

Tip: Always turn saucepan and skillet handles toward the back of the range to prevent accidents.

DEVILED SWISS STEAK

¼ cup all-purpose flour
1½ teaspoons dry mustard
1½ pounds top round steak, 1 inch thick
Salt and pepper
3 tablespoons hot vegetable oil
1 cup sliced onion
1 carrot, diced
1 (16-ounce) can whole tomatoes
1 tablespoon light brown sugar
2 tablespoons Worcestershire sauce

Combine flour and mustard, stirring well. Dredge steak in flour mixture; pound flour into steak with a meat mallet. Sprinkle with salt and pepper.

Brown steak on both sides in oil in a medium skillet. Transfer to a 13- x 9- x 2-inch baking dish; add onion and carrot. Combine tomatoes, sugar, and Worcestershire sauce; pour over steak. Then cover and bake at 350° for 1½ hours. Yield: 6 servings.

Mrs. E. W. Hanley,
Elberton, Georgia.

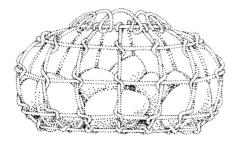

Delicate Quiche From The Microwave

A microwave oven cooks quiche in about half the time required conventionally, and the result is the same—a delicate, creamy custard. Because the technique for microwaved quiche is almost identical to the conventional method, recipes are easy to adapt.

When converting a quiche recipe to microwave cooking, you may need to reduce the liquid slightly. This is due to the greater expansion that occurs in the microwave oven. The amount of liquid needed will depend on the type and amount of filling used, but a general rule of thumb is to reduce the liquid between ¼ and ½ cup. If you have a problem with a converted quiche boiling over, simply reduce the liquid further when preparing the recipe again.

Whether cooked conventionally or by microwaves, quiche requires about 10 minutes standing time after cooking has finished. The center of a microwaved quiche will be slightly soft at the end of the cooking cycle, but will continue to cook during standing time. Stop microwaving when a knife inserted off-center comes out clean. Do not cook it until the center is set.

When microwaving quiche, give the dish a half turn after half of the cooking time has elapsed. This promotes even cooking of the custard. If your oven has an uneven cooking pattern, you may need to turn the dish two or even three times during the cooking cycle.

The recipes included here will acquaint you with the ease of preparing quiche in the microwave oven. Since the wattage of microwave ovens varies, the cooking times will vary. A time range is given in our recipes to allow for the difference. To prevent overcooking, always check for doneness at the lower end of the range.

Preparing the Pastry

For a microwaved quiche, the pastry is microwaved before the custard mixture is added. This allows the pastry to crisp and dry, preventing soggy crust. Microwave the pastry until it is opaque and the bottom is dry.

The pastry will not brown during microwave cooking. Adding a few drops of yellow food coloring to the dough will give it a golden appearance. Before microwaving, place a piece of heavy-duty plastic wrap over the pastry, and cover with dried beans or peas. Do not use metallic weights.

QUICHE PASTRY

1 cup all-purpose flour
½ teaspoon salt
⅓ cup plus 1 tablespoon shortening
2 to 3 tablespoons cold water
3 to 4 drops yellow food coloring (optional)

Combine flour and salt in a medium bowl; cut in shortening with pastry blender until mixture resembles coarse meal. Combine water and food coloring if extra color is desired (pastry will not brown in microwave oven). Sprinkle water evenly over flour mixture; stir with a fork until all ingredients are moistened.

Shape into a ball. Roll dough on a lightly floured surface to a circle 2 inches larger than inverted 9½-inch quiche dish. Fit pastry loosely into dish. Trim edges, and fold under to form a standing rim; then flute.

Place a piece of heavy-duty plastic wrap over pastry; cover with dried beans or peas. Microwave at HIGH for 5½ to 7 minutes or until pastry is opaque and bottom is dry. Yield: pastry for one 9½-inch quiche.

BENEDICT QUICHE

1 cup diced Canadian bacon or ham (about 5 ounces)
¼ cup chopped green pepper
¼ cup sliced ripe olives
2 tablespoons chopped pimiento
1 cup (4 ounces) shredded Cheddar cheese
1 (9½-inch) quiche pastry, microwaved
3 eggs, beaten
1½ cups half-and-half
½ teaspoon salt
⅛ teaspoon pepper
Hollandaise sauce (recipe follows)

Combine Canadian bacon, green pepper, olives, and pimiento in a 1-quart casserole. Cover with heavy-duty plastic wrap; microwave at HIGH for 2 to 4 minutes or until green pepper is crisp-tender. Drain well on paper towels. Sprinkle cheese in microwaved pastry shell; top with Canadian bacon mixture.

Combine eggs, half-and-half, salt, and pepper in a medium bowl; mix well. Pour egg mixture into quiche shell; microwave at MEDIUM HIGH for 12 minutes. Give dish a half turn; microwave at MEDIUM HIGH for 7 to 12 minutes or until a knife inserted off-center comes out clean (center will be slightly soft). Let stand 10 minutes before serving. Serve quiche with hollandaise sauce. Yield: one 9½-inch quiche.

Hollandaise Sauce:

½ cup butter or margarine
3 egg yolks
1 tablespoon plus 1½ teaspoons lemon juice
¼ teaspoon salt
Dash of white pepper

Place butter in a medium bowl; microwave at HIGH for 45 seconds to 1 minute or until melted (do not allow butter to boil). Set aside.

Combine remaining ingredients in container of electric blender; blend until thick and lemon colored. Add melted butter in a slow, steady stream, and continue to process until thick. Yield: about ⅔ cup.

SPICY SAUSAGE QUICHE

½ pound bulk pork sausage
½ cup sliced fresh mushrooms
½ cup chopped onion
1 (4-ounce) can whole green chiles,
  drained, seeded, and chopped
¼ teaspoon whole basil leaves
¼ teaspoon chili powder
1 cup (4 ounces) shredded Cheddar cheese
1 (9½-inch) quiche pastry, microwaved
3 eggs, beaten
1½ cups half-and-half
½ teaspoon salt
⅛ teaspoon pepper
Paprika

Crumble sausage into a 1½-quart casserole; add mushrooms, onion, chiles, basil, and chili powder, mixing well. Cover with heavy-duty plastic wrap; microwave at HIGH for 4 to 6 minutes or until meat is done, stirring once. Drain off drippings. Sprinkle Cheddar cheese in microwaved pastry shell; top with the sausage mixture.

Combine eggs, half-and-half, salt, and pepper in a medium bowl; mix well. Pour egg mixture into quiche shell; sprinkle with paprika. Microwave at MEDIUM HIGH for 12 minutes. Give dish a half turn; microwave at MEDIUM HIGH for 7 to 13 minutes or until a knife inserted off-center comes out clean (center will be slightly soft). Let stand 10 minutes before serving. Yield: one 9½-inch quiche.

QUICHE LORRAINE

8 slices bacon
1 cup (4 ounces) shredded Swiss cheese
½ cup finely chopped onion
1 (9½-inch) quiche pastry, microwaved
4 eggs, beaten
2 cups half-and-half
½ teaspoon salt
¼ teaspoon pepper
Ground nutmeg

Place bacon on a bacon rack in a 12- x 8- x 2-inch baking dish; cover with paper toweling. Microwave at HIGH for 6 to 8 minutes or until bacon is done; crumble bacon. Sprinkle cheese, bacon, and onion into microwaved pastry shell.

Combine eggs, half-and-half, salt, and pepper in a medium bowl; mix well. Pour egg mixture into quiche shell; sprinkle with nutmeg. Microwave at MEDIUM HIGH for 8 minutes. Give dish a half turn; microwave at MEDIUM HIGH for 6 to 13 minutes or

until knife inserted off-center comes out clean (center will be slightly soft). Let stand 10 minutes before serving. Yield: one 9½-inch quiche.

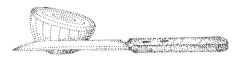

Fry A Batch Of Onion Rings

Crispy fried onion rings—what could be better with a thick, juicy steak or hamburger? You can serve them fresh from your own kitchen by following one of these easy recipes.

While all four recipes begin with a large onion, the batter makes each one special. For French-Fried Onion Rings Supreme, simply dip the rings in evaporated milk, then in a mixture of salt and self-rising flour before frying. Cornmeal gives Deluxe Fried Onion Rings a special crunchy texture.

Combine just 6 simple ingredients in a blender to make the batter for Crispy Fried Onion Rings. And Easy Onion Rings are just that—easy to prepare and a golden-brown delight.

CRISPY FRIED ONION RINGS

1 extra-large Spanish onion
1¼ cups all-purpose flour
1 teaspoon baking powder
¼ teaspoon salt
1 cup beer
1 egg, beaten
1 tablespoon vegetable oil
Vegetable oil

Peel onion; cut into ⅜-inch slices, and separate into rings.

Combine dry ingredients, beer, egg, and 1 tablespoon vegetable oil in container of electric blender; process until smooth. Place batter in a shallow pan; using a fork, dip onion rings into batter, coating both sides well.

Fry in deep hot oil (375°) until golden brown on both sides (3 to 5 minutes). Drain well on paper towels. Yield: 4 to 6 servings.

Note: These onion rings may be frozen in a single layer on baking sheets for later use. When frozen, package rings as desired in foil. To reheat, place onion rings on baking sheets; bake at 400° for 7 minutes. *Mrs. Ernest Ivey, Shreveport, Louisiana.*

DELUXE FRIED ONION RINGS

1 extra-large Spanish onion
1 cup all-purpose flour
1 tablespoon cornmeal
2 teaspoons salt
¼ teaspoon pepper
1½ teaspoons baking powder
1 egg, divided
⅔ cup milk
1 tablespoon vegetable oil
Vegetable oil

Peel onion; cut into ¼-inch slices, and separate into rings. Place onion rings in a large bowl, and cover with ice water. Let stand 30 minutes. Drain on paper towels.

Combine flour, cornmeal, salt, pepper, and baking powder in a medium bowl. Combine egg yolk, milk, and 1 tablespoon vegetable oil; beat well. Stir egg mixture into flour mixture, mixing thoroughly.

Beat egg white until stiff but not dry; fold egg white into batter. Heat 1 inch of vegetable oil to 375°; dip onion rings into batter, and fry in hot oil until golden brown on both sides (about 3 to 5 minutes). Drain well on paper towels. Yield: 4 to 6 servings. *Mary Shelby, Kansas City, Missouri.*

EASY ONION RINGS

1 large Spanish onion
1 cup all-purpose flour
1 teaspoon baking powder
1 teaspoon salt
2 eggs
½ cup milk
1 teaspoon vegetable oil
Vegetable oil

Peel onion; cut into ¼-inch slices, and separate into rings.

Combine dry ingredients; stir well. Add eggs, milk, and 1 teaspoon oil; beat until smooth.

Dip onion rings into batter; fry in deep hot oil (375°) until golden brown. Drain on paper towels. Yield: 4 to 6 servings. *Margaret Connelly, Fort Worth, Texas.*

Tip: To prevent grease from spattering while frying, invert a colander over skillet to catch grease and allow steam to escape.

FRENCH-FRIED ONION RINGS SUPREME

1 large Spanish onion or 3 large Bermuda onions
1⅓ cups self-rising flour
½ teaspoon salt
1 (5.33-ounce) can evaporated milk, undiluted
Vegetable oil

Peel onion; cut into ¼-inch slices, and separate into rings.

Combine flour and salt; stir well.

Dip onion rings into milk, and then into flour mixture; repeat. Set aside on paper towels 10 minutes. Fry in deep hot oil (375°) until golden brown. Drain on paper towels. Yield: 4 to 6 servings. *Mrs. Blair Cunnyngham, Cleveland, Tennessee.*

Something Cool And Creamy For Dessert

These cool, creamy desserts are four of the most luscious ways to end a meal. Although they vary in flavor from apple and coffee to chocolate and crème de menthe, it's marshmallows that make them all velvety smooth.

Soft, puffy marshmallows are melted with milk, flavored with crème de menthe, then beaten with whipped cream for a quick, impressive Crème de Menthe Mousse. Coffee Mallow is made by a similar procedure, but depends on strong coffee for melting the marshmallows and adding distinctive flavor.

For Cool Chocolate-Mint Dessert, marshmallows are mixed with crushed peppermint candy, nuts, cookie crumbs, and whipped cream as the topping for a rich chocolate filling. And Apple Delight combines orange juice and pineapple juice with marshmallows and apples.

APPLE DELIGHT

1 cup orange juice
1 cup pineapple juice
1 (10.5-ounce) package miniature marshmallows
2 cups grated apple
1½ cups whipped topping
3 dozen vanilla wafers
¼ cup crushed vanilla wafers

Combine juice and marshmallows in a saucepan; cook over low heat, stirring constantly, until marshmallows melt. Chill until thick. Stir grated apple into marshmallow mixture, and fold in the whipped topping.

Line a 9-inch square baking pan with whole vanilla wafers. Pour apple mixture over vanilla wafers, spreading evenly. Chill; sprinkle with crushed vanilla wafers. Yield: 9 servings.
Mrs. William S. Bell, Chattanooga, Tennessee.

CRÈME DE MENTHE MOUSSE

20 large marshmallows, cut in pieces
¼ cup milk
2 to 3 tablespoons crème de menthe
1 cup whipping cream, whipped
Whipped cream
Grated chocolate
Mint sprigs

Combine marshmallows and milk in a saucepan; cook over low heat, stirring constantly, until marshmallows melt. Stir in crème de menthe. Chill until thick.

Combine marshmallow mixture and 1 cup whipped cream, beating until well blended. Spoon into individual dessert dishes; chill. Top with a dollop of whipped cream, grated chocolate, and mint sprigs. Yield: 4 servings.
H. Joyce De Long, Annandale, Virginia.

COFFEE MALLOW

32 large marshmallows, cut in pieces
1 cup strong coffee
2 teaspoons vanilla extract
1 cup whipping cream, whipped
Maraschino cherries

Combine marshmallows and coffee in a saucepan; cook over low heat, stirring constantly, until marshmallows melt. Chill just until mixture is thickened.

Stir vanilla into coffee mixture; fold in whipped cream. Spoon into individual dessert dishes; chill. Garnish with a maraschino cherry. Yield: 6 servings.
Mrs. E. F. Bastable, Chevy Chase, Maryland.

Tip: Marshmallows do not dry out if stored in the freezer. Cut them while frozen to add to salads and desserts; kitchen shears don't get sticky either.

COOL CHOCOLATE-MINT DESSERT

1 cup powdered sugar
½ cup butter
2 egg yolks
2 (1-ounce) squares unsweetened chocolate
1 cup chopped nuts, divided
2 egg whites, stiffly beaten
2 cups crushed chocolate sandwich cookies, divided
8 ounces hard peppermint candy, crushed
12 large marshmallows, cut in small pieces
1 cup whipping cream, whipped

Combine sugar and butter, creaming until light and fluffy. Add egg yolks, mixing well. Melt chocolate in top of double boiler. Gradually add chocolate to creamed mixture, beating constantly; stir in ½ cup nuts, and fold in egg whites.

Press 1 cup cookie crumbs into bottom of an 8-inch square baking dish; gently spread chocolate mixture over crumbs. Chill until firm.

Combine candy, marshmallows, ½ cup nuts, and ½ cup cookie crumbs; mix well. Gently stir in whipped cream. Spread whipped cream mixture over chocolate layer; sprinkle remaining ½ cup cookie crumbs over top. Chill. Yield: 9 servings. *Mrs. Otto Murphy, Springfield, Tennessee.*

Ham—The Versatile Entrée

If you're trying to select an entrée for a special occasion and also want to have plenty of leftovers, we suggest a ham.

For a special meal, serve Plum Ham, a ham baked with a sweet plum glaze. Then enjoy the leftovers in a variety of ways. Combine strips of ham with a fruited curry sauce, and serve it over rice. Grind the leftover ham and bake it in patties or a spicy loaf. Or dice it for the cheesy Ham Quiche.

When buying ham, compare price per pound of various cuts. The shank portion is usually priced much lower than other selections. And although the shank contains more bone than other cuts, it is still a very good buy.

PLUM HAM

1 (6- to 7-pound) uncooked ham
1 (1-pound) can plums
⅔ cup firmly packed brown sugar
¼ cup water
1 tablespoon plus 1 teaspoon dry mustard

Place ham, fat side up, in a 13- x 9- x 2-inch baking pan. Drain plums, reserving juice; set plums aside. Combine plum juice, brown sugar, water, and dry mustard; mix well. Pour half of glaze mixture over ham. Wrap foil loosely around ham. Bake at 325° for 3 to 3½ hours (about 30 minutes per pound).

Remove ham from oven about 30 minutes before cooking time is up. Score ham in a diamond pattern, making cuts ¼ inch deep in ham fat. Spoon remaining glaze mixture over ham, and return ham to oven. Bake, uncovered, at 400° for 30 minutes, basting frequently. Garnish with plums. Yield: 12 to 14 servings. *Ginger Barker, Mesquite, Texas.*

SPICY HAM LOAF

¾ cup dark corn syrup
2 teaspoons dry mustard
⅓ cup vinegar
3 cups ground ham (about 1½ pounds)
2 cups ground pork (1 pound)
1 cup fine dry breadcrumbs
2 eggs
½ cup apple juice
1 tablespoon minced onion
½ teaspoon dry mustard
½ teaspoon Worcestershire sauce
¼ teaspoon pepper

Combine corn syrup, 2 teaspoons dry mustard, and vinegar in a small saucepan; bring to a boil. Boil 2 minutes, stirring occasionally. Remove syrup from heat, and set aside.

Combine remaining ingredients; mix well. Place meat mixture in a greased 13- x 9- x 2-inch baking pan; shape into 12- x 4-inch loaf. Bake at 300° for 1½ to 2 hours, basting every 15 minutes with syrup mixture. Yield: 6 to 8 servings. *Mrs. William B. Moore, Selma, Alabama.*

Tip: Remember that preheating the oven is generally wasteful except for "quick-bake" items such as cookies, pizza, and frozen entrées. Cut down on this habit.

One of the nicest things about baked ham is all the wonderful ways you can serve the leftovers.

HAM QUICHE

Pastry for 9-inch quiche dish or piepan
½ cup mayonnaise
2 tablespoons all-purpose flour
4 eggs, beaten
½ cup milk
1 cup diced fully cooked ham
1 cup (4 ounces) shredded Cheddar cheese
1 cup (4 ounces) shredded Swiss cheese

Line a 9-inch quiche dish or piepan with pastry; trim excess pastry around edges. Fold edges under and flute. Bake at 400° for 3 minutes; remove from oven, and gently prick with a fork. Bake 5 minutes longer. Let cool on rack.

Combine mayonnaise, flour, eggs, and milk; mix thoroughly. Stir in ham and cheese. Pour into quiche shell, and bake at 350° for 45 to 50 minutes. Yield: one 9-inch quiche.

Lynne Weeks, Midland, Georgia.

PINEAPPLE-HAM PATTIES

1 (15¼-ounce) can unsweetened sliced pineapple
1 pound ground ham
½ pound ground lean pork
1 cup cooked rice
1 egg, slightly beaten
1 teaspoon monosodium glutamate
1 teaspoon Worcestershire sauce
2 tablespoons cornstarch
⅛ teaspoon ground cloves
2 tablespoons water
1 tablespoon lemon juice
¼ cup light corn syrup

Drain pineapple slices, reserving juice. Set aside.

Combine meats, rice, egg, monosodium glutamate, and Worcestershire sauce in a medium bowl; mix well, and shape into 8 patties. Place patties in a lightly greased shallow baking dish; press a pineapple slice into each patty. Bake at 350° for 25 minutes.

Combine cornstarch, cloves, and water in a small saucepan; stir until cornstarch is dissolved. Stir in reserved pineapple juice, lemon juice, and corn syrup; cook over low heat, stirring constantly, until smooth and thickened.

Spoon pineapple sauce over ham patties, and bake an additional 10 minutes. Yield: 8 servings. *Mrs. Loren Martin, Knoxville, Tennessee.*

CURRIED HAM WITH RICE

1 (8¼-ounce) can pineapple chunks
2 tablespoons butter or margarine
1 medium onion, cut into strips
1 medium-size green pepper, cut into strips
1 cup diced celery
1 teaspoon curry powder
1 tablespoon cornstarch
½ cup orange juice
1½ to 2 cups fully cooked ham strips (2 inches long)
½ cup slivered almonds, toasted
3 or 4 water chestnuts, sliced
Hot cooked rice

Drain pineapple chunks, reserving juice. Add enough water to juice to make 1 cup. Set aside.

Melt butter in a large heavy skillet. Stir in onion, green pepper, celery, and curry powder. Cover and cook over low heat 20 minutes. Blend in cornstarch. Gradually stir in pineapple juice, orange juice, and pineapple; cook over low heat, stirring constantly, until thickened and bubbly. Cook 1 additional minute.

Stir in ham, almonds, and water chestnuts; heat thoroughly. Serve over hot cooked rice. Yield: 6 servings.
Mrs. S. D. Thomas, Dothan, Alabama.

Best Of Barbecued Ribs

Whether you enjoy ribs barbecued on an outdoor grill or baked in the oven, you'll enjoy these recipes.

Included is a recipe for oven-baked ribs with real barbecue flavor. And the outdoor cook will want to try Apple Barbecued Ribs; applesauce is added to the basting sauce for extra flavor.

BARBECUED RIBS

2 pounds spareribs
1 lemon, sliced
1 medium onion, finely chopped
½ cup catsup
1½ tablespoons Worcestershire sauce
½ teaspoon chili powder
½ teaspoon salt
Dash of hot sauce
½ cup water

Cut ribs into serving-size pieces; place in a 13- x 9- x 2-inch baking pan. Place a slice of lemon on each rib. Bake at 425° for 30 minutes.

Combine remaining ingredients; mix well. Spoon over ribs. Reduce heat to 350°; bake an additional 1½ hours or until tender, basting occasionally. Yield: 2 servings. *Lorraine Simpler, Selbyville, Delaware.*

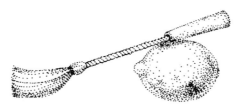

APPLE BARBECUED RIBS

5 to 6 pounds spareribs
4 quarts water
½ cup chopped onion
¼ cup vegetable oil
½ cup catsup
⅓ cup chopped parsley
2 tablespoons honey
2 tablespoons lemon juice
1 tablespoon Worcestershire sauce
1 teaspoon salt
1 teaspoon prepared mustard
½ teaspoon ground ginger
¼ teaspoon pepper
1 clove garlic, minced
1 (16-ounce) can applesauce

Cut ribs into serving-size pieces; place in a large Dutch oven. Add water; cover, and simmer 30 minutes.

Sauté onion in hot oil until tender. Add next 11 ingredients; simmer 15 minutes.

Place spareribs on grill over slow coals. Grill about 40 minutes, turning frequently. Brush with sauce, and cook an additional 20 minutes, basting and turning frequently. Baste with remaining sauce before serving. Yield: 4 to 6 servings. *Margaret Cotton, Franklin, Virginia.*

SMOKY BARBECUED RIBS

3 pounds spareribs
1 (3½-ounce) bottle liquid smoke
1 cup catsup
¼ cup Worcestershire sauce
1 cup water
2½ tablespoons lemon juice
1 teaspoon salt
1 teaspoon chili powder
1 teaspoon celery seeds

Cut ribs into serving-size pieces; place in a 13- × 9- × 2-inch baking pan. Brush liquid smoke over each piece. Bake at 425° for 30 minutes.

Combine remaining ingredients; pour over ribs. Bake at 350° about 1 hour, turning and basting every 20 minutes. Yield: 2 to 3 servings.

Make-Ahead Salads Highlight The Menu

Round out your luncheon menus with one of these refreshing vegetable salads. All three can be made ahead and chilled until the last minute, leaving you time to enjoy with your guests.

CREAMY PEA SALAD

1 (10-ounce) package frozen green peas, thawed
¼ cup chopped onion
¼ cup chopped celery
¼ teaspoon salt
⅛ teaspoon pepper
⅛ teaspoon whole basil leaves
½ cup commercial sour cream
9 slices bacon, cooked and crumbled
½ cup cashews, coarsely chopped
Lettuce leaves

Combine first 7 ingredients, stirring gently. Chill 3 to 4 hours. Stir in bacon and cashews; serve on lettuce leaves. Yield: 4 servings. *Patsy Hull, Montgomery, Alabama.*

Tip: After using a gas barbecue grill, turn the burner up to high for about 10 minutes to burn off residue on the rack.

BLACK-EYED PEA SALAD

2 (15-ounce) cans black-eyed peas,
   drained
½ cup chopped red onion
½ cup chopped green pepper
½ clove garlic
¼ cup vinegar
¼ cup sugar
¼ cup vegetable oil
½ teaspoon salt
Dash of pepper
Dash of hot sauce

Combine first 4 ingredients; toss
lightly. Combine remaining ingredients;
mix well and pour over pea mixture.
Cover and refrigerate at least 12 hours.
Remove garlic before serving. Yield: 6
to 8 servings.   *Alice Zunker,*
San Antonio, Texas.

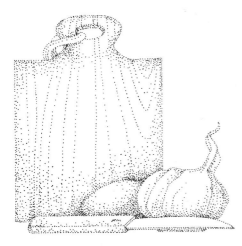

SPINACH AND MUSHROOM SALAD

1 pound fresh spinach, torn
⅔ cup sliced fresh mushrooms
6 slices bacon, cooked and crumbled
2 hard-cooked eggs, chopped
Mustard Dressing

Combine spinach, mushrooms, bacon,
and eggs in a large salad bowl. Serve
with Mustard Dressing. Yield: about 6
servings.

Mustard Dressing:

2 tablespoons Dijon mustard
¼ cup vegetable oil
1 egg, slightly beaten
2 tablespoons lemon juice
1 tablespoon grated Parmesan cheese
1 teaspoon sugar
1 teaspoon Worcestershire sauce
½ teaspoon salt
Dash of pepper

Combine all ingredients; mix well.
Yield: about ⅔ cup. *H. Joyce Delong,*
Annandale, Virginia.

Steps To A Perfect Caesar Salad

Many great recipes have been created
by sheer accident, and such is the case
with Caesar salad. The story goes that
Caesar Cardini, a well-known restaura-
teur in Mexico, was overwhelmed with
guests one holiday weekend. By Sun-
day, only a few crates of romaine, several dozen eggs, Parmesan cheese, some
lemons, and dry bread were left. But
instead of closing shop, Caesar de-
lighted the diners with a new salad prepared from the rather limited
ingredients he had on hand.

He added a dressing of garlic-flavored
salad oil, wine vinegar, fresh lemon
juice, and seasonings to the romaine.
Then he tossed in a coddled egg to bind
the ingredients together, and sprinkled
the salad with grated Parmesan cheese.
The final touch was the bread, seasoned
and cubed for croutons.

To add a special touch to the im-
promptu creation, Caesar had his wait-
ers prepare the salad at the diners'
tables. And therein lies the secret to the
delightfully fresh taste of Caesar salad:
The ingredients are never combined in
advance.

With the recipe that follows and the
step-by-step instructions shown in the
photographs, you can make a Caesar
salad as spectacular as the original.

CAESAR SALAD

1 cup olive oil
3 cloves garlic, peeled and halved
1 large head romaine
3 (¾-inch-thick) slices French bread
2 tablespoons grated Parmesan cheese
1 egg
3 tablespoons red wine vinegar
1 teaspoon Worcestershire sauce
¾ teaspoon salt
¼ teaspoon dry mustard
1 lemon, halved
Freshly ground pepper
¼ cup grated Parmesan cheese
½ (2-ounce) can anchovy fillets (optional)

Combine olive oil and garlic in a jar
with a tight-fitting lid. Chill several
hours or overnight.

Wash romaine under cold, running
water. Trim core, and separate stalk
into leaves; discard wilted or discolored
portions. Shake leaves well to remove
moisture, or dry on paper towels. Place
romaine in a large plastic bag; chill at
least 2 hours or overnight.

Brush both sides of bread slices with
garlic-olive oil mixture, and cut into ¾-
inch cubes. Place on a baking sheet,
and bake at 350° for 15 minutes or until
croutons are dry and crisp. Place in a
bowl, and toss with 2 tablespoons Parmesan cheese. Let croutons cool; then
store in an airtight container.

Pour water to a depth of 2 inches into
a medium saucepan; bring water to a
rapid boil, and turn off heat. Carefully
lower egg into water, using a slotted
spoon; let stand 1 minute. Remove egg
from water, and set aside to cool.

Discard garlic from olive oil mixture
in jar. Add vinegar, Worcestershire
sauce, salt, and dry mustard to jar.
Shake dressing well.

Cut coarse ribs from large leaves of
romaine; tear leaves into bite-size
pieces, and place in a large salad bowl.
Shake dressing well, and pour over romaine; toss lightly until well coated.

Break coddled egg over romaine;
then squeeze on juice from lemon
halves. Grind a generous amount of
pepper over salad, and sprinkle with ¼
cup Parmesan. Toss lightly. Top with
croutons; garnish with anchovies, if desired. Yield: 6 servings.

*Step 1—Wash romaine under cold, running
water. Trim core, and separate stalk into
leaves; discard wilted or discolored portions.
Shake leaves to remove moisture, or dry on
paper towels. Combine olive oil and garlic
in jar with tight lid. Chill romaine and olive
oil mixture.*

Step 2—Brush both sides of bread slices with garlic-olive oil mixture, and cut into ¾-inch cubes. Bake croutons at 350° until brown and crisp; toss with Parmesan cheese.

Step 3—Bring water to a rapid boil, and turn off heat; carefully lower egg into water, using a slotted spoon. Let stand 1 minute; remove from water, and set aside to cool.

Step 4—Remove garlic from olive oil mixture. Add vinegar, Worcestershire sauce, salt, and dry mustard to jar. Shake dressing well.

Step 5—Tear romaine into bite-size pieces; add dressing, tossing lightly. Break coddled egg over romaine; then squeeze on juice from lemon halves. Grind pepper over salad, and sprinkle with Parmesan cheese. Toss lightly, and top with croutons.

Caesar salad is a fresh-tasting combination of romaine, coddled egg, lemon juice, and Parmesan tossed with a garlic-flavored dressing. Crisp croutons are the final touch, and you can garnish with anchovies if you wish.

Bake The Potatoes In A Casserole

There's more than one way to enjoy baked potatoes—and that means baking them in a bubbly casserole layered with cheese and other ingredients. That's what you do to Potatoes Gourmet, which also calls for sour cream and green onions, and Two-Cheese Potatoes, made with cottage cheese and Cheddar cheese.

POTATO-BROCCOLI-CHEESE BAKE

2 tablespoons butter or margarine
2 tablespoons all-purpose flour
2 cups milk
1 (3-ounce) package cream cheese, cubed
½ cup shredded Swiss cheese
1 teaspoon salt
⅛ teaspoon ground nutmeg
⅛ teaspoon pepper
1 (16-ounce) package frozen shredded hash brown potatoes, thawed
1 (10-ounce) package frozen chopped broccoli, cooked and drained
¼ cup dry breadcrumbs
1 tablespoon melted butter or margarine

Melt 2 tablespoons butter in a heavy Dutch oven over low heat; add flour and cook 1 minute, stirring constantly. Gradually add milk; cook over medium heat, stirring constantly, until thickened and bubbly. Add cream cheese, Swiss cheese, salt, nutmeg, and pepper; cook over low heat, stirring constantly, until cheese melts. Add potatoes, and stir well.

Spoon one-half of potato mixture into a lightly greased 9-inch square baking dish; spread broccoli evenly over potatoes. Spoon remaining potatoes over broccoli layer. Cover and bake at 350° for 35 minutes.

Combine breadcrumbs and 1 tablespoon melted butter, stirring to coat breadcrumbs; sprinkle over casserole. Bake, uncovered, an additional 10 to 15 minutes. Yield: 8 servings.
Opal M. Rogers,
Tempe, Arizona.

Tip: When a sauce curdles, remove pan from heat and plunge into a pan of cold water to stop cooking process. Beat sauce vigorously or pour into a blender and beat.

OLIVE POTATOES

¾ cup evaporated milk
¾ cup water
3 tablespoons butter or margarine
3 tablespoons all-purpose flour
4 ounces sharp Cheddar cheese, diced
½ teaspoon salt
Dash of pepper
4 cups diced cooked potatoes
½ cup sliced ripe olives
½ cup soft breadcrumbs
2 tablespoons melted butter or margarine

Combine milk and water; stir well, and set aside.

Melt 3 tablespoons butter in a heavy saucepan over low heat; add flour and cook 1 minute, stirring constantly. Gradually add milk mixture. Add cheese and cook over medium heat, stirring constantly, until thickened and bubbly. Stir in salt and pepper.

Combine potatoes and olives; spoon into a lightly greased deep 1½-quart casserole. Pour cheese sauce over the potatoes.

Combine breadcrumbs and 2 tablespoons melted butter, stirring to coat breadcrumbs; sprinkle evenly over casserole. Bake at 350° for 35 minutes or until breadcrumbs are golden. Yield 8 servings.
Mrs. Bill Duke,
Corpus Christi, Texas.

POTATOES GOURMET

6 medium potatoes
¼ cup melted butter or margarine
2 cups (8 ounces) shredded Cheddar cheese
1 (8-ounce) carton commercial sour cream
3 green onions, chopped
1 teaspoon salt
¼ teaspoon pepper
2 tablespoons butter or margarine

Cover potatoes with salted water, and bring to a boil; reduce heat, and cook about 30 minutes or until tender. Cool slightly. Peel and coarsely shred potatoes; set aside.

Combine ¼ cup melted butter and cheese in a heavy saucepan; cook over low heat, stirring constantly, until cheese is partially melted.

Combine potatoes, cheese mixture, sour cream, onion, salt, and pepper; stir well. Spoon potato mixture into a greased 2-quart shallow casserole; dot with 2 tablespoons butter. Cover and bake at 300° for 25 minutes. Yield: 6 to 8 servings.
Mrs. Bobby Greever,
Mountain City, Tennessee.

TWO-CHEESE POTATOES

6 medium potatoes
2 cups small-curd cottage cheese
1 cup commercial sour cream
2 tablespoons finely chopped onion
2 tablespoons finely chopped fresh parsley
1 to 2 teaspoons dried dillweed
1½ teaspoons salt
½ cup shredded Cheddar cheese

Cover potatoes with salted water, and bring to a boil; reduce heat, and cook about 30 minutes or until tender. Cool slightly. Peel and thinly slice potatoes; place in a large bowl.

Combine next 6 ingredients; add to potatoes, stirring gently. Spoon potato mixture into a lightly greased 1½-quart casserole; sprinkle casserole with shredded cheese. Bake at 350° for 30 to 40 minutes or until bubbly. Yield: 6 to 8 servings.
Irene Haverland,
Deepwater, Missouri.

EASY POTATO CASSEROLE

1 (32-ounce) package frozen shredded hash brown potatoes, thawed
1 medium onion, chopped
½ cup chopped green pepper
1 (10¾-ounce) can cream of potato soup, undiluted
1 (10¾-ounce) can cream of celery soup, undiluted
1 (8-ounce) carton commercial sour cream
½ teaspoon salt
⅛ teaspoon pepper
1 cup (4 ounces) shredded Monterey Jack cheese

Combine all ingredients except cheese; stir well. Spoon potato mixture into a greased shallow 2-quart casserole. Bake at 325° for 1 hour and 15 minutes. Sprinkle with cheese, and bake an additional 15 minutes. Yield: 8 servings.
Diana Curtis,
Albuquerque, New Mexico.

A Menu Made For Two

Here's a delightful menu that's proportioned just right to serve two.

The main dish is Cheesy Chicken Skillet, a quick and appealing entrée that makes four portions; freeze two for another meal. Rounding out the menu are special salad, vegetable, and rice dishes. And for a spectacular finish—flaming Bananas Foster for Two.

CHEESY CHICKEN SKILLET

2 whole chicken breasts, split
2 tablespoons melted butter or margarine
1 (11-ounce) can Cheddar cheese soup, undiluted
¼ cup water
2 medium potatoes, peeled and quartered
2 stalks celery, cut into 2-inch slices
½ cup sliced carrots
1 bay leaf
¼ teaspoon poultry seasoning

Brown chicken on both sides in butter; add remaining ingredients to skillet. Bring to a boil; cover and simmer 30 minutes, stirring occasionally. Remove bay leaf.

For 2 servings, serve 2 chicken pieces and half the sauce immediately.

To freeze remainder, line a 1-quart casserole with aluminum foil; spoon remaining mixture into prepared dish.

Wrap foil securely around mixture, and place in freezer. After mixture is frozen, remove from dish and return the wrapped portion to freezer.

To serve, unwrap mixture; return to a 1-quart casserole dish, and thaw in refrigerator. When thawed, bake at 350° for 30 to 35 minutes or until bubbly. Yield: 4 servings. *Mrs. Bruce Fowler, Woodruff, South Carolina.*

MIXED VEGETABLE SALAD

1 cup sliced cauliflower flowerets
½ cup shredded carrots
½ cup chopped celery
1 tablespoon minced green pepper
¼ cup mayonnaise
2 tablespoons milk
1 teaspoon vinegar
1 teaspoon frozen or dried chives
¼ teaspoon salt
Dash of pepper
Lettuce leaves (optional)

Combine first 4 ingredients; chill. Combine remaining ingredients except lettuce leaves; mix well, using a wire whisk. Chill.

Pour dressing over vegetables; toss well. Serve on lettuce leaves, if desired. Yield: 2 servings. *Mrs. R. Weisman, Kingsville, Texas.*

HONEY-GLAZED CARROTS

5 medium carrots, peeled
⅓ cup water
¼ teaspoon salt
2 tablespoons honey
2 teaspoons lemon juice
¼ teaspoon ground cinnamon

Cut carrots into ½-inch slices. Combine carrots, water, and salt in a small saucepan; cook until crisp-tender. Drain.

Combine carrots, honey, lemon juice, and ground cinnamon in a small saucepan; cook over medium heat, stirring gently, until carrots are glazed (about 5 minutes). Yield: 2 servings. *Mrs. James Tuthill, Virginia Beach, Virginia.*

BACON FRIED RICE

3 slices bacon
½ cup chopped onion
1 egg, beaten
1½ to 2 cups cooked rice

Fry bacon in a 10-inch skillet until crisp; remove from pan and drain well, reserving 1 tablespoon bacon drippings. Crumble bacon, and set aside.

Sauté onion in bacon drippings over low heat until tender. Add egg and scramble until slightly set. Stir in cooked rice and bacon; heat thoroughly. Yield: 2 servings. *Peggy S. Barnes, Richardson, Texas.*

BANANAS FOSTER FOR TWO

2 tablespoons butter
3 tablespoons brown sugar
⅛ teaspoon ground cinnamon
1 banana, peeled, halved, and sliced lengthwise
1 tablespoon lemon juice
¼ cup rum
2 tablespoons banana-flavored liqueur
Vanilla ice cream

Melt butter in a chafing dish or small skillet. Add sugar and cinnamon; cook syrup over medium heat until bubbly. Add bananas and lemon juice; heat 3 to 4 minutes, basting constantly with syrup.

Combine rum and liqueur in a small long-handled pan; heat just until warm. Ignite, and pour over bananas. Baste bananas with sauce until flames die down. Serve immediately over ice cream. Yield: 2 servings. *Mrs. J. W. Waits, Shreveport, Louisiana.*

Flavor The Rolls With Honey

Traditional dinner rolls take a flavorful twist in this recipe. Add a hint of honey to the basic roll dough, and we think you'll like the combination.

Tender and moist right from the oven, these rolls will retain their freshness in an airtight container in the refrigerator for several days.

SUPER HONEY ROLLS

2 packages dry yeast
1 cup warm water (105° to 115°)
About 3¾ to 4 cups all-purpose flour, divided
1 teaspoon salt
½ cup butter or margarine, melted
1 egg, beaten
3 tablespoons honey
2 tablespoons butter or margarine, melted

Dissolve yeast in water in a large mixing bowl. Combine 2½ cups flour and salt; add to yeast mixture, stirring well. Add ½ cup butter, egg, and honey; stir well. Add enough flour to form a stiff dough. Place in a well-greased bowl, turning to grease top. Cover and let rise in a warm place (85°), free from drafts, until doubled in bulk (about 1 hour).

Punch dough down; turn dough out on a lightly floured surface, and turn to coat with flour. Shape into ¾-inch balls; place 3 balls in each cup of well-greased muffin pans. Cover and let rise in a warm place 20 to 25 minutes. Brush tops of rolls with 2 tablespoons butter. Bake at 400° for 10 to 12 minutes or until golden brown. Yield: 2 dozen rolls. *Mrs. Wilda Bell, Chattanooga, Tennessee.*

Green Beans Take On A New Look

Fresh green beans are delicious cooked Southern-style—tossed with butter or flavored with ham hocks. But when simmered with tomatoes, baked with a sour cream or cheese sauce, or tossed with a variety of seasonings, fresh green beans take on a whole new taste.

Be sure to use fresh green beans as soon as possible, and remember that 1 pound will yield 3 cups of cooked beans.

SPANISH GREEN BEANS

1 pound fresh green beans
1 onion, chopped
1 clove garlic, minced
2 tablespoons butter or margarine, melted
1½ teaspoons salt
¼ teaspoon pepper
5 tomatoes, diced
2 green peppers, chopped

Remove strings from green beans; cut beans into 1½-inch pieces, and wash thoroughly. Drain and set aside.

Sauté onion and garlic in butter until tender. Add beans, salt, and pepper; cover and continue to cook over low heat for 10 minutes, stirring frequently. Stir in tomatoes and green pepper. Cover and simmer 25 to 30 minutes or until beans are tender, stirring frequently. Yield: 4 to 6 servings.
Pauline Snider,
Fort Worth, Texas.

DILLY GREEN BEANS

2 hard-cooked eggs
1½ pounds fresh green beans
1 cup chopped onion
¼ cup butter or margarine, melted
1½ teaspoons salt
1½ teaspoons dillseeds
Dash of pepper

Cut hard-cooked eggs in half and remove yolk. Chop egg whites and sieve egg yolks; set aside.

Remove strings from beans; cut beans into 2-inch pieces, and wash thoroughly. Cook beans, covered, in lightly salted water until tender (about 20 to 25 minutes); drain well and set aside.

Sauté onion in butter until tender. Add green beans and seasonings, tossing lightly. Cook over medium heat until heated thoroughly. Remove from heat; garnish with chopped egg whites and sieved egg yolks before serving. Yield: 4 to 6 servings.
Mrs. C. D. Marshall,
Culpeper, Virginia.

GREEN BEANS IN SOUR CREAM

2 pounds fresh green beans
1 medium onion, thinly sliced
2 tablespoons finely chopped parsley
2 tablespoons butter or margarine, melted
2 tablespoons all-purpose flour
2 teaspoons grated lemon rind
1 teaspoon salt
¼ teaspoon pepper
1 cup commercial sour cream
1 cup buttered breadcrumbs

Remove strings from green beans; cut beans into 1½-inch pieces, and wash thoroughly. Cook beans, covered, in lightly salted water until tender (about 20 to 25 minutes); drain and set aside.

Sauté onion and parsley in butter; reduce heat and add flour, lemon rind, salt, and pepper. Cook, stirring, until bubbly. Add sour cream, and cook just until heated thoroughly.

Combine sour cream mixture and beans; stir well. Spoon beans into a greased 2-quart casserole. Sprinkle breadcrumbs over beans. Bake at 350° for 20 minutes. Yield: 6 to 8 servings.
Sandra Moore,
Bowling Green, Kentucky.

GREEN BEANS AU GRATIN

1 pound fresh green beans
¼ cup butter or margarine
¼ cup all-purpose flour
1 teaspoon salt
⅛ teaspoon dry mustard
1½ cups milk
½ cup shredded Swiss cheese
1½ tablespoons grated Parmesan cheese
Paprika
½ cup slivered almonds

Remove strings from green beans; cut beans into 1½-inch pieces, and wash thoroughly. Cook beans, covered, in lightly salted water until tender (about 20 to 25 minutes); drain and set aside.

Melt butter in a heavy saucepan over low heat. Blend in flour, salt, and mustard; cook 1 minute, stirring constantly. Gradually add milk; cook over medium heat, stirring, until thickened and bubbly. Stir in Swiss cheese; cook over low heat until cheese is melted.

Combine cheese sauce and beans; spoon into a lightly greased 1½-quart casserole. Sprinkle with Parmesan cheese and paprika.

Bake at 350° for 20 minutes. Top with almonds, and bake 5 to 10 minutes or until bubbly. Yield: 6 servings.
Sue West,
Sulphur Springs, Texas.

Make This Cake For Morning

For a quick morning sweet, good with coffee or for brunch, try this coffee cake. A fig mixture, made from crumbled fig cookies, is layered between the batter and sprinkled on top in a lattice fashion.

EASY FIG COFFEE CAKE

½ cup firmly packed brown sugar
2 tablespoons butter or margarine, softened
½ teaspoon ground cinnamon
10 fig-filled bar cookies, crumbled
2 eggs
¾ cup sugar
⅓ cup melted butter or margarine
1½ cups all-purpose flour
1½ teaspoons baking powder
½ teaspoon salt
½ cup milk
1 teaspoon vanilla extract

Combine brown sugar, 2 tablespoons butter, cinnamon, and crumbled fig cookies; mix well, and set aside.

Beat eggs in a large mixing bowl until frothy; add sugar and melted butter. Beat well. Combine flour, baking powder, and salt; gradually add flour mixture to egg mixture alternately with milk, mixing well. Stir in vanilla.

Pour half of batter into a greased and floured 8-inch square pan; top with half of fig mixture. Pour remainder of batter over fig layer. Sprinkle remaining fig mixture on top in a lattice fashion. Bake at 350° for 40 to 45 minutes or until cake tests done. Yield: 9 servings.
Jackie Denisco,
Indiantown, Florida.

June

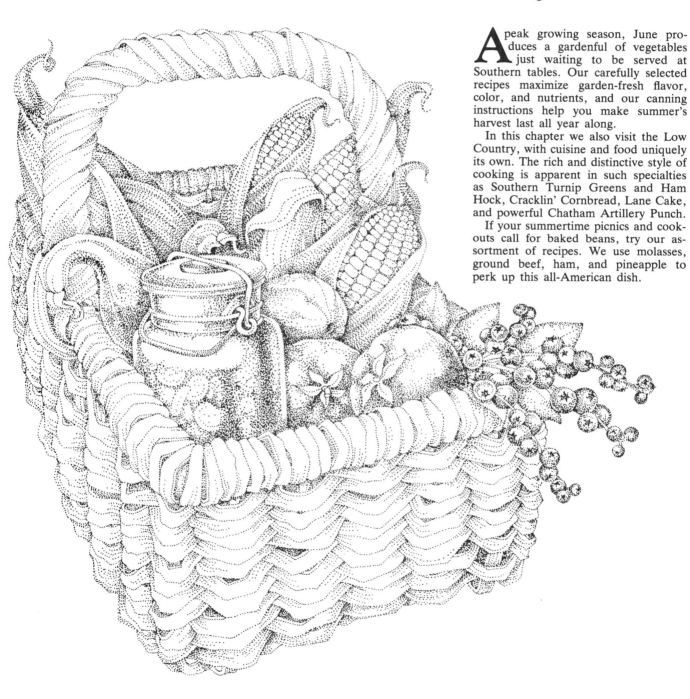

A peak growing season, June produces a gardenful of vegetables just waiting to be served at Southern tables. Our carefully selected recipes maximize garden-fresh flavor, color, and nutrients, and our canning instructions help you make summer's harvest last all year along.

In this chapter we also visit the Low Country, with cuisine and food uniquely its own. The rich and distinctive style of cooking is apparent in such specialties as Southern Turnip Greens and Ham Hock, Cracklin' Cornbread, Lane Cake, and powerful Chatham Artillery Punch.

If your summertime picnics and cookouts call for baked beans, try our assortment of recipes. We use molasses, ground beef, ham, and pineapple to perk up this all-American dish.

The Low Country Way With Food

Miles of marshlands, hundreds of sea islands, and a winding shoreline are main ingredients of the rich coastal stew known as the Low Country. This vast area, encompassing the eastern reaches of South Carolina and Georgia, is filled with picturesque coastal towns, sprawling plantations, broad beaches, and a rich heritage that comes right down to the food on your plate.

Towering oaks weighted with Spanish moss line narrow highways, and water lies everywhere teeming with seafood ready for the taking. And beyond what you can see comes a distinctive flavor combining native Indian, English, and African influence. This tidal wash of the past can be found in the architecture, dialect, social customs, and, thankfully for our taste buds, the food.

Perhaps it's the great availability of seafood or the fresh vegetables and rice grown in the marshlands that give the Low Country its unique cultivation of flavors, but it's more than just that. Margaret DeBolt, author of *Savannah Sampler Cookbook*, says, "The food of this area is a reflection of our heritage; it's so much more than food; it's a way of life."

Benne seed cakes and cookies are as popular today as when first baked by plantation cooks, and so are Low Country picnics featuring large pots of seafood boiled with selected seasonings. Not only do the foods of this area reflect a varied heritage, but they also capture the traditions that are so much a part of the Old South.

Rice was one of the first sources of great economic wealth for this area. Plantation homes built among the low-lying coastal areas, so perfect for rice cultivation, reflect this era of affluence. Many popular Southern favorites, such as Hoppin' John, are a result of the rice boom. But red rice, a delicately seasoned tomato-flavored rice, belongs solely to the Low Country. Ginny Lentz of Charleston comments, "In the Low Country we eat tomatoes in every way imaginable." Ginny, a native of Columbia, South Carolina, moved to this area about seven years ago and is caught up in the lore and beauty of it all. "I moved to the coast, got salt water in my veins, and just can't leave. I love the marshlands, and I love the seafood." Ginny's love for seafood led to the writing of a cookbook featuring seafood specialties of the Low Country.

An Emphasis on Seafood

Beaufort, South Carolina, a charming town, is filled with classic historical homes from the days when rice, indigo, and cotton flourished. Today, shrimp boats trawl the sounds and coastal waters for a thriving seafood industry. The seafood served in this area is fresh from the ocean. Popular local seafood restaurants offer the finest in Low Country seafood: she-crab soup, boiled shrimp, and oyster stew.

One regional distinction of Low Country cooking is that seafood is enjoyed any time of day—even at breakfast. Tiny shrimp are often served in a spicy stew that's spooned over grits. Crispy Fried Crab Cakes are also a breakfast specialty. And don't forget the ham, eggs, and Southern Cracklin' Cornbread.

The emphasis on fish and seafood also varies according to season. Informal outdoor gatherings range from a wintertime oyster roast to a summertime Low Country seafood boil. The warm ocean breeze stirs up an appetite for a pot of fresh seafood served with Savannah Red Rice, Old-Fashioned Coleslaw, Buttermilk Corn Sticks, and ice-cold watermelon.

"I think of the friendliness and the graciousness of the Old South when I think of Low Country entertaining," comments Margaret DeBolt. "There are just so many possibilities for outdoor gatherings, from the informal seafood feasts and plantation barbecues to the more elegant courtyard receptions."

Punch That Packs a Punch

Savannah has traditionally been known for its warm hospitality and social events. The beautiful formal gardens of the historic townhouses and city squares of Savannah beckon guests into a dream world. But if you're served some of the famous Chatham Artillery Punch, you'll soon be shocked back to reality. This beverage, named for the Chatham Artillery, Georgia's oldest military organization, has been served for generations. It is said that military functions seemed to liven up when the punch was served. The original recipe calls for 2 gallons wine, 2 gallons rum, and 1 gallon each of brandy, gin, and rye added to a base of green tea, brown sugar, and fruit juices. Ten quarts of champagne were added at serving time to accommodate about 200 people. We offer a variation of the original with a warning—"serve with caution."

Benne seeds or sesame seeds were first brought to this area by the slaves.

Believed to hold the secret to health and good luck, the seeds were planted near the slave quarters of the early plantations. They have traditionally been used in cakes, cookies, and candies since the days of early plantation cooks.

Desserts from the Low Country portray the elegance and richness of its sophisticated style. Savannah Trifle is a luscious version made with pound cake, a sherry flavored custard, and whipped cream. Lane Cake is made in three layers with a rich, buttery, raisin filling, then covered in a creamy sweet frosting.

The intriguing mixture of tradition and varied heritage continues to flavor Low Country cooking today. Enjoy its special taste with our recipes.

Low Country Fare: Rich In Tradition And Flavor

Tradition and a varied heritage give the Low Country a flavor of its own and a cuisine of its own. These recipes offer a taste of that rich and distinctive style of cooking.

■ Sample the best of Low Country flavor with this hearty breakfast:

Fresh Melon
Shrimp Stew and Grits
Country Ham   Scrambled Eggs
Crispy Fried Crab Cakes
Southern Cracklin' Cornbread

SHRIMP STEW AND GRITS

1½ cups chopped celery
¾ cup chopped green pepper
1 cup chopped onion
2 tablespoons melted butter or margarine
3 pounds small shrimp, peeled and deveined
2 tablespoons cornstarch
3 tablespoons Worcestershire sauce
1 teaspoon salt
½ to 1 teaspoon pepper
1 teaspoon seafood seasoning
1 cup water
1 cup chopped radishes
Hot cooked grits

Sauté celery, green pepper, and onion in butter until just tender. Add shrimp, cornstarch, Worcestershire sauce, salt, pepper, and seafood seasoning; stir gently. Add water; cook over medium heat, stirring constantly, until thickened. Reduce heat and simmer 15 to 20 minutes, stirring occasionally. Add radishes; heat thoroughly. Serve over hot cooked grits. Yield: 10 to 12 servings.

■ Fresh seafood and vegetables are popular fare for a Low Country picnic. This menu includes other area favorites:

Low Country Seafood Boil
Savannah Red Rice
Southern Turnip Greens and Ham Hock
Old-Fashioned Coleslaw   Rosy Chutney
Buttermilk Corn Sticks
Old-South Carrot Cake   Watermelon
Iced Tea

This will expose hard, semi-transparent membrane covering the edible crabmeat. On each half, use a knife to remove the membrane covering the meat; or slice lengthwise through each half without removing membrane. Large chunks of meat will be exposed; remove with knife or fingers. Crack the claws with a mallet, nutcracker, or knife handle, and remove meat. Yield: 8 to 12 servings.

CRISPY FRIED CRAB CAKES

1 cup chopped onion
1 cup chopped celery
½ cup chopped green pepper
¼ cup melted butter or margarine
½ pound fresh crabmeat, drained and flaked
1 (8-ounce) package herb-seasoned stuffing mix
½ cup self-rising flour
3 eggs, well beaten
2 tablespoons vinegar
1 teaspoon salt
1 teaspoon dry mustard
2 to 3 teaspoons pepper
2 cups vegetable oil

Sauté onion, celery, and green pepper in butter until vegetables are tender.

Combine all ingredients except vegetable oil, stirring well. Form into patties 3 inches in diameter and ½ inch thick. Fry in hot oil (360°) until golden brown, turning once. Drain on paper towels. Yield: 8 to 10 servings.

SOUTHERN CRACKLIN' CORNBREAD

4 cups cornmeal
2 teaspoons soda
1½ teaspoons salt
4 eggs, beaten
4 cups buttermilk
⅓ cup bacon drippings
1 cup cracklings

Combine cornmeal, soda, and salt; stir in eggs and buttermilk. Heat bacon drippings in a 13- x 9- x 2-inch baking pan until very hot; add drippings and cracklings to batter, mixing well.

Pour batter into hot pan; bake at 450° for 25 minutes or until bread is golden. Cut into squares. Yield: 15 to 20 servings.

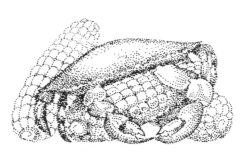

LOW COUNTRY SEAFOOD BOIL

6 large potatoes, halved
4 large sweet onions, halved
1 tablespoon salt
1 dozen live blue crabs
1 (3-ounce) package crab boil
3 whole buds garlic
4 to 6 lemons, halved
1 cup vinegar
1 dozen ears fresh corn
5 pounds unpeeled shrimp
Melted butter
Cocktail sauce

Fill a 5- or 6-gallon pot about two-thirds full of water; bring water to a boil. Add potatoes, onions, and salt; cover and cook over high heat 20 minutes. Stir in crabs, crab boil, garlic, lemons, and vinegar; cook an additional 10 minutes. Reduce heat, and add corn; simmer 5 minutes. Remove from heat, and add shrimp; let stand in water 5 minutes.

Drain off water; arrange crab, shrimp, ears of corn, and potatoes on serving platter. Serve with melted butter and cocktail sauce.

To remove meat from crab, pry off apron flap on underside of crab with thumb or knife. Lift off top shell, using thumb or knife. Then break off large claws, and set aside for eating later. Peel off the spongy substance on each side of crab body. Remove digestive organs and other parts in center body.

SAVANNAH RED RICE

¾ cup diced onion
⅓ to ½ cup diced green pepper
2 tablespoons vegetable oil
1½ pounds cooked ham, finely chopped
2 (8-ounce) cans tomato sauce
2 cups water
2 tablespoons sugar
½ teaspoon salt
2 cups uncooked regular rice

Sauté onion and green pepper in oil in a Dutch oven until tender. Stir in ham; cook over medium heat about 3 minutes.

Add tomato sauce, water, sugar, and salt; stir well. Bring mixture to a boil, and add rice. Reduce heat; cover and simmer 15 minutes.

Cut a circle of brown paper large enough to fit over top of Dutch oven, allowing 2-inch overlap around edge of pot. Remove lid from Dutch oven, and place paper over pot. Replace lid over paper; continue to simmer 15 to 20 minutes. Yield: 8 to 10 servings.

SOUTHERN TURNIP GREENS AND HAM HOCK

About 1¾ pounds ham hock
2 quarts water
2 bunches (about 10 pounds) turnip greens with roots
1 teaspoon salt
1 tablespoon sugar

Wash ham hocks and place in an 8-quart Dutch oven; add water, and bring to a boil. Reduce heat, and simmer 30 to 45 minutes or until meat is tender.

Pick and wash turnip greens. Peel turnip roots; cut in half.

Add greens, roots, salt, and sugar to Dutch oven; bring to a boil. Reduce heat; cover and simmer about 30 to 45 minutes or until greens and roots are tender. Yield: 8 to 12 servings.

OLD-FASHIONED COLESLAW

10 cups shredded cabbage
2 cups shredded carrots
½ cup sweet pickle salad cubes
½ cup mayonnaise or salad dressing
½ teaspoon salt
½ teaspoon sugar
½ teaspoon dry mustard
½ teaspoon pepper

Combine cabbage, carrots, and pickles; set aside.

Combine remaining ingredients; mix well. Spoon over cabbage mixture, and toss gently. Chill until serving time. Yield: 12 to 15 servings.

ROSY CHUTNEY

1 (3-inch) cinnamon stick, broken into pieces
2 tablespoons mustard seeds
10 whole cloves
1½ cups red wine vinegar
2¾ cups sugar
2 teaspoons salt
2 cups (about 2 large) peeled, seeded, and minced tomatoes
2 cups (about 1 large) unpeeled, minced, tart apple
1 cup minced onion
1 cup minced green pepper
1 cup minced celery

Tie spices in a cheesecloth bag. Place in a 6-quart saucepan. Add vinegar, sugar, and salt; bring to a rolling boil. Reduce heat, and simmer 10 to 15 minutes. Remove spice bag, and add remaining ingredients; return mixture to a boil. Reduce heat; simmer about 30 minutes, stirring constantly, until thick and clear. Cool. Place in a covered container, and refrigerate. Yield: 1 quart.

Tip: Milk cartons make splendid freezing containers for stocks, soups, etc. They also serve well for freezing fish, shrimp, or any foods that should be frozen in water.

BUTTERMILK CORN STICKS

1⅓ cups cornmeal
⅓ cup all-purpose flour
1 teaspoon baking powder
½ teaspoon soda
½ teaspoon salt
1 tablespoon sugar
1 cup buttermilk
1 egg, beaten
2 tablespoons melted shortening

Combine first 6 ingredients; stir in buttermilk and egg just until dry ingredients are moistened. Stir in shortening.

Place a well-greased cast-iron corn-stick pan in a 400° oven for 3 minutes or until hot. Remove pan from oven; spoon batter into pan, filling two-thirds full. Bake at 400° for 12 to 15 minutes or until lightly browned. Yield: 15 corn sticks.

OLD-SOUTH CARROT CAKE

2 cups all-purpose flour
2 cups sugar
1 teaspoon baking powder
¼ teaspoon soda
¼ teaspoon salt
1 teaspoon ground cinnamon
4 eggs
1 cup vegetable oil
2 cups grated carrots
Deluxe Cream Cheese Frosting

Combine dry ingredients. Stir gently; set aside. Combine eggs and oil, beating well. Fold in the dry ingredients and carrots.

Spoon batter into 3 greased and floured 9-inch cakepans; bake at 375° for 25 minutes or until cake tests done. Cake layers will be thin. Cool 10 minutes in pans; remove from pans, and cool completely. Spread Deluxe Cream Cheese Frosting between layers and on top and sides of cake. Yield: one 3-layer cake.

Deluxe Cream Cheese Frosting:

½ cup butter or margarine, softened
1 (8-ounce) package cream cheese, softened
1 (16-ounce) package powdered sugar
2 teaspoons vanilla extract
1 cup chopped pecans
1 cup flaked coconut

Combine butter and cream cheese; cream until light and fluffy. Add sugar and vanilla, mixing well. Stir in pecans and coconut. Yield: enough frosting for one 3-layer cake.

■ Wilkop's Whitehall Inn in Beaufort, South Carolina, shares a recipe for one of its seafood specialties.

CRAB-STUFFED FLOUNDER

¾ cup minced celery
½ cup minced onion
½ cup minced fresh parsley
¼ cup minced shallots
¼ cup minced green pepper
1 clove garlic, minced
½ cup melted butter or margarine
1 tablespoon all-purpose flour
½ cup milk
½ cup dry white wine
8 ounces fresh lump crabmeat
1¼ cups seasoned dry breadcrumbs
¼ teaspoon salt
Dash of pepper
6 (10-ounce) flounder fillets
Mornay Sauce
Paprika
Hot cooked mashed potatoes (optional)
Fresh minced parsley (optional)

Sauté celery, onion, parsley, shallots, green pepper, and garlic in butter in a large skillet over medium heat; cook until vegetables are tender. Add flour and cook 1 minute, stirring constantly. Gradually add milk and wine; cook over medium heat, stirring constantly, until slightly thickened. Remove mixture from heat; stir in crabmeat, breadcrumbs, salt, and pepper.

Place 3 fillets in a greased 15- x 10- x 1-inch jellyroll pan; spoon about 1 cup crabmeat stuffing on each fillet. Cut remaining fillets in half lengthwise; place a fillet half on either side of stuffed fillets in baking pan, pressing gently into stuffing mixture. Top each portion with Mornay Sauce; sprinkle with paprika. Bake at 425° for 15 to 20 minutes or until fish fillets flake easily when tested with a fork.

Pipe or spoon hot cooked mashed potatoes around each portion, if desired. Garnish with additional paprika and parsley, if desired. Cut each portion in half to serve. Yield: 6 servings.

Mornay Sauce:

¼ cup butter
¼ cup all-purpose flour
2 cups milk
½ teaspoon salt
⅛ teaspoon white pepper
2 egg yolks
1 tablespoon whipping cream
¼ cup shredded Swiss cheese

Melt butter in a heavy 2-quart saucepan over low heat; add flour and cook 1 minute, stirring constantly. Gradually add milk; cook over medium heat, stirring constantly, until thickened and bubbly. Stir in salt and pepper.

Beat egg yolks until thick and lemon colored; stir in cream. Stir some of hot mixture into yolks; add to remaining hot mixture, stirring constantly. Cook over medium heat, stirring constantly, until thickened (about 2 to 3 minutes). Add cheese; stir until melted. Remove from heat. Yield: about 2 cups.

■ A favorite appetizer throughout the Low Country area combines benne seeds with sharp cheese.

BENNE CHEESE BITES

½ cup benne seeds (sesame seeds)
4 cups (1 pound) shredded sharp Cheddar cheese
½ cup butter, softened
2 cups all-purpose flour
½ teaspoon salt
¼ teaspoon cayenne pepper

Spread benne seeds evenly in an 8-inch square baking pan. Bake at 350°, stirring occasionally, for 10 to 15 minutes or until seeds are golden.

Combine cheese and butter; mix well. Stir in benne seeds. Combine flour, salt, and cayenne pepper; add to creamed mixture, mixing well.

Divide dough in half; shape each half into an 8- x 1½-inch roll. Wrap each in waxed paper, and chill at least 2 hours.

Cut rolls into ¼-inch slices. Bake at 350° for 15 to 17 minutes. Yield: about 4½ dozen.

■ Our English heritage is evident in such delicacies as Savannah Trifle.

SAVANNAH TRIFLE

6 cups milk
1½ cups sugar
2 tablespoons cornstarch
6 eggs
½ cup cream sherry
1½ pounds sliced pound cake
2 cups whipping cream, whipped
Maraschino cherries

Scald milk in top of double boiler. Combine sugar and cornstarch, stirring well. Add eggs to sugar mixture; beat with an electric mixer until well blended. Stir some of hot milk into egg mixture; add to remaining hot milk in double boiler, stirring constantly. Cook, stirring constantly, until custard thickens and coats a metal spoon. Cool completely. Stir sherry into custard.

Place half of pound cake evenly in a 5-quart serving bowl. Pour half of custard over pound cake. Spread half of whipped cream over custard. Repeat layers. Garnish top of trifle with cherries. Yield: 12 to 14 servings.

■ Generation after generation continues to enjoy spectacular Lane Cake. This version of the original recipe was updated by the late Emma Rylander Law, a granddaughter of Emma Rylander Lane, developer of the cake.

LANE CAKE

1 cup butter or margarine, softened
2 cups sugar
3¼ cups sifted cake flour
2 teaspoons baking powder
Pinch of salt
1 cup milk
2 teaspoons vanilla extract
8 egg whites, stiffly beaten
Filling (recipe follows)
Frosting (recipe follows)

Cream butter; gradually add sugar, beating with electric mixer until light and fluffy. Combine dry ingredients; stir well. Add dry ingredients to creamed mixture alternately with milk, beating well after each addition. Stir in vanilla. Fold in egg whites.

Pour batter into 3 greased and floured 9-inch cakepans. Bake at 375° for 20 minutes or until cake tests done. Cool in pans 10 minutes; remove from pans, and cool completely.

Spread filling between layers; spread top and sides of cake with frosting. Yield: one 3-layer cake.

Filling:

8 large egg yolks
1 cup sugar
½ cup butter or margarine
1 cup golden raisins, finely chopped
⅓ cup bourbon or brandy
1 teaspoon vanilla extract

Combine egg yolks, sugar, and butter in a 2-quart saucepan. Cook over medium heat, stirring constantly, until thickened (about 20 minutes).

Remove from heat, and stir in remaining ingredients. Let cool before spreading on cake. Yield: enough filling for one 3-layer cake.

Frosting:

½ cup sugar
¼ cup light corn syrup
2 tablespoons water
⅛ teaspoon salt
2 egg whites
½ teaspoon vanilla extract

Combine sugar, corn syrup, water, and salt in a heavy saucepan. Cook over medium heat, stirring constantly, until mixture is clear. Cook, stirring frequently, until candy thermometer reaches 242°.

Beat egg whites until soft peaks form; continue to beat egg whites while slowly adding syrup mixture. Add vanilla; continue beating until stiff peaks form and frosting is thick enough to spread. Yield: enough for one 3-layer cake.

■ This variation of Savannah's most noted drink includes all the necessary ingredients in smaller amounts. Plan ahead because the stock needs to ferment for 2 to 6 weeks—the longer the better.

CHATHAM ARTILLERY PUNCH

1 (4-ounce) can gunpowder green tea
2 quarts cold water
Juice of 9 oranges
Juice of 9 lemons
1 (1-pound) package light brown sugar
½ cup firmly packed light brown sugar
2 (10-ounce) jars maraschino cherries, drained
2 (50.7-ounce) bottles Rhine or Catawba wine
1 quart light rum
1 quart rye whisky
1 quart gin
1 (25.4-ounce) bottle brandy
½ cup Benedictine
Champagne or club soda, chilled

Combine tea and water; let stand overnight. Stir fruit juices into tea; strain.

Combine tea and remaining ingredients except champagne in a 3-gallon crock or glass container. Cover lightly, and let stock ferment 2 to 6 weeks.

Strain stock; discard cherries and pour liquid into bottles. Chill as needed. At serving time, dilute each gallon chilled stock with 1 quart champagne and pour over ice. Yield: about 2½ gallons stock.

Cook Vegetables With A Light Touch

Southerners are known for their expertise in cooking fresh vegetables. Many favorites, such as green beans, are traditionally simmered for hours. While these are delicious, there are some excellent alternative cooking methods.

Three methods that give gentle treatment to vegetables are steaming, stir-frying, and microwaving. Since these methods require minimum amounts of liquid and a relatively short cooking period, the maximum amount of flavor, color, and nutrients will be preserved.

Steaming

Steaming vegetables noticeably enhances their vibrant color and reduces nutrient loss to a minimum. To steam, you will need a pot with a tight-fitting lid and a steaming rack. There are several styles of steaming pots on the market, some with multiple racks so more than one food can be steamed at a time. But you don't have to buy a complete steaming pot; you can purchase a flexible steaming rack to fit inside a pot or wok you already have on hand.

The amount of water needed depends on the type steaming utensil used. Usually about 1 inch of water is sufficient; just be sure the boiling water does not touch the rack. Arrange vegetables in the steaming rack, and place over water; cover, and let the water boil over medium-high heat. The cooking times will vary from about 10 minutes for delicate broccoli up to about 40 minutes for large whole potatoes. (With longer cooking times, check the water level, and add more as needed.)

Foods at the center of the steaming rack will cook more rapidly than at the outer edge. Therefore, vegetables with tough stalks should be arranged with the stalk toward the center. Splitting thick stalks will ensure that they will cook as rapidly as the tender buds.

Stir-Frying

Stir-fried vegetables are cooked only until they are crisp-tender, preserving their natural flavor, color, and food value. The vegetables are cooked with a small amount of oil over high heat in a wok or heavy skillet. They are stirred continuously to ensure even cooking. Because the temperature used is high, and the vegetables are left crunchy, stir-frying is a rapid cooking method.

Vegetables should be prepared completely—sliced or chopped—before you heat the wok. Slice less tender vegetables, such as celery, diagonally to expose the largest possible area to the heat. Use this same method for fibrous vegetables like celery.

When stir-frying a delicate vegetable, such as mushrooms, with a fibrous vegetable, cut the delicate vegetable into larger pieces or add it later to prevent it from overcooking. If some vegetables are cooking faster than others, push them up the sides of the wok to slow their cooking.

Microwaving

Because microwaved vegetables require little or no added moisture, they retain flavor and nutrients. Vegetables with a high water content will actually cook in their own juices, thereby enhancing their natural flavor. For example, young sweet corn on the cob may be wrapped in heavy-duty plastic wrap and microwaved without any added water.

Microwaves enter food at the outside edges, which causes the outer portions to cook faster than the center. Stir small, loose vegetables once or twice during microwaving to distribute heat. Arrange whole or halved vegetables in a ring, leaving the center open so microwaves can enter; rotate the dish part way through microwaving to promote even cooking. Thick, dense vegetables, such as potatoes and acorn squash, will continue to cook after the microwave cycle is completed. Allow about 5 minutes standing time and check for doneness. If microwaved until the center is tender, the edges will be overcooked.

The time required to microwave vegetables depends on the quantity and type vegetable cooked, and the wattage of your oven. Microwaving time increases with the amount of food cooked. Likewise, sturdier vegetables require more time than tender vegetables. The higher the wattage of the microwave, the faster it cooks. Check your manufacturer's directions for the wattage of your oven and approximate vegetable cooking times.

GARDEN MEDLEY SALAD

¾ pound fresh green beans
4 ears fresh corn
1 (8-ounce) package fresh mushrooms
½ pint cherry tomatoes
Leaf lettuce
Herb dressing (recipe follows)

Remove ends from green beans, and cut diagonally into 1-inch pieces; steam for 8 minutes or until they are crisp-tender. Plunge into cold water. Cut corn from cob; steam 5 minutes or until crisp-tender. Plunge into cold water.

Arrange green beans, corn, mushrooms, and tomatoes on six lettuce-lined salad plates. Serve with herb dressing. Yield: 6 servings.

Herb Dressing:

½ cup vegetable oil
¼ cup tarragon vinegar
1 tablespoon finely chopped green onion
1 teaspoon sugar
½ teaspoon dry mustard
⅛ teaspoon salt
¼ teaspoon dillweed

Combine all ingredients in a small jar; screw lid tightly, and shake well. Yield: about ¾ cup.

STEAMED BROCCOLI

1 (2-pound) bunch fresh broccoli
Water
Salt and pepper to taste
Pimiento strips

Trim off large leaves of broccoli. Remove tough ends of lower stalks, and wash broccoli thoroughly. Make lengthwise slits in thick stalks. Arrange broccoli in steaming rack with stalks to center of rack. Steam 10 to 15 minutes or to desired degree of doneness.

Season broccoli to taste with salt and pepper. Arrange broccoli on serving plate. Garnish with strips of pimiento. Yield: 4 to 5 servings.

MICROWAVED CORN ON THE COB

Remove shucks and silk from corn. Butter corn lightly; wrap in heavy-duty plastic wrap or waxed paper. Microwave on HIGH according to the following times: 1 ear, 2 to 3 minutes; 2 ears, 4 to 5 minutes; 3 ears, 6 to 7 minutes; 4 ears, 8 to 9 minutes.

STIR-FRIED SQUASH MEDLEY

3 tablespoons peanut oil
¾ pound zucchini, sliced
¾ pound yellow squash, sliced
½ cup chopped onion
1 clove garlic, crushed
1 cup diced tomatoes
1 tablespoon Worcestershire sauce
2 tablespoons tomato paste
1½ teaspoons salt

Pour oil around top of preheated wok, coating sides; allow to heat at medium high (325°) for 2 minutes. Add squash, onion, and garlic; stir-fry 2 minutes. Add remaining ingredients; simmer 8 to 10 minutes or until vegetables are crisp-tender, stirring occasionally. Yield: about 6 servings.

ITALIAN-STYLE ZUCCHINI

2 tablespoons peanut oil
½ cup chopped onion
4 medium zucchini, thinly sliced
1 (16-ounce) can stewed tomatoes
¼ teaspoon salt
⅛ teaspoon dried whole oregano leaves
2 tablespoons grated Parmesan cheese

Pour oil around top of preheated wok, coating sides; allow to heat at medium high (325°) for 2 minutes. Add onion and zucchini; stir-fry 3 minutes. Add tomatoes, salt, and oregano; simmer 6 to 8 minutes or until zucchini is crisp-tender, stirring occasionally. Remove to serving bowl, and sprinkle with Parmesan cheese. Yield: 4 to 6 servings.

STIR-FRIED MUSHROOMS WITH BACON

4 slices bacon, cut into ½-inch pieces
½ pound fresh mushrooms, sliced
¼ cup dry red wine

Preheat wok at medium high (325°); add bacon, and stir-fry 3 minutes or until bacon is crisp. Remove bacon with a slotted spoon, reserving drippings in wok. Add mushrooms; stir-fry 2 minutes or until mushrooms are barely tender. Add wine and bacon. Reduce heat to low; simmer 3 minutes. Yield: 2 to 3 servings.

Tip: To slice firm fresh mushrooms faster, use an egg slicer.

ASPARAGUS IN LEMON BUTTER

1 pound young asparagus
¼ cup water
3 tablespoons butter or margarine
¾ teaspoon lemon juice

Wash asparagus; snap off tough ends. Remove scales with knife or vegetable peeler. Arrange whole spears in an 8-inch square dish with largest spears to outside of dish. Add water, and cover with heavy-duty plastic wrap. Microwave at HIGH for 5 to 7 minutes. Let stand, covered, while preparing lemon butter.

Place butter in a 1-cup glass measure. Melt at HIGH for 30 to 45 seconds. Stir in lemon juice. Drain excess liquid from asparagus, if desired. Drizzle lemon butter over asparagus. Yield: 4 servings.

BACON-TOPPED GREEN BEANS

1 pound fresh green beans
3 slices bacon, coarsely chopped
½ cup chopped onion
¼ cup water
½ teaspoon salt

Remove strings from beans; cut beans into 1- to 1½-inch pieces. Set aside.

Sprinkle bacon into a 2-quart casserole; cover with paper toweling. Microwave at HIGH for 2 minutes; stir. Microwave an additional 1 to 2 minutes or until done. Remove bacon and set aside, reserving drippings in casserole.

Add beans, onion, and water to drippings; stir well. Cover with heavy-duty plastic wrap. Microwave at HIGH for 5 minutes; stir well. Cover and microwave at HIGH for 9 to 12 minutes or until beans are the desired tenderness. Stir in salt, and sprinkle with cooked bacon. Yield: about 4 servings.

CARROT-LIMA-SQUASH MEDLEY

½ cup sugar
1 tablespoon plus 1 teaspoon cornstarch
2 teaspoons salt
¼ teaspoon dillweed
1⅓ cups orange juice
1 pound carrots, peeled and diagonally sliced (about 3 cups)
2 cups fresh lima beans
1 medium zucchini, sliced
1 medium yellow squash, sliced

Combine sugar, cornstarch, salt, and dillweed in a small saucepan; mix well. Stir in orange juice. Cook over medium heat, stirring constantly, until thickened and bubbly. Reduce heat to low to keep sauce warm.

Steam carrots 10 minutes; add limas and squash. Steam 10 to 15 minutes or until tender. Serve sauce over vegetables. Yield: 10 to 12 servings.

Start The Day With An Omelet

For a special way to start the morning, try a cheesy ham-filled omelet. Egg whites are beaten separately to give this Ham and Cheese Omelet a light and airy texture. Complete the menu with fresh fruit for a breakfast that looks as good as it tastes.

HAM AND CHEESE OMELET

4 eggs, separated
½ teaspoon all-purpose flour
2 tablespoons milk
½ medium onion, chopped
1 tablespoon chopped fresh parsley
½ teaspoon salt
Dash of pepper
3 tablespoons butter or margarine, divided
3 slices cooked ham, cut into pieces
3 slices process American cheese

Beat egg whites until stiff but not dry. Beat egg yolks until thick and lemon colored. Combine yolks, flour, milk, onion, parsley, salt, and pepper; mix well. Fold into egg whites.

For each omelet, melt 1 tablespoon of butter in an 8-inch skillet until just hot enough to sizzle a drop of water; pour in one-third of egg mixture. As mixture starts to cook, gently lift edges of omelet and tilt pan to allow uncooked portion to flow underneath. When mixture is set and no longer flows freely, sprinkle one-third of ham on half of omelet; cover ham with 1 slice of cheese. Fold omelet in half, and place on a warm platter. Repeat procedure with remaining ingredients. Yield: 3 servings.
Pat Mestayer,
Raceland, Louisiana.

Give Everyday Entrées A Lift

Are you and your family tired of your usual round of weekly entrées? This assortment of economical main dishes will give your menus a lift.

Turn diced cooked ham into a casserole with pineapple, raisins, green pepper, and a sweet-and-sour sauce; this Raisin Ham is colorful and delicious served over rice. Chicken goes spicy in Mexican Chicken, while Roast in Beer-and-Onion Sauce is a change from the usual pot roast.

MEXICAN CHICKEN

1 (2½- to 3-pound) broiler-fryer, cut up
Salt
Pepper
½ cup all-purpose flour
1 tablespoon chili powder
⅓ cup vegetable oil
1 medium onion, chopped (about ½ cup)
1 medium-size green pepper, chopped (about ½ cup)
1 clove garlic, chopped
1 cup uncooked regular rice
1 (14½-ounce) can tomatoes, chopped
2 cups water

Sprinkle chicken with salt and pepper. Combine flour and chili powder; stir well. Dredge chicken in flour mixture, and brown in hot oil in an electric skillet.

Remove chicken from skillet. Add onion, green pepper, and garlic to skillet; sauté until tender. Stir in rice, tomatoes, and water. Arrange chicken over rice and vegetables; cover and simmer 35 minutes. Yield: 4 to 6 servings.
Mrs. C. W. Kennard,
Anderson, Texas.

Add some south-of-the-border flavor to everyday meals with Mexican Chicken. It's quick and easy to prepare.

Brown roast on all sides in oil in a Dutch oven. Combine beer, tomato sauce, and onion soup mix; mix well. Pour beer mixture over roast. Cover and cook 2 hours.

Place green pepper on roast, and cook an additional 45 minutes or until roast is tender. Serve roast with sauce. Yield: 6 to 8 servings.
Mrs. Farmer L. Burns,
New Orleans, Louisiana.

ROAST IN BEER-AND-ONION SAUCE

1 (3- to 5-pound) boneless chuck roast
Vegetable oil
1 (8-ounce) can beer
1 (8-ounce) can tomato sauce
1 (1.375-ounce) package onion soup mix
1 small green pepper, thinly sliced

Tip: Buy meat in bulk. Be it half of a ham, a large pot roast, or a family-size package, cut it and freeze it in serving-size portions. As a general rule, the larger the cut, the less expensive the individual serving.

RAISIN HAM

1 (15¼-ounce) can pineapple chunks
3 to 3½ cups diced cooked ham
½ cup golden raisins
1 medium onion, thinly sliced and separated into rings
1 small green pepper, sliced into rings
⅓ cup vinegar
2 teaspoons dry mustard
½ cup firmly packed brown sugar
2 tablespoons cornstarch
¼ teaspoon salt
1 tablespoon soy sauce
1 teaspoon Worcestershire sauce
Hot cooked rice

Drain pineapple, reserving liquid; add enough water to liquid to measure 1 cup. Set pineapple and liquid aside.

Place ham in a lightly greased 12- x 8- x 2-inch baking pan; sprinkle raisins over ham. Layer onion, green pepper, and pineapple over ham and raisins.

Combine reserved pineapple liquid, vinegar, mustard, sugar, cornstarch, and salt in a small saucepan, stirring until cornstarch is dissolved. Cook mixture over low heat, stirring constantly, until thickened. Stir in soy sauce and Worcestershire sauce; pour over ham and vegetables. Bake at 350° for 45 minutes. Serve over hot cooked rice. Yield: 6 servings. *Mrs. M. L. Shannon, Fairfield, Alabama.*

He's Now A Full-Time Gourmet

"Cooking was just a hobby until it turned into my vocation," explains Charles Williams of Atlanta. "I first learned to cook when I went to college, but it was mostly things like grits and cornbread. Then one Christmas I was given a set of basic French cooking lessons as a gift."

That was almost five years ago. Since then, Charles has expanded his interest in food to include a career managing two gourmet cookware shops in Atlanta. Charles says that he enjoys working in the shops because he can sit in on all the cooking classes and see the new kitchen equipment when it first comes out.

By altering recipes to suit his tastes, Charles comes up with his own creations. Here he shares three of his specialties, including La Tarte Aux Pommes, a delicious apple tart baked with an almond-flavored custard. His recipes are followed by recipes from other men who also enjoy cooking.

BEEF ELEGANTE

1 (10-ounce) package frozen chopped
    spinach
1 clove garlic
2 tablespoons melted butter or margarine
2 tablespoons whipping cream
1 pound cooked ham, finely chopped
¼ cup soft breadcrumbs
1 egg, beaten
Dash of pepper
1 (1- to 1½-pound) boneless round steak,
    ½ inch thick
Salt and pepper
1 teaspoon ground thyme
½ cup Chablis or other dry white wine
1 (⅞-ounce) package béarnaise sauce mix

Cook spinach according to package directions; drain well and set aside.

Cook garlic in butter until garlic is lightly browned. Discard garlic. Add spinach to butter and cook over medium heat, stirring constantly, 1 to 2 minutes. Remove from heat, and stir in whipping cream; set aside.

Combine ham, breadcrumbs, egg, and pepper, stirring well; set aside.

Trim excess fat from steak; sprinkle with salt, pepper, and thyme. Spread spinach mixture over steak, leaving a 1-inch border; top with ham mixture. Starting with long side, roll steak jelly-roll fashion; tie with string at 1½-inch intervals. Place steak, seam side down, in a shallow roasting pan; pour wine over top. Cover and bake at 350° for 1 hour. Uncover steak, and bake an additional 30 minutes. Remove and discard string before serving.

Prepare béarnaise sauce mix according to package directions; spoon over beef roll. Yield: 6 to 8 servings.

LA TARTE AUX POMMES

½ cup apricot preserves
1½ cups all-purpose flour
½ teaspoon salt
1½ tablespoons sugar
¼ cup plus 2 tablespoons unsalted butter
2 tablespoons shortening
1 tablespoon vinegar
3 to 4 tablespoons cold water
4 medium cooking apples
3 tablespoons lemon juice
3 tablespoons butter
3 tablespoons sugar
1 teaspoon vanilla extract
3 egg yolks
¼ cup sugar
3 tablespoons ground almonds
¼ cup whipping cream

Cook apricot preserves over medium heat, stirring constantly, just until melted; strain, discarding pulp. Set aside.

Combine flour, salt, and 1½ tablespoons sugar in a small mixing bowl; cut in ¼ cup plus 2 tablespoons butter and shortening with pastry blender until mixture resembles coarse meal. Sprinkle vinegar and water evenly over surface; stir with a fork until all dry ingredients are moistened. Shape into a ball; chill.

Roll out dough to fit a 10-inch tart pan. Brush pastry with 2 tablespoons strained apricot preserves; chill. Prick bottom of pastry with a fork. Bake shell at 375° for 15 minutes.

Peel and core apples; sprinkle with lemon juice. Cut apples in half vertically; place cut side down on a chopping board, and cut into thin lengthwise slices. Keeping slices together, transfer halves to a lightly greased 12- x 8- x 2-inch baking dish; dot with 3 tablespoons butter. Sprinkle with 3 tablespoons sugar and vanilla; bake at 375° for 30 minutes or until tender. Carefully transfer halves, keeping slices together, to prepared pastry shell; set aside.

Combine egg yolks and ¼ cup sugar; beat until light and lemon colored. Stir in almonds and whipping cream; pour over apples in pastry shell. Bake at 375° for 20 to 25 minutes or until firm. Remove tart from pan; brush remaining preserves over top. Yield: 8 to 10 servings.

CARROTS MADEIRA

¼ cup butter or margarine
1½ pounds carrots, peeled and cut into
    thin sticks
1 teaspoon sugar
1 teaspoon salt
¼ cup Madeira wine
6 sprigs fresh parsley, minced
⅛ teaspoon dried tarragon leaves

Melt butter in a heavy saucepan; add carrots, sugar, salt, and wine. Bring to a boil; cover and simmer 15 to 20 minutes or until carrots are tender. Drain well; sprinkle with parsley and tarragon. Yield: 6 servings.

Tip: Keep small packages of leftovers from getting lost in the freezer by placing them in a large nylon-mesh or plastic bag.

MACKEREL CREOLE

2½ to 3 pounds mackerel fillets
1 teaspoon salt
1 teaspoon pepper
1 (16-ounce) can tomatoes, quartered
1 medium-size green pepper, chopped
1 medium onion, chopped
1 cup chopped celery
¼ cup water
Hot cooked rice

Place fish in a large skillet; sprinkle with salt and pepper.

Combine remaining ingredients except rice; spoon over fish. Bring to a boil. Reduce heat; cover and simmer 20 minutes or until fish flakes easily. Serve over hot cooked rice. Yield: 4 to 5 servings.   F. P. Pridgen,
Fayetteville, North Carolina.

JALAPENO HOT RICE

1 medium onion, chopped (about ½ cup)
1 medium-size green pepper, chopped
2 jalapeño peppers, seeded and finely
    chopped
¼ cup butter or margarine, melted
1 (4-ounce) can mushroom stems and
    pieces, undrained
1 (10¾-ounce) can chicken broth,
    undiluted
1 cup uncooked rice

Sauté onion, green pepper, and jalapeño pepper in butter in a medium saucepan until tender. Add mushrooms, chicken broth, and rice; cover and simmer 15 to 20 minutes or until rice is tender. Yield: 4 servings.

Charles Burris,
Lafayette, Louisiana.

EASY TOMATO RELISH

1 teaspoon whole cloves
1 teaspoon ground nutmeg
1 teaspoon whole allspice
1 tablespoon whole mustard seeds
1 tablespoon plus 2 teaspoons crushed red
    pepper
1½ teaspoons celery seeds
2 dozen medium tomatoes, peeled and cut
    into eighths
8 medium-size green peppers, cut into
    eighths
8 medium onions, cut into eighths
3 cups sugar
1 tablespoon salt
2 quarts vinegar

Combine first 6 ingredients; tie in a cheesecloth bag and set aside.

Position knife blade in processor bowl; place about one-eighth of the vegetables in bowl. Place cover on top; process until finely chopped (stop processor and scrape down sides, if necessary). Place chopped vegetables in a large Dutch oven; repeat procedure until all of the vegetables are chopped.

Add spice bag, sugar, salt, and vinegar to vegetables; bring to a boil. Reduce heat; simmer, uncovered, 2 to 2½ hours or until desired degree of thickness, stirring often. Remove and discard spice bag. Spoon tomato mixture into hot sterilized jars, leaving ½-inch headspace. Adjust lids; process in boiling-water bath 5 minutes. Yield: about 12 pints.   John Lewis,
Simpsonville, South Carolina.

MAUNA LOA SUNDAES

1 (20-ounce) can pineapple chunks
¼ cup firmly packed brown sugar
2 teaspoons cornstarch
1 tablespoon butter or margarine
2 tablespoons finely chopped crystallized
    ginger (optional)
¼ cup brandy or Cognac
1 quart vanilla ice cream
Toasted flaked coconut

Drain pineapple, reserving ½ cup juice. Combine reserved juice, sugar, and cornstarch in a medium saucepan; cook over medium heat, stirring constantly, until thickened. Add butter, pineapple, and ginger; cook, stirring often, until thoroughly heated. Set aside.

Heat brandy in a small saucepan over medium heat; do not boil. Ignite with a long match, and pour over pineapple sauce. Spoon sauce over ice cream; top with coconut. Yield: 6 to 8 servings.

James Strieber,
Odenton, Maryland.

Tip: When squeezing fresh lemons or oranges for juice, first grate the rind by rubbing the washed fruit against surface of grater, taking care to remove only the outer colored portion of the rind. Wrap in plastic in teaspoon portions and freeze for future use.

Make Summer's Harvest Last Year-Round

One of the best things about summer is the abundance of fresh vegetables straight out of the garden—as well as all those plump, juicy peaches and berries. And canning is one of the best ways to ensure a continuous enjoyment of summer's harvest. Putting up beans, peas, tomatoes, squash, okra, and corn while they are at their peak of flavor pays dividends during the colder months.

The boiling-water-bath method of canning proves safe for fruits and tomatoes, but higher temperatures reached only by the steam-pressure method are imperative for canning most vegetables.

And you should always boil home-canned vegetables vigorously for 10 minutes before serving to eliminate possible contamination; then home-canned fruits should be safe to eat straight from the jar.

GREEN BEANS

Wash beans, trim ends, and string if necessary; cut into 1-inch lengths.

Hot pack: Cover beans with boiling water, and boil 5 minutes. Pack hot beans loosely in hot sterilized jars, leaving ½-inch headspace. Add ½ teaspoon salt to pints, 1 teaspoon to quarts. Cover with boiling liquid, leaving ½-inch headspace. Cover at once with metal lids, and screw metal bands tight. Process in pressure canner at 10 pounds pressure (240°). Process pint jars for 20 minutes and quart jars for 25 minutes.

Cold pack: Pack beans tightly into hot sterilized jars, leaving ½-inch headspace. Add ½ teaspoon salt to pints, 1 teaspoon to quarts. Cover with boiling water, leaving ½-inch headspace. Cover at once with metal lids, and screw metal bands tight. Process in pressure canner at 10 pounds pressure (240°). Process pints for 20 minutes and quarts for 25 minutes.

BLACK-EYED, FIELD, AND CROWDER PEAS

Select young, tender peas. Shell and wash peas.

Hot pack: Cover peas with boiling water, and bring to a boil; boil 3 minutes. Drain. Pack hot peas loosely into hot sterilized jars, leaving 1-inch headspace. (Do not shake or press peas down.) Add ½ teaspoon salt to pints, 1 teaspoon to quarts. Cover with boiling water, leaving 1-inch headspace. Cover at once with metal lids, and screw metal bands tight. Process in pressure canner at 10 pounds pressure (240°). Process pints for 35 minutes and quarts for 40 minutes.

Cold pack: Pack peas loosely into hot sterilized jars, leaving 1-inch headspace. (Do not shake or press peas down.) Add ½ teaspoon salt to pints, 1 teaspoon to quarts. Cover with boiling water, leaving 1-inch headspace. Cover at once with metal lids, and screw metal bands tight. Process in pressure canner at 10 pounds pressure (240°). Process pints for 35 minutes and quarts for 40 minutes.

CREAM-STYLE CORN

Husk corn and remove silks; wash. Cut corn from cob at about center of the kernel; scrape cob.

Hot pack: Add 2 cups water and 1 teaspoon salt to 4 cups corn; bring to a boil, and boil 3 minutes. Pack loosely into hot sterilized pint jars, leaving 1-inch headspace. Cover with boiling liquid, leaving 1-inch headspace. Cover at once with metal lids, and screw metal bands tight. Process in pressure canner at 10 pounds pressure (240°). Process pints for 85 minutes.

Cold pack: Pack corn loosely into hot sterilized pint jars, leaving 1½-inches headspace. Add ½ teaspoon salt to each pint. Cover with boiling water, leaving ½-inch headspace. Cover jars at once with metal lids, and screw metal bands tight. Process in pressure canner at 10 pounds pressure (240°). Process pints for 95 minutes.

OKRA

Select young, tender pods of okra. Wash okra; trim stem ends. Cook for 1 minute in boiling water; drain. Leave pods whole or cut into 1-inch slices. Use hot-pack method only.

Hot pack: Pack okra into hot sterilized jars, leaving ½-inch headspace. Add ½ teaspoon salt to pints and 1 teaspoon to quarts. Cover with boiling water, leaving ½-inch headspace. Cover at once with metal lids, and screw metal bands tight. Process in pressure canner at 10 pounds pressure (240°). Process pints for 25 minutes and quarts for 40 minutes.

SUMMER SQUASH

Wash and trim squash: do not peel. Cut squash into ½-inch slices; then cut

Enjoy the flavor of summer all year long by canning homemade vegetable soup.

slices into uniform pieces. Use hot-pack method only.

Hot pack: Add just enough water to squash to cover; bring to boiling point; steam or boil 2 to 3 minutes. Pack hot squash loosely into hot sterilized jars, leaving 1-inch headspace. Add ½ teaspoon salt to pints, 1 teaspoon to quarts.

Cover with boiling liquid, leaving 1-inch headspace. Cover at once with metal lids, and screw metal bands tight. Process in pressure canner at 10 pounds pressure (240°). Process pints for 30 minutes and quarts for 40 minutes.

Tip: Remember to cut your vegetables before cooking rather than cooking them whole. This speeds the process. Legumes or dried fruits should be soaked also to reduce cooking time. Soaking returns them to their natural state or consistency.

LIMA BEANS

Shell and wash beans just before time to can.

Hot pack: Cover beans with boiling water, and boil 3 minutes. Pack hot beans loosely in hot sterilized jars, leaving 1-inch headspace. Add ½ teaspoon salt to pints, 1 teaspoon to quarts. Cover with boiling liquid, leaving 1-inch headspace. Cover at once with metal lids, and screw metal bands tight. Process in pressure canner at 10 pounds pressure (240°). Process pint jars for 40 minutes and quart jars for 50 minutes.

Cold pack: Pack beans loosely in hot sterilized jars, leaving 1-inch headspace. (Do not shake or press beans down.) Add ½ teaspoon salt to pints, 1 teaspoon to quarts. Cover with boiling water, leaving 1-inch headspace. Cover at once with metal lids, and screw metal bands tight. Process in pressure canner at 10 pounds pressure (240°). Process pints for 40 minutes and quarts for 50 minutes.

TOMATOES

Peel tomatoes; leave whole or cut them as desired.

Hot pack: Bring tomatoes to a boil, stirring to keep from sticking; boil 5 minutes. Pack hot tomatoes into hot sterilized jars, leaving 1-inch headspace. Add ½ teaspoon salt to pints, 1 teaspoon to quarts. Cover with boiling juice, leaving ½-inch headspace. Cover at once with metal lids, and screw metal bands tight. Process pints for 10 minutes and quarts for 15 minutes in boiling-water bath.

Cold pack: Pack raw tomatoes into hot sterilized jars, leaving ½-inch headspace. Press gently to fill spaces. Do not add water. Add ½ teaspoon salt to pints, 1 teaspoon to quarts. Cover at once with metal lids, and screw metal bands tight. Process pints for 35 minutes and quarts for 45 minutes in boiling-water bath.

Note: If unsure of high-acid content of the tomatoes, use the steam-pressure canning method.

VEGETABLE SOUP

1½ quarts water
8 cups peeled, cored, chopped tomatoes
6 cups peeled, cubed potatoes
4 cups lima beans
4 cups cut corn
6 cups sliced carrots
2 cups sliced celery
2 cups chopped onion
Salt

Combine water and vegetables; bring to a boil, and boil 5 minutes. Pour into hot sterilized jars, leaving 1-inch headspace. Add ¼ teaspoon salt to pints and ½ teaspoon to quarts. Cover at once with metal lids, and screw metal bands tight. Process in pressure canner at 10 pounds pressure (240°). Process pints for 55 minutes and quarts for 85 minutes. Yield: about 14 pints or 7 quarts.

Tip: Placing a jar of jam, jelly, syrup, or honey in a pan of simmering water dissolves the sugar crystals on top.

PEACHES

Select ripe, firm peaches. Peel and cut into halves or slices. Remove pits. To prevent fruit from darkening during preparation, use an ascorbic-citric mixture according to the manufacturer's directions, or drop peaches into a mild salt solution (2 tablespoons salt and 2 tablespoons vinegar or lemon juice per gallon of water). If using salt solution, rinse and drain fruit before packing.

Make a medium syrup: Combine 3 cups sugar and 1 quart water; cook until sugar dissolves. Yield will be 5½ cups. It usually takes 1 to 1½ cups syrup for each quart of fruit.

Hot pack: Heat peaches thoroughly in hot syrup. Pack peaches into hot sterilized jars, leaving ½-inch headspace. Cover with boiling syrup, leaving ½-inch headspace. Cover at once with metal lids, and screw metal bands tight. Process pints for 20 minutes and quarts for 25 minutes in boiling-water bath.

Cold pack: Pack raw peaches into hot sterilized jars, leaving ½-inch headspace. Cover with boiling syrup, leaving ½-inch headspace. Cover at once with metal lids, and screw metal bands tight. Process pints for 25 minutes and quarts for 30 minutes in boiling-water bath.

BERRIES (EXCEPT STRAWBERRIES)

Select fully ripened berries. Handle as little as possible. Wash and cap berries; drain well.

Hot pack: (Use for blackberries and others that hold their shape well.) Add ¼ to ½ cup sugar to each 4 cups berries; let stand 2 hours. Cook until sugar dissolves and mixture comes to a boil, stirring gently to keep berries from sticking. Pack hot berries into hot sterilized jars, leaving ½-inch headspace. (If there is not enough syrup to cover berries, add boiling water, leaving ½-inch headspace.) Cover at once with metal lids, and screw metal bands tight. Process pints for 10 minutes and quarts for 15 minutes in boiling-water bath.

Cold pack: (Use for red raspberries or others that do not hold their shape well.) Make a medium syrup: Combine 3 cups sugar and 1 quart water; cook until sugar dissolves. Yield will be 5½ cups. It usually takes 1 to 1½ cups syrup for each quart of fruit. Pack raw berries into hot sterilized jars, leaving ½-inch headspace. Shake jars as berries are added to get a full pack. Cover with boiling syrup, leaving ½-inch headspace. Cover jars at once with metal lids; screw metal bands tight. Process

pints for 15 minutes and quarts for 20 minutes in boiling-water bath.

Without sugar: Pour hot water into Dutch oven, barely covering the bottom. Add berries; simmer until thoroughly heated. Pack hot berries into hot sterilized jars, leaving ½-inch headspace. If there is not enough juice to cover berries, add boiling water, leaving ½-inch headspace. Cover at once with metal lids, and screw metal bands tight. Process pints for 10 minutes and quarts for 15 minutes in boiling-water bath.

Beverages For A Summer Day

Fresh fruits and juices, ginger ale and rum combine in these recipes and add up to lots of new ideas for summer coolers. All are as appealing to the eye as they are to the taste.

If you want to fill the punch bowl for a crowd, try Bubbling Jade Punch or refreshing Pineapple Punch. For a thicker, icier punch filled with bananas, cherries, and crushed pineapple, try Tropical Ice.

If you enjoy the taste of rum, serve Easy Rum Slush; its light, tart taste will make it an all-summer favorite.

PINK COCONUT FROST

1 (6-ounce) can frozen pink lemonade concentrate, undiluted
¾ to 1½ cups gin
3 tablespoons cream of coconut
1 to 2 tablespoons maraschino cherry juice
16 to 20 ice cubes
Maraschino cherries

Combine all ingredients except cherries in container of electric blender; process until frothy. Garnish each serving with a maraschino cherry. Yield: about 4 cups. *Mrs. William Evans, Birmingham, Alabama.*

PINEAPPLE PUNCH

1 (46-ounce) can pineapple juice, chilled
3 cups cranberry juice cocktail, chilled
1 (33.8-ounce) bottle ginger ale, chilled
1 cup light rum (optional)
1 lemon, thinly sliced

Combine pineapple juice, cranberry juice cocktail, and ginger ale in a punch bowl, stirring gently. Stir in light rum, if desired. Add lemon slices. Yield: about 12 cups.
Mrs. Leisa Kilgore,
Gardendale, Alabama.

TROPICAL ICE

2 cups mashed bananas
1 (20-ounce) can crushed pineapple, undrained
1 (4-ounce) jar maraschino cherries, drained and chopped
2 cups orange juice
1 tablespoon lemon juice
1 cup sugar
1 (33.8-ounce) bottle ginger ale

Combine first 6 ingredients; stir well, and freeze until firm.

To serve, partially thaw fruit mixture. Place in punch bowl, and break into chunks. Add ginger ale; stir until slushy. Yield: 12 cups. *Becky Barnett,*
West Point, Mississippi.

BUBBLING JADE PUNCH

1 (3-ounce) package lime-flavored gelatin
1 cup boiling water
2 cups cold water
1 (6-ounce) can frozen lemonade concentrate, thawed and undiluted
1 cup pineapple juice, chilled
1 (33.8-ounce) bottle ginger ale, chilled
Whole fresh strawberries (optional)

Dissolve gelatin in boiling water; stir in cold water, lemonade concentrate, and pineapple juice; chill well.

Pour mixture into punch bowl; add ginger ale. Garnish with strawberries, if desired. Yield: about 10 cups.
Mrs. Kathryn M. Elmore,
Demopolis, Alabama.

EASY RUM SLUSH

1 (6-ounce) can frozen orange juice concentrate, undiluted
1 (6-ounce) can frozen lemonade concentrate, undiluted
1 to 1¼ cups light rum
Ice cubes

Combine orange juice concentrate, lemonade concentrate, and rum in container of electric blender. Add ice to within 1 inch of container top; blend well. Yield: about 5½ cups.
Mrs. Paul E. Kline,
Palm Beach Gardens, Florida.

FOUR-FRUIT REFRESHER

3 cups cranberry juice, chilled
1½ cups apple juice, chilled
¾ cup orange juice, chilled
¼ cup plus 2 tablespoons lemon juice, chilled
1½ (33.8-ounce) bottles ginger ale, chilled
Orange slices (optional)

Combine fruit juice and ginger ale; stir gently. Serve over ice cubes, and garnish with orange slices, if desired. Yield: 12 cups. *Susanne L. Webb,*
Roanoke, Virginia.

Try A Self-Filled Cupcake

Serve a platter of cupcakes and watch them disappear. Baked in their own paper liners, each little cake is a perfect snack or dessert.

A delicious cream cheese and chocolate morsel filling makes Self-Filled Cupcakes a winner with all age groups. For a more traditional cupcake, try Happy Day Cupcakes. Topped with a simple butter frosting, they are sure to create smiling faces.

SELF-FILLED CUPCAKES

1 (18.5-ounce) package devil's food cake mix
1 (8-ounce) package cream cheese, softened
⅓ cup sugar
1 egg
Dash of salt
1 (6-ounce) package semisweet chocolate morsels

Prepare cake mix according to package directions. Spoon batter into paper-lined muffin pans, filling two-thirds full.

Combine cream cheese and sugar, creaming until light and fluffy. Add egg and salt, beating well; stir in chocolate morsels. Spoon 1 heaping teaspoon cream cheese mixture into center of each cupcake. Bake at 350° for 25 minutes. Cool in pan 10 minutes; remove to wire rack to complete cooling. Yield: 2½ dozen cupcakes.
Maybelle Pinkston,
Corryton, Tennessee.

HAPPY DAY CUPCAKES

¼ cup shortening
⅔ cup sugar
1 egg
1 cup plus 2 tablespoons all-purpose flour
1¼ teaspoons baking powder
½ teaspoon salt
½ cup plus 1 tablespoon milk
½ teaspoon vanilla extract
Butter frosting (recipe follows)

Cream shortening; gradually add sugar, beating with electric mixer until light and fluffy. Add egg, beating well. Combine flour, baking powder, and salt; add to creamed mixture, mixing well. Add milk and vanilla; beat for 1 minute.

Spoon batter into paper-lined muffin pans, filling half full. Bake at 375° for 20 to 25 minutes or until cupcakes test done. Cool and frost with butter frosting. Yield: 1 dozen cupcakes.

Butter Frosting:

3 tablespoons butter, softened
1½ cups sifted powdered sugar, divided
Pinch of salt
1 tablespoon milk
¾ teaspoon vanilla extract

Combine butter, ½ cup sugar, and salt, creaming with electric mixer until light and fluffy. Add remaining sugar alternately with milk, beating until smooth enough to spread. Add vanilla; beat well. Yield: enough for 1 dozen cupcakes. *Linda E. Whitt,*
Missouri City, Texas.

Tip: For ingredients listed in recipes: If the direction comes before the ingredient—for example, sifted flour—first sift the flour, then measure. If the direction comes after the ingredient—for example, pecans, chopped—first measure pecans, then chop.

BANANA-COCOA CUPCAKES

½ cup butter or margarine, softened
1 cup sugar
1 egg
1½ cups all-purpose flour
1¼ teaspoons soda
¼ cup cocoa
½ teaspoon ground cinnamon
1¼ cups mashed ripe bananas (about 3 medium)
Sifted powdered sugar

Cream butter; gradually add sugar, beating with electric mixer until light and fluffy. Add egg, beating well. Combine flour, soda, cocoa, and cinnamon; add to creamed mixture alternately with banana, beating after each addition.

Spoon batter into paper-lined muffin pans, filling half full. Bake at 350° for 20 to 25 minutes or until cupcakes test done. Cool in pan 10 minutes; remove to wire rack. Sprinkle with powdered sugar. Yield: 1½ dozen cupcakes.

Mrs. H. J. Sherrer,
Bay City, Texas.

Summer Is Sandwich Time

Sandwiches are fun to serve, especially during the summer when meals tend to be more relaxed. But if you serve them often, you may find it a challenge to create new ways to prepare them. If you need inspiration, here are recipes you'll want to try. We offer a variety of fillings that include meat, cheese, vegetables, and fruit.

BAKED CHICKEN SANDWICHES

1 (10¾-ounce) can cream of chicken soup, undiluted
1½ cups diced cooked chicken
1 (4-ounce) jar chopped pimiento
¾ cup milk
3 tablespoons all-purpose flour
2 tablespoons minced onion
18 slices sandwich bread
Butter or margarine, softened
3 eggs, well beaten
3 cups finely crushed potato chips

Combine soup, chicken, pimiento, milk, flour, and onion in a medium saucepan. Cook over low heat until thickened and bubbly. Cool thoroughly.

Trim crust from bread. (Reserve crust for use in another recipe.) Spread butter on both sides of bread. Spread about ¼ cup chicken mixture on each of 9 slices of bread; top with the remaining 9 slices. Wrap each sandwich tightly with aluminum foil and freeze until ready to serve.

Remove sandwiches from freezer; unwrap and slice in half diagonally. Dip each half in egg, and dredge in potato chips. Arrange on a baking sheet; bake at 325° for 30 minutes. Yield: 9 servings.

Mrs. James S. Tiffany,
Dallas, Texas.

EGGSCLUSIVE SANDWICHES

4 hard-cooked eggs, chopped
½ cup finely chopped celery
1 tablespoon chopped parsley
1½ teaspoons chopped pimiento
¼ teaspoon salt
⅛ teaspoon pepper
⅓ cup mayonnaise or salad dressing
12 slices buttered toast
2 tomatoes, sliced
8 slices bacon, cooked
4 lettuce leaves

Combine eggs, celery, parsley, pimiento, salt, and pepper; add mayonnaise, and mix well. Spread 4 slices of toast with egg mixture; top each with another slice of toast. Arrange tomato, bacon, and lettuce on toast. Top with remaining toast. Cut into quarters to serve, using wooden picks to hold layers together. Yield: 4 sandwiches.

Mrs. James L. Twilley,
Macon, Georgia.

ASPARAGUS GRILL SANDWICHES

8 slices sandwich bread
Butter or margarine
8 slices cooked ham or 16 slices cooked bacon
4 slices onion
4 slices tomato
16 asparagus spears, cooked
4 slices process American cheese
Cheese sauce (recipe follows)

Spread one side of each slice of bread with butter. Place 4 slices of bread, buttered side down, on a hot griddle. On each slice place 2 slices of ham or 4 slices of bacon, 1 slice of onion and tomato, 4 asparagus spears, and 1 slice of cheese. Place remaining 4 slices of bread, buttered side up, on top of cheese. Cook until sandwiches are golden brown on bottom; turn to brown top slices of bread. Pour hot cheese sauce over the sandwiches before serving. Yield: 4 sandwiches.

Cheese Sauce:

2 tablespoons butter or margarine
2 tablespoons all-purpose flour
1 cup milk
1 cup (4 ounces) shredded sharp Cheddar cheese

Melt butter in a heavy saucepan over low heat. Add flour, and cook 1 minute, stirring constantly. Gradually add milk; cook over medium heat, stirring constantly, until thickened and bubbly. Add cheese, and stir until melted. Yield: about 1 cup.

Mrs. Ginger McVay,
Miami, Florida.

APPLE SANDWICHES

2 apples, finely chopped
¼ cup raisins
6 to 8 ounces cooked ham, finely diced
¼ cup (1 ounce) shredded mild Cheddar cheese
½ cup mayonnaise
2 teaspoons lemon juice
12 slices hot buttered toast
6 lettuce leaves

Combine apple, raisins, ham, cheese, mayonnaise, and lemon juice; mix well. Spread about ½ cup of apple mixture on each of 6 slices of toast. Top with lettuce leaves and remaining toast. Cut sandwiches in half, and serve immediately. Yield: 6 servings.

Mrs. Harvey Kidd,
Hernando, Mississippi.

Right: *Two of summer's favorite melons and slices of other fresh fruits add up to Fruit Rhapsody (page 158). Orange-Coconut Dressing provides the crowning touch.*

Page 134: *Lane Cake (page 121) and Savannah Trifle (page 121) are traditional Low Country desserts.*

Above: *Cucumber, carrot, and crabmeat combine as a delicious filling for Crab-Stuffed Tomato Salad (page 148).*

Left: *Steamed Broccoli (page 122) turns a vibrant green—a welcome change from the dull color that results from overcooking.*

Far Left: *These dishes embody the true flavor of the Low Country: (front) Low Country Seafood Boil (page 119); (center) Southern Turnip Greens and Ham Hock (page 119), Savannah Red Rice (page 119), and Rosy Chutney (page 120); (back) Buttermilk Corn Sticks (page 120), Old-Fashioned Coleslaw (page 120), and Old-South Carrot Cake (page 120).*

Microwave Appetizers For A Crowd

Any hostess will tell you that serving hot appetizers to a crowd takes lots of advance planning and preparation. But with the help of a microwave oven, it's easier than you might think. The appetizers can be made ahead, refrigerated on microwave-safe serving platters, and microwaved as needed. To show you just how easy it is to microwave hot appetizers, we suggest you try our kitchen-tested recipes.

When preparing these appetizers, remember that the cooking times will vary because wattage of microwave ovens varies. A time range is given in our recipes to allow for the difference. To prevent overcooking, always check for doneness at the lower end of the range. Here are some other pointers.

—Before refrigerating appetizers prepared in advance, place them on serving platters that are microwave safe. This will eliminate the need to transfer them after microwaving.

—Arrange individual appetizers about ¼ inch apart in a doughnut pattern on the microwave dish. That way, microwaves will enter on every side of the appetizers, allowing more even heating.

—When covering with plastic wrap during microwaving, use only the heavy-duty type. Lighter weight plastic wraps may melt in the microwave. Turn back one corner of the wrap to allow excess steam to escape.

—Follow recipe instructions for stirring, turning, and covering. These techniques promote even cooking.

—The amount of food being microwaved affects the cooking time. Our recipes recommend cooking a dozen appetizers at a time. If the number is increased, the time required will increase and cooking may be uneven. If few appetizers are microwaved, decrease cooking time slightly.

SHRIMP-STUFFED MUSHROOMS

1 (6-ounce) can medium shrimp
½ pound large fresh mushrooms
2 tablespoons butter or margarine
¼ cup finely chopped onion
2 tablespoons chopped fresh parsley
¼ cup seasoned dry breadcrumbs

Prepare shrimp according to label directions; finely chop, and set aside.

Clean mushrooms with damp paper towels. Remove mushroom stems, and finely chop. Set mushroom caps aside.

Place butter in a 1-quart casserole. Microwave at HIGH for 25 to 45 seconds or until melted. Add onion and chopped mushroom stems; cover with heavy-duty plastic wrap. Microwave at HIGH for 3 to 4 minutes or until onion is transparent. Stir in parsley, breadcrumbs, and shrimp. Spoon mixture into mushroom caps. Place on a glass pizza plate or microwave-safe platter; cover and chill.

To serve, remove cover and microwave at HIGH for 2 to 4 minutes or until appetizers are hot, giving platter one half-turn. Yield: about 1 dozen.

Note: To microwave without chilling, reduce time to 1½ to 3 minutes.

CREAMY CRAB DIP

6 tablespoons butter or margarine
¼ cup finely chopped onion
1 clove garlic, minced
2 tablespoons chopped fresh parsley
2 (3-ounce) packages cream cheese, cut into cubes
1 to 2 teaspoons Worcestershire sauce
¼ teaspoon hot sauce
⅛ teaspoon salt
2 (6-ounce) packages frozen crabmeat, thawed, drained, and flaked

Place butter in a 2-quart casserole. Microwave at HIGH for 45 seconds or until butter melts. Add onion, garlic, and parsley; cover with heavy-duty plastic wrap. Microwave at HIGH for 2½ to 3½ minutes or until onion is tender. Add cream cheese; cover and microwave at HIGH for ½ to 1 minute, stirring once.

Stir in Worcestershire sauce, hot sauce, and salt; mix well. Gently stir in crabmeat. Microwave at HIGH for 1½ to 2½ minutes or until thoroughly heated. Serve with crackers. Yield: 2¼ cups.

Note: Dip may be made ahead and chilled. Serve cold, or microwave on HIGH about 2 to 3 minutes or until hot, stirring once.

MAKE-AHEAD NACHOS

2 tablespoons butter or margarine
1 medium tomato, chopped (about 1 cup)
½ cup finely chopped onion
1 clove garlic, minced
1 (4-ounce) can chopped green chiles
1 (16-ounce) can refried beans
½ teaspoon chili powder
½ cup (2 ounces) shredded mozzarella cheese
2 (7½-ounce) packages round tortilla chips
2 cups (8 ounces) shredded sharp Cheddar cheese
3 jalapeño peppers, sliced into rings

Place butter in a 2-quart casserole; microwave at HIGH for 25 to 45 seconds or until melted. Brush some melted butter on sides of dish to prevent sticking. Add tomato, onion, garlic, and green chiles to casserole; cover with heavy-duty plastic wrap. Microwave at HIGH for 2 minutes; stir mixture well, and give dish a half-turn. Microwave, covered, at HIGH for 2 to 3 minutes or until onion and tomato are tender.

Stir beans and chili powder into tomato mixture. Cover and microwave at HIGH for 1 to 3 minutes or until thoroughly heated, giving dish a half-turn and stirring once. Stir in mozzarella cheese. Microwave, covered, at HIGH for 30 seconds to 1 minute or until cheese is melted, stirring once. Chill well.

Select unbroken chips, and place about 1 dozen on a glass pizza plate or microwave-safe platter. Top each with a heaping teaspoonful of bean mixture; sprinkle with Cheddar cheese, and top with a slice of jalapeño pepper. Cover with heavy-duty plastic wrap and chill. Repeat the procedure with remaining ingredients.

Before microwaving, turn back one side of plastic wrap. Microwave each platter of appetizers at HIGH for 30 to 55 seconds or until Cheddar cheese is melted, giving platter one half-turn. Yield: about 8 dozen.

Note: Bean mixture may be stored in refrigerator several days.

Tip: "Light meat" tuna is less expensive than "white meat" tuna. Prices also descend according to the pack—from fancy or solid, to chunks, to flaked or grated. When you intend to use tuna for salads, sandwich fillings, creamed dishes, or even casserole dishes, you can save money by buying the less-expensive packs.

RUMAKI

About ½ pound chicken livers
¼ cup soy sauce
1½ tablespoons dry white wine
2 cloves garlic, minced
⅛ teaspoon ground ginger
1 (6-ounce) can water chestnuts, drained
12 slices bacon, cut into thirds

Cut chicken livers in about 1-inch pieces. Combine soy sauce, wine, garlic, and ginger in an 8-inch square baking dish; stir well. Place chicken livers in soy sauce mixture. Cover and marinate in refrigerator 2 to 3 hours.

Cut water chestnuts in half. Place a water chestnut half and a piece of chicken liver on each piece of bacon. Roll up, and secure with a wooden pick. Arrange on paper-towel-lined glass pizza plates or microwave-safe platters, placing no more than a dozen appetizers on each. Cover and refrigerate up to 2 hours.

When ready to microwave, cover platters with paper toweling. Microwave each platter of appetizers on HIGH for 4½ to 7 minutes or until bacon is crisp and liver is done, giving dish one half-turn. Yield: about 3 dozen.

Note: Rumaki may be microwaved without final chilling. Microwaving time will not be changed.

Baked Beans For Your Cookout

One item sure to be on the menu for picnics and cookouts is baked beans. Perhaps one reason they are so popular is that there are so many delicious ways to prepare them. Quick Baked Beans has the flavor of molasses, while pineapple and brown sugar lend a tropical flavor to Hawaiian Baked Beans and Franks. And ground beef is a hearty addition to Beefy Baked Beans.

QUICK BAKED BEANS

1 (16-ounce) can Boston-style baked beans
1 (8-ounce) can tomato sauce
1 (4½-ounce) can deviled ham
1 tablespoon molasses
1 teaspoon prepared mustard
¼ teaspoon salt
1 (3-ounce) can French-fried onions

Combine first 6 ingredients; stir well, and spoon into a 1-quart casserole. Top with onions. Bake, uncovered, at 350° for 20 to 30 minutes. Yield: 4 servings. *Mrs. W. J. Scherffius, Mountain Home, Arkansas.*

BAKED BEANS WITH HAM

½ cup finely chopped onion
½ pound fully cooked ham, chopped
1½ tablespoons vegetable oil
1 (28-ounce) can pork and beans
1 (8-ounce) can tomato sauce
2 tablespoons brown sugar
1 tablespoon Worcestershire sauce
1 teaspoon prepared mustard

Sauté onion and ham in oil until onion is tender. Combine ham mixture and remaining ingredients; stir well. Spoon bean mixture into a 2-quart casserole. Bake, uncovered, at 350° for 40 minutes. Yield: 4 to 6 servings. *Kristie Grimes Gareis, Winchester, Virginia.*

BEEFY BAKED BEANS

1 pound ground beef
½ cup chopped onion
1 (28-ounce) can pork and beans
½ cup catsup
1 to 2 tablespoons vinegar
1 tablespoon Worcestershire sauce
½ teaspoon salt
¼ teaspoon pepper
¼ teaspoon hot sauce

Cook ground beef and onion until meat is browned, stirring to crumble meat. Drain well.

Combine beef mixture and remaining ingredients; stir well. Spoon bean mixture into a 1½-quart casserole. Bake, uncovered, at 350° for 30 minutes. Yield: 4 to 6 servings. *Zenna Mae Phipps, Independence, Virginia.*

Tip: Save the divided TV-dinner trays; assemble your own dinners from left-over meat and vegetables. Freeze and use when you have enough to serve and surprise the family.

HAWAIIAN BAKED BEANS AND FRANKS

2 (16-ounce) cans baked beans
1 (16-ounce) package frankfurters, cut into 1-inch pieces
1½ cups drained crushed pineapple
2 tablespoons finely chopped onion
2 tablespoons brown sugar
1 tablespoon catsup
1 teaspoon prepared mustard

Combine all ingredients; stir well. Spoon mixture into a 2-quart casserole. Bake, uncovered, at 350° for 50 to 60 minutes. Yield: 6 to 8 servings. *Mrs. O. V. Elkins, Raleigh, North Carolina.*

Brighten The Meal With Beets

Whether prepared fresh as a side dish or pickled for year-round enjoyment, garden-fresh beets perk up any meal.

To retain the color in fresh beets during cooking, don't cut the stems or roots too close; leave 1 inch on both roots and stems. Do not peel the beets before cooking; when partially cool, the skin, stem, and root will slip off easily.

CREAMY BEETS

1¼ pounds fresh beets
3 tablespoons sliced green onion
1 tablespoon lemon juice
1 teaspoon sugar
½ teaspoon salt
3 drops of hot sauce
⅓ cup commercial sour cream

Leave root and 1 inch of stem on beets; scrub with a brush. Place beets in a saucepan; add water to cover. Bring to a boil; cover and cook 35 to 40 minutes or until tender. Drain; pour cold water over beets, and drain. Cool. Trim off beet stems, and rub off skins. Dice.

Combine beets with remaining ingredients except sour cream in a medium saucepan. Cook over medium heat until very hot, stirring occasionally; cover, remove from heat, and let stand 5 minutes. Add sour cream; cook over low heat, stirring constantly, until heated (do not boil beets). Yield: 4 servings. *Mrs. Eunice Palmer, Morris Chapel, Tennessee.*

BEETS AND APPLES

1 pound fresh beets
2 medium apples, peeled, cored, and cut
    into rings
½ cup firmly packed light brown sugar
1 tablespoon all-purpose flour
1 teaspoon salt
1 tablespoon vinegar
3 tablespoons butter or margarine

Leave root and 1 inch of stem on beets; scrub with a brush. Place beets in a saucepan; add water to cover. Bring to a boil; cover and cook 35 to 40 minutes or until tender. Drain, reserving ½ cup juice; pour cold water over beets, and drain.

Trim off beet stems and roots, and rub off skins; cut beets into ¼-inch slices. Place half the beets in a 2-quart shallow baking dish; spread half the apples on top. Repeat layers, and set aside.

Combine sugar, flour, salt, vinegar, butter, and reserved beet juice in a small saucepan; cook over medium heat until sugar is melted. Pour over apples and beets; bake at 350° for 20 minutes. Yield: 8 servings.   *Connie Weathers,*
Dalton, Georgia.

EASY PICKLED BEETS

8 to 9 pounds fresh small beets
1 teaspoon celery seeds
1 tablespoon mustard seeds
3½ cups vinegar
3 cups sugar
1½ teaspoons salt

Leave root and 1 inch of stem on beets; scrub with a brush. Place beets in a saucepan; add water to cover. Bring to a boil; cover and cook 35 to 40 minutes or until tender. Drain, reserving 2½ cups liquid; pour cold water over beets, and drain. Trim off the beet root and stems; then rub off skins; set beets aside.

Combine celery seeds and mustard seeds in a cheesecloth bag. Combine vinegar, reserved beet liquid, sugar, salt, and spice bag in a Dutch oven. Bring to a boil; reduce heat, and simmer liquid 15 minutes.

Pack beets into hot sterilized jars, leaving ½-inch headspace. Pour syrup over beets to within ½ inch of top of jar. Top with lids, and screw metal bands tight. Process in boiling-water bath for 30 minutes. Yield: 7 to 8 pints.
Paul P. Dayhoff, Jr.,
Lisbon, Maryland.

CHILLED BEETS AND CAULIFLOWER

2 medium heads cauliflower
1 pound fresh beets
Russian Mayonnaise
Minced parsley

Wash cauliflower, and break into flowerets. Cook, covered, in a small amount of boiling salted water about 10 minutes or until done; drain and cool.

Leave root and 1 inch of stem on beets; scrub with a brush. Place beets in a saucepan; add water to cover. Bring to a boil; cover and cook 35 to 40 minutes or until tender. Drain; pour cold water over beets, and drain. Cool. Trim off beet roots and stems, and rub off skins. Dice and add Russian Mayonnaise. Mix well, and set aside.

Place cauliflower in a serving bowl; spoon beet mixture over top. Sprinkle with parsley, and chill at least 30 minutes before serving. Yield: 8 servings.

Russian Mayonnaise:

2 hard-cooked egg yolks
1 teaspoon salt
⅛ teaspoon freshly ground pepper
1 teaspoon dry mustard
1 teaspoon sugar
1½ cups commercial sour cream
3 tablespoons olive oil
1 teaspoon lemon juice
1 tablespoon vinegar

Press egg yolks through a sieve; add salt, pepper, dry mustard, sugar, and sour cream, mixing well. Add oil in a slow, steady stream, stirring constantly. Add lemon juice and vinegar, stirring until blended. (Dressing should be thick.) Yield: about 2 cups.
Sandra Huff,
Oak Ridge, Tennessee.

ORANGE-GINGER BEETS

½ pound fresh beets
½ teaspoon grated orange rind
¾ cup orange juice
1 tablespoon cornstarch
2 teaspoons sugar
½ teaspoon ground ginger
⅛ teaspoon salt
1 tablespoon butter or margarine

Leave root and 1 inch of stem on beets; scrub with a brush. Place beets in a saucepan; add water to cover. Bring to a boil; cover and cook 35 to 40 minutes or until tender. Drain; pour cold water over beets, and drain. Trim off beet roots and stems, and rub off skins; cut beets into julienne strips, and set aside.

Combine orange rind, orange juice, cornstarch, sugar, ginger, and salt in a small bowl, mixing well. Melt butter in a medium skillet; add beets and orange juice mixture. Place over medium heat; bring to a boil, and cook 1 minute, stirring constantly. Yield: 4 servings.
Mrs. Rex S. Clements, Jr.,
Leeds, Alabama.

Fruit Salads Give A Light Touch

If you want to add a refreshing touch to your springtime meals, serve one of these fruit salads. One is tossed with a poppy seed dressing; another—Sunny Salad—is left plain so you can add the dressing of your choice. Crunchy Apple Salad combines apples, bananas, pineapple, and raisins. Chopped pecans add the crunch.

For a special sweet salad, try Ambrosia Bowl. Fresh juicy orange slices are layered with bananas, pineapple chunks, coconut, and powdered sugar. A mixture of pineapple syrup and Cointreau is poured over the fruit before it's garnished with maraschino cherries.

FRESH FRUIT SALAD WITH POPPY-SEED DRESSING

1 (11-ounce) can mandarin oranges, drained
2 apples, cored and chopped
1 pint fresh strawberries, halved
2 bananas, sliced
1 to 2 avocados, peeled and chopped
½ cup chopped dates
⅓ cup orange juice
⅓ cup vegetable oil
¼ cup honey
1 teaspoon lemon juice
1 tablespoon poppy seeds
½ teaspoon salt
½ teaspoon prepared mustard

Combine first 6 ingredients in a large mixing bowl. Combine remaining ingredients, mixing well. Pour over fruit, and toss gently to coat; chill 1 to 2 hours. Yield: 6 to 8 servings.

Jennifer Kimmel,
Nashville, Tennessee.

SUNNY SALAD

2 heads Bibb lettuce, torn
1 (16-ounce) can grapefruit sections,
  drained
1 (16-ounce) can prune plums, drained,
  pitted, and halved
2 bananas, sliced
¼ cup chopped pecans or walnuts

Combine all ingredients in a large
bowl. Toss lightly with desired dressing.
Yield: 8 servings. *Aimee A. Goodman,*
Knoxville, Tennessee.

AMBROSIA BOWL

1 (15¼-ounce) can pineapple chunks
2 tablespoons Cointreau, light rum, or
  orange juice
4 large oranges, peeled and sliced
  crosswise
¼ cup powdered sugar, divided
4 medium bananas, diagonally sliced
1 (3½-ounce) can flaked coconut
Maraschino cherries

Drain pineapple, reserving syrup; set
pineapple aside.
Combine reserved pineapple syrup
and Cointreau, mixing well; set aside.
Layer half the orange slices in a large
serving bowl; sprinkle with 2 tablespoons powdered sugar. Layer half the
banana slices and half the pineapple;
sprinkle with half the coconut. Repeat
layers of orange slices, sugar, banana,
and pineapple; pour syrup mixture over
fruit. Sprinkle with remaining coconut.
Garnish with maraschino cherries;
chill 3 to 4 hours. Yield: 8 to 10
servings. *Miss Carolyn Brantley,*
Greenville, Mississippi.

CRUNCHY APPLE SALAD

1 cup chopped apple
1 cup sliced banana
1 (8-ounce) can pineapple chunks, drained
½ cup raisins
½ cup chopped pecans
1 tablespoon lemon juice
⅓ cup mayonnaise
Lettuce leaves

Combine all ingredients except lettuce; toss gently to coat, and chill 1 to 2
hours. Serve on lettuce leaves. Yield: 4
servings. *Claude Thomas,*
Sweetwater, Tennessee.

SOUR CREAM FRUIT SALAD

1 (15½-ounce) can pineapple chunks,
  drained
1 (11-ounce) can mandarin oranges,
  drained
1 cup miniature marshmallows
1 cup flaked coconut
1 cup commercial sour cream
1 large apple, cored and cubed
12 dates, pitted and cut into ¼-inch slices
1 cup walnuts, coarsely chopped
12 maraschino cherries, sliced
Lettuce leaves

Combine all ingredients except lettuce; toss salad gently. Chill 6 to 8
hours or overnight; serve salad on lettuce leaves. Yield: 8 servings.
Mrs. James Tuthill,
Virginia Beach, Virginia.

Make The Best
Chicken Salad Ever

Versatile chicken teams with a variety
of fruits, nuts, and vegetables to make
superb main-dish salads—either hot or
cold. The chilled salads include the delightful Chicken-Avocado Salad, Pineapple-Chicken Salad Pie, and
Macadamia Chicken Salad, which is
served in tomato wedges and has Rum
Dressing spooned over it.
The salad goes into a casserole as Hot
Chicken Salad Pinwheel, which is sprinkled with cheese and bacon, and
Crunchy Hot Chicken Salad, rich with
almonds and celery.

PINEAPPLE-CHICKEN SALAD PIE

1 (20-ounce) can pineapple chunks,
  drained
3 cups diced cooked chicken
1 cup chopped celery
¼ cup finely chopped green onion
2 tablespoons lemon juice
1½ to 2 teaspoons seasoned salt
¼ cup chopped cashew nuts
½ cup mayonnaise
1 baked 9-inch pastry shell, cooled

Combine half of pineapple chunks
and next 7 ingredients; stir well. Spoon

salad into pastry shell, pressing firmly.
Garnish with remaining pineapple
chunks; chill before serving. Yield: 6
servings.
Note: Pastry shell may be omitted;
salad may be served on lettuce leaves, if
desired. *Doris Garton,*
Shenandoah, Virginia.

CRUNCHY HOT CHICKEN SALAD

3 cups diced cooked chicken
1 cup finely chopped celery
2 teaspoons chopped onion
½ cup sliced almonds
1 (10¾-ounce) can cream of chicken soup,
  undiluted
1½ cups cooked rice
1 tablespoon lemon juice
½ teaspoon salt
¼ teaspoon pepper
¾ cup mayonnaise
¼ cup water
3 hard-cooked eggs, sliced
2 cups crushed potato chips
¾ cup shredded Cheddar cheese

Combine first 9 ingredients; toss
gently and set aside.
Combine mayonnaise and water; beat
with a wire whisk until smooth. Pour
over chicken mixture; stir well. Add
eggs, and toss gently. Spoon into a
greased 2-quart shallow baking dish;
cover and refrigerate 8 hours or overnight.
Bake at 450° for 10 to 15 minutes or
until thoroughly heated. Sprinkle with
potato chips and cheese; bake an additional 5 minutes. Yield: 6 to 8
servings. *Margaret H. Dabbs,*
Birmingham, Alabama.

MACADAMIA CHICKEN SALAD

3 cups diced cooked chicken
1 cup finely chopped celery
½ cup mayonnaise
Salt
⅛ teaspoon white pepper
8 medium tomatoes
Lettuce leaves
Rum Dressing
¼ cup chopped macadamia nuts

Combine first 5 ingredients; stir
well. Cover and chill 2 hours.
Place tomatoes in boiling water for 1
minute. Drain and immediately plunge
into cold water. Gently remove skins.

With stem end up, cut each tomato into 6 wedges, cutting to, but not through, base of tomato. Spread wedges slightly apart; sprinkle inside of wedges with salt. Cover and chill 1½ hours.

Place each tomato on lettuce leaves; spoon chicken mixture into shells. Spoon Rum Dressing over salad, and sprinkle with nuts. Yield: 8 servings.

Rum Dressing:

2 tablespoons pineapple juice
¼ cup plus 2 tablespoons mayonnaise
½ teaspoon rum extract

Combine all ingredients; mix well. Chill 1 to 2 hours. Yield: about ½ cup.
Lilly S. Bradley,
Salem, Virginia.

The perfect warm-weather entrée: Chicken-Avocado Salad, served on a bed of lettuce and garnished with egg quarters.

HOT CHICKEN SALAD PINWHEEL

1½ cups diced cooked chicken
¼ cup chopped celery
¼ cup chopped green pepper
¼ cup chopped onion
½ cup frozen English peas, thawed
Salt and pepper to taste
⅓ cup mayonnaise
1 (8-ounce) can crescent dinner rolls
¼ cup shredded sharp Cheddar cheese
4 slices cooked bacon, crumbled, or ¼ cup imitation bacon
1 egg, beaten
1 (10½-ounce) can asparagus tips, drained (optional)

Combine first 7 ingredients; mix well and set aside. Separate crescent rolls into triangles. Arrange 4 triangles on a greased baking sheet with the points outward and the bases forming a square in the center of the pan.

Arrange remaining 4 triangles over the first 4 triangles with the points outward and the bases forming a second square at a 45° turn over the first square. Press overlapping part of triangles slightly to mesh bases and form a 2-inch circle in the center of the pan.

Spoon chicken mixture onto crescent pinwheel, forming a ring. Sprinkle with cheese and bacon. Bring points of triangles over the chicken mixture, and secure tips under the edges of the circle, stretching triangles slightly as necessary. Brush with beaten egg. Bake at 350° for 25 minutes or until crust is golden brown; place on a warm serving platter.

If desired, heat the asparagus tips, and arrange in center of pinwheel. Yield: 4 to 6 servings.

CHICKEN-AVOCADO SALAD

1 medium-size ripe avocado, peeled and cubed
2 to 3 tablespoons lemon or lime juice
1 teaspoon salt
1 (3.5-ounce) can pitted ripe olives, drained and sliced
4 to 5 stalks celery, chopped (about 2 cups)
2 cups diced cooked chicken
½ cup mayonnaise
1 tablespoon lemon or lime juice
Lettuce leaves
3 hard-cooked eggs, quartered
Pimiento strips

Sprinkle avocado with 2 to 3 tablespoons lemon juice and salt; toss well.

Combine avocado, olives, celery, and chicken; stir gently. Combine mayonnaise and 1 tablespoon lemon juice; mix well. Stir mayonnaise mixture into chicken mixture. Serve salad on lettuce; garnish with egg quarters and pimiento strips. Yield: 6 servings.
Mrs. Fred Hays,
Mansfield, Georgia.

Tip: Always measure accurately. Level dry ingredients in a cup with a knife edge or a spoon handle. Measure liquids in a cup so that the fluid is level with the top of the measuring line. Measure solid shortening by packing it firmly in a graduated measuring cup.

A Quick Sauerbraten

When traditional sauerbraten is made, the meat may marinate several days to take on its characteristic sour flavor. But this shortcut recipe will help you duplicate that same spicy taste in just a few hours.

QUICK SAUERBRATEN

1 (4-pound) chuck roast
2 tablespoons vegetable oil
3 tablespoons brown sugar
1 teaspoon ground ginger
⅛ teaspoon ground cloves
⅛ teaspoon ground allspice
1 bay leaf
1½ teaspoons salt
1 teaspoon coarsely ground pepper
¾ cup chopped onion
1½ cups water, divided
⅔ cup red wine vinegar
2 to 4 tablespoons all-purpose flour

Brown roast on both sides in hot oil in a large Dutch oven. Combine sugar, ginger, cloves, allspice, bay leaf, salt, pepper, onion, 1 cup water, and vinegar; mix well, and pour over roast. Cover and simmer 1½ to 2 hours or until roast is tender, turning once. Remove roast to serving platter.

Stir remaining water into flour; stir into pan drippings. Cook, stirring constantly, until thickened. Pour over roast. Yield: 5 to 6 servings.
Linette Walther,
Palatka, Florida.

Cake, The Ideal Dessert

If cake is your idea of an ideal dessert, be sure to try Regal Cream Cheese Cake, a fruit-filled cake with a cream cheese frosting. Our layer cake and chocolate cake are also outstanding.

COCONUT-PINEAPPLE LAYER CAKE

1 cup butter, softened
2 cups sugar
4 eggs
3 cups all-purpose flour
2 teaspoons baking powder
1 teaspoon salt
1 cup milk
1 teaspoon lemon juice
1 teaspoon vanilla extract
½ teaspoon almond extract
Pineapple Filling
Heavenly Frosting
1⅓ cups flaked coconut

Cream butter; gradually add sugar, beating until light and fluffy and sugar is dissolved. Add eggs, one at a time, beating well after each addition.

Combine flour, baking powder, and salt; add to creamed mixture alternately with milk, beginning and ending with flour mixture. Beat on low speed of electric mixer just until blended. Stir in lemon juice and flavorings.

Pour batter into 3 greased and floured 9-inch round cakepans. Bake at 350° for 25 to 30 minutes or until cake tests done. Cool in pans 10 minutes; remove from pans.

Spread Pineapple Filling between warm layers; let cool. Spread top and sides of cake with Heavenly Frosting; sprinkle with coconut. Yield: one 9-inch layer cake.

Pineapple Filling:

3 tablespoons all-purpose flour
½ cup sugar
⅛ teaspoon salt
1 (20-ounce) can crushed pineapple, undrained
2 tablespoons butter or margarine

Combine flour, sugar, and salt in a small saucepan; add pineapple and butter. Cook over medium heat, stirring constantly, until thickened. Yield: filling for one 3-layer cake.

Heavenly Frosting:

1½ cups sugar
Pinch of salt
½ cup water
1 teaspoon vinegar
3 egg whites

Combine all ingredients except egg whites in a heavy saucepan. Cook over medium heat, stirring constantly, until mixture is clear. Cook without stirring until the syrup spins a 4- to 6-inch thread.

Beat egg whites until soft peaks form. Continue beating egg whites while slowly adding syrup mixture; beat until stiff peaks form and frosting is thick enough to spread. Yield: frosting for one 3-layer cake. *Mrs. Walter Perdue, Collinsville, Virginia.*

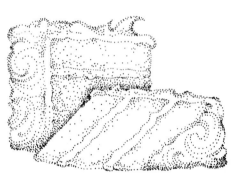

REGAL CREAM CHEESE CAKE

3 cups all-purpose flour
2 cups sugar
1 teaspoon soda
1 teaspoon salt
1 teaspoon ground cloves
3 eggs, beaten
1 cup vegetable oil
1 teaspoon almond extract
1 (8-ounce) can crushed pineapple, undrained
1 cup chopped toasted almonds
2 cups mashed banana
Cream Cheese Frosting

Combine first 5 ingredients in a large mixing bowl; add eggs and oil, stirring until dry ingredients are moistened. Do not beat. Stir in the almond extract, pineapple, almonds, and banana.

Spoon batter into a greased and floured 10-inch tube pan. Bake at 300° for 1 hour and 35 minutes or until done. Cool in pan 10 minutes; remove cake from pan, and cool completely.

Frost cake with Cream Cheese Frosting. Yield: one 10-inch cake.

Cream Cheese Frosting:

½ cup butter or margarine, softened
1 (8-ounce) package cream cheese, softened
1 (16-ounce) package powdered sugar
1 tablespoon instant tea
⅛ teaspoon salt

Cream butter and cream cheese; gradually add sugar, tea, and salt, beating until light and fluffy. Yield: enough for one 10-inch cake.
Mrs. Bernice Bartlett, Gallatin, Tennessee.

EASY CHOCOLATE CAKE

1 cup water
½ cup shortening
½ cup butter or margarine
3½ tablespoons cocoa
2 cups all-purpose flour
2 cups sugar
½ cup buttermilk
2 eggs, beaten
1 teaspoon soda
1 teaspoon vanilla extract
Chocolate Nut Frosting

Combine water, shortening, butter, and cocoa in a medium saucepan; cook over medium heat, stirring frequently, until mixture comes to a boil.

Combine flour and sugar in a large mixing bowl. Add cocoa mixture, stirring well. Stir in buttermilk, eggs, soda, and vanilla. Pour batter into a greased and floured 15- x 10- x 1-inch jellyroll pan. Bake at 400° for 20 minutes. Cool cake in pan completely. Spread Chocolate Nut Frosting on top of cake. Cut into squares. Yield: 24 servings.

Chocolate Nut Frosting:

½ cup butter or margarine
⅓ cup milk
3½ tablespoons cocoa
1 (16-ounce) package powdered sugar
1 cup chopped pecans

Combine butter, milk, and cocoa in a medium saucepan; cook over medium heat, stirring frequently, just until mixture comes to a boil. Remove saucepan from heat, and add sugar; stir with a wire whisk until smooth. Stir in pecans. Use immediately. If necessary, gradually add a small amount of milk, about 2 tablespoons at a time, to make spreading consistency. Yield: enough for one 15- x 10- x 1-inch cake.
Mrs. Elizabeth Moore, Huntsville, Alabama.

July

Tackle the long hot days of July with food dedicated to summer. Equipped with dishes to prepare ahead, grill outdoors, or take with you, our fourth annual *Summer Suppers* special section offers the most delicious ways yet to help you make the most of the South's favorite season.

If our cool desserts and frosty beverages aren't enough to satisfy your summer appetites, take a look at the unbeatable things our readers have done with peaches. You won't want to miss the regal Peaches and Cream Cake—as luscious as the fruit itself!

And enjoy the bounty of fresh produce by stuffing your favorite vegetables with savory meat fillings. They're a great luncheon idea for the peak of the summer season.

Summer Glows With Peaches

Fresh juicy peaches. Just one bite lets you know you've discovered one of summer's golden delights. With the bounty of this fruit from the peach-growing South come specialties as luscious as the fruit itself.

Layers of cake and peach filling are frosted with whipped cream, then topped with fresh peach slices for a delicious Peaches and Cream Cake. An old-fashioned dumpling tastes best when the center is a juicy ripe peach, unbeatable when served hot with cream.

The special flavor of peaches welcomes being mixed with other fruits. Peaches and blueberries are a tasty combination for both a cobbler and a salad. When combined with bananas, peaches make a special summertime jam.

Selecting good-quality peaches is the first step to making these peach favorites. Don't buy peaches with even a touch of green; they were immature when picked and will never ripen properly. The best ripe peaches have a creamy or yellow background and are fairly firm.

BRANDY SPICED PEACHES

1 (1-inch) cube gingerroot, sliced
2 (4-inch) sticks cinnamon
1 tablespoon whole allspice
1 tablespoon whole cloves
5 cups sugar, divided
3 cups vinegar
2 cups water
24 small, firm, ripe peaches, peeled
3 tablespoons pure brandy flavor

Place gingerroot, cinnamon sticks, allspice, and cloves on a piece of cheesecloth; tie ends securely. Combine spice bag, 2 cups sugar, vinegar, and water in a large Dutch oven; bring to a boil. Add peaches; simmer 2 minutes or until thoroughly heated. Carefully remove peaches, and set aside.

Add brandy flavor to syrup in Dutch oven; bring to a boil. Remove from heat, and add peaches; let stand 3 to 4 hours. Carefully remove peaches from syrup; set peaches aside. Add 2 cups sugar to syrup, and bring to a boil. Remove mixture from heat, and add peaches; cover and let stand 24 hours.

Heat peaches thoroughly in hot syrup. Pack peaches into hot sterilized jars, leaving ½-inch headspace.

Add remaining 1 cup sugar to syrup; bring to a boil. Cover peaches with boiling syrup, leaving ½-inch headspace. Adjust lids; process pints for 20 minutes and quarts for 25 minutes in boiling-water bath. Yield: about 6 pints or 3 quarts.
Paul P. Dayhoff, Jr.,
Lisbon, Maryland.

GEORGIA PEACH SALAD

2¼ cups orange juice, divided
1 (6-ounce) package orange-flavored gelatin
¼ cup plus 2 tablespoons sugar
1 teaspoon grated lemon rind
2 cups buttermilk
1 cup coarsely chopped fresh peaches
1 cup fresh blueberries
Lettuce
Fresh peach slices (optional)
Fresh blueberries (optional)
1 cup commercial sour cream

Bring 2 cups orange juice to a boil in a medium saucepan. Add gelatin, sugar, and lemon rind; stir until gelatin is dissolved. Chill until mixture is the consistency of unbeaten egg white. Gradually add buttermilk, and mix well. Fold in peaches and blueberries. Pour mixture into a 6-cup mold; refrigerate until set.

Unmold on lettuce-lined serving plate. Garnish with peach slices and blueberries, if desired. Combine sour cream and remaining ¼ cup orange juice; mix well. Serve dressing over salad. Yield: 10 to 12 servings.
Mrs. Loyd Davenport,
West Palm Beach, Florida.

ROSY PEACH-BANANA JAM

3¼ cups mashed peaches (about 2 pounds)
1 cup mashed banana (about 3 medium)
½ cup coarsely chopped maraschino cherries
2 tablespoons lemon juice
1 (1¾-ounce) package powdered fruit pectin
6 cups sugar

Combine peaches, banana, cherries, lemon juice, and fruit pectin in a large Dutch oven; stir well. Place over high heat and bring to a boil, stirring frequently. Quickly stir in sugar; bring to a boil; boil 1 minute or until mixture reaches 220° on candy thermometer, stirring constantly. Remove from heat; skim off foam with a metal spoon.

Quickly ladle jam into hot sterilized jars, leaving ⅛-inch headspace; cover at once with metal lids, and screw metal bands tight. Process in boiling-water bath for 5 minutes. Yield: 7 cups.
Mrs. Vaden Calvary,
Dodd City, Texas.

CREOLE PEACH DIP

2 cups pureed fresh peaches
½ cup sugar
1 teaspoon lemon juice
Dash of salt
2 cups frozen whipped topping, thawed

Combine peaches, sugar, lemon juice, and salt; stir well. Fold in whipped topping. Chill until serving time. Serve with thin wafers or lightly flavored cookies. Yield: about 4 cups.
T. O. Davis,
Waynesboro, Mississippi.

PEACHES AND CREAM CAKE

1 (18.5-ounce) package butter-flavor cake mix
1½ cups sugar
4 tablespoons cornstarch
4 cups chopped fresh peaches
½ cup water
2 cups whipping cream
2 to 3 tablespoons powdered sugar
1 cup commercial sour cream
Fresh sliced peaches

Prepare cake according to package directions, using two 8-inch cakepans. Cool and split each layer.

Combine sugar and cornstarch in a saucepan. Add peaches and water; cook over medium heat, stirring constantly, until smooth and thickened. Cool mixture completely.

Combine whipping cream and powdered sugar in a medium mixing bowl; beat until stiff peaks form.

Spoon one-third of peach filling over split layer of cake; spread ⅓ cup sour cream over filling. Repeat procedure with remaining cake layers, peach filling, and sour cream, ending with remaining cake layer. Frost with sweetened whipped cream, and garnish with fresh peach slices. Store in refrigerator. Yield: one 8-inch cake.

Emma Coleman,
Ruston, Louisiana.

PEACHY BLUEBERRY COBBLER

1 cup sugar
1 cup all-purpose flour
2 teaspoons baking powder
1 teaspoon salt
1 cup milk
½ cup butter or margarine, melted
3 medium peaches, peeled, sliced, and lightly sugared
⅔ cup fresh or frozen blueberries
Vanilla ice cream (optional)

Combine dry ingredients in a medium mixing bowl. Combine milk and butter; pour over dry ingredients, and mix until smooth. Pour into a greased 12- x 8- x 2-inch glass baking dish.

Spread peaches evenly over top of batter; sprinkle with blueberries. Bake at 350° for 50 minutes or until batter rises through the fruit and top is golden brown. Serve cobbler warm and topped with vanilla ice cream, if desired. Yield: 8 to 10 servings.

Note: Two (10-ounce) packages frozen peaches, thawed and drained, may be substituted for fresh peaches.

Mrs. Nancy Bluhm,
Winston-Salem, North Carolina.

PEACH DUMPLINGS

2 to 2½ cups all-purpose flour
2 teaspoons baking powder
1 teaspoon salt
¾ cup shortening
½ cup milk
4 medium peaches, peeled and halved
Sugar
Ground cinnamon
⅔ cup sugar
1½ cups water
2 tablespoons butter or margarine
¼ teaspoon ground cinnamon
Dash of ground nutmeg
Whipping cream

Combine flour, baking powder, and salt; cut in shortening with pastry blender until mixture resembles coarse meal. Gradually add milk, stirring to

make a soft dough. Roll dough into a 14-inch square (¼-inch thickness) on a lightly floured surface; then cut dough into four 7-inch squares.

Place 2 peach halves on each square. Sprinkle each with 2 teaspoons sugar and ⅛ teaspoon cinnamon. Moisten edges of each dumpling with water; bring corners to center, pinching edges to seal.

Place dumplings 1 inch apart in a lightly greased shallow baking pan.

Combine remaining ingredients except whipping cream in a medium saucepan; place over low heat, stirring until butter melts and sugar dissolves. Pour syrup over dumplings. Bake at 425° for 40 to 45 minutes or until golden brown. Serve with cream. Yield: 4 servings.

Mrs. Grant Adkins,
Wichita Falls, Texas.

Use Juicy Blueberries To Your Advantage

In midsummer when plump blueberries make their appearance at the market, it's time to bake them in pies, muffins, and cobblers. You'll love our Fresh Blueberry Cream Pie, rich with sour cream, or our Blueberry Kuchen—blueberries baked in a thick, buttery crust. And it's hard to resist Fresh Blueberry Cobbler, served warm with whipped cream.

Like all berries, blueberries are highly perishable, so they should be stored in the coldest part of the refrigerator and used as soon as possible. Before using, rinse the blueberries briefly with water, and drain well in a colander or on absorbent towels.

BLUEBERRY KUCHEN

1 cup all-purpose flour
2 tablespoons sugar
Pinch of salt
½ cup butter or margarine, softened
1 tablespoon vinegar
2 tablespoons all-purpose flour
1 cup sugar
⅛ teaspoon ground cinnamon
3 cups fresh blueberries, divided
Powdered sugar

Combine first 3 ingredients; cut in butter with pastry blender until mixture resembles coarse meal. Sprinkle vinegar evenly over surface; stir with a fork until all dry ingredients are moistened. Press pastry in bottom and 1 inch up sides of a 9-inch springform pan.

Combine 2 tablespoons flour, 1 cup sugar, and cinnamon, mixing well. Stir in 2 cups blueberries; spread evenly over pastry. Bake at 400° for 45 minutes. Remove from oven, and sprinkle remaining 1 cup blueberries evenly over top. Chill well before removing from pan. Sprinkle with powdered sugar. Yield: about 6 servings.

Susan Settlemyre,
Chapel Hill, North Carolina.

BLUEBERRY MUFFINS

⅔ cup shortening
1 cup sugar
3 eggs
3 cups all-purpose flour
2½ teaspoons baking powder
1 teaspoon salt
1 cup milk
1 cup fresh blueberries

Cream shortening; gradually add sugar, beating until light and fluffy. Add eggs, one at a time, beating well after each addition. Combine flour, baking powder, and salt; add to creamed mixture alternately with milk, beginning and ending with flour mixture. Stir in blueberries. Spoon batter into greased muffin pans, filling two-thirds full. Bake at 375° for 20 to 25 minutes. Yield: about 2 dozen.

Note: Batter may be stored in refrigerator 2 weeks before baking.

Nan Fountain,
Greenville, Mississippi.

Fresh Blueberry Cream Pie is rich with juicy berries, thick sour cream filling, and streusel topping.

BLUEBERRY SAUCE

2 cups fresh blueberries
⅓ cup sugar
⅓ cup water

Combine all ingredients in a medium saucepan; mix well, and bring to a boil. Reduce heat and simmer 4 minutes, stirring occasionally. Serve warm. Yield: about 2 cups. *Charlotte Baker, Charlottesville, Virginia.*

FRESH BLUEBERRY COBBLER

2 cups fresh blueberries
¼ cup water
⅔ cup sugar
1 cup whole wheat flour
½ cup firmly packed brown sugar
½ teaspoon salt
1 teaspoon baking powder
Pinch of ground nutmeg
⅓ cup butter, softened
Whipped cream

Combine blueberries, water, and sugar in a medium saucepan. Bring to a boil; reduce heat and simmer 2 minutes, stirring constantly. Pour into an 8-inch square baking dish.

Combine flour, brown sugar, salt, baking powder, and nutmeg in a small mixing bowl, mixing well; cut in butter with pastry blender until mixture resembles coarse meal. Sprinkle over blueberry mixture. Bake at 350° for 25 minutes. Serve warm with whipped cream. Yield: 6 servings. *Linda Clark, Elizabethton, Tennessee.*

Tip: During the week, keep a shopping list handy to write down items as you need them. This will eliminate unnecessary trips to the store. Before your weekly shopping trip, make a complete shopping list. If the list is arranged according to the layout of the store, you'll save time and steps.

FRESH BLUEBERRY CREAM PIE

1 cup commercial sour cream
2 tablespoons all-purpose flour
¾ cup sugar
1 teaspoon vanilla extract
¼ teaspoon salt
1 egg, beaten
2½ cups fresh blueberries
1 unbaked 9-inch pastry shell
3 tablespoons all-purpose flour
1½ tablespoons butter or margarine
3 tablespoons chopped pecans or walnuts

Combine first 6 ingredients; beat 5 minutes at medium speed of an electric mixer or until smooth. Fold in the blueberries. Pour filling into pastry shell; bake at 400° for 25 minutes. Remove from oven.

Combine remaining ingredients, stirring well; sprinkle over top of pie. Bake 10 additional minutes. Chill before serving. Yield: one 9-inch pie.

Betsy Highsmith, Wilmington, North Carolina.

summer Suppers

Our Summer Dreams: Charcoal Smoke, Crisp Greens, Melting Desserts

Summer is a time for dreaming, day or night, and if you need a little inspiration, how about Marinated Tenderloin, Fresh Corn Pudding, or Pineapple Dessert Soufflé? These are just a few of the recipes that you'll find included in this *Summer Suppers* special section.

Most of the selections are geared to the season—dishes to prepare ahead, grill outdoors, or take advantage of summer fruits and vegetables. Dreams meant to become reality.

We also share the menus and ideas for entertaining of several Southerners. There is a gracious dinner built around the annual walking horse events in Middle Tennessee. The menu featured at J. W. and Caroline Cross' Tuck-A-Way Farm includes an old family recipe for Asparagus Cutlets.

Away to the lake we go, Smith Mountain Lake in Virginia with several families from Roanoke for a day of outdoor activities. As the sun begins to get low it's time for food, starting with Clam Crisps and Cheese Wafers, followed by a main course of Grilled Flank Steak, Broiled Tomatoes, Asparagus and Peas Casserole, Sweet and Sour Potato Salad, Lettuce and Fruit Salad, and hot rolls. Then, what the children have been waiting for, Lemon Ice Cream Tarts.

We also take a hayride, but not just any hayride. This is a hayride-with-dinner donated by Capt. and Mrs. Quentin Crommelin to the Landmarks Foundation of Montgomery, Alabama, for a fund-raising auction. This outing for ten couples starts at the Crommelins' country home followed by the hayride to Fort Toulouse, where there is a narrated tour. A picnic supper features Cream Cheese Pâté, Crispy Fried Chicken Breasts, Virginia Ham Sandwiches (with Priscilla Crommelin's homemade mayonnaise), Deluxe Potato Salad, Tangy Romaine Salad, Parson's Tipsy Pudding, white wine, and coffee.

Other features for *Summer Suppers* help you make the season more enjoyable: fresh vegetable side dishes to let you bring your vegetable garden harvest to the table with flair; light and refreshing salads that seem so right during warm months; a whole range of appetizers to serve for all those summer occasions; cool beverages; and light, dreamy desserts.

Fire up the grill, pack the basket, call your friends. Don't let summer go by without some delicious occasions.

A Show Of Horses And Hospitality

During the summer in Middle Tennessee, the heartland of walking horse country, all talk is of the International Grand Championship Walking Horse Show, sponsored by the Walking Horse Owners Association. Horse owners and trainers are caught in the excitement of preparing for the five-day festival. Held annually in Murfreesboro, the show welcomes horse owners from around the world to compete for various championships.

In true Tennessee style, J. W. and Caroline Cross open their home to friends to celebrate this special event. "I really enjoy planning a round of parties that feature horse-related activities," says Caroline. And Tuck-A-Way Farm, the family residence located outside Franklin, provides the perfect setting for a gracious dinner served alfresco.

Caroline and J. W. welcome their guests beneath sprawling shade trees that overlook the lush pasture. Here guests sip Fruit Slushy or Bloodless Marys and nibble on a Sparkling Fresh Fruit Bowl and the Zesty Artichoke Appetizer.

Inside, an impressive buffet table is beautifully set with Caroline's favorite menu. The main feature of the buffet is the Marinated Tenderloin. This melt-in-your-mouth meat is marinated overnight before being baked to perfection. Fresh Spinach Salad Delight is tossed with hearts of palm, artichoke hearts, bacon, onions, tomatoes, and eggs and is topped with Tangy Salad Dressing.

Side dishes carefully chosen to complement the entrée and salad include a delicately flavored Squash and Egg Casserole and an old family recipe for Asparagus Cutlets. "This cutlet recipe was given to me by my aunt many years ago, and I've never seen it in any cookbook," Caroline proudly tells us.

Once plates are filled, guests move back outdoors to attractively arranged tables. There's plenty of room for everyone to visit and discuss their participation in the upcoming events.

Even though everything is delicious, guests always save room for dessert, a choice of Raspberry Sauce Dessert or Lemon Angel Cake.

BLOODLESS MARY

2 (46-ounce) cans tomato juice, chilled
2 teaspoons garlic salt
2 teaspoons celery salt
1 teaspoon pepper
2 tablespoons Worcestershire sauce
Juice of 2 lemons (about 4 to 6 tablespoons)
6 to 8 dashes of hot sauce
⅛ teaspoon sugar

Combine all ingredients; stir well. Chill several hours before serving. Yield: about 3 quarts.

SPARKLING FRESH FRUIT BOWL

3 cantaloupes, halved
3 honeydew melons, halved
½ watermelon
2 pineapples, peeled, cored, and cubed
½ cup drained red maraschino cherries
½ cup drained green maraschino cherries
¾ cup sugar
1 cup lime juice

Scoop out melon balls, or peel melons and cut into cubes.
Combine melon balls, pineapple cubes, and cherries in a large salad bowl; chill until serving time.
Combine sugar and lime juice; stir well. Set mixture aside until sugar dissolves. Pour over fruit, and toss gently before serving. Yield: 24 servings.

FRUIT SLUSHY

2 (6-ounce) cans frozen lemonade concentrate, thawed and undiluted
2 (6-ounce) cans frozen limeade concentrate, thawed and undiluted
2 (6-ounce) cans frozen orange juice concentrate, thawed and undiluted
2 (6-ounce) cans frozen pineapple juice concentrate, thawed and undiluted
Cracked ice

Combine half of each of the first 4 ingredients in container of electric blender; add enough cracked ice to fill blender. Process until mixture is slushy. Empty blender container.
Repeat procedure with remaining ingredients. Serve immediately. Yield: about 2 quarts.

ZESTY ARTICHOKE APPETIZER

2 (14-ounce) cans artichoke hearts, drained and chopped
1 cup grated Parmesan cheese
1 cup mayonnaise
Dash of garlic salt
Dash of Worcestershire sauce
Dash of hot sauce
Fresh parsley (optional)

Combine first 6 ingredients, stirring well. Spoon into a lightly greased 1-quart casserole or soufflé dish. Bake at 350° for 20 minutes. Garnish with parsley, if desired; serve with toast points or melba rounds. Yield: 3 cups.

Marinated Tenderloin
Fresh Spinach Salad Delight
Tangy Salad Dressing
Squash and Egg Casserole
Asparagus Cutlets
Rolls
Raspberry Sauce Dessert
Lemon Angel Cake
Wine

MARINATED TENDERLOIN

12 to 16 pounds beef tenderloin
Garlic salt
Red pepper
Coarsely ground black pepper
1 (16-ounce) bottle olive oil
1 (16-ounce) bottle red wine vinegar
3 cups Burgundy
3 cloves garlic, minced
Fresh parsley (optional)
Radish roses (optional)

Sprinkle tenderloin with garlic salt, red pepper, and black pepper; place in a deep roasting pan.
Combine olive oil, vinegar, Burgundy, and garlic; stir well. Pour marinade over tenderloin; cover with foil, and refrigerate overnight.
Cover and bake tenderloin (do not drain marinade) at 425° until meat thermometer registers 140° (rare) or 160° (medium rare). Garnish with fresh parsley and radish roses, if desired. Yield: 18 to 24 servings.

FRESH SPINACH SALAD DELIGHT

1 pound fresh spinach, torn into bite-size pieces
1 cup thinly sliced hearts of palm
1 (14-ounce) can artichoke hearts, drained and diced
6 slices bacon, cooked and crumbled
4 green onions, thinly sliced
2 to 3 tomatoes, cut into wedges
2 hard-cooked eggs, chopped
Tangy Salad Dressing

Combine all ingredients except dressing in a large salad bowl; toss lightly. Cover salad, and chill until serving time. Serve with Tangy Salad Dressing. Yield: about 16 servings.

Tangy Salad Dressing:

1 small onion, minced
¾ cup sugar
½ cup vinegar
⅓ cup catsup
¼ cup vegetable oil
2 tablespoons Worcestershire sauce

Combine all ingredients in container of electric blender; blend well. Chill before serving. Yield: 2 cups.

SQUASH AND EGG CASSEROLE

2 pounds yellow squash, thinly sliced
2 medium onions, thinly sliced
Thick white sauce (recipe follows)
6 hard-cooked eggs, finely chopped
½ cup soft breadcrumbs
2 tablespoons melted butter or margarine
Parsley (optional)

Cook squash and onion in a small amount of boiling water until tender (about 8 to 10 minutes); drain. Combine squash, onion, thick white sauce, and eggs; stir well. Spoon into a lightly greased deep 2½-quart casserole. Combine breadcrumbs and butter; sprinkle over casserole. Bake at 350° for 20 to 25 minutes or until hot and bubbly. Garnish with parsley, if desired. Yield: 8 servings.

Thick White Sauce:
¼ cup plus 2 tablespoons butter or
  margarine
¼ cup plus 2 tablespoons all-purpose
  flour
2 cups milk
½ teaspoon salt

Melt butter in a heavy saucepan over low heat; add flour and cook 1 minute, stirring constantly. Gradually add milk; cook over medium heat, stirring constantly, until thickened and bubbly. Stir in salt. Yield: about 2¼ cups.

Note: To serve a crowd, prepare two separate casseroles.

ASPARAGUS CUTLETS

2 (10½-ounce) cans asparagus tips
Asparagus White Sauce
4 cups cracker crumbs, divided
2 cups (8 ounces) shredded sharp
  Cheddar cheese
2 eggs, beaten
Vegetable oil
Fresh parsley (optional)
Lemon slices (optional)

Drain asparagus, reserving liquid. Combine asparagus, Asparagus White Sauce, 2 cups cracker crumbs, and cheese in a large bowl; cover and chill overnight.

Shape asparagus mixture into 14 flat patties; dip in beaten egg, then roll in remaining cracker crumbs.

Heat 1 inch oil to 375° in a large skillet. Add patties, and cook until golden brown. Drain on paper towels; garnish patties with parsley and lemon slices, if desired. Yield: 14 servings.

Asparagus White Sauce:
¼ cup plus 2 tablespoons butter or
  margarine
¼ cup plus 2 tablespoons all-purpose
  flour
1 cup reserved asparagus liquid
1 cup milk
½ teaspoon salt

Melt butter in a heavy saucepan over low heat; add flour and cook 1 minute, stirring constantly. Gradually add asparagus liquid and milk; cook over medium heat, stirring constantly, until sauce is thickened and bubbly. Stir in salt. Yield: about 2¼ cups.

RASPBERRY SAUCE DESSERT

1 (10-ounce) package frozen raspberries,
  thawed
1 tablespoon cornstarch
1 tablespoon water
¼ cup sugar
½ cup red currant jelly
¼ cup Cointreau or other orange-flavored
  liqueur
Vanilla ice cream

Place raspberries in container of electric blender, and puree; strain, discarding the seeds.

Combine cornstarch and water; stir well. Combine raspberry puree and cornstarch mixture in a small saucepan; cook over low heat, stirring constantly, until thickened (about 5 minutes). Add sugar and jelly, stirring constantly, until dissolved. Stir in liqueur. Remove from heat; chill. Serve over vanilla ice cream. Yield: about 2 cups.

Note: Sauce may be prepared ahead and frozen; thaw before serving.

LEMON ANGEL CAKE

2 envelopes unflavored gelatin
1 cup lemon juice
6 large eggs, separated
2 cups sugar, divided
1 (19¼-ounce) angel food cake, cut into
  1-inch pieces
1 cup whipping cream
¼ cup sifted powdered sugar
Yellow food coloring

Soften gelatin in lemon juice; let stand 5 minutes.

Beat egg yolks until thick and lemon colored. Combine egg yolks, 1 cup sugar, and gelatin mixture in a small saucepan; cook over low heat until thickened. Set aside to cool.

Beat egg whites (at room temperature) until soft peaks form. Gradually add 1 cup sugar; continue beating until peaks are stiff and glossy. Fold lemon mixture into egg whites.

Gently fold cake pieces into lemon mixture, coating all pieces well. Spoon into a lightly greased 10-inch tube pan; chill overnight.

Remove cake from pan by gently running a knife between sides of cake and edge of pan; invert onto platter.

Combine whipping cream and powdered sugar; beat until stiff peaks form. Add a few drops of yellow food coloring, mixing well. Spread on top and sides of cake. Store cake in refrigerator until serving time. Yield: one 10-inch cake.

A Rainbow Of Summer Salads

These salads can be a summer cook's best friend. They add a light, refreshing touch to the menu, and their cheerful colors brighten any table.

Start with lots of leafy green spinach; add cabbage, almonds, and raisins, and you end up with spectacular Crunchy Spinach Salad. Or scoop out fresh pineapple and stuff it with a shrimp-and-fruit mixture for Pineapple Boats Ahoy.

CRUNCHY SPINACH SALAD

½ pound fresh spinach, torn into bite-size
  pieces
2 tablespoons toasted slivered almonds
¾ cup shredded purple cabbage
¼ cup raisins
Dressing (recipe follows)

Combine all ingredients except dressing in a large bowl. Toss and serve with dressing. Yield: 6 to 8 servings.

Dressing:
¼ cup sugar
¾ teaspoon dry mustard
¾ teaspoon salt
½ teaspoon celery seeds
1½ tablespoons minced onion
¼ cup vinegar
½ cup vegetable oil

Combine all ingredients in a jar. Cover tightly, and shake vigorously. Chill several hours. Shake dressing again before serving over salad. Yield: 1 cup.
  Mrs. Mary D. Ahl,
  New Orleans, Louisiana.

MEDITERRANEAN SPRING SALAD

½ pound new potatoes
½ cup olive oil
2 tablespoons lemon juice
1 clove garlic, crushed
2 teaspoons dried oregano leaves
¼ teaspoon salt
6 cups torn mixed salad greens
1 large tomato, cut into wedges
1 medium-size green pepper, thinly sliced
    into rings
1 small purple onion, thinly sliced and
    separated into rings
1 small cucumber, thinly sliced
½ cup crumbled feta cheese
1 (2-ounce) can anchovy fillets (optional)

Cook potatoes in boiling salted water about 25 minutes or until tender; drain well, and cool slightly. Peel and thinly slice potatoes; place in a shallow bowl. Combine oil, lemon juice, garlic, oregano, and salt; mix well. Pour over potatoes; marinate 1 hour. Drain potatoes, reserving marinade.

Place salad greens in a large bowl. Arrange potatoes, tomato, green pepper, onion, cucumber, cheese, and anchovies (if desired) over salad greens. Serve with reserved marinade. Yield: 6 servings.
Sandra Smith,
Talbott, Tennessee.

VEGETABLE-RICE SALAD

1¼ cups uncooked regular rice
1 cucumber, peeled and chopped
Salt
1 large carrot, peeled and diced
⅓ pound fresh green beans, cut into
    ½-inch pieces (about 1 cup)
1 cup frozen English peas
1 red pepper, chopped
2 medium tomatoes, peeled, seeded, and
    cut into lengthwise strips
2 tablespoons tarragon vinegar
½ teaspoon salt
½ teaspoon pepper
¼ cup plus 2 tablespoons olive oil
Lettuce leaves

Cook rice according to package directions; chill.

Sprinkle cucumber generously with salt; cover and let stand 30 minutes. Rinse well.

Combine carrot, beans, and peas in a medium saucepan; cover with water, and cook 8 to 10 minutes or until crisp-tender; drain and rinse in cold water.

Combine cucumber, carrot, beans, peas, rice, red pepper, and tomatoes. Combine vinegar, ½ teaspoon salt, and pepper; gradually add oil, beating with a wire whisk until blended. Pour dressing over salad, and toss gently. Serve on lettuce leaves. Yield: 6 servings.
Ruth E. Cunliffe,
Lake Placid, Florida.

VEGETABLE-CORNED BEEF SALAD

1 (6-ounce) package lemon-flavored gelatin
½ teaspoon salt
1 cup boiling water
¼ cup vinegar
½ cup cold water
¼ cup sliced pimiento-stuffed olives
1½ teaspoons minced onion, divided
1½ cups shredded cabbage
1 cup diced celery, divided
2 tablespoons diced pimiento
2 tablespoons finely chopped green pepper
1 envelope unflavored gelatin
¼ cup cold water
1 cup chicken broth
Dash of hot sauce (optional)
2 tablespoons lemon juice
½ teaspoon prepared mustard
Salt to taste
1 (8-ounce) carton commercial sour cream
1 (12-ounce) can corned beef, diced
¼ cup chopped sweet pickle
Cucumber slices (optional)
Parsley (optional)

Dissolve lemon-flavored gelatin and ½ teaspoon salt in boiling water; stir in vinegar and ½ cup cold water. Spoon about 3 tablespoons gelatin mixture into bottom of a lightly oiled 1½-quart mold; chill until slightly thickened. Press olives into thickened gelatin; return to refrigerator. Chill remaining gelatin mixture until consistency of unbeaten egg white; fold in 1 teaspoon

onion, cabbage, ½ cup celery, pimiento, and green pepper. Spoon mixture over olive layer, and chill until firm.

Soften unflavored gelatin in ¼ cup cold water. Bring chicken broth to a boil; stir in softened gelatin. Cool. Stir in ½ teaspoon onion, hot sauce, if desired, lemon juice, mustard, salt, and sour cream. Chill until consistency of unbeaten egg white. Fold in ½ cup celery, corned beef, and sweet pickle.

Spoon mixture over vegetable layer. Chill until firm. Unmold and garnish with cucumber slices and parsley, if desired. Yield: 8 servings. *Bird Helmick,*
Vici, Oklahoma.

CRAB-STUFFED TOMATO SALAD

4 large tomatoes
1 (6½-ounce) can crabmeat, drained and
    flaked
¾ cup shredded carrot
½ cup peeled, diced cucumber
1 tablespoon mayonnaise
½ teaspoon salt
Lettuce leaves
Fresh parsley

Slice off top of each tomato, and scoop out pulp, leaving shells intact. Invert tomatoes to drain. Dice enough tomato pulp to make ½ cup; reserve remaining pulp for use in other recipes.

Combine ½ cup tomato pulp, crabmeat, carrot, cucumber, mayonnaise, and salt; stir well. Chill until serving time.

Spoon crabmeat mixture into tomato shells; serve on lettuce leaves. Garnish with parsley. Yield: 4 servings.
Mrs. M. L. Shannon,
Fairfield, Alabama.

PINEAPPLE BOATS AHOY

4½ cups water
1½ pounds fresh shrimp
1 large fresh pineapple
1 medium orange
1 medium grapefruit
1 medium avocado
Juice of 1 lime (2 to 3 tablespoons)
Dressing (recipe follows)

Bring water to a boil. Add shrimp; return to a boil. Lower heat, and simmer 3 to 5 minutes. Drain shrimp well; rinse with cold water. Chill. Peel and devein shrimp; set aside.

Cut pineapple in half lengthwise. Scoop out pulp, leaving shells ½ to ¼ inch thick. Cut pineapple pulp into bite-size pieces, discarding core. Set aside 1 cup pineapple pieces; reserve remaining pieces for use in other recipes.

Peel, seed, and section orange and grapefruit; combine fruit sections with 1 cup pineapple pieces and shrimp. Cover; chill until ready to serve.

Before serving, peel and dice avocado; sprinkle with lime juice to prevent discoloration. Combine avocado and shrimp mixture; spoon into reserved pineapple shells. Pour dressing over top before serving. Yield: 3 to 4 servings.

Dressing:

½ cup vegetable oil
2 tablespoons Chablis or other dry white wine
2 tablespoons lime juice
½ teaspoon salt
½ teaspoon paprika
1 teaspoon honey

Combine all ingredients in container of electric blender; blend well. Serve immediately. Yield: ¾ cup.

Mrs. Archer Yates,
Dunwoody, Georgia.

SUMMER APPLE SALAD

3 envelopes unflavored gelatin
1 cup cold water
¾ cup sugar
1½ teaspoons salt
3 cups boiling water
⅓ cup vinegar
¼ cup lime juice
2 large apples, unpeeled and finely chopped (about 2½ cups)
1 cup finely chopped green pepper
½ cup chopped green onion
Lettuce
Apple wedges (optional)

Soften gelatin in cold water; stir well. Add sugar and salt. Gradually add boiling water, stirring until gelatin is dissolved. Add vinegar and lime juice.

Chill until consistency of unbeaten egg white. Fold in apple, green pepper, and onion. Spoon into 12 (½-cup) individual molds, and chill until set. Unmold on lettuce-lined plate, and garnish with apple wedges, if desired. Yield: 12 servings.

Mrs. Janis Moyer,
Farmersville, Texas.

Party Starters To Munch And Spread

Inside, outside, or around the pool, parties and appetizers go hand in hand. Since the general rule seems to be the more, the merrier, that means putting out a variety of appetizers for your guests to munch, dip, or spread.

For a savory surprise, broil pineapple, shrimp, bacon, and green pepper threaded on skewers. Quiche is always popular, and Miniature Cheese Quiches will be a crowd pleaser. And there's lots more cheese to be enjoyed in Cheesy Chili Dip, Cheese Straws, and Tipsy Cheese Spread.

SAUCY PARTY MEATBALLS

1½ pounds ground beef
1 egg, slightly beaten
½ cup soft breadcrumbs
1 small onion, grated
½ teaspoon salt
⅛ teaspoon pepper
⅛ teaspoon monosodium glutamate
1 (16-ounce) can whole cranberry sauce
2 (8-ounce) cans tomato sauce
1 (8-ounce) can whole cranberry sauce

Combine first 7 ingredients; mix well, and shape into 1-inch balls. Combine 16-ounce can of cranberry sauce and tomato sauce in a large saucepan; heat thoroughly. Add meatballs; cover and simmer 50 to 55 minutes or until done. Add remaining cranberry sauce; heat thoroughly. Transfer to chafing dish, and keep warm. Yield: about 3 dozen.

Ethel Evans,
St. Petersburg, Florida.

BROILED CHICKEN WINGS

1 pound chicken wings
3 tablespoons lemon juice
3 tablespoons soy sauce
⅛ teaspoon onion powder
Salt and pepper to taste
1 tablespoon honey
1 tablespoon catsup

Remove tips from wings; cut wings into 2 pieces, and place in a shallow dish.

Combine lemon juice, soy sauce, and onion powder; pour over chicken. Cover and marinate wings in refrigerator several hours or overnight.

Drain chicken wings, reserving 1 tablespoon marinade; place wings on a foil-lined broiler pan. Sprinkle with salt and pepper. Combine reserved marinade, honey, and catsup, stirring well; brush half of mixture on chicken wings. Broil 6 to 7 inches from broiler for 7 minutes. Turn and brush with remaining sauce; broil 7 additional minutes. Yield: about 1½ dozen.

Mrs. W. J. Scherffius,
Mountain Home, Arkansas.

SALMON BALL

1 (15½-ounce) can red salmon, drained and flaked
1 tablespoon lemon juice
1 tablespoon dried minced onion flakes
1 (8-ounce) package cream cheese, softened
½ teaspoon Worcestershire sauce
1 teaspoon prepared horseradish
¼ teaspoon salt
½ teaspoon liquid smoke
⅓ cup finely chopped pecans or walnuts

Combine first 8 ingredients; mix well. Shape mixture into a ball; chill about 2 hours or until firm. Roll ball in pecans. Serve with crackers or chips. Yield: one 5-inch salmon ball.

Mary Anne Pusey,
Mount Airy, Maryland.

Tip: For just a squirt of lemon, poke a hole in one end and squeeze.

SHRIMP KABOBS

1 (15½-ounce) can pineapple chunks
¼ cup lemon juice
1 cup soy sauce
3 pounds large fresh shrimp, peeled and deveined
1 pound bacon
1 green pepper, cut into 1-inch pieces

Drain pineapple, reserving juice. Combine pineapple juice, lemon juice, soy sauce, and shrimp. Cover tightly, and marinate in refrigerator 1 hour or more.

Cut bacon slices in half; cook until limp but not crisp. Drain and set aside.

Drain shrimp; alternate pineapple chunks, shrimp, bacon, and green pepper on skewers. Broil until bacon is crisp and shrimp is done (about 2 to 3 minutes). Yield: about 2 dozen servings.
Mrs. Bernie Benigno,
Gulfport, Mississippi.

ZESTY SHRIMP DIP

1 (3-ounce) package cream cheese, softened
1 (8-ounce) carton commercial sour cream
2 teaspoons lemon juice
1 (0.6-ounce) package Italian salad dressing mix
2 tablespoons finely chopped green pepper
1 (4¼-ounce) can medium shrimp, drained, rinsed, and chopped

Beat cream cheese until light and fluffy. Stir in remaining ingredients. Chill at least 1 hour. Serve with fresh vegetables. Yield: 1⅔ cups.
Mrs. Raymond F. McHugh,
Fallston, Maryland.

CHEESE STRAWS

1 pound sharp Cheddar cheese, shredded
½ cup butter or margarine, softened
2 teaspoons Worcestershire sauce
1½ cups all-purpose flour
1 teaspoon salt
1 teaspoon paprika
¾ teaspoon red pepper

Combine cheese, butter, and Worcestershire sauce; beat well. Combine next 4 ingredients, mixing well. Gradually add flour mixture to cheese mixture, mixing until dough is no longer crumbly. Form into a ball.

Use a cookie gun to shape dough into straws, following manufacturer's instructions, or use the following procedure: Divide dough into fourths; on waxed paper, roll each piece into a rectangle ⅓ inch thick. Use a pastry wheel to cut dough into 4- x ½-inch strips.

Place strips on ungreased cookie sheets; bake at 375° for 10 to 12 minutes or until lightly browned. Store in airtight containers, placing waxed paper between layers. Yield: about 8 dozen.
Mrs. Steve Toney,
Helena, Arkansas.

MINIATURE CHEESE QUICHES

2 eggs, beaten
½ cup milk
1½ tablespoons butter, melted
1 cup (4 ounces) shredded Cheddar cheese
Pastry shells (recipe follows)
Red pepper or paprika (optional)

Combine first 4 ingredients; stir well, and pour into pastry shells. Sprinkle with red pepper, if desired. Bake at 350° for 25 minutes or until set. Yield: 2 dozen.

Pastry Shells:

1¼ cups all-purpose flour
1 teaspoon salt
3 tablespoons butter, melted
1 egg yolk
3 to 4 tablespoons cold water

Combine flour and salt; add butter, mixing well. Add egg yolk and water; stir with a fork until all dry ingredients are moistened. Shape dough into 24 (1-inch) balls. Place in lightly greased 1¾-inch muffin pans, shaping each into a shell. Yield: 2 dozen.
Mrs. Thomas Hamlin,
Richmond, Virginia.

TIPSY CHEESE SPREAD

2 pounds sharp Cheddar cheese, shredded
2 cloves garlic, crushed
1 tablespoon Worcestershire sauce
½ teaspoon dry mustard
1 cup beer
Salt to taste

Beat cheese (at room temperature) until creamy, using an electric mixer or food processor. Add garlic, Worcestershire sauce, and mustard; mix well. Gradually add beer, mixing until well blended. Add salt to taste. Store in refrigerator. Serve at room temperature with rye bread or crackers. Yield: about 3½ cups cheese spread.
Elizabeth Kraus,
Louisville, Kentucky.

CHEESY CHILI DIP

1 (10-ounce) can tomatoes and green chilies
1 (4-ounce) can chopped green chilies
1 tablespoon cornstarch
1 medium onion, diced
1 clove garlic, minced
½ teaspoon salt
½ teaspoon pepper
¼ to ½ teaspoon crushed red pepper
1 cup (4 ounces) diced Colby cheese
Tortilla chips

Drain tomatoes and chopped green chilies, reserving liquid. Set vegetable mixture aside.

Combine reserved liquid and cornstarch in a 1-quart saucepan; cook over medium heat, stirring constantly, until thickened. Stir in tomatoes, chilies, onion, garlic, and seasonings. Cook, stirring constantly, until onion is tender. Stir in cheese; cook over low heat until melted. Serve warm with tortilla chips. Yield: 2¼ cups.
Patsy M. Smith,
Lampasas, Texas.

Tip: Keep soft cheese—American, Swiss, etc.—from sticking to grater by first rubbing grater with a dab of butter applied with a paper towel.

ZUCCHINI HORS D'OEUVRES

1 cup biscuit mix
½ cup finely chopped onion
½ cup grated Parmesan cheese
2 tablespoons chopped fresh parsley
½ teaspoon salt
½ teaspoon seasoned salt
½ teaspoon ground oregano
⅛ teaspoon pepper
1 clove garlic, minced
¼ cup vegetable oil
4 eggs, beaten
3 cups thinly sliced zucchini

Combine all ingredients except zucchini, mixing well. Stir in zucchini. Spread evenly in a lightly greased 13- x 9- x 2-inch baking pan. Bake at 350° for 30 minutes. Cut into 1½-inch squares. Serve warm. Yield: about 4 dozen.
Mildred Sherrer,
Bay City, Texas.

A Lively Menu For A Day At The Lake

Summer's the time for easy living, and that's exactly what Barbara and Bill Rakes keep in mind when it comes to entertaining. On weekends, the Rakes invite other families to join them for a leisurely gathering at their summer home on Smith Mountain Lake, a short drive from Roanoke, Virginia.

After a day of water skiing, sailing, and sunning, everyone congregates on the Rakes' deck for relaxing. Barbara has Pink Lemonade Slush ready for the children and Cheese Wafers and Clam Crisps for everyone to munch on. The appetizers are a snap to serve because they can be prepared in advance. The dough for Cheese Wafers may be frozen, making them readily available for many weekend lake gatherings.

Dinner is centered around Grilled Flank Steak, a good way to prepare steak for a large group. Bill grills four flank steaks and serves them in thin, savory slices. While Bill tends to the grilling, Barbara puts the last-minute touches to the rest of the meal: grilled

tomatoes (fresh from Bill's garden), a vegetable casserole, and salads.

Dessert is Lemon Ice Cream Tarts. The recipe yields more than enough for one get-together, leaving a few for snacking on hot summer days.

Dinner is served on the deck, with the adults sitting around the deck eating from individual trays while the children have their special eating area on a quilt spread out on the lawn.

Pink Lemonade Slush
Clam Crisps   Cheese Wafers
Grilled Flank Steak
Broiled Tomatoes
Asparagus and Peas Casserole
Lettuce and Fruit Salad
With Poppy Seed Dressing
Sweet and Sour Potato Salad
Hot Rolls
Lemon Ice Cream Tarts
Burgundy

PINK LEMONADE SLUSH

2 (6-ounce) cans frozen pink lemonade
    concentrate, undiluted
6 cups crushed ice
Maraschino cherries (optional)

Combine 1 can pink lemonade concentrate and 1 cup ice in container of electric blender; process until thick and smooth. Gradually add 2 more cups of ice, blending thoroughly. Pour into serving pitcher.

Repeat process using remaining concentrate and ice. Garnish with cherries, if desired. Yield: about 6 cups.

CLAM CRISPS

2 tablespoons chopped onion
1 tablespoon butter or margarine, melted
1½ tablespoons all-purpose flour
¼ teaspoon Worcestershire sauce
Dash of garlic powder
1 (7½-ounce) can minced clams,
    undrained
14 slices bread, crusts removed
½ cup butter or margarine, melted

Sauté onion in butter until transparent; remove from heat. Stir in flour, Worcestershire sauce, and garlic powder. Gradually stir in clams. Cook over medium heat, stirring constantly, until mixture is thickened and bubbly; let cool.

Flatten bread slices with a rolling pin; spread 1½ teaspoons filling on each slice, and roll jellyroll fashion. Cut into thirds, and place seam-side down on greased cookie sheets. Brush with melted butter, and bake at 425° for 8 to 10 minutes or until lightly browned. Yield: 3½ dozen.

Note: Bread rolls may be prepared a day ahead and refrigerated. At serving time, slice rolls and bake.

CHEESE WAFERS

1 pound butter or margarine, softened
4 cups (1 pound) shredded sharp Cheddar
    cheese
4 cups all-purpose flour
⅛ teaspoon salt
1½ to 2 teaspoons red pepper
½ teaspoon paprika
Powdered sugar (optional)

Cream butter and cheese; add flour, salt, red pepper, and paprika, mixing well. Chill. Shape dough into 4 rolls, 1 inch in diameter; wrap each roll in foil. Refrigerate 24 hours.

Slice rolls ¼ inch thick, and place on ungreased baking sheets. Bake at 350° for 15 minutes; cool. Sift a small amount of powdered sugar over wafers before removing from baking sheet, if desired. Yield: about 16 dozen.

Note: Dough may be shaped into rolls and frozen. Cheese Wafers also freeze well after baking.

GRILLED FLANK STEAK

4 (1¼- to 1½-pound) flank steaks
Garlic powder
1 cup soy sauce
½ cup Worcestershire sauce
½ cup vegetable oil

Sprinkle flank steak lightly on both sides with garlic powder. Prick both sides of steak with fork, and place in a large shallow pan.

Combine remaining ingredients; pour over steak. Cover and marinate steak 8 hours or overnight in refrigerator, turning occasionally.

Remove steak from marinade. Grill over medium coals 7 to 9 minutes on each side, or until desired degree of doneness is reached. To serve, slice steak across grain in thin slices. Yield: 12 to 14 servings.

BROILED TOMATOES

1½ cups herb-seasoned stuffing mix
2 tablespoons butter or margarine, melted
½ cup grated Parmesan cheese
Dijon mustard
8 tomatoes, halved

Combine stuffing mix, butter, and cheese; mix well.

Spread mustard over surface of tomatoes. Spoon stuffing mixture over mustard. Broil 4 inches from heat about 7 minutes or until topping is lightly browned. Yield: 16 servings.

ASPARAGUS AND PEAS CASSEROLE

2 (14½-ounce) cans asparagus spears
2 (17-ounce) cans green peas
4 hard-cooked eggs, peeled and sliced
Cheese sauce (recipe follows)
½ cup buttered breadcrumbs

Drain asparagus spears and peas, reserving liquid. Cut asparagus into 1-inch pieces. Arrange half of vegetables in a 3-quart casserole; place two sliced eggs on top. Pour half of cheese sauce over eggs. Repeat layers. Sprinkle breadcrumbs on top. Bake at 350° for 30 minutes. Yield: 14 to 16 servings.

Cheese Sauce:

6 tablespoons butter or margarine
¼ cup plus 3 tablespoons all-purpose flour
1 cup reserved liquid from asparagus and peas
1 pound process American cheese, cut into 1-inch cubes

Melt butter in a heavy saucepan over low heat; add flour and cook 1 minute, stirring constantly. Gradually add 1 cup reserved liquid from asparagus and peas. Cook over medium heat, stirring constantly, until thickened. Add cheese, and stir until smooth. Yield: about 2 cups.

LETTUCE AND FRUIT SALAD WITH POPPY SEED DRESSING

3 (11-ounce) cans mandarin oranges, drained
3 pink grapefruit, peeled, seeded, and sectioned
6 heads Bibb lettuce, torn into bite-size pieces
Poppy seed dressing (recipe follows)

Combine mandarin oranges, grapefruit sections, and lettuce in a large salad bowl; toss lightly. Serve with poppy seed dressing. Yield: 14 to 16 servings.

Poppy Seed Dressing:

¼ to ½ cup chopped onion
¾ cup tarragon vinegar
2 tablespoons vegetable oil
2½ tablespoons poppy seeds
1 tablespoon sugar
1 teaspoon salt
1 teaspoon dry mustard
¾ cup vegetable oil

Combine first 7 ingredients in container of electric blender; blend well. Slowly add ¾ cup vegetable oil, continuing to blend until thick. Pour into a jar with a tight-fitting lid, and chill. Shake well before serving. Yield: 2 cups.

SWEET AND SOUR POTATO SALAD

16 medium potatoes
5 hard-cooked eggs, chopped
2 to 2½ cups chopped sweet pickles
2 teaspoons celery seeds
1 teaspoon dry mustard
1 teaspoon salt
¼ teaspoon pepper
Dressing (recipe follows)
Parsley sprigs (optional)

Peel and quarter potatoes; cook in a Dutch oven in boiling salted water to cover until done. Drain and cool.

Cube potatoes; add eggs, pickles, celery seeds, mustard, salt, pepper, and dressing. Stir gently. Refrigerate 24 hours. Garnish with parsley sprigs before serving, if desired. Yield: about 16 servings.

Dressing:

3 egg yolks
½ cup sugar
½ cup vinegar
2 tablespoons butter or margarine
1½ cups mayonnaise

Place egg yolks and sugar in a small saucepan; gradually add vinegar, mixing well. Add butter and place over medium heat, stirring constantly, until mixture comes to a boil. Remove from heat, and chill. Add mayonnaise, and mix well. Yield: about 2¼ cups.

LEMON ICE CREAM TARTS

½ gallon vanilla ice cream
1 (12-ounce) can frozen lemonade concentrate, undiluted
21 (3-inch) graham cracker tart shells
Chocolate shavings (optional)

Place half of ice cream and half of lemonade concentrate in container of electric blender; blend until smooth. Pour into tart shells. Repeat with remaining ice cream and lemonade. Freeze until firm. Carefully remove filled crusts from tart pans about 5 minutes before serving. Top with chocolate shavings, if desired. Yield: 21 (3-inch) tarts.

Desserts That Melt In Your Mouth

Summertime party menus call for desserts that are light and refreshing as well as elegant. These chilled and frozen selections are just that—the perfect ending to a special meal.

Whipped cream and beaten egg whites give a light texture to luscious Pineapple Dessert Soufflé, while crushed peppermint candy puts the mint flavor in Peppermint Bavarian.

Frozen delights include a rich chocolate pie—a mousse-like filling in a graham cracker crust; delicately flavored orange tarts; and frosty lime-flavored parfaits.

PINEAPPLE DESSERT SOUFFLE

2 envelopes unflavored gelatin
½ cup cold water
6 egg yolks
2 tablespoons grated lemon rind
¼ cup lemon juice
1 cup sugar
½ teaspoon salt
1⅓ cups drained crushed pineapple
6 egg whites
1 cup whipping cream, whipped
Pineapple chunks (optional)
Fresh mint leaves (optional)

Combine gelatin and water; let mixture stand 5 minutes.

Beat egg yolks slightly in the top of a double boiler; stir in lemon rind, juice, sugar, and salt. Cook over boiling water, stirring constantly, until the mixture thickens. Remove from heat; add gelatin, and stir until dissolved. Add pineapple; set aside to cool until slightly thickened (about 30 minutes).

Beat egg whites (at room temperature) until stiff peaks form. Fold egg whites and whipped cream into yolk mixture. Pour into a lightly oiled 6-cup ring mold. Chill overnight. Unmold on a serving platter; garnish with pineapple chunks and fresh mint leaves, if desired. Yield: 8 servings.
Mrs. John R. Taylor, Jr.,
Jonesboro, Tennessee.

PEPPERMINT BAVARIAN

About 1 cup vanilla wafer crumbs
3 tablespoons sugar
3 tablespoons butter or margarine, melted
About 16 vanilla wafers
1 envelope unflavored gelatin
¼ cup cold water
1 cup milk
¾ cup crushed peppermint candy
Dash of salt
1 cup whipping cream
Whipped cream
Crushed peppermint candy (optional)

Combine vanilla wafer crumbs and sugar; add butter, mixing well with a fork. Press mixture onto bottom of an 8-inch springform pan. Bake at 350° for 8 minutes; cool on a wire rack. Line sides of pan with vanilla wafers; set aside.

Combine gelatin and cold water; let stand 5 minutes.

Combine milk, ¾ cup crushed peppermint candy, and salt in a small saucepan. Cook over low heat, stirring occasionally, until candy dissolves; remove from heat. Add gelatin, and stir until dissolved. Chill until partially set (about 35 minutes).

Beat whipping cream until soft peaks form; fold into chilled mixture, and pour into wafer-lined springform pan. Chill at least 5 hours. Garnish with whipped cream; sprinkle with additional crushed peppermint candy, if desired. Yield: 6 to 8 servings.
Mrs. Carl Ramay,
Englewood, Colorado.

LIME PARFAITS

½ cup sugar
1 cup milk
½ cup light corn syrup
2 egg yolks, beaten
1 cup half-and-half
⅓ cup lime juice
1 teaspoon grated lime rind
2 egg whites
1 pint fresh strawberries
1 cup whipping cream, whipped

Combine sugar, milk, corn syrup, and egg yolks in top of a double boiler;

cook, stirring constantly, until slightly thickened (8 to 10 minutes). Remove from heat; cool. Stir half-and-half, lime juice, and lime rind into the custard mixture.

Beat egg whites (at room temperature) until stiff peaks form; gently fold into lime mixture. Spoon into an 8- or 9-inch square pan. Freeze until firm.

Thaw lime mixture slightly; break into chunks. Place chunks in a chilled large bowl; beat at medium speed of an electric mixer until fluffy. Return to pan; freeze until firm.

Rinse and hull strawberries. Set aside 6 to 8 whole strawberries; slice the remaining berries.

Thaw lime mixture slightly. Spoon alternate layers of lime mixture, sliced strawberries, and whipped cream into chilled parfait glasses. Top with whipped cream; garnish with whole berries. Serve immediately. Yield: 6 to 8 servings.
Margaret W. Cotton,
Franklin, Virginia.

PEACH MACAROON MOUSSE

2 envelopes unflavored gelatin
½ cup cold water
¼ cup sugar
¼ cup Cointreau or other orange-flavored liqueur
1 quart vanilla ice cream, softened
1 cup macaroon crumbs
1½ cups sliced fresh peaches
1 cup whipping cream
Sliced fresh peaches (optional)
Whipped cream (optional)

Combine gelatin and cold water in top of a double boiler; let stand 5 minutes. Place over boiling water and cook, stirring constantly, until dissolved. Remove from heat; stir in sugar and liqueur. Add ice cream, crumbs, and 1½ cups peaches; stir well. Beat whipping cream until soft peaks form; fold into gelatin mixture. Pour into an oiled 7-cup mold. Freeze until firm.

Unmold on a serving platter, and garnish with additional peaches and whipped cream, if desired. Yield: 8 to 10 servings.
Mrs. William Strieber,
Crofton, Maryland.

CRANBERRY-CREAM CHEESE TARTS

1 (3-ounce) package cream cheese, softened
1 (16-ounce) can jellied cranberry sauce
¼ cup sifted powdered sugar
¼ teaspoon salt
12 large marshmallows, diced
½ cup chopped pecans
1 cup whipping cream
15 (3-inch) baked pastry shells or graham cracker tart shells
Whipped cream (optional)

Beat cream cheese, cranberry sauce, sugar, and salt at high speed of electric mixer until fluffy; stir in marshmallows and pecans.

Beat whipping cream until soft peaks form; fold into cranberry mixture. Chill 3 to 4 hours. To serve, spoon cranberry mixture into pastry shells; garnish with additional whipped cream, if desired. Yield: 15 tarts.

Note: Cranberry mixture may be stored in refrigerator 2 days.

Mary Ann Ferguson,
Union City, Tennessee.

FROZEN ORANGE TARTS

2 cups vanilla wafer crumbs
¼ cup finely chopped walnuts
6 tablespoons butter or margarine, melted
½ cup sugar
¼ cup frozen orange juice concentrate, thawed
1 egg white
1 (8-ounce) carton commercial sour cream
Whipped cream (optional)

Combine crumbs and walnuts; add butter, mixing well with a fork.

Place paper liners in 12 muffin cups; press about 3 tablespoons crumb mixture onto bottom and sides of each cup.

Combine sugar, orange juice concentrate, and egg white (at room temperature); beat at medium speed of an electric mixer until soft peaks form (about 7 minutes). Fold sour cream into the orange mixture.

Spoon orange mixture into prepared muffin cups; freeze. Let tarts stand at room temperature 10 to 15 minutes before serving. Garnish with whipped cream, if desired. Yield: 12 servings.

Sandra Moore,
Bowling Green, Kentucky.

FROZEN CHOCOLATE PIE

2 (4-ounce) bars sweet cooking chocolate
4 eggs, separated
1 envelope unflavored gelatin
2 tablespoons water
1 teaspoon vanilla extract
Dash of salt
1 cup sugar
2 cups whipping cream, whipped
1 cup chopped pecans
2 (9-inch) graham cracker crusts
2 tablespoons graham cracker crumbs, divided

Melt chocolate in top of a double boiler, stirring constantly. Stir some of chocolate into egg yolks; add yolk mixture to remaining chocolate, stirring constantly. Remove from heat.

Soften gelatin in water. Add gelatin to chocolate mixture; stir until gelatin is completely dissolved.

Beat egg whites (at room temperature) until frothy; add vanilla and salt, beating slightly. Gradually add sugar, beating well after each addition; continue beating until the whites are stiff and glossy. Do not underbeat.

Fold meringue, whipped cream, and pecans into chocolate mixture; spoon equal portions into crusts. Sprinkle 1 tablespoon crumbs over each pie. Freeze 3 hours or until firm. To serve, let stand at room temperature 10 minutes before slicing. Yield: two 9-inch pies.

Mrs. J. T. Ballard,
Wichita Falls, Texas.

Tip: Unused or extra egg whites may be frozen and used as needed. Make meringues or angel pies with the whites later. Egg whites freeze well.

A Hayride For History's Sake

Nothing generates excitement quite like a summertime picnic and hayride. And when the occasion doubles as a fundraiser for preserving and restoring local historic sites, the gathering becomes even more special. Such was the party hosted by Capt. and Mrs. Quentin Crommelin of Wetumpka, Alabama, and Mrs. Henry Crommelin of Montgomery, Alabama.

The Crommelins donated the party to the Landmarks Foundation of Montgomery for their annual auction. "A picnic supper and hayride to historic Fort Toulouse for 10 couples," was the promise the Crommelins made to the highest bidder. And they delivered in grand style.

Guests arrived at Quentin and Priscilla's beautiful country home to begin the hayride. The short trip led to Fort Toulouse, located near the junction of the Coosa and Tallapoosa Rivers, just south of Wetumpka. Now a park with camping facilities under construction, the fort area has served as home for explorers, armies, and early Indian tribes. Guests were treated to a brief history of the area while enjoying appetizers and champagne on the riverbank.

A Southern-style picnic supper greeted the travelers back at the Crommelin home. Fried chicken breasts, along with sandwiches made with thin slices of Virginia ham and homemade mayonnaise, were the entrée offerings. Priscilla's homemade mayonnaise also flavored the stuffed eggs that garnished her Deluxe Potato Salad. Tangy Romaine Salad rounded out the main course, and Parson's Tipsy Pudding ended the meal.

CREAM CHEESE PATE

1 (8-ounce) package cream cheese, softened
1 teaspoon curry powder
¼ teaspoon onion juice
¼ teaspoon Worcestershire sauce
1 (9-ounce) jar chutney

Combine first 4 ingredients, mixing well. Shape into a flat 6-inch circle on serving dish. Chill until firm. Top with chutney, and chill well. Serve with crackers. Yield: about 2 cups.

Note: Consistency of chutney varies among brands. If chutney contains excess liquid, drain before placing on cream cheese mixture. Chop large pieces of chutney, if necessary.

CRISPY FRIED CHICKEN BREASTS

1 cup all-purpose flour
¾ teaspoon salt
½ teaspoon pepper
24 whole chicken breasts, boned and quartered
Vegetable oil

Combine flour, salt, and pepper. Wash chicken pieces, and pat dry; dredge in flour mixture.

Heat oil to 375° in a large skillet; add chicken, and fry until golden brown. Drain. Yield: 24 servings.

VIRGINIA HAM SANDWICHES

28 thin slices baked Virginia ham (about 1 pound)
2 (16-ounce) packages very thin sandwich bread
Homemade mayonnaise (recipe follows)

Place 1 slice ham on half of bread slices. Spread remaining bread slices with homemade mayonnaise; place over ham. Yield: 28 sandwiches.

Homemade Mayonnaise:

½ teaspoon dry mustard
½ teaspoon salt
½ teaspoon pepper
2 egg yolks
2 tablespoons lemon juice
1 tablespoon vinegar
1 cup olive oil

Allow all ingredients to reach room temperature.

Combine dry mustard, salt, and pepper. Beat egg yolks at medium-high

speed of electric mixer 1 to 2 minutes or until thickened. Add mustard mixture, lemon juice, and vinegar; beat an additional 30 seconds.

Very slowly (only a drop at a time) add ⅓ to ½ cup oil to egg yolk mixture, beating constantly at medium-high speed. Be sure that oil is thoroughly combined in egg yolk mixture before adding another drop.

Then add remaining oil, 1 tablespoon at a time, being sure oil is thoroughly combined in egg yolk mixture before adding another tablespoon. Scrape mixer bowl frequently during entire procedure, which will take about an hour. Spoon mayonnaise into a jar with a tight-fitting lid; store in refrigerator. Yield: about 1¼ cups.

DELUXE POTATO SALAD

3 green peppers
5 pounds potatoes, cooked, peeled, and cubed
1 bunch celery, chopped
2½ teaspoons salt
1 teaspoon pepper
¾ cup mayonnaise
1 tablespoon Dijon mustard
Stuffed eggs (recipe follows)
4 (8½-ounce) cans artichoke hearts, chilled and drained
2 tablespoons pimiento-stuffed olive slices
Small whole sweet pickles
Fresh parsley sprigs

Chop 2 green peppers; cut remaining pepper into rings. Combine chopped green pepper, potatoes, celery, salt,

pepper, mayonnaise, and mustard; mix well, and chill thoroughly.

Spoon potato salad onto a large serving platter. Arrange stuffed eggs and artichoke hearts around edge of platter. Garnish salad with green pepper rings, olive slices, pickles, and parsley. Yield: 24 servings.

Stuffed Eggs:

1½ dozen hard-cooked eggs
¼ cup homemade mayonnaise (*see* this page)
2 tablespoons minced onion
¼ teaspoon curry powder
½ teaspoon salt
⅛ teaspoon pepper
Paprika
Fresh parsley sprigs
18 slices pimiento-stuffed olives

Cut eggs in half lengthwise; remove yolks. Mash yolks; stir in mayonnaise, onion, curry powder, salt, and pepper.

Fill egg whites with yolk mixture; chill. Sprinkle half of stuffed eggs with paprika, and top with a small sprig of fresh parsley. Top remaining stuffed eggs with pimiento-stuffed olive slices. Yield: 18 servings.

TANGY ROMAINE SALAD

3 heads romaine, torn
4 cups cherry tomatoes
2 cucumbers, sliced
2 avocados, coarsely chopped
1 cup vegetable oil
½ cup tarragon vinegar
¾ teaspoon dry mustard
¾ teaspoon salt
½ teaspoon pepper

Combine first 4 ingredients in a large salad bowl; set aside. Combine remaining ingredients in a jar; cover and shake vigorously. Pour over salad; toss gently. Yield: 24 servings.

Tip: To speed up salad making, wash, trim and dry all ingredients as soon as you buy them, and tie together in a plastic bag. At mealtime, just pull out the bag and make the salad.

PARSON'S TIPSY PUDDING

Custard (recipe follows)
40 ladyfingers
1 (2¾-ounce) package slivered almonds, toasted
1 cup cream sherry, divided
3 cups whipping cream
¾ cup powdered sugar

Prepare custard; chill at least 8 hours. Split 28 ladyfingers, and use to line bottom and sides of a 13- x 9- x 2-inch baking dish; sprinkle with almonds. Pour ½ cup sherry over ladyfingers, covering entire surface. Cover and let soak 1 hour.

Split remaining ladyfingers, and place in a 13- x 9- x 2-inch pan. Sprinkle with remaining sherry, and let soak 1 hour.

Pour chilled custard over almond-topped layer; then top with remaining sherry-soaked ladyfingers.

Beat whipping cream until foamy; gradually add powdered sugar, beating until stiff peaks form. Spoon over ladyfingers. Chill until serving time. Yield: 24 servings.

Custard:

6 cups milk
6 eggs
1½ cups sugar
1½ teaspoons vanilla extract

Heat milk in a heavy 5-quart Dutch oven. Beat eggs with electric mixer until thick and lemon colored; add sugar, mixing well. Gradually stir about ¾ cup hot milk into egg mixture; add to remaining hot mixture, stirring constantly.

Cook over low heat, stirring constantly, until mixture thickens and coats a metal spoon (about 15 minutes). Remove from heat, and set Dutch oven in cold water; stir custard gently until slightly cool. Stir in vanilla. Chill 8 hours or overnight. Yield: 6 cups.

Tip: Use up extra heavy cream by whipping until stiff, then drop by dollops onto cookie sheet. Freeze until firm, pack into boxes, and return to freezer. Use as garnish for puddings or cakes.

Fire Up The Grill For Summer Flavor

Just about anything tastes better when cooked outdoors over glowing coals. Beef, chicken, ham, and even fish take on that irresistible grilled flavor as the air fills with a tantalizing aroma.

For a complete meal cooked on the grill, try Chicken-Mushroom Bundles. Potatoes and carrots cook along with chicken breasts and mushrooms for a delicious blend of flavors. And burgers get a new twist when flavored with red wine, green onion, egg, and hamburger seasoning.

MARINATED BARBECUED CHUCK STEAK

1 tablespoon chili powder
2 teaspoons ground ginger
1 teaspoon salt
1 clove garlic, minced
2 tablespoons minced onion
⅓ cup lemon juice
¼ cup olive oil
1 (2-pound) chuck steak (about 1 inch thick)

Combine first 7 ingredients; stir. Place steak in a large shallow bowl; pour marinade over steak. Turn steak to coat both sides with marinade; cover and refrigerate 10 hours or overnight.

Remove steak from marinade; place on grill over hot coals. Cook 8 to 10 minutes on each side or until desired degree of doneness. Yield: 2 servings.
Mrs. Bill Anthony,
North Little Rock, Arkansas.

BURGUNDY BURGERS

4 green onions
1 pound ground beef
1 egg
¼ cup Burgundy
1 teaspoon hamburger seasoning
¼ cup Burgundy
¼ cup butter or margarine

Thinly slice green onions, including 1 inch of green tops.

Combine half of green onion with beef, egg, ¼ cup Burgundy, and hamburger seasoning; mix well. Shape into 4 patties about ¾ inch thick.

Combine remaining onion, ¼ cup Burgundy, and butter in a small saucepan; cook until heated thoroughly.

Place patties on grill 3 to 5 inches from coals; cook 4 to 8 minutes on each side or to desired degree of doneness, basting occasionally with sauce. Serve remaining sauce with burgers. Yield: 4 servings.
Mrs. Bob Stockfleth,
Memphis, Tennessee.

HONEY HAM KABOBS

1 cup firmly packed brown sugar
½ cup honey
½ cup orange juice
1 (1½-pound) fully cooked ham steak, cut into 1-inch cubes
1 small pineapple, peeled, cored, and cut into 1-inch chunks
16 large pimiento-stuffed olives

Combine brown sugar, honey, and orange juice; mix well, and set aside.

Alternate ham, pineapple, and olives on skewers. Grill over medium heat 10 to 12 minutes, turning often. Baste liberally with honey mixture after each turn. Yield: 4 servings.
Mrs. David A. Gibson,
Martin, Tennessee.

CHICKEN-MUSHROOM BUNDLES

3 whole chicken breasts, split
Salt and pepper
2 potatoes, cut into ½-inch slices
5 carrots, cut into ¾-inch slices
12 mushrooms, thinly sliced
¾ teaspoon salt, divided
6 tablespoons butter or margarine
6 tablespoons dry sherry
Fresh parsley sprigs

Place each chicken breast on a large piece of heavy-duty aluminum foil. Sprinkle with salt and pepper. Divide potato slices, carrot slices, and mushroom slices equally among bundles. Salt vegetables in each packet with ⅛ teaspoon salt; dot each with 1 tablespoon butter. Pour 1 tablespoon sherry into each bundle. Seal foil tightly. Cook on grill about 1 hour. Unwrap bundles, and place on serving plates. Garnish with parsley sprigs. Yield: 6 servings.

Note: Two tablespoons cream of chicken soup may be added to each bundle instead of sherry.

*Marlan Hornburg,
Melbourne, Florida.*

BARBECUED CATFISH

6 (1-pound) catfish
⅛ teaspoon paprika
¼ teaspoon salt
¼ teaspoon pepper
2 tablespoons sugar
1 teaspoon Worcestershire sauce
¼ cup vinegar
¼ cup catsup
½ cup vegetable oil

Clean, skin, and fillet fish. Combine remaining ingredients. Baste fish with sauce. Place fish in a well-greased, hinged fish basket. Place on grill about 3 to 4 inches from coals. Cook 7 to 8 minutes on each side or until fish flakes easily, brushing frequently with the sauce. Yield: 6 servings.

*Cynthia D. Harper,
Snow Hill, North Carolina.*

Tip: To keep mushrooms fresh longer, refrigerate in a brown paper bag.

Side Dishes Fresh From The Garden

What better way to enjoy the bounty of the season than with vegetable and fruit side dishes from the garden. Bright-red tomatoes, crisp zucchini, and juicy melons team with other fruits and vegetables in savory combinations like Mexican Corn, Tomato-Zucchini Stir-Fry, and Fruit Rhapsody. They're great for family meals or to round out a summer party menu.

CHEESY GREEN BEANS

1 pound fresh green beans, cut into
  2-inch pieces
1 (1⅜-ounce) envelope dry onion soup mix
1 cup water
3 tablespoons butter or margarine, melted
⅓ cup toasted slivered almonds
3 tablespoons grated Parmesan cheese
½ teaspoon paprika

Combine green beans, onion soup mix, and water in a medium saucepan. Cook over low heat until beans are tender, about 15 minutes; drain. Stir in butter, almonds, and cheese. Spoon beans into a serving dish; sprinkle with paprika. Yield: 4 servings.

*Lynn Nelson,
Biloxi, Mississippi.*

FRESH CORN PUDDING

3 eggs, beaten
1 cup milk
1 cup half-and-half
1 tablespoon sugar
1 teaspoon salt
2 cups fresh corn, cut from the cob
¼ cup dry breadcrumbs
2 tablespoons butter or margarine, melted

Combine eggs, milk, half-and-half, sugar, and salt, mixing well. Stir in remaining ingredients. Pour into a greased 1½-quart casserole, and place in a baking pan on oven rack; pour 1 to 1½ inches boiling water into pan. Bake at 350° for 1 hour or until pudding is firm. Yield: 6 to 8 servings.

*Mrs. Russell Spear,
Hilliard, Florida.*

MEXICAN CORN

¼ cup butter or margarine, melted
2 cups fresh corn, cut from the cob
¼ cup chopped green pepper
¼ cup chopped red pepper
1 teaspoon salt
1 cup commercial French-fried onions
1 cup cubed fresh tomatoes
¼ teaspoon ground oregano

Combine first 5 ingredients in a heavy skillet. Cover and cook over medium heat 7 minutes, stirring occasionally. Stir in French-fried onions, tomatoes, and oregano. Cook, uncovered, 2 minutes or until tomatoes are thoroughly heated. Yield: 4 to 6 servings.

*Mrs. Huston King,
Vale, North Carolina.*

Tip: When canning non-acid vegetables, such as turnip greens and mustard greens, remember that they should be processed in a pressure cooker. Some bacteria do not begin to grow until air is excluded, and it takes a temperature higher than boiling to kill them. Ten pounds' pressure in a pressure cooker puts the temperature at 240°. There are some handy family-size pressure cookers on the market, which make home canning more convenient.

STUFFED EGGPLANT

1 medium eggplant
½ cup chopped onion
¼ cup chopped green pepper
2 tablespoons margarine, melted
¼ teaspoon salt
⅛ teaspoon pepper
1 cup (4 ounces) shredded Cheddar cheese
1 cup chopped ripe olives
½ cup soft breadcrumbs

Wash eggplant, and cut in half length-wise. Cover and cook in a small amount of boiling water 10 minutes; drain. Remove pulp, leaving a ½-inch shell. Chop pulp, and set aside.

Sauté onion and green pepper in margarine until tender. Add chopped eggplant, salt, pepper, cheese, and olives; mix lightly. Stuff shells with eggplant mixture; top with breadcrumbs. Bake at 375° for 30 minutes. Yield: 2 servings.
Mrs. Virginia Mathews,
Jacksonville, Florida.

TOMATO-ZUCCHINI STIR-FRY

6 medium zucchini, thinly sliced
½ cup chopped onion
2 tablespoons chopped fresh parsley
1 clove garlic, minced
1 tablespoon salt
⅛ teaspoon pepper
1 teaspoon dried oregano leaves
¼ cup vegetable oil
3 medium tomatoes, peeled and cut into wedges
½ cup grated Parmesan cheese
Chopped fresh parsley (optional)

Sauté zucchini, onion, 2 tablespoons parsley, garlic, salt, pepper, and oregano in hot oil, stirring frequently, until zucchini is tender. Add tomatoes; cook 5 minutes or until thoroughly heated. Spoon into a serving dish, and sprinkle with Parmesan cheese. Sprinkle with additional chopped parsley, if desired. Yield: 6 to 8 servings. *Lucille Hall,*
Bakersfield, Missouri.

Tip: Mix liquid from canned fruit in a jar as you acquire it; then use it in a gelatin dessert or as a punch drink.

SHERRIED FRUIT MELANGE

2 cups halved fresh strawberries
2 cups watermelon balls
2 cups cantaloupe balls
1 cup sliced fresh peaches
1 cup cubed fresh pineapple
1 cup seedless white grapes
½ cup dry sherry
2 to 4 tablespoons sugar
1 teaspoon grated orange rind
1 teaspoon ground coriander
½ teaspoon dried mint

Combine fruit in a large mixing bowl. Combine remaining ingredients; pour over fruit mixture, tossing lightly. Cover; chill 2 to 3 hours. Yield: 8 servings. *Jan Wisland,*
Whitefish Bay, Wisconsin.

FAVORITE SUMMER SALAD

1 fresh pineapple
6 apricots, halved
1 banana, sliced
1 cup cantaloupe balls
1 cup watermelon balls
1 cup seedless white grapes
1 cup flaked coconut
1 (16-ounce) carton commercial sour cream
¼ cup chopped pecans

Chill pineapple overnight. Peel and core pineapple; cut into bite-size chunks. Combine fruit; add flaked coconut, and toss gently.

Combine sour cream and pecans; spoon over fruit. Chill at least 2 hours before serving. Yield: 8 to 10 servings.
Mrs. Gerald Duncan,
Jacksonville, Florida.

FRUIT RHAPSODY

1 cup seedless green grapes
1 banana, peeled and sliced
½ cantaloupe, peeled and cut in wedges
½ honeydew melon, peeled and cut in wedges
1 orange, peeled and sliced
Lettuce leaves
Fresh mint sprigs
Orange-Coconut Dressing

Arrange first 5 ingredients on a bed of lettuce. Garnish orange slices with mint. Serve with Orange-Coconut Dressing. Yield: 4 to 6 servings.

Orange-Coconut Dressing:

1 teaspoon grated orange rind
¼ cup flaked coconut
1 cup mayonnaise
½ cup whipping cream, whipped

Combine orange rind, flaked coconut, and mayonnaise, mixing well. Fold in whipped cream. Chill dressing several hours. Yield: 1⅓ cups.
Linda P. Sayers,
Winston-Salem, North Carolina.

Serve This Supper In A Basket

If you're looking for a prepare-ahead menu and an imaginative way to serve it, look at what we've done with the popular picnic fare of fried chicken, ham biscuits, and deviled eggs. We've put individual servings together as a supper-in-a-basket, with no knives or forks required.

Bite-size pieces of chicken dipped in batter and fried to a golden brown substitute for the usual fried chicken. With Golden Chicken Nuggets you eliminate the fork as well as the mess.

Ham-filled biscuits couldn't be easier with our recipe, which allows the biscuit dough to be made up to a week in advance. And for an easy-to-eat fruit salad, serve Fruit on Picks: banana, pineapple, and grapes threaded on skewers.

To make your basket supper even more appealing, use an assortment of baskets with colorful napkins as liners.

Golden Chicken Nuggets
Ham-Filled Angel Biscuits
Best Deviled Eggs   Fruit on Picks
Chocolate-Banana Brownies
Chablis

These individual basket suppers are as appealing to the eye as to the taste: Golden Chicken Nuggets, Ham-Filled Angel Biscuits, Best Deviled Eggs, Fruit on Picks, Chocolate-Banana Brownies, and Chablis.

(about 8 to 10 minutes). Roll dough to ¼-inch thickness, and brush with melted butter. Cut with a 2-inch biscuit cutter, and place ½ inch apart on a greased baking sheet; top each with a second biscuit. Bake at 400° for 12 to 15 minutes. Fill with sliced ham. Yield: about 3 dozen.

Note: Dough may be refrigerated up to 1 week before rolling out.

Florence L. Costello,
Chattanooga, Tennessee.

BEST DEVILED EGGS

6 hard-cooked eggs
¼ cup mayonnaise
2 tablespoons chopped onion
1 tablespoon chopped green olives
1 teaspoon vinegar
1 teaspoon prepared mustard
⅛ teaspoon salt
Dash of pepper
Paprika

Slice eggs in half lengthwise, and carefully remove yolks. Mash yolks with mayonnaise. Add remaining ingredients except paprika; stir well. Stuff egg whites with yolk mixture. Garnish eggs with paprika. Yield: 6 to 8 servings.

Margot Fostee,
Hubbard, Texas.

GOLDEN CHICKEN NUGGETS

3 whole chicken breasts, skinned and boned
½ cup all-purpose flour
¾ teaspoon salt
2 teaspoons sesame seeds
1 egg, slightly beaten
½ cup water
Hot vegetable oil

Cut chicken into 1- x 1½-inch pieces; set aside. Combine next 5 ingredients. Dip chicken into batter, and fry in hot oil (375°) until golden brown. Drain on paper towels. Yield: 6 to 8 servings.

Tip: For best results in browning food, dry the food first on paper towels.

HAM-FILLED ANGEL BISCUITS

4½ cups all-purpose flour
1 tablespoon sugar
1 teaspoon soda
1 tablespoon baking powder
1½ teaspoons salt
1 cup shortening
2 packages dry yeast
¼ cup warm water (105° to 115°)
2 cups buttermilk
Melted butter or margarine
Sliced ham

Combine first 5 ingredients; mix well. Cut in shortening. Dissolve yeast in water; add yeast mixture and buttermilk to flour mixture, mixing well.

Turn dough out on a floured surface, and knead until smooth and elastic

FRUIT ON PICKS

3 bananas, cut into ¾-inch slices
3 tablespoons orange juice concentrate, undiluted
1 cup toasted coconut
2 (6-ounce) jars maraschino cherries, drained
1 (15¼-ounce) can pineapple chunks, drained
1 cup seedless grapes

Dip banana slices in orange juice; roll in coconut. Place fruit on 10-inch wooden skewers, alternating cherries, pineapple chunks, grapes, and banana slices until skewers are filled. Yield: 6 to 8 servings.

Mrs. Charles Price,
Houston, Texas.

CHOCOLATE-BANANA BROWNIES

1 (6-ounce) package semisweet chocolate
  morsels
¼ cup butter or margarine
½ cup sugar
¼ cup butter or margarine, softened
1 egg
¼ cup milk
1½ cups mashed banana
1¼ cups all-purpose flour
1 teaspoon salt
½ teaspoon baking powder
½ teaspoon ground cinnamon
¼ teaspoon soda
½ cup chopped nuts

Melt chocolate and ¼ cup butter in a small saucepan over low heat; stir to blend. Cool.

Combine sugar and softened butter; cream well. Beat in egg, milk, and banana. Combine dry ingredients; add to banana mixture, and stir well.

Divide batter in half. Add nuts and the melted chocolate to one half; stir well. Spread half of chocolate batter in a greased and floured 9-inch square baking pan; pour plain batter over chocolate layer, and top with remaining chocolate batter. Marble batter with a knife. Bake at 350° for 25 to 30 minutes. Cool. Cut into 3-inch squares. Yield: 6 to 8 servings.
*Mrs. Harvey Kidd,
Hernando, Mississippi.*

Keep The Beverages Light And Frosty

Cool, refreshing beverages are just what's needed to perk up a hot summer day. Whether you're looking for a frosty drink to serve at a party or just for the family, you can't go wrong with one of these summer coolers.

We've added fresh strawberries to lemonade, stirred up pitchers of Punchy Sangría, and whipped up a batch of Frozen Margaritas Supreme.

PUNCHY SANGRIA

2 (6-ounce) cans frozen pink lemonade
  concentrate, thawed and undiluted
4½ cups rosé, chilled
Juice of 1 lime
2 cups club soda, chilled
1 lemon, thinly sliced
1 orange, thinly sliced

Combine lemonade, rosé, and lime juice; stir until blended. Slowly stir in club soda. Garnish with lemon and orange slices. Serve over ice. Yield: 2¼ quarts.
*Gail Hatter,
McGregor, Texas.*

GIN PUNCH

6 cups water
2 cups sugar
1 (48-ounce) can pineapple juice
1 (48-ounce) can grapefruit juice
1 (8-ounce) jar maraschino cherries,
  undrained
2 cups gin
1 (33.8-ounce) bottle ginger ale, chilled

Combine water and sugar in a large saucepan; bring to a boil, and stir until dissolved. Cool.

Combine sugar mixture, juice, and cherries; chill. Add gin and ginger ale just before serving. Yield: 6½ quarts.
*Jo Anne Mattke,
Edmond, Oklahoma.*

FROZEN MARGARITAS SUPREME

Lime wedge
Salt
1 (6-ounce) can frozen limeade
  concentrate, thawed and undiluted
¾ cup tequila
¼ cup Triple Sec or other orange-flavored
  liqueur
Crushed ice
Lime slices (optional)

Rub rim of 4 cocktail glasses with wedge of lime. Place salt in saucer; spin rim of each glass in salt. Set prepared glasses aside.

Combine limeade, tequila, and Triple Sec in container of electric blender; blend well. Add crushed ice to fill blender three-fourths full; blend well.

Pour beverage into prepared glasses; garnish with a slice of lime, if desired. Yield: 4 servings. *John R. Nelson, Jr.,
Richardson, Texas.*

SUMMERTIME FRUIT PUNCH

Grated rind of 1 orange
Grated rind of 1 lemon
2 cups water
2 cups sugar
2 teaspoons almond extract
3 cups fresh orange juice, strained
1½ cups fresh lemon juice, strained
1 (48-ounce) bottle cranberry juice
  cocktail
1 quart ginger ale

Combine orange and lemon rind, water, and sugar in a medium saucepan. Bring to a boil, and simmer 5 minutes; let cool. Stir in almond extract and fruit juice. Pour over ice; stir in ginger ale. Yield: about 1 gallon.
*Mrs. J. E. Sypher,
Charlotte, North Carolina.*

STRAWBERRY LEMONADE

2 pints fresh strawberries
1½ cups sugar
3 cups water
1½ cups lemon juice

Place strawberries in container of food processor or electric blender; process until smooth.

Combine sugar and water in a saucepan; cook over medium heat until sugar is dissolved. Combine sugar mixture, strawberries, and lemon juice; mix well. Chill; serve over ice. Garnish as desired. Yield: about 1½ quarts.
*Leticia R. Eppink,
Keswick, Virginia.*

Slice Tomatoes Into Something Tasty

With juicy, vine-ripened tomatoes now at their peak of flavor, you can enjoy them in a variety of zesty summer side dishes. One of the best is Jiffy Tomato Stack-Ups, thick tomato slices topped with chopped broccoli, Swiss cheese, and onion, then broiled. Or try broiled tomato halves with a special dill sauce spooned over them.

BAKED TOMATOES WITH CORN

6 small firm tomatoes
½ teaspoon salt
½ teaspoon sugar
Dash of paprika
2 eggs, beaten
2 cups cooked fresh corn
1 teaspoon salt
⅛ teaspoon pepper
3 tablespoons melted butter or margarine, divided
1 cup soft breadcrumbs

Cut tops from tomatoes; scoop out pulp, leaving shells intact. Reserve pulp for use in other recipes. Combine ½ teaspoon salt, sugar, and paprika; sprinkle over tomato shells.

Combine eggs, corn, 1 teaspoon salt, pepper, and 2 tablespoons butter; spoon into tomato shells. Combine breadcrumbs and remaining butter; spoon over corn mixture. Place tomatoes in a shallow baking dish. Bake at 375° for 35 to 40 minutes. Yield: 6 servings.
Mrs. Ray S. Duff,
Hurricane, West Virginia.

PARMESAN TOMATOES

4 pounds (about 15 or 16 small) fresh tomatoes, peeled and sliced
½ cup melted butter
1 teaspoon dried oregano leaves
½ teaspoon dried basil leaves
1 cup grated Parmesan cheese
½ teaspoon dried parsley flakes

Arrange tomatoes in a 13- x 9- x 2-inch baking dish. Pour butter over tomatoes; sprinkle with oregano, basil, cheese, and parsley flakes. Bake at 325° for 25 to 30 minutes. Yield: 10 to 12 servings.
Martha Ann Rabon,
Stapleton, Alabama.

CHEESY STUFFED TOMATOES

6 large firm tomatoes
Salt
1 cup instant rice
½ clove garlic
2 tablespoons vegetable oil
1 cup (4 ounces) shredded process cheese spread
2 tablespoons olive oil

Remove stems from tomatoes, and cut a ¼-inch slice from the top of each. Scoop out pulp and reserve. Sprinkle inside of each shell with ⅛ teaspoon salt; invert on paper towels and set aside.

Press reserved pulp through a food mill or sieve, and reserve 6 tablespoons liquid. Cook instant rice according to package directions.

Sauté garlic in vegetable oil until lightly browned; remove from heat, and stir in cheese and rice. Fill tomatoes with mixture; spoon 1 tablespoon reserved tomato liquid into each, and replace tops. Place tomatoes in a greased 8-inch square baking dish; spoon olive oil over top. Bake at 375° for 20 to 25 minutes. Yield: 6 servings.
Mrs. Rose Naquin,
Melville, Louisiana.

BROILED TOMATOES WITH DILL SAUCE

1 cup commercial sour cream
½ cup mayonnaise
¼ cup finely chopped onion
2 teaspoons minced fresh dillweed
½ teaspoon salt
8 large firm tomatoes
Salt and pepper
8 teaspoons butter or margarine, divided

Combine first 5 ingredients; chill.

Remove stems from tomatoes; cut in half crosswise. Sprinkle cut side with salt and pepper. Dot each half with ½ teaspoon butter. Broil 3 to 5 inches from heat about 5 minutes. Serve hot with dill mixture. Yield: 8 servings.
Ann Elsie Schmetzer,
Madisonville, Kentucky.

JIFFY TOMATO STACK-UPS

1 (10-ounce) package frozen chopped broccoli
1 cup (4 ounces) shredded Swiss cheese
2 tablespoons finely chopped onion
4 large tomatoes

Cook broccoli according to package directions; drain. Add cheese and onion, stirring well.

Cut tomatoes into 1-inch slices, and place on baking sheet. Spoon broccoli mixture onto each tomato slice; broil 3 to 5 inches from heat 8 minutes or until cheese melts. Yield: 4 to 6 servings.
Mrs. Carl Ramay,
Plano, Texas.

Stuff Vegetables With Savory Meat Fillings

Summer's favorite vegetables become the main course when they're scooped out and stuffed with savory meat fillings. All you need to add is a salad and bread for a nutritious meal.

Bacon-and-Egg-Stuffed Tomatoes are ideal for a cool summer luncheon. It's a bacon-and-egg salad served in tomato shells. For hot entrées, try Stuffed Yellow Squash With Cheese Sauce or Savory Stuffed Zucchini, both filled with ground beef. Ham-Stuffed Eggplant is filled with a mixture of ham, onion, celery, and olives.

SAVORY STUFFED ZUCCHINI

3 medium zucchini
Salt and pepper
1 tablespoon butter or margarine
½ pound lean ground beef
½ cup chopped celery
¼ cup chopped onion
1 (8-ounce) can tomato sauce
½ cup soft breadcrumbs
¼ cup grated Parmesan cheese

Wash squash thoroughly; cook in boiling salted water 5 minutes. Cut squash in half lengthwise; scoop out and discard seeds. Sprinkle cavities with salt and pepper; set aside.

Melt butter in a large skillet; add beef, celery, and onion. Cook, stirring constantly, until beef is browned. Add tomato sauce and breadcrumbs; stir well. Spoon mixture into squash cavities; place squash in a shallow baking dish. Sprinkle with cheese; bake, uncovered, at 375° for 30 minutes. Yield: 6 servings.
Mrs. Ervin M. Leeman,
Decatur, Arkansas.

STUFFED YELLOW SQUASH WITH CHEESE SAUCE

3 large (about 2 pounds) yellow squash
½ pound ground beef
1 clove garlic, pressed
½ cup uncooked regular rice
1 teaspoon salt
⅛ teaspoon pepper
1 (16-ounce) can stewed tomatoes
½ cup water
Parmesan Cheese Sauce

Wash squash thoroughly; cook in boiling salted water for 8 to 10 minutes or until tender but still firm. Drain and cool slightly. Trim stems. Cut squash in half lengthwise; remove and discard seeds. Set aside.

Cook ground beef and garlic in a large skillet over medium heat until beef is browned, stirring to crumble meat. Add rice, salt, and pepper; cook 2 minutes, stirring constantly. Add tomatoes and water; stir well. Cover; reduce heat to low, and simmer 20 minutes or until rice is done and liquid is absorbed.

Place squash shells in a 13- x 9- x 2-inch baking pan. Spoon meat mixture into shells; spoon Parmesan Cheese Sauce over meat mixture. Cover tightly with aluminum foil. Bake at 375° for 15 minutes or until squash are heated thoroughly. Yield: 6 servings.

Parmesan Cheese Sauce:
1 tablespoon butter or margarine
1 tablespoon all-purpose flour
½ cup milk
2 tablespoons grated Parmesan cheese
¼ teaspoon dry mustard
⅛ teaspoon salt
Dash of pepper
Dash of red pepper

Melt butter in a small heavy saucepan over low heat; add flour, stirring until smooth. Cook 1 minute, stirring constantly. Gradually add milk; cook over medium heat, stirring constantly, until thickened and bubbly. Stir in cheese, mustard, salt, and pepper; cook, stirring constantly, until cheese is melted. Yield: about ½ cup.

Margaret W. Cotton,
Franklin, Virginia.

Tip: Use a blender or food processor to make crumbs from crackers or stale bread. If you don't have stale bread on hand, dry fresh bread in a microwave or toaster oven.

HAM-STUFFED EGGPLANT

1 large eggplant
½ cup chopped onion
½ cup thinly sliced celery
¼ cup butter or margarine, melted
1 cup diced cooked ham
1 (8-ounce) can tomato sauce
1 cup ripe olives, sliced
½ teaspoon salt
Dash of pepper
¼ cup grated Parmesan cheese

Wash eggplant, and cut in half lengthwise. Remove pulp, leaving a ¼-inch shell; set shells aside. Dice pulp.

Sauté eggplant pulp, onion, and celery in butter until tender. Stir in next 5 ingredients. Stuff shells with ham mixture, and place in a 9-inch square baking pan. Sprinkle Parmesan cheese on each eggplant half. Bake at 400° for 20 to 25 minutes. Yield: 2 servings.

Mrs. Bruce Fowler,
Woodruff, South Carolina.

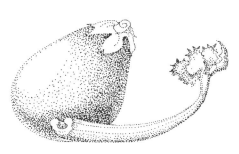

BACON-AND-EGG-STUFFED TOMATOES

6 large tomatoes
Salt and pepper
6 hard-cooked eggs, chopped
¾ cup diced celery
⅓ cup mayonnaise
6 slices bacon, cooked and crumbled
2 tablespoons chopped fresh parsley
¼ teaspoon salt
¼ teaspoon pepper
Paprika

Wash tomatoes thoroughly. Cut tops from tomatoes; scoop out pulp, leaving shells intact. Chop tomato pulp. Drain tomato shells, and sprinkle cavities with salt and pepper.

Combine tomato pulp, eggs, celery, mayonnaise, bacon, parsley, ¼ teaspoon salt, and ¼ teaspoon pepper; stir well. Fill tomato shells with bacon-and-egg mixture. Sprinkle with paprika. Yield: 6 servings. *Jane Mollenkamp, Atlanta, Georgia.*

CHICKEN-STUFFED MUSHROOMS

12 large fresh mushrooms
¼ cup butter or margarine
1 cup finely chopped cooked chicken breast
3 to 4 tablespoons chicken broth
1 egg, beaten
1 cup soft breadcrumbs, divided
1 teaspoon dried parsley flakes
1 tablespoon minced onion
½ to 1 teaspoon salt
¼ teaspoon pepper

Rinse mushrooms; remove and chop stems. Set mushroom caps aside. Melt butter in a large skillet; add stems, and sauté until tender. Stir in chicken. Stir chicken broth and egg into ¾ cup breadcrumbs; add breadcrumb mixture, parsley, onion, salt, and pepper to skillet, stirring well.

Spoon chicken mixture into mushroom caps, and sprinkle with remaining ¼ cup breadcrumbs. Place mushrooms in a 9-inch square baking pan; add ½ inch of water. Bake at 350° for 30 to 35 minutes. Yield: 4 servings.

Wilma H. Knick,
Lexington, Virginia.

SHRIMP-STUFFED PEPPERS

3 cups water
1 pound small or medium shrimp
6 medium-size green peppers
3 quarts water
3 cloves garlic
1 teaspoon salt
1 (10¾-ounce) can cream of mushroom soup, undiluted
2 tablespoons chopped onion
2 tablespoons butter or margarine
Juice of 1 lemon
¼ to ½ teaspoon pepper
1½ cups cooked rice
1 teaspoon chopped fresh parsley
1 cup (4 ounces) shredded Swiss cheese
Paprika

Bring 3 cups water to a boil; add shrimp, and return to a boil. Lower heat, and simmer 3 to 5 minutes. Drain well; rinse with cold water. Chill. Peel and devein shrimp; set aside.

Cut off top of each pepper; remove membrane and seeds.

Combine 3 quarts water, garlic, and salt in a Dutch oven; bring to a boil. Add green peppers, and boil 8 to 10 minutes or until crisp-tender (do not overcook); drain.

Combine soup, onion, butter, lemon juice, and pepper in a Dutch oven;

cook over medium heat, stirring occasionally, until butter melts. Add rice, shrimp, and parsley to soup mixture; stir well.

Stuff green peppers with shrimp mixture; place in a shallow baking dish. Add water to barely cover bottom of baking dish. Bake, uncovered, at 350° for 30 minutes. Sprinkle cheese on top of shrimp mixture; sprinkle with paprika. Bake an additional 10 minutes or until cheese melts. Yield: 6 servings.

Mrs. C. W. Kennard,
Anderson, Texas.

Deep-Dish Pizza, The Easy Way

A good example of the versatility of the food processor is Ouida Marie Kelly's Deep-Dish Mediterranean Pizza. The processor mixes and kneads dough for the crust; then it chops, slices, and shreds ingredients for the sauce and toppings.

DEEP-DISH MEDITERRANEAN PIZZA

¾ cup warm water (105° to 115°)
2 packages dry yeast
3 cups unbleached flour
1 teaspoon salt
½ cup warm water (105° to 115°)
1 tablespoon olive oil
Pizza sauce (recipe follows)
1 green pepper, seeded
16 fresh mushrooms
18 ripe olives, drained
1 (8-ounce) package pepperoni
2 (8-ounce) packages mozzarella cheese

Combine ¾ cup warm water and yeast. Let stand 5 minutes.

Position knife blade in processor bowl; top with cover. Add flour, salt, ½ cup water, and oil; process 5 seconds or until mixture resembles coarse crumbs.

With processor running, pour yeast mixture through food chute. Stop processor immediately when dough forms a loose ball (after about 10 seconds).

Dough will be sticky.

Grease hands; shape dough into a ball and place in a well-greased bowl, turning twice to coat well. Cover and let rise in a warm place (85°), free from drafts, 1 hour or until doubled in bulk.

Punch dough down, and divide in half. Roll each half into a 16- x 11-inch rectangle. Place each half in a lightly greased 15½- x 10- x 1-inch jellyroll pan. Turn edges up slightly to form a ridge around pan. Cover and let rise in a warm place (85°), free from drafts, 1 hour.

Prepare pizza sauce; set aside.

Quarter green pepper. Position knife blade in dry bowl; top with cover; add green pepper. Pulse until pepper is chopped (scrape bowl once during chopping if necessary). Drain; set aside.

Position slicing disc in processor bowl; top with cover. Stack mushrooms sideways in food chute, alternating caps and stems. Slice, applying firm pressure with food pusher. Set aside.

Position slicing disc in processor bowl; top with cover. Place olives in food chute and slice, applying moderate pressure with food pusher. Remove and set aside.

Position slicing disc in processor bowl; top with cover; wedge pepperoni in food chute. Slice, applying firm pressure with food pusher. Set aside.

Position shredding blade in processor bowl; top with cover; put cheese in food chute. Shred, applying moderate pressure with food pusher. Set aside.

Spread half of pizza sauce evenly over each dough half; top each with half of shredded cheese. Arrange green pepper, mushrooms, olives, and pepperoni over cheese layers.

Bake at 350°, on the lowest rack of the oven, for 35 to 40 minutes or until crust is lightly browned. Yield: two 15½- x 10- x 1-inch pizzas.

Pizza Sauce:

2 cloves garlic, peeled
1 onion, peeled
1 tablespoon olive oil
2 (14½-ounce) cans Italian-style tomatoes, chopped
1 (6-ounce) can tomato paste
1 tablespoon dried oregano leaves
1 tablespoon dried basil leaves
1 teaspoon dried thyme leaves
1 teaspoon salt

Position knife blade in dry processor bowl; top with cover. Drop garlic through food chute with processor running; process 3 to 5 seconds or until garlic is minced. Remove garlic, and set aside.

Cut onion into quarters. Position knife blade in processor bowl; top with cover; add the onion. Pulse 3 to 4 times or until onion is chopped (scrape bowl once during chopping if necessary).

Heat oil in a heavy 10-inch skillet over low heat. Add garlic and onion; cook over low heat, stirring frequently, until onion is tender. Add remaining ingredients, stirring well. Bring to a boil; reduce heat and simmer 1 hour, stirring occasionally. Yield: 3 cups.

Ouida Marie Kelly,
Tulsa, Oklahoma.

Scallops Are A Great Catch

Year-round availability and speed of preparation make scallops a great spur-of-the-moment menu idea. This seafood treasure is equally good broiled simply on skewers or simmered in wine and baked in a rich Mornay sauce.

When purchasing scallops, count on 40 to the pound. Since they are highly perishable, cook scallops within two days of purchase. Always wash them well before cooking to remove all the sand and grit.

SCALLOPS EN BROCHETTE WITH VEGETABLES

1 pound scallops
1 pound bacon
1 (8-ounce) bottle oil and vinegar dressing
4 medium tomatoes, cut into quarters
2 large green peppers, cut into eighths
16 mushroom caps

Rinse scallops; drain.

Cut bacon in half crosswise. Wrap 1 strip bacon around each scallop, and thread on skewers, leaving ½ inch between scallops. Place skewers on a broiler rack; brush with dressing.

Alternate vegetables on skewers, and place on a broiler rack; brush with oil and vinegar dressing.

Broil 4 inches from heat, about 5 minutes for scallop skewers and 3 to 5 minutes for vegetable skewers (until vegetables are crisp-tender). Turn skewers often, and baste with dressing frequently. Yield: 6 to 8 servings.

Jean Goodwin,
Athens, Georgia.

BROILED SCALLOPS WITH TARTAR SAUCE

2 pounds scallops
Salt and pepper
Paprika
Butter or margarine
Fresh parsley sprigs (optional)
Lemon wedges (optional)
Creamy Tartar Sauce

Rinse scallops; place in a 13- x 9- x 2-inch baking pan. Sprinkle with salt, pepper, and paprika; dot with butter. Broil 3 inches from heat 5 to 8 minutes, basting with pan drippings several times.

Arrange scallops on serving dish; garnish with parsley and lemon wedges, if desired. Serve with Creamy Tartar Sauce. Yield: 4 servings.

Creamy Tartar Sauce:

1 cup mayonnaise
1 tablespoon minced onion
2 tablespoons minced fresh parsley
1 tablespoon chopped pimiento-stuffed
   olives
2 tablespoons sweet pickle relish

Combine all ingredients, mixing well; chill sauce at least 3 hours. Yield: about 1½ cups.
Perle I. Caldwell,
Knoxville, Tennessee.

SCALLOPS MORNAY

¾ cup water
½ cup Sauterne or Sauterne cooking wine
¼ teaspoon salt
¼ teaspoon instant minced onion
Dash of pepper
½ pound scallops
½ cup sliced fresh mushrooms
1 tablespoon butter or margarine
1½ tablespoons all-purpose flour
½ cup milk
¼ teaspoon salt
⅛ teaspoon pepper
½ cup (2 ounces) shredded process Swiss
   cheese
2 to 3 tablespoons chopped fresh parsley

Combine first 5 ingredients in a medium saucepan; simmer 5 minutes.

Rinse scallops; drain. Stir scallops and mushrooms into liquid mixture; cover, and simmer 5 minutes.

Remove scallops and mushrooms from liquid with a slotted spoon; set aside. Boil remaining liquid until reduced to ½ cup (about 10 minutes).

Melt butter in a heavy saucepan over low heat; add flour and cook 1 minute, stirring constantly. Combine reduced liquid and milk; gradually add to flour mixture. Cook over medium heat, stirring constantly, until thickened and bubbly. Stir in ¼ teaspoon salt and ⅛ teaspoon pepper. Add Swiss cheese, and stir until melted.

Remove sauce from heat. Stir scallops and mushrooms into sauce. Spoon scallop mixture into 6 greased (6-ounce) custard cups or other individual serving dishes. Bake at 375° for 15 to 20 minutes. Sprinkle with parsley. Yield: 6 servings.
Hedy Samuels,
Southern Pines, North Carolina.

HOT SEAFOOD SALAD

½ pound scallops, coarsely chopped
   (about 1 cup)
½ pound small shrimp, peeled and
   deveined (about 1 cup)
1 cup dry white wine
2 cups (5½ ounces) sliced fresh
   mushrooms
1 tablespoon butter or margarine, melted
1 (8-ounce) carton commercial sour cream
1 cup chopped celery
¼ cup sliced almonds, toasted
¼ cup (1 ounce) crumbled blue cheese
¼ cup chopped green pepper
2 tablespoons minced onion
1 to 2 tablespoons lemon juice
1 teaspoon salt
½ cup seasoned dry breadcrumbs
2 tablespoons butter or margarine, melted
Lemon wedges

Rinse scallops and shrimp. Combine scallops, shrimp, and wine in a saucepan; simmer 3 minutes. Drain.

Sauté mushrooms in 1 tablespoon butter 2 to 3 minutes or just until tender. Combine scallops, shrimp, mushrooms, sour cream, celery, almonds, cheese, green pepper, onion, lemon juice, and salt; stir well. Spoon scallop mixture into 6 (10-ounce) custard cups or other individual serving dishes. Combine breadcrumbs and remaining butter, stirring well. Sprinkle breadcrumbs over scallop mixture. Bake at 300° for 10 to 15 minutes. Garnish with lemon wedges. Yield: 6 servings.
Helen J. Seine,
Austin, Texas.

The Sweetest Corn Of Summer

Golden corn on the cob, that old Southern favorite, is just one of many ways to enjoy this delicious vegetable. When the plump, juicy kernels are cut from the cob, you have the basis for puffy fritters, Easy Succotash, a sweet pudding, or moist cornbread.

The yield of kernels cut from the cob will depend on the size of the ears. Generally, two average-size ears will yield about 1 cup kernels.

SCALLOPED CORN

2 cups cooked fresh corn cut from cob
2 eggs, slightly beaten
¼ cup minced green pepper
½ teaspoon salt
1 cup cracker crumbs, divided
2 tablespoons butter, divided
⅔ cup half-and-half
Paprika
Parsley (optional)

Combine corn, eggs, green pepper, and salt; mix well. Spoon half of mixture into a greased 1½-quart casserole. Sprinkle with half of cracker crumbs, and dot with 1 tablespoon butter. Repeat layers; pour half-and-half over top.

Bake at 325° for 30 to 35 minutes. Remove from oven, and sprinkle with paprika. Garnish with parsley, if desired. Yield: 5 to 6 servings.
Ann Elsie Schmetzer,
Madisonville, Kentucky.

Tip: Do not thaw fish at room temperature or in warm water; it will lose moisture and flavor. Instead, place in refrigerator to thaw; allow 18 to 24 hours for thawing a 1-pound package. Do not refreeze thawed fish.

MEXICAN CORN

2 cups fresh corn cut from cob (about 4 ears)
¼ cup butter or margarine, melted
¼ cup chopped green pepper
¼ cup chopped red pepper
1 cup sliced onion, separated into rings
1 teaspoon salt
1 large tomato, peeled and diced (about 1 cup)
¼ teaspoon dried oregano leaves

Combine first 6 ingredients in a large skillet; cover and cook over medium heat 7 minutes, stirring occasionally. Add tomato and oregano; cook, uncovered, 2 minutes or until tomato is heated thoroughly. Yield: 4 to 5 servings. *Rena Nixon, Mount Airy, North Carolina.*

FRESH CORN PUDDING

6 to 8 ears fresh corn
1 egg, separated
2 tablespoons sugar
1 teaspoon salt
3 tablespoons butter or margarine, softened
¼ cup milk
1 teaspoon vanilla extract

Cut corn from cob, scraping cob to remove the pulp. Measure 3 cups of corn and pulp.

Combine corn, egg yolk, sugar, salt, butter, milk, and vanilla in a medium mixing bowl; stir well.

Beat egg white until stiff but not dry; fold into corn mixture. Spoon into a lightly greased 8-inch square baking dish. Bake at 350° for 30 to 40 minutes or until set. Yield: 6 servings.
Judy Cunningham, Roanoke, Virginia.

FOILED CORN ON THE COB

12 ears fresh corn
Herb Spread
Salt and pepper to taste

Husk corn right before cooking. Place each ear on a piece of aluminum foil. Brush corn with Herb Spread; sprinkle with salt and pepper. Wrap foil tightly around corn. Bake at 450° for 25 minutes, turning several times. Yield: 12 servings.

Herb Spread:

½ cup margarine, softened
½ teaspoon dried rosemary leaves
½ teaspoon dried marjoram leaves

Combine all ingredients, stirring well. Yield: ½ cup. *Edna J. Chadsey, Cleveland, Tennessee.*

EASY SUCCOTASH

2 cups fresh lima beans (about 1 pound)
4 cups fresh corn cut from cob (about 8 ears)
3 tablespoons butter or margarine
½ cup whipping cream
½ teaspoon salt
⅛ teaspoon pepper

Cook beans in boiling salted water about 15 minutes or until almost tender; drain. Add corn, butter, whipping cream, salt, and pepper; mix well. Cook over low heat, stirring often, 7 to 10 minutes, or until corn is done. Yield: 6 servings. *Charlotte J. Frolick, Birmingham, Alabama.*

GOLDEN CORN FRITTERS

1 cup self-rising flour
1 teaspoon sugar
1 teaspoon salt
½ teaspoon pepper
2 eggs, beaten
1½ cups fresh corn cut from cob (about 3 ears)
½ cup milk
2 teaspoons vegetable oil
Hot vegetable oil

Combine first 4 ingredients in a large mixing bowl; mix well, and set aside.

Combine eggs, corn, milk, and 2 teaspoons vegetable oil; mix well. Stir corn mixture into dry ingredients.

Drop mixture by rounded teaspoonfuls into vegetable oil heated to 375°; cook fritters until golden, turning once. Yield: about 3 dozen. *Lynne Weeks, Midland, Georgia.*

Tip: Leftover vegetables may be folded into cream sauce to serve over a plain omelet; added to fritter batter; or marinated with French dressing for a salad.

FRESH CORN CASSEROLE

6 slices bacon
4 cups fresh corn cut from cob (about 8 ears)
1 cup chopped green pepper
½ cup chopped onion
2 medium tomatoes, peeled and chopped
1 teaspoon salt
¼ teaspoon pepper

Cook bacon until crisp; drain and crumble. Reserve 2 tablespoons bacon drippings in skillet; add corn, green pepper, and onion. Cook over high heat 5 minutes, stirring often; stir in bacon, tomatoes, salt, and pepper. Spoon mixture into a lightly greased 2-quart shallow baking dish; bake at 350° for 15 minutes. Yield: 8 servings.
Sheila J. Heatwole, Virginia Beach, Virginia.

CORN SAUTE

4 cups fresh corn cut from cob (about 8 ears)
¼ cup butter or margarine, melted
½ cup half-and-half
½ teaspoon salt
Pepper to taste

Combine corn and butter in a large skillet; cover and cook over low heat 1 minute. Add remaining ingredients; cook, uncovered, over low heat 5 to 7 minutes or until liquid is absorbed, stirring frequently. Yield: 6 to 8 servings.
Mrs. Carlysle Sayre, Lexington, Kentucky.

FRESH CORNBREAD

1 cup cornmeal
½ cup all-purpose flour
1 tablespoon plus 1 teaspoon baking powder
1 tablespoon sugar
1 teaspoon salt
1 cup fresh corn cut from cob (about 2 ears)
1 egg, slightly beaten
¼ cup bacon drippings or vegetable oil
1 cup buttermilk

Combine first 5 ingredients; add corn, egg, bacon drippings, and buttermilk, stirring well. Pour into a greased 9-inch cast-iron skillet or a 9-inch square baking pan. Bake at 475° for 20 to 25 minutes or until brown. Yield: about 8 servings.
Clova Brown, Milton, West Virginia.

Serve Franks For Family Pleasers

Frankfurters can be combined with a multitude of ingredients for family-pleasing results that are economical as well. For a one-dish dinner, we suggest Frankfurter-Cabbage Skillet; a hint of nutmeg adds a special touch. Spanish Frankfurters is a tangy main dish that's served over rice. And for a special family treat, fry a batch of Crusty Franks for some of the best corn dogs you'll ever taste.

FRANKFURTER-CABBAGE SKILLET

1 small head cabbage, coarsely shredded
¼ teaspoon ground nutmeg
2 large carrots, coarsely shredded
2 large green onions with tops, sliced
¾ teaspoon salt
¼ teaspoon pepper
2 tablespoons butter or margarine
1 cup water
1 pound frankfurters, scored
Mustard and catsup (optional)

Place cabbage in a large skillet; sprinkle with nutmeg. Add carrot, onion, salt, and pepper. Dot with butter. Add water; cover, and bring to a boil over high heat. Reduce heat to low and simmer 10 minutes, stirring once. Place frankfurters on vegetables; simmer, covered, 10 minutes or until vegetables are tender and frankfurters are heated thoroughly. Serve with mustard and catsup, if desired. Yield: 6 to 8 servings.
Jennifer Fowler,
Woodruff, South Carolina.

FRANKS AND HASH BROWNS

1 large onion, chopped
6 frankfurters, sliced
¼ cup plus 2 tablespoons bacon drippings or margarine, melted
6 medium potatoes, cooked and sliced
1 or 2 large carrots, shredded

Sauté onion and franks in bacon drippings. Add potatoes; cook 10 to 15 minutes or until potatoes are golden brown, stirring frequently. Add carrot; continue cooking until heated thoroughly. Yield: 6 servings. *Mrs. Fay Hatfield,*
Garden City, Kansas.

CRUSTY FRANKS

12 frankfurters, cut into halves or thirds
2 cups pancake or waffle mix
¼ cup yellow cornmeal
1 teaspoon dry mustard
½ teaspoon onion salt
½ teaspoon garlic powder
1½ cups water
Hot vegetable oil
Mustard and catsup

Wipe frankfurters dry. Combine next 6 ingredients in a medium mixing bowl; stir just until moistened.

Dip franks in batter. Fry in deep hot oil (375° to 400°) 2 to 3 minutes or until brown, turning once. Drain on paper towels. Serve with mustard and catsup. Yield: 6 servings. *Martha Ann Rabon,*
Stapleton, Alabama.

SPANISH FRANKFURTERS

¼ cup minced onion
¼ cup minced green pepper
2 tablespoons bacon drippings
½ cup chili sauce
½ cup water
2 tablespoons vinegar
2 tablespoons sugar
⅛ teaspoon red pepper
1 pound frankfurters, cut into thirds
Hot cooked rice

Combine first 8 ingredients in a large skillet; simmer 7 to 10 minutes. Add frankfurters; simmer, covered, 10 additional minutes. Serve over hot rice. Yield: 4 servings. *Mrs. Jack Fuqua,*
Roanoke, Virginia.

FRANKFURTER SKILLET DINNER

2 cups chopped onion
¼ cup butter or margarine, melted
1 pound frankfurters, quartered
1 (14½-ounce) can whole tomatoes, undrained
5 or 6 medium potatoes, cut into 1-inch cubes
1 teaspoon salt
1 teaspoon caraway seeds

Sauté onion in butter until golden. Add frankfurters; cook 5 minutes, stirring occasionally. Chop tomatoes; add with liquid to frankfurters. Add remaining ingredients. Simmer, covered, 30 minutes or until potatoes are tender; stir occasionally. Yield: 6 servings.
Doris Garton,
Shenandoah, Virginia.

Snack On A Date-Nut Sweet

The flavors of dates and nuts naturally go together, and this recipe for Date-Nut Bars is no exception. Flavored with cinnamon and topped with a powdered sugar glaze, they are great for dessert or for just plain snacking.

DATE-NUT BARS

1 cup chopped dates
1 cup water
1 cup sugar
7 tablespoons butter or margarine
2 teaspoons ground cinnamon
1 teaspoon soda
3 tablespoons boiling water
¾ cup chopped nuts
2 cups all-purpose flour
1 teaspoon salt
1 teaspoon baking powder
Glaze (recipe follows)

Combine first 5 ingredients in a large saucepan; simmer, stirring frequently, for 5 minutes. Combine soda and boiling water; stir into date mixture. Add nuts; stir well. Cool.

Combine flour, salt, and baking powder; add to date mixture, blending well. Spread mixture evenly into a greased 15- x 10- x 1-inch jellyroll pan. Bake at 375° for 20 minutes. Spread evenly with glaze while still warm. Cool for 10 minutes; then cut into bars. Yield: about 36 bars.

Glaze:

1 cup powdered sugar
2 tablespoons milk
1 tablespoon butter, melted
1 teaspoon vanilla extract

Combine all ingredients, stirring until smooth. Yield: about ⅔ cup.
Mrs. Julius L. Feinberg,
Albuquerque, New Mexico.

Right: *Tantalize summer appetites with grilled Chicken-Mushroom Bundles (page 157). Just add salad and rolls for a complete meal.*

Pages 168 and 169: *To cool off on a hot summer day bring out the freezer and crank up some Chocolate Ice Cream (page 176), Straw-Ba-Nut Ice Cream (page 177), or Vanilla Ice Cream (page 176).*

Page 170: *Elegant Crab Soup (page 188) is rich and creamy with milk and whipping cream—and a generous dash of Scotch.*

Cool Off With Cucumber Soup

For quick summertime refreshment, Creamy Cucumber Soup is easily made in the blender.

You can serve the soup as an appetizer, or enjoy it with crackers and salad for a light lunch.

CREAMY CUCUMBER SOUP

1 (10¾-ounce) can cream of celery soup, undiluted
1 cup milk
1 small cucumber, cut into pieces
1 small green pepper, cut into pieces
¼ cup sliced pimiento-stuffed olives
Dash of hot sauce
1 cup commercial sour cream
1 tablespoon lemon juice
Cucumber slices (optional)

Combine soup, milk, cucumber, green pepper, olives, and hot sauce in container of electric blender; process 2 minutes. Add sour cream and lemon juice; stir well. Chill at least 4 hours. Garnish with cucumber slices, if desired. Yield: about 5 cups.

Mrs. Robert Deleot,
Decatur, Georgia.

Bar Cookies From The Microwave

If bar cookies are a favorite at your house, consider preparing them in your microwave oven. While some recipes cannot be adapted for microwaving, and the results of others may vary in texture and color from conventionally baked bar cookies, you can get good results by using proper microwave techniques and an adapted recipe.

Avoid recipes with a high proportion of shortening or butter. The high fat content of these foods attracts microwave energy, causing overcooking in spots. Since bar cookies will not brown in the microwave oven, frost the cookies or use ingredients with natural color, such as chocolate, brown sugar, or dark spices.

The recipes here are geared specifically for the microwave oven, and each

gives a time range. To prevent overcooking, always check for doneness at the lower end of the time range. Here are some other helpful tips.

Shielding the Corners

Corners of bar cookies cook faster than the center. Shielding corners with aluminum foil reduces energy received and slows the cooking process. But before shielding, check your manufacturer's directions; some of the older microwave ovens can be damaged by the use of foil. If your oven does not allow shielding, bake cookies in a round dish.

To shield bar cookies, cut triangles of foil and place over the top corners of dish, keeping foil smooth and close to dish. Be sure the foil is at least 1 inch from the walls of the oven. If foil is not smooth or touches oven walls, it may cause an arc (spark of electricity). If an arc does occur, flatten foil and continue microwaving.

For most bar cookies, shields should be left in place during the entire microwave cycle. However, remove the shields earlier if the cycle is almost complete and the corners are not cooking as rapidly as the center.

Testing for Doneness

The wooden pick test used for conventional baking is not accurate for most microwave baking. Microwaved bar cookies are done even when they are fairly firm to the touch and almost dry on top. (A few wet spots will dry while the cookies cool.)

When bar cookies test done, remove shields and place dish on a sheet of foil on a heat-resistant surface. The foil reflects heat onto the dish to complete cooking on the bottom.

NUTTY FUDGE BROWNIES

2 (1-ounce) squares unsweetened chocolate
¼ cup butter or margarine
1 cup sugar
2 eggs
¼ cup milk
½ teaspoon vanilla extract
⅔ cup all-purpose flour
½ teaspoon baking powder
¼ teaspoon salt
½ cup finely chopped pecans
Chocolate frosting (recipe follows)

Place chocolate squares in a small bowl; microwave at HIGH for 1½ to 2½ minutes or until melted. Set chocolate aside to cool.

Place butter in a small bowl; microwave at LOW for 40 to 50 seconds or until softened.

Cream butter with electric mixer until fluffy; gradually add sugar, beating well. Add eggs, milk, and vanilla; beat well. Stir in chocolate.

Combine flour, baking powder, and salt; stir well. Add to creamed mixture; mix well. Stir in pecans.

Spread mixture in a well-greased 8-inch square baking dish. Shield corners with triangles of foil, keeping foil smooth and close to dish. Microwave at MEDIUM HIGH for 4 minutes. Give dish a half turn, and microwave at HIGH for 3½ to 5½ minutes or until top is almost dry. Remove from oven, and place on a sheet of foil. Cool. Spread with chocolate frosting, if desired. Cut into 2-inch squares. Yield: 16 squares.

Chocolate Frosting:

1 (1-ounce) square unsweetened chocolate
2 tablespoons butter or margarine
1½ teaspoons water
1¼ cups sifted powdered sugar
1 egg yolk
¼ teaspoon vanilla extract

Place chocolate in a small bowl; microwave at HIGH for 1½ to 2 minutes or until chocolate melts.

Place butter in a small bowl; microwave at LOW for 40 seconds or until softened. Combine all ingredients; beat with an electric mixer until smooth. Yield: enough frosting for 8-inch square pan of bar cookies.

Tip: Ideal conditions for storing chocolate are a temperature of 60° to 70° and a humidity reading of 50%. Keep chocolate away from moisture, and do not store in the refrigerator. During hot weather keep chocolate in a cool place.

Bar cookies cook in a microwave oven in a fraction of the time required for conventional preparation. Clockwise from back: Chewy Peanut Bars, Date-Oat Bars, Peanut Butter-and-Fudge Bars.

CHEWY PEANUT BARS

¼ cup plus 2 tablespoons butter or
  margarine
1 cup firmly packed brown sugar
¼ cup creamy peanut butter
¾ cup chopped salted peanuts, divided
2 eggs
1 cup all-purpose flour
½ teaspoon baking powder
½ teaspoon salt
1 teaspoon vanilla extract
2 (1.2-ounce) chocolate bars, broken into
  pieces

Place butter in a large bowl; microwave at HIGH for 45 to 60 seconds or until melted. Add brown sugar and peanut butter, mixing well. Add ½ cup peanuts, eggs, flour, baking powder, salt, and vanilla; stir well. Spoon batter into a greased 8-inch square baking dish. Shield corners with triangles of foil, keeping foil smooth and close to dish. Microwave at MEDIUM HIGH for 4 minutes; give dish a half turn. Microwave at HIGH for 3 to 6 minutes or until top is almost dry. Remove from microwave, and place on a sheet of foil. Top immediately with chocolate pieces. Let stand 5 minutes; spread melted chocolate evenly over top, and sprinkle with remaining nuts. Cool. Cut into squares. Yield: 16 squares.

PEANUT BUTTER-AND-FUDGE BARS

½ (12-ounce) package peanut butter
  morsels (about 1¼ cups)
½ cup light corn syrup
2 tablespoons butter or margarine
4 cups crisp rice cereal
2 (6-ounce) packages semisweet chocolate
  morsels
¼ cup butter or margarine
1 cup sifted powdered sugar
2 tablespoons milk
½ teaspoon vanilla extract

Combine peanut butter morsels, corn syrup, and 2 tablespoons butter in a large bowl. Microwave at HIGH for 1½ to 2 minutes or until morsels begin to melt. Stir until morsels melt. Add cereal, and mix well. Press half the mixture into a buttered 12- x 8- x 2-inch baking dish; chill. Set remainder aside while preparing chocolate layer.

Place chocolate morsels and butter in a 1-quart casserole. Microwave at HIGH for 1½ to 2 minutes or until morsels begin to melt. Stir until morsels melt. Add powdered sugar, milk, and vanilla, stirring until blended. Spread chocolate mixture over chilled layer. Spread remaining cereal mixture over chocolate layer; press firmly. Chill until set. Cut into squares. Yield: 24 squares.

DATE-OAT BARS

2 (8-ounce) packages pitted dates, coarsely
  chopped
1 tablespoon all-purpose flour
½ cup water
½ cup butter or margarine
1½ cups shredded coconut
¼ cup honey
⅛ teaspoon salt
2½ cups quick-cooking oats, uncooked
½ cup finely chopped pecans
½ teaspoon vanilla extract

Combine dates and flour in a large bowl. Toss lightly, and set aside.

Measure water in a 1-cup glass measure; microwave at HIGH for 2 to 3 minutes or until boiling. Pour water over dates. Add butter, coconut, honey, and salt; stir well. Microwave at HIGH for 2 to 3 minutes or until thick, stirring at 1-minute intervals.

Add oats, pecans, and vanilla to date mixture, mixing well. Spoon mixture into a buttered 9-inch square baking pan; press gently. Chill until set. Cut into bars, and store in refrigerator in an airtight container. Yield: 24 bars.

Tip: Use soda on a damp cloth to shine up your kitchen appliances.

August

Nothing beats the heat of a sultry August day better than home-made ice cream. Whether you prefer chocolate, fruit-flavored, or nutty Butter Pecan, you'll find no greater variety than that offered in our recipes for homemade ice cream. The foods staff's favorite? Flavor-packed Straw-Ba-Nut!

While the ice cream ripens, fire up the grill for some meaty kabobs, all flavored with special marinades that keep them juicy and tender. Choose beef, shrimp, or lamb, all threaded on skewers among chunks of fruit or vegetables.

We all have our favorite ways to prepare potato salad and coleslaw, but be sure to try some of the new combinations our readers have created for these special summer salads.

Summertime Menu:
Tennis, Golf, And
Light Dining

For Judd and Betty Farr, having a party means simply inviting some friends over for an afternoon of outdoor recreation. Because of the resort-like quality of the Farrs' home, their guests can take part in their choice of tournaments—on the court with tennis or on the greens with golf.

The Farrs had their Laykold tennis court built to overlook the 18th hole of the Greenville Country Club so that their family of nine and friends would have an activity to get involved in. "I find the tennis court far more pleasing than something like a swimming pool, and it can be used year-round," Judd points out.

It's a rare occasion when you can't find at least one member of the Farr family with a tennis racket or golf club in hand. Weekdays, Betty will often have a group of her friends over for a round robin of tennis; Judd will invite the men over in the evening. When the weekend rolls around, the men take to the golf course, while the women take advantage of the tennis court.

Hamburgers are the usual fare for these get-togethers, but occasionally Betty will combine her efforts with those of her friend and neighbor, Rene Fridy, to make the menu something special.

The first thing Betty and Rene do is get out their cookbooks and recipe files and plan a menu that they think everyone will enjoy.

The result of this planning is a menu that appeals to guests and is easy to serve from colorful tables arranged on the terrace near the tennis courts.

Score Points With
This Menu

To feed their hungry crowd of friends, Betty and Rene came up with this casual menu.

Guests cool off with refreshing Health-Kick Punch and nibble on marinated shrimp, a cheese appetizer, a molded chicken salad, and beef or pork tenderloin sandwiches. Even the centerpiece is part of the meal: an assortment

of fresh vegetables that guests can dip into their choice of dressings. Dessert is Crema, a Greek vanilla-flavored pudding served with fresh strawberries.

Health-Kick Punch
Fresh Vegetables
Romano Dressing   Pepper Dressing
Three-Cheese Appetizer
Mediterranean Shrimp Bowl
Chicken-Cucumber Mold
Beef and Pork Tenderloin Sandwiches
Crema

HEALTH-KICK PUNCH
Juice of 10 oranges
Juice of 6 lemons
6 medium or 4 large bananas, sliced
½ cup crushed pineapple
1½ cups light rum
1 cup honey
1 cup banana-flavored liqueur
⅔ cup grenadine syrup
6 drops Angostura bitters
Lemon slices

Combine first 9 ingredients in a large bowl, stirring well. Pour punch mixture, one-third at a time, into container of electric blender; blend until smooth. Pour punch into large serving container; stir well. Float lemon slices on top of punch; serve over crushed ice. Yield: about 3 quarts.

ROMANO DRESSING
2 cups (½ pound) grated Romano cheese
1⅓ cups vegetable oil
⅓ cup olive oil
Juice of 2 lemons
2 cloves garlic

Combine all ingredients in a small mixing bowl; stir well. Chill overnight; remove garlic. Pour mixture into container of electric blender; blend well. Serve with fresh vegetables. Yield: 2¼ cups.

PEPPER DRESSING
1 (8-ounce) carton commercial sour cream
¼ cup whipping cream
2 teaspoons dried green pepper flakes
½ teaspoon paprika
½ teaspoon salt
½ teaspoon pepper
¼ teaspoon instant minced garlic
1 teaspoon instant onion flakes
¼ teaspoon dehydrated chives

Combine all ingredients in a small mixing bowl; stir well. Refrigerate dressing overnight. Serve with fresh vegetables. Yield: 1¼ cups.

THREE-CHEESE APPETIZER
1 envelope unflavored gelatin
¼ cup cold water
¼ cup chopped pecans
¾ cup mayonnaise
½ teaspoon salt
1½ teaspoons prepared mustard
Dash of hot sauce
2 cups (8 ounces) shredded sharp Cheddar cheese
½ cup grated Parmesan cheese
¼ cup (1 ounce) crumbled blue cheese
1 cup whipping cream
Mayonnaise
Chopped parsley (optional)
Cherry tomatoes (optional)

Soften gelatin in water in a small saucepan; place over low heat, stirring until dissolved. Combine next 9 ingredients in a medium bowl, stirring well; stir in gelatin mixture. Lightly coat a 4-cup mold with mayonnaise; pour cheese mixture into mold; chill overnight or until firm. Unmold on serving plate; garnish with chopped parsley and cherry tomatoes, if desired. Serve with crackers. Yield: about 3¼ cups.

MEDITERRANEAN SHRIMP BOWL
⅔ cup olive oil
⅓ cup wine vinegar
1 teaspoon salt
¼ teaspoon pepper
1 clove garlic, crushed
1 teaspoon dried oregano leaves
Juice of 1 lemon
1 medium onion, thinly sliced and separated into rings
2 pounds shrimp, cooked, peeled, and deveined
Cherry tomatoes (optional)
Endive (optional)
Fresh mushrooms (optional)

Combine first 8 ingredients in a medium mixing bowl; stir well. Add shrimp; toss. Cover tightly, and refrigerate 2 hours, tossing occasionally.

Drain shrimp. Pour shrimp into a serving bowl; garnish with cherry tomatoes, endive, and mushrooms, if desired. Yield: 12 servings.

CHICKEN-CUCUMBER MOLD

2 (2½-pound) broiler-fryers, quartered
1 teaspoon salt
¼ teaspoon pepper
3 bay leaves
1 bunch green onions, cut into 1-inch pieces
2 carrots, peeled and cut into 1-inch pieces
2 sprigs fresh parsley
1 envelope unflavored gelatin
2 cucumbers, thinly sliced
Sauce (recipe follows)

Place chicken in a Dutch oven; cover with water, and bring to a boil. Add salt, pepper, bay leaves, onion, carrots, and parsley. Cover and simmer 1 hour.

Remove chicken; let cool. Bone chicken, and chop meat; place in a lightly oiled 4-cup ring mold. Set aside. Strain broth; refrigerate. Skim and discard fat from cold broth.

Combine ¼ cup broth and gelatin in a small saucepan; bring to a boil, stirring to dissolve gelatin. Add 1½ cups broth, mixing well. Pour gelatin mixture over chicken. Chill overnight.

Unmold on serving plate. Place cucumber slices overlapping on top of mold. Serve with sauce and crackers. Yield: about 24 servings.

Sauce:

½ cup mayonnaise
½ teaspoon dried tarragon leaves
Juice of ½ lemon

Combine mayonnaise, tarragon, and lemon juice in a small mixing bowl; stir well. Yield: ½ cup.

Tip: Fresh meat, poultry, and fish should be loosely wrapped and refrigerated; use in a few days. Loosely wrap fresh ground meat, liver, and kidneys; use in one or two days. Wieners, bacon, and sliced sandwich meats can be stored in original wrapping in refrigerator. Store all meat in the coldest part of the refrigerator.

■ Marinate these beef and pork tenderloins together, but cook them separately. Sandwiches can be prepared from either or both types of meat.

BEEF AND PORK TENDERLOIN SANDWICHES

1 (6- to 7-pound) beef tenderloin, trimmed
2 (⅔-pound) pork tenderloins, trimmed
Marinade (recipe follows)
Vegetable oil
Party rye bread
Endive
Mayonnaise (optional)
Commercial barbecue sauce (optional)
Prepared horseradish (optional)

Place tenderloins in a large pan or dish; pour marinade over top, and cover tightly. Refrigerate overnight, turning meat several times; drain.

Place beef tenderloin, fat side up, on rack in a shallow roasting pan; rub with 1 tablespoon vegetable oil. Bake at 450° for 15 minutes. Turn oven off; do not open door. Let roast remain in oven 45 minutes (roast will be medium rare).

Place pork tenderloins, fat side up, on rack in a shallow roasting pan; rub with 1 teaspoon vegetable oil. Bake at 325° for 1 hour or until well done.

Slice tenderloins, and place on serving platter. Serve on party rye bread with endive; top with mayonnaise, barbecue sauce, or horseradish, if desired. Yield: about 24 servings.

Marinade:

½ cup port wine
½ cup brandy
½ teaspoon dried tarragon leaves
½ teaspoon dried whole thyme
2 bay leaves
1¼ teaspoons salt
½ teaspoon pepper
½ teaspoon dry mustard

Combine all ingredients in a small mixing bowl, mixing well. Yield: 1 cup.

CREMA

1 quart milk
¾ cup sugar, divided
4 egg yolks, beaten
¼ cup cornstarch
1 teaspoon vanilla extract
Fresh strawberries

Combine milk and ½ cup sugar in a medium saucepan; bring to boiling point, stirring occasionally (do not boil). Remove from heat.

Combine egg yolks and remaining ¼ cup sugar in a medium mixing bowl; gradually add cornstarch, stirring well. Gradually stir half of hot milk into the egg mixture; add to remaining hot milk, stirring constantly. Cook over medium heat, stirring constantly, until smooth and thickened. Stir in vanilla. Pour custard into serving bowl and chill. To serve, top with fresh strawberries. Yield: 6 to 8 servings.

Note: Recipe may be doubled or tripled if desired.

Ice Cream: Make It Rich And Creamy

No sound is more welcome on a warm summer day than the cranking of an ice cream freezer. From the moment the activity starts, family and friends gather around to share the fun and wait for the dasher to be lifted.

The South's bountiful fruit crop is just about the best thing that can happen to a freezer of homemade ice cream. Just imagine the flavor of Straw-Ba-Nut, a luscious combination of strawberries, bananas, and pecans. Peach lovers will want to freeze a gallon of our Deluxe Peach Ice Cream.

Before starting your ice cream preparation, get acquainted with your freezer by reading the manufacturer's instructions carefully. Freezers are made of different materials, which can make a difference in the ice-salt ratio recommended. For most 1-gallon freezers, you should use about 3 to 4 cups rock salt and 20 pounds crushed ice.

Fill the freezer can only as full as recommended by the manufacturer. Most should be filled no more than two-thirds of their capacity. For electric freezers, let the motor run about 1 minute before adding ice and salt in layers. Hand-turned freezers should be turned about 1 minute to stir the mixture before freezing.

Let the ice cream ripen to harden and blend flavors. Push the ice cream down from the top sides of the can, and blend soft with firm portions. Cover with foil and replace lid. Pack the freezer bucket with ice and salt, using a higher ratio of salt to ice than for freezing. Wrap well, and let stand in a cool place for one to three hours. Drain off brine and check the ice and salt frequently, adding more as needed.

VANILLA ICE CREAM

8 eggs, separated
2 cups sugar
1 pint whipping cream
2 tablespoons vanilla extract
⅛ teaspoon all-purpose flour
⅛ teaspoon cream of tartar
Dash of salt
About 2½ cups milk
Fresh mint sprigs (optional)
Fresh strawberries (optional)

Beat egg yolks with electric mixer at medium speed until frothy. Gradually add sugar, beating until thick and lemon colored. Add whipping cream, vanilla, flour, and cream of tartar to egg yolk mixture; mix well.

Combine egg whites and salt; beat until stiff peaks form. Fold the egg white mixture into egg yolk mixture; then pour into freezer can of a 1-gallon hand-turned or electric freezer.

Add enough milk to fill can three-fourths full. Freeze according to manufacturer's instructions. Let ripen at least 1 hour. Garnish each serving with mint sprigs and strawberries, if desired. Yield: about 1 gallon.

Therese Livingston,
Oneonta, Alabama.

CHOCOLATE ICE CREAM

3 eggs
1 cup sugar
1 quart half-and-half
1 pint whipping cream
1 cup chocolate syrup
1 tablespoon vanilla extract
About 3 cups milk

Beat eggs with electric mixer at medium speed until frothy. Gradually add sugar, beating until thick. Add next 4 ingredients; mix well. Pour mixture into freezer can of a 1-gallon hand-turned or electric freezer.

Add enough milk to fill can about three-fourths full. Freeze according to manufacturer's instructions. Let ripen at least 1 hour. Yield: about 1 gallon.

Mrs. H. Davis Collier, Jr.,
Jacksonville, Florida.

PEPPERMINT ICE CREAM

1 quart milk
1 pound peppermint candy
1 pint half-and-half
1 pint whipping cream, whipped

Combine milk and candy; cover and refrigerate 12 hours. (Candy will dissolve.) Combine candy mixture, half-and-half, and whipped cream. Pour into freezer can of a 1-gallon hand-turned or electric freezer.

Freeze according to manufacturer's instructions. Let ripen at least 1 hour. Yield: about 1 gallon.

Mrs. James W. Elliott, Jr.,
Roanoke, Virginia.

BUTTER PECAN ICE CREAM

2 cups chopped pecans
3 tablespoons butter or margarine, melted
3 (14½-ounce) cans evaporated milk
2 (3¾-ounce) packages instant vanilla
   pudding mix
2½ cups sugar
1 teaspoon vanilla extract
2 quarts milk

Sauté chopped pecans in butter, stirring constantly, about 5 minutes or until toasted. Set aside to cool.

Combine remaining ingredients; mix well. Pour mixture into freezer can of a 1½- to 2-gallon hand-turned or electric freezer. Freeze about 10 minutes or until ice cream is thick. Remove dasher, and add pecans to ice cream mixture. Return dasher; freeze until firm according to manufacturer's instructions. Let ripen at least 1 hour. Yield: about 1½ gallons.

Jean Park,
LaGrange, Georgia.

BANANA SPLIT ICE CREAM

4 eggs
1¼ cups sugar
6 cups milk
½ teaspoon salt
1 (14-ounce) can sweetened condensed
   milk
2 cups half-and-half
1 tablespoon vanilla extract
2 bananas, chopped
1 (10-ounce) jar maraschino cherries,
   drained and chopped

Beat eggs with electric mixer at medium speed until frothy. Gradually add sugar, beating until thick. Add 6 cups milk and salt; mix well. Pour egg mixture into a large saucepan, and place over low heat; cook, stirring constantly, until thoroughly heated.

Combine egg mixture, sweetened condensed milk, half-and-half, and vanilla; stir well. Add bananas and cherries.

Pour mixture into freezer can of a 1-gallon hand-turned or electric freezer. Freeze according to manufacturer's instructions. Let ripen at least 1 hour. Yield: about 1 gallon.

Mrs. Bill Anthony,
North Little Rock, Arkansas.

DELUXE PEACH ICE CREAM

6 cups mashed peaches
1 cup sugar
3 eggs
1½ cups sugar
2 tablespoons all-purpose flour
½ teaspoon salt
1 quart milk
1 cup whipping cream
1 tablespoon vanilla extract

Combine peaches and 1 cup sugar; stir well, and set aside.

Beat eggs with electric mixer at medium speed until frothy. Combine 1½ cups sugar, flour, and salt; stir well. Gradually add sugar mixture to eggs, beating until thick. Add milk; mix well.

Pour egg mixture into a large saucepan. Cook over low heat, stirring constantly, until mixture thickens and coats a metal spoon (about 15 minutes). Remove from heat, and set pan in cold water; stir gently until cool. Stir in cream and vanilla. Add peaches, stirring well.

Pour mixture into freezer can of a 1-gallon hand-turned or electric freezer. Freeze according to manufacturer's instructions. Let ripen at least 1 hour. Yield: about 1 gallon.

Florence L. Costello,
Chattanooga, Tennessee.

RASPBERRY ICE CREAM

1 (10-ounce) package frozen raspberries,
   thawed
½ cup sugar
2½ cups milk
1½ cups whipping cream
1½ teaspoons vanilla extract

Process undrained raspberries with food mill to remove seeds.

Combine raspberries and remaining ingredients; stir until sugar is dissolved.

Pour mixture into freezer can of a 1-gallon hand-turned or electric freezer. Freeze according to manufacturer's instructions. Let ripen at least 1 hour. Yield: about 2 quarts.

Peggy Fowler Revels,
Woodruff, South Carolina.

STRAW-BA-NUT ICE CREAM

6 eggs
2 cups sugar
1 (14-ounce) can sweetened condensed
  milk
1½ teaspoons vanilla extract
1 pint fresh strawberries, sliced
2 bananas, mashed
1 cup chopped pecans
1 (8-ounce) container frozen whipped
  topping, thawed
Red food coloring (optional)
About 1 cup milk

Beat eggs with electric mixer at medium speed until frothy. Gradually add sugar, beating until thick. Stir in sweetened condensed milk and vanilla.

Combine strawberries, bananas, and pecans; fold in whipped topping. Add fruit mixture to egg mixture; stir gently. Add food coloring, if desired, until mixture reaches preferred color. Pour into freezer can of a 1-gallon hand-turned or electric freezer.

Add enough milk to fill can three-fourths full. Freeze according to manufacturer's instructions. Let ripen at least 1 hour. Yield: about 1 gallon.

Note: One 10-ounce bag frozen strawberries, thawed, may be substituted for fresh ones.
Ardella Welch,
Duke, Oklahoma.

STRAWBERRY ICE CREAM

1 quart strawberries, mashed
¼ to ½ cup sugar
2 eggs
1 cup sugar
3 cups whipping cream
3 cups milk
½ teaspoon almond extract
⅛ teaspoon salt

Combine strawberries and ¼ to ½ cup sugar; stir well. Set aside.

Beat eggs with electric mixer at medium speed until frothy. Gradually add 1 cup sugar, beating until thick. Add cream, milk, almond extract, and salt; mix well. Stir in strawberry mixture.

Pour mixture into freezer can of a 1-gallon hand-turned or electric freezer. Freeze according to manufacturer's instructions. Let ripen at least 1 hour. Yield: about 1 gallon.
Mrs. Andy Jackson,
Live Oak, Florida.

Tip: Use muffin pans to make extra-large ice cubes for punch.

Add something new to your next family picnic with Refreshing Macaroni Salad and Creamy Potato Salad.

Give Summer Salads A New Twist

For your next family cookout or picnic, try one of these variations of favorite summer salads. Although it seems that everyone has a special way of preparing potato salad and coleslaw, our recipes give them a new twist.

Creamy Potato Salad is flavored with crumbled bacon, chopped eggs, and green onions; sour cream and Italian salad dressing give it a rich, creamy texture. Traditional coleslaw gets a flavor boost from chili sauce and pimientos, while fresh chives add a nice touch to Cucumbers in Sour Cream.

REFRESHING MACARONI SALAD

2 (8-ounce) packages shell macaroni
2 medium cucumbers, peeled
  and chopped
2 bunches green onions, chopped
1 pint cherry tomatoes, halved
1 cup salad dressing or mayonnaise
1 tablespoon garlic salt
¼ teaspoon pepper
Fresh parsley sprigs (optional)

Cook macaroni according to package directions; drain and let cool. Add remaining ingredients except parsley; stir gently. Cover and chill at least 2 hours. Garnish with parsley, if desired. Yield: 12 servings.
Vulane Phillips,
Springfield, Missouri.

ARTICHOKE-RICE SALAD

2 cups chicken broth
1 cup uncooked regular rice
¼ cup chopped green onion
¼ cup chopped green pepper
¼ cup sliced pimiento-stuffed olives
1 (6-ounce) jar marinated artichoke
  hearts, drained and halved
½ cup mayonnaise
¼ to ½ teaspoon dried dillweed
½ teaspoon salt
⅛ teaspoon pepper
Lettuce leaves (optional)
Sliced pimiento-stuffed olives (optional)

Place broth in a medium saucepan; bring to a boil, and stir in rice. Return to a boil; reduce heat and simmer, covered, 20 minutes or until done. Cool. Stir in onion, green pepper, ¼ cup olives, artichoke hearts, mayonnaise, dillweed, salt, and pepper; chill.

Spoon salad into lettuce-lined bowl; garnish with additional sliced olives, if desired. Yield: 4 to 5 servings.

Mrs. B. E. Burch,
Decatur, Georgia.

CHILLED BEAN SALAD

1 (10-ounce) package frozen sliced green
  beans
1 (10-ounce) package frozen lima beans
1 (10-ounce) package frozen English peas
½ cup chopped onion
2 hard-cooked eggs, chopped
1 (8-ounce) can water chestnuts, drained
  and chopped
½ cup mayonnaise
1 teaspoon prepared mustard
¼ teaspoon salt

Cook beans and peas according to package directions; drain and let cool. Add onion, eggs, and water chestnuts. Combine mayonnaise, mustard, and salt, mixing well; stir into bean mixture. Cover and chill 8 hours or overnight. Yield: 6 to 8 servings. *Diana Curtis, Albuquerque, New Mexico.*

CUCUMBERS IN SOUR CREAM

3 large cucumbers, peeled and thinly
  sliced
1 tablespoon salt
2 tablespoons vinegar
1 (8-ounce) carton commercial sour cream
½ teaspoon chopped fresh chives
½ teaspoon pepper

Place cucumbers in a medium bowl; sprinkle with salt, and let stand 1 hour. Drain cucumbers on paper towels, pressing to remove excess liquid. Return to bowl; stir in remaining ingredients. Chill at least 1 hour. Yield: 6 to 8 servings. *Mrs. Velva Ross, Barboursville, West Virginia.*

SHREDDED CARROT SALAD

½ cup raisins
1 cup boiling water
2 pounds carrots, shredded
½ cup flaked coconut
½ cup crushed pineapple, drained
1 cup mayonnaise

Combine raisins and water; let stand 15 minutes. Drain. Add remaining ingredients; toss gently. Chill at least 1 hour before serving. Yield: 10 servings.
Mrs. Grant Adkins,
Wichita Falls, Texas.

CHILI COLESLAW

4 to 5 cups finely shredded cabbage
1 cup thinly sliced celery
2 tablespoons minced onion
1 (6-ounce) can sliced pimiento, drained
½ cup mayonnaise or salad dressing
¼ cup chili sauce
½ teaspoon salt

Combine cabbage, celery, onion, and pimiento; set aside.

Combine mayonnaise, chili sauce, and salt; stir well. Pour dressing over cabbage mixture; toss well. Chill several hours. Yield: 8 to 10 servings.
Mrs. Charles Carper,
Portland, Texas.

CREAMY POTATO SALAD

9 medium potatoes
3 hard-cooked eggs
⅔ cup mayonnaise
1 teaspoon prepared mustard
¾ cup commercial sour cream
1 teaspoon salt
¼ teaspoon pepper
11 slices bacon
¼ cup chopped green onion
½ cup chopped celery
¼ cup commercial Italian salad dressing

Cook potatoes in boiling salted water about 30 minutes or until tender. Drain well, and cool slightly. Peel and cut potatoes into ¾-inch cubes.

Remove yolks from eggs and mash; set whites aside. Stir mayonnaise, mustard, sour cream, salt, and pepper into yolks; set aside.

Cook bacon until crisp; drain on paper towels, and crumble.

Chop egg whites; add bacon, potatoes, onion, celery, and Italian dressing. Fold in mayonnaise mixture; chill at least 2 hours. Yield: 12 servings.
Lynette L. Walther,
Palatka, Florida.

SAUERKRAUT SALAD

2 cups chopped sauerkraut, drained
½ cup sugar
½ cup thinly sliced celery
½ green pepper, cut into thin strips
½ cup grated carrots
½ cup chopped onion
1 (2-ounce) jar chopped pimiento, drained

Combine sauerkraut and sugar, mixing well; let stand 30 minutes. Add remaining ingredients; stir well. Cover and chill at least 12 hours. Yield: 8 servings. *Mrs. T. J. Compton, Austin, Texas.*

Pick Tomatoes While They Are Green

Tomatoes are one of summer's most versatile vegetables. And Southerners know they are as delicious green as when ripened. Here are three good ways to enjoy them, ranging from old-fashioned fried green tomatoes to a relish that preserves the flavor of green tomatoes for year-round enjoyment.

FRIED GREEN TOMATOES

4 medium-size green tomatoes, cut into
  ¼-inch slices
1 teaspoon onion salt
½ teaspoon pepper
¼ cup cornmeal
½ cup bacon drippings

Sprinkle tomatoes with onion salt and pepper; dredge in cornmeal. Fry tomato

slices in hot bacon drippings until browned, turning once. Drain well on paper towels. Serve hot. Yield: 6 to 8 servings.   *Mrs. Robert Collins,*
Fairfax, Missouri.

END-OF-THE-GARDEN RELISH

8 quarts (about ¼ bushel) green tomatoes, thinly sliced
12 medium onions, thinly sliced
1 cup salt
3 quarts cider vinegar
4 (1-pound) packages brown sugar
2 tablespoons dry mustard
2 tablespoons whole cloves
2 (3½-inch) cinnamon sticks
2 tablespoons ground ginger
1 tablespoon celery seeds
4 medium-size green peppers, coarsely chopped
8 medium-size red sweet peppers, coarsely chopped

Sprinkle tomatoes and onion with salt; let stand overnight. Drain well, and rinse with cold water; set aside.

Combine vinegar and sugar in a large, deep kettle, stirring until sugar is dissolved. Tie mustard, cloves, cinnamon, ginger, and celery seeds in a cheesecloth bag; add to vinegar mixture, and bring to a boil. Add tomato-onion mixture and peppers; cook over low heat about 1 hour or until the tomato slices are transparent.

Fill hot sterilized jars, leaving ⅛-inch headspace. Cover with metal lids, and screw metal bands tight; process 10 minutes in boiling-water bath. Yield: about 10 quarts.

HOME-STYLE SANDWICH SPREAD

2 quarts green tomatoes, cored and sliced
1 pint green peppers, seeded and quartered
1 pint red peppers, seeded and quartered
½ cup chopped onion
1½ teaspoons salt
1 cup vinegar
3 cups sugar
1 (16-ounce) jar salad dressing
⅓ cup prepared mustard

Grind tomatoes, peppers, and onion; add salt, and stir well. Place vegetable mixture in a colander; drain overnight at room temperature.

Combine vegetables, vinegar, and sugar in a Dutch oven; bring to a boil,

and boil 20 minutes. Let stand until cold. Add salad dressing and mustard, stirring well. Spoon sandwich spread into sterilized jars, leaving ⅛-inch headspace; cover with metal lids, and screw metal bands tight. Store in refrigerator. Yield: 7½ cups.   *Rosella Michael,*
Bluefield, Virginia.

A Catch Of Fish Favorites

Whether you prefer flounder, haddock, trout, or halibut, there are probably as many fish recipes as there are fish in the sea. And our readers have shared some of their favorites.

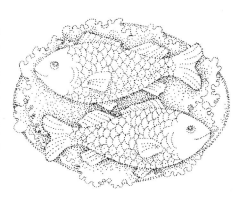

FILLET OF FLOUNDER IN WINE SAUCE

3 tablespoons butter or margarine
3 tablespoons all-purpose flour
1 (10¾-ounce) can cream of mushroom soup, undiluted
¾ cup dry white wine
3 tablespoons grated Parmesan cheese
2 tablespoons chopped fresh parsley
½ teaspoon salt
⅛ teaspoon pepper
1 pound flounder fillets
Grated Parmesan cheese (optional)

Melt butter over low heat; add flour, stirring until smooth. Add soup and wine, stirring constantly until thickened. Stir in cheese, parsley, salt, and pepper.

Arrange fish in a lightly greased 13- x 9- x 2-inch baking dish. Pour sauce over fish. Sprinkle additional Parmesan cheese on top, if desired. Bake, uncovered, at 375° for 30 minutes. Yield: 4 servings.   *Helen Boatman,*
Chapel Hill, North Carolina.

CHINESE-STYLE FRIED HALIBUT

½ cup vinegar
1 cup sugar
1⅓ cups water
3 chicken bouillon cubes
1 large green pepper, cut into strips
1 (15¼-ounce) can pineapple chunks, drained
1½ tablespoons cornstarch
1½ teaspoons soy sauce
1½ teaspoons water
2 pounds halibut steaks or fillets
½ cup all-purpose flour
1 teaspoon salt
Hot vegetable oil

Combine vinegar, sugar, 1⅓ cups water, bouillon cubes, green pepper, and pineapple in a medium saucepan; simmer 10 minutes. Combine cornstarch, soy sauce, and 1½ teaspoons water; stir well. Gradually add cornstarch mixture to pineapple mixture; cook over low heat, stirring constantly, until thickened.

Rinse fish, and pat dry. Combine flour and salt; stir well. Dredge fish in flour mixture; fry in ⅛ inch hot oil (375°) until golden brown. Do not overcook; drain on paper towels. Serve pineapple sauce over fish. Yield: 6 to 8 servings.   *Cynthia Harper,*
Snow Hill, North Carolina.

BAKED HADDOCK

2 pounds fresh or frozen haddock fillets, thawed
1 large tomato, chopped
1 small green pepper, finely chopped
⅓ cup lemon juice
1 tablespoon vegetable oil
2 teaspoons instant minced onion
¾ to 1 teaspoon dried basil leaves
2 teaspoons salt
¼ teaspoon pepper
4 drops hot sauce

Arrange fillets in a single layer in a lightly greased 13- x 9- x 2-inch baking dish. Combine remaining ingredients; mix well, and spoon over fish. Bake 5 to 8 minutes at 500° or until fish flakes easily with a fork. Yield: 6 servings.
Doris Garton,
Shenandoah, Virginia.

Tip: Roll lemons, oranges, and grapefruits on a counter before cutting to soften; you'll get more juice.

TROUT IN WINE SAUCE

½ pound medium shrimp
1½ cups boiling salted water
4 trout fillets (about 1 pound)
1 cup all-purpose flour
½ teaspoon salt
¼ teaspoon pepper
¼ cup butter or margarine, melted
4 green onions, chopped
¼ cup all-purpose flour
1½ cups milk
½ teaspoon salt
Pinch of white pepper
½ cup dry vermouth

Add shrimp to boiling salted water; return to a boil. Lower heat, and simmer 3 to 5 minutes. Drain well; rinse with cold water. Let cool. Peel and devein shrimp, and set aside.

Rinse trout fillets, and pat dry. Combine 1 cup flour, ½ teaspoon salt, and ¼ teaspoon pepper; dredge fish in seasoned flour. Sauté fish in butter in a large skillet until lightly browned, turning once. Remove fish; drain on paper towels, and set aside. Reserve butter in skillet.

Stir onion into butter; coat completely. Add ¼ cup flour and cook 1 minute, stirring constantly. Gradually add milk; cook over medium heat, stirring constantly, until sauce is thickened and bubbly. Remove from heat and set aside.

Add shrimp, ½ teaspoon salt, white pepper, and vermouth to sauce; stir well.

Carefully place trout fillets in wine sauce; simmer until thoroughly heated. Yield: 4 servings. *Mrs. Pierre J. Bouis, Kenner, Louisiana.*

A Special Chocolate Pie

Easier than it looks, this Chocolate-Amaretto Mousse Pie can be made in a matter of minutes. The filling is a creamy blend of whipped topping mix, chocolate pudding, and almond-flavored liqueur.

CHOCOLATE-AMARETTO MOUSSE PIE

2 (1.5-ounce) envelopes whipped topping mix
1½ cups milk
2 (4⅛-ounce) packages chocolate instant pudding and pie filling mix
¼ cup amaretto or other almond-flavored liqueur
1 baked 9-inch pastry shell, cooled
1 (8-ounce) container frozen whipped topping, thawed (optional)
Chocolate shavings (optional)

Prepare topping mix according to package directions. Add milk, pudding mix, and amaretto; beat 2 minutes at high speed of electric mixer. Spoon mixture into pastry shell. Top with whipped topping and chocolate shavings, if desired. Chill at least 4 hours. Yield: one 9-inch pie. *Barbara Bartolomeo, Houston, Texas.*

Blanch Vegetables In The Microwave

Small amounts of vegetables can be blanched in the microwave oven with a minimum of time and effort. This means that the home gardener can pick produce at its peak, even if only a few servings, and quickly prepare it for freezing. An added bonus of microwave blanching is the elimination of pots of boiling water that require constant attention and heat up the kitchen.

The general procedure for microwave blanching follows. Refer to the chart for specific information on each vegetable.

—The key to good results when blanching in the microwave is to work with small amounts of vegetables at a time. The chart gives specific amounts of each vegetable to use. If you have larger quantities, just repeat the blanching process, using only the amount specified each time.

—Prepare the vegetables for blanching according to the method described in the chart; place in a microwave-safe utensil, such as a casserole dish. Add water if specified, but do not add salt. Cover with the lid of the utensil or with heavy-duty plastic wrap.

—Because wattage of microwave ovens varies, the blanching times will vary. We give a time range in the chart to allow for the difference. Stir the vegetable halfway through blanching time,

Vegetables should be stirred halfway through blanching time to ensure uniform heating.

After blanching, immediately plunge vegetables into ice water to stop the cooking process.

and check at the lower end of the range. Blanching is complete when the vegetable is evenly heated and has a uniformly bright color.

—After blanching, immediately plunge the vegetables into ice water to stop the cooking process. When thoroughly cooled, drain well on paper towels; pat with additional paper towels to remove excess moisture.

—Place the vegetables in freezer cartons or freezer bags; seal. Label with contents and date. Freeze immediately at 0° or below. To ensure rapid freezing, spread containers out evenly in freezer.

MICROWAVE BLANCHING CHART

VEGETABLE	AMOUNT	WATER	DISH SIZE	SETTING	MINUTES	METHOD
Beans, green or wax	1 lb. (5 cups)	½ cup	1½ quart	HIGH	4 to 6	Wash beans, and remove ends; cut beans into 1- to 2-inch pieces. Place beans and water in dish. Cover and blanch, stirring once. Plunge beans immediately into ice water. When cool, spread on paper towels; blot with additional towels. Place in freezer containers, and freeze.
Broccoli	1¼ lbs. (1 bunch, 6 cups)	½ cup	2 quart	HIGH	3 to 5	Wash broccoli. Remove and discard outer leaves and tough ends of stalks; cut broccoli into 1-inch pieces. Place broccoli and water in dish. Cover and blanch, stirring once. Plunge broccoli immediately into ice water. When cool, spread on paper towels; blot with additional towels. Place in freezer containers, and freeze.
Carrots	1 lb. (3½ cups sliced)	¼ cup	1½ quart	HIGH	3½ to 5½	Wash and peel carrots; cut into ½-inch-thick slices. Place carrots and water in dish. Cover and blanch, stirring once. Plunge carrots immediately into ice water. When cool, spread on paper towels; blot with additional towels. Place in freezer containers, and freeze.
Cauliflower	1½ lbs. (1 head, 5 cups)	½ cup	2 quart	HIGH	3 to 5	Wash cauliflower. Remove and discard outer leaves; cut cauliflower into flowerets. Place flowerets and water in dish. Cover and blanch, stirring once. Plunge flowerets immediately into ice water. When cool, spread on paper towels; blot with additional towels. Place in freezer containers, and freeze.
Corn	2 lbs. (4 ears, 2½ cups)	¼ cup	1 quart	HIGH	4 to 5	Remove husks, and wash corn; cut kernels from cob. Place corn and water in dish. Cover and blanch, stirring once. Plunge corn immediately into ice water. When cool, spread on paper towels; blot with additional towels. Place in freezer containers, and freeze.
Peas, black-eyed, crowder, or English	2 lbs., unshelled	¼ cup	1 quart	HIGH	3 to 5	Shell and wash peas. Place peas and water in dish. Cover and blanch, stirring once. Plunge peas immediately into ice water. When cool, spread on paper towels; blot with additional towels. Place in freezer containers, and freeze.
Spinach	1 lb.	none	3 quart	HIGH	2½ to 3½	Wash spinach thoroughly; trim leaves. Place spinach in dish. Cover and blanch, stirring once. Plunge spinach immediately into ice water. When cool, spread on paper towels; blot with additional towels. Place in freezer containers, and freeze.
Squash, yellow or zucchini	1 lb. (4 cups sliced)	¼ cup	1½ quart	HIGH	2½ to 4	Wash squash, and cut into ½-inch-thick slices. Place squash and water in dish. Cover and blanch, stirring once. Plunge squash immediately into ice water. When cool, spread on paper towels; blot with additional towels. Place in freezer containers, and freeze.

Melons Offer A Cool Taste Of Summer

When cantaloupe, watermelon, and honeydew are served in chilled salads, a cold soup, or a citrusy julep, you know you're in for something light and refreshing—custom designed for a summer day. Watermelon balls become an elegant first course when served in a compote with creamy Celery-Nut Dressing as a topping. Melon Soup, made with either cantaloupe or honeydew melon, tastes of summer with orange juice and sparkling wine. And Rainbow Melon Julep calls for melon balls chilled in orange juice and lime juice.

To get the best results with these melon pleasers, buy only quality melons. Plugging is the best way to judge the quality of a melon, but skin color is also a good indicator. A ripe cantaloupe will have a gray netting on the rind, with a light green to yellow background. The skin of a honeydew melon should be a creamy color and velvety smooth to the touch. A fresh green or gray color with a white to yellow underside indicates a good choice for watermelon. All melons should have a faint, characteristic aroma.

Watermelon Salad With Celery-Nut Dressing is an elegant way to begin a meal.

WATERMELON SALAD WITH CELERY-NUT DRESSING

½ (8-ounce) package cream cheese, softened
2 tablespoons mayonnaise
⅓ cup whipping cream
1⅓ cups finely diced celery
3 to 4 cups watermelon balls, chilled
Lettuce leaves (optional)
½ cup chopped pecans

Beat cream cheese until light and fluffy. Add mayonnaise; beat until smooth and well blended.

Beat whipping cream until soft peaks form; fold into cream cheese mixture. Fold in celery.

Spoon watermelon balls into sherbet or champagne glasses (or onto lettuce, if desired). Spoon dressing over melon; top with pecans. Yield: 6 servings.

Betty Chason,
Tallahassee, Florida.

Tip: Use the syrup from canned fruits in gelatin salads or desserts. Chances are it won't make the dish too sweet, but the best rule is to taste and judge.

MINTED FRUIT MEDLEY

1 cantaloupe, peeled, seeded, and cut into bite-size pieces
1 (15¼-ounce) can pineapple chunks, drained
10 to 15 maraschino cherries, quartered
2 drops peppermint extract
Fresh mint sprigs

Combine cantaloupe, pineapple, cherries, and peppermint extract; toss lightly. Chill mixture thoroughly. Garnish with mint sprigs before serving. Yield: 4 to 6 servings.

Mrs. Ken Vincent,
Monroe, Louisiana.

MELON SOUP

4 cups finely chopped cantaloupe or honeydew melon, divided
1½ cups orange juice
¼ cup lime juice
1 tablespoon honey or sugar
1½ cups sweet sparkling wine or ginger ale

Combine 2 cups melon, orange juice, lime juice, and honey in container of electric blender; process until smooth. Stir in remaining 2 cups melon and wine; chill thoroughly. Yield: about 4 servings.

Peggy Fowler Revels,
Woodruff, South Carolina.

FRESH FRUIT CUP WITH MINT DRESSING

1 cantaloupe, peeled, seeded, and cut into bite-size pieces
1 cup cubed honeydew melon
1 cup cubed watermelon
1 cup green grapes
1 cup fresh strawberries
1 cup sliced fresh peaches
Mint Dressing

Combine fruit in a large bowl; cover tightly, and chill. Serve with Mint Dressing. Yield: 8 to 10 servings.

Mint Dressing:

1 (8-ounce) carton commercial sour cream
1 to 2 tablespoons chopped fresh mint or mint extract to taste
2 tablespoons powdered sugar
¼ teaspoon ground cardamom
1 drop green food coloring (optional)

Combine all ingredients, mixing well. Cover and chill for at least 30 minutes. Yield: 1 cup.   *Mrs. R. W. Turnbull,*
Atlantic Beach, Florida.

VANILLA FRUIT CUP

½ cup sugar
2 to 4 tablespoons light brown sugar
½ cup water
½ cup orange juice
¼ cup lemon juice
1½ teaspoons vanilla extract
8 cups assorted fresh fruit (melon balls, strawberries, peach slices, green grapes, and banana slices)

Combine first 5 ingredients in a medium saucepan. Bring to a boil; reduce heat, and simmer 5 to 8 minutes. Remove from heat, and stir in vanilla. Arrange fruit in a large bowl; pour syrup over fruit and toss gently. Chill several hours or overnight. Yield: 12 servings.
Mrs. Terry Tolle,
Waynesville, North Carolina.

Tip: Evaporated milk and sweetened condensed milk are two forms in which milk is sold. They are different and cannot be interchanged in a recipe. Using evaporated milk in a recipe calling for sweetened condensed milk will result in disaster. Evaporated milk is unsweetened milk thickened by removing some of its water content. Sweetened condensed milk is sweetened with sugar and thickened by evaporation of some of its water content.

RAINBOW MELON JULEP

8 cups assorted melon balls (watermelon, cantaloupe, honeydew)
½ cup orange juice
½ cup lime juice
1 to 2 tablespoons chopped fresh mint
2 teaspoons grated orange rind
2 teaspoons grated lime rind
2 tablespoons sugar (optional)
1 cup lemon-lime carbonated beverage
Fresh mint sprigs (optional)

Combine first 6 ingredients; add sugar, if desired. Chill at least 2 hours. Just before serving, add carbonated beverage. Garnish with mint sprigs, if desired. Yield: 10 to 12 servings.
Jane White,
Jacksonville, Florida.

Season's Best Squash Offerings

The delicate flavors of yellow squash and zucchini are enhanced with a variety of seasonings and other vegetables in these recipes. For a colorful combination, stir-fry them together in a wok; cook just until tender before adding tomatoes and cheese to create Squash Stir-Fry.

Light, airy, and creamy are all ways to describe Cheesy Squash Bake. It's a combination of stiffly beaten egg whites, sour cream, cheese, bacon, and squash. And Zucchini Mexican Style calls for taco sauce, seasonings, and a medley of garden vegetables.

ZIPPY SQUASH CASSEROLE

5 large yellow squash
2 tablespoons butter or margarine, softened
1 cup (4 ounces) shredded Cheddar cheese
1 medium onion, chopped
½ cup chopped celery
3 slices bacon, cooked, drained, and crumbled
1 (2-ounce) jar diced pimiento
1 tablespoon chopped green chiles
½ teaspoon salt
¼ teaspoon garlic salt
⅛ teaspoon pepper
½ cup soft breadcrumbs
1 tablespoon butter or margarine, melted

Wash squash thoroughly; trim off ends. Place in boiling salted water to

cover. Cook 15 to 20 minutes or until tender; drain and mash.

Combine next 10 ingredients; add squash, stirring well. Spoon squash mixture into a buttered 1½-quart casserole. Combine breadcrumbs and 1 tablespoon melted butter; sprinkle over squash mixture. Bake at 350° for 20 minutes. Yield: 4 to 6 servings.
Paula Patterson,
Houston, Texas.

CHEESY SQUASH BAKE

7 medium-size yellow squash
½ teaspoon salt
2 eggs, separated
1 (8-ounce) carton commercial sour cream
2 tablespoons all-purpose flour
1¾ cups (7 ounces) shredded Cheddar cheese
8 slices bacon, cooked, drained, and crumbled
⅓ cup fine, dry breadcrumbs
1 tablespoon butter or margarine, melted

Wash squash thoroughly; trim off ends. Place in boiling salted water to cover. Cook 15 to 20 minutes or until tender. Drain and cool slightly. Thinly slice squash; sprinkle with salt.

Beat egg yolks until thick and lemon colored; stir in sour cream and flour. Beat egg whites until stiff peaks form; fold into yolk mixture.

Layer half the squash, egg mixture, and cheese in a 12- x 8- x 2-inch baking dish. Sprinkle with all the bacon. Layer remaining squash, egg mixture, and cheese. Combine breadcrumbs and butter, and sprinkle over top. Bake at 350° for 20 to 25 minutes. Yield: 8 to 10 servings.
Donna Callaway,
Tallahassee, Florida.

SQUASH STIR-FRY

2 tablespoons vegetable oil or peanut oil
1 clove garlic, minced
1 large onion, sliced and separated into
    rings
3 medium zucchini, thinly sliced
3 medium-size yellow squash, thinly sliced
3 tomatoes, cut into wedges
¾ teaspoon salt
½ teaspoon pepper
1 cup (4 ounces) shredded process
    American cheese

Pour oil around top of hot wok, coating sides until bottom is covered with oil. Add garlic; stir-fry briefly. Add onion; stir-fry 1 minute. Stir in zucchini and yellow squash; cook 2 to 3 minutes or until crisp-tender. Add tomatoes, salt, and pepper; stir well. Sprinkle cheese over vegetables, stirring just until cheese melts. Yield: about 6 servings.
Shirley Hastings,
Stillwater, Oklahoma.

ZUCCHINI MEXICAN STYLE

4 cups grated zucchini (about 3 to 4
    medium squash)
1 medium onion, thinly sliced and
    separated into rings
¾ cup celery, thinly sliced
1 medium carrot, grated
½ green pepper, cut into strips
¼ cup vegetable oil
⅓ cup commercial taco sauce
2 teaspoons prepared mustard
¼ teaspoon dried basil leaves
¼ teaspoon salt
⅛ teaspoon pepper
3 tomatoes, cut into wedges

Sauté first 5 ingredients in hot oil in a large skillet for 5 minutes, stirring occasionally. Stir in taco sauce, mustard, basil, salt, and pepper. Add tomatoes; cook 5 minutes. Yield: 6 to 8 servings.
Mrs. Ralph Berger,
Cushing, Oklahoma.

Marinades Make Kabobs Even Better

Kabobs are so good when cooked out, and the ones we feature here are even better because of a marinade or a special sauce. Steak-and-Shrimp Kabobs, Marinated Steak Kabobs, and Savory Lamb Kabobs all marinate for hours before they go on the grill. The marinade is brushed on while they cook.

A spicy sauce is brushed on Liver Kabobs, slices of liver and bacon threaded with onion and pepper.

MARINATED STEAK KABOBS

1 cup chopped onion
½ cup vegetable oil
¼ cup lemon juice
¼ cup soy sauce
1 tablespoon Worcestershire sauce
1 teaspoon prepared mustard
1 pound sirloin steak, cut into 2-inch
    cubes
1 large green pepper, cut into 1-inch
    pieces
2 medium onions, quartered
2 medium tomatoes, quartered

Sauté onion in oil; remove from heat. Stir in lemon juice, soy sauce, Worcestershire sauce, and mustard; pour over meat and vegetables. Cover and marinate overnight in refrigerator.

Remove meat and vegetables from marinade, reserving marinade. Alternate meat and vegetables on skewers. Grill 5 minutes on each side over medium coals or until desired degree of doneness, brushing frequently with marinade. Yield: 4 servings.
Louanne Lyles,
Columbia, South Carolina.

STEAK-AND-SHRIMP KABOBS

½ cup soy sauce
½ cup honey
¼ cup cream sherry
1 teaspoon grated orange rind
½ teaspoon garlic powder
2 to 2½ pounds sirloin steak, cut into
    1½-inch cubes
20 large fresh shrimp, peeled and
    deveined (about 1 pound)
1 small fresh pineapple
20 large mushrooms
1 tablespoon cornstarch

Combine first 5 ingredients; stir well. Add steak and shrimp; cover and marinate in the refrigerator for 3 to 4 hours or overnight.

Cut a thick slice from top and bottom of pineapple. Quarter pineapple lengthwise; remove rind and core. Cut into 1½-inch-thick chunks. Set aside.

Remove steak and shrimp from marinade, reserving liquid. Alternate steak, shrimp, pineapple, and mushrooms on skewers for grilling.

Gradually stir cornstarch into reserved marinade in a small saucepan; cook over medium heat, stirring constantly, until thickened and bubbly.

Grill kabobs 3 minutes over medium coals; turn and brush with marinade. Grill 5 minutes or until desired degree of doneness, brushing with marinade as needed. Yield: 6 to 8 servings.
Mrs. James S. Tiffany,
Dallas, Texas.

SHRIMP KABOBS

1 large green pepper, cut into 1-inch
    pieces
1 (8-ounce) can pineapple chunks in
    unsweetened juice
¼ cup prepared mustard
1 tablespoon brown sugar
1 pound fresh medium shrimp, peeled
    and deveined
4 slices bacon, cut into thirds
1 (4-ounce) can button mushrooms,
    drained

Pour boiling water over green pepper pieces; let stand 5 minutes. Drain.

Drain pineapple, reserving juice. Combine pineapple juice, mustard, and sugar in a small bowl; stir until well blended.

Alternate pineapple chunks, shrimp, bacon, mushrooms, and green pepper on skewers. Brush with sauce. Broil 4 inches from heat 5 minutes on each side, brushing often with sauce. Yield: 4 servings.
Norma Patelunas,
St. Petersburg, Florida.

SAVORY LAMB KABOBS

1 (4-pound) leg of lamb
½ cup soy sauce
½ cup wine vinegar
1 cup vegetable oil
6 cloves garlic, minced
1½ tablespoons sugar
¾ teaspoon pepper
2 large green peppers, cut into 1-inch
    pieces
18 to 24 cherry tomatoes
18 to 24 small onions

Remove fell (tissue-like covering) from leg of lamb; cut meat into 1-inch cubes, and set aside.

Combine soy sauce, vinegar, oil, garlic, sugar, and pepper. Add lamb; cover and marinate overnight in refrigerator. Remove meat from marinade, reserving marinade. Alternate meat and vegetables on skewers. Grill 15 to 20 minutes over medium coals or until desired degree of doneness, brushing often with marinade. Yield: 6 servings.
Michelle Dumford,
Atlantic Highlands, New Jersey.

LIVER KABOBS

2 tablespoons Worcestershire sauce
¼ cup vinegar
3 tablespoons prepared mustard
3 tablespoons molasses
½ cup catsup
1 pound beef or calf's liver
6 slices bacon
1 large sweet red pepper, cut into 12 pieces
1 large green pepper, cut into 12 pieces
8 small onions

Combine first 5 ingredients in a small saucepan; simmer over low heat 3 minutes. Set aside.

Cut liver into bacon-size strips. Lay a liver strip on each bacon slice. Alternate vegetables and meat on skewers, lacing meat accordion style. Brush with sauce, and grill 15 to 20 minutes over hot coals or until bacon is crisp and liver is cooked to desired doneness. Yield: 4 servings. *Susan Settlemyre,*
Raleigh, North Carolina.

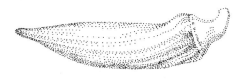

Okra In Your Favorite Ways

From our readers come an assortment of their favorite ways to enjoy fresh okra. For a very traditional dish, serve Old-Time Fried Okra; or for a delicious variation, try Okra With Cheese.

Okra combines well with other vegetables for dishes such as Okra and Tomatoes. And because okra is so popular in Creole cookery, we've included Quick Okra Chowder from Louisiana.

OKRA WITH CHEESE

1 pound okra
All-purpose flour
2 teaspoons paprika
2 eggs, beaten
Vegetable oil
1 cup (4 ounces) shredded Cheddar cheese
Salt and pepper to taste

Wash okra well; drain. Cut off tip and stem ends; cut okra into ½-inch slices. Combine flour and paprika. Dip okra in egg, then in flour mixture. Fry in hot oil until golden brown and crisp; drain okra slightly.

Add cheese, salt, and pepper to okra; stir gently to coat. Serve immediately. Yield: 4 to 5 servings.

OKRA AND TOMATOES

1 pound okra
3 slices bacon, chopped
1 large onion, chopped
1 medium-size green pepper, finely chopped
1 (16-ounce) can tomatoes, chopped
¼ teaspoon salt
¼ teaspoon pepper

Wash okra well; drain. Cut off tip and stem ends; cut okra into ½-inch slices; set aside.

Fry bacon in a Dutch oven until crisp; drain on paper towels, reserving 2 tablespoons drippings.

Cook okra in drippings 5 minutes or until lightly browned. Add onion and green pepper; cook, stirring occasionally, until tender. Stir in tomatoes, salt, and pepper. Cover, and simmer 20 minutes. Stir in bacon, and heat thoroughly. Yield: 6 to 8 servings.
Mrs. Kathleen A. Wilson,
Orange, Texas.

QUICK OKRA CHOWDER

12 slices bacon, chopped
1 medium onion, minced
1 medium-size green pepper, cut into strips
1 quart sliced okra
1 (16-ounce) can whole tomatoes, undrained and cut into eighths
1 cup canned lima beans, undrained
1 cup canned corn, undrained
1 teaspoon salt
¼ teaspoon parsley flakes
2 cups water

Fry bacon in a large Dutch oven until limp; add onion and green pepper; cook, stirring constantly, until tender. Add remaining ingredients; simmer, covered, 30 minutes. Yield: 10 servings.
Suzanne Clark,
Alexandria, Louisiana.

OLD-TIME FRIED OKRA

1 quart okra
½ cup all-purpose flour
½ cup cornmeal
½ teaspoon salt
⅛ teaspoon pepper
1 egg, well beaten
1 cup shortening

Wash okra well; drain. Cut off tip and stem ends; cut okra into ½-inch slices, and set aside.

Combine flour, cornmeal, salt, and pepper, mixing well. Stir egg into okra; dredge in flour mixture.

Heat shortening in a large skillet until hot; add okra, and fry until brown and crisp. Drain well. Yield: 6 servings.
Mrs. William S. Bell,
Chattanooga, Tennessee.

OKRA PILAF

4 slices bacon, chopped
1 medium onion, chopped
½ cup chopped green pepper
2 tomatoes, peeled, seeded, and chopped
1 cup thinly sliced okra
⅛ teaspoon pepper
1 cup hot cooked rice

Fry bacon until crisp; remove from skillet, and set aside. Add onion and green pepper to drippings in skillet; cook over medium heat, stirring constantly, until tender. Add tomatoes and okra; cook, stirring often, until liquid is absorbed. Remove from heat, and stir in pepper and rice.

Spoon mixture into top of double boiler; place over boiling water, and cook 15 minutes. Stir in reserved bacon. Yield: 6 servings. *Ruth E. Cunliffe,*
Lake Placid, Florida.

Tip: To reheat cooked pasta or rice, place it in a strainer over a pan of boiling water. Cover and steam 10 to 15 minutes.

Pamper Yourself With Bread For Breakfast

Waking up to a fresh coffee cake or homemade biscuits can make any breakfast extra special. Bake Banana-Sour Cream Coffee Cake one evening, and it will stay fresh and moist for several days when stored in an airtight container. Hot Cheesy Biscuits can be whipped up in minutes.

HOT CHEESY BISCUITS

2 cups all-purpose flour
2 teaspoons baking powder
½ teaspoon salt
½ to ¾ teaspoon red pepper
¼ cup shortening
1 cup (4 ounces) shredded sharp Cheddar cheese
1 cup buttermilk

Combine flour, baking powder, salt, and red pepper; cut in shortening and cheese until mixture resembles coarse meal. Add buttermilk, stirring until dry ingredients are moistened.

Drop dough by heaping teaspoonfuls about 2 inches apart on lightly greased baking sheets. Bake at 450° for 10 to 12 minutes. Yield: about 3 dozen.
Mrs. John D. Gibson,
Mount Pleasant, Tennessee.

BANANA-SOUR CREAM COFFEE CAKE

½ cup chopped pecans
¼ cup sugar
½ teaspoon ground cinnamon
½ cup shortening
1 cup sugar
2 eggs
1 cup mashed bananas
1 teaspoon vanilla extract
½ cup commercial sour cream
2 cups all-purpose flour
1 teaspoon baking powder
1 teaspoon soda
¼ teaspoon salt

Combine pecans, ¼ cup sugar, and cinnamon; stir well, and set aside.

Combine shortening and 1 cup sugar; cream until light and fluffy. Beat in eggs, bananas, and vanilla; stir in sour cream.

Combine remaining dry ingredients; add to creamed mixture, and stir just enough to blend.

Sprinkle half of reserved cinnamon mixture into bottom of a well-greased 10-inch Bundt pan; spoon half of batter into pan. Sprinkle remaining cinnamon mixture over batter; spoon remaining batter into pan. Bake at 350° for 40 to 45 minutes or until cake tests done.

Cool cake 5 minutes in pan on a wire rack. Loosen edges of cake, if necessary. Invert cake on serving plate; serve warm or cold. Yield: one 10-inch coffee cake.
Mrs. William V. White,
Charlotte, North Carolina.

Blackberries Bring A Cobbler

Served warm or cold, mounded with ice cream, or drenched in milk or cream, fruit cobblers are a favorite summertime dessert, dear to any Southerner's heart. And we think you'll like this deep-dish blackberry cobbler particularly delicious.

DEEP-DISH BLACKBERRY COBBLER

4 cups fresh blackberries or 2 (16-ounce) packages frozen blackberries, thawed
1 cup sugar
2 tablespoons all-purpose flour
2 tablespoons lemon juice
⅛ teaspoon salt
Triple-crust pastry (recipe follows)
1½ tablespoons butter or margarine, divided

Combine berries, sugar, flour, lemon juice, and salt; stir well.

Prepare pastry, and divide dough in half. Roll half of dough to ⅛-inch thickness to fit sides and bottom of a lightly greased 2-quart baking dish. Spoon half of berry mixture into pastry-lined dish; dot with half of butter.

Divide remaining dough in half. Roll one portion of dough into a rectangle; place over berries, making a few slits in pastry. Top with remaining berry mixture, and dot with remaining butter.

Roll out remaining portion of dough to fit top of baking dish. Cover dish, and seal pastry edges. Make slits along the top.

Bake at 450° for 10 minutes; reduce heat to 350°, and bake 45 minutes longer or until bubbly and golden brown. Serve warm. Yield: 6 servings.

Triple-Crust Pastry:

2 cups all-purpose flour
¾ teaspoon salt
⅔ cup shortening
3 tablespoons ice water

Combine flour and salt; cut in shortening until mixture resembles coarse crumbs. Sprinkle water over mixture, and stir with a fork; shape dough into a ball. Yield: crust for 1 cobbler.
Mrs. Ann Upshaw,
Memphis, Tennessee.

Spaghetti In A Squash?

Slice into a spaghetti squash, and it may surprise you. Once this oblong, golden-colored squash is cooked and sliced, the flesh comes out in strands just like spaghetti. This special squash makes a delicious pie; the sweet combination is similar to old-fashioned coconut custard pie.

SPAGHETTI SQUASH PIE

1 medium spaghetti squash
½ cup sugar
½ cup firmly packed brown sugar
2 tablespoons all-purpose flour
1 cup evaporated milk
1 cup water
3 egg yolks, beaten
5 tablespoons butter or margarine, melted
1 teaspoon coconut extract
1 unbaked 10-inch pastry shell

Wash squash; cut in half, and discard seeds. Place squash, cut side down, in a Dutch oven; add 2 inches of water. Bring to a boil and cook, covered, 25 to 30 minutes or until squash is tender. Drain squash; cool.

Using a fork, remove spaghetti-like strands from inside of squash. Measure 1½ cups of squash strands to be used in the pie.

Combine next 8 ingredients, mixing well; stir in reserved squash strands. Pour mixture into pastry shell. Bake at 450° for 5 minutes; reduce oven to 350°, and bake 40 additional minutes or until the pie is set. Serve pie warm or cool. Yield: one 10-inch pie.
Mrs. L. L. Livingston,
Hopewell, Virginia.

September

Afternoon school bells ring in September, sending hungry children home wanting an afterschool snack. You won't be defenseless with our slice-and-bake cookies on hand. Serve them warm from the oven with a tall glass of milk.

Brisk fall evenings call for something special, and our Texas readers came up with just that. We chose from recipes they submitted to create *Mexican Food Fest* and now offer this spectacular feast of flavors to all our readers. From tacos to tamales, we know you will enjoy sampling the rich regional cuisine as much as we did. Only those with true Mexican spirit should try Cheesy Jalapeño Peppers—they're hot!

From mild-mannered cream cheese to the nutty flavor of Gruyère, you'll enjoy the unmistakable flavor cheese gives to many foods in this chapter.

For Starters, Serve Soup

If you have dinner guests ready to sit down for a full-course meal, you'll want to begin by teasing their appetites. An appetizer soup does just that—it can be as suited to a formal table and starched linen napkins as Elegant Crab Soup, or as casual as a crock of French Onion Soup.

The creamy, more filling soups, like Tasty Fish Chowder, should be served in small portions. Lighter soups like Fire Water—not quite the scorcher it sounds since it's served cold—can fill a mug without filling a guest. It's great for sipping leisurely on the deck before being seated at the table.

Remember that the flavor of the soup should always complement the entrée. How about a cup of Cream of Broccoli to lead you to a juicy prime rib?

FIRE WATER

2 teaspoons beef-flavored bouillon granules
1 cup water
3 cups tomato juice
¼ cup plus 1 tablespoon lemon juice
1 medium onion, grated
1 medium cucumber, peeled and grated
1 medium-size green pepper, minced
½ cup chopped celery
1 clove garlic, minced
2 tablespoons chopped parsley

Combine bouillon granules and water; stir to dissolve bouillon. Stir in remaining ingredients. Cover and chill 24 hours. Yield: 5½ cups.

Mrs. Harvey Kidd,
Hernando, Mississippi.

TASTY FISH CHOWDER

2 slices bacon, chopped
1 medium onion, chopped
1 (16-ounce) package frozen haddock fillets, partially thawed
1 cup chopped celery
1 large potato, peeled and diced
2½ cups water
1½ teaspoons salt
¼ teaspoon pepper
3 tablespoons butter or margarine
¼ cup all-purpose flour
2 cups evaporated milk

Cook bacon until limp; add onion, and sauté until bacon is crisp and onion is tender. Cut haddock into bite-size

pieces. Stir haddock, celery, potato, water, salt, and pepper into sautéed mixture. Bring to a boil; reduce heat, and simmer, covered, 15 to 20 minutes or until potatoes are tender.

Melt butter in a heavy saucepan over low heat; add flour, and cook 1 minute, stirring constantly. Gradually stir in milk; cook over medium heat, stirring constantly, until sauce is thickened and bubbly. Gradually stir white sauce into fish mixture; cook over medium heat, stirring constantly, until chowder is thoroughly heated. Yield: about 8 cups chowder.

Mrs. Jack Land,
Live Oak, Florida.

ELEGANT CRAB SOUP

¼ cup finely chopped onion
¼ cup plus 2 tablespoons butter or margarine, melted
2 tablespoons all-purpose flour
2 (12-ounce) packages frozen crabmeat, thawed
1 teaspoon salt
⅛ teaspoon pepper
1 quart plus 2 cups milk
1 cup whipping cream
¼ cup Scotch
Chopped parsley

Sauté onion in butter until tender. Add flour, and cook 1 minute, stirring constantly. Add crabmeat, salt, and pepper; cook over low heat, stirring occasionally, about 10 minutes.

Gradually add milk; cook over low heat 15 minutes. Add cream and Scotch; stir well. Sprinkle with parsley just before serving. Yield: about 8 cups.

Claire A. Bastable,
Chevy Chase, Maryland.

CREAM OF BROCCOLI SOUP

4 cups water
2 cups chopped fresh or frozen broccoli
2 cups chopped ham
1 medium onion, chopped
1 medium potato, chopped
3 tablespoons butter or margarine
1½ teaspoons whole dried basil
1 teaspoon pepper
1 chicken-flavored bouillon cube
½ teaspoon dried thyme leaves
½ teaspoon salt
1 cup milk
Grated Parmesan cheese (optional)

Combine first 11 ingredients in a Dutch oven; bring to a boil. Reduce

heat, and simmer 30 minutes or until broccoli is tender, stirring occasionally.

Spoon a third of broccoli mixture into container of electric blender; blend 20 seconds. Repeat until all ingredients have been blended. Pour mixture back into Dutch oven. Stir in milk, and simmer 20 minutes. Garnish each serving with cheese, if desired. Yield: about 7 cups.

Mrs. John J. O'Neill,
Welaka, Florida.

FRENCH ONION SOUP

2 pounds yellow onions, thinly sliced
1 tablespoon olive oil
3 tablespoons butter or margarine
1 teaspoon brown sugar
2 tablespoons molasses
1 teaspoon salt
1 teaspoon pepper
3 tablespoons all-purpose flour
2 quarts beef broth
¾ cup vermouth
5 (¾-inch-thick) slices French bread, toasted and halved
2 cups (8 ounces) shredded Swiss cheese

Combine onion, oil, and butter in a large saucepan; cook, covered, over medium heat 15 minutes, stirring occasionally. Stir in brown sugar, molasses, salt, and pepper. Simmer, covered, 35 minutes, stirring occasionally. Add flour and cook 1 minute, stirring constantly. Gradually add beef broth and vermouth; cook over medium heat, stirring constantly, until thickened and bubbly. Reduce heat and simmer an additional 20 minutes, stirring occasionally.

Ladle soup into 10 individual baking dishes. Top each with a half slice of bread, and sprinkle with cheese. Place under broiler 2 to 3 minutes or until cheese melts. Yield: 10 cups.

Lynne Weeks,
Midland, Georgia.

Cheese In, Flavor Up

Parmesan cheese keeps its flavor locked in a hard brick until grated. Gruyère looks mild, but adds a robust spark to its companion. Cheddar cheese casts a warm glow over whatever it touches, and timid cream cheese hides behind its smoothness.

Cheese has as many personalities as there are types to enjoy. Flavors range from subtle to sharp, but even the mildest cheese adds an unmistakable punch to the food it accompanies.

Explore the many types of cheese, but approach each with delicacy. If overcooked, cheese turns into a tough, stringy mass. So use low heat when preparing dishes that contain cheese; when it tops a dish, add it the last few minutes of the cooking period.

Soft, unripened cheeses, such as cream cheese and cottage cheese, demand refrigerator storage in airtight containers. Their shelf life is short, usually five to seven days from date of purchase.

Hard, ripened cheeses are much sturdier and can be stored for longer periods. Once cheese is cut, wrap it in plastic wrap or store in a plastic bag in the refrigerator. Don't worry about mold that forms on cured cheese—it's unappetizing rather than harmful and can just be cut away.

SEASHELL-PROVOLONE CASSEROLE

3 medium onions, finely chopped
¼ cup butter or margarine, melted
1½ to 2 pounds ground beef
1 (15½-ounce) jar plain spaghetti sauce
1 (16-ounce) can stewed tomatoes
1 (4-ounce) can mushroom stems and pieces, drained
1 teaspoon garlic salt
1 (8-ounce) package seashell macaroni
1 (8-ounce) package provolone cheese, sliced
3 cups commercial sour cream
1 cup (4 ounces) shredded mozzarella cheese

Sauté onion in butter in a large skillet just until tender. Add ground beef; cook until browned, stirring to crumble meat. Add spaghetti sauce, tomatoes, mushrooms, and garlic salt to meat mixture; stir well, and simmer 20 minutes.

Cook macaroni according to package directions except reduce salt to 1½ teaspoons; drain.

Place half of macaroni in a deep 4-quart greased casserole; layer with half of meat sauce, half of provolone, and half of sour cream. Repeat layers, and top with mozzarella cheese. Cover and bake at 350° for 30 minutes; uncover and bake 15 minutes. Yield: about 12 servings.
Caroline Jackson,
Johnson City, Tennessee.

REUBEN MEAT PIE

1 unbaked 9-inch pastry shell
1 (4-ounce) package plus 1 (2.5-ounce) package sliced corned beef, shredded
1 cup (4 ounces) shredded Swiss cheese
½ cup well-drained chopped sauerkraut
2 tablespoons all-purpose flour
¼ teaspoon salt
Dash of ground nutmeg
2 eggs, beaten
1 cup half-and-half

Prick bottom and sides of pastry shell with a fork. Bake at 425° for 7 minutes.

Sprinkle corned beef in pastry shell; add cheese, and top with sauerkraut.

Combine remaining ingredients, mixing well. Pour over sauerkraut in pastry shell. Bake at 325° for 35 to 40 minutes or until set. Let pie stand 10 minutes before serving. Yield: one 9-inch pie.
Mrs. Steve Garvin,
Wilkesboro, North Carolina.

SWISS SCHNITZEL

6 (¼-inch-thick) veal cutlets
3 eggs
1½ teaspoons salt
¾ teaspoon coarsely ground pepper
¾ cup all-purpose flour
1½ cups soft breadcrumbs
¾ cup butter or margarine
5 ounces Gruyère cheese, thinly sliced
3 tablespoons parsley flakes (optional)
Lemon slices
Fresh parsley sprigs (optional)

Place cutlets on a sheet of waxed paper. Using a meat mallet or rolling pin, flatten to ⅛-inch thickness.

Combine eggs, salt, and pepper; beat well. Dredge cutlets in flour; dip in egg, and coat with breadcrumbs.

Melt butter in a large skillet over medium heat; add cutlets, and sauté 4 to 5 minutes. Turn cutlets, and top with cheese. Cover and cook an additional 3 to 4 minutes. Sprinkle with parsley flakes, if desired. Serve cutlets with lemon slices; garnish with parsley sprigs, if desired. Yield: 6 servings.
Philip R. Rast,
Charlotte, North Carolina.

Tip: Make an effort to thaw foods at least partially before cooking. Don't try to incorporate thawing time into cooking time. This is a sure energy waster.

SWISS OVEN OMELET

6 slices bacon, cut into halves
⅓ cup finely chopped onion
8 eggs
1 cup milk
1 teaspoon salt
¼ teaspoon pepper
1 (8-ounce) package sliced Swiss cheese, cut lengthwise into 1-inch strips

Cook bacon until transparent and partially brown. Remove bacon from skillet, reserving 1 tablespoon drippings in skillet. Drain bacon on paper towels, and set aside. Sauté onion in reserved bacon drippings just until tender.

Combine onion, eggs, milk, salt, and pepper; mix well. Pour egg mixture into a lightly buttered shallow 1½-quart casserole. Top with cheese strips and bacon. Bake at 350° for 40 minutes or until set. Serve immediately. Yield: 6 to 8 servings.
Marie Bloodworth,
Macon, Georgia.

CHICKEN BREASTS GRUYERE

2 whole chicken breasts, split, boned, and skinned
Garlic salt
Pepper
¼ cup plus 2 tablespoons butter or margarine, melted
4 slices Spanish onion, separated into rings
20 large fresh mushrooms, sliced
⅔ cup dry sherry, divided
⅔ cup commercial sour cream
1½ cups (6 ounces) shredded Gruyère cheese
2 tablespoons chopped fresh chives

Sprinkle chicken liberally with garlic salt and pepper. Sauté in butter in a large skillet until lightly golden. Transfer chicken to a broiler-proof serving dish, reserving drippings in skillet.

Sauté onion in drippings until transparent; add mushrooms, and sauté 3 to 5 minutes. Remove skillet from heat.

Add ⅓ cup sherry, sour cream, and cheese to mushroom mixture; stir until cheese melts. Add remaining sherry, mixing well. Spoon sauce over chicken. Broil 3 to 3½ inches from broiler element until sauce just begins to brown. Sprinkle with chopped chives, and serve immediately. Yield: 4 servings.
Robert G. Vance,
Sarasota, Florida.

CHICKEN PARMIGIANA

3 whole chicken breasts, split, boned,
    and skinned
2 eggs, slightly beaten
1 teaspoon salt
⅛ teaspoon pepper
¾ cup fine, dry breadcrumbs
½ cup vegetable oil
1 (15-ounce) can tomato sauce
¼ teaspoon dried whole basil
⅛ teaspoon garlic powder
1 tablespoon butter or margarine
½ cup grated Parmesan cheese
8 ounces mozzarella cheese, thinly sliced
    and cut into triangles

Place each chicken breast on a sheet of waxed paper. Flatten to ¼-inch thickness, using a meat mallet or rolling pin.

Combine eggs, salt, and pepper. Dip chicken breasts into egg mixture, and roll each in breadcrumbs. Brown chicken in hot oil in a large skillet; drain on paper towels. Place chicken in a lightly greased 13- x 9- x 2-inch baking dish.

Drain oil from skillet. Combine tomato sauce, basil, and garlic powder in skillet. Bring to a boil, and simmer 10 minutes or until thickened. Stir in butter. Pour mixture over chicken, and sprinkle with Parmesan cheese.

Cover and bake at 350° for 30 minutes. Uncover and arrange mozzarella cheese slices on top. Bake 10 additional minutes. Yield: 6 servings.

Mrs. W. J. Scherffius,
Mountain Home, Arkansas.

INDIVIDUAL SOUFFLES

¼ cup butter or margarine
¼ cup all-purpose flour
¼ teaspoon salt
Dash of red pepper
1 cup milk
2 cups (8 ounces) shredded Cheddar
    cheese
6 eggs, separated
¼ teaspoon cream of tartar

Melt butter in a heavy saucepan. Blend in flour, salt, and pepper; cook 1 minute, stirring constantly. Gradually stir in milk; cook over medium heat, stirring constantly, until thickened and bubbly. Remove from heat. Add cheese, stirring until melted.

Beat egg yolks until thick and lemon colored. Gradually stir about one-fourth of hot mixture into yolks; add to remaining hot mixture, stirring constantly.

Beat egg whites (at room temperature) until foamy; add cream of tartar. Continue beating until soft peaks form; gently fold into cheese sauce. Spoon mixture into 5 lightly greased 10-ounce soufflé dishes. Bake at 350° for 30 minutes. Serve immediately. Yield: 5 servings.

Marie Lazelle,
Grove, Oklahoma.

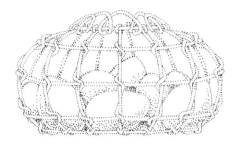

CREPES FLORENTINE

3 eggs
1½ cups milk
1⅓ cups all-purpose flour
½ teaspoon salt
1½ tablespoons vegetable oil
Additional vegetable oil
Spinach filling (recipe follows)
Mushroom filling (recipe follows)
Béchamel sauce (recipe follows)

Combine first 5 ingredients in container of an electric blender; process until smooth. Refrigerate batter 1 hour (this allows flour particles to swell and soften so crepes are light in texture).

Brush the bottom of a 10-inch crêpe pan or nonstick skillet with vegetable oil; place pan over medium heat until oil is just hot, not smoking.

Pour about 2 tablespoons batter into pan; quickly tilt pan in all directions so batter covers pan in a thin film. Cook about 1 minute.

Lift edge of crêpe to test for doneness. Crêpe is ready for flipping when it can be shaken loose from the pan. Flip the crêpe, and cook about 30 seconds on the other side (this side is rarely more than spotty brown).

When the crêpes are done, place on a towel to cool. Stack between layers of waxed paper to prevent sticking.

Place one crêpe in a buttered shallow 2-quart casserole. Spoon about 1 tablespoon spinach filling over crêpe, spreading evenly. Place one crêpe over spinach filling, and spread with about 2 tablespoons mushroom filling. Repeat procedure with remaining crêpes and fillings, ending with a crêpe. Pour béchamel sauce over top.

Bake at 350° for 25 to 30 minutes. To serve, cut stacked crêpes into wedges. Yield: 8 to 10 servings.

Spinach Filling:

1 (10-ounce) package frozen chopped
    spinach
1 tablespoon chopped onion
2 tablespoons butter or margarine, melted
¼ teaspoon salt
⅔ cup béchamel sauce (recipe follows)

Cook spinach according to package directions; drain well. Sauté onion in butter until tender. Combine all ingredients, mixing well. Yield: 1 cup.

Mushroom Filling:

1 tablespoon chopped onion
2 tablespoons butter or margarine, melted
1 egg, beaten
1 cup small-curd cottage cheese
1 (4-ounce) can plus 1 (2-ounce) can
    sliced mushrooms, drained
¼ teaspoon salt
⅛ teaspoon pepper

Sauté onion in butter until tender. Combine remaining ingredients, mixing well; stir in onion mixture. Yield: 2 cups.

Béchamel Sauce:

¼ cup butter or margarine
¼ cup plus 1 tablespoon all-purpose flour
½ teaspoon salt
⅛ teaspoon pepper
2¼ cups milk
½ cup half-and-half
2 cups (8 ounces) shredded Swiss cheese

Melt butter in a heavy saucepan over low heat; blend in flour, salt, and pepper. Cook 1 minute. Gradually add milk and half-and-half; cook over medium heat, stirring constantly, until thickened and bubbly. Add cheese, stirring until melted. Yield: 3⅔ cups.

Mrs. Marshall Marvelli,
Winston-Salem, North Carolina.

Tip: To combine egg yolks with a hot mixture and have a smooth product, follow this procedure: beat the egg yolks; then add a small amount of the hot liquid to the yolks, beating briskly. When enough of the hot liquid has been added to raise the temperature of the yolks, add to the hot mixture and continue stirring and cooking until mixture is of consistency desired. The mixture will curdle if beaten yolks are added directly to the hot mixture.

BAVARIAN CHEESE PUFFS

1 cup milk
¼ cup butter or margarine
½ teaspoon salt
1 cup all-purpose flour
4 eggs
1 cup (4 ounces) shredded Muenster
  cheese

Combine milk, butter, and salt in a medium saucepan; bring to a boil. Add flour all at once, stirring vigorously over medium heat until mixture leaves sides of pan and forms a ball. Remove from heat, and allow to cool slightly.

Add eggs, one at a time, beating with a wooden spoon after each addition. (After the second egg, the mixture will appear to be separating into lumps. Continue beating until mixture is smooth and glossy.) Beat in cheese.

Drop heaping tablespoonfuls of batter 2 to 3 inches apart onto a greased baking sheet. Bake at 375° for 30 to 35 minutes or until golden brown and puffed. Yield: 10 to 12 servings.

Marshall Carter,
Arlington, Virginia.

GRASSHOPPER CHEESECAKE

1½ cups chocolate wafer crumbs (about
  26 chocolate wafers)
¼ cup butter or margarine, melted
3 (8-ounce) packages cream cheese,
  softened
1½ cups sugar
4 eggs
1 egg yolk
¼ cup plus 2 tablespoons white or green
  crème de menthe
3 tablespoons white crème de cacao
4 (1-ounce) squares semisweet chocolate
½ cup commercial sour cream

Combine chocolate wafer crumbs and butter, stirring well. Press onto bottom of a 9-inch springform pan; set aside.

Beat cream cheese at medium speed of electric mixer until light and fluffy. Gradually add sugar, beating well. Add eggs, one at a time, beating well after each addition. Add egg yolk, and beat well.

Stir crème de menthe and crème de cacao into cream cheese mixture; spoon into crust. Bake at 350° for 55 to 60 minutes or until set. Cool thoroughly.

Melt chocolate in top of a double boiler, and allow to cool; stir in sour cream. Spread chocolate mixture over top of cheesecake; chill well before serving. Yield: one 9-inch cheesecake.

Mrs. J. Russell Buchanan,
Prospect, Kentucky.

Limas, Sauced And Spicy

Lima beans go from spicy to mild and cheesy with these three recipes. Rancho Lima Beans combines limas and ground beef with garlic, red pepper, and chili powder—hearty enough for a main dish. Lima Beans Creole simmers limas with onion, green pepper, bacon, and tomatoes. On the milder side, there's Swiss Lima Bean Casserole, topped with a creamy Swiss cheese sauce and sliced toasted almonds.

For maximum plumpness and flavor, shell limas just before cooking them. Remember, 1 pound of unshelled limas yields 2 cups of shelled beans.

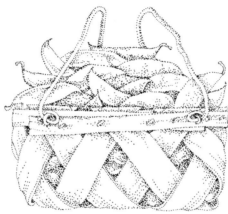

SWISS LIMA BEAN CASSEROLE

4 cups fresh lima beans
¼ cup butter or margarine
3 tablespoons all-purpose flour
2½ cups milk
2 cups (8 ounces) shredded Swiss cheese
1 (4-ounce) can sliced mushrooms,
  drained
3 tablespoons grated onion
½ cup sliced almonds, lightly toasted

Cook beans in boiling salted water until tender (20 to 30 minutes); drain.

Melt butter in a heavy saucepan over low heat; add flour and cook 1 minute, stirring constantly. Gradually add milk. Cook over medium heat, stirring constantly, until thickened and bubbly. Add cheese; stir until cheese melts.

Combine beans, mushrooms, and onion in a deep 2-quart casserole; stir gently. Pour cheese sauce over bean mixture, and sprinkle with almonds. Bake at 350° for 20 to 30 minutes or until bubbly. Yield: 8 servings.

Mrs. William F. Britt,
Bowling Green, Kentucky.

LIMA BEANS CREOLE

3½ cups fresh lima beans
6 slices bacon
¼ cup finely chopped onion
2 tablespoons chopped green pepper
1 (16-ounce) can whole tomatoes,
  undrained
½ teaspoon salt
⅛ teaspoon pepper

Cook beans in boiling salted water in a Dutch oven until tender (20 to 30 minutes); drain. Return beans to Dutch oven, and set aside.

Cook bacon until crisp. Remove from skillet, reserving 2 tablespoons drippings; crumble bacon, and set aside. Sauté onion and green pepper in reserved drippings until tender.

Stir onion mixture, bacon, and remaining ingredients into beans; cover and simmer 15 minutes. Yield: 6 servings.

Margaret L. Hunter,
Princeton, Kentucky.

RANCHO LIMA BEANS

2 cups fresh lima beans
½ pound ground beef
2 medium onions, sliced
1 clove garlic, pressed
1 (28-ounce) can whole tomatoes, drained
1 teaspoon crushed red pepper
1 teaspoon salt
1 teaspoon chili powder
½ cup (2 ounces) shredded Cheddar
  cheese

Cook beans in boiling water until tender (20 to 30 minutes); drain, reserving 1 cup liquid.

Cook ground beef, onion, and garlic in a small Dutch oven until meat is browned. Add lima beans, reserved liquid, tomatoes, red pepper, salt, and chili powder. Cover and simmer 50 minutes; stir cheese into bean mixture. Cover and cook an additional 10 minutes. Yield: about 6 servings.

Margaret Ryalls,
Troy, Virginia.

Tip: Grills or pans with a non-stick finish may become scratched or lose their finish with use. Spray the damaged surface with a non-stick vegetable spray to prevent food from sticking.

Kick Off With These Appetizers

Now that it's football season, you'll want to kick off your before-the-game (or after) gatherings with a winning assortment of appetizers.

Cheese-Garlic Dip—good with chips, assorted crackers, or crisp raw vegetables—can be prepared in minutes with a food processor or blender. Fresh broccoli marinated in a tangy garlic mixture is made the day before to allow the flavors to blend.

For a hearty appetizer, you'll find Party Pizzettes deliciously satisfying. Refrigerated biscuits are rolled out for the crust, then layered with a spicy deviled ham and tomato sauce mixture, sliced mushrooms, and shredded mozzarella cheese.

Treat your football guests to Party Pizzettes, Cheese-Garlic Dip, and Cocktail Broccoli.

COCKTAIL BROCCOLI

1½ pounds fresh broccoli
1½ cups olive oil
¼ cup white wine vinegar
2 teaspoons monosodium glutamate
   (optional)
¼ to ½ teaspoon garlic powder
Pepper to taste

Wash broccoli, and cut off flowerets; reserve stems for use in another recipe. Combine remaining ingredients, and pour over flowerets. Marinate 24 hours before serving. Yield: 8 to 10 servings.

Mrs. Robert Harrell, Jr.,
Ellenwood, Georgia.

CHEESE-GARLIC DIP

1 (8-ounce) package cream cheese,
   softened
1 (5.33-ounce) can evaporated milk
1 (8-ounce) container sharp Cheddar cold
   pack cheese food
¼ teaspoon garlic powder
Dash of garlic salt
Dash of Worcestershire sauce

Combine all ingredients in container of electric blender or processor; blend until smooth. Serve with crackers, chips, or raw vegetables. Yield: about 2 cups.

Betty Ann Lichner,
Savannah, Georgia.

TINY CHEESE BISCUITS

1½ cups all-purpose flour
1 cup (4 ounces) shredded sharp Cheddar
   cheese
½ teaspoon ground red pepper
3 tablespoons sesame seeds
½ cup butter or margarine, softened
1 egg, beaten
¼ teaspoon water

Combine first 4 ingredients, mixing well; cut in butter until mixture resembles coarse crumbs. Add egg and water; mix well with hands, and shape into 1-inch balls. Place on greased baking sheet; bake at 400° for 15 minutes. Yield: about 2½ dozen.

Gloria Duncan,
Jackson, Tennessee.

PARTY PIZZETTES

1 (11-ounce) package refrigerated biscuits
1 (8-ounce) can tomato sauce
1 (4½-ounce) can deviled ham
½ teaspoon whole oregano
10 fresh mushrooms, cleaned and sliced
1½ cups (6 ounces) shredded mozzarella
   cheese

Roll each biscuit into a 4-inch circle; place on baking sheet. Combine next 3 ingredients, stirring well. Spread a small amount on each biscuit; top with mushrooms and cheese. Bake at 450° about 10 minutes or until golden brown. Cool on baking sheet about 5 minutes. Yield: 10 (4-inch) pizzas.

Mrs. Gene Coleman,
Whispering Pines, North Carolina.

MEXICAN FOOD FEST

Taste Mexico Without Leaving Home

Mexico is an ideal place to be hungry. From spicy appetizers to cooling desserts, Mexican cuisine offers a variety of dishes as rich and colorful as the country itself.

Most Southerners think of Mexican food as highly seasoned, filled with cheese, and topped with sour cream. While this Tex-Mex style of cooking is undeniably delicious, it's only a hint of what awaits south of the border.

The diversity of the land of Mexico greatly influences the food from region to region. Veracruz with its abundance of seafood contributes such specialties as Huachinango a la Veracruzana (Veracruz-Style Red Snapper).

Calabaza, a small, sweet pumpkin, is a staple in the cooking of Oaxaca. Here you'll find a traditional recipe combining the pumpkin with pork for Calabaza Guisada Con Puerco. (If calabaza is unavailable, you can substitute zucchini.)

From other regions of Mexico come such specialties as Ceviche, an appetizer of raw fish marinated in lime juice. You'll also find a delicious chicken entrée baked in peanut mole sauce and a spicy beef and raisin combination.

HUACHINANGO A LA VERACRUZANA
(Veracruz-Style Red Snapper)

3 pounds red snapper fillets
Salt and pepper
¼ cup lime juice
Jalapeño Sauce
Limes (cut in tulip shape)
Radish roses
Parsley sprigs
Pimiento-stuffed olives

Place fillets in a lightly oiled 13- x 9- x 2-inch baking dish. Sprinkle with salt and pepper. Pour lime juice over fish; refrigerate, covered, 1 hour. Drain fillets, and pour Jalapeño Sauce over them. Bake, uncovered, at 350° for 30 minutes. Garnish with limes, radish roses, parsley sprigs, and stuffed olives. Yield: 6 to 8 servings.

Jalapeño Sauce:

3 cups tomatoes, peeled and diced
¾ cup chopped onion
2 cloves garlic, minced
2 tablespoons vegetable oil
3 medium-size pickled jalapeño peppers, seeded, rinsed, and chopped
¼ cup pimiento-stuffed olives, sliced
1 teaspoon salt
Pinch of ground cinnamon
Pinch of ground cloves

Puree tomatoes in blender. Sauté onion and garlic in hot oil until tender. Add tomatoes and remaining ingredients; simmer 5 minutes. Yield: 4 cups.
Peggy C. Schoolfield,
Waxahachie, Texas.

PICADILLO
(Spicy Beef Over Rice)

2 pounds ground beef
2 medium onions, chopped
1 clove garlic, minced
2 tablespoons olive oil
2 apples, peeled, cored, and chopped
3 canned jalapeño peppers, seeded and sliced into thin strips
½ cup raisins
¼ cup pimiento-stuffed olives, sliced
⅛ teaspoon ground cinnamon
⅛ teaspoon ground cloves
¼ teaspoon salt
⅛ teaspoon pepper
¼ cup slivered almonds
2 tablespoons olive oil
Hot cooked rice

Brown ground beef, onion, and garlic in 2 tablespoons hot olive oil. Add next 8 ingredients; simmer 20 minutes.

Sauté almonds in 2 tablespoons olive oil until golden brown. Drain almonds, and sprinkle over meat mixture. Serve over hot cooked rice. Yield: 6 servings.

Note: Meat mixture freezes well. To reheat, combine thawed meat mixture and 2 tablespoons water in a medium saucepan. Cook over low heat until thoroughly heated. *Mrs. R. Ledyard,*
Beaumont, Texas.

CALABAZA GUISADA CON PUERCO
(Pumpkin Cooked With Pork)

2 pounds pork chops, boned and cubed
2 tablespoons vegetable oil
2 small calabaza or 2 large zucchini, peeled and diced
¼ teaspoon ground cumin
¼ teaspoon pepper
2 cloves garlic, minced
½ teaspoon salt
1 (14½-ounce) can tomatoes, drained
1 small onion, chopped
Hot cooked rice (optional)

Cook pork in hot oil until browned. Add remaining ingredients except rice. Cover; simmer 30 minutes or until squash is tender. Serve over hot cooked rice, if desired. Yield: 4 servings.
Pat Sanders,
Austin, Texas.

POLLO EN MOLE DE CACAHUATE
(Chicken With Peanut Mole Sauce)

1 (3-pound) broiler-fryer, cut up and skinned
Salt
1 teaspoon paprika
All-purpose flour
1 cup vegetable oil
¼ cup all-purpose flour
3 tablespoons smooth peanut butter
2 cloves garlic, pressed
2 tablespoons chili powder
1 teaspoon ground cumin
2½ cups water
1 teaspoon Worcestershire sauce
¼ teaspoon salt
Parsley sprigs

Rinse chicken, and pat dry. Season with salt and paprika; dredge with flour. Brown chicken in hot oil in a large skillet. Remove chicken from skillet, and drain on paper towels; reserve ⅓ cup of pan drippings. Place chicken in a 13- x 9- x 2- inch baking dish.

Return reserved pan drippings to skillet; stir in ¼ cup flour, and cook 1 minute, stirring constantly. Add peanut butter, garlic, chili powder, and cumin; cook, stirring constantly, until bubbly. Gradually add water; cook over medium heat, stirring until thickened. Stir in Worcestershire sauce and ¼ teaspoon salt.

Pour sauce over chicken; bake, uncovered, at 350° for 30 minutes. Garnish with parsley sprigs. Yield: 4 servings.
Betty J. Moore,
Temple, Texas.

Tip: Use the water-displacement method for measuring shortening if the water that clings to the shortening will not affect the product. Do not use this method for measuring shortening for frying. To measure ¼ cup shortening using this method, put ¾ cup water in a measuring cup; add shortening until the water reaches the 1-cup level. Be sure that the shortening is completely covered with water. Drain off the water before using shortening.

CEVICHE
(Marinated Raw Fish)

1 pound trout, mackerel, or pompano fillets
¾ cup lime juice or lemon juice
1 large onion, finely chopped
2 tomatoes, peeled, seeded, and chopped
½ large green pepper, diced
2 tablespoons plus 2 teaspoons dried cilantro or ½ cup fresh coriander leaves, minced
2 large cloves garlic, pressed
1 teaspoon salt
½ teaspoon pepper
¼ cup pimiento-stuffed olives, sliced
¼ cup olive oil
2 tablespoons fresh lime juice or vinegar
1 small avocado, peeled, seeded, and diced
Tortilla chips (optional)

Cut fish into 1- x ¼-inch strips, and place in a glass or earthenware bowl (do not use metal); cover fish with ¾ cup lime juice. Refrigerate, covered, 2 to 4 hours. Drain fish; press out excess juice, and place fish in bowl.

Combine next 10 ingredients; stir into fish. Refrigerate until ready to serve. Top fish with avocado just before serving. Serve with tortilla chips, if desired. Yield: 6 servings.
Note: Fresh parsley may be substituted for cilantro. *Bertha Y. Ivaldi,*
Brownsville, Texas.

Appetizers Mean A Spicy Start

A tray of these south-of-the-border appetizers will transform your party into a real fiesta.

For Jalapeño Cheese Squares, chopped jalapeño peppers are baked in a simple cheese and egg mixture—the result is moderately hot. Those with true Mexican spirit should try Cheesy Jalapeño Peppers.

Chile con Queso and Prairie Fire Bean Dip introduce green chiles and chili powder in some thick and creamy dips.

TAMALE MEATBALLS

1½ pounds ground beef
2 cups crumbled cornbread
1 (10-ounce) can mild enchilada sauce
½ teaspoon salt
1 (8-ounce) can tomato sauce
½ cup (2 ounces) shredded Monterey Jack cheese

Combine ground beef, cornbread, ½ cup enchilada sauce, and salt; mix well. Shape meat mixture into 1-inch meatballs. Place meatballs in a 15- x 10- x 1-inch jellyroll pan; bake at 350° for 18 to 20 minutes or to desired doneness. Drain meatballs on paper towels, and place in a chafing dish.

Combine remaining enchilada sauce and tomato sauce in a small saucepan; cook over low heat until thoroughly heated. Pour sauce over meatballs; sprinkle with cheese. Serve meatballs with toothpicks. Yield: about 7 dozen.
Mrs. J. H. Jackson,
Cleveland, Texas.

CHILE CON QUESO

1 large onion, chopped
1 clove garlic, minced
1 tablespoon vegetable oil
1 tablespoon all-purpose flour
1 tablespoon chili powder
1 (10-ounce) can tomatoes and green chiles
1 pound process cheese spread, cut into ½-inch cubes
1 canned jalapeño pepper, seeded and chopped (optional)

Sauté onion and garlic in oil in a Dutch oven until tender but not brown. Stir flour and chili powder into onion mixture; cook over low heat 1 minute, stirring constantly. Add tomatoes and green chiles; cook over low heat, stirring constantly, until thickened and bubbly. Add cheese and jalapeño pepper, if desired; cook over low heat, stirring frequently, until cheese is melted. Serve warm with taco or tortilla chips. Yield: about 3½ cups.
Mrs. Don H. Eldridge,
Houston, Texas.

PRAIRIE FIRE BEAN DIP

1 (16-ounce) can refried beans
1 cup (4 ounces) shredded provolone
    cheese
⅔ cup water or beer
¼ cup butter or margarine
2 tablespoons minced onion
2 cloves garlic, minced
1 tablespoon plus 1 teaspoon chili powder
Dash of hot sauce

Combine all ingredients in a large saucepan. Cook over low heat, stirring constantly, until cheese melts and mixture is thoroughly heated. Transfer mixture to a chafing dish; serve with taco chips. Yield: 2 cups.   *Linda Allie, Smithfield, Texas.*

CHEESY JALAPENO PEPPERS

1 (11-ounce) jar pickled jalapeño peppers,
    drained
1 (8-ounce) package cream cheese,
    softened
½ small onion, grated
4 slices bacon, cooked, drained, and
    crumbled
Dash of celery salt
Sliced pitted ripe olives (optional)
Sliced pimiento-stuffed olives (optional)
Pimiento strips (optional)
Cooked crumbled bacon (optional)

Rinse peppers; remove stem end. Cut peppers in half lengthwise; remove seeds. (Wear rubber gloves when working with peppers.)

Beat cream cheese until fluffy; stir in onion, 4 slices crumbled bacon, and celery salt. Spread each jalapeño pepper half with cream cheese mixture; garnish with olives, pimiento, or additional crumbled bacon, if desired. Yield: about 2½ dozen.   *Margot Foster, Hubbard, Texas.*

JALAPENO CHEESE SQUARES

4 cups (16 ounces) shredded Cheddar
    cheese
4 eggs, beaten
1 teaspoon minced onion
4 canned jalapeño peppers, seeded and
    chopped

Combine all ingredients, stirring well. Spread cheese mixture into an ungreased 8-inch square pan. Bake at 350° for 30 minutes; cut into 1-inch squares. Yield: 64 squares.   *Annette Crane, Dallas, Texas.*

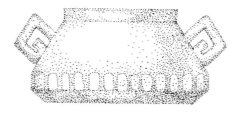

Tex-Mex, A Fiesta Of Tacos And Tamales

From tacos and tamales to burritos and chalupas, Tex-Mex foods offer a fiesta of tastes and colors. A different style from authentic Mexican cooking, Tex-Mex calls for lots of cheese, chiles, tomatoes, onions, and sour cream. Most Tex-Mex favorites are made with corn or flour tortillas, and many are topped with taco sauce or picante sauce.

TAMALES

1½ pounds boneless chuck roast
½ pound boneless lean pork
1 tablespoon vinegar
1 teaspoon salt
½ teaspoon pepper
4 cups water
2 to 3 dozen corn husks
2 cloves garlic, crushed
1 tablespoon cumin seeds
3 tablespoons shortening, melted
1 tablespoon chili powder
1½ teaspoons salt
½ teaspoon pepper
2 cups plus 2 tablespoons instant corn
    masa
1½ teaspoons chili powder
¾ teaspoon salt
1½ tablespoons shortening, melted

Combine beef, pork, vinegar, 1 teaspoon salt, ½ teaspoon pepper, and 4 cups water in a Dutch oven; cook over low heat about 2½ hours or until meat is tender. Drain, reserving liquid. Shred meat with a fork.

Cover dried corn husks with hot water; let stand 1 to 2 hours or until softened. Drain well, and pat with paper towels to remove excess water. (If husks are too narrow, overlap 2 husks to make a wide one. If husks are too wide, tear off one side.) Use an 8- x 8-inch aluminum foil square for each tamale if the dried corn husks are not available.

Sauté garlic and cumin seeds in 3 tablespoons shortening for 5 minutes. Add shredded meat, 1 cup reserved meat broth, 1 tablespoon chili powder, 1½ teaspoons salt, and ½ teaspoon pepper. Cook, uncovered, over low heat 30 minutes, stirring occasionally.

Combine corn masa, 1½ teaspoons chili powder, and ¾ teaspoon salt in a large mixing bowl; stir well. Add 1¼ cups reserved meat broth and 1½ tablespoons shortening; mix dough well.

Place 1 tablespoon of dough in the center of each husk, spreading to within ½ inch of edge. Place 1 tablespoon meat mixture on dough, spreading evenly. Fold sides of husk to center, enclosing the filling completely. Fold pointed end under; tie with string or narrow strips of softened corn husk.

Place a coffee cup in the center of a rack in a large pot. Add just enough water to fill pot below rack level in order to keep tamales above water.

Stand tamales on folded ends around the cup. Bring water to a boil. Cover, and steam 1½ hours or until tamale dough pulls away from husk, adding more water as needed. Yield: 1½ dozen.   *Mrs. L. L. Gray, Fort Worth, Texas.*

Tip: Look for meat cuts that are the most lean for the money. Buy less expensive cuts of meat, but make sure you're not paying for large amounts of gristle, fat, and bone.

MEXICAN FOOD FEST

TACOS

1 (16-ounce) can whole tomatoes
1 tablespoon hot sauce
½ teaspoon dried whole oregano
Salt
Pepper
1 pound ground beef
12 taco shells
1 bunch green onions, chopped
1 small head iceberg lettuce, shredded
2 cups (8 ounces) shredded American
  cheese

Drain tomatoes, reserving liquid; finely chop tomatoes. Combine tomatoes, reserved liquid, hot sauce, oregano, ½ teaspoon salt, and ¼ teaspoon pepper in a medium saucepan. Cook over low heat 10 to 15 minutes or until thickened.

Combine ground beef, 1 teaspoon salt, and ¼ teaspoon pepper in a skillet; cook until browned, stirring to crumble. Drain ground beef well.

Place a heaping tablespoon of meat in a taco shell. Top meat with green onion, tomato sauce, lettuce, and cheese. Repeat procedure with remaining ingredients. Yield: 6 servings.

Bobbye Crane,
Dallas, Texas.

BURRITOS

1½ pounds boneless pork roast
1 cup finely chopped onion
2 tablespoons vegetable oil
1 clove garlic, crushed
1 teaspoon salt
1½ cups water
4 canned jalapeño peppers, seeded and
  chopped
1 (16-ounce) can refried beans
1 tablespoon vegetable oil
1 cup (4 ounces) shredded Cheddar cheese
12 flour tortillas
Commercial taco sauce

Remove fat from pork, and cut pork into ½-inch cubes. Cook pork and onion in 2 tablespoons vegetable oil until meat is no longer pink. Add garlic, salt, and water; bring to a boil over medium heat. Reduce heat to low;

cover and simmer about 1½ to 2 hours or until the meat is tender.

Shred meat with a fork. Add peppers; cook, uncovered, about 30 minutes or until liquid evaporates.

Heat refried beans in 1 tablespoon oil in a medium skillet. Add cheese to beans, and stir mixture until cheese melts.

Wrap tortillas tightly in foil; bake at 350° for 15 minutes. Spread 2 tablespoons bean mixture on each tortilla. Spoon 2 heaping tablespoons of meat mixture off center of tortilla. Fold the edge nearest meat filling up and over filling just until mixture is covered. Fold in sides of tortilla to center; roll up. Repeat with remaining ingredients.

Place burritos on a baking sheet; cover with aluminum foil. Bake at 325° for 15 minutes. Serve immediately with taco sauce. Yield: 6 servings.

Elizabeth J. Hill,
Port Arthur, Texas.

EGGS SONORA

6 flour tortillas
8 eggs, scrambled
3 cups (12 ounces) shredded Cheddar
  cheese
1 pound bacon, cooked, drained, and
  crumbled
1 medium onion, finely chopped
1 cup guacamole
¼ cup sliced ripe olives
Commercial sour cream
Salsa (recipe follows)

Wrap tortillas tightly in foil; bake at 350° for 15 minutes.

Layer eggs, cheese, bacon, onion, guacamole, and olives evenly on each warm tortilla. Top with sour cream and salsa. Yield: 6 servings.

Salsa:

1 (28-ounce) can whole tomatoes
1 (4-ounce) can green chiles, drained and
  chopped
1 large onion, finely chopped
2 tablespoons vegetable oil
1 teaspoon salt
¼ teaspoon dried whole oregano (optional)
1 clove garlic, minced
¼ teaspoon sugar

Drain tomatoes, reserving liquid; finely chop tomatoes. Combine tomatoes, reserved liquid, and remaining ingredients; mix well. Cover salsa and place in refrigerator to chill for at least 2 hours. Yield: about 5 cups.

Mrs. C. E. Owens,
Houston, Texas.

TEXAS TURKEY CHALUPAS

3 cups diced, cooked turkey
1 small onion, minced
½ teaspoon salt
¼ teaspoon pepper
¼ teaspoon dried whole oregano
Dash of garlic salt
½ medium head lettuce, shredded
1 medium tomato, diced
2 tablespoons taco sauce
½ teaspoon lemon juice
1 (8-ounce) package corn tortillas
Vegetable oil
1 (16-ounce) carton commercial sour
  cream
1 cup guacamole
2 cups (8 ounces) shredded Cheddar
  cheese
Commercial taco sauce

Combine turkey, onion, salt, pepper, oregano, and garlic salt; stir well.

Combine shredded lettuce, tomato, 2 tablespoons taco sauce, and lemon juice; stir well.

Fry tortillas, one at a time, in ¼ inch of hot oil about 5 seconds on each side or just until softened. Drain tortillas well on paper towels.

Spoon an equal amount of turkey mixture on each tortilla. Carefully spread about 2½ tablespoons sour cream over turkey mixture; spoon guacamole over sour cream, spreading evenly. Top with lettuce mixture and cheese. Serve with additional taco sauce. Yield: 6 servings.

Geneva Emswiler,
Porter, Texas.

VEGETABLE BURRITOS

12 flour tortillas
1 large onion, thinly sliced
2 cloves garlic, crushed
2 tablespoons vegetable oil
½ pound mushrooms, sliced
1 large green pepper, cut into thin strips
2 medium carrots, thinly sliced
4 medium zucchini, cut into ½-inch slices
2 large tomatoes, peeled and cut into ½-inch wedges
2 (4-ounce) cans diced green chiles, drained
¼ cup sliced ripe olives
1 teaspoon chili powder
1 teaspoon salt
½ teaspoon ground cumin
½ teaspoon dried whole oregano
1½ cups (6 ounces) shredded Cheddar cheese
1½ cups (6 ounces) shredded Monterey Jack cheese or Monterey Jack cheese with jalapeño peppers
1 cup guacamole
1 (8-ounce) carton commercial sour cream
Chopped green onion (optional)
Commercial taco sauce (optional)

Wrap tortillas tightly in foil; bake at 350° for 15 minutes.

Sauté onion and garlic in hot oil in a large skillet until onion is limp. Reduce heat to medium, and stir in next 11 ingredients. Cook, uncovered, 10 minutes or until vegetables are crisp-tender, stirring occasionally. Remove to a lightly greased shallow 2-quart casserole, using a slotted spoon. Stir in half the cheese; sprinkle with remaining cheese. Broil 6 inches from heat until cheese melts.

Spoon a small amount of vegetable mixture off center of each tortilla. Spread with a small amount of guacamole and sour cream. Top with green onion and taco sauce, if desired. Fold edge nearest filling up and over filling just until mixture is covered. Fold in sides of tortilla to center; roll up. Repeat with remaining ingredients. Serve immediately. Yield: 12 vegetable burritos.

Phoebe Auld,
Port Neches, Texas.

The Best Of The Breads From Mexico

In Texas or south of the border, bread is as basic to the meal as *salsa* and chiles. The flour tortilla is the best known bread because it can be used in the creation of many dishes besides being eaten alone spread with butter. But sopaipillas, cornbread, and flatbread are as much a part of traditional Mexican breads as tortillas.

SOPAIPILLAS

1 package dry yeast
¼ cup warm water (105° to 115°)
4 cups all-purpose flour
1½ teaspoons salt
1 teaspoon baking powder
2 tablespoons sugar
1 tablespoon shortening
1½ cups milk, scalded
Vegetable oil
Honey or powdered sugar (optional)

Dissolve yeast in warm water; let stand 5 minutes.

Combine flour, salt, baking powder, and sugar; cut in shortening. Make a well in center of mixture. Add yeast mixture and milk, mixing well. (The dough will be sticky.)

Turn dough out on a lightly floured surface, and knead 15 to 20 times. Roll dough to ¼-inch thickness; cut into 3-inch squares.

Heat ½ inch of oil in a large skillet to about 370°. Gently place dough squares in oil, a few at a time, lightly pressing down with the back of a fork until dough starts to bubble and puffs up; turn and cook on other side until barely golden in color. Drain on absorbent towels. Serve with honey or sprinkle with powdered sugar, if desired. Yield: about 3 dozen.

Note: When frying sopaipillas, rather than removing all from oil at one time, leave a few in skillet while adding additional sopaipillas; the ones left in the skillet will absorb the heat of the oil and keep it from overheating.

Sylbia Ransberger,
Coleman, Texas.

MEXICAN FLATBREAD

2 cups all-purpose flour
½ cup yellow cornmeal
½ teaspoon salt
¼ cup butter or margarine
⅔ cup warm water

Combine flour, cornmeal, and salt; stir well. Cut in butter with pastry blender until mixture resembles coarse meal. Sprinkle water evenly over surface; stir with a fork until ingredients are moistened. Shape dough into a ball; chill.

Shape dough into 1-inch balls; roll each ball out into circles about 4 inches in diameter. Place circles on ungreased cookie sheets. Bake at 375° for 9 minutes or until lightly browned. Cool flatbread on racks. Yield: about 3 dozen.

LaVonda Calaway,
Pampa, Texas.

Tip: With an electric blender it's easy to make breadcrumbs from dry bread slices and leftover hamburger and hot-dog buns. Break up bread and buns, and blend at medium speed for a few seconds. Store crumbs in an airtight container and freeze.

MEXICAN CORNBREAD

1 cup self-rising cornmeal
½ teaspoon soda
½ teaspoon salt
½ teaspoon sugar
3 eggs, beaten
1 cup milk
3 jalapeño peppers, seeded and chopped
½ cup chopped onion
1½ cups (6 ounces) shredded Cheddar
  cheese
1 teaspoon garlic powder
1 (7-ounce) can whole kernel corn,
  drained
1 (2-ounce) jar chopped pimiento, drained
⅓ cup bacon drippings

Combine cornmeal, soda, salt, and sugar; stir in remaining ingredients. Spoon into a greased 10-inch iron skillet. Bake at 350° for 45 minutes or until golden brown. Yield: 12 to 15 servings.
Mary Ann Curry,
Tyler, Texas.

NEVER-FAIL FLOUR TORTILLAS

3½ cups all-purpose flour
1¼ teaspoons salt
¾ teaspoon baking powder
⅓ cup shortening
1 cup warm milk (105° to 115°)

Combine flour, salt, and baking powder; stir well. Cut in shortening with pastry blender until mixture resembles coarse meal. Stir in milk, and mix well. Turn dough out on a smooth surface, and knead about 3 minutes.

Divide dough into 10 equal portions. Roll out each portion with a rolling pin into a very thin circle, about 8 inches in diameter, turning dough and rolling on both sides.

Heat an ungreased skillet over medium heat; cook tortillas about 2 minutes on each side or until lightly browned, being careful not to let tortillas wrinkle. Pat tortillas lightly with spatula while browning the second side. Serve hot. Yield: 10 tortillas.
Norma Fair,
Portland, Texas.

Mexican-Style Sauces

Salsas, or sauces, are the bases for many Mexican dishes, whether they bind the dish together or give extra flavor as a topping. They are also good as a dip for corn chips.

Sauces are generally referred to as red or green, depending on either a tomato or avocado base. To vary the degree of hotness, the use of chiles and amount of spices may be altered.

AVOCADO SAUCE

1 avocado, peeled and sliced
¼ cup commercial sour cream
¼ cup milk
1 teaspoon instant minced onion
1 clove garlic, pressed
1 teaspoon salt
1 teaspoon dried cilantro leaves or 1
  tablespoon fresh cilantro
½ teaspoon hot sauce
2 to 3 tablespoons lemon juice

Combine all ingredients in container of electric blender. Blend until smooth; chill well. Yield: about 1¼ cups.
Note: Place avocado seed in the sauce to prevent mixture from darkening.
Barbara Bartolomeo,
Houston, Texas.

MEXICAN SAUCE

2 medium onions, chopped
1 medium-size green pepper, chopped
5 stalks celery, chopped
2 tablespoons vegetable oil
1 (28-ounce) can tomatoes
2 (4-ounce) cans green chiles, chopped
2 teaspoons chili powder
Pinch of sugar
Dash of ground cumin
Dash of garlic powder
Dash of salt
Dash of pepper

Sauté onion, green pepper, and celery in hot oil in a large skillet. Drain tomatoes, reserving liquid. Chop tomatoes; add tomatoes, reserved liquid, and chiles to skillet. Stir in remaining ingredients. Simmer, covered, 1 hour, stirring occasionally. Yield: 4 cups.
Mary Anderson,
Odessa, Texas.

Desserts Are Light And Cool

End a spicy meal with one of these authentic Mexican desserts. Light and cool, they range from simple buñuelos to elegant flan.

Nothing could be easier than buñuelos. Simply cut tortillas in strips, fry them until crisp, and toss them in a cinnamon and sugar mixture. Try them once, and you may find them habit-forming.

Then for an elegant end to your meal, try baking Flan Almendra, a luscious caramel-coated custard. Ground almonds are blended with the custard mixture but settle to the bottom during baking to leave a crunchy almond crust beneath a creamy-smooth custard.

CREAMY PRALINES

2½ cups sugar
¾ cup evaporated milk
2 tablespoons butter
2 tablespoons light corn syrup
2 cups pecan halves

Combine sugar, milk, butter, and corn syrup in a heavy Dutch oven, mixing well; bring to a boil. Stir in pecans; cook, stirring occasionally, until mixture reaches soft-ball stage (234°).

Remove from heat; beat 2 to 3 minutes or until mixture is creamy and begins to thicken. Working rapidly, drop mixture by rounded tablespoonfuls onto lightly buttered waxed paper; let cool. Yield: about 1½ dozen.
Sylvia Pettit,
Austin, Texas.

BUNUELOS

1 cup sugar
1 teaspoon ground cinnamon
¼ teaspoon ground nutmeg
12 (8-inch) flour tortillas
Hot vegetable oil

Combine first 3 ingredients in a large plastic bag, mixing well; set aside.

Cut tortillas into 3- x 2-inch strips; fry a few at a time in 1 inch hot oil (375°) until crisp and golden brown, turning once. Drain on paper towels. While still warm, place a few at a time in sugar mixture in bag; shake gently to coat. Store in airtight container. Yield: about 5 dozen.
Billie Duncan,
Quanah, Texas.

FLAN ALMENDRA

½ cup sugar
1⅔ cups sweetened condensed milk
1 cup milk
3 eggs
3 egg yolks
1 teaspoon vanilla extract
1 cup slivered almonds, coarsely ground

Sprinkle sugar evenly in a 9-inch cakepan; place over medium heat. Using oven mitts, caramelize sugar by shaking pan occasionally until sugar is melted and a light golden brown; cool. (Mixture may crack slightly as it cools.)

Combine remaining ingredients in container of electric blender; blend at high speed 15 seconds. Pour over caramelized sugar; cover pan with aluminum foil, and place in a larger shallow pan. Pour about 1 inch of hot water in larger pan. Bake at 350° for 55 minutes or until a knife inserted near center comes out clean.

Remove pan from water and uncover; let cool on wire rack at least 30 minutes. Loosen edges with a spatula. Place serving plate upside down on top of cakepan; quickly invert flan onto serving plate. Yield: 6 to 8 servings.

Note: A little stirring may be necessary when caramelizing the sugar if a gas burner is used.
Ana Rosa Albelais Foster,
Austin, Texas.

Glossary Of Mexican Cookery

Eager to try your hand at preparing a Mexican or Tex-Mex recipe? Then keep this glossary of basic Mexican cookery terms handy.

Aguacate: avocado
Almendra: almond
Arroz: rice
Buñuelos: fritters; dessert pastries sprinkled with cinnamon and sugar
Burritos: flour tortillas filled with a vegetable or meat mixture, folded up, and often topped with a sauce
Calabaza: Mexican pumpkin or squash (may substitute zucchini)
Cerveza: beer
Ceviche: cold, raw, marinated seafood
Chalupa: tostadas spread with an assortment of toppings
Chayote: delicate-flavored, pear-shaped, light-green squash (pattypan squash may be substituted)
Chilaquiles: any dish that calls for fried stale tortillas
Chile con queso: chiles with cheese, served with beans or used as a dip
Chiles rellenos: green chiles stuffed with cheese, vegetables, or meat
Chorizo: spicy Spanish sausage
Cilantro: coriander (use fresh parsley as a substitute for fresh cilantro)
Empanada: turnover filled with meat, vegetable, or sweet filling
Enchiladas: tortillas filled with any combination of fillings and rolled, stacked, or folded before being topped with a sauce and baked
Flan: caramel custard dessert topped with caramelized sugar
Frijoles: beans
Frijol negro: black bean
Frito: fried
Garbanzos: chick peas
Guacamole: avocados mashed with a variety of seasonings
Helado: ice cream
Huachinango: red snapper
Huevos: eggs
Jalapeños: hot, green peppers often seeded and pickled
Largo: extremely hot green chile
Leche: milk
Maíz: corn
Masa: corn flour used to make tortillas and tamales
Mole: a highly seasoned sauce frequently served with chicken
Nachos: cheese-topped corn chips often served as an appetizer
Picadillo: a spicy beef mixture often served with rice
Plátanos: plantains (may substitute bananas for plantains)
Pollo: chicken
Quesadillas: tortillas filled with cheese and then fried
Queso: cheese
Refritos: cooked, mashed, fried beans
Sal: salt
Salsa: red or green chile sauce
Serrano: a hot green chile
Sopaipillas: puffy, deep-fried bread traditionally served with honey
Tacos: tortillas that are folded and filled with meat, refried beans, or vegetables before being topped with a sauce
Tamales: cornmeal or masa dough filled with meat and wrapped in cornhusks and steamed; dessert tamales may be filled with fresh or dried fruit
Tomatillo: small, firm green tomato-like fruit covered with a papery husk; tastes similar to a slightly green plum
Tortilla: thin, flat pancake made of flour or corn
Tostada: fried tortilla
Verde: green; usually indicates a dish prepared with green chiles

Versatile, Affordable Chicken Livers

One of the best ways to relieve your food budget is by serving chicken livers as an entrée. Distinctive in flavor, they combine well with ingredients like bacon, mushrooms, and onions.

Try Chicken Livers With Rice for a quick and easy family dish, or Sautéed Chicken Livers—an entrée special enough for any occasion. You can also enjoy livers in appetizer servings. For Chicken Liver and Bacon Roll-Ups the livers are dipped in Dijon mustard and then baked until crisp in a coating of cracker crumbs.

SAUTEED CHICKEN LIVERS

1 pound chicken livers, cut into bite-size pieces
3 tablespoons butter or margarine, melted
½ pound fresh mushrooms, sliced
½ cup sliced onion
1 teaspoon all-purpose flour
½ teaspoon salt
1 (14½-ounce) can tomatoes, undrained
½ cup dry white wine
2 teaspoons chopped fresh parsley
½ teaspoon Worcestershire sauce
Hot cooked rice or toast points

Sauté chicken livers in butter 5 minutes or until brown. Remove livers, and drain on paper towels, reserving drippings in skillet. Sauté mushrooms and onion in drippings until onion is golden. Stir in flour and salt. Add tomatoes, wine, parsley, and Worcestershire sauce; bring to a boil. Reduce heat and cook 5 minutes, stirring often. Add chicken livers; simmer 5 additional minutes. Serve over rice or toast points. Yield: 4 servings. *Sarah J. Phelps, Baltimore, Maryland.*

CHICKEN LIVERS STROGANOFF

¾ pound chicken livers
1 (4-ounce) can sliced mushrooms, drained
1 medium onion, chopped
¾ cup vermouth
½ teaspoon dried rosemary, crushed
¼ teaspoon dried whole thyme
1 teaspoon salt
¾ cup commercial sour cream
Hot cooked noodles

Combine first 7 ingredients in a medium saucepan; bring to a boil. Reduce heat and simmer, covered, 20 minutes. Stir in sour cream; cook over medium heat, stirring constantly, until thoroughly heated. Serve over hot cooked noodles. Yield: 4 servings.
Sam Jones, Tallahassee, Florida.

CHICKEN LIVER AND BACON ROLL-UPS

1 pound chicken livers
3 tablespoons Dijon mustard
10 to 12 slices bacon, cut in half
½ cup cracker crumbs

Dip chicken livers lightly in mustard. Wrap a half slice of bacon around each, and secure with a toothpick; coat livers with crumbs. Place in an 8-inch square baking dish; bake at 425° for 25 minutes. Yield: 6 to 8 appetizer servings.
Mrs. H. J. Sherrer, Bay City, Texas.

CHICKEN LIVERS WITH RICE

1 (4-ounce) can sliced mushrooms
1 pound chicken livers
¼ cup chopped green pepper
1½ tablespoons butter or margarine, melted
2 tablespoons catsup
Hot cooked rice

Drain mushrooms, reserving liquid. Add enough water to liquid to make ¾ cup; set aside.
Sauté chicken livers and green pepper in butter until livers are browned. Stir in mushrooms, reserved liquid, and catsup; bring to a boil. Reduce heat. Cover and simmer 10 minutes, stirring occasionally. Serve over rice. Yield: 4 servings.
Esther Hench, Fort Lauderdale, Florida.

Tip: Bent or dented measuring utensils give inaccurate measures. Use only standard measuring cups and spoons that are in good condition.

Microwave Sandwiches With Ease

Hot sandwiches in mere minutes. That's what your microwave oven has to offer, not to mention ease of preparation and a quick cleanup.

As for flavor, these recipes offer choices ranging from Pizza Burgers and grilled Reubens to Hot Brown Sandwiches—all developed by the *Southern Living* test kitchens to acquaint you with the ease of microwaving sandwiches. Because wattage of microwave ovens varies, the cooking times will vary. Each recipe gives a time range to allow for the difference. To prevent overcooking, always check for doneness at the lower end of the range. Here are some other pointers.

Using a browning container: A browning container gives a grilled flavor to microwaved sandwiches. The container should be preheated according to manufacturer's directions, usually about 4 minutes for a browning dish and 7 minutes for a browning grill. To save time, preheat the container.

Should you have to microwave the sandwiches in several batches, the container will need to be preheated between each batch; however, this preheating usually takes about half as long as the first. Be sure to read the manufacturer's directions carefully for complete instructions.

Warming sliced meat: Spread slices of meat on a microwave-safe platter, and cover with heavy-duty plastic wrap. A half-pound of most meats will microwave in 1 to 1½ minutes. For larger amounts, allow slightly more time. If microwaving more than 2 pounds of meat, rearrange slices once during the cooking period.

To save time on cleanup, you can microwave up to 1 pound of sliced meat without a dish. Simply divide the slices into two or three stacks, and wrap all with one sheet of heavy-duty plastic wrap. If heating more than 1 pound, repeat process with remaining meat.

Heating bread: Bread becomes tough or soggy unless microwaved properly. Be sure to toast bread slices before using them for sandwiches that will be heated in the microwave; otherwise, they will become soggy. Untoasted bread will toughen if microwaved too long; microwave only until it is slightly warm. Heat from the sandwich filling will complete the warming process.

Grilled Reubens, Pizza Burgers, and Hot Brown Sandwiches are three delicious reasons for microwaving sandwiches.

Before microwaving, wrap bread in a paper towel to absorb moisture. A single hamburger bun or hot dog bun will heat in 10 to 15 seconds at HIGH. If the bun is frozen, microwave at HIGH for 25 to 30 seconds.

REUBEN SANDWICHES

2 tablespoons butter or margarine, softened
8 slices rye or pumpernickel bread
⅓ cup commercial Thousand Island dressing
1 (3-ounce) package thinly sliced corned beef
4 slices Swiss cheese
1¼ cups sauerkraut, well drained

Spread butter on one side of each slice of bread; spread other side with Thousand Island dressing. On 4 slices, arrange corned beef, cheese, and sauerkraut evenly over Thousand Island dressing. Top with remaining bread, placing buttered side out.

Preheat browning dish at HIGH for 4 minutes or according to manufacturer's directions. Add sandwiches; microwave at HIGH for 1 minute. Turn sandwiches, and microwave at HIGH for 1 minute or until browned and cheese begins to melt. Yield: 4 servings.

Note: If your browning dish will only hold 2 sandwiches, preheat browning dish 2 minutes or according to manufacturer's directions before you microwave the remaining sandwiches.

PIZZA BURGERS

¾ pound bulk pork sausage
¾ pound ground beef
¼ cup finely chopped green onion
¼ cup finely chopped green pepper
1 (8-ounce) can pizza sauce
¼ teaspoon garlic salt
8 small hamburger buns
1 cup (4 ounces) shredded mozzarella cheese

Crumble sausage and beef in a 2-quart casserole; stir in onion and green pepper. Microwave at HIGH for 6 to 7 minutes or until meat is brown, stirring every 2 minutes. Drain well. Add pizza sauce and garlic salt, mixing well. Microwave at HIGH for 2 to 3 minutes or until hot, stirring once.

Spoon meat mixture on bottom of hamburger buns; sprinkle with cheese. Microwave at HIGH for 1 minute 15 seconds to 1 minute 45 seconds or until cheese begins to melt. Cover with bun tops; microwave at HIGH for 30 to 45 seconds or until tops are warm. Serve immediately. Yield: 8 servings.

Tip: Packaged meat should always be rewrapped before it's put in the freezer. Remove the plastic wrap and plastic or cardboard tray from meat; rewrap with heavy-duty aluminum foil or freezer wrapping paper, or put in a heavy plastic bag. Seal the package securely; label and freeze at once.

HOT BROWN SANDWICHES

6 slices bacon
2 tablespoons butter or margarine
3 tablespoons all-purpose flour
⅛ teaspoon salt
⅛ teaspoon pepper
½ cup turkey or chicken broth
½ cup milk
⅓ cup grated Parmesan cheese
About ½ pound sliced turkey or chicken
6 slices bread, toasted
6 slices tomato
Salt and pepper
Paprika
Fresh parsley sprigs (optional)

Cut bacon slices in half crosswise; place on a microwave roasting rack set in a 12- x 8- x 2-inch baking dish. Cover with paper towel, and microwave at HIGH for 5 to 7 minutes or until done. Drain and set aside.

Place butter in a 4-cup glass measure. Microwave at HIGH for 30 to 45 seconds or until butter is melted. Blend in flour, salt, and pepper. Gradually stir in chicken broth and milk. Microwave at HIGH for 3 to 4½ minutes, stirring at 1-minute intervals, until thickened and bubbly. Stir in cheese; microwave at HIGH for 1 to 2 minutes or until smooth. Stir well. Cover by pressing a piece of heavy-duty plastic wrap directly on top of sauce. Set aside.

Wrap turkey slices in heavy-duty plastic wrap. Microwave at HIGH for 1 to 1½ minutes or until thoroughly heated.

Arrange turkey slices evenly on toast slices. Cover with cheese sauce. Top each with 1 slice tomato, and sprinkle with salt and pepper; place 2 pieces bacon on each tomato slice. Sprinkle lightly with paprika; garnish with parsley, if desired. Yield: 6 servings.

Super Is The Word For These Eggplant Dishes

If you're looking for ways to dress up eggplant, you'll probably be tempted to prepare all of these recipes because they offer such a variety of flavors.

If you are a cookout enthusiast, try cooking sliced eggplant on the grill. While the eggplant cooks, soaking up a charcoal flavor, an Italian-seasoned butter is brushed on.

In a casserole, eggplant combines with sausage for a quick standby dish. And be sure to try the casserole in which the eggplant is layered with sliced tomatoes, Cheddar cheese, and a ground beef-vegetable mixture. Our foods staff thinks it's best described by its title: super.

EASY EGGPLANT CASSEROLE

1 small eggplant
½ pound bulk sausage
1 small onion, chopped
1 egg, well beaten
½ cup dry breadcrumbs
1 tablespoon butter or margarine, melted
¼ cup cracker crumbs

Peel eggplant, and cut into 1-inch cubes; cook in a small amount of boiling water 10 minutes or until tender. Drain. Let cool slightly.

Cook sausage and onion until onion is tender and sausage is brown. Combine eggplant, sausage mixture, egg, and breadcrumbs. Mix well, and spoon into a greased 1-quart casserole. Combine butter and cracker crumbs; sprinkle over casserole. Bake at 350° for 25 minutes. Yield: 4 servings.

Louise Spraggins,
Birmingham, Alabama.

GRILLED EGGPLANT

1 large eggplant
⅓ cup butter or margarine, melted
½ teaspoon garlic salt
½ teaspoon Italian seasoning
¼ teaspoon salt
⅛ teaspoon pepper

Peel the eggplant, and then cut into ¾-inch slices.

Combine butter, garlic salt, and Italian seasoning; stir well. Brush eggplant slices with butter mixture, and sprinkle with salt and pepper.

Place eggplant about 3 to 4 inches from coals. Grill over medium coals 10 minutes or until tender, turning and basting occasionally. Yield: 6 to 8 servings.

Cathy Darling,
Maidsville, West Virginia.

Tip: Reheat single servings in a microwave or toaster oven; these use less energy than a standard range.

SUPER EGGPLANT CASSEROLE

1 large eggplant
½ cup salt
3 quarts water
2 eggs, well beaten
2 tablespoons milk
1½ cups bacon-flavored cracker crumbs
½ cup margarine, melted
1 pound ground chuck
1 large onion, chopped
1 large green pepper, chopped
1 teaspoon seasoned salt
½ teaspoon pepper
1 teaspoon dried whole oregano
1 bay leaf, crumbled
2 medium tomatoes, cut into ½-inch slices
1 cup (4 ounces) shredded extra sharp Cheddar cheese, divided
½ cup grated Parmesan cheese
2 eggs, well beaten
½ cup milk

Peel eggplant, and cut into ½-inch slices. Dissolve ½ cup salt in water; add eggplant, and soak for 30 minutes. Drain well, and pat dry.

Combine 2 eggs and 2 tablespoons milk, mixing well. Dip eggplant in mixture, and coat with cracker crumbs. Fry a few at a time in ½ cup margarine, just until browned, turning once. Repeat until all are browned; drain on paper towels.

Sauté ground chuck with chopped onion and green pepper until beef is lightly browned. Stir in seasoned salt, pepper, oregano, and bay leaf.

Layer one-third of eggplant, half each of beef mixture, tomato slices, and Cheddar cheese in a greased 13- x 9- x 2-inch baking dish. Repeat layers. Place remaining eggplant on top, and sprinkle with Parmesan cheese.

Combine 2 eggs and ½ cup milk, mixing well; pour over casserole. Bake at 375° for 35 minutes. Yield: about 8 servings.

Mrs. Victor J. Seine,
Austin, Texas.

Right: Try these special breads of Mexico to liven up any meal. Clockwise: Sopaipillas (page 197), Never-Fail Flour Tortillas (page 198), and Mexican Cornbread (page 198).

Page 206: Bring the taste and color of fall to your table with Glazed Acorn Rings (page 214) and Sausage-Stuffed Turban Squash (page 214).

Above: *In Swiss Schnitzel (page 189), the veal cutlets are smothered in a melting layer of Gruyère.*

Right: *These appetizers will get your taste buds tingling: Cheesy Jalapeño Peppers (page 195), Jalapeño Cheese Squares (page 195), and Chile con Queso (page 194).*

Far Right: *Spinach Soufflé Roll (page 215) is a delicate soufflé baked in a jellyroll pan, then rolled around a well-seasoned filling of spinach, cheese, and mushrooms.*

Chocolate Cups Waiting To Be Filled

Chocolate lovers will delight over these tempting homemade dessert cups. Chocolate morsels, coconut, and chopped nuts are combined and shaped in muffin tins to form the petite treats.

Use your imagination to create the finishing touch with a special filling. We suggest adding a scoop of ice cream and garnishing with a cherry—and maybe adding your favorite topping for a spectacular sundae. Or, for a less filling dessert, fill the cups with your favorite fruit.

CHOCOLATE CUPS

⅔ cup semisweet chocolate morsels
2 cups flaked coconut
½ cup chopped nuts
Ice cream or fruit

Melt chocolate morsels over low heat, stirring constantly; remove from heat. Stir in coconut and nuts, mixing well.

Line a muffin tin with 8 paper baking cups. Spoon chocolate mixture evenly into paper cups; press mixture firmly on bottom and sides of cups, forming a shell. Let stand at room temperature for 2 hours or until hardened.

To serve, gently peel paper cups from chocolate shells. Fill with ice cream or fruit or as desired. Yield: 8 servings.
Mrs. Harvey Kidd,
Hernando, Mississippi.

The Sauce Is The Secret

Have you ever wondered what Worcestershire or teriyaki sauce adds to a recipe? The secret lies in the flavor-enhancing abilities of these sauces.

Soy sauce, with its distinctive salty taste, is perfect with meat and chicken. Worcestershire sauce has a sweeter flavor, ideal in a zesty barbecue sauce. If grilled meats are your specialty, give them an extra-special touch by marinating and basting with teriyaki sauce.

POLYNESIAN MEATBALLS

1 pound ground round steak
½ cup milk
¼ cup cornmeal
1 egg, beaten
2 tablespoons chopped onion
2 tablespoons chopped green pepper
1¼ teaspoons dry mustard
1 teaspoon salt
1 teaspoon chili powder
¼ teaspoon pepper
2 tablespoons vegetable oil
1 (10½-ounce) can beef broth
1 (15¼-ounce) can pineapple chunks, drained
½ cup chopped green pepper
¼ cup sugar
¼ cup red wine vinegar
2 tablespoons soy sauce
½ teaspoon salt
½ cup water
3 tablespoons cornstarch

Combine first 10 ingredients, stirring well; shape into 1-inch meatballs. Cook in oil over medium heat for 15 to 20 minutes.

Combine next 7 ingredients in a medium saucepan; simmer 15 minutes, stirring frequently. Slowly add water to cornstarch, stirring until smooth. Stir cornstarch mixture into broth mixture; cook until thickened and bubbly.

Combine meatballs and sauce; stir to coat meatballs. Serve in a chafing dish. Yield: about 6 dozen.
Mrs. Hugh F. Mosher,
Huntsville, Alabama.

SAUCY OVEN SPARERIBS

4 pounds spareribs
1 tablespoon vegetable oil
1½ teaspoons salt
¼ teaspoon pepper
1 cup catsup
1 cup water
¼ cup vinegar
¼ cup Worcestershire sauce
3 tablespoons brown sugar
1 teaspoon salt
1 teaspoon celery seeds
1 teaspoon chili powder
¼ teaspoon pepper
Dash of hot sauce
Parsley (optional)

Cut ribs into serving-size pieces (3 to 4 ribs per person). Cook ribs in oil until browned on both sides; sprinkle with 1½ teaspoons salt and ¼ teaspoon pepper. Place spareribs in a 13- x 9- x 2-inch baking pan.

Combine remaining ingredients, except parsley, in a small saucepan; stir well. Bring sauce to a boil; reduce heat, and simmer 10 minutes. Pour the sauce over ribs.

Cover and bake at 325° for 2 hours or until well done. Uncover and bake at 350° for 15 minutes. Garnish with parsley, if desired. Yield: 4 to 6 servings.
Mrs. Parke LaGourgue Cory,
Neosho, Missouri.

TERIYAKI BEEF KABOBS

2½ pounds boneless sirloin steak, cut into 1½-inch cubes
1 cup teriyaki sauce
10 large fresh mushroom caps
1 small fresh pineapple
10 small onions
2 large green peppers, cut into 1-inch pieces
Hot cooked brown and wild rice (optional)

Combine steak and teriyaki sauce; cover and marinate 3 to 3½ hours in refrigerator. Add mushroom caps to marinade for last hour.

Cut a thick slice from top and bottom of pineapple. Remove rind from pineapple; quarter and remove core. Cut into 1½-inch thick chunks. Set aside.

Cook onion and green pepper in boiling water to cover 5 minutes; drain. Remove steak and mushrooms from marinade, reserving sauce. Alternate steak, pineapple, onions, and green pepper on skewers.

Grill kabobs 5 minutes over medium coals; turn and brush with sauce. Grill 5 minutes or until desired degree of doneness, brushing with sauce as needed. Serve on bed of rice, if desired. Yield: 6 to 8 servings.
Craig Weinbrenner,
Dallas, Texas.

Tip: Chocolate must be treated delicately. It should always be stored at a temperature under 75°. If a gray color develops, this is a sign that the cocoa butter has risen to the surface. Flavor and quality will not be lessened, and the gray color will disappear when the chocolate is melted. Temperature, time, and stirring are important when melting chocolate. Chocolate will scorch at too high a temperature; heating too long and stirring too much will cause chocolate to separate into particles that will not melt and blend together.

PORK CHOW MEIN

3 pounds lean pork, cubed
2 cups diced celery
2 cups diced onion
2 tablespoons vegetable oil
1 (16-ounce) can bean sprouts, drained
1 (8-ounce) can bamboo shoots, drained
1 (8-ounce) can sliced water chestnuts, drained
2 cups water
1 cup soy sauce
½ cup water
¼ cup cornstarch
Hot cooked rice
1 (3-ounce) can Chinese noodles

Sauté pork, celery, and onion in oil in a Dutch oven until browned. Cover and simmer 45 to 55 minutes or until pork is tender; drain off drippings.

Stir next 5 ingredients into pork mixture; bring to a boil. Lower heat. Combine ½ cup water and cornstarch; stir until smooth, and add to pork mixture. Cook, stirring constantly, until thickened and bubbly. Serve over rice, and garnish with noodles. Yield: 8 to 10 servings.
Viola Broadaway,
Fort Valley, Georgia.

ORIENTAL CHICKEN

2 cloves garlic, minced
2 tablespoons vegetable oil
1 (2½- to 3-pound) broiler-fryer, cut up and skinned
2 (4-ounce) cans sliced mushrooms, undrained
1 cup beef broth
⅓ cup soy sauce
2 tablespoons instant minced onion
1 teaspoon sugar
⅛ teaspoon curry powder
Pinch of ground ginger
2 stalks celery, cut into ½-inch pieces
1 (8-ounce) can bamboo shoots, drained
1 medium-size green pepper, diced
½ cup fresh bean sprouts
Hot cooked rice

Sauté garlic in oil in a large skillet 1 minute. Add chicken, and cook until browned (about 10 minutes).

Combine next 7 ingredients; pour over chicken. Cover and simmer 35 minutes. Add next 4 ingredients; cook, uncovered, 5 to 7 minutes or until vegetables are crisp-tender. Serve over rice. Yield: 5 to 6 servings.
Gloria Pedersen,
Corinth, Mississippi.

Cookies To Slice And Bake

With these recipes, a full cookie jar is only minutes away. That's because the dough is prepared ahead, shaped into rolls, and chilled. Then when the urge for homemade cookies strikes, it's just a matter of slicing the dough and baking.

Lemon Pecan Dainties, Oatmeal Nut Crispies, and Double Peanut Butter Cookies are among the choices—all too tempting to resist. So tempting, in fact, they won't last long unless you make more than one batch.

CHEWY CHOCOLATE COOKIES

1½ cups butter or margarine, softened
1 cup sugar
1 cup firmly packed brown sugar
3 eggs
2 teaspoons vanilla extract
4½ cups all-purpose flour
2 teaspoons soda
½ teaspoon salt
1 cup chopped pecans
1 (6-ounce) package semisweet chocolate morsels

Cream butter; gradually add sugar, beating until light and fluffy. Add eggs and vanilla, beating well.

Combine flour, soda, and salt; add to creamed mixture, beating just until blended. Stir in chopped pecans and chocolate morsels.

Shape dough into 3 long rolls, 2 inches in diameter. Wrap each in waxed paper, and freeze overnight.

Unwrap rolls, and cut into ¼-inch slices; place on ungreased cookie sheets. Bake at 350° for 12 to 14 minutes or until lightly browned. Yield: about 7 dozen.
Annette Teague,
Memphis, Tennessee.

OATMEAL NUT CRISPIES

1 cup shortening
1 cup sugar
1 cup firmly packed light brown sugar
2 eggs, slightly beaten
1 teaspoon lemon extract
1½ cups all-purpose flour
1 teaspoon soda
½ teaspoon salt
2 teaspoons ground cinnamon
3 cups quick-cooking oats, uncooked
½ cup chopped pecans

Cream shortening; gradually add sugar, beating until light and fluffy. Add eggs, one at a time, beating well after each addition. Add lemon extract, beating well.

Combine flour, soda, salt, and cinnamon; add to creamed mixture, beating well. Stir in oats and pecans.

Shape dough into 2 long rolls, 2 inches in diameter; wrap each in waxed paper, and chill 2 to 3 hours or until firm.

Unwrap rolls, and cut into ¼-inch slices; place 2 to 3 inches apart on lightly greased cookie sheets. Bake at 350° for 10 to 12 minutes. Yield: about 7 dozen.
Mrs. Dene Elmore,
Demopolis, Alabama.

LEMON PECAN DAINTIES

½ cup shortening
1 cup sugar
1 egg, beaten
1 tablespoon lemon juice
1 tablespoon grated lemon rind
2 cups all-purpose flour
1 teaspoon baking powder
Pinch of salt
1 cup chopped pecans

Cream shortening; gradually add sugar, beating until light and fluffy. Add egg, lemon juice, and grated lemon rind; beat well.

Combine flour, baking powder, and salt; add to creamed mixture, beating just until blended. Stir in pecans.

Shape dough into a long roll, 2 inches in diameter; wrap in waxed paper, and chill 2 to 3 hours or until firm.

Unwrap roll, and cut into ¼-inch slices; place on lightly greased cookie sheets. Bake at 350° for 10 to 12 minutes. Yield: about 3 dozen.
Joan B. Piercy,
Memphis, Tennessee.

EASY PECAN COOKIES

1 teaspoon soda
1 tablespoon hot water
1 cup butter or margarine, softened
1 cup sugar
1 cup firmly packed brown sugar
2 eggs
½ teaspoon vanilla extract
3¾ cups all-purpose flour
1 cup chopped pecans

Combine soda and water; mix well, and set aside.

Cream butter; gradually add sugar, beating until light and fluffy. Add eggs, beating well; stir in soda mixture and vanilla. Add flour, beating just until blended. Stir in pecans.

Shape dough into 2 long rolls, 1¼ inches in diameter. Wrap each in waxed paper, and chill 2 to 3 hours or until firm.

Unwrap rolls, and cut into ¼-inch slices; place on ungreased cookie sheets. Bake at 350° for 10 to 12 minutes. Yield: about 6½ dozen.

Alberta Pinkston,
Knoxville, Tennessee.

DOUBLE PEANUT BUTTER COOKIES

1½ cups all-purpose flour
½ cup sugar
½ teaspoon baking soda
¼ teaspoon salt
½ cup shortening
¾ cup creamy peanut butter, divided
¼ cup light corn syrup
1 tablespoon milk

Combine flour, sugar, soda, and salt; cut in shortening and ½ cup peanut butter with pastry blender until mixture resembles coarse meal. Stir in corn syrup and milk.

Shape dough into a long roll, 2 inches in diameter; wrap in waxed paper, and chill 2 to 3 hours or until firm.

Unwrap roll, and cut into ¼-inch slices; place half of slices on ungreased cookie sheets. Spread each with ½ teaspoon peanut butter. Top with remaining cookie slices, and seal edges with fork. Bake at 350° for 10 to 12 minutes. Yield: about 2 dozen.

Mrs. Joe D. Wilson,
Radford, Virginia.

Sausage Links These Great Dishes

For generations, sausage was a standby among German, Polish, and Italian cooks because it didn't need refrigeration. That's no problem today, but Southerners still love to turn plain links or bulk sausage into appetizers, main dishes, and breakfast casseroles.

A mild sausage is used for Swiss Sausage Casserole. In this dish, the sausage and Swiss cheese are baked between bread slices in an egg-rich custard.

In Sausage Jambalaya, Polish sausage is combined with lots of fresh tomatoes, shrimp, and chopped chicken for a potpourri that's flavorful and substantial.

SWISS SAUSAGE CASSEROLE

2 pounds mild bulk pork sausage
1 teaspoon prepared mustard
12 slices thin-sliced sandwich bread, crusts removed
6 sandwich-size slices Swiss cheese
3 eggs
1¼ cups milk
¾ cup half-and-half
¼ teaspoon salt
1 teaspoon Worcestershire sauce
Dash of pepper
Dash of ground nutmeg

Cook sausage until browned, stirring to crumble; drain well. Combine sausage and mustard, stirring until blended. Cut bread slices in half diagonally. Space half of bread evenly in a greased 12- x 8- x 2-inch baking dish. Sprinkle sausage over bread; top with cheese slices. Space remaining bread halves evenly on top of cheese slices.

Combine remaining ingredients; beat until blended. Pour egg mixture over bread in baking dish. Cover and refrigerate overnight.

Bake, uncovered, at 350° for 35 to 40 minutes or until egg mixture is set. Yield: 8 to 10 servings.

Nyla W. Smith,
Jackson, Alabama.

SALAMI-CORN CASSEROLE

2 cups chopped salami
½ cup chopped onion
2 tomatoes, diced
½ cup diced green pepper
12 eggs, slightly beaten
1 teaspoon salt
¼ teaspoon pepper
1 (17-ounce) can whole kernel corn, drained

Combine all ingredients in a large bowl, stirring well. Pour into a greased 13- x 9- x 2-inch baking dish. Bake at 350° for 30 to 40 minutes or until mixture is set. Yield: 10 to 12 servings.

Mrs. R. P. Hotaling,
Martinez, Georgia.

SAUSAGE PINWHEELS

2 cups all-purpose flour
1 tablespoon baking powder
1 teaspoon salt
¼ cup shortening
⅔ cup milk
1 pound hot bulk pork sausage

Combine flour, baking powder, and salt; cut in shortening until mixture resembles coarse meal. Add milk, stirring until well blended. Turn dough out onto a lightly floured surface; knead lightly 3 or 4 times.

Roll dough into an 18- x 12-inch rectangle. Spread sausage (at room temperature) over dough, leaving a ½-inch margin on all sides. Carefully roll dough lengthwise, jellyroll fashion; pinch seam and ends to seal. Cover and refrigerate at least 1 hour.

Slice dough into ¼-inch slices. Arrange 1 inch apart on baking sheets. Bake at 350° for 20 minutes or until browned. Yield: about 3½ dozen pinwheels.

Nancy H. Aden,
Midlothian, Virginia.

SAUSAGE AND OKRA SOUP

1 pound Polish sausage, cut in ¼-inch slices and halved
Vegetable oil
3 tablespoons all-purpose flour
1 medium onion, chopped
1 clove garlic, minced
2 quarts chicken broth
3 tablespoons tomato paste
2 cups sliced okra, fresh or frozen
1 (10-ounce) package frozen whole kernel corn
½ cup minced green or red pepper
¼ cup chopped fresh parsley
Salt and pepper to taste

Brown sausage in oil in a heavy Dutch oven; drain sausage, reserving drippings in pan. Add enough oil to drippings to make 3 tablespoons. Add flour to drippings, stirring until smooth. Cook 1 minute, stirring constantly. Add onion and garlic; cook an additional minute, stirring constantly.

Gradually add about 1 cup chicken broth; cook over medium heat, stirring constantly, until thickened and bubbly. Add tomato paste; stir until blended. Add sausage, remaining chicken broth, and all other ingredients. Bring to a boil; reduce heat and simmer 15 to 20 minutes or until vegetables are tender, stirring occasionally. Yield: 8 to 10 servings.

Ella Stivers,
Abilene, Texas.

SAUSAGE JAMBALAYA

½ cup chopped onion
½ cup coarsely chopped green pepper
1 clove garlic, minced
2 tablespoons butter or margarine, melted
2 tablespoons all-purpose flour
2½ cups water
½ cup dry white wine
2 tablespoons chopped fresh parsley
1 bay leaf, crushed
½ teaspoon dried whole thyme
½ teaspoon red pepper
1¼ teaspoons salt
Pepper to taste
5 cups peeled, diced tomatoes
2 cups uncooked regular rice
1 pound Polish sausage, cut into ¼-inch
    slices
4 whole chicken breasts, boned, skinned,
    and cut into bite-size pieces
½ pound fresh shrimp, peeled and
    deveined

Sauté onion, green pepper, and garlic in butter in a large Dutch oven until tender. Add flour, stirring until smooth. Gradually add water and wine, stirring until blended.

Add remaining ingredients except shrimp. Bring to a boil, stirring occasionally. Cover and simmer 25 minutes, stirring occasionally. Add shrimp, and simmer 5 minutes or until shrimp are pink. Yield: 12 to 14 servings.

Chuck Morgan, Jr.,
Winston-Salem, North Carolina.

Smoked German sausage makes a surprising stuffing to liven up chicken in Chicken Rolls Elégante.

CHICKEN ROLLS ELEGANTE

½ pound Mettwurst or other smoked
    German sausage
1 small onion, minced
⅓ cup minced celery
¼ teaspoon dried whole thyme
6 whole chicken breasts, split, boned,
    and skinned
1 egg, beaten
½ cup soft breadcrumbs
2 tablespoons shredded Swiss cheese
12 strips pimiento
2 eggs
2 tablespoons lemon juice
2 cups cracker crumbs
½ teaspoon lemon-pepper seasoning
1 teaspoon salt
1 teaspoon paprika
Vegetable oil
3 tablespoons butter or margarine
1½ tablespoons all-purpose flour
1 cup milk
¼ teaspoon salt
¼ teaspoon season-all

Remove casings and dice sausage. Cook sausage, onion, celery, and thyme in a large skillet over medium heat until meat is browned. Set aside to cool.

Place each chicken breast on a sheet of waxed paper. Flatten to ¼-inch thickness, using a meat mallet or rolling pin. Combine 1 egg and breadcrumbs; add reserved sausage mixture; mix well. Spoon 1 tablespoon sausage mixture on top of each chicken breast; top with ½ teaspoon of cheese and a pimiento strip. Fold sides of chicken breast over stuffing, and secure with a toothpick.

Combine remaining 2 eggs and lemon juice; beat until blended. Combine cracker crumbs, lemon-pepper seasoning, 1 teaspoon salt, and paprika; blend well. Dip stuffed chicken breasts in egg mixture; coat with cracker mixture. Brown chicken on all sides in hot oil; drain chicken, reserving 2 tablespoons plus 1 teaspoon pan drippings.

Melt butter in a 13- x 9- x 2-inch baking dish. Add chicken breasts in a single layer; baste with melted butter from the dish. Bake at 350° for 30 minutes or until chicken is done.

Heat reserved pan drippings in a heavy saucepan over low heat; add flour, stirring until smooth. Cook 1 minute, stirring constantly. Gradually add milk; cook over medium heat, stirring constantly, until thickened and bubbly. Stir in ¼ teaspoon salt and season-all. Serve gravy with chicken. Yield: 12 servings.

Lee Ann Ray,
Pilot Point, Texas.

Tip: Always try to match pan size with the burner. A pan that is smaller in diameter than its accompanying burner will allow heat to escape.

SAUSAGE-EGGPLANT MAIN DISH

1 pound mild bulk pork sausage
1 medium onion, sliced
2 small green peppers, chopped
1 large eggplant, peeled and cubed
1 (28-ounce) can tomatoes, undrained and
    chopped
⅓ cup tomato paste
Salt and pepper to taste
½ cup (2 ounces) grated Romano cheese

Cook sausage, onion, and green pepper in a large skillet until sausage is browned; drain on paper towels, and return to skillet. Add remaining ingredients, except cheese. Simmer about 20 minutes or until eggplant is tender. Sprinkle cheese on top. Yield: 6 servings.   *Mrs. J. L. Springfield,
            Cottageville, South Carolina.*

His Specialty Is Homemade Pasta

All it takes is spending one afternoon in George Gambrill's sunny Birmingham kitchen, watching him crank out row upon row of homemade noodles, to realize that there's more to good Italian pasta than emptying a box of noodles into boiling water.

After spending over a year in Italy researching local food customs, George returned to Birmingham intrigued with noodlemaking. "It's not unusual to walk into some restaurants there and see homemade noodles hanging from the rafters to dry," George explains as he laps his own freshly prepared product over a broomstick to dry.

One of his specialties is Straw and Hay Pasta, which calls for combining regular white noodles with spinach noodles and tossing them with a creamy sauce of sautéed mushrooms and Parmesan cheese. When describing his recipe, George reminds beginning noodlemakers that mixing up the dough and preparing the sauce is the easy part. He quickly points out that it requires time and patience to knead the pasta dough until it is thin and pliable enough to be cut into noodles.

Following George's recipe for Straw and Hay Pasta are specialties from other men who enjoy cooking.

STRAW AND HAY PASTA

¼ cup butter
1 pound medium-size fresh mushrooms,
    finely chopped
¼ cup minced onion
Green noodles (recipe follows)
White noodles (recipe follows)
6 quarts boiling water, divided
2 tablespoons salt, divided
2 tablespoons olive oil, divided
¼ cup plus 2 tablespoons freshly grated
    Parmesan cheese
½ cup whipping cream
1 teaspoon salt
1 teaspoon freshly ground black pepper
Additional freshly grated Parmesan cheese
    (optional)

Melt butter in a large skillet; add mushrooms and onion. Sauté until tender, and set aside.

Prepare green noodles and white noodles according to recipes that follow. Combine 3 quarts boiling water, 1 tablespoon salt, and 1 tablespoon olive oil in each of 2 large Dutch ovens. Add green noodles to one Dutch oven and white noodles to other; cook 2 to 3 minutes or until tender.

While noodles are cooking, add cheese, whipping cream, 1 teaspoon salt, and pepper to mushroom-onion mixture. Place over low heat until warm, stirring well. Drain noodles, and combine the two kinds; immediately toss with mushroom sauce. Sprinkle with additional Parmesan cheese, if desired. Serve at once. Yield: 8 servings.

Green Noodles:

1 (10-ounce) package frozen chopped
    spinach
3 eggs
3 to 4 cups all-purpose flour
½ teaspoon salt
3 to 4 tablespoons water

Cook spinach according to package directions; drain. Place spinach on paper towels; squeeze until barely moist.

Beat eggs in a large mixing bowl, using a wire whisk. Add spinach, one-fourth of flour, and salt; beat with wire whisk until blended. Work in remaining flour and water (add a tablespoon at a time) to form dough.

To shape pasta by machine: Pass dough through smooth rollers of pasta machine on widest setting. Generously dust dough with flour, and fold in half. Repeat rolling, dusting, and folding procedure about 10 times or until dough becomes smooth and pliable.

Cut dough into 3 pieces. Pass each piece of dough through rollers. Continue moving width gauge to narrower settings; pass dough through rollers once at each setting, dusting with flour if needed.

Roll dough to thinness desired, about 1/16 inch. Pass each dough sheet through the cutting rollers of machine. Hang noodles on a wooden drying rack (dry no longer than 30 minutes).

White Noodles:

3 eggs
3 to 4 cups all-purpose flour
1 teaspoon salt
2 to 4 tablespoons water

Beat eggs in a large mixing bowl, using a wire whisk. Add one-fourth of flour and salt; beat with wire whisk until blended. Work in remaining flour and water (add a tablespoon at a time) to form dough.

Shape, cut, and dry according to procedure given for green noodles.

FRUIT-GLAZED CHICKEN

1 (12-ounce) can frozen orange juice
    concentrate, thawed and undiluted
½ cup catsup
¼ cup lemon juice
2 tablespoons soy sauce
2 tablespoons melted butter or margarine
1 teaspoon ground allspice
½ teaspoon garlic powder
¼ teaspoon ground ginger
Salt to taste
Freshly ground pepper to taste
6 whole chicken breasts, split, boned, and
    skinned
3 bananas, peeled and quartered
Lemon juice
1 (11-ounce) can mandarin orange
    sections, drained

Combine first 10 ingredients in a small mixing bowl, stirring well. Place chicken breasts in an ungreased 13- x 9- x 2-inch baking dish. Pour orange juice mixture over chicken. Cover and marinate several hours or overnight in the refrigerator.

Drain chicken, reserving marinade. Bake at 350° for 50 minutes or until done, basting occasionally with marinade. Dip bananas in lemon juice. Place bananas and orange sections around chicken breasts; bake an additional 5 minutes. Yield: 12 servings.

            *Emmett Ramey,
            Austin, Texas.*

Tip: Rub hands with parsley to remove any odor.

CHICKEN SALTIMBOCCA ALLA ROMANA

6 whole chicken breasts, split, boned, and skinned
6 (1-ounce) Swiss cheese slices, halved
6 thin slices prosciutto or smoked ham, halved
3 tablespoons all-purpose flour
3 tablespoons dry breadcrumbs
3 tablespoons grated Parmesan cheese
¼ teaspoon garlic salt
¼ teaspoon dried whole tarragon
1 egg, beaten
¼ cup plus 2 tablespoons butter or margarine, divided
12 small fresh mushrooms, halved
¼ cup dry sherry
¼ cup white wine
½ cup chicken broth
1 tablespoon cornstarch
1 tablespoon water

Place each half of chicken breast on waxed paper; flatten to ¼-inch thickness, using a meat mallet or rolling pin.

Place a piece of Swiss cheese and prosciutto in center of each half of chicken breast. Roll up lengthwise, and secure with toothpick.

Combine flour, breadcrumbs, Parmesan cheese, garlic salt, and tarragon in a shallow dish. Dip each chicken breast in egg; then coat with breadcrumb mixture. Brown chicken on all sides in ¼ cup melted butter, and place in a 13- x 9- x 2-inch baking dish.

Sauté mushrooms in 2 tablespoons butter; spoon over chicken. Add sherry, white wine, and chicken broth. Bake at 350° for 30 minutes or until done. Remove chicken to serving platter, reserving pan drippings.

Combine cornstarch and water in a small saucepan, stirring until smooth; stir in pan drippings. Cook over medium heat, stirring constantly, until thickened. Serve over chicken. Yield: 12 servings. *Paul Fransway, Houston, Texas.*

QUICK-AND-EASY RATATOUILLE

1 large onion, chopped
2 cloves garlic, minced
½ cup olive oil
1 large eggplant, peeled and cubed
1 teaspoon salt
⅛ teaspoon pepper
¼ teaspoon dried whole basil
1 large zucchini, sliced
2 medium-size green peppers, cut into ½-inch pieces
6 unpeeled tomatoes, cut into ½-inch cubes

Sauté onion and garlic in oil until crisp-tender. Add eggplant, salt, pepper, and basil; cover and cook 5 minutes over medium heat. Stir in zucchini and green pepper; cover and cook 5 minutes. Add tomatoes; cook until thoroughly heated. Serve hot or cold. Yield: 6 servings. *George Irvin, Euless, Texas.*

SOUTHERN OYSTERS ROCKEFELLER

Rock salt
¼ cup plus 2 tablespoons butter
¼ cup finely chopped scallions or green onions
¼ cup finely chopped celery
6 cups chopped fresh spinach
3 tablespoons finely chopped parsley
¼ teaspoon garlic powder
½ teaspoon salt
¼ teaspoon pepper
¼ cup plus 2 tablespoons fine dry breadcrumbs
2 dozen oysters on the half shell, drained
¼ cup dry sherry
Lemon juice
Hot sauce
6 slices bacon, cooked and crumbled
2 tablespoons chopped pimiento

Sprinkle a thin layer of rock salt in 2 (12-inch) pizza plates or piepans.

Melt butter, and add scallions and celery; sauté until tender. Stir in spinach, parsley, garlic powder, salt, and pepper. Cook, uncovered, 10 minutes, stirring occasionally. Remove from heat; add breadcrumbs, stirring well.

Arrange oysters (in shells) over salt. Brush each oyster with sherry, and sprinkle with a few drops of lemon juice and hot sauce; then top with spinach mixture. Garnish with bacon and chopped pimiento.

Bake at 350° for 15 minutes. Place under broiler (about 5 inches from source of heat) for 1 minute. Yield: 4 servings. *Bill Walker, Miami, Florida.*

Tip: Experiment with new cooking methods. Oriental stir-fry cooking is not only intriguing as a change-of-pace menu idea, it's more energy efficient and nutritious than boiling or steaming. Cut food into small pieces so that they can cook quickly.

Fresh Bread From New Orleans

New Orleans is known for its delicious French bread, and much of the French bread that is served widely throughout the Crescent City is baked nightly at the G. H. Leidenheimer Baking Co., Ltd. So that you can enjoy its special flavor without leaving home, our test kitchens have adapted this version based on a Leidenheimer recipe.

NEW ORLEANS FRENCH BREAD

6½ cups all-purpose flour
2¼ cups water
4 packages dry yeast
¾ teaspoon sugar
1½ teaspoons lard
4⅓ cups all-purpose flour
1½ cups water
2½ teaspoons salt
2 tablespoons plus 1½ teaspoons sugar
2 tablespoons lard

Combine first 5 ingredients in a large mixing bowl; mix with heavy-duty electric mixer at high speed for 5 minutes. Place dough in a lightly greased large bowl, turning to grease top. Cover dough and let rise in a warm place (85°), free from drafts, 4 hours.

Return dough to large mixing bowl. Add remaining ingredients; beat at high speed 10 to 12 minutes.

Turn dough out onto a floured surface, and divide into 5 equal portions; shape each portion into a 14-inch loaf. Place loaves on greased baking sheets. Place a pan of boiling water on the lower rack of oven to obtain steam. Bake at 425° for 25 to 30 minutes or until done. Yield: 5 loaves.

October

Sportsmen know October as the height of football season. Rally team spirit before the game with one of our tail-gate picnics packed to keep those anxious fans happy.

October also yields the fall and winter varieties of squash. Take a look at all of the menu possibilities created around the acorn, butternut, hubbard, and turban squash recipes included in this chapter. Their mild sweet flavor will surprise you.

Other fall harvest crops naturally bake into traditional Southern desserts, often seasoned with a careful blend of spices. Our favorites include Sweet Potato Pudding and Butter Pecan Cake, and you won't want to miss them.

You Can't Judge A Squash By Its Cover

What vegetable comes in sizes from small to large, shapes as varied as an elongated pear or a turban-topped bowl, and a medley of orange, yellow, red, and green as exuberant as fall itself? Squash—the hard-shelled types—give you these choices and more.

On the outside, acorn, butternut, hubbard, and turban squash appear very different, but a closer look inside reveals the linking similarity—a slightly sweet pulp. Regardless of shape, these squash are prepared in much the same way and are perfect for stuffing.

Acorn squash, which is small and green with deep ridges, becomes the main course when it's stuffed with a mixture of ground pork, apples, and spices for Deluxe Acorn Squash. As a side dish, Glazed Acorn Rings are brushed with a brown sugar-orange glaze that accents its essentially sweet nature.

Sausage adds flavor to two other types of squash—butternut, a cream colored squash with a straight neck and a bulbous base, and turban, a squash shaped like its name. Harvest Squash and Sausage-Stuffed Turban Squash are both baked and served in their own shells.

And don't forget hubbard, that bulky squash with wrinkled skin. It can range from dark green to orange and can grow as large as a pumpkin. Combine it with cranberries for Tart Hubbard Squash.

SAUSAGE-STUFFED TURBAN SQUASH

1 (3-pound) turban squash
Salt
1 pound mild bulk sausage
1 cup chopped celery
¼ cup chopped onion
½ cup sliced fresh mushrooms
1 egg, slightly beaten
½ cup commercial sour cream
¼ cup grated Parmesan cheese
¼ teaspoon salt
Parsley sprigs (optional)
Fresh mushroom slices (optional)

Remove small upper portion of squash, cutting down to seeds. Remove seeds to form a cavity; discard upper portion of squash and seeds. Sprinkle cavity with salt. Place squash, cut side down, in a 9-inch square baking pan. Fill pan with 1 inch water. Bake at 375° for 1 hour or until tender. Remove squash from pan, reserving water.

Combine sausage, celery, and onion in a heavy skillet; cook 5 minutes, stirring to crumble sausage. Stir in ½ cup mushrooms, and continue to cook until meat is browned. Drain well.

Combine egg, sour cream, cheese, and ¼ teaspoon salt; stir well. Add egg mixture to sausage mixture, and blend well; spoon into cavity of squash. Place squash, stuffing side up, into same pan with reserved water. Bake 20 to 25 minutes. Before serving, garnish with parsley and mushrooms, if desired. Yield: about 6 servings. *Margaret Hunter, Princeton, Kentucky.*

TART HUBBARD SQUASH

2 medium hubbard squash
2 eggs, beaten
⅓ cup melted butter or margarine, divided
1½ cups fresh cranberries, coarsely chopped
¼ cup sugar
½ teaspoon salt
⅛ teaspoon pepper
Ground nutmeg

Cut squash in half and remove seeds; pare and cube. Cover and cook in a small amount of boiling salted water for 15 minutes or until tender. Drain; mash pulp.

Combine pulp, eggs, and 3 tablespoons butter; mix well. Stir in cranberries, sugar, salt, and pepper.

Spoon mixture into a lightly greased 1½-quart casserole; top with remaining butter. Sprinkle nutmeg over top. Bake at 350° for 30 minutes or until bubbly. Yield: 8 servings. *Mozelle Dome, New Braunfels, Texas.*

HARVEST SQUASH

1 large butternut squash
1 cup water
1 pound mild bulk sausage
1 small onion, chopped
1 cup soft breadcrumbs
1 cup tomato juice
¼ teaspoon salt
⅛ teaspoon pepper

Cut squash in half lengthwise; remove seeds. Place cut side down in a large baking dish. Add water; bake at 350° for 30 minutes.

Partially cook sausage over low heat, stirring to crumble; drain well.

Carefully scoop pulp from shells, leaving shells intact; mash pulp. Combine sausage, pulp, onion, breadcrumbs, tomato juice, salt, and pepper; mix well. Stuff shells with mixture. Place in a baking dish, and bake at 375° for 20 to 25 minutes. Yield: 4 to 6 servings. *Hazel Slucher, Taylorsville, Kentucky.*

GLAZED ACORN RINGS

1 large acorn squash
⅓ cup orange juice
½ cup firmly packed brown sugar
¼ cup light corn syrup
¼ cup butter or margarine
2 teaspoons grated lemon rind
⅛ teaspoon salt
Orange slices (optional)
Parsley (optional)

Cut squash into ¾-inch-thick slices; remove seeds and membrane. Arrange squash in lightly greased shallow baking dish. Pour orange juice over squash. Cover; bake at 350° for 30 minutes.

Combine next 5 ingredients in a saucepan. Bring to a boil; reduce heat, and simmer 5 minutes. Pour sugar mixture over squash. Bake, uncovered, an additional 15 to 20 minutes or until squash is tender, basting occasionally. Garnish with orange slices and parsley, if desired. Yield: 4 to 6 servings. *Rhonda Harrell, Titusville, Florida.*

DELUXE ACORN SQUASH

1 large acorn squash
¼ pound ground pork
1 large apple, peeled, cored, and chopped
1 tablespoon brown sugar
¼ teaspoon ground nutmeg
¼ teaspoon ground cinnamon
½ teaspoon salt
Butter or margarine

Cut squash in half, and remove seeds. Cook, covered, in boiling water for 10 minutes. Scoop pulp from shells.

Cook pork until brown; stir in apple and pulp. Cook over medium heat for 10 minutes, stirring often. Add sugar, nutmeg, cinnamon, and salt; mix well. Spoon into squash shells; dot with butter. Place shells in a shallow pan; bake at 350° for 30 minutes. Yield: 2 to 4 servings.
Mrs. A. G. Eichelberg,
Sykesville, Maryland.

Soufflés That Don't Fall?

If you're hesitant about trying the usual baked soufflé for fear it will fall before serving, we have an uncommonly delicious solution: Prepare a soufflé roll.

Soufflé rolls are light and puffy, much like the more familiar soufflé. But because they're baked in a shallow jellyroll pan rather than the deeper soufflé dish, they don't rise as high. Consequently, they fall only slightly after baking, which doesn't affect the delicate texture. Another plus for soufflé rolls is the extra flavor that comes from the filling that's rolled inside.

In addition to a light-as-a-feather cheese soufflé roll filled with a spinach-mushroom mixture, we also offer Chocolate-Mocha Roulage, a delectable chocolate roll wrapped around a liqueur-flavored whipped cream filling.

To ensure your success with soufflé rolls, use the tips that follow and refer to the procedure for preparing Spinach Soufflé Roll on page 216.

—Separate the eggs when cold, being sure there is no trace of yolk in the egg whites.

—Allow egg whites to come to room temperature before beating; otherwise, they won't reach maximum volume.

—Make sure the bowl and beaters used for beating the egg whites are clean and dry; if not, this will decrease foaming and volume.

—Avoid overbeating the egg whites; beat just until stiff (not dry) peaks form.

—Use the proper technique when folding beaten egg whites into other mixtures. Take a rubber spatula, and cut down through the center of the mixture; then come up on the side of the bowl, turning the bowl slightly before repeating the folding motion.

—Since proper baking time is critical in preventing overcooking or undercooking the soufflé, you'll need to check the temperature of your oven with an accurate oven thermometer.

SPINACH SOUFFLE ROLL

¼ cup plus 2 tablespoons all-purpose flour
¼ teaspoon salt
Dash of red pepper
⅓ cup butter or margarine
1¼ cups milk
¾ cup (3 ounces) shredded Cheddar cheese
¼ cup Parmesan cheese
7 eggs, separated
¼ teaspoon cream of tartar
¼ teaspoon salt
Additional grated Parmesan cheese
Spinach-Mushroom Filling
4 ounces sliced Cheddar cheese, cut diagonally
Fresh spinach (optional)

Grease bottom and sides of a 15- x 10- x 1-inch jellyroll pan with vegetable oil. Line with waxed paper, allowing paper to extend beyond ends of pan; grease waxed paper with vegetable oil.

Combine flour, ¼ teaspoon salt, and red pepper; stir well.

Melt butter in a large, heavy saucepan over low heat; add flour mixture, stirring with a wire whisk until smooth. Cook 1 minute, stirring constantly with whisk. Gradually add milk; cook over medium heat, stirring constantly with whisk, until very thick and mixture leaves sides of pan. Remove from heat; beat in ¾ cup Cheddar and ¼ cup Parmesan cheese.

Place egg yolks in a large bowl; beat at high speed of electric mixer until thick and lemon colored. Gradually stir in one-fourth of hot cheese mixture; add remaining cheese mixture, beating well.

Combine egg whites (at room temperature) and cream of tartar; beat at high speed of electric mixer until foamy. Add ¼ teaspoon salt, and beat until

stiff peaks form. Fold one-third of egg whites into cheese mixture; then carefully fold in remaining egg whites.

Pour cheese mixture into jellyroll pan, spreading evenly. Bake on center rack of oven at 350° for 15 minutes or until puffed and firm to the touch (do not allow to overcook).

Loosen edges of soufflé with a metal spatula, but do not remove from pan; place on wire rack. Let cool 15 minutes.

Place 2 lengths of waxed paper (longer than jellyroll pan) on a smooth, slightly damp surface; overlap edge of paper nearest you over second sheet. Sprinkle additional Parmesan cheese over the waxed paper.

Quickly invert jellyroll pan onto waxed paper, with long side nearest you; remove pan, and carefully peel waxed paper from soufflé. Spoon Spinach-Mushroom Filling over surface, spreading to edges.

Starting at long side, carefully roll the soufflé jellyroll fashion; use the waxed paper to help support the soufflé as you roll. Using your hands, gently smooth and shape the roll.

Carefully slide the roll, seam side down, onto a large ovenproof platter or cookie sheet. Arrange cheese slices on top. Place 3 inches from broiler element, and broil until cheese melts and is lightly browned. If desired, garnish with fresh spinach. Yield: 8 servings.

Spinach-Mushroom Filling:

2 (10-ounce) packages frozen chopped spinach
¼ cup finely chopped onion
¼ cup melted butter or margarine
½ cup diced fresh mushrooms
¾ cup (3 ounces) shredded Cheddar cheese
¼ cup grated Parmesan cheese
½ cup commercial sour cream
¼ teaspoon salt
¼ teaspoon ground nutmeg

Cook spinach according to package directions; drain and press dry.

Sauté onion in butter until transparent. Add mushrooms, and sauté 3 minutes. Stir in remaining ingredients. Yield: about 1¾ cups.

Note: The soufflé is very fragile and may crack or break during rolling.
Mrs. Gary Willcox,
Austin, Texas.

Tip: To mince parsley and other herbs, hold firmly in tight bunch and cut with kitchen shears or on a board with sharp knife.

Step 1—*Combine flour, salt, and red pepper. Melt butter over low heat; add flour mixture, stirring with wire whisk until smooth. Cook 1 minute, stirring constantly. Gradually add milk; cook over medium heat, stirring with whisk, until mixture thickens and leaves sides of pan. Remove from heat, and beat in cheese.*

Step 2—*After beating egg yolks until thick and lemon colored, stir in a fourth of the hot cheese sauce; add remaining sauce, beating well. Beat egg whites, cream of tartar, and salt until stiff peaks form; gently fold into cheese mixture.*

Step 3—*Spread cheese mixture evenly in a waxed paper-lined and oiled jellyroll pan. Bake at 350° for 15 minutes. Loosen edges of soufflé, and let cool in pan 15 minutes; invert pan onto waxed paper sprinkled with Parmesan cheese. Carefully peel off paper.*

Step 4—*Spoon filling over soufflé, spreading to edges. Starting at long side, carefully roll the soufflé jellyroll fashion. Use the waxed paper to help support soufflé as you roll.*

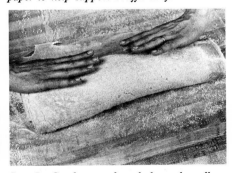

Step 5—*Gently smooth and shape the roll with your hands; carefully slide it onto an ovenproof platter or cookie sheet. Arrange cheese slices on top, and broil (3 inches from element) until cheese melts and is lightly browned.*

CHOCOLATE-MOCHA ROULAGE

1 (6-ounce) package semisweet chocolate
   morsels
2 tablespoons plus 1 teaspoon strong
   black coffee
5 eggs, separated
1¼ cups sugar, divided
1 teaspoon vanilla extract
2 teaspoons cocoa
1 cup whipping cream
2 tablespoons powdered sugar
2 to 3 tablespoons green crème de menthe
   or Kahlúa or other coffee-flavored
   liqueur
Additional powdered sugar

Grease bottom and sides of a 15- x 10- x 1-inch jellyroll pan with vegetable oil; line with waxed paper, and also grease waxed paper with vegetable oil.

Combine chocolate morsels and coffee in top of a double boiler; bring water to a boil. Reduce heat to low; cook, stirring occasionally, until chocolate melts.

Place egg yolks in a large bowl, and beat until foamy at high speed of electric mixer; gradually add ¾ cup sugar, beating until mixture is thick and lemon colored. (The mixture will look much like cake batter.)

Gradually stir about one-fourth of hot chocolate mixture into yolk mixture; fold in remaining chocolate mixture.

Beat egg whites (at room temperature) at high speed of electric mixer until foamy. Gradually add ½ cup sugar, beating until stiff peaks form. Fold egg whites into chocolate mixture; gently fold in vanilla extract.

Pour chocolate mixture into jellyroll pan, spreading evenly. Bake on center rack of oven at 350° for 15 to 18 minutes; do not overcook (surface will shine when done). Immediately cover top with a damp linen towel or 2 layers of damp paper towels; place on a wire rack, and let cool 20 minutes. Carefully remove towel. Loosen edges of soufflé with a metal spatula, and sift cocoa over top.

Place 2 lengths of waxed paper (longer than jellyroll pan) on a smooth, slightly damp surface; overlap edge of paper nearest you over second sheet. Quickly invert jellyroll pan onto waxed paper, with long side nearest you; remove pan, and carefully peel paper from soufflé.

Beat whipping cream until foamy; gradually add 2 tablespoons powdered sugar and crème de menthe, beating until soft peaks form.

Spoon whipped cream mixture over soufflé, spreading it so there is more on the side facing you (mixture will spread out as you roll); leave a 1-inch margin on all sides.

Starting at long side, carefully roll the soufflé jellyroll fashion; use the waxed paper to help support the soufflé as you roll. Secure the waxed paper around the roulage; then smooth and shape it with your hands.

Carefully slide roulage onto a large cookie sheet, seam side down; store in refrigerator until serving time. Before serving, sift additional powdered sugar over roulage; carefully transfer to serving dish, using the waxed paper to lift and slide it. Trim away excess waxed paper. Yield: 12 to 14 servings.

Note: The roulage is very fragile and may crack or break during rolling.

Spirits Will Rally For This Menu

Avid football fans know that the real way to enjoy a football game is to arrive at the stadium early and bring plenty to eat. If you're planning to pack a tailgate picnic and need some inspiration, here are two menus to choose from.

For variety, the first menu features Imperial Chicken Rollups. Boned chicken breasts are buttered and breaded, then rolled up to bake and serve. Accompany the chicken with a vegetable salad and deviled eggs, and top off the menu with Cocoa Drop Cookies.

If sandwiches are more your style, our other menu calls for Meal-In-One Sandwiches. A salad, cookies, and beverage complete the picnic.

Imperial Chicken Rollups
Crunchy Vegetable Salad
Nippy Deviled Eggs
Cocoa Drop Cookies

IMPERIAL CHICKEN ROLLUPS

¾ cup butter or margarine, melted
2 cloves garlic, pressed
1 cup fine dry breadcrumbs
⅔ cup grated Parmesan cheese
¼ cup minced fresh parsley
1 teaspoon salt
¼ teaspoon pepper
4 whole chicken breasts, split, skinned, and boned
Juice of 2 lemons
Paprika

Combine butter and garlic; stir well, and set aside.

Combine breadcrumbs, cheese, parsley, salt, and pepper; stir well. Dip chicken in butter mixture, and coat with breadcrumb mixture.

Fold long sides of chicken together; bring short ends over and secure with a toothpick. Place chicken rolls seam side down in a greased 13- x 9- x 2-inch pan; sprinkle with lemon juice and paprika. Bake at 350° for 1 hour or until done. Yield: 8 servings.
Mrs. J. W. Riley, Jr.,
Kingsport, Tennessee.

CRUNCHY VEGETABLE SALAD

1 pound fresh broccoli
1 small head cauliflower
2 to 3 large carrots, sliced
2 small zucchini, sliced
2 small onions, sliced and separated into rings
⅔ cup mayonnaise or salad dressing
⅓ cup vegetable oil
⅓ cup apple cider vinegar
¼ cup sugar
1 tablespoon salt

Trim off large leaves of broccoli. Remove tough ends of lower stalks, and wash broccoli thoroughly. Cut into bite-size pieces.

Wash cauliflower, and remove green leaves. Separate cauliflower into flowerets, slicing large flowerets into bite-size pieces.

Combine vegetables in a large bowl. Combine remaining ingredients; stir well. Add mayonnaise mixture, tossing to coat vegetables. Chill salad several hours before serving. Yield: 8 to 10 servings.
Mrs. Frank Tetrault,
Southlala, Texas.

NIPPY DEVILED EGGS

8 hard-cooked eggs
¼ cup mayonnaise
1 teaspoon prepared mustard
½ to 1 teaspoon prepared horseradish
¼ teaspoon salt
¼ teaspoon pepper
Paprika

Cut eggs in half lengthwise; remove yolks. Mash yolks; stir in mayonnaise, mustard, horseradish, salt, and pepper.

Fill egg halves with mixture; chill. Sprinkle with paprika before serving. Yield: 8 servings.
Mrs. Parke LaGourgue Cory,
Neosho, Missouri.

COCOA DROP COOKIES

½ cup shortening
1 cup sugar
1 egg
¾ cup buttermilk
1 teaspoon vanilla extract
1¾ cups all-purpose flour
½ teaspoon soda
½ teaspoon salt
½ cup cocoa
1 cup chopped pecans or walnuts

Cream shortening; gradually add sugar, beating until light and fluffy. Add egg, beating well. Stir in buttermilk and vanilla extract.

Combine flour, soda, salt, and cocoa; add to creamed mixture, beating well. Stir in pecans. Chill dough 1 hour.

Drop dough by teaspoonfuls, 2 inches apart, on greased cookie sheets. Bake at 400° for 8 to 10 minutes. Yield: about 5 dozen.
Mrs. Russell Rehkemper,
Tampa, Florida.

Tip: When boiling eggs, add 1 teaspoon salt to the water. This prevents a cracked egg from draining into the water.

**Meal-In-One Sandwiches
Eight-Vegetable Marinated Salad
Oatmeal-Coconut Cookies
Easy Citrus Sangría**

MEAL-IN-ONE SANDWICHES

¼ cup mayonnaise
2 tablespoons chili sauce
1 teaspoon instant minced onion
1 teaspoon lemon juice
1 cup finely shredded cabbage
1 pound sliced corned beef
1 pound sliced ham
1 pound sliced turkey
1 pound sliced Swiss cheese
8 slices rye bread

Combine first 5 ingredients; cover coleslaw, and refrigerate 4 hours.

Place one-fourth pound each of corned beef, ham, turkey, and cheese on 4 slices of rye bread; top each with equal amounts of coleslaw. Cover with remaining slices of rye bread. Yield: 4 servings.
*Barbara Stelter,
Cincinnati, Ohio.*

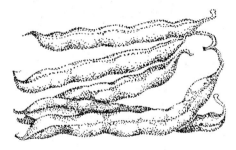

EIGHT-VEGETABLE MARINATED SALAD

1 (16-ounce) can cut green beans, drained
1 (16-ounce) can cut wax beans, drained
1 (15½-ounce) can kidney beans, drained
1 cup cooked and drained baby lima beans
1 cup drained canned whole kernel corn
1 cup sliced carrots
3 medium onions, chopped
2 medium-size green peppers, chopped
1 cup vinegar
1 cup sugar
½ cup vegetable oil

Combine vegetables in a large bowl, and toss lightly.

Combine vinegar, sugar, and oil in a small saucepan; bring to a boil. Pour hot marinade over vegetables; stir gently. Cover and chill salad overnight. Yield: 12 servings. *Lora Blocker,
Dade City, Florida.*

OATMEAL-COCONUT COOKIES

1 cup sugar
1 cup firmly packed brown sugar
1 cup shortening, melted
2 eggs
1 teaspoon vanilla extract
1 cup all-purpose flour
1 teaspoon soda
½ teaspoon salt
4 cups regular oats, uncooked
1 cup flaked coconut

Combine sugar and shortening, beating until light and fluffy. Add eggs, one at a time, beating well after each addition. Stir in vanilla.

Combine flour, soda, and salt; add to creamed mixture, beating well. Stir in oats and coconut. Chill dough 1 hour.

Shape dough into 1-inch balls. Place 2 inches apart on ungreased cookie sheets. Bake at 325° for 12 to 15 minutes. Yield: about 7 dozen cookies.
*Nancy Mulkey,
Tullahoma, Tennessee.*

EASY CITRUS SANGRIA

1 (50.7-ounce) bottle Burgundy or other dry red wine, chilled
1½ cups brandy or bourbon
1 (6-ounce) can frozen orange juice concentrate, thawed and undiluted
Grated rind of 4 lemons
Juice of 4 lemons
¾ to 1 cup sugar
1 (33.8-ounce) bottle club soda, chilled

Combine first 6 ingredients in a large pitcher, stirring to dissolve sugar. Add club soda before serving. Serve over ice. Yield: about 3½ quarts.
*Mrs. George Sellers,
Albany, Georgia.*

Pears Add Sparkle To Meals

Enjoying the sunny goodness of fresh ripe pears isn't difficult. Poach them in a simple sugar syrup flavored with orange and lemon juice. Or bake them into a quick bread to be enjoyed with breakfast or afternoon coffee. And if you've never baked pears in a pie, we recommend Deep-Dish Pear Pie; it's topped with a Cheddar cheese-flavored pastry.

ORANGE POACHED PEARS

1½ cups sugar
½ cup water
½ cup orange juice
2 tablespoons lemon juice
6 pears, peeled, halved, and cored
Whipped cream (optional)
Twist of orange rind (optional)

Combine first 4 ingredients in a large skillet; bring to a boil over medium heat, stirring until sugar dissolves. Boil gently 5 minutes. Add pears. Cover; reduce heat and cook 15 minutes, turning pears once.

Transfer pears and syrup to a medium bowl; cover and refrigerate until thoroughly chilled.

Spoon pears and syrup into dessert dishes; top with whipped cream and a twist of orange rind, if desired. Yield: 6 servings. *Peggy Fowler Revels,
Woodruff, South Carolina.*

SPICED PEAR BUTTER

6 pounds (about 12 medium) pears, peeled and chopped
1¼ cups water
¼ cup lemon juice
2 teaspoons ground cinnamon
4 cups firmly packed brown sugar
½ cup port wine

Combine pears, water, and lemon juice in a Dutch oven; cover and cook over medium heat 30 minutes. Drain and mash pears. Add remaining ingredients; cook over low heat 1 hour or until thickened, stirring occasionally.

Pour hot pear mixture into sterilized jars, leaving ⅛-inch headspace; cover at once with metal lids, and screw metal bands tight. Process in boiling-water bath for 10 minutes. Yield: 3 pints.
*Eva G. Key,
Isle of Palms, South Carolina.*

PEAR BREAD

3 cups all-purpose flour
1 teaspoon soda
¼ teaspoon baking powder
1 teaspoon salt
1 tablespoon ground cinnamon
1 cup chopped pecans
¾ cup vegetable oil
3 eggs, slightly beaten
2 cups sugar
2 cups peeled and grated pears
2 teaspoons vanilla extract

Combine first 6 ingredients in a large bowl; make a well in center of mixture. Combine oil, eggs, sugar, pears, and vanilla; add to dry ingredients, stirring just until moistened. Spoon mixture into 2 greased 8½- x 4½- x 3-inch loafpans. Bake at 325° for 1 hour and 15 minutes or until bread tests done. Cool 10 minutes before removing from pans. Yield: 2 loaves. *Carole Bunge, Mountain Home, Arkansas.*

DEEP-DISH PEAR PIE

2 pounds (about 4 medium) pears, peeled, halved, and cored
1 tablespoon lemon juice
3 tablespoons all-purpose flour
1 cup sugar
Dash of salt
½ teaspoon ground cinnamon
½ teaspoon ground nutmeg
1 tablespoon butter
Cheddar Cheese Pastry
Whipped cream (optional)

Place pear halves in a 1½-quart casserole or deep-dish 9-inch pieplate. Sprinkle with lemon juice. Combine flour, sugar, salt, cinnamon, and nutmeg; sprinkle over pears. Dot with butter. Cover with Cheddar Cheese Pastry, crimping pastry to sides of dish. Cut slits in top of pastry for steam to escape. Bake at 350° for 30 to 40 minutes. Serve with whipped cream, if desired. Yield: 6 servings.

Cheddar Cheese Pastry:

1 cup all-purpose flour
½ teaspoon salt
⅓ cup shortening
¼ cup (1 ounce) shredded sharp Cheddar cheese
2 to 3 tablespoons cold water

Combine flour and salt; cut in shortening with pastry blender until mixture resembles coarse meal. Stir in cheese. Sprinkle cold water evenly over surface; stir with a fork until all dry ingredients are moistened. Shape dough into a ball.

Roll out dough on a floured surface; cut dough to cover top of a deep-dish 9-inch pieplate. Yield: pastry for one 9-inch pie. *Florence L. Costello, Chattanooga, Tennessee.*

Tip: Slip a cookie sheet or a sheet of foil under a casserole or fruit pie in the oven to catch bubble-over.

Parfaits And Custard For Two

Sometimes the hardest part of planning a meal for two is preparing a dessert that won't leave you with lots of leftovers. But with these recipes, the problem is solved because they yield exactly two servings. Choose a flavorful parfait, baked custard, crème de menthe tarts, or Mint Patty Alaska.

MOCHA-MALLOW PARFAITS

12 large marshmallows
½ cup water
1½ teaspoons instant coffee powder
½ cup whipping cream, whipped
¼ cup chocolate wafer crumbs

Combine marshmallows, water, and coffee powder in a small saucepan; cook over medium heat until marshmallows are melted, stirring occasionally. Cool mixture thoroughly. Fold in whipped cream. (Chill until slightly thickened if mixture is thin.)

Alternate layers of coffee mixture and wafer crumbs in parfait glasses, beginning and ending with coffee mixture. Place the parfaits in the refrigerator to chill until serving time. Yield: 2 servings. *Mrs. C. D. Marshall, Culpeper, Virginia.*

MINT PATTY ALASKA

2 egg whites
¼ teaspoon cream of tartar
¼ teaspoon vanilla extract
Dash of salt
¼ cup sugar
2 individual dessert sponge cakes
2 (2-ounce) chocolate-coated peppermint ice cream patties

Beat egg whites (at room temperature), cream of tartar, vanilla, and salt until foamy. Gradually add sugar, beating until stiff peaks form.

Place sponge cakes on an ovenproof wooden board or serving dish. Top each cake with an ice cream patty. Quickly spread meringue over entire surface, making sure edges are sealed.

Bake at 500° for 1 or 2 minutes or until meringue peaks are browned. Serve immediately. Yield: 2 servings.

Sandy Wallace, Mobile, Alabama.

BAKED CUSTARD

2 eggs, slightly beaten
2 tablespoons sugar
⅛ teaspoon salt
1 teaspoon vanilla extract
Dash of ground nutmeg
1½ cups milk, scalded

Combine first 5 ingredients, stirring until blended. Gradually add scalded milk, stirring constantly. Pour mixture into two 10-ounce custard cups. Set custard cups in a 9-inch square pan; pour hot water into pan to a depth of 1 inch.

Bake at 350° for 30 minutes or until knife inserted in center comes out clean. Remove custard cups from water; cool. Chill thoroughly. Yield: 2 servings. *Nancy M. Wheless, Gainesville, Florida.*

CHILLED ORANGE PARFAITS

1 teaspoon unflavored gelatin
3 tablespoons cold water
1½ teaspoons cornstarch
½ cup milk, divided
3 tablespoons sugar
Pinch of salt
3 tablespoons orange juice
¼ teaspoon grated orange rind
1 egg, separated
4 ladyfingers

Soften gelatin in cold water; set aside. Dissolve cornstarch in 2 tablespoons milk; set aside.

Scald remaining milk in a medium saucepan; stir in sugar, salt, and cornstarch mixture. Cook over low heat, stirring constantly, 15 to 20 minutes or until thickened. Add gelatin mixture, orange juice, and orange rind; stir until the gelatin dissolves.

Beat egg yolk until thick and lemon colored. Gradually stir about one-fourth of hot mixture into egg yolk; add to remaining hot mixture, stirring constantly. Cook over low heat, stirring constantly, for 5 minutes. Cool.

Beat egg white until stiff peaks form; fold into cooked mixture. Chill until slightly thickened.

Crumble 1 ladyfinger into each parfait glass; stand 1 ladyfinger on end in each glass. Fill glasses with custard mixture; chill until firm. Yield: 2 servings.

Eleanor Glading, Snow Hill, Maryland.

GRASSHOPPER TARTS

½ cup chocolate wafer crumbs
2 tablespoons butter, melted
1 cup marshmallow creme
1 tablespoon green crème de menthe
1 tablespoon white crème de cacao
½ cup whipping cream, whipped

Combine wafer crumbs and butter, stirring well; press firmly into bottom of two 5-inch tart pans.

Combine marshmallow creme and liqueur in a small mixing bowl; beat 1 minute at high speed of electric mixer. Fold in whipped cream; spoon mixture into crusts. Freeze. Yield: 2 servings.
Alice McNamara,
Eucha, Oklahoma.

Tired of chips and dip and looking for something new to munch on? Try Crispy Fried Cauliflower, coated with cracker crumbs and deep fried.

Call On Cauliflower For Flavor

Start with a fresh, solid head of cauliflower, separate the tightly clustered white flowerets, and you have the beginning of the three delicious dishes in the following recipes.

The tender buds make a popular snack when deep fried until golden brown for Crispy Fried Cauliflower. Try stir-frying beef and cauliflower seasoned with soy sauce for an Oriental-style main dish. As a side dish topped with a cheese sauce, Cauliflower Medley (with brussels sprouts and onions) becomes a colorful accompaniment for ham or poultry.

CRISPY FRIED CAULIFLOWER

1 medium head cauliflower
½ cup round buttery cracker crumbs
½ cup corn flake crumbs
Salt and pepper to taste
½ teaspoon sugar
1 tablespoon grated Parmesan cheese
2 eggs
2 tablespoons half-and-half
¼ teaspoon hot sauce
Vegetable oil

Wash cauliflower, and break into flowerets. Cook, covered, in a small amount of boiling salted water about 10 minutes or until crisp-tender; drain.

Combine cracker crumbs, corn flake crumbs, salt, pepper, sugar, and Parmesan cheese; stir well. In a separate bowl combine eggs, half-and-half, and hot sauce; beat well.

Dip each floweret into egg mixture; then dredge in cracker crumbs. Repeat procedure. Deep fry in hot oil (375°) until golden brown. Yield: 6 servings.
Mrs. Bernie Benigno,
Gulfport, Mississippi.

CAULIFLOWER MEDLEY

1 large head cauliflower
1 (10-ounce) package frozen brussels sprouts
1 (9-ounce) package frozen creamed small onions
2 tablespoons margarine
2 tablespoons all-purpose flour
1 cup milk
½ teaspoon salt
¼ teaspoon white pepper
1 teaspoon Worcestershire sauce
2 cups (8 ounces) shredded sharp Cheddar cheese
1 (2-ounce) jar diced pimiento, drained
¼ cup seasoned breadcrumbs

Wash cauliflower, and break into flowerets. Cook, covered, in a small amount of boiling salted water about 10 minutes or until crisp-tender; drain.

Cook brussels sprouts and onions according to individual package directions. Drain brussels sprouts.

Combine vegetables in a lightly greased 2-quart casserole, and set aside.

Melt margarine in a heavy saucepan over low heat; add flour, stirring until smooth. Cook 1 minute, stirring constantly. Gradually stir in milk; cook over medium heat, stirring constantly, until thickened and bubbly. Stir in salt, pepper, and Worcestershire sauce. Add cheese, stirring until melted.

Spoon sauce over vegetables, and top with pimiento and breadcrumbs. Bake at 375° for 20 minutes or until bubbly. Yield: 8 servings.   *Leola Wenley,*
Arlington, Virginia.

BEEF AND CAULIFLOWER ORIENTAL

1 pound boneless round steak
1 small head cauliflower
2 tablespoons butter or margarine, melted
½ green pepper, coarsely chopped
1 (10½-ounce) can beef broth, undiluted
2 tablespoons cornstarch
¼ cup soy sauce
½ cup chopped green onion
1 (4-ounce) can sliced mushrooms, drained (optional)
Hot cooked rice

Partially freeze steak; slice across grain into 3- x ¼-inch strips. Set aside. Wash cauliflower, and break into flowerets.

Cook steak in butter in a heavy skillet until browned. Add cauliflower and green pepper; cover and simmer 10 minutes. Combine broth and cornstarch, mixing well. Stir broth mixture, soy sauce, and onion into skillet. Cook over medium heat, stirring constantly, until thickened. Stir in mushrooms, if desired. Serve over rice. Yield: 4 servings.

Delores Garry,
Houston, Texas.

An Outdoorsman Prepares A Special Brunch

For Bill Sandy, growing up along the shores of the Chesapeake Bay just naturally instilled a love for the outdoors. An avid hunter and fisherman, he brings his catch home and prepares it himself in his Roanoke, Virginia, kitchen.

Bill and his wife, Charlotte, especially enjoy entertaining friends for brunch. According to Bill, "The main course for breakfast or brunch shouldn't be just eggs and sausage; I always include wild game, chicken, or seafood on the menu." Oyster stew and Marinated Quail are among his favorites.

Freshly shucked oysters in their own juice are the secret to Bill's oyster stew. "Cooking oysters without the liquor is like wringing all the juices out of a piece of meat before cooking it," he comments.

For his special quail dish, Bill marinates the quail overnight. The birds are baked for a short time, then grilled briefly over hot coals. Since Bill enjoys cooking outdoors, he prepares much of the wild game in a smoker.

Bill's brunch guests also enjoy his personalized Bloody Marys. "They're just not the same when I make them by the pitcher; some like them hotter than others, so I prefer to season each to suit individual tastes," he says.

Along with Bill's recipes, we've included favorite dishes from other men who enjoy cooking.

OYSTER STEW

¼ cup butter
1 pint freshly shucked oysters and oyster liquor
¼ teaspoon salt
⅛ teaspoon celery salt
¼ teaspoon pepper
1½ cups milk
¼ cup dry white wine (optional)

Melt butter in a heavy saucepan; add oysters and liquor. Cook over medium heat, stirring often, until hot (do not boil); add salt, celery salt, and pepper. Gradually add milk, stirring constantly. Continue cooking over medium heat, stirring constantly, until heated through and oyster edges curl. Stir in wine, if desired. Yield: about 4 cups.

MARINATED QUAIL

½ cup white wine vinegar
¼ cup plus 2 tablespoons red burgundy
½ teaspoon celery salt
½ teaspoon lemon pepper seasoning
¼ teaspoon onion salt
¼ teaspoon ground allspice
Pinch of ground sage
2 teaspoons bacon drippings
12 quail, cleaned
Melted butter

Combine first 8 ingredients, mixing well; add quail. Cover and marinate in refrigerator at least 24 hours, turning quail several times.

Bake at 300° for 20 minutes, basting with marinade. Remove quail from marinade; grill over hot coals 10 to 20 minutes, basting often with melted butter. Yield: 6 servings.

BLOODY MARY

⅓ cup tomato juice
⅔ cup clam and tomato juice cocktail
¼ teaspoon fresh lemon juice
⅓ teaspoon Worcestershire sauce
⅛ teaspoon celery salt
⅛ teaspoon salt
⅛ teaspoon pepper
2 drops of hot sauce
1½ to 2 ounces vodka
Celery stick

Combine the first 9 ingredients in a 14-ounce glass; stir well. Add ice cubes, and garnish with a celery stick. Yield: 1 serving.

PEPPERY HUSH PUPPIES

2 cups yellow cornmeal
½ cup plus 3 tablespoons all-purpose flour
1½ teaspoons sugar
1 teaspoon salt
2 teaspoons baking powder
½ teaspoon soda
1 teaspoon creole seasoning
½ cup buttermilk
⅔ cup water
½ cup melted margarine
1 egg, well beaten
1 cup grated onion
1 medium-size green pepper, finely chopped
2 jalapeño peppers, seeded and finely chopped

Combine dry ingredients; add buttermilk, water, margarine, and egg. Mix well. Stir in onion and peppers. Carefully drop batter by teaspoonfuls into hot oil (375°). Fry 3 to 5 minutes, turning once, until hush puppies are golden brown. Drain well on paper towels. Yield: about 2½ dozen.

Col. Bob F. Wilson,
Shreveport, Louisiana.

EASY FRUIT SALAD

1 (17-ounce) can salad fruit, drained
1 orange, peeled, seeded, and sectioned
1 banana, peeled and thinly sliced
Lettuce leaves
Lime Sherbet Dressing

Combine fruit; toss gently. Cover and chill 30 minutes. Spoon onto lettuce leaves. Serve with Lime Sherbet Dressing. Yield: 2 servings.

Lime Sherbet Dressing:

½ cup lime sherbet, softened
½ cup mayonnaise
½ tablespoon poppy seeds

Combine all ingredients; mix well. Yield: 1 cup.

Roger Young,
Nashville, Tennessee.

Tip: Bananas that have passed their prime are still useful. Remove any brown portions, and puree the rest for baby food or to make banana cake or banana bread.

BLACK BEANS AND RICE

1 pound dried black beans
2 tablespoons olive oil
1 medium tomato, peeled
1 bay leaf
1 small onion
½ medium-size green pepper
2 cloves garlic, minced
½ cup olive oil
¼ cup chopped onion
½ cup chopped green pepper
1 teaspoon ground oregano
¼ teaspoon ground cumin
1 tablespoon salt
2 tablespoons wine vinegar
½ teaspoon hot pepper sauce
Hot cooked rice
Chopped onion
⅔ cup vegetable oil
⅓ cup vinegar

Sort and wash beans. Place in a large Dutch oven, and cover with water 2 inches above beans; let soak overnight. Add 2 tablespoons olive oil, tomato, bay leaf, 1 onion, ½ green pepper, and half of garlic to beans. Bring to a boil. Reduce heat; cover and simmer 2 to 3 hours or until desired degree of doneness, adding more water if necessary. Remove and discard bay leaf and any remaining tomato, onion, green pepper, and garlic.

Heat ½ cup olive oil in a medium skillet; sauté ¼ cup chopped onion and ½ cup chopped green pepper until tender. Add remaining garlic, oregano, cumin, salt, and wine vinegar; cook over low heat, stirring constantly, 2 minutes. Stir mixture into beans; add pepper sauce, stirring gently. Serve over hot cooked rice; top with chopped onion.

Combine vegetable oil and vinegar in a jar. Cover tightly, and shake vigorously. Spoon a small amount over each serving. Yield: 8 to 10 servings.
Scott Peeler,
Valrico, Florida.

MUSTARD CHICKEN

2 tablespoons dry mustard
1½ cups soft breadcrumbs
4 whole chicken breasts, split
2 tablespoons lemon juice
1 to 2 tablespoons olive oil
Mustard sauce (recipe follows)

Combine dry mustard and breadcrumbs; set aside.
Rub chicken with lemon juice and oil. Dredge chicken in breadcrumb mixture,

and place skin side up in a 15- x 10- x 1-inch jellyroll pan. Bake at 425° for 35 minutes in upper third of oven; bake an additional 10 minutes in lower third of oven. Serve chicken with mustard sauce. Yield: 8 servings.

Mustard Sauce:

3 tablespoons butter or margarine
1 tablespoon instant minced onion
¼ cup all-purpose flour
2 cups milk
2 tablespoons Dijon mustard
¼ teaspoon salt
Dash of white pepper

Melt butter in a heavy saucepan over low heat; sauté onion in butter until onion is browned. Add flour and cook 1 minute, stirring constantly, until bubbly. Gradually add milk; cook over medium heat, stirring constantly, until thickened and bubbly. Stir in mustard, salt, and pepper. Yield: about 2 cups.
Dale Barr,
Birmingham, Alabama.

MUSHROOM QUICHE

Pastry for 9-inch pie shell
1 small onion, chopped
½ pound fresh mushrooms, sliced
2 tablespoons olive oil
3 eggs, beaten
½ cup evaporated milk
1 (8-ounce) carton commercial sour cream
½ teaspoon ground nutmeg
1 teaspoon salt
½ teaspoon pepper
½ pound Swiss cheese, diced
1 tablespoon all-purpose flour

Line a 9-inch quiche dish or piepan with pastry; trim excess pastry around edges. Prick bottom and sides of quiche shell with a fork; bake at 425° for 6 to 8 minutes. Let cool on rack.
Sauté onion and mushrooms in olive oil until tender. Combine next 6 ingredients in a large bowl; stir well. Combine cheese and flour; add to egg mixture. Stir in onion and mushrooms. Pour into pastry shell, and bake at 350° for 45 minutes or until set. Yield: one 9-inch quiche.
J. Michael Grant,
Danville, Virginia.

Spice Up Some Dried Beans

Do dried beans have a way of just sitting on your kitchen shelf, never being noticed or cooked? Well, get out the bean pot, because cooler weather means it's time to stir up some hearty, nutritious dried bean dishes.

Most dried beans benefit from a good bit of seasoning. Red beans, for example, take on the flavors of salt pork, garlic, red pepper, and smoked sausage in Creole Beans and Rice.

For an even spicier possibility, try a bowl of Hot Texas Chili. Dried pinto beans, ground beef, green chiles, and jalapeño pepper give this chili both flavor and bite.

CAPITOL HILL BEAN SOUP

1 pound dried navy beans
1 (about 1-pound) ham bone
½ cup mashed potatoes
3 cups chopped celery
3 cups chopped onion
¼ cup chopped fresh parsley
1 clove garlic, minced
2 teaspoons salt
Pepper to taste

Sort and wash beans; place in a Dutch oven. Cover with water, and soak overnight. Drain beans. Add ham bone, and cover with water. Cover and bring to a boil; reduce heat, and simmer 1 hour. Add remaining ingredients; simmer 1 hour or until beans are tender. Remove ham and dice; return to soup. Yield: 12 to 15 servings. *Lois Wilson,*
Ackerly, Texas.

HOT TEXAS CHILI

1 pound dried pinto beans
2 pounds ground beef
2 large onions, chopped
2 cloves garlic, minced
1 jalapeño pepper, seeded, rinsed, chopped
3 to 5 tablespoons chili powder seasoning blend
1 tablespoon ground cumin
1 teaspoon celery salt
1 teaspoon pepper
1 (4-ounce) can green chiles, undrained and chopped
1 (28-ounce) can tomatoes, undrained and chopped
1 (15-ounce) can tomato sauce
4 cups cocktail vegetable juice

Sort and wash beans; place in a Dutch oven. Cover with water, and bring to a boil; cover and cook 2 minutes. Remove from heat, and let stand 1 hour. Bring to a boil; reduce heat, and simmer 1 hour or until beans are tender. Drain beans, and set aside.

Combine ground beef, onion, garlic, and jalapeño pepper in a large Dutch oven; cook over medium heat, stirring to crumble meat, until meat is browned and onion is tender. Drain off pan drippings. Add beans and remaining ingredients; stir well. Cover and simmer 1 hour. Yield: 10 to 12 servings.

Patsy M. Smith,
Lampasas, Texas.

CREOLE BEANS AND RICE

1 pound dried red beans
½ pound salt pork
3 cups chopped onions
1 bunch green onions, chopped
1 cup chopped fresh parsley
1 cup chopped green pepper
2 cloves garlic, pressed
1 tablespoon salt
1 teaspoon red pepper
1 teaspoon pepper
3 dashes of hot sauce
1 tablespoon Worcestershire sauce
1 (8-ounce) can tomato sauce
¼ teaspoon dried whole oregano
¼ teaspoon dried whole thyme
2 pounds Mettwurst or other smoked German sausage, cut into bite-size pieces
Hot cooked rice

Sort and wash beans; place in a Dutch oven. Cover with water, and soak overnight. Drain beans. Add pork, and cover beans with water. Cover and cook over low heat 45 minutes. Add all remaining ingredients except sausage and rice; cover and cook over low heat 1 hour, stirring occasionally. Add sausage; cook, uncovered, over low heat 45 minutes, stirring occasionally. Serve over rice. Yield: about 12 servings.

Jewel McDougal,
Crane, Texas.

Tip: When you're out of canned tomatoes for your recipe—don't panic! Try substituting a can of tomato paste plus a cup of water. In most recipes you'll never know the difference.

BEAN CHALUPA

1 pound dried pinto beans
1 (3-pound) boneless pork or beef roast
2 cloves garlic, minced
1 large onion, chopped
2 tablespoons chili powder
1 tablespoon ground cumin
1 teaspoon salt
1 (4-ounce) can chopped green chiles, undrained
1 teaspoon dried whole oregano
1 (15-ounce) package corn chips
1 small head lettuce, shredded
3 to 4 medium tomatoes, peeled and chopped
2 to 3 ripe avocados, peeled and chopped
1 large onion, chopped
3 cups (12 ounces) shredded sharp Cheddar cheese
Commercial taco sauce

Sort and wash beans; place in a large Dutch oven. Cover with water; add next 7 ingredients. Cover and simmer about 3 hours or until meat is tender. Add oregano; cook, uncovered, 30 minutes. Remove meat; shred and return to beans.

For each serving, spoon bean mixture over corn chips. Add layers of lettuce, tomato, avocado, onion, and cheese. Top chalupas with taco sauce. Yield: 12 to 14 servings. *Mrs. V. L. Walters,*
Houston, Texas.

Stretch Beef With Foo Yong Patties

Take a break from routine main dishes with savory Foo Yong Patties. Chop suey vegetables and mushrooms stretch a pound of ground beef to serve six, making the dish as economical as it is unusual. Foo Yong Sauce adds the finishing touch.

FOO YONG PATTIES

1 pound ground beef
6 eggs, well beaten
1 (16-ounce) can chop suey or chow mein vegetables, drained
1 (2-ounce) can sliced mushrooms, drained
1 teaspoon salt
Fresh parsley sprigs (optional)
Foo Yong Sauce

Cook ground beef until browned in a large skillet, stirring until meat is crumbled. Remove beef, reserving drippings in skillet.

Combine beef and next 4 ingredients in a large bowl; stir well.

For each patty, pour ⅓ cup egg mixture into skillet over medium heat; retain patty shape by pushing egg back into patties. Cook until browned, turning once. Drain on paper towels. Garnish with parsley, if desired. Serve hot with Foo Yong Sauce. Yield: 6 servings.

Foo Yong Sauce:
1 tablespoon cornstarch
2 teaspoons sugar
1 cup water
2 tablespoons soy sauce
1 teaspoon vinegar

Combine cornstarch and sugar in a small saucepan.

Combine remaining ingredients; gradually add liquid mixture to cornstarch mixture, stirring constantly. Cook over medium heat, stirring constantly, until thickened and bubbly. Reduce heat, and simmer 1 minute. Yield: about 1 cup. *Mrs. Roland Guest, Jr.,*
Jackson, Mississippi.

A Flavor Lift For Leftover Roast

Leftover roast beef can be as special as the first time around with these two recipes. Carry-Along Beef Pies calls for chopped roast beef and vegetables to be baked in a flaky turnover pastry. And Roast Beef Salad can be spread between bread slices or, for a lighter meal, stuffed into a tomato.

ROAST BEEF SALAD

4 cups ground cooked roast beef
½ cup chopped celery
½ cup chopped sweet pickle
1 tablespoon prepared mustard
1 cup mayonnaise
¼ teaspoon salt

Combine all ingredients, mixing well; chill 1 to 2 hours. Yield: 8 servings.

Gloria Pedersen,
Corinth, Mississippi.

CARRY-ALONG BEEF PIES

½ teaspoon instant beef bouillon granules
2 tablespoons boiling water
1¾ cups chopped cooked roast beef
½ cup chopped cooked potatoes
½ cup chopped cooked carrots
1 medium onion, chopped
2 tablespoons sweet pickle relish
2 tablespoons catsup
⅛ teaspoon ground savory
¼ teaspoon salt
Dash of pepper
Flaky Pastry

Dissolve bouillon in boiling water, and set aside.

Combine next 9 ingredients; pour bouillion over top. Stir gently to mix, and set aside.

Divide pastry dough in half; roll one part out to ⅛-inch thickness on a lightly floured surface. Cut into four 5½-inch squares; repeat with remaining dough. Place about ⅓ cup meat mixture in center of each square, and fold pastry in half diagonally to make a triangle. Moisten edges with water, and press with a fork to seal. Prick tops with fork.

Place beef pies on lightly greased baking sheets, and bake at 425° for 25 to 30 minutes or until lightly browned. Yield: 8 servings.

Flaky Pastry:

3 cups all-purpose flour
1½ teaspoons salt
1 cup plus 3 tablespoons shortening
About ¾ cup cold water

Combine flour and salt; cut in shortening with pastry blender until mixture resembles coarse meal. Sprinkle cold water by tablespoonfuls evenly over surface; stir with a fork until all ingredients are moistened. Add more water, if necessary. Shape dough into a ball. Yield: enough for 8 beef pies.

Pam Snellgrove,
La Grange, Georgia.

Simplify Cream Soups With Microwaves

If you've ever attempted to prepare a cream soup and found it sticking, scorching, or lumping, you know it can be tricky. A microwave oven eliminates these problems, and you don't have to constantly stir the soup, either.

Here we present some basic tips, along with a variety of recipes designed to acquaint you with the ease of microwaving cream soups. A time range is given in each recipe to allow for the difference in wattage of microwave ovens. To prevent overcooking, always check for doneness at the lower end of the range.

—Almost any soup will convert to microwaving. Since less liquid evaporates than during conventional cooking, you may need to increase the thickening agent or decrease the liquid.

—Microwaved liquids boil higher than conventionally cooked liquids, so select a container twice as large as the volume of the soup; this will prevent boilovers.

—If a recipe specifies covering, use the container's lid (if it's microwave safe), heavy-duty plastic wrap, or waxed paper. If the cooking time is long, plastic wrap and waxed paper may need to be replaced during the cooking cycle.

—Cream soups made with milk can be microwaved at HIGH power. If made with cream, microwave at MEDIUM to prevent curdling unless the soup contains a thickening agent, such as flour or cornstarch, to stabilize the mixture. Use MEDIUM for soups thickened with eggs.

—Microwaved soups need to be stirred occasionally to blend ingredients and ensure even cooking. Stirring at 2-minute intervals is sufficient for most soups that contain a thickening agent. Those without thickening agents require less frequent stirring.

—Cheese attracts microwave energy and will cook more rapidly than foods with a lower fat content. Since overcooking will cause cheese to become tough and stringy, always add it to soup toward the end of the microwave cycle.

BACON-TOPPED CHEESE SOUP

6 slices bacon, chopped
½ cup finely chopped celery
½ cup finely chopped carrot
½ cup finely chopped onion
½ cup finely chopped green pepper
⅓ cup all-purpose flour
½ teaspoon salt
¼ teaspoon pepper
2 cups half-and-half
1 cup milk
1 (14½-ounce) can clear chicken broth
2 cups (8 ounces) shredded sharp
    Cheddar cheese

Place bacon in a 3-quart casserole; cover and microwave at HIGH 6 to 9 minutes or until done. Remove bacon with a slotted spoon, reserving drippings in casserole; set bacon aside.

Add vegetables to drippings; microwave at HIGH 6 to 8 minutes or until tender. Blend in flour, salt, and pepper; stir well. Gradually stir in half-and-half, milk, and chicken broth. Cover and microwave at HIGH 7 to 11 minutes or until thickened and bubbly, stirring at 2-minute intervals. Add cheese, stirring until melted. Cover and microwave at MEDIUM 2 minutes. Top each serving with bacon. Yield: 9 cups.

CREAMY CRAB SOUP

1 (6-ounce) package frozen crabmeat
2 (10¾-ounce) cans cream of celery soup, undiluted
2½ cups milk
1 cup half-and-half
2 tablespoons butter or margarine
2 hard-cooked eggs, chopped
½ teaspoon Old Bay seasoning
½ teaspoon Worcestershire sauce
⅛ teaspoon garlic salt
¼ teaspoon white pepper
¼ cup dry sherry
Fresh parsley sprigs (optional)

Thaw crabmeat according to package directions; drain and flake. Set aside.

Combine next 10 ingredients in a 3-quart casserole. Cover and microwave at HIGH 4 minutes; stir well. Cover and microwave at MEDIUM 5 minutes. Stir in crabmeat; cover and microwave at MEDIUM 6 to 8 minutes or until thoroughly heated. Garnish each serving with a parsley sprig, if desired. Yield: about 2 quarts.

CREAM OF POTATO SOUP

3 cups diced potatoes
1 cup sliced celery
¾ cup chopped onion
1 tablespoon chopped fresh parsley
½ cup water
2 tablespoons butter or margarine
1 teaspoon instant chicken bouillon
    granules
½ teaspoon salt
¼ teaspoon pepper
2 cups half-and-half
2 tablespoons all-purpose flour

Combine first 9 ingredients in a 3-quart casserole. Cover and microwave at HIGH 4 minutes; stir well. Cover and microwave at HIGH 7 to 9 minutes or until vegetables are tender, stirring once.

Combine ¼ cup half-and-half and flour in a jar. Cover tightly, and shake vigorously until combined. Combine flour mixture and remaining half-and-half; gradually stir into vegetable mixture. Cover and microwave at HIGH for 3 minutes; stir well. Cover and microwave at HIGH 2 to 4 minutes or until thickened and bubbly, stirring at 2-minute intervals. Yield: 1 quart.

CREAM OF BROCCOLI SOUP

1 (14½-ounce) can chicken broth
2 (10-ounce) packages frozen chopped
  broccoli, thawed
½ cup chopped onion
½ teaspoon Worcestershire sauce
¼ teaspoon celery salt
¼ teaspoon white pepper
⅛ teaspoon salt
⅛ teaspoon garlic powder
2 cups half-and-half
2 tablespoons cornstarch

Combine first 8 ingredients in a 3-quart casserole. Cover with heavy-duty plastic wrap; microwave at HIGH for 3 to 5 minutes or until broccoli is crisp-tender.

Combine 1 cup half-and-half and cornstarch in a small bowl, blending well; stir in remaining half-and-half. Gradually stir cornstarch mixture into broccoli mixture. Cover and microwave at HIGH for 3 minutes; stir well. Cover and microwave at HIGH for 6 to 9 minutes or until thickened and bubbly, stirring at 2-minute intervals. Yield: 6½ cups.

Loaf Breads Can Be Quick Or Yeasty

Bite into a still-warm slice of Country Crust Bread, and you'll know it was well worth the time spent in kneading the yeast dough and allowing it to rise.

That's not to say, however, that delicious loaf breads can't be prepared in a hurry. Hawaiian Loaf and Orange Nut Loaf prove that point. Both are quick breads, ready to enjoy in just the time it takes to mix and bake.

HAWAIIAN LOAF

1 cup margarine, softened
2 cups sugar
4 eggs
1 cup mashed ripe banana
4 cups all-purpose flour
2 teaspoons baking powder
1 teaspoon soda
¾ teaspoon salt
1 (15¼-ounce) can crushed pineapple,
  undrained
1 cup flaked coconut

Cream margarine; gradually add sugar, beating until light and fluffy. Add eggs, beating well; stir in banana.

Combine flour, baking powder, soda, and salt; add to creamed mixture, mixing just until smooth. Fold in pineapple and coconut. Spoon into 2 greased and floured 9- x 5- x 3-inch loafpans. Bake at 350° for 1 hour or until bread tests done. Yield: 2 loaves. *Cindy Murphy, Cleveland, Tennessee.*

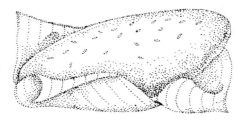

COUNTRY CRUST BREAD

2 packages dry yeast
2 cups warm water (105° to 115°)
½ cup sugar
1 tablespoon salt
2 eggs, beaten
¼ cup vegetable oil
6 cups unbleached flour
Vegetable oil
Melted butter

Dissolve yeast in water, and let stand 5 minutes; add sugar, salt, eggs, ¼ cup vegetable oil, and 3 cups flour. Mix well, and gradually stir in remaining flour.

Turn dough out on a floured surface, and knead until smooth and elastic (about 8 to 10 minutes). Shape dough into a ball; place in a well-greased bowl, turning to grease top. Cover and let rise in a warm place (85°), free from drafts, 1½ to 2 hours or until doubled in bulk.

Punch dough down; divide in half, and place on a floured surface. Roll each half into an 18- x 9-inch rectangle.

Beginning at narrow edge, roll up dough; press firmly as you roll to eliminate air pockets. Pinch seam and ends together to seal. Place loaves, seam side down, in well-greased 9- x 5- x 3-inch loafpans. Brush top of each with vegetable oil.

Cover loaves and let rise until doubled in bulk. Bake on lower rack of oven at 375° for 30 to 35 minutes or until loaves sound hollow when tapped. Remove from pans, and brush with melted butter. Yield: 2 loaves.
Mrs. E. F. Bastable, Chevy Chase, Maryland.

POTATO LIGHTBREAD

1 (2-ounce) package or 1 cup instant
  potato flakes
2 packages dry yeast
2 cups water (105° to 115°)
¼ cup plus 2 tablespoons sugar
1 teaspoon salt
6 tablespoons margarine, melted
2 cups milk
2 eggs, well beaten
12 cups all-purpose flour, divided

Prepare instant potatoes according to package directions.

Dissolve yeast in warm water in a large bowl; let stand 5 minutes. Add sugar, salt, margarine, milk, and potatoes; mix well. Add eggs, mixing well. Gradually beat in 8 cups flour; add remaining flour, mixing well.

Turn dough out on a floured surface, and knead until smooth and elastic (about 8 to 10 minutes). Place in a well-greased bowl, turning to grease top. Cover and let rise in a warm place (85°), free from drafts, 1½ to 2 hours or until doubled in bulk.

Punch dough down; divide into 4 portions, and shape each into a loaf. Place in well-greased 9- x 5- x 3-inch loafpans. Let rise until doubled in bulk; bake at 425° for 10 minutes. Reduce heat to 350°; bake an additional 35 to 40 minutes or until loaves sound hollow when tapped. Yield: 4 loaves.
Mrs. Hugh F. Mosher, Huntsville, Alabama.

Tip: When you use a lot of nonfat dry milk, measure the easy way: Mark the level of powder and water on side of a plastic container with an indelible marker. No need to measure next time.

ORANGE NUT LOAF

½ cup shortening
1¼ cups sugar
2 eggs
2 cups all-purpose flour
1½ teaspoons baking powder
1 teaspoon salt
½ cup orange juice
1 tablespoon grated orange rind
½ cup chopped pecans

Cream shortening; gradually add sugar, beating until light and fluffy. Add eggs, one at a time, beating well after each addition.

Combine flour, baking powder, and salt; add to creamed mixture, mixing until smooth. Gradually add orange juice, beating just until blended. Stir in orange rind and pecans.

Spoon batter into a greased and floured 9- x 5- x 3-inch loafpan; bake at 350° for 60 to 65 minutes or until bread tests done. Yield: 1 loaf.

Mrs. S. Sealy Wilbanks, Jr.,
Alexander City, Alabama.

Get Your "Apple A Day" In Cake, Bread

It's hard to beat the taste of a plump, juicy apple, but you'll find that these apple specialties will make a good thing even better.

It'll be easy to have your "apple a day" with Apple Coconut Cake. It includes lots of chopped apples, pecans, and coconut and is drizzled with a caramel glaze.

Apple Bread, chock full of apples, raisins, and walnuts, is perfect for a special breakfast bread or for after-school snacks. And for a spectacular fall dessert, try Apple Baked Alaska, a new version of an old classic. Apples baked with sugar and spices are topped with vanilla ice cream and meringue.

APPLE-NUT SALAD

2 eggs, well beaten
½ cup sugar
½ cup vinegar
6 large apples, peeled and diced
1 cup pecans, coarsely chopped
2 tablespoons whipping cream

Combine eggs, sugar, and vinegar; cook over medium heat, stirring constantly, until thickened. Remove from heat, and beat until smooth; cool.

Combine apples and pecans. Add whipping cream to cooled egg mixture. Pour over the apple-pecan mixture; stir gently to mix. Yield: 6 servings.

Charlotte A. Pierce,
Greensburg, Kentucky.

APPLE BREAD

½ cup butter or margarine, softened
1 cup sugar
2 eggs
1 teaspoon soda
2 tablespoons buttermilk
2 cups all-purpose flour
1 teaspoon vanilla extract
2 cups peeled, diced cooking apples
½ cup walnuts, chopped
½ cup raisins
1 tablespoon butter or margarine, melted
¼ cup firmly packed brown sugar
¼ teaspoon ground cinnamon

Cream ½ cup butter, gradually adding sugar; beat until light and fluffy. Add eggs, one at a time, beating well after each addition.

Dissolve soda in buttermilk; add to batter, mixing well. Stir in flour. Add vanilla, and stir well. Stir in apples, walnuts, and raisins. Spoon into 2 greased and floured 7½- x 3- x 2-inch loafpans. Drizzle melted butter over loaves. Combine brown sugar and cinnamon; stir well, and sprinkle over loaves. Bake at 350° for about 40 to 45 minutes. Cool in pan 5 minutes; turn out on wire rack. Yield: 2 loaves.

Gladys Johnston,
Elberton, Georgia.

APPLE COCONUT CAKE

3 cups all-purpose flour
1 teaspoon soda
1 teaspoon salt
1 cup vegetable oil
3 eggs
2¼ cups sugar
2 teaspoons vanilla extract
2 cups chopped pecans
3 cups peeled, chopped cooking apples
½ cup flaked coconut
Glaze (recipe follows)

Combine flour, soda, and salt; mix well, and set aside.

Combine oil, eggs, sugar, and vanilla; beat at medium speed of electric mixer

for 2 minutes. Add flour mixture; mix at low speed just until blended. Fold in pecans, apples, and coconut. (Batter will be stiff.)

Spoon into a greased and floured 10-inch tube pan. Bake at 350° for 1 hour and 20 minutes or until cake tests done. Cool in pan 10 minutes. Remove from pan; immediately drizzle glaze over cake. Yield: one 10-inch cake.

Glaze:

½ cup firmly packed light brown sugar
¼ cup milk
½ cup butter or margarine

Combine all ingredients in a heavy saucepan; bring to a full boil and cook, stirring constantly, for 2 minutes. Let cool to lukewarm. Yield: about 1 cup.

Peggy Hester,
Russellville, Alabama.

APPLE BAKED ALASKA

4 cups thinly sliced cooking apples
½ cup raisins
¼ cup water
½ cup firmly packed brown sugar
1 teaspoon ground cinnamon
¼ teaspoon ground nutmeg
1 pint vanilla ice cream
4 egg whites
⅛ teaspoon salt
½ cup sugar

Combine apples, raisins, and water. In a separate bowl, combine brown sugar, cinnamon, and nutmeg; stir well. Add brown sugar mixture to apple mixture, and stir well. Spoon apple mixture into a 2½-quart baking dish. Bake at 350° for 35 minutes, stirring occasionally. Refrigerate until well chilled.

Spoon rounded tablespoons of ice cream evenly over apple mixture. Place dish in freezer while preparing the meringue.

Beat egg whites (at room temperature) until frothy; add salt, and continue beating. Gradually add sugar, beating well after each addition; continue beating until stiff and glossy. Do not underbeat.

Remove ice cream-topped apples from freezer. Quickly spread meringue over entire surface, making sure the edges are sealed.

Bake at 450° for 2 to 3 minutes or until meringue peaks are browned. Serve immediately. Yield: 8 servings.

Mrs. W. P. Chambers,
Louisville, Kentucky.

Cornish Hens, Stuffed And Baked To Perfection

When the occasion calls for a sophisticated entrée, nothing fills the bill like a beautifully garnished platter of baked Cornish hens. Here are two delicious versions that both feature a rich, moist stuffing of rice and mushrooms. Elegant Cornish Hens are basted with a seasoned soy sauce mixture during baking, while Cornish Hens Flambé are flamed in brandy for their final touch.

A note on how to flambé the hens. To produce enough fumes to ignite, the brandy must be heated quickly. Warm the brandy, ignite it, and pour the flaming liquid evenly over the food.

An alternate method is to warm the spirit, pour it over the food, and then ignite. But in testing this method, we found that the alcohol dispersed and diluted when poured over the food, making it more difficult to ignite.

ELEGANT CORNISH HENS

1 (6-ounce) package long grain and wild
   rice mix
1 chicken bouillon cube
4 (1- to 1½-pound) Cornish hens
½ cup chopped onion
½ cup chopped celery
1 tablespoon butter or margarine, melted
¼ pound fresh mushrooms, sliced
1 teaspoon grated lemon rind
1 teaspoon poultry seasoning
¼ cup vegetable oil
¼ cup lemon juice
2 tablespoons soy sauce
1 teaspoon paprika
½ teaspoon garlic salt
Dash of white pepper
Lemon slices (optional)
Parsley (optional)

Cook rice according to package directions, adding bouillon cube with rice and seasoning.

Remove giblets from hens; reserve for another use. Rinse hens with cold water, and pat dry.

Sauté onion and celery in butter; add mushrooms, and cook 1 to 2 minutes. Combine rice, vegetables, lemon rind, and poultry seasoning, stirring well.

Stuff hens lightly with the rice mixture. Close cavities, and secure with toothpicks; truss.

Combine next 6 ingredients, stirring well. Brush hens with soy sauce mixture, and place breast side up in 13- x 9- x 2-inch baking pan. Bake at 325° for 1¼ to 1½ hours, depending on size of hens; baste often with soy sauce mixture. Garnish with lemon slices and parsley, if desired. Yield: 4 servings.
Mrs. Leo Cole,
Lake Charles, Louisiana.

CORNISH HENS FLAMBE

1 large onion, minced
2 tablespoons butter or margarine, melted
2 cups mushrooms, sliced
½ cup diced cooked ham
1½ cups cooked wild rice
2 to 4 tablespoons brandy
¼ teaspoon dried whole marjoram
¼ teaspoon dried whole thyme
6 (1- to 1½-pound) Cornish hens
Salt
Coarsely ground black pepper
2 to 4 tablespoons dry sherry
¼ cup chicken broth
¼ cup brandy

Sauté onion in butter until tender. Add mushrooms and ham; cook 3 to 5 minutes or until mushrooms are tender. Combine mushroom mixture, rice, 2 to 4 tablespoons brandy, marjoram, and thyme.

Remove giblets from hens; reserve for another use. Rinse hens with cold water, and pat dry; sprinkle with salt and pepper. Stuff hens lightly with rice mixture. Close cavities, and secure with toothpicks; truss. Place hens breast side up in a 15- x 10- x 1-inch jellyroll pan. Bake hens at 350° for 1¼ to 1½ hours, depending on size of hens.

Place hens on serving platter. Combine sherry and chicken broth; brush over hens. Heat ¼ cup brandy in a small saucepan over medium heat. (Do not boil.) Ignite with a long match, and pour over hens. After flames die down, serve immediately. Yield: 6 servings.
Mrs. H. S. Wright,
Leesville, South Carolina.

Tip: Always try to use a meat thermometer when roasting. This can usually prevent overcooking. Get in the habit of using a minute-timer for precise cooking. Do follow your recipes; they were meant as a guide.

Stir-Fry A Crowd Pleaser

Even people who think they don't like Chinese food like Sweet-and-Sour Pork. None of the ingredients is mysterious or "foreign," but the stir-fry method of cooking is decidedly Oriental. Each chunk of pork and piece of pepper is bathed in a smooth, sweet sauce, which should suit even the most confirmed American in the family.

SWEET-AND-SOUR PORK

2 tablespoons peanut oil
1¼ pounds boneless pork shoulder, cut
   into 1-inch cubes (about 2½ cups)
1 teaspoon garlic salt
⅛ teaspoon pepper
1¾ cups water
2 medium-size green peppers, cut into
   1-inch pieces
½ cup raisins
⅓ cup sugar
⅓ cup vinegar
2 tablespoons cornstarch
¼ cup soy sauce
3 cups hot cooked rice

Pour oil around top of preheated wok, coating sides; allow to heat at medium high (325°) for 2 minutes. Add pork, and stir-fry about 5 to 6 minutes. Add garlic salt, pepper, and water. Reduce heat to low (225°); cover and simmer about 25 minutes or until pork is very tender.

Add green pepper; cook, uncovered, about 4 minutes. Stir in raisins, sugar, and vinegar. Dissolve cornstarch in soy sauce, and add to pork mixture. Cook, stirring constantly, until thickened and bubbly. Serve over rice. Yield: 4 to 5 servings.
Lois Rodriquez,
Henryetta, Oklahoma.

Enjoy A Colorful Corn Chowder

A steaming bowl of chowder—filled with corn and cheese and served with a crisp salad and bread—is a perfect choice for lunch or a light supper.

The creamy base of Corn and Cheese Chowder is thick with cream-style corn and melting Cheddar; bits of tomato give additional flavor and color.

CORN AND CHEESE CHOWDER

2 cups water
2 cups diced potatoes
½ cup chopped onion
½ cup diced celery
2 tablespoons margarine
½ teaspoon dried whole basil
1 large bay leaf
1 (17-ounce) can cream-style corn
2 cups milk
1 cup canned tomatoes, chopped
2 teaspoons salt
⅛ teaspoon pepper
½ cup (2 ounces) shredded Cheddar cheese
1 tablespoon minced fresh parsley

Combine first 7 ingredients in a large Dutch oven; bring to a boil. Reduce heat, and simmer about 10 minutes or until potatoes are tender. Discard bay leaf. Stir in corn, milk, tomatoes, salt, and pepper; heat thoroughly. Add cheese; cook over low heat, stirring constantly, until cheese is melted. Sprinkle parsley over chowder. Yield: 8 to 10 servings.
Lily Jo Drake,
Melbourne Beach, Florida.

Feast On Fall's Sweet Harvest

Turn fall's harvest of crunchy pecans, sweet persimmons, and cool, crisp apples into luscious Southern baked goods. Other harvest crops, like sweet potatoes and pumpkins, add moistness and robust flavor to this temptation of recipes.

SWEET POTATO PUDDING

2 eggs, beaten
¾ to 1 cup sugar
2 cups grated raw sweet potatoes
1 (13-ounce) can evaporated milk
½ cup milk
½ teaspoon ground cinnamon
½ teaspoon ground nutmeg
½ teaspoon salt
⅓ cup butter or margarine, melted
1 cup flaked coconut

Combine eggs and sugar in a large mixing bowl, beating well; stir in remaining ingredients. Pour into a greased 1½-quart casserole. Bake at 350° for 1 hour. Yield: 6 to 8 servings.
Thelma M. Skelton,
Manassas, Virginia.

PUMPKIN PANCAKES

1 small pumpkin
1½ cups pancake mix
¼ cup wheat germ
2 tablespoons sugar
¼ teaspoon ground cinnamon
¼ teaspoon ground nutmeg
¼ teaspoon ground ginger
2 eggs, separated
1½ cups milk
2 tablespoons vegetable oil
Maple-Nut Syrup or Orange Syrup

Wash pumpkin, and cut in half crosswise. Place halves, cut side down, in a 15- x 10- x 1-inch jellyroll pan. Bake at 325° for 45 minutes or until tender; cool.

Peel pumpkin, and discard seeds. Puree pulp in food processor, or mash thoroughly. Set aside ½ cup pumpkin; store remainder in refrigerator for other uses for up to 5 days. (If desired, substitute ½ cup canned mashed pumpkin.)

Combine pancake mix, wheat germ, sugar, and spices in a large mixing bowl. Beat egg yolks. Stir in milk, pumpkin, and oil; add to dry ingredients all at once, stirring just until moistened (batter will be lumpy). Beat egg whites until stiff; fold into batter.

Cook pancakes on a hot, lightly greased griddle using about ¼ cup batter for each. Turn pancakes when tops are covered with bubbles and edges look cooked. Serve with Maple-Nut Syrup or Orange Syrup. Yield: 4 to 5 servings.

Note: To serve these pancakes as a dessert, substitute 5 to 6 tablespoons brown sugar for regular sugar. Top with whipped cream or ice cream.

Maple-Nut Syrup:

1 cup maple or maple-flavored syrup
1 tablespoon butter or margarine
½ cup chopped walnuts or pecans

Combine syrup and butter in a saucepan; bring to a boil. Remove from heat; stir in walnuts. Serve hot. Yield: about 1½ cups.

Orange Syrup:

½ cup orange juice
⅓ cup light corn syrup
1 tablespoon butter or margarine

Combine all ingredients; cook over medium heat 5 minutes. Serve hot. Yield: about 1 cup. *James L. Strieber,*
Crofton, Maryland.

PERSIMMON BREAD

2 cups all-purpose flour
2 teaspoons baking powder
½ teaspoon soda
½ teaspoon salt
1 teaspoon ground cinnamon
½ teaspoon ground nutmeg
1 cup sugar
1 cup persimmon pulp
½ cup milk
2 eggs, slightly beaten
¼ cup butter, softened
1 cup chopped pecans or walnuts

Combine flour, baking powder, soda, salt, cinnamon, and nutmeg; stir lightly, and set aside.

Combine sugar, persimmon pulp, milk, and eggs; mix well. Add flour mixture and butter, mixing well. Stir in pecans. Spoon batter into a greased and floured 9- x 5- x 3-inch loafpan. Bake at 350° for 45 minutes or until bread tests done. Yield: one loaf.
Captain Hugh Poole,
Conyers, Georgia.

APPLE-NUT COOKIES

¾ cup shortening
1 cup firmly packed brown sugar
1 egg
1 teaspoon water
1½ cups all-purpose flour
1 teaspoon baking powder
½ teaspoon soda
½ teaspoon salt
1 teaspoon ground cinnamon
¼ teaspoon ground nutmeg
1 cup finely chopped apple
1½ cups regular oats, uncooked
½ cup raisins
½ cup chopped walnuts

Toasting pecans in butter brings out the full flavor of the nut in Butter Pecan Cake.

Cream shortening; gradually add sugar, beating until light and fluffy and sugar is dissolved. Beat in egg and water. Add next 6 ingredients, beating 2 minutes on medium speed of electric mixer. Stir in apple, oats, raisins, and walnuts.

Drop dough by heaping teaspoonfuls onto lightly greased baking sheets. Bake at 375° for 10 to 12 minutes. Yield: about 5 dozen.   *Betty R. Butts,*
Kensington, Maryland.

Tip: For perfectly shaped round cookies, pack homemade refrigerator cookie dough into clean 6-ounce juice cans (don't remove bottoms) and freeze. Thaw about 15 minutes, open bottom and push up, using the top edge as a cutting guide.

BUTTER PECAN CAKE

3 tablespoons butter or margarine
1⅓ cups chopped pecans
⅔ cup butter or margarine, softened
1⅓ cups sugar
2 eggs
2 cups all-purpose flour
1½ teaspoons baking powder
¼ teaspoon salt
⅔ cup milk
1½ teaspoons vanilla extract
Butter Pecan Frosting

Melt 3 tablespoons butter in a 13- x 9- x 2-inch baking pan. Stir in pecans, and bake at 350° for 10 minutes. Cool.

Cream softened butter in a large mixing bowl; gradually add sugar, beating until light and fluffy and sugar is dissolved. Add eggs, one at a time, beating well after each addition.

Combine flour, baking powder, and salt; add to creamed mixture alternately with milk, beginning and ending with flour mixture. Stir in vanilla and 1 cup pecans, reserving remaining pecans for Butter Pecan Frosting.

Pour batter into 2 greased and floured 9-inch cakepans. Bake at 350° for 30 minutes or until cake tests done. Cool layers in pans 10 minutes; remove from pans, and cool completely.

Spread Butter Pecan Frosting between layers and on top and sides of cake. Yield: one 2-layer cake.

Butter Pecan Frosting:

3 tablespoons butter or margarine, softened
3 cups powdered sugar
3 tablespoons plus 1 teaspoon milk
¾ teaspoon vanilla extract
Reserved toasted pecans

Cream butter; add sugar, milk, and vanilla, beating until light and fluffy. Stir in reserved toasted pecans. Yield: enough frosting for one 2-layer cake.
Mrs. Donald C. Vanhoy,
Salisbury, North Carolina.

Meet A New Vegetable

In the South, you'll find chayotes growing in Louisiana and Florida, but they may be known by other names. In Louisiana, they're known as mirlitons, and Floridians call them vegetable pears. Regardless of what you call them, they're one of the most versatile vegetables in the kitchen.

CHAYOTES AND SHRIMP CASSEROLE

2 or 3 large chayotes
½ cup chopped onion
1 cup chopped green onion
¾ cup chopped fresh parsley
2 stalks celery, chopped
⅔ cup chopped green pepper
2 or 3 cloves garlic, minced
1 small bay leaf
2 tablespoons melted butter or margarine
1½ pounds medium shrimp, peeled and deveined
1 egg, beaten
1 cup soft breadcrumbs
Butter or margarine

Peel chayotes, and cut in half lengthwise; remove seeds. Cut into 1-inch cubes; cook in boiling salted water to cover until tender, about 15 to 20 minutes. Drain well, and set aside.

Sauté onion, parsley, celery, green pepper, garlic, and bay leaf in 2 tablespoons butter until tender; stir in shrimp and chayotes. Simmer, stirring occasionally, 3 to 5 minutes or until shrimp turn pink. Remove bay leaf. Quickly stir in egg and breadcrumbs.

Spoon shrimp mixture into a buttered 2-quart shallow baking dish. Dot with butter; bake at 350° for 25 to 30 minutes. Yield: 6 to 8 servings.

Patti Buckley,
Kenner, Louisiana.

FRIED CHAYOTES

2 chayotes, peeled
1 egg, well beaten
¾ to 1 cup cracker crumbs
½ cup melted butter or margarine

Cook chayotes in boiling salted water 20 to 30 minutes or until tender. Drain and allow to cool.

Cut chayotes crosswise into ½-inch slices; remove seeds. Dip slices into egg; coat with cracker crumbs. Sauté chayotes in butter over medium heat until golden brown, turning once. Drain on paper towels. Serve hot. Yield: 4 to 6 servings.

Florence L. Costello,
Chattanooga, Tennessee.

CHAYOTE-CHEESE BAKE

5 to 6 medium chayotes
6 slices bacon
1 large onion, finely chopped
½ green pepper, finely chopped
1 (10¾-ounce) can cream of mushroom soup, undiluted
1 cup (4 ounces) shredded American cheese
⅛ to ¼ teaspoon garlic powder
Salt and pepper to taste
½ cup Italian-style breadcrumbs
2 tablespoons melted butter or margarine

Peel chayotes, and cut in half; remove seeds. Dice chayotes. Cook in boiling salted water to cover until tender, about 20 minutes. Drain well.

Cook bacon until crisp; remove bacon and drain on paper towels, reserving drippings. Crumble bacon, and set aside. Sauté onion and green pepper in bacon drippings until tender. Remove from heat; stir in soup, cheese, garlic powder, salt, and pepper. Add cooked chayotes, mashing slightly with a fork. Stir in half of crumbled bacon, and pour into a greased 2-quart casserole.

Combine breadcrumbs and butter; mix well. Sprinkle crumbs over casserole, and top with the remaining bacon. Bake at 350° for 20 minutes or until bubbly. Yield: 8 servings. *Pat Andrus,*
Scott, Louisiana.

This Bread Swirls With Flavor

If your family quibbles over their preference for white bread, whole wheat, and rye, here is just the solution. It's a unique Marble Loaf, with separate whole wheat-rye and white bread doughs kneaded together into a loaf that literally swirls with flavor.

MARBLE LOAF

Whole Wheat-Rye Dough:

2 cups whole wheat flour
2 cups rye flour
2½ cups all-purpose flour
1 tablespoon sugar
1 tablespoon salt
2 packages dry yeast
2¼ cups water
¾ cup cornmeal
⅓ cup molasses
3 tablespoons butter or margarine
1 tablespoon caraway seeds

Combine all flour, stirring well. Combine sugar, salt, yeast, and 1½ cups flour in a large mixing bowl; stir well.

Combine water, cornmeal, molasses, butter, and caraway seeds; place over low heat until butter melts, stirring occasionally. Cool liquid mixture to 120° to 130°.

Gradually add liquid mixture to flour-yeast mixture, beating well at high speed of electric mixer. Beat 2 additional minutes at medium speed. Gradually add enough of remaining flour to form a moderately stiff dough, beating well after each addition.

Turn dough out onto a lightly floured surface, and knead until smooth and elastic (about 10 minutes). Shape into a ball, and place in a well-greased bowl; turn to grease top. Cover and let rise in a warm place (85°), free from drafts, for 1½ hours or until doubled in bulk.

White Dough:

About 6 cups all-purpose flour, divided
3 tablespoons sugar
2½ teaspoons salt
1 package dry yeast
1½ cups water
½ cup milk
3 tablespoons butter or margarine
1 egg white, slightly beaten

Combine 2 cups flour, sugar, salt, and yeast in a large mixing bowl; stir well. Combine water, milk, and butter; place over low heat until butter melts, stirring occasionally. Cool liquid mixture to 120° to 130°.

Gradually add liquid mixture to flour mixture, beating well at high speed of electric mixer. Beat 2 additional minutes at medium speed. Gradually add ¾ cup flour, beating 2 minutes at medium speed. Gradually add enough of remaining flour to form a soft dough, beating well after each addition.

Turn dough out onto a floured surface, and knead until smooth and elastic (about 10 minutes). Shape into a ball, and place in a well-greased bowl; turn to grease top. Cover and let rise in a warm place (85°), free from drafts, for 1 hour or until doubled in bulk.

Shaping the Loaf:

Punch whole wheat-rye dough down; divide into 2 equal portions. Place each portion on a lightly floured surface. Cover and let rest 15 minutes.

Repeat procedure with white dough.

Combine 1 portion whole wheat-rye dough and 1 portion white dough; lightly knead 12 to 15 times.

Roll combined dough into a 16- x 9-inch rectangle. Roll up rectangle crosswise; pinch seam and ends to seal. Place loaf, seam side down, on a greased baking sheet. Cover and let rise in a warm place (85°), free from drafts, 1 hour or until doubled in bulk.

Brush loaf with half of egg white. Bake at 400° for 40 minutes or until loaf sounds hollow when tapped. Transfer loaf to wire rack to cool.

Repeat procedure with remaining dough. Yield: 2 loaves.

Sue-Sue Hartstern,
Louisville, Kentucky.

Salads With Rice And More

Once you taste Rice Salad With Fresh Mushrooms, we think you'll agree that a rice salad is an excellent alternative to a potato dish. A rice and vegetable mixture is marinated in a commercial salad dressing, making the preparation time short, too.

Shrimp and Rice Salad has added zip when the shrimp are cooked in a crab-boil mix.

Rice is cooked with bouillon cubes, combined with vegetables, and then marinated in creamy Italian dressing for Rice Salad With Fresh Mushrooms.

RICE SALAD WITH FRESH MUSHROOMS

1 (7-ounce) package instant rice
5 chicken bouillon cubes
1 cup chopped onion
1 cup chopped green pepper
1 cup chopped celery
½ pound fresh mushrooms, sliced
1 (4-ounce) jar diced pimiento
1 (8-ounce) bottle creamy Italian dressing

Cook rice according to package directions, except omit salt and add bouillon cubes. Cool.

Combine rice and remaining ingredients; stir well. Chill thoroughly. Yield: 8 to 10 servings. *Jane Grace,* *Cyril, Oklahoma.*

SHRIMP AND RICE SALAD

6 cups water
1½ pounds unpeeled medium shrimp
1 (3-ounce) package crab-boil mix
2 cups cooked rice
½ cup commercial French dressing
½ cup diced celery
Lettuce leaves
Green pepper rings
Olives
Cherry tomatoes
Russian dressing

Bring water to a boil; add shrimp and crab-boil mix, and return to a boil.

Lower heat, and simmer 3 to 5 minutes. Drain well; rinse with cold water. Chill. Peel and devein shrimp.

Combine rice and French dressing; stir well, and let marinate in refrigerator 30 to 45 minutes. Stir shrimp and celery into rice mixture; stir well. Chill thoroughly.

Spoon salad onto lettuce; garnish with green pepper, olives, and tomatoes. Serve with Russian dressing. Yield: 4 to 6 servings. *Anna May Simmons,* *Gainesville, Florida.*

Tip: When cooking cabbage, shrimp, or other foods that cause unpleasant odors, put a dozen cloves in a small pan of boiling water and let simmer. The odor of the cloves will counteract the unpleasant odor with a delightful fragrance. (It's cheaper than commercial deodorant sprays.)

CONFETTI RICE SALAD

1 (10-ounce) package frozen English peas
2 cups cooked rice
1 medium zucchini, shredded
2 tablespoons chopped pimiento
⅔ cup vegetable oil
3 to 4 tablespoons vinegar
½ teaspoon salt
¼ teaspoon sugar
¼ teaspoon dried whole basil
Lettuce leaves (optional)

Cook peas according to package directions; drain. Combine peas, rice, zucchini, and pimiento; stir well.

Combine next 5 ingredients, stirring well; pour over rice mixture, and stir gently to combine. Drain salad; serve on lettuce leaves, if desired. Yield: 6 to 8 servings.   *Bertha Fowler,*
Woodruff, South Carolina.

RICE SALAD WITH ARTICHOKE HEARTS

1 (8-ounce) package chicken-flavored rice
1 (6-ounce) jar marinated artichoke hearts
⅔ cup mayonnaise
1 teaspoon curry powder
⅓ cup chopped green pepper
4 green onions, chopped
8 pimiento-stuffed olives, sliced

Cook rice according to package directions, except omit butter. Cool.

Drain artichokes, reserving liquid. Slice artichokes, and set aside. Combine artichoke liquid, mayonnaise, and curry powder; stir well.

Combine rice, green pepper, onion, olives, and sliced artichokes; pour mayonnaise mixture over rice mixture, and stir well. Chill thoroughly. Yield: 6 to 8 servings.   *Eloise Haynes,*
Greenville, Mississippi.

Look What Yogurt's Into

Everyone's into yogurt, and yogurt is turning up in everything. As adventuresome cooks experiment with this light, tart dairy product, the results range from refreshing breakfast drinks to rich desserts.

For instance, plain yogurt is folded into a heady blend of onion, garlic, herring, and horseradish for a vegetable and cracker dip. A rich concoction of yogurt, cream cheese, sour cream, and honey is turned into a graham cracker crust for Strawberry Yogurt Pie.

STRAWBERRY YOGURT PIE

2 cups graham cracker crumbs
⅓ cup butter, melted
¼ cup honey
1 (8-ounce) package cream cheese, softened
1 (8-ounce) carton strawberry-flavored yogurt
1 (8-ounce) carton commercial sour cream
1 teaspoon vanilla extract
⅓ cup honey
½ cup sliced fresh strawberries

Combine graham cracker crumbs, butter, and honey; blend well, and press on bottom and sides of a 9-inch pie-plate. Freeze at least 30 minutes.

Beat cream cheese on medium speed of an electric mixer until smooth and fluffy. Combine yogurt and sour cream, mixing well; add to cream cheese. Blend until smooth; stir in vanilla and honey. Pour mixture into prepared crust; freeze pie until firm.

Remove from freezer 30 minutes before serving; garnish with sliced strawberries. Yield: one 9-inch pie.

STRAWBERRY YOGURT SALAD

1 (6-ounce) package strawberry-flavored gelatin
2 cups boiling water
2 (10-ounce) packages frozen strawberries, thawed
1 (8-ounce) carton strawberry-flavored yogurt

Dissolve gelatin in boiling water. Drain strawberries, reserving juice; set strawberries aside.

Combine gelatin, reserved strawberry juice, and yogurt in container of electric blender; blend until smooth. Pour mixture into a bowl; fold in strawberries. Pour into a 12- x 8- x 2-inch dish, and chill until firm. Yield: 12 servings.
Brenda Clifford,
Shelbyville, Tennessee.

TROPICAL COFFEE CAKE

1½ cups all-purpose flour
1 cup sugar
2 teaspoons baking powder
½ teaspoon salt
1 (8-ounce) carton peach-flavored yogurt
½ cup vegetable oil
2 eggs
1 cup flaked coconut
⅓ cup sugar
1 teaspoon ground cinnamon

Combine first 7 ingredients; beat 3 minutes at medium speed of an electric mixer. Pour into a greased and floured 9-inch square pan.

Combine coconut, ⅓ cup sugar, and cinnamon; sprinkle over top. Bake at 350° for 40 minutes or until cake tests done. Yield: 9 servings.   *Nelda Hase,*
Gainesville, Georgia.

ORANGE PICK-ME-UP

1 (8-ounce) carton orange-flavored yogurt
1 cup milk
1 cup fresh orange sections
1 egg
¼ teaspoon vanilla extract
2 teaspoons sugar
2 to 3 ice cubes

Combine first 6 ingredients in container of electric blender; blend on high speed until frothy. Add ice cubes one at a time, blending until crushed. Serve immediately. Yield: about 3½ cups.
Doris Amonette,
Tulsa, Oklahoma.

YOGURT HERRING DIP

1 (8-ounce) package Neufchâtel cheese, softened
1 small onion, quartered
1 small clove garlic
1 (3¼-ounce) can kippered herring, drained
¼ teaspoon salt
⅛ teaspoon pepper
1 tablespoon prepared horseradish, undrained
1 (8-ounce) carton plain yogurt

Combine first 7 ingredients in container of food processor or electric blender; process until smooth. Remove mixture to a bowl; fold in yogurt. Serve with fresh vegetables or assorted crackers. Yield: about 2½ cups.

Marie Hayman,
Lake Worth, Florida.

The Best Pizza Is Homemade

If your yen for pizza keeps you going back to the local pizza parlor, consider making your own. No question, making pizza from scratch takes some time, but you'll be rewarded with a bubbling-hot creation with a flavor unsurpassed outside your own kitchen. To master the techniques, use the recipe that follows and the step-by-step instructions illustrated in the photographs on page 234.

Good pizza begins with the crust. In Best Ever Homemade Pizza, it's a light, crusty foundation for homemade tomato sauce and ground beef. Toppings may vary according to taste—pepperoni, ripe olives, and mushrooms—but we suggest freshly shredded Cheddar and mozzarella, with a final sprinkling of Parmesan after baking.

Take one bite of Best Ever Homemade Pizza, and you'll never settle for bought pizza again.

BEST EVER HOMEMADE PIZZA

2 (1-pound) cans tomatoes, undrained and chopped
2 small green peppers, chopped
2 small onions, chopped
2 bay leaves
2 teaspoons salt
2 teaspoons sugar
1 teaspoon dried whole oregano
⅛ teaspoon pepper
Pizza crust (recipe follows)
1½ pounds ground beef
1 teaspoon salt
1 (3½-ounce) package sliced pepperoni (optional)
1½ cups sliced ripe olives (optional)
1 (4-ounce) can sliced mushrooms, drained (optional)
3 cups (12 ounces) shredded Cheddar cheese
3 cups (12 ounces) shredded mozzarella cheese
½ cup grated Parmesan cheese

Combine first 8 ingredients in a large saucepan. Simmer over low heat 1 hour or until thickened, stirring occasionally. Remove bay leaves. Spread sauce evenly over each pizza crust, leaving a ½-inch border around edges.

Combine ground beef and 1 teaspoon salt in a skillet; cook over medium heat until meat is no longer pink, stirring to crumble. Drain well on paper towels.

Spoon meat over tomato sauce. If desired, top with pepperoni, olives, and mushrooms. Bake pizza at 450° for 10 minutes.

Sprinkle pizzas with Cheddar and mozzarella cheese. Bake an additional 10 minutes. Remove from oven, and sprinkle with Parmesan cheese. Yield: two 12-inch pizzas.

Pizza Crust:

1 cup boiling water
2 tablespoons shortening
¼ teaspoon salt
1 package dry yeast
3 to 4 cups all-purpose flour

Combine water, shortening, and salt in a large mixing bowl; stir until shortening is melted. Let cool to lukewarm (105° to 115°). Sprinkle yeast over water mixture; stir until dissolved. Gradually add flour to yeast mixture, mixing well after each addition.

Turn dough out on a lightly floured surface; knead until smooth and elastic. Shape into a ball; place in a greased bowl, turning once to grease top. Cover and let rise in a warm place (85°), free from drafts, 1 hour or until doubled.

Punch dough down, and divide in half. Lightly grease hands, and pat dough evenly into two 12-inch pizza pans. Yield: 2 pizza crusts.

Mrs. Ray Harp,
Shawnee, Oklahoma.

Tip: For best results, sauté fresh mushrooms before freezing. Thaw and add to recipe.

Step 1—*While the tomato sauce is simmering, prepare the pizza dough. Knead the dough until smooth and elastic, and let rise about 1 hour.*

Step 3—*Spread sauce over crusts. Top with cooked and drained ground beef. If desired, sprinkle with pepperoni, ripe olives, and mushrooms. Bake at 450° for 10 minutes.*

Step 2—*Punch pizza dough down, and divide in half. Lightly grease hands, and evenly pat each portion of dough into a 12-inch pizza pan.*

Step 4—*Sprinkle pizzas with Cheddar and mozzarella, and bake 10 additional minutes. Remove from oven, and top with Parmesan.*

November

Frosty November marks the start of a season filled with holiday celebrations. Our *Holiday Dinners* special section is custom-designed with your needs in mind, whether you want to host an open house for everyone or a small dinner for close family members.

As November days grow cooler, you'll need hot and hearty foods to keep you warm. Choose one of our pasta variations, rich with meat or thick sauces, or a piping hot soup or stew. We found Hamburger Soup especially easy to make, and flavorful, too.

For dessert, slice into a luscious homemade pie. Whether your weakness is for nuts, fruit, or chocolate, you'll find several pies here to please you.

No Wonder Pasta's A Favorite

The pasta family is one of the biggest, most versatile groups you'd ever hope to meet. Spaghetti, macaroni, and their lesser known cousins get along equally well with a variety of companions. To prove our point, we've selected recipes using the South's favorite pastas in deliciously imaginative ways.

Wide egg noodles get dressed up with veal sauce, and macaroni gets similar elegant treatment when combined with cottage cheese and sour cream in Macaroni and Cheese Deluxe.

Layering lasagna noodles with meat sauce and cheese is not the only way to enjoy these wide noodles. For Sausage-Lasagna Rollups, the noodles are coiled around a rich three-cheese mixture and topped with a spicy sauce made with hot Italian sausage.

SAUSAGE-LASAGNA ROLLUPS

1 pound hot Italian link sausage, cut into ½-inch pieces
¾ cup chopped onion
1 clove garlic, minced
1 (24-ounce) can tomato juice
1 (6-ounce) can tomato paste
½ cup water
2 teaspoons sugar
½ teaspoon salt
1 bay leaf
2 cups cream-style cottage cheese
1 egg, slightly beaten
½ cup grated Parmesan cheese, divided
2 cups (8 ounces) shredded mozzarella cheese, divided
¼ teaspoon salt
¼ teaspoon white pepper
8 lasagna noodles

Cook sausage in a large, heavy skillet until browned; remove sausage, reserving ¼ cup drippings in skillet. (If sausage does not yield ¼ cup drippings, add oil to make ¼ cup.)

Sauté onion and garlic in drippings until onion is crisp-tender. Add sausage, tomato juice, tomato paste, water, sugar, ½ teaspoon salt, and bay leaf; simmer, uncovered, 1 hour, stirring occasionally. Remove bay leaf.

Combine cottage cheese, egg, ¼ cup Parmesan cheese, 1 cup mozzarella cheese, ¼ teaspoon salt, and pepper. Chill thoroughly.

Cook lasagna noodles according to package directions; drain. Rinse noodles, and cool.

Spread about 1 cup meat sauce in a lightly greased 13- x 9- x 2-inch baking dish. Spread ¼ cup cheese mixture on each lasagna noodle; roll up jellyroll fashion from narrow end. Arrange lasagna rolls, seam side down, in pan. Pour remaining meat sauce over rolls; top with remaining Parmesan and mozzarella cheese. Bake at 350° for 30 to 40 minutes or until bubbly. Yield: 8 servings.
Barbara Stelter, Cincinnati, Ohio.

NOODLES WITH VEAL SAUCE

2 pounds boneless veal or beef, cut into ½-inch cubes
¼ cup vegetable oil
1 cup sliced celery
2 small onions, sliced and separated into rings
2 (8-ounce) cans tomato sauce
½ cup water
2 teaspoons sugar
1½ teaspoons paprika
1 teaspoon salt
1 (8-ounce) package wide egg noodles
¼ cup finely chopped parsley

Cook veal in oil in a large skillet until browned. Add celery and onion; cook until crisp-tender. Add tomato sauce, water, sugar, paprika, and salt; cover and simmer 1 hour or until meat is tender.

Cook noodles according to package directions; drain. Arrange noodles in a serving dish. Spoon meat sauce over noodles, and sprinkle with parsley. Yield: 6 servings.
Jean Barr, Baltimore, Maryland.

FETTUCCINE ALFREDO

1 (8-ounce) package fettuccine
6 tablespoons butter or margarine, melted
½ cup grated Parmesan cheese
2 tablespoons half-and-half
Freshly ground pepper to taste

Cook fettuccine according to package directions. Drain. Combine remaining ingredients, mixing well. Add fettuccine, and toss gently. Serve immediately. Yield: 4 servings.
Lynn Lloyd, Birmingham, Alabama.

SPAGHETTI WITH PARSLEY

2 cups firmly packed fresh parsley
1 tablespoon dried whole basil
1 teaspoon salt
½ teaspoon pepper
1 teaspoon chopped garlic
½ cup olive oil
½ cup grated Parmesan cheese
1 (7-ounce) package thin spaghetti
⅓ cup finely chopped walnuts or pine nuts
Additional Parmesan cheese

Combine parsley, basil, salt, pepper, garlic, and oil in container of an electric blender; process until pureed. Remove from blender container, and stir in ½ cup Parmesan cheese.

Prepare spaghetti according to package directions; drain. Combine spaghetti and sauce, tossing well. Sprinkle with walnuts. Serve immediately with Parmesan cheese. Yield: 6 servings.
Virginia J. Thompson, Ocean Ridge, Florida.

MACARONI AND CHEESE DELUXE

1 (8-ounce) package elbow macaroni
2 cups cream-style cottage cheese
1 (8-ounce) carton commercial sour cream
1 egg, slightly beaten
¾ teaspoon salt
Dash of pepper
2 cups (8 ounces) shredded sharp Cheddar cheese
Paprika

Cook macaroni according to package directions; drain. Rinse macaroni, and set aside.

Combine next 6 ingredients; add macaroni, and stir well. Spoon mixture into a lightly greased 2-quart casserole. Sprinkle with paprika, and bake at 350° for 45 minutes. Yield: 6 to 8 servings.
Mrs. Deann Reed, Staunton, Virginia.

Our Pies Are Full Of Sweet Surprises

Remember when pies were once cooled on the windowsill and sometimes mysteriously disappeared? The story is old, but homemade pies are still too tempting to resist. But if you think that there's nothing new in pies, take a look at some fresh ideas from our readers.

Gone are the days when meringue adorned only the top of a pie. Add graham cracker crumbs and chopped pecans to meringue and turns it into a crust and filling in one. A dollop of whipped cream and a maraschino cherry are the crowning touch for each luscious slice of Angel Pie.

Give the richness of Southern pecan pie a different twist by adding semi-sweet chocolate morsels. Macadamia Pie is also a delectable variation of this old favorite.

As an alternative to traditional fruit-cake, try this delicious Fruitcake Pie. It's skillfully spiced with ginger, nutmeg, and cloves and is chock full of dates, nuts, cherries, and pineapple.

And who said all pies have to be baked in a piepan? We made Cheery Cherry Tarts in individual pastry shells to make it easier to serve pie to a crowd.

FRUITCAKE PIE

Pastry (recipe follows)
½ cup chopped pecans
½ cup dates, chopped
½ cup candied cherries, chopped
¼ cup candied pineapple, chopped
6 tablespoons butter or margarine, softened
½ cup firmly packed brown sugar
3 eggs, slightly beaten
½ cup light corn syrup
¼ teaspoon ground ginger
¼ teaspoon ground nutmeg
¼ teaspoon ground cloves
Dash of salt
¼ cup candied cherries, halved
¼ cup pecan halves

Line a 10-inch piepan with pastry; set aside.

Combine chopped pecans, dates, and chopped candied fruit; sprinkle over pastry shell.

Cream butter and sugar until light and fluffy; add eggs, corn syrup, spices, and salt. Beat at medium speed of electric mixer until well blended. Pour filling over fruit mixture in pastry shell.

Decorate top of filling as desired with halves of candied cherries and pecans. Bake at 350° for 40 to 45 minutes or until filling is set. Cool before serving. Yield: one 10-inch pie.

Pastry:

1¼ cups all-purpose flour
1 teaspoon salt
½ cup shortening
⅓ cup ice water

Combine flour and salt; cut in shortening with pastry blender until mixture resembles coarse meal. Sprinkle ice water evenly over surface; stir with a fork until dry ingredients are moistened. Shape into a ball; chill. Roll pastry to fit a 10-inch pieplate. Yield: one 10-inch pastry shell.
Mrs. Jack Sterne,
Columbia, South Carolina.

ORANGE AMBROSIA PIE

3 tablespoons cornstarch
¾ cup sugar
Salt
¼ cup cold water
¾ cup boiling water
Grated rind, juice, and pulp of 1 large orange
2 eggs, separated
1 teaspoon lemon juice
½ cup flaked coconut
1 baked 9-inch pastry shell
3 tablespoons cold water
1 teaspoon baking powder
6 tablespoons sugar

Combine cornstarch, ¾ cup sugar, and a pinch of salt; add ¼ cup cold water, stirring until smooth. Add boiling water, mixing well. Stir in orange rind, juice, and pulp. Beat egg yolks, and add to orange mixture. Cook over medium heat, stirring constantly, until smooth and thickened. Remove from heat; stir in lemon juice and coconut. Pour into pastry shell.

Beat egg whites (at room temperature) until foamy; gradually add 3 tablespoons cold water, beating until soft peaks form. Add baking powder and a pinch of salt. Gradually add 6 tablespoons sugar, beating until stiff peaks form. Spread meringue over filling, sealing to edge of pastry. Bake at 325° for 15 minutes or until golden brown. Yield: one 9-inch pie.
Virginia Thompson,
Ocean Ridge, Florida.

PINEAPPLE PIE

Pastry for double-crust 9-inch pie
1 (20-ounce) can crushed pineapple, undrained
2 tablespoons cornstarch
¼ teaspoon salt
½ cup sugar
½ cup evaporated milk
2 tablespoons margarine
2 tablespoons lemon juice

Roll half of pastry to ⅛-inch thickness, and fit into a 9-inch piepan.

Combine pineapple, cornstarch, salt, sugar, and evaporated milk; cook over medium heat, stirring constantly, until thickened. Remove from heat; add margarine and lemon juice, stirring until margarine melts. Pour into pastry-lined piepan.

Roll out remaining pastry to ⅛-inch thickness, and cut into ten 10- x ½-inch strips. Using a canapé cutter or knife, cut out small leaf shapes from remaining pastry. Arrange strips in lattice design over pie, and trim pastry overhang even with piepan. Lightly moisten leaf-shaped cutouts and place around rim, overlapping slightly; gently press cutouts in place. Bake at 400° for 25 minutes or until filling is set and crust is golden brown. Yield: one 9-inch pie.
Note: Pie may be covered with a complete top crust rather than lattice strips, if desired.
Mrs. Ray Harp,
Shawnee, Oklahoma.

CHOCOLATE PECAN PIE

⅔ cup evaporated milk
2 tablespoons margarine
1 (6-ounce) package semisweet chocolate morsels
2 eggs, beaten
1 cup sugar
2 tablespoons all-purpose flour
¼ teaspoon salt
1 teaspoon vanilla extract
1 cup chopped pecans
1 unbaked 9-inch pastry shell

Combine evaporated milk, margarine, and chocolate morsels in a small saucepan; place over low heat until chocolate melts, stirring constantly. Remove from heat.

Combine next 6 ingredients; stir in chocolate mixture. Pour into pastry shell. Bake at 375° for 35 to 40 minutes. Yield: one 9-inch pie.
Mrs. V. O. Walker,
Pennington, Texas.

JAPANESE FRUIT PIE

2 eggs, beaten
1 cup sugar
½ cup butter or margarine, melted
1 teaspoon vinegar
1 cup raisins
1 cup chopped pecans
1 cup flaked coconut
1 unbaked 9-inch deep-dish pastry shell

Combine first 7 ingredients, mixing well. Pour into pastry shell. Bake at 325° for 45 minutes. Yield: one 9-inch pie. *Mrs. James S. Tiffany, Dallas, Texas.*

CHEERY CHERRY TARTS

½ cup sugar
4½ teaspoons cornstarch
1 (16-ounce) can red tart pitted cherries
3 to 4 drops red food coloring (optional)
⅛ teaspoon almond extract
16 medium or 32 small baked tart shells
Sweetened whipped cream (optional)

Combine sugar and cornstarch in a small saucepan, stirring well to remove lumps.

Drain cherries, reserving ½ cup juice. Stir juice into sugar mixture; add food coloring, if desired. Cook over low heat until thickened and clear, stirring constantly. Add cherries; simmer 10 to 15 minutes, stirring gently once or twice. Stir in almond extract; cool.

Spoon filling into tart shells; garnish with whipped cream, if desired. Yield: 16 medium or 32 small tarts.

COCONUT CREAM PIE

3 egg yolks
Pinch of salt
2½ cups milk
¾ cup sugar
¼ cup all-purpose flour
1 teaspoon vanilla extract
1 cup flaked coconut
1 baked 9-inch pastry shell
Sweetened whipped cream

Combine egg yolks, salt, and milk; mix well. Place over low heat, stirring constantly, until warm. Combine sugar and flour, mixing well; gradually add to milk mixture, stirring constantly. Cook over low heat, stirring constantly, until thickened. Remove from heat; stir in vanilla and coconut.

Pour filling into pastry shell; chill thoroughly. Top with whipped cream before serving. Yield: one 9-inch pie. *Mrs. Bill Murphy, Big Spring, Texas.*

ANGEL PIE

3 egg whites
1 teaspoon vanilla extract
1 cup sugar
1 cup graham cracker crumbs
1 cup chopped pecans
1 teaspoon baking powder
Sweetened whipped cream
Maraschino cherries

Combine egg whites and vanilla, beating until soft peaks form. Gradually add sugar, and beat until stiff peaks form.

Combine graham cracker crumbs, pecans, and baking powder; fold into egg white mixture. Spread evenly in a well-greased and floured 9-inch pieplate. Bake at 325° for 25 minutes. Cool. Top each serving with a dollop of whipped cream and a maraschino cherry. Yield: one 9-inch pie.

Mrs. Earl L. Faulkenberry, Lancaster, South Carolina.

CHOCOLATE MERINGUE PIE

3 eggs, separated
2 cups milk
1½ cups sugar
½ cup cocoa
¼ cup cornstarch
½ teaspoon vanilla extract
1 baked 9-inch pastry shell
6 tablespoons sugar
Flaked coconut (optional)

Beat egg yolks until thick and lemon colored; combine with milk in a large, heavy saucepan. Stir well.

Combine 1½ cups sugar, cocoa, and cornstarch; mix well to remove lumps. Add sugar mixture to milk mixture, stirring well. Cook over medium heat, stirring constantly, until thickened (about 20 minutes). Remove from heat, and stir in vanilla. Pour filling into pastry shell. Let cool completely before topping with meringue.

Beat egg whites (at room temperature) until soft peaks form. Gradually add 6 tablespoons sugar, 1 tablespoon at a time, beating until stiff peaks form. Spread meringue over filling, sealing to edge of pastry; sprinkle with coconut, if desired.

Bake at 425° for 5 to 8 minutes or until golden brown. Cool completely before serving. Yield: one 9-inch pie. *Mrs. Roy Carlisle, Columbus, Georgia.*

MACADAMIA PIE

3 eggs, slightly beaten
⅔ cup sugar
1 cup light corn syrup
1½ cups salted macadamia nuts, chopped
2 tablespoons butter or margarine, melted
1 teaspoon vanilla extract
1 unbaked 9-inch pastry shell

Combine eggs, sugar, and corn syrup, mixing well; stir in macadamia nuts, melted butter, and vanilla. Pour filling into pastry shell.

Bake at 325° for 55 to 60 minutes or until filling is set. Cool on a wire rack; chill before serving. Yield: one 9-inch pie. *Mrs. Charles R. Simms, Palestine, Illinois.*

TRANSPARENT PIE

1 cup butter or margarine, melted
1 (16-ounce) package light brown sugar
5 eggs
2 unbaked 8-inch pastry shells
Sweetened whipped cream (optional)

Combine butter and sugar, mixing well. Add eggs, one at a time, beating well after each addition; pour into pastry shells. Bake at 350° for 40 minutes. Cool. Top with whipped cream, if desired. Yield: two 8-inch pies. *Mrs. Otto Murphy, Springfield, Tennessee.*

Right: *Noodles with Veal Sauce (page 236), Sausage-Lasagna Rollups (page 236), and Macaroni and Cheese Deluxe (page 236) are three delicious reasons for exploring the versatility of pasta.*

Page 240: *Festive beverages are a specialty at the Red Apple Inn. Clockwise: Creamy Eggnog (page 259), Café Royal (page 259), Café Diablo (page 259), Red Apple Cider (page 259), Hot Buttered Rum (page 259), and King Alfonso (page 259).*

Stir Up The Holiday Spirit

There's a chill in the air, but the warmth of Southern traditions fills the room as the holiday season unfolds again. Family and friends gather to celebrate these special times and feast upon an array of favorite foods. In our own holiday tradition, we have prepared this special section laden with recipes, menus, and suggestions to help you make this season even better.

To start things off right, enjoy hot appetizers and holiday beverages. Festive fruit and vegetable side dishes suggest ways to round out any meal. Yeast breads, filled with candied fruits and nuts, add a fresh aroma as they bake. And regardless of the gathering, there's always room for dessert—and ours all have that special holiday touch. Our menus include a traditional family meal, an open house, and a sophisticated New Year's Eve black-tie dinner.

When seven couples in Louisville gather in celebration of the holidays, it's not just another party—it's their way of ending the season and welcoming the new year.

Weary from the rush of public festivities, the group of friends decided they'd break away from the hubbub of the holidays for an intimate New Year's Eve party. They concluded that the food would need to be exceptional and the setting formal. It was agreed that everyone would dress the part—black-tie for the men and holiday evening attire for the women.

Sound exhausting? It wasn't, because everyone shared in the planning and preparation. Like many holiday celebrations, the event has become a tradition over the past six years, but the menu hasn't. It's new and exciting each year.

According to Cheeky Bahe, one of the original party planners, a different house is chosen each year for a change of setting so each of the seven couples can serve as host and hostess. The women meet well in advance of the party to plan a menu appropriate for the occasion, and each is responsible for providing at least one specialty for the meal.

The tinkle of fine crystal, the glow of candlelight, and the crackle of logs burning in the fireplace welcomed guests as they arrived at the home of John and Phyllis Kirwan for last year's party. Everyone gathered in front of the fire for cocktails and appetizers before dinner.

Crackers were dipped into Hot Artichoke-Seafood Dip while Brie, wrapped and baked in pastry, was sliced and served with fresh fruit.

Dinner was served from the buffet. Guests helped themselves to pork roast glazed with an herb-orange sauce; Pesto, spaghetti tossed with olive oil, fresh parsley, and seasonings; and Icebox Rolls, a family recipe of Laurie Mercke. (The rolls were prepared a day in advance, then baked and served piping hot.)

The salads awaited guests at each place setting, so there was no fuss with extra salad plates on the buffet. Wine glistening through fine cut crystal accompanied the meal.

Mocha Meringue Pie, drizzled with Kahlúa, was served with hot coffee to end the meal as distinctively as it began.

The complete menu and recipes follow to help guide you in planning your own special gathering.

Brie Wrapped in Pastry
Hot Artichoke-Seafood Dip
Porc à l'Orange
Pesto
Buttered Peas With Onions
Curry Spinach Salad
Icebox Rolls
Mocha Meringue Pie

BRIE WRAPPED IN PASTRY

4 patty shells, thawed
2 (4½-ounce) cans Brie cheese

Shape 2 patty shells into a ball; roll out to ⅛-inch thickness. Cut out an 8-inch circle. Place cheese in center of pastry; wrap pastry around cheese, pinching edges to seal. Repeat procedure using remaining patty shells and cheese. Decorate tops with scraps of pastry cut into decorative shapes.

Place pastries on ungreased baking sheet in a 450° oven; immediately reduce temperature to 400°. Bake for 20 to 25 minutes or until golden brown. Serve with fresh sliced apples and pears. Yield: 12 to 14 servings.

Susan Kannapell,
Louisville, Kentucky.

HOT ARTICHOKE-SEAFOOD DIP

2 (14-ounce) cans artichoke hearts, drained and chopped
2 cups mayonnaise
2 cups grated Parmesan cheese
2 (6-ounce) packages frozen crabmeat with shrimp, thawed, drained, and flaked
½ cup dry seasoned breadcrumbs

Combine first 4 ingredients, mixing well. Spoon into a lightly greased 1½-quart casserole. Top with breadcrumbs. Bake at 325° for 15 to 20 minutes. Serve with crackers. Yield: 12 to 14 servings.

Susan Kannapell,
Louisville, Kentucky.

PORC A L'ORANGE

1 (6- to 7-pound) pork loin roast
1 clove garlic, sliced
1 teaspoon rosemary
½ teaspoon salt
¼ teaspoon pepper
2 tablespoons Dijon mustard
2 tablespoons orange marmalade
1 tablespoon light brown sugar
⅔ cup orange juice, divided
2 oranges, thinly sliced (optional)
Fresh parsley (optional)
1 to 2 tablespoons Grand Marnier or
    other orange-flavored liqueur

When buying roast, ask the butcher to saw across the rib bones at the base of the backbone of roast, to separate ribs from backbone. Cut small slits in fat of loin and insert slivers of garlic. Rub with rosemary, salt, and pepper.

Place meat, fat side up, on rack in open shallow roasting pan; roast at 325° until done, allowing 30 to 35 minutes per pound (170° on meat thermometer).

Combine mustard, marmalade, brown sugar, and 2 tablespoons orange juice, mixing well. About 15 minutes before roast is done, brush with mustard mixture to glaze. Continue roasting 15 minutes. Remove roast to serving platter. Garnish with orange slices and parsley, if desired.

Skim fat from roasting pan; add remaining orange juice and Grand Marnier to pan drippings, mixing well. Serve with roast. Yield: 12 to 14 servings.   *Ward Tabler,*
Louisville, Kentucky.

PESTO

1 cup chopped fresh parsley
¼ cup dried whole basil
1 clove garlic, pressed
¾ to 1 cup olive oil
1 (16-ounce) package spaghetti
2 tablespoons butter or margarine
1 cup grated Parmesan cheese
Fresh parsley sprigs (optional)

Combine parsley and basil; mix well. Stir in garlic. Add olive oil, mixing well. Set aside.

Prepare spaghetti according to package directions; drain. Add butter; mix well. Toss spaghetti with olive oil mixture. Add Parmesan cheese; toss. Garnish with fresh parsley sprigs, if desired. Yield: 14 servings.   *Gretchen Clark,*
Louisville, Kentucky.

BUTTERED PEAS WITH ONIONS

3 (10-ounce) packages frozen green peas
2 (16-ounce) jars onions, undrained
1 teaspoon salt
⅔ cup melted butter or margarine
Pepper
¼ cup chopped parsley (optional)

Combine peas, onions, and salt in a large saucepan; cook over medium heat until peas are tender; drain. Pour butter over vegetables, and season with pepper. Sprinkle with parsley, if desired. Yield: 14 servings.   *Phyllis Kirwan,*
Louisville, Kentucky.

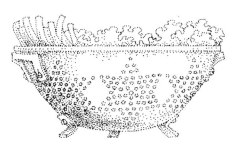

CURRY SPINACH SALAD

1½ pounds fresh spinach, torn
¼ cup slivered almonds
¾ cup chopped dates
1 large banana, peeled and chopped
1 Bermuda onion, sliced
Curry Dressing

Combine first 5 ingredients in a large bowl; toss. Serve with Curry Dressing. Yield: 12 to 14 servings.

Curry Dressing:

¾ cup olive oil
3½ tablespoons wine vinegar
1 clove garlic, crushed
1 teaspoon curry powder
⅛ teaspoon white pepper

Combine all ingredients, mixing well. Store in refrigerator until ready to use. Yield: 1 cup. *Mary Henderson Hulbert,*
Anchorage, Kentucky.

ICEBOX ROLLS

2 packages dry yeast
¼ cup warm water (105° to 115°)
1 tablespoon sugar
1 cup boiling water
¾ cup shortening
¾ cup cold water
¼ cup sugar
1 teaspoon salt
2 eggs, beaten
6 cups all-purpose flour
Melted butter or margarine

Dissolve yeast in warm water; add 1 tablespoon sugar, and set aside. Pour boiling water over shortening in a large bowl, stirring to melt shortening. Stir in cold water, ¼ cup sugar, and salt. Add eggs and yeast mixture, mixing well. Gradually add flour, mixing well. Cover and chill 24 hours.

Turn dough out on a lightly floured surface; knead 2 to 3 minutes. Shape dough into 1½-inch balls; dip in melted butter, and place on greased baking sheets. Let rise in a warm place (85°), free from drafts, about 1 hour or until doubled in bulk.

Bake at 400° for 12 to 15 minutes. Yield: about 3 dozen.   *Laurie Mercke,*
Louisville, Kentucky.

MOCHA MERINGUE PIE

3 egg whites
½ teaspoon baking powder
¾ cup sugar
Pinch of salt
1 cup chocolate wafer crumbs
½ cup chopped pecans
1 teaspoon vanilla extract
1 quart coffee ice cream, softened
1 cup whipping cream
½ cup powdered sugar
Sweet chocolate curls
½ to ⅔ cup Kahlúa or other
    coffee-flavored liqueur

Beat egg whites (at room temperature) until frothy; add baking powder, beating slightly. Gradually add sugar and salt; continue beating until stiff and glossy. Fold in chocolate wafer crumbs, pecans, and vanilla.

Spoon meringue into a buttered 9-inch piepan; use spoon to shape meringue into a pie shell, swirling sides high. Bake at 350° for 30 minutes; cool.

Spread the ice cream evenly over the meringue crust; cover and freeze overnight.

Combine whipping cream and powdered sugar, beating until light and fluffy; spread on pie. Garnish with chocolate curls; freeze until firm.

Let pie stand at room temperature 10 minutes before slicing. Pour 1 tablespoon Kahlúa over each serving. Yield: one 9-inch pie.

Note: This pie is thick and rich. It will easily yield 8 servings.

Cheeky Johnston Bahe,
Louisville, Kentucky.

These Side Dishes Might Steal The Show

Southerners so pride themselves on holiday menus that they serve side dishes as rich and as lavish as the dessert. These fruit and vegetable recipes feature new combinations and traditional favorites as spectacular as any creamy chocolate mousse you'll ever taste.

Delicately flavored Honey Apple Rings provide a perfect flavor accompaniment and garnish when nestled around a holiday ham or turkey. But serve Broccoli With Orange Sauce on a platter all its own—the lush green flowerets and creamy orange sauce make a truly inviting dish. A simple twist of orange provides an attractive garnish.

Winter Fruit Delight calls for frozen blueberries to highlight fresh grapefruit sections. We substituted fresh cranberries for the blueberries and found the flavor a bit more tart but just as delicious. Add extra sugar if you prefer the sweeter taste. Serve the combo in individual compotes to be sure to get every drop of the fruit-flavored syrup.

HONEY APPLE RINGS

½ cup honey
2 tablespoons vinegar
¼ teaspoon salt
¼ teaspoon ground cinnamon
4 medium cooking apples, unpeeled, cored, and cut into ½-inch rings

Combine honey, vinegar, salt, and cinnamon in a large skillet; bring to a boil. Add apple rings; reduce heat and simmer 8 to 10 minutes, turning apples once. Yield: 8 servings.

Louise Spraggins,
Birmingham, Alabama.

CRANBERRY CHUTNEY

1 pound fresh cranberries
1 cup sugar
½ cup firmly packed brown sugar
½ cup golden raisins
2 teaspoons ground cinnamon
1½ teaspoons ground ginger
½ teaspoon ground cloves
¼ teaspoon ground allspice
1 cup water
1 cup chopped onion
1 cup chopped cooking apple
½ cup chopped celery

Combine first 9 ingredients in a Dutch oven; cook over medium heat, stirring frequently, until juice is released from cranberries, about 15 minutes. Stir in remaining ingredients; reduce heat and simmer, uncovered, about 15 minutes or until thickened, stirring occasionally. Chill before serving. Chutney will keep in refrigerator in airtight container for up to 2 weeks. Yield: about 1 quart.

Mrs. Loye W. Cromer,
Anderson, South Carolina.

WINTER FRUIT DELIGHT

4 medium grapefruit
1 cup sugar
½ cup orange marmalade
2 cups frozen whole blueberries or fresh cranberries
3 medium bananas

Peel and section grapefruit, reserving juice. Add enough water to juice to measure 1 cup.

Combine juice, sugar, and marmalade in a large saucepan; bring to a boil, stirring occasionally. Add blueberries; boil 5 to 8 minutes or until skins pop. Cool. Stir in grapefruit; cover and chill. Slice bananas, and stir into chilled grapefruit mixture just before serving. Serve in individual compotes. Yield: 8 servings.

Note: When substituting cranberries for blueberries, increase sugar to 1¼ cups, if desired. *Mrs. David A. Sabo,*
Covington, Georgia.

BROCCOLI WITH ORANGE SAUCE

1 bunch fresh broccoli
2 tablespoons butter or margarine
2 tablespoons all-purpose flour
½ cup orange juice
½ teaspoon grated orange rind
½ cup orange sections
¼ teaspoon dried whole tarragon
¼ teaspoon salt
½ cup plain yogurt

Trim off large leaves of broccoli. Remove tough ends of lower stalks, and wash broccoli thoroughly; separate into spears. Cook broccoli, covered, in a small amount of boiling water 10 minutes or until crisp-tender.

Melt butter in a heavy saucepan over low heat; add flour and cook 1 minute, stirring constantly. Gradually stir in orange juice. Stir in next 4 ingredients; cook over medium heat, stirring constantly, until thickened and bubbly. Stir in yogurt.

Drain broccoli, and arrange on a serving platter. Spoon sauce over top. Yield: 6 servings. *Kathie Koerwer,*
Augusta, Georgia.

Tip: Use slivered orange and lemon peel to season stews and other meat dishes.

CHEESY POTATO CASSEROLE

6 medium potatoes
1 cup (4 ounces) shredded mild Cheddar
  cheese
½ cup milk
2 tablespoons butter or margarine
1 (8-ounce) carton commercial sour cream
¼ cup chopped onion
1 teaspoon salt
¼ teaspoon pepper
Butter or margarine
Paprika

Cook potatoes in boiling salted water about 30 minutes or until tender. Chill. Peel and grate potatoes.

Combine cheese, milk, and 2 tablespoons butter in a small saucepan; cook over low heat until butter and cheese melt, stirring occasionally. Remove from heat; stir in sour cream, onion, salt, and pepper. Fold cheese mixture into potatoes. Pour into a greased 2-quart casserole; dot with butter, and sprinkle with paprika. Bake at 350° for 45 minutes. Yield: 6 servings.
Joan B. Piercy,
Memphis, Tennessee.

CORN-CHEESE PUDDING

1 (17-ounce) can whole kernel corn,
  drained
1 (2-ounce) jar pimiento, drained and
  chopped
1 cup (4 ounces) shredded medium
  Cheddar cheese
1 medium-size green pepper, chopped
2 eggs, slightly beaten
½ cup milk
2 tablespoons all-purpose flour
2 tablespoons sugar
2 tablespoons butter or margarine, melted
1 teaspoon salt

Combine all ingredients; mix well. Pour into a greased 1½-quart casserole. Bake at 350° for 45 to 50 minutes. Yield: 4 to 6 servings.
Florence L. Costello,
Chattanooga, Tennessee.

Tip: Cut raw turnips into strips and serve as a snack or hors d'oeuvre. They're good served with a dip.

FESTIVE SWEET POTATOES

3 cups cooked, mashed sweet potatoes
½ cup sugar
¼ cup milk
⅓ cup margarine, melted
1 teaspoon vanilla extract
2 eggs, beaten
1 cup flaked coconut
1 cup firmly packed brown sugar
⅓ cup all-purpose flour
⅓ cup margarine, melted
1 cup chopped pecans

Combine first 6 ingredients, mixing well. Spoon into a lightly greased 8-inch square baking dish.

Combine remaining ingredients; sprinkle over top of sweet potatoes. Bake at 375° about 25 minutes or until golden brown. Yield: 6 servings.
Marilyn Griner,
Marietta, Georgia.

Pumpkin Bakes Into Something Sweet

After the time for carving jack-o'-lanterns is over, pumpkins can take on new faces in a tempting array of baked goods. The season's most versatile vegetable adds a rich, sweet flavor to our Moist Pumpkin Bread, Pumpkin Cake Bars, and crunchy Pumpkin Layer Cake.

Small pumpkins are best for cooking since they contain more tender flesh and less water. To prepare fresh pumpkin, wash it well, and cut in half crosswise. Place halves, cut-side down, on a 15- x 10- x 1-inch jellyroll pan. Bake at 325° for 45 minutes or until fork tender; cool 10 minutes. Peel pumpkin, and discard seeds. Puree the pulp in a food processor, or mash thoroughly.

While canned pumpkin can't match the distinctive flavor of fresh, you can substitute 1 (16-ounce) can of pumpkin for 2 cups mashed fresh pumpkin to make these treats year-round.

PUMPKIN PRALINE PIE

2 cups cooked, mashed pumpkin
1 (14-ounce) can sweetened condensed
  milk
2 eggs
1 teaspoon ground cinnamon
½ teaspoon ground nutmeg
½ teaspoon ground ginger
½ teaspoon salt
1 unbaked 9-inch pastry shell
12 to 14 pecan halves
3 tablespoons dark brown sugar
3 tablespoons whipping cream

Combine pumpkin, condensed milk, eggs, spices, and salt; beat on medium speed of an electric mixer 1 minute or until smooth. Pour into pastry shell; bake at 375° for 50 minutes or until knife inserted halfway between center and edge of pie comes out clean. Let cool slightly; arrange pecan halves in a circle on top of pie, and set aside.

Combine sugar and whipping cream in a small saucepan; cook over medium heat, stirring constantly, until sugar dissolves. Reduce heat, and simmer 5 minutes; let cool 5 minutes. Spoon over pecan halves. Yield: one 9-inch pie.
Shirley Hodge,
Delray Beach, Florida.

BAKED PUMPKIN PUDDING

¼ cup butter or margarine, melted
2 cups sugar
5 eggs, beaten
½ cup all-purpose flour
½ cup evaporated milk
2 cups cooked, mashed pumpkin
1 teaspoon ground cinnamon
½ teaspoon ground nutmeg
½ teaspoon ground ginger
½ teaspoon ground mace
½ teaspoon ground cloves
2 teaspoons vanilla extract
Pecan halves

Combine butter and sugar; mix well. Add eggs, mixing well; stir in flour and milk. Add pumpkin, spices, and vanilla; mix until smooth. Pour batter into a well-greased 2-quart casserole; bake at 350° for 55 minutes or until firm. Top with pecan halves. Yield: 8 to 10 servings. *Martha Macdonald Boelt,*
Toano, Virginia.

PUMPKIN LAYER CAKE

2 cups sugar
4 eggs, well beaten
1 cup corn oil
2 cups cooked, mashed pumpkin
2 cups all-purpose flour
2 teaspoons baking powder
2 teaspoons soda
1 teaspoon salt
1 teaspoon ground cinnamon
1 teaspoon ground allspice
Frosting (recipe follows)

Combine sugar, eggs, oil, and pumpkin, mixing well. Combine dry ingredients; add to pumpkin mixture, and beat 1 minute at medium speed of an electric mixer. Pour batter into 3 greased and floured 9-inch round cakepans. Bake at 325° for 25 to 30 minutes or until cake tests done. Cool in pans 10 minutes; remove cake from pans; cool completely. Spread frosting between layers and on top of cake. Yield: one 3-layer cake.

Note: Cake slices best when chilled.

Frosting:

1 cup firmly packed dark brown sugar
½ cup sugar
2 teaspoons all-purpose flour
1 cup milk
2 tablespoons butter
½ cup chopped pecans or walnuts
1 cup flaked coconut
1 teaspoon vanilla extract

Combine sugar, flour, and milk in a medium saucepan; cook over medium heat, stirring constantly, until thickened (225° on candy thermometer). Add butter, stirring until melted; stir in pecans, coconut, and vanilla. Yield: enough for one 3-layer cake. *Thelma Woffard, New Castle, Delaware.*

PUMPKIN CAKE BARS

2 cups sugar
2 cups all-purpose flour
2 teaspoons baking powder
1 teaspoon soda
½ teaspoon salt
2 teaspoons ground cinnamon
¾ cup corn oil
2 cups cooked, mashed pumpkin
4 eggs
Fluffy Cream Cheese Frosting

Combine first 6 ingredients. Add oil, pumpkin, and eggs; beat 1 minute at medium speed of an electric mixer. Spoon batter into a greased 15- x 10- x 1-inch jellyroll pan; bake at 350° for 20 to 25 minutes. Cool completely; frost with Fluffy Cream Cheese Frosting. Cut into bars. Yield: 4 dozen.

Fluffy Cream Cheese Frosting:

1 (3-ounce) package cream cheese, softened
¼ cup plus 2 tablespoons margarine, softened
1 tablespoon orange juice or whipping cream
1 teaspoon vanilla extract
1¾ cups sifted powdered sugar

Beat cream cheese and margarine until light and fluffy; add orange juice and vanilla, and mix well. Gradually add powdered sugar, mixing until light and fluffy. Yield: about 1 cup.
Geraldine Lipka, Annapolis, Maryland.

MOIST PUMPKIN BREAD

⅔ cup shortening
2⅔ cups sugar
4 eggs
2 cups cooked, mashed pumpkin
⅔ cup water
3⅓ cups all-purpose flour
½ teaspoon baking powder
2 teaspoons soda
1½ teaspoons salt
1 teaspoon ground cinnamon
1 teaspoon ground cloves
⅔ cup pecans or walnuts, ground
⅔ cup raisins

Cream shortening; gradually add sugar, beating well. Add eggs; mix well. Stir in pumpkin and water.
Combine flour, baking powder, soda, salt, cinnamon, and cloves; add to creamed mixture, mixing well. Fold in pecans and raisins. Spoon into 2 well-greased and floured 9- x 5- x 3-inch loafpans; bake at 350° for 1 hour and 10 minutes or until bread tests done. Yield: 2 loaves. *Mrs. H. S. Wright, Leesville, South Carolina.*

Family Dinner Highlights The Holidays

When Jane Jerden announces that her holiday meal is ready, eager cries of "I wanna sit next to Grandma" echo through the house. A crackling fire provides a cheerful background and generates a warm sense of togetherness as this Atlanta family gathers at the table. Once the coveted spot by Grandma has been decided upon, the family settles down to the serious business of eating.

"With three busy children, J. L. and I keep our holiday celebrations simple. The recipes are usually quick and easy," Jane says. They're also delightful, beginning with Sour Cream-Topped Tomato Soup. For the main dish, an impressive standing rib roast was selected. "I prefer to have turkey at either Thanksgiving or Christmas, but not for both occasions," Jane explains.

Festive side dishes are an important part of holiday fare, and the three on the Jerden menu are exceptional. Plain white rice is turned into beef-flavored Consommé Rice; and crisp celery is combined with almonds, water chestnuts, and mushrooms to make Jane's Celery Casserole. But, of all three side dishes, the individual Bean Bundles are the most popular. Wrapped with bacon, the tiny bundles of green beans are topped with commercial French dressing and marinated before being baked.

Also special to this dinner is a superb salad and bread.

Everyone, especially the children, looks forward to dessert. Once the French Silk Pie is sliced and served, it is easy to see why. This chocolate-filled meringue crust pie is an annual tradition with the Jerden family, a perfect ending to an important meal.

Sour Cream-Topped Tomato Soup
Orange Walnut Salad
Standing Rib Roast   Bean Bundles
Consommé Rice   Celery Casserole
Feather Light Biscuits
French Silk Pie

SOUR CREAM-TOPPED TOMATO SOUP

2 (46-ounce) cans tomato juice
6 beef-flavored bouillon cubes
4 stalks celery with leaves, chopped
2 bay leaves
6 peppercorns
2 medium onions, cut into ½-inch slices
Commercial sour cream
Chopped chives

Combine first 6 ingredients in a large Dutch oven. Cover and simmer 2 hours. Strain. Garnish soup with dollops of sour cream and chopped chives. Yield: 10 to 12 servings.

ORANGE WALNUT SALAD

2 small heads Bibb lettuce, torn into bite-size pieces
1 pound fresh spinach, torn into bite-size pieces
2 oranges, peeled, seeded, and sectioned
½ medium onion, sliced and separated into rings
½ cup coarsely chopped walnuts
2 teaspoons butter or margarine, melted
Sweet-Sour Dressing

Place first 4 ingredients in a large bowl. Sauté walnuts in butter until lightly browned; then add to lettuce mixture. Toss with Sweet-Sour Dressing. Yield: 6 to 8 servings.

Sweet-Sour Dressing:
1 teaspoon paprika
1 teaspoon celery seeds
1 teaspoon dry mustard
1 teaspoon salt
1 teaspoon grated onion
½ cup sugar
1 cup vegetable oil
½ cup vinegar

Combine all ingredients in a jar. Cover tightly, and shake vigorously. Chill several hours. Shake again before serving over salad. Yield: 1¾ cups.

Tip: After removing a roast from the oven, let it rest at least 15 minutes for easier carving.

STANDING RIB ROAST

1 (6- to 8-pound) standing rib roast
Salt and pepper

Sprinkle roast with salt and pepper. Place roast, fat side up, on rack in a shallow roasting pan. Insert meat thermometer, making certain end of thermometer does not touch fat or bone.
Roast at 325° as follows: rare, 27 minutes per pound or 140° on thermometer; medium, 30 minutes per pound or 160°; well done, 36 minutes per pound or 170°.
Let stand at room temperature about 15 minutes before carving. Yield: 12 to 16 servings.

BEAN BUNDLES

2 (16-ounce) cans whole green beans, drained
12 to 16 slices bacon, cut in half
1 (8-ounce) bottle commercial French dressing
4 to 5 whole pimientos, cut into strips

Arrange green beans in bunches of 8, wrapping a half slice of bacon around each bunch; place beans in a 13- x 9- x 2-inch baking dish. Pour dressing over beans. Cover and chill 3 hours.
Bake, uncovered, at 350° for 40 minutes, turning beans after the first 20 minutes of cooking.
Remove beans from baking dish with a slotted spoon. Garnish bean bunches with strips of pimiento before serving. Yield: 8 servings.

CONSOMME RICE

2 cups uncooked regular rice
¼ cup plus 2 tablespoons butter or margarine, melted
2 (10½-ounce) cans beef consommé, undiluted
1¼ cups water
Parsley sprigs

Combine first 4 ingredients in a 3-quart casserole. Bake, uncovered, at 350° for 1 hour. Garnish with parsley before serving. Yield: 8 to 10 servings.

CELERY CASSEROLE

3 cups diced celery
¼ cup slivered almonds
½ cup sliced water chestnuts
1 (4-ounce) can sliced mushrooms, drained
¼ cup plus 1 tablespoon butter or margarine
3 tablespoons all-purpose flour
1 cup chicken broth
¾ cup half-and-half
½ cup grated Parmesan cheese
½ cup soft breadcrumbs
3 tablespoons butter or margarine, melted
Parsley sprigs

Cook celery in a small amount of boiling water just until tender (about 5 minutes); drain. Combine celery, almonds, water chestnuts, and mushrooms; mix well and pour into a greased 12- x 8- x 2-inch baking dish.
Melt ¼ cup plus 1 tablespoon butter in a heavy saucepan over low heat; blend in flour and cook 1 minute, stirring constantly. Gradually add chicken broth and half-and-half; cook over medium heat, stirring constantly, until thickened and bubbly. Pour sauce over celery mixture.
Combine cheese and breadcrumbs; sprinkle over casserole. Drizzle melted butter over top.
Bake at 350° for 25 minutes. Garnish with parsley. Yield: 8 servings.

FEATHER LIGHT BISCUITS

1 package dry yeast
2 tablespoons warm water (105° to 115°)
5 cups all-purpose flour
1 tablespoon baking powder
1 teaspoon soda
1½ teaspoons salt
2 tablespoons sugar
1 cup shortening
2 cups buttermilk
Melted butter or margarine

Dissolve yeast in warm water; set aside. Combine flour, baking powder, soda, salt, and sugar in a large mixing bowl; cut in shortening until mixture resembles coarse meal. Add buttermilk, mixing well. Stir in yeast mixture.
Turn dough out on a lightly floured surface, and knead 1 to 2 minutes. Roll

dough to ½-inch thickness; cut with a 2-inch biscuit cutter. Place biscuits on a lightly greased baking sheet; brush tops with melted butter. Bake at 400° for 15 minutes. Yield: about 2 dozen.

FRENCH SILK PIE

3 egg whites
¼ teaspoon cream of tartar
⅛ teaspoon salt
¾ cup sugar
½ cup chopped pecans
½ teaspoon vanilla extract
1 (4-ounce) package sweet baking chocolate
3 tablespoons water
1 tablespoon brandy
2 cups whipping cream, divided
Grated sweet chocolate

Beat egg whites (at room temperature), cream of tartar, and salt until foamy. Gradually add sugar, beating until stiff peaks form. Fold in chopped pecans and vanilla.

Spoon meringue into a well-greased 9-inch piepan. Use a spoon to shape meringue into a pie shell, swirling sides high. Bake at 300° for 1 hour. Cool.

Combine chocolate and water in a medium saucepan; place over low heat. Cook, stirring often, until chocolate melts. Let cool. Stir in brandy. Beat 1 cup whipping cream until stiff peaks form; fold into chocolate mixture. Pour chocolate mixture into cooled meringue shell; chill at least 3 hours.

Beat remaining whipping cream until stiff peaks form; spread evenly over top of pie. Garnish with grated chocolate. Yield: one 9-inch pie.

Salads Get Special Attention

When planning a menu for a holiday occasion, it's sometimes hard to decide on the salad. You want one that will complement the main course and have a festive look. This varied array of salads

should help you select the perfect one for that special meal.

As for color, Festive Spinach Salad will brighten any menu. Crisp spinach is tossed with bits of cauliflower, bright pimiento, onion, and bacon and topped with a tangy sweet-and-sour dressing. To save time, prepare all the ingredients ahead and store them in separate plastic bags in the refrigerator. Immediately before serving, you can assemble and dress the salad quickly.

We've included two congealed salads that have a holiday look and taste. Cranberry Salad Ring is rich in color and is filled with fruit and nuts. Frosted Apricot Salad conceals pineapple and bananas and has a special cream cheese topping.

CORN SALAD

2 (16-ounce) cans white shoepeg corn, drained
1 (2-ounce) jar pimiento, drained
½ cup chopped green pepper
½ cup chopped onion
2 stalks celery, chopped
½ cup sugar
½ cup vegetable oil
½ cup vinegar
1 teaspoon salt
½ teaspoon pepper

Combine vegetables, tossing lightly. Combine remaining ingredients; mix well. Pour over vegetables, and toss lightly. Cover and chill overnight. Drain well before serving. Yield: 8 servings.
Wanda Elliott,
Rockdale, Texas.

FESTIVE SPINACH SALAD

2 pounds fresh spinach, torn
1 small head cauliflower, broken into flowerets
1 (4-ounce) jar pimiento, chopped
1 medium onion, sliced
Sweet-and-Sour Dressing
6 slices bacon, cooked and crumbled

Combine spinach, cauliflower, pimiento, and onion in a large salad bowl; toss lightly. Pour ½ cup Sweet-and-Sour

Dressing over the vegetables, tossing lightly. Sprinkle bacon over salad. Yield: 8 to 10 servings.

Sweet-and-Sour Dressing:
¾ to 1 cup sugar
½ cup vinegar
1 cup vegetable oil
1 teaspoon celery seeds
1 teaspoon paprika
¾ teaspoon salt

Combine sugar and vinegar in a medium saucepan. Bring to a boil; remove from heat. Add remaining ingredients, mixing well. Chill. Yield: about 2 cups.
Mrs. George Sellers,
Albany, Georgia.

CRANBERRY SALAD RING

4 (3-ounce) packages black raspberry-flavored gelatin
2 cups boiling water
½ cup cold water
2 cups fresh cranberries, ground
2 oranges, unpeeled, seeded, and ground
2 apples, unpeeled, cored, and ground
1 (15¼-ounce) can crushed pineapple, undrained
2 cups sugar
1 cup chopped pecans
Lettuce leaves (optional)
Mayonnaise or salad dressing (optional)
Orange slices (optional)

Dissolve gelatin in boiling water. Add cold water, and chill until consistency of unbeaten egg white.

Combine next 6 ingredients; mix well. Fold fruit mixture into gelatin mixture. Pour into a lightly oiled 10-cup ring mold; chill until set. Unmold on lettuce leaves. Fill center of ring with mayonnaise, and garnish with orange slices, if desired. Yield: 18 to 20 servings.
Lena Russell Wray,
Des Arc, Arkansas.

Tip: Compare costs of fresh, frozen, canned, and dried foods. To compute the best buy, divide the price by the number of servings. The lower price per serving will be the thriftiest buy.

WINTER FRUIT SALAD

1 (20½-ounce) can pineapple chunks
½ cup sugar
2 tablespoons all-purpose flour
2 egg yolks
1 (16-ounce) can sliced peaches, drained
    and diced
1 (16-ounce) can pear halves, drained and
    chopped
1 (16-ounce) jar Queen Anne cherries,
    drained and pitted
1½ cups miniature marshmallows
2 to 3 medium bananas

Drain pineapple, reserving 1 cup juice. Set pineapple aside.

Combine reserved juice, sugar, and flour in a small saucepan; mix well. Cook over medium heat until mixture is thick.

Beat egg yolks until thick and lemon colored. Gradually stir about one-fourth of hot mixture into yolks; add to remaining hot mixture, stirring constantly. Cook 2 additional minutes, stirring constantly. Cool.

Add remaining ingredients, except bananas, to custard; mix well. Chill. Just before serving, slice bananas and add to custard; mix well. Yield: 8 to 10 servings.   Mrs. Marshall Marvelli,
    Winston-Salem, North Carolina.

FROSTED APRICOT SALAD

2 (3-ounce) packages apricot-flavored
    gelatin
1 cup miniature marshmallows
2 cups boiling water
2 cups cold water
1 (20-ounce) can crushed pineapple
2 bananas, diced
½ cup sugar
2 tablespoons all-purpose flour
2 tablespoons butter or margarine
1 egg, beaten
1 (3-ounce) package cream cheese,
    softened
1 cup whipping cream, whipped

Dissolve gelatin and marshmallows in boiling water. Add cold water, and chill until mixture is consistency of unbeaten egg white. Drain pineapple, reserving ½ cup juice. Fold pineapple and banana into gelatin mixture. Pour into a lightly oiled 9-inch square baking dish. Chill until set.

Combine sugar, reserved pineapple juice, flour, butter, and egg in a small saucepan; cook over medium-low heat, stirring constantly, until thickened. Remove from heat. Add cream cheese; beat until smooth. Chill.

Fold whipped cream into chilled mixture. Spread topping over salad. Chill at least 2 hours. Yield: about 9 servings.
    Mrs. James F. Crowell,
    Princeton, Kentucky.

Say "Hello" With Hot Appetizers

There are lots of nice greetings at holiday time: a quick hug, a kiss on the cheek, a brightly wrapped package. Another way to say "hello" is with a savory assortment of hot appetizers.

Get out your chafing dish, and keep Hot Spinach Dip or Cheesy Pineapple Dip at just the right temperatures for enjoying with crackers or crusty chunks of French bread.

Use sausage to fill mushroom caps or as the surprise center for plump balls of cheese pastry. (When preparing Sausage Balls in Cheese Pastry in our *Southern Living* test kitchens, our foods staff found that the easiest way to work the dough around the sausage was with our fingers.)

For a hot mini-sandwich, we suggest Beefy Party Snacks. And instead of serving chicken wings or small drumsticks, try Chicken Little Fingers—tender strips of boned chicken just right for dipping in a tangy plum sauce.

SAUSAGE-STUFFED MUSHROOMS

1 pound fresh mushrooms
1 pound bulk pork sausage
1 teaspoon minced garlic
2 tablespoons chopped parsley
1½ cups (6 ounces) shredded sharp
    Cheddar cheese

Rinse mushrooms and pat dry; remove stems. Chop stems, and combine with sausage, garlic, and parsley; cook until sausage is browned, stirring to crumble. Drain off pan drippings. Stir in cheese, mixing well.

Spoon mixture into mushroom caps, and place in a 13- x 9- x 2-inch baking dish. Bake at 350° for 20 minutes. Yield: about 2 dozen.   Barbara Wells,
    Amissville, Virginia.

SAUSAGE BALLS IN CHEESE PASTRY

1 pound mild or hot bulk pork sausage
¾ cup dry breadcrumbs
⅓ cup chicken broth
⅛ teaspoon ground nutmeg
¼ teaspoon poultry seasoning
1½ cups all-purpose flour
¼ teaspoon salt
1 teaspoon paprika
2 cups (8 ounces) shredded sharp
    Cheddar cheese
½ cup butter or margarine, softened

Combine first 5 ingredients, mixing well. Shape into 1-inch balls. Cook over low heat until done, turning to brown on all sides. Drain on paper towels.

Combine flour, salt, paprika, and cheese; cut in butter with pastry blender (mixture will be dry). Mix with hands until dough is smooth. Shape 1 tablespoon of dough around each sausage ball, covering sausage completely. Place on greased baking sheets. Bake at 350° for 15 to 20 minutes. Yield: about 4 dozen.

Note: After pastry has been shaped around sausage balls, they may be frozen. To serve, thaw and bake.
    Pauline Lester,
    Saluda, South Carolina.

HOT BACON APPETIZERS

½ pound bacon, cooked and crumbled
¾ cup (6 ounces) shredded process
    American cheese
¼ cup butter or margarine, softened
2 teaspoons caraway seeds
50 melba toast rounds

Combine first 4 ingredients, mixing well; spread evenly on toast rounds. Place on baking sheet, and broil 2 minutes or until cheese melts. Serve hot. Yield: 50 appetizers.

Mrs. John R. Allen,
Dallas, Texas.

BEEFY PARTY SNACKS

½ pound ground chuck
½ medium onion, finely chopped
2 tablespoons catsup
1 tablespoon prepared mustard
½ teaspoon salt
¼ teaspoon pepper
1 loaf party rye bread

Combine first 6 ingredients, mixing well; spread evenly on bread slices. Broil 3 to 4 minutes or until done. Serve immediately. Yield: about 2 dozen. *Virginia Mathews,*
Jacksonville, Florida.

CHICKEN LITTLE FINGERS

6 whole chicken breasts, boned
1½ cups buttermilk
2 tablespoons lemon juice
2 teaspoons Worcestershire sauce
1 teaspoon soy sauce
1 teaspoon paprika
1 tablespoon Greek seasoning
1 teaspoon salt
1 teaspoon pepper
2 cloves garlic, minced
4 cups soft breadcrumbs
½ cup sesame seeds
¼ cup butter or margarine, melted
¼ cup melted shortening
Plum Sauce

Cut chicken into ½-inch strips. Combine next 9 ingredients; add chicken, mixing until well coated. Cover and refrigerate overnight.

Drain chicken thoroughly. Combine breadcrumbs and sesame seeds, mixing well. Add chicken, and toss to coat. Place chicken in 2 greased 13- x 9- x 2-inch baking dishes. Combine butter and shortening; brush on chicken. Bake at 350° for 35 to 40 minutes. Serve with Plum Sauce. Yield: 12 to 14 appetizer servings.

Plum Sauce:

1½ cups red plum jam
1½ tablespoons prepared mustard
1½ tablespoons prepared horseradish
1½ teaspoons lemon juice

Combine all ingredients in a small saucepan, mixing well. Place over low heat just until warm, stirring constantly. Yield: about 1¾ cups.

Frances Elizabeth Morgan,
Rison, Arkansas.

HOT SPINACH DIP

2 (10-ounce) packages frozen chopped spinach
¼ cup butter or margarine, melted
2 tablespoons chopped onion
3 tablespoons all-purpose flour
½ cup evaporated milk
1 (6-ounce) roll jalapeño cheese, softened
½ teaspoon pepper
¾ teaspoon celery salt
¾ teaspoon garlic salt
1 tablespoon Worcestershire sauce
Dash of red pepper

Cook spinach according to package directions; drain well, reserving ½ cup liquid. Set spinach aside.

Combine butter, onion, and flour; stir well, and cook about 1 minute. Gradually add reserved spinach liquid and evaporated milk; cook until slightly thickened, stirring constantly.

Add cheese and seasonings to sauce, stirring until cheese is melted. Add spinach, mixing well. Serve hot with crackers. Yield: about 1¾ cups.

Note: Dip may be frozen. Thaw and heat before serving.

Mrs. C. W. Kennard,
Anderson, Texas.

CHEESY PINEAPPLE DIP

½ cup chopped green pepper
½ cup butter or margarine, melted
1 (16-ounce) jar process cheese spread
1 (15¼-ounce) can crushed pineapple, drained
¼ cup slivered almonds, toasted

Sauté green pepper in butter until tender; stir in cheese, pineapple, and almonds. Place over low heat until cheese melts, stirring constantly. Serve hot, with cubes of French bread as dippers. Yield: about 3 cups.

Mary Vaughn,
Dallas, Texas.

Welcome Friends To An Open House

Having friends and family over for an open house is one of the best ways we know to celebrate the holiday season. To help you plan your open house, the *Southern Living* foods staff has selected a variety of recipes designed for carefree holiday entertaining.

Foods that can be made ahead are the key to entertaining with ease. The sweets we've selected—Apricot-Stuffed Dates, Coconut Candy, and Yellow Sponge Cake—can all be made the day before serving. Hot Spiced Punch and Zesty Meatballs can be assembled early and heated just before guests arrive.

The dip we've chosen is flavored with cabbage, carrot, green pepper, and onion. Center it on a serving tray with your choice of fresh vegetables for dipping, and you have a dish so colorful that it can serve as a centerpiece.

FRESH VEGETABLE DIP

¼ cup shredded cabbage
⅓ cup shredded carrot
2 tablespoons finely chopped green pepper
1 tablespoon finely chopped onion
1 (8-ounce) carton commercial sour cream
2 tablespoons mayonnaise
1 teaspoon tarragon vinegar
¾ teaspoon garlic salt
Fresh vegetables for dipping

Combine cabbage, carrot, green pepper, and onion; mix well. Stir in sour cream, mayonnaise, vinegar, and garlic salt. Cover and chill. Serve with vegetables. Yield: 8 to 10 servings.

ZESTY MEATBALLS

3 pounds ground chuck
3 medium onions, finely chopped
1½ cups soft breadcrumbs
1½ teaspoons salt
¾ teaspoon pepper
1½ teaspoons chili powder
¼ cup plus 2 tablespoons milk
Vegetable oil
¾ cup Worcestershire sauce
¾ cup sugar
¼ cup plus 2 tablespoons vinegar
3 (8-ounce) cans tomato sauce
Fresh chopped parsley

Combine the first 7 ingredients, mixing well; shape into 1-inch balls. Cook meatballs in hot oil until they are lightly browned; drain. Place meatballs in a 13- x 9- x 2-inch baking dish.

Combine remaining ingredients except parsley in a medium saucepan; bring to a boil. Cook over low heat for 1 minute, stirring constantly. Pour sauce over meatballs. Bake at 325° for 30 minutes. Garnish with parsley, if desired. Yield: about 6 dozen.

Elizabeth H. Hall,
Memphis, Tennessee.

CREAM CHEESE PASTRIES

½ cup butter, softened
½ cup margarine, softened
1 (8-ounce) package cream cheese, softened
¼ cup sugar
2½ cups all-purpose flour
2 teaspoons ground cinnamon, divided
½ cup sugar, divided
½ cup chopped pecans, divided

Combine first 5 ingredients, mixing well; cover and chill 24 hours. Divide dough into 4 equal portions. Turn each portion out onto a lightly floured surface, and roll into a 12-inch circle. Sprinkle each circle with ½ teaspoon cinnamon, 2 tablespoons sugar, and 2 tablespoons pecans. Cut each circle into 12 wedges. Roll up each wedge, beginning at wide end. Place, seam side down, on greased baking sheets; bake at 325° for 20 minutes. Yield: 4 dozen.

Gwen Louer,
Roswell, Georgia.

APRICOT-STUFFED DATES

½ cup dried apricots
⅓ cup flaked coconut
¼ cup chopped pecans
1 tablespoon orange juice
1 (8-ounce) package pitted dates
Powdered sugar

Steam apricots over boiling water 5 minutes. Put apricots, coconut, and pecans through a food chopper. Combine ground mixture and orange juice, mixing well.

Make a lengthwise slit in dates. Stuff dates with apricot mixture; dust with powdered sugar, as desired. Yield: about 4 dozen.

Maybelle Pinkston,
Corryton, Tennessee.

COCONUT CANDY

2 cups firmly packed brown sugar
2 cups sugar
¼ cup light corn syrup
1⅓ cups half-and-half
¼ cup melted butter or margarine
¼ teaspoon salt
1 teaspoon vanilla extract
1½ cups flaked coconut

Combine sugar, corn syrup, and half-and-half in a large Dutch oven. Cook over medium heat to soft ball stage (238°), stirring constantly. Remove from heat; add butter and salt without stirring. Cool to lukewarm (110°).

Add vanilla to candy, and beat with a wooden spoon until mixture is creamy and loses its gloss; fold in coconut. Pour mixture into a greased 9-inch square pan; cut into 1-inch squares. Yield: about 6 dozen squares.

Mrs. W. P. Chambers,
Louisville, Kentucky.

YELLOW SPONGE CAKE

6 eggs, separated
¼ cup water
1 teaspoon vanilla extract
1 cup sugar
½ teaspoon salt
1¼ cups sifted all-purpose flour
½ teaspoon baking powder
1 teaspoon cream of tartar
½ cup sugar

Place egg yolks in a small mixing bowl; beat 6 minutes at high speed of electric mixer or until thick and lemon colored. Combine water and vanilla; add to egg yolks. Beat on low speed until thoroughly blended. Turn mixer to medium speed, and beat 4 minutes or until thick.

Gradually beat in 1 cup sugar and salt; continue beating about 5 to 6 minutes or until mixture feels smooth between two fingers.

Combine flour and baking powder. Sprinkle about one-fourth of flour mixture over yolk mixture; carefully fold in. Repeat procedure with remaining flour, using one-fourth at a time; set aside.

Beat egg whites (at room temperature) until foamy; add cream of tartar, and beat until soft peaks form. Gradually add ½ cup sugar, 2 tablespoons at a time, beating until stiff peaks form (about 4 to 5 minutes).

Remove about 1 cup of stiffly beaten egg whites, and gently fold into yolk mixture. Gently fold yolk mixture into remaining egg whites.

Pour batter into an ungreased 10-inch tube pan, spreading evenly with a spatula. Bake at 350° for 50 minutes or until cake springs back when lightly touched. Remove from oven; invert pan and cool completely (about 40 minutes) before removing from pan. Yield: one 10-inch cake.

Mrs. Sue-Sue Hartstern,
Louisville, Kentucky.

HOT SPICED PUNCH

1 cup firmly packed brown sugar
1 cup water
¼ teaspoon salt
½ teaspoon ground cinnamon
½ teaspoon ground cloves
¼ teaspoon ground nutmeg
¼ teaspoon ground allspice
2 (16-ounce) cans jellied cranberry sauce
3½ cups water
6 cups apple juice
Butter
Cinnamon sticks (optional)

Combine sugar, 1 cup water, salt, and spices in a large Dutch oven; heat to boiling. Reduce heat, and simmer.

Combine cranberry sauce and 3½ cups water; mix well. Gradually add

cranberry mixture and apple juice to simmering sugar syrup; heat to just below simmering.

Pour punch into mugs, and dot with butter; garnish with cinnamon sticks, if desired. Yield: about 1 gallon.

Ruth Hormanski,
Melbourne Beach, Florida.

Elegant Entrées For Your Holiday Table

To be really perfect, holiday meals call for the just-right entrée. With the entrée decided on, the rest of the menu falls into place.

For a change of pace, consider a country ham baked in apple cider and then glazed with mustard and brown sugar, or fill a pork crown roast with a luscious fruit-rice dressing.

And for something really elegant, we suggest Holiday Duckling or perhaps a standing rib roast served with a fluffy Yorkshire pudding.

ROAST TURKEY WITH OYSTER STUFFING

1 (12- to 15-pound) turkey
Salt and pepper
2 pints oysters
½ cup chopped celery
½ cup chopped onion
1 bay leaf
¼ cup butter or margarine, melted
6 cups cornbread crumbs
2 eggs, beaten
1 tablespoon chopped fresh parsley
1 teaspoon poultry seasoning
About ⅓ cup butter or margarine, melted
Whole spiced peaches (optional)
Fresh parsley sprigs (optional)

Remove giblets and neck from turkey; reserve for giblet gravy, if desired. Rinse turkey thoroughly with cold water; pat dry. Sprinkle cavity with salt and pepper.

Drain 2 pints oysters, reserving 1½ cups liquid.

Sauté celery, onion, and bay leaf in ¼ cup butter until vegetables are tender. Remove bay leaf, and discard.

Combine sautéed vegetables, cornbread crumbs, eggs, chopped parsley, poultry seasoning, 1 teaspoon salt, dash of pepper, and reserved oyster liquid in a large mixing bowl; stir well.

Gently stir oysters into cornbread mixture. Stuff dressing into cavity of turkey, and close cavity with skewers. Tie ends of legs to tail with cord or string, or tuck them under flap of skin around tail. Lift wingtips up and over back so they are tucked under bird.

Brush entire bird with about ⅓ cup melted butter; place, breast side up, on a rack in roasting pan. Insert meat thermometer in breast or meaty part of thigh, making sure it does not touch bone.

Bake at 325° until meat thermometer registers 185° (about 4½ to 5½ hours); baste turkey frequently with pan drippings. If turkey starts to get too brown, cover lightly with aluminum foil. Turkey is done when drumsticks are easy to move. Garnish turkey with spiced peaches and parsley, if desired. Yield: 20 to 24 servings. *Mrs. Mary Dishon,*
Stanford, Kentucky.

HOLIDAY DUCKLING

1 (3- to 5-pound) dressed duckling
1 teaspoon salt
3 cups toasted breadcrumbs
2 cups finely diced celery
⅔ cup chopped orange sections
1 tablespoon grated orange rind
¾ teaspoon salt
½ teaspoon poultry seasoning
⅛ teaspoon pepper
1 egg, beaten
¼ cup butter or margarine, melted
2 tablespoons honey
1 teaspoon bottled brown bouquet sauce
Watercress (optional)
Orange slices (optional)

Cut wings of duckling off at first joint; rub cavity with salt. Do not prick skin. Set aside.

Combine next 7 ingredients, tossing lightly; add egg and butter, stirring gently until well mixed. Spoon dressing into cavity of duckling. Spoon remaining dressing into a shallow casserole; set aside. Close the cavity of duckling with skewers.

Combine honey and bouquet sauce, mixing well; set aside. Place duckling, breast side up, on a rack in roasting pan. Bake, uncovered, at 325° for 2 to 2½ hours or until drumsticks and thighs move easily; during last 30 minutes of cooking time, brush duckling often with honey mixture. Bake extra dressing at 325° for 15 to 20 minutes. Place duckling on serving platter; garnish with watercress and orange slices, if desired. Yield: 3 to 5 servings.

Florence L. Costello,
Chattanooga, Tennessee.

COUNTRY HAM IN APPLE CIDER

1 (12- to 14-pound) country ham
2 quarts apple cider
1 tablespoon whole cloves
½ cup firmly packed brown sugar
2 tablespoons prepared mustard
Fresh parsley sprigs (optional)

Place ham in a very large container; cover with cold water, and soak overnight. Scrub ham thoroughly with a stiff brush. Place ham, skin side down, in a large roasting pan. Pour cider over ham, and sprinkle with cloves. Cover and bake at 325° for 6 to 7 hours (allow 30 minutes per pound).

Carefully remove ham from pan juices; remove skin. Place ham, fat side up, on a cutting board; score fat in a diamond design. Return ham to roaster, fat side up. Combine brown sugar and mustard, stirring well. Coat exposed portion of ham with sugar mixture. Continue baking, uncovered, for 30 minutes.

Remove ham from roaster; discard pan drippings. Cool ham thoroughly; place on a carving board or serving platter. To serve, thinly slice ham; garnish with parsley, if desired. Yield: 24 to 28 servings.

Eva G. Key,
Isle Of Palms, South Carolina.

ROYAL CROWN ROAST OF PORK

1 (16-rib) crown roast of pork
Salt and pepper
¼ cup chopped onion
2 tablespoons butter or margarine, melted
⅔ cup uncooked instant rice
¾ cup water
⅛ teaspoon poultry seasoning
½ cup chopped dried prunes
¼ cup chopped dried apricots
Canned apricot halves, drained (optional)

Sprinkle roast on all sides with ½ teaspoon salt and ⅛ teaspoon pepper; place, bone ends up, in a shallow roasting pan. Insert meat thermometer, making sure it does not touch fat or bone.

Sauté onion in butter until tender but not browned. Add rice, water, ½ teaspoon salt, ⅛ teaspoon pepper, and poultry seasoning to onion; stir to moisten rice. Bring rice mixture to a boil; remove from heat. Cover tightly, and let stand 10 minutes. Stir dried prunes and dried apricots into the rice mixture.

Fill center of roast with rice mixture. Place a folded strip of aluminum foil over exposed ends of ribs. Bake at 350° for 25 to 30 minutes per pound or until meat thermometer registers 170°. Garnish with apricot halves, if desired. Yield: about 8 servings.

Mrs. M. L. Shannon,
Fairfield, Alabama.

STANDING RIB ROAST WITH YORKSHIRE PUDDING

Yorkshire pudding (recipe follows)
1 (6½-pound) standing rib roast
Salt and pepper
Spiced crabapples (optional)
Fresh parsley sprigs (optional)

Prepare batter for Yorkshire pudding 8 hours before time to bake to allow time for required chilling.

Sprinkle roast with salt and pepper. Place roast, fat side up, on rack in a shallow roasting pan. Insert meat thermometer, making certain end of thermometer does not touch fat or bone.

Bake roast at 325° as follows, depending on the desired degree of doneness: rare, 27 minutes per pound or 140° on

Standing rib roast gets a special touch when served with delicate Yorkshire pudding.

meat thermometer; medium, 30 minutes per pound or 160°; well done, 36 minutes per pound or 170°.

Remove roast to serving platter, reserving ¼ cup clear pan drippings for Yorkshire pudding. Garnish roast with spiced crabapples and parsley, if desired. Serve roast with Yorkshire pudding. Yield: 12 servings.

Yorkshire Pudding:

1 cup all-purpose flour
Pinch of salt
2 eggs
2 cups milk
¼ cup clear beef drippings

Combine flour and salt in a large mixing bowl. Add eggs and ½ cup milk; beat at low speed of electric mixer until dry ingredients are moistened. Gradually add ½ cup milk, beating constantly; continue beating until batter is smooth. Stir in remaining 1 cup milk; cover and refrigerate 8 hours.

Pour beef drippings into a 1½-quart clear baking dish; heat at 400° for 5

minutes. Pour batter into baking dish; bake 45 to 50 minutes or until puffed and golden brown. Serve immediately. Yield: 12 servings.

Note: Yorkshire pudding may also be baked in a 9-inch round cakepan. Increase oven temperature to 425°, and bake pudding 45 to 50 minutes.

Joan Mainor,
Columbus, Georgia.

Tip: Read labels to learn the weight, quality, and size of food products. Don't be afraid to experiment with new brands. Store brands can be equally good in quality and nutritional value, yet lower in price. Lower grades of canned fruits and vegetables are as nutritious as higher grades. Whenever possible, buy most foods by weight or cost per serving rather than by volume or package size.

These Desserts Put The Emphasis On Festive

Give a Southern cook a variety of fruits and nuts, sugar and spices, and such seasonal favorites as eggnog and mincemeat, and you'll get Holiday Cherry Dessert, Black Walnut Cake, Eggnog Pie, Mincemeat-Cheese Pie, and a whole array of sinfully rich holiday desserts.

Add ice cream as an ingredient, and there are other irresistible possibilities. Tipsy Mud Pie, for example, is a chocolate cookie-crumb crust layered with sliced bananas and filled with chocolate ice cream that's been laced with brandy and Kahlúa. After freezing, it's spread with whipped topping, drizzled with chocolate syrup, and sprinkled with chopped pecans.

Or you may be tempted by Amber Bombe, a mound of coffee and vanilla ice cream sprinkled with Almond Brittle Candy. The slices are served with a dollop of Rum Cream Topping.

BLACK WALNUT CAKE

½ cup butter, softened
½ cup shortening
2 cups sugar
5 eggs, separated
1 cup buttermilk
1 teaspoon soda
2 cups all-purpose flour
1 teaspoon vanilla extract
1½ cups chopped black walnuts
1 (3-ounce) can flaked coconut
½ teaspoon cream of tartar
Cream Cheese Frosting
Chopped black walnuts

Cream butter and shortening; gradually add sugar, beating until light and fluffy and sugar is dissolved. Add egg yolks, beating well.

Combine buttermilk and soda; stir until soda dissolves.

Add flour to creamed mixture alternately with buttermilk mixture, beginning and ending with flour. Stir in vanilla. Add 1½ cups walnuts and coconut, stirring well.

Beat egg whites (at room temperature) with cream of tartar until stiff peaks form. Fold egg whites into batter.

Pour batter into 3 greased and floured 9-inch round cakepans. Bake at 350° for 30 minutes or until cake tests done. Cool layers in pans 10 minutes; remove from pans, and cool completely. Frost cake with Cream Cheese Frosting; sprinkle remaining walnuts on top of cake. Yield: one 9-inch layer cake.

Cream Cheese Frosting:

¾ cup butter, softened
1 (8-ounce) package cream cheese, softened
1 (3-ounce) package cream cheese, softened
6¾ cups sifted powdered sugar
1½ teaspoons vanilla extract

Cream butter and cream cheese; gradually add sugar, beating until light and fluffy. Stir in vanilla. Yield: enough for one 9-inch 3-layer cake.

Mrs. Leslie L. Jones,
Richmond, Kentucky.

CRANBERRY APPLE DESSERT

1 (7¼-ounce) package vanilla wafers, finely crushed
¼ cup butter or margarine, melted
½ cup butter or margarine, softened
1 cup sifted powdered sugar
1 egg
2 cups cranberries, chopped
3 medium-size cooking apples, peeled and finely chopped
1 (8¼-ounce) can crushed pineapple, drained
1 cup sugar
1 cup miniature marshmallows
1 cup whipping cream
1 tablespoon powdered sugar

Combine crumbs and melted butter, stirring well. Press half of mixture into a 13- x 9- x 2-inch dish (crumb mixture will be loose).

Cream butter; gradually add 1 cup powdered sugar, beating until light and fluffy and sugar is dissolved. Add egg, and beat 7 to 8 minutes. Carefully spread creamed mixture evenly over the crumb mixture.

Combine cranberries, apples, pineapple, sugar, and marshmallows; stir well. Spoon fruit mixture evenly over creamed mixture.

Beat whipping cream until foamy; gradually add remaining powdered sugar, beating until soft peaks form. Spread whipped cream over fruit; sprinkle with remaining crumbs, and press lightly. Yield: 15 servings.

Mrs. John W. Stevens,
Lexington, Kentucky.

MINCEMEAT-CHEESE PIE

4 (3-ounce) packages cream cheese, softened
½ cup sugar
2 eggs, beaten
1 tablespoon grated lemon rind
1 tablespoon lemon juice
½ teaspoon vanilla extract
1½ cups prepared mincemeat
1 unbaked 9-inch pastry shell

Beat cream cheese at medium speed of electric mixer until smooth. Add sugar, eggs, lemon rind, lemon juice, and vanilla, beating well.

Spread mincemeat in pastry shell. Spoon cream cheese mixture evenly over mincemeat. Bake at 375° for 35 minutes or until cheese layer is firm when lightly touched in center. Cool to room temperature; then chill until serving time. Yield: one 9-inch pie.

Evelyn L. Beall,
Annapolis, Maryland.

Tip: To loosen cake layers or cookies left in the pan too long, return to 350° oven 2 minutes, then remove food from pan immediately.

PUMPKIN CHEESECAKE

1½ cups biscuit mix
2 tablespoons sugar
¼ cup butter or margarine
1 (8-ounce) package cream cheese, softened
¾ cup sugar
3 eggs
2 tablespoons all-purpose flour
1 teaspoon ground cinnamon
¼ teaspoon ground ginger
¼ teaspoon ground nutmeg
1 (16-ounce) can pumpkin
¼ teaspoon vanilla extract
1½ cups commercial sour cream
2 tablespoons sugar
½ teaspoon vanilla extract

Combine biscuit mix and 2 tablespoons sugar, stirring well; cut in butter with pastry blender until mixture resembles coarse meal. Press mixture into a 9-inch square baking pan.

Beat cream cheese; gradually add ¾ cup sugar, beating until light and fluffy and sugar is dissolved. Add eggs, one at a time, beating well after each addition.

Combine flour, cinnamon, ginger, and nutmeg; stir well. Add to creamed mixture, beating well. Add pumpkin and ¼ teaspoon vanilla to creamed mixture, mixing well. Pour batter over crust. Bake at 350° for 55 minutes or until set.

Beat sour cream on medium speed of electric mixer for 2 minutes. Add 2 tablespoons sugar and remaining vanilla; beat 1 minute longer. Spread over the cheesecake while hot. Refrigerate at least 6 hours. Yield: 9 servings.

Jeanne Lee Smith,
Louisville, Kentucky.

EGGNOG PIE

1 envelope unflavored gelatin
¼ cup cold water
1½ cups commercial eggnog
3 cups miniature marshmallows
¼ cup bourbon
1 cup whipping cream, whipped
1 (8-inch) chocolate crumb crust
1 tablespoon chocolate shavings

Dissolve gelatin in water; set aside.
Combine eggnog and marshmallows in top of a double boiler; bring water to a boil. Reduce heat to low; cook, stirring occasionally, until marshmallows melt and mixture is smooth. Stir gelatin into eggnog mixture. Cool.

Add bourbon, and stir well. Chill mixture until the consistency of unbeaten egg white. Fold half of whipped cream into eggnog mixture.

Pour filling into crumb crust, and chill until set. Top with remaining whipped cream, and sprinkle with chocolate shavings. Yield: one 8-inch pie.

H. W. Asbell,
Leesburg, Florida.

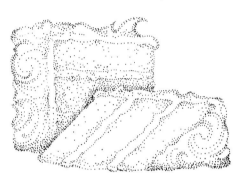

ORANGE-NUT BUTTER CAKE

¾ cup butter or margarine, softened
1 cup sugar
3 eggs
1 cup orange marmalade
4 cups all-purpose flour
1½ teaspoons soda
1 teaspoon salt
½ cup orange juice
½ cup evaporated milk
1 teaspoon vanilla extract
1 tablespoon grated orange rind
1 cup chopped pecans or walnuts
Whipped Orange Topping
Fresh orange sections (optional)

Cream butter; gradually add sugar, beating until light and fluffy and sugar is dissolved. Add eggs, one at a time, beating well after each addition. Add marmalade, and mix well.

Combine flour, soda, and salt; stir well. Combine orange juice and milk, stirring well. Add dry ingredients to batter alternately with juice mixture, beginning and ending with dry ingredients. Stir in vanilla. Add grated orange rind and pecans; stir well.

Pour batter into a greased and floured 10-inch tube pan. Bake at 350° for 1 hour and 5 minutes or until cake tests done. Cool in pan 10 minutes; remove from pan, and cool completely. Frost cake with Whipped Orange Topping; garnish with orange sections, if desired. Yield: one 10-inch cake.

Whipped Orange Topping:

1 cup whipping cream
2 tablespoons sugar
1 tablespoon grated orange rind

Beat whipping cream until foamy; gradually add sugar, beating until soft peaks form. Stir in rind. Yield: 2 cups.

Mrs. Robert E. Peeples,
Yulee, Florida.

ORANGE CREAM DESSERT

1 envelope unflavored gelatin
¼ cup cold water
¾ cup fresh orange juice, unstrained
2 tablespoons lemon juice
6 tablespoons sugar, divided
½ teaspoon grated orange rind
1 egg white
¼ teaspoon salt
1 cup whipping cream, whipped
Fresh orange slices (optional)
Mint leaves (optional)
Whipped cream (optional)
Grated orange rind (optional)

Dissolve gelatin in cold water, and set aside.

Combine orange juice and lemon juice, 3 tablespoons sugar, and orange rind in a small saucepan; bring to a boil, stirring frequently. Stir gelatin into juice mixture. Chill until the consistency of unbeaten egg white.

Beat egg white (at room temperature) and salt until foamy. Gradually add remaining 3 tablespoons sugar, beating until stiff peaks form.

Fold egg white and whipped cream into juice mixture. Pour into an oiled 1-quart mold; chill until set. To serve, unmold and garnish with orange slices and mint. Top with a dollop of whipped cream and grated orange rind, if desired. Yield: 6 to 8 servings.

Mrs. Ed Bates,
Fort Worth, Texas.

TIPSY MUD PIE

1 (15-ounce) package chocolate
  cream-filled cookies, crushed
5 tablespoons butter or margarine, melted
1 banana, thinly sliced
1 tablespoon lemon juice
1 pint chocolate ice cream, softened
½ teaspoon vanilla extract
1 tablespoon instant coffee powder
1 (12-ounce) carton frozen whipped
  topping, thawed and divided
2 tablespoons brandy
2 tablespoons Kahlúa or other
  coffee-flavored liqueur
½ cup plus 2 tablespoons chopped pecans
2 tablespoons chocolate syrup

Combine cookie crumbs and butter, mixing well. Press mixture firmly into a 10-inch pieplate. Combine banana slices and lemon juice; arrange banana slices in a single layer on chocolate crust. Cover and freeze.

Combine ice cream, vanilla, coffee powder, ¼ cup whipped topping, brandy, Kahlúa, and ½ cup pecans; mix well. Spread evenly on chocolate crust. Cover and freeze overnight.

Spread remaining whipped topping on pie; drizzle chocolate syrup over top. Sprinkle with 2 tablespoons pecans. Yield: one 10-inch pie.

Mrs. E. Lamar McMath,
Jacksonville, Florida.

HOLIDAY CHERRY DESSERT

2 eggs
1 cup sugar
1 teaspoon vanilla extract
1 cup all-purpose flour
1 teaspoon baking powder
½ teaspoon salt
½ cup chopped pecans or walnuts
1 (16-ounce) can pitted tart cherries
¾ cup sugar
2 tablespoons cornstarch
½ teaspoon almond extract
Whipped cream or vanilla ice cream

Beat eggs until thick and lemon colored; gradually add 1 cup sugar, beating well. Add vanilla; mix well.

Combine flour, baking powder, and salt; stir well. Add dry ingredients to egg mixture, and mix well. Stir in pecans. Pour ⅔ cup batter into a greased and floured 9-inch square baking pan, spreading evenly.

Drain cherries, reserving juice. Stir cherries into remaining batter. Pour batter evenly over first layer. Bake at 350° for 45 to 50 minutes. Cool; cut cake into 3-inch squares.

Add water to cherry juice to equal 1 cup. Combine remaining sugar and cornstarch in a saucepan; stir well. Add cherry juice, stirring well. Cook over low heat until clear and thickened. Stir in almond extract.

Serve squares with a dollop of whipped cream or a scoop of ice cream. Spoon cherry topping over each serving. Yield: 9 servings.   *Eunice M. Davies,*
Sarasota, Florida.

AMBER BOMBE

½ gallon vanilla ice cream, slightly
  softened
1 quart coffee ice cream, slightly softened
Almond Brittle Candy
Rum Cream Topping

Lightly brush inside of a 12-cup mold or bowl with unflavored oil. Place in freezer until thoroughly chilled. Using a chilled spoon, spread vanilla ice cream evenly on bottom and sides of mold, leaving center hollow. Freeze about 4 hours or until ice cream is firm.

Spoon coffee ice cream into center of ice cream-lined mold, filling coffee ice cream even with edge of vanilla ice cream. Cover tightly with lid of mold or aluminum foil. Freeze until very firm (at least 5 hours).

Using the tip of a knife, loosen the edges of the ice cream from the mold. Invert mold onto a chilled serving plate. Wrap a warm towel around the mold for 30 seconds. Remove the towel, and firmly hold the plate and mold together. Shake gently, and slowly lift off the mold. Sprinkle top and sides of ice cream with Almond Brittle Candy. Immediately return ice cream bombe to freezer.

To serve, cut bombe into slices and top each with a dollop of Rum Cream Topping. Yield: 12 servings.

Almond Brittle Candy:

1 cup sugar
¾ cup finely chopped almonds
Pinch of salt

Sprinkle sugar evenly in a heavy skillet. Cook slowly over very low heat, stirring occasionally, just until sugar melts to a golden syrup. (If cooked too long or at a higher temperature, syrup becomes too dark and burns.)

Remove from heat, and stir in almonds and salt. Immediately pour syrup into a buttered 9-inch pan, spreading as thinly as possible. Cool thoroughly.

Break candy into pieces, and put into container of electric blender or food processor; process until finely chopped. Yield: enough to cover top and sides of ice cream bombe.

Rum Cream Topping:

1 cup whipping cream
1 teaspoon sugar
1 tablespoon rum

Beat whipping cream until foamy; gradually add sugar and rum, beating until soft peaks form. Yield: 1 cup.

Mrs. Robert W. Deleot,
Decatur, Georgia.

Yeast Breads Herald The Season

When kitchen shelves fill up with nuts and spices and colorful candied fruits, and the smell of yeast fills the kitchen, you'll know the festive baking season has begun. Nothing quite translates the holiday feeling like a loaf of home-baked yeast bread fresh from the oven and topped with a glaze.

Two of our loaves, Chocolate Pinwheel Loaf and Cocoa-Nut Swirl Bread, have swirled centers of chocolate and nuts. Our glazed, sweet Sugar Plum Bread is full of candied fruits, raisins, and walnuts. And once you've satisfied your sweet tooth, be sure to try a loaf of our Dark Caraway Seed Bread; it's made with three kinds of flour and a generous sprinkling of caraway seeds.

SUGAR PLUM BREAD

¼ cup sugar
1 cup milk, scalded
¼ cup shortening
1 teaspoon salt
2 packages dry yeast
2 eggs, beaten
4 cups all-purpose flour
1 cup chopped walnuts
¾ cup raisins
¼ cup chopped red candied cherries
¼ cup chopped candied pineapple
1 teaspoon chopped candied lemon peel
1 teaspoon ground cardamom
Glaze (recipe follows)

Combine sugar, milk, shortening, and salt in a large bowl; stir until shortening melts. Cool to 105° to 115°. Add yeast, eggs, and 2 cups flour; mix well. Gradually stir in remaining flour.

Turn dough out on a floured surface. Knead walnuts, fruit, and cardamom into dough; continue kneading until smooth and elastic (about 8 to 10 minutes). Place in a well-greased bowl, turning to grease top. Cover and let rise in a warm place (85°), free from drafts, 40 to 50 minutes or until doubled in bulk. Punch dough down; cover and let rest 15 minutes.

Divide dough in half, and shape each half into a smooth ball. Place each on a greased baking sheet, and lightly press to flatten bottom. Cover; let rise in a warm place (85°), free from drafts, 40 to 50 minutes or until doubled in bulk. Bake at 350° for 25 minutes or until loaves are golden brown. Remove from baking sheets to wire racks. Drizzle glaze over warm loaves. Yield: 2 loaves.

Glaze:

1½ cups sifted powdered sugar
2 tablespoons water
½ teaspoon vanilla extract

Combine all ingredients, mixing well. Yield: about ¾ cup.
Mrs. Earl L. Faulkenberry,
Lancaster, South Carolina.

Tip: If breads, cakes, or pies are browning too fast, put a piece of aluminum foil over top and finish baking.

CLOVERLEAF REFRIGERATOR ROLLS

½ cup sugar
2 cups water
1 cup shortening
1 tablespoon salt
3 packages dry yeast
½ cup warm water (105° to 115°)
2 eggs, beaten
7 to 7½ cups all-purpose flour

Combine sugar, 2 cups water, shortening, and salt in a medium saucepan; place over medium heat, stirring until shortening melts. Cool to 105° to 115°.

Dissolve yeast in ½ cup warm water. Combine sugar mixture, eggs, and half of flour in a large mixing bowl; add yeast mixture, mixing well. Stir in enough remaining flour to make a soft dough. Cover tightly with plastic wrap, and refrigerate overnight.

Remove dough from refrigerator; punch down. Let rise in a warm place (85°), free from drafts, for 2 hours or until doubled in bulk. Turn dough out on a floured surface, and knead 3 or 4 times (dough will be sticky).

Lightly grease muffin pans. Shape dough into 1-inch balls; place 3 balls in each muffin cup. Cover and let rise in a warm place (85°), free from drafts, for 40 to 50 minutes or until doubled in bulk. Bake at 400° for 12 to 15 minutes or until golden brown. Yield: 4 dozen rolls.
Mrs. W. Harold Groce,
Arden, North Carolina.

CHOCOLATE PINWHEEL LOAF

½ cup milk, scalded
¼ cup butter
¼ cup sugar
1 teaspoon salt
1 package dry yeast
¼ cup warm water (105° to 115°)
2 eggs, beaten
3 cups all-purpose flour
1 (1-ounce) square unsweetened chocolate, melted and cooled
Glaze (recipe follows)

Combine scalded milk, butter, sugar, and salt; stir until butter melts. Cool to 105° to 115°.

Dissolve yeast in warm water in a large mixing bowl. Stir in milk mixture, eggs, and 2 cups flour; beat until smooth. Stir in remaining flour to make a soft dough.

Divide dough in half, and set one half aside. Turn one portion of dough out on a floured surface, and knead until smooth and elastic (about 8 to 10 minutes). Place in a well-greased bowl, turning to grease top. Cover and let rise in a warm place (85°), free from drafts, 1 hour or until doubled in bulk.

Pour melted chocolate over remaining dough; knead into dough until it has a marbled appearance (about 8 to 10 minutes). Place in a well-greased bowl, turning to grease top. Cover and let rise in a warm place (85°), free from drafts, 1 hour or until doubled in bulk.

Punch each dough down, and turn out on a floured surface; roll each into an 18- x 10-inch rectangle. Position chocolate dough on top of plain dough. Roll halves up together, jellyroll fashion, beginning at short end. Fold under ends, and place seam side down in a greased 9- x 5- x 3-inch loafpan. Cover and let rise in a warm place (85°), free from drafts, 50 to 60 minutes or until doubled in bulk. Bake at 350° for 30 minutes or until golden brown. Remove loaf from pan, and transfer to a wire rack. Drizzle glaze over warm loaf. Yield: 1 loaf.

Glaze:

1 cup sifted powdered sugar
1½ tablespoons milk
½ teaspoon vanilla extract

Combine all ingredients, mixing well. Yield: about ½ cup.
Mrs. Robert Collins,
Fairfax, Missouri.

DARK CARAWAY SEED BREAD

2 packages dry yeast
3 cups warm water (105° to 115°)
About 4 cups unbleached all-purpose flour
About 4 cups whole wheat flour
About 1 cup rye flour
2 teaspoons salt
¼ cup caraway seeds

Dissolve yeast in warm water in a large mixing bowl; set mixture aside.

Combine flour, stirring well. Gradually add about 1 cup flour mixture, salt, and caraway seeds to yeast mixture; mix well. Stir in enough remaining flour to make a soft dough.

Turn dough out on a floured surface, and knead until smooth and elastic (about 5 minutes). Place in a well-greased bowl, turning to grease top. Cover and let rise in a warm place (85°), free from drafts, 1½ hours or until doubled in bulk.

Punch dough down; turn out on a floured surface, and knead 1 minute. Place in a well-greased bowl, turning to grease top. Cover and let rise in a warm place (85°), free from drafts, 1 hour or until doubled in bulk.

Punch dough down; divide in half, and shape each half into a smooth ball. Place on a greased baking sheet, and lightly press to flatten bottom. Cover and let rise 20 minutes.

Cut ¼-inch-deep crisscross slashes in top of each loaf with a sharp knife. Place a pan of water on lower oven rack. Bake at 400° for 5 minutes. Reduce oven temperature to 375°, and bake an additional hour or until loaves sound hollow when tapped. Remove from baking sheet; cool on wire racks. Yield: 2 loaves. *Ella C. Stivers, Abilene, Texas.*

FROSTED HOT ORANGE ROLLS

¾ cup milk, scalded
½ cup margarine
½ cup sugar
2 teaspoons salt
2 packages dry yeast
½ cup warm water (105° to 115°)
1 egg, beaten
4 cups all-purpose flour
1 cup sugar
¼ cup grated orange rind
½ cup raisins (optional)
¼ cup margarine, melted
Orange glaze (recipe follows)

Combine milk, ½ cup margarine, ½ cup sugar, and salt; stir until margarine melts. Cool to 105° to 115°.

Dissolve yeast in warm water in a large mixing bowl. Stir in milk mixture, egg, and half the flour; beat until smooth. Stir in remaining flour to make a soft dough.

Place dough in a well-greased bowl, turning to grease top. Cover and refrigerate at least 2 hours.

Combine 1 cup sugar, orange rind, and raisins; set aside. Punch dough down, and divide in half. Turn dough out on a lightly floured surface. Roll each half into an 18- x 9-inch rectangle. Brush each rectangle with melted margarine; sprinkle with sugar mixture. Roll up jellyroll fashion, beginning at long side; pinch long edges to seal. Cut each roll into 1½-inch slices. Place slices in 2 well-greased 9-inch square pans. Cover and let rise in a warm place (85°), free from drafts, for 50 to 60 minutes or until doubled in bulk. Bake at 375° for 25 minutes. Spoon glaze over warm rolls. Yield: about 2 dozen.

Orange Glaze:

2 cups sifted powdered sugar
3 tablespoons orange juice

Combine sugar and orange juice, mixing well. Yield: about 1 cup.
*Mrs. Russell Wagoner,
Kerrville, Texas.*

COCOA-NUT SWIRL BREAD

About 6½ cups all-purpose flour
2 packages dry yeast
1 cup sugar, divided
2 cups milk
½ cup shortening
1½ teaspoons salt
2 eggs
2 tablespoons cocoa
2 tablespoons milk
1 (2½-ounce) package slivered almonds, chopped
Butter or margarine
Glaze (recipe follows)

Combine 3½ cups flour and yeast in a large mixing bowl; stir well.

Combine ½ cup sugar, 2 cups milk, shortening, and salt in a small saucepan; heat until liquids are very warm (120° to 130°). Gradually add to flour mixture, stirring well. Add eggs, and beat dough at low speed of an electric mixer 1 minute; increase to high speed, and beat 3 minutes. Stir in enough remaining flour to make a soft dough.

Turn dough out on a lightly floured surface, and knead until smooth and elastic (about 8 to 10 minutes). Place in a well-greased bowl, turning to grease top. Cover and let rise in a warm place (85°), free from drafts, 40 to 50 minutes or until doubled in bulk.

Punch dough down, and divide in half. Turn out on a lightly floured surface. Roll each half of dough into a 15- x 7-inch rectangle. Brush each rectangle lightly with water.

Combine remaining ½ cup sugar, cocoa, and 2 tablespoons milk; mix until smooth, adding additional milk if necessary. Spread half the cocoa mixture evenly over each rectangle; sprinkle with almonds, and dot with butter. Roll up jellyroll fashion, beginning at short end. Fold under ends, and place in a greased 9- x 5- x 3-inch loafpan. Cover and let rise in a warm place (85°), free from drafts, 40 to 50 minutes, or until doubled in bulk. Bake at 375° for 30 to 35 minutes or until loaves sound hollow when tapped. Remove loaves from pans, and transfer to wire racks. Drizzle glaze over warm loaves. Yield: 2 loaves.

Glaze:

1 cup sifted powdered sugar
1½ tablespoons milk
¼ teaspoon vanilla extract

Combine all ingredients, mixing well. Yield: about ½ cup. *Alice McNamara, Eucha, Oklahoma.*

Tip: To know when yeast is doubled in bulk, press dough flat in bowl, mark level on outside of bowl, then mark a measure on outside of bowl that is double the first.

Have A Ball With Cheese

Keep these special cheese balls in mind as the calendar fills with all the festive occasions that call for appetizers. Each cheese ball has a distinctively different appearance and flavor, but all are equally successful on the party buffet.

PIMIENTO CHEESE BALL

1 (3-ounce) package cream cheese, softened
¼ cup mayonnaise
1 cup (4 ounces) shredded Swiss cheese
1 cup (4 ounces) shredded American cheese
2 tablespoons chopped pimiento
1 teaspoon Worcestershire sauce
½ teaspoon onion powder
¼ teaspoon hot sauce
½ cup crushed potato chips
1½ teaspoons grated Parmesan cheese

Combine cream cheese and mayonnaise; blend until smooth. Add Swiss and American cheese; beat well. Add pimiento, Worcestershire sauce, onion powder, and hot sauce; beat well. Chill at least 1 hour; shape into a ball.

Combine potato chips and Parmesan cheese; roll ball in mixture. Chill until firm. Yield: 1 cheese ball.

Janet M. Filer,
Arlington, Virginia.

Deviled ham, pimiento, and hot sauce spice up Deviled Pecan Ball.

OLIVE CHEESE BALL

2 (8-ounce) packages cream cheese, softened
4 cups (1 pound) shredded mild Cheddar cheese
1 (.06-ounce) envelope Italian salad dressing mix
¼ cup chopped pimiento-stuffed olives
2 teaspoons olive juice
1 cup chopped pecans or walnuts

Combine all ingredients except pecans; mix well. Shape into a ball, and coat with pecans. Yield: 1 cheese ball.

Freda Lovelace,
Wytheville, Virginia.

DEVILED PECAN BALL

2 (8-ounce) packages cream cheese, softened
2 cups (8 ounces) shredded sharp Cheddar cheese
1 (2¼-ounce) can deviled ham
2 tablespoons chopped pimiento
2 teaspoons Worcestershire sauce
2 teaspoons grated onion
1 teaspoon dried parsley flakes
1 teaspoon lemon juice
1 teaspoon dry mustard
¼ teaspoon salt
½ teaspoon seasoned salt
¾ teaspoon paprika
2 to 4 drops of hot sauce
2 cups pecans, chopped

Combine first 3 ingredients, blending well. Stir in remaining ingredients except pecans. Chill 2 hours. Divide cheese mixture in half, and shape into 2 balls; roll in pecans. Serve with crackers. Yield: 2 cheese balls.

Mrs. Ray Sorrells,
Elizabethton, Tennessee.

Tip: To determine the size or capacity of a utensil, fill a liquid measure with water; then pour into utensil. Repeat until utensil is full, noting amount of water used. To determine a utensil's dimensions, measure from the inside edges.

BLUE CHEESE BALL

2 cups (8 ounces) shredded mild Cheddar
  cheese
2 ounces blue cheese, crumbled
1 cup grated Parmesan cheese
1 (3-ounce) package cream cheese,
  softened
½ teaspoon dry mustard
⅔ cup evaporated milk
2 cups potato chips, crushed

Combine first 6 ingredients; blend
until smooth. Chill 2 hours. Shape
cheese mixture into a ball; roll in potato
chips. Serve with crackers. Yield: 1
cheese ball. *Mrs. Charles DeHaven,*
Owensboro, Kentucky.

Sip Beverages From A Country Inn

Neatly tucked away in the Ozark
Mountains, the Red Apple Inn in
Heber Springs, Arkansas, has developed quite a flair with holiday beverages. The inn is known for its
traditional Hot Buttered Rum and a
thick, rich eggnog, as well as two flaming coffees—all as festive as the season.

You can bring the flavor of this country inn to your own holiday entertaining
with their special recipes.

CREAMY EGGNOG

12 eggs, separated
2 cups sugar
1 to 1½ pints bourbon
1 quart whipping cream, whipped
Ground nutmeg

Beat egg yolks in a large mixing bowl
until thick and lemon colored; gradually
add sugar, beating well. Slowly stir in
bourbon; cover and chill at least 1 hour.

Beat egg whites in a large mixing
bowl until stiff. Pour chilled mixture
into punch bowl, and fold in egg whites;
then fold in whipped cream. Sprinkle
with nutmeg. Yield: about 1 gallon.

KING ALFONSO

1½ ounces dark crème de cacao
1 teaspoon half-and-half
1 maraschino cherry

Pour crème de cacao into a cordial
glass; carefully spoon half-and-half over
liqueur, allowing it to float. Pierce
cherry with a toothpick, and use as garnish. Yield: 1 serving.

RED APPLE CIDER

1 quart hard cider
2 tablespoons grenadine
6 whole cloves
¼ teaspoon ground nutmeg
Dark rum or Cognac
Cinnamon sticks

Combine cider, grenadine, cloves,
and nutmeg in a medium saucepan.
Heat mixture until hot (do not boil).
Ladle into mugs; add about 1 tablespoon rum to each. Garnish each serving with a cinnamon stick. Yield: about
1 quart.

HOT BUTTERED RUM

1 (16-ounce) package brown sugar
½ cup butter, softened
½ teaspoon ground cinnamon
½ teaspoon ground nutmeg
½ teaspoon ground cloves
Dash of salt
Rum
Cinnamon sticks
Lemon slices (optional)

Combine sugar, butter, spices, and
salt in a medium mixing bowl. Beat at
medium speed of electric mixer until
well mixed. Store butter mixture in a
covered container in refrigerator.

To serve, place 1 heaping tablespoon
butter mixture, 1 jigger (1½ ounces)
rum, and 1 cinnamon stick in a mug; fill
with boiling water. Stir well. Garnish
with lemon slice, if desired. Yield:
about 18 cups.

CAFE DIABLO

3 cups hot coffee
¼ cup plus 2 tablespoons brandy
¼ cup Triple Sec or other orange-flavored
  liqueur
8 whole cloves
4 orange twists
4 lemon twists
4 (2-inch) cinnamon sticks (optional)

Fill 4 mugs with ¾ cup hot coffee
each; set aside.

Combine next 3 ingredients in a medium saucepan. Heat mixture until hot
(do not boil). Ignite and pour 2½ tablespoons into each mug; place 1 orange
twist and 1 lemon twist into each mug.
Garnish each serving with a cinnamon
stick, if desired. Yield: 4 servings.

CAFE ROYAL

¼ cup brandy or Cognac
2⅔ cups hot strong coffee
Whipped cream

Place brandy in a small saucepan, and
heat until warmed; remove from heat
and ignite. When flames die, pour 1 tablespoon brandy into each of 4 mugs.
Add ⅔ cup coffee to each, and top with
whipped cream. Yield: 4 servings.

Make-Aheads Make It Easy

If you're planning a busy day of holiday shopping, take a few minutes the
night before to prepare one of these
overnight refrigerator casseroles. After
that busy day, treat your family to a
bubbling-hot casserole in just the time it
takes to bake.

Ham, broccoli, cheese, and eggs
make a colorful combination in Ham
and Broccoli Strata. Our Macaroni and
Chicken Casserole is different from
most versions in that the uncooked macaroni is stirred in and baked with the
rest of the ingredients. Like our other
casseroles, preparation time is minimal.

FIRECRACKER ENCHILADA CASSEROLE

2 pounds ground beef
1 large onion, chopped
2 tablespoons chili powder
2 to 3 teaspoons ground cumin
1 teaspoon salt
1 (15-ounce) can ranch-style beans
6 frozen corn tortillas, thawed
1½ cups (6 ounces) shredded Monterey
    Jack cheese
1½ cups (6 ounces) shredded Cheddar
    cheese
1 (10-ounce) can tomatoes and green
    chiles
1 (10¾-ounce) can cream of mushroom
    soup, undiluted

Cook ground beef and onion in a large skillet until meat is brown and onion is tender; discard pan drippings. Add chili powder, cumin, and salt; stir well. Cook meat mixture over low heat 10 minutes.

Spoon meat mixture into a 13- x 9- x 2-inch baking pan. Layer beans, tortillas, and cheese over meat mixture. Pour tomato liquid over cheese; chop tomatoes, and spread tomatoes and chiles over cheese. Spread soup over top of casserole.

Cover baking pan; refrigerate overnight. Bake, uncovered, at 350° for 1 hour. Yield: 8 to 10 servings.
Patricia Pashby,
Memphis, Tennessee.

CHICKEN AND RICE CASSEROLE

3 cups diced cooked chicken
2 cups cooked rice
4 hard-cooked eggs, chopped
2 (10¾-ounce) cans cream of mushroom
    soup, undiluted
1½ cups chopped celery
1 small onion, chopped
1 cup mayonnaise
2 tablespoons lemon juice
1 (2¾-ounce) package sliced almonds
    (optional)
1 cup soft breadcrumbs
2 tablespoons butter or margarine, melted

Combine first 9 ingredients, stirring well. Spoon mixture into a lightly greased shallow 2-quart casserole.

Combine breadcrumbs and butter, stirring well; sprinkle over top of casserole. Cover and refrigerate overnight.

Remove from refrigerator, and allow to sit at room temperature 1 hour. Bake, uncovered, at 350° for 40 to 45 minutes or until bubbly. Yield: about 6 servings.
Hattie Truesdale,
Camden, South Carolina.

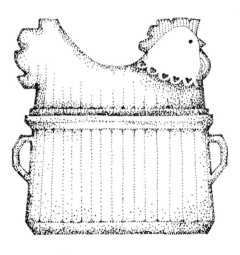

MACARONI AND CHICKEN CASSEROLE

1 cup uncooked elbow macaroni
1 cup diced cooked chicken or turkey
1 (10¾-ounce) can cream of mushroom
    soup, undiluted
1 cup milk
½ (8-ounce) package process cheese
    spread, diced
2 hard-cooked eggs, chopped
2 tablespoons chopped pimiento

Combine all ingredients, stirring well. Spoon mixture into a buttered 1½-quart casserole; cover dish, and place in refrigerator overnight.

Remove casserole from refrigerator, and allow to sit at room temperature 1 hour. Cover and bake at 350° for 1 hour and 15 minutes. Yield: 6 servings.
Lillian Blunt,
Louisville, Kentucky.

GROUND BEEF AND SAUSAGE CASSEROLE

1 (8-ounce) package spaghetti
1½ cups (6 ounces) shredded Cheddar
    cheese
1 pound ground chuck
1 pound hot bulk sausage
¼ cup chopped onion
1 clove garlic, crushed
1 (15-ounce) can tomato sauce
½ cup catsup
3 tablespoons Worcestershire sauce
1 teaspoon dried whole basil
¼ teaspoon salt

Cook spaghetti according to package directions; drain. Place in a buttered 11- x 7- x 2-inch baking dish; cover spaghetti with cheese.

Cook ground chuck, sausage, onion, and garlic until meat is browned, stirring to crumble. Drain off pan drippings. Stir in tomato sauce, catsup, Worcestershire sauce, basil, and salt. Simmer 5 minutes, stirring occasionally.

Pour meat mixture over cheese, spreading evenly. Refrigerate overnight. Bake, uncovered, at 350° for 25 to 30 minutes. Yield: 8 servings.
Nancy S. Register,
Columbus, Georgia.

CRAB-EGG CASSEROLE

6 slices white bread, crusts removed
1½ cups mayonnaise
1⅓ cups half-and-half
1 (6-ounce) package frozen crabmeat,
    thawed, drained, and flaked
1 (4-ounce) can sliced mushrooms,
    drained
1 (2-ounce) jar diced pimiento
8 hard-cooked eggs, thinly sliced
½ cup finely chopped celery
½ cup chopped green pepper
¼ cup chopped onion
3 tablespoons dry sherry
½ cup soft breadcrumbs
2 tablespoons butter or margarine, melted

Cut bread into small cubes; set aside.

Combine mayonnaise and half-and-half in a large bowl; stir well. Fold bread cubes and next 8 ingredients into mayonnaise mixture. Spoon crab mixture into a lightly greased shallow 2-quart casserole. Cover and refrigerate overnight.

Cut bread into small cubes. Layer bread cubes, broccoli, and ham in a buttered 12- x 8- x 2-inch baking dish. Combine eggs, milk, onion, mustard, and cheese; stir well. Pour over casserole; cover and refrigerate 24 hours. Bake, uncovered, at 325° for 55 to 60 minutes. Garnish with parsley, egg slices, and paprika, if desired. Yield: 6 to 8 servings. *Mrs. Jim Caughman, Charlotte, North Carolina.*

Serve Eggnog With A Spoon

Thick and Creamy Eggnog is so thick you'll want to eat it with a spoon. While more traditional eggnog recipes call for milk or cream, this one is made with whipped topping. The result is an extra-thick holiday treat.

THICK AND CREAMY EGGNOG

6 eggs, separated
½ cup sugar, divided
1 (1.5-ounce) envelope whipped topping mix
¼ cup plus 2 tablespoons bourbon
Ground nutmeg

Beat egg whites (at room temperature) until foamy. Gradually add ¼ cup sugar, beating until stiff peaks form; set aside.

Prepare whipped topping mix according to package directions; set aside.

Beat egg yolks until thick and lemon colored. Gradually add remaining sugar and bourbon, beating well.

Fold yolk-bourbon mixture and prepared whipped topping into egg whites. Spoon eggnog into individual serving glasses and sprinkle with nutmeg. Yield: about 2 quarts. *Alma Durden, Pelham, Georgia.*

Made a day ahead, Ham and Broccoli Strata is ideal for serving when your schedule is the busiest.

Combine breadcrumbs and butter, stirring well; sprinkle over top of casserole. Bake at 325° for 1 hour or until bubbly. Yield: 8 servings.
Mrs. Ron Walker, Garland, Texas.

Tip: Plan your menus for the week, but stay flexible enough to substitute good buys when you spot them. By planning ahead, you can use leftovers in another day's meal.

HAM AND BROCCOLI STRATA

12 slices white bread, crusts removed
1 (10-ounce) package frozen chopped broccoli, cooked and drained
2 cups diced cooked ham
6 eggs, slightly beaten
3½ cups milk
1 tablespoon instant minced onion
¼ teaspoon dry mustard
3 cups (12 ounces) shredded sharp Cheddar cheese
Parsley sprigs (optional)
Hard-cooked egg slices (optional)
Paprika (optional)

Choose A Dressing For The Turkey

If you're planning on turkey as the centerpiece of your holiday dinner, you'll want to count on serving one that is roasted to perfection. To guide you in preparation, here is our test kitchen method for roasting turkey.

And, of course, turkey just isn't complete without the dressing. Here's where the variety begins.

Cornbread dressing is a Southern basic, and one of our foods staff's favorite versions is Cornbread-Sage Dressing, rich with eggs, onion, celery, and buttermilk. Fruited Cornbread Dressing, a delicious variation, calls for apples, raisins, and prunes to be stirred into the cornbread base.

For a change from a cornbread base, try Pecan-Sage Dressing. It's based on breadcrumbs and ground pecans.

ROAST TURKEY

1 (12- to 14-pound) turkey
Salt
Melted butter, margarine, or vegetable oil

Remove giblets, and rinse turkey thoroughly with cold water; pat dry. Sprinkle cavity with salt. Tie ends of legs to tail with cord or string, or tuck them under flap of skin around tail. Lift wingtips up and over back so they are tucked under bird.

Brush entire bird with melted butter; place on a roasting rack, breast side up. Insert meat thermometer in breast or meaty part of thigh, making sure it does not touch bone. Bake at 325° until meat thermometer reaches 185° (about 4½ to 5 hours). If turkey starts to brown too much, cover loosely with aluminum foil.

When turkey is two-thirds done, cut the cord or band of skin holding the drumstick ends to the tail; this will ensure that the inside of the thighs is cooked. Turkey is done when drumsticks are easy to move up and down. Let stand 15 minutes before carving. Yield: 20 to 24 servings.

CORNBREAD-SAGE DRESSING

3 cups self-rising cornmeal
¼ cup all-purpose flour
1 tablespoon sugar
1 teaspoon salt
Pinch of soda
3 cups buttermilk
2 eggs, well beaten
1 cup chopped celery
¾ cup chopped onion
3 tablespoons bacon drippings
1¾ cups herb-seasoned stuffing mix
½ teaspoon rubbed sage
1 (10¾-ounce) can cream of chicken soup, undiluted
3 cups turkey or chicken broth

Combine cornmeal, flour, sugar, salt, and soda, stirring lightly; add buttermilk and eggs, mixing well. Stir in chopped celery and onion.

Heat bacon drippings in a 10-inch iron skillet until very hot; add 1 tablespoon drippings to batter, mixing well.

Pour batter into hot skillet, and bake at 450° about 30 minutes or until bread is lightly browned. Crumble into a large mixing bowl; add stuffing mix and sage. Set aside.

Place soup in a medium saucepan; gradually stir broth into soup. Cook over medium heat, stirring constantly, until thoroughly heated. Pour over crumb mixture; stir well. Spoon into a well-greased 13- x 9- x 2-inch baking dish; bake at 375° for 35 to 40 minutes or until thoroughly heated. Yield: 12 to 15 servings. *Bertha Stutts, Waynesboro, Tennessee.*

PECAN-SAGE DRESSING

2 (1-pound) loaves stale bread
3 cups chopped onion
4 cups chopped celery
1 cup butter or margarine, melted
½ cup ground pecans
1½ teaspoons salt
½ teaspoon pepper
½ teaspoon rubbed sage
3¼ to 3½ cups hot chicken or turkey broth

Place several slices of bread in container of electric processor or blender;

process until finely crumbed. Repeat procedure until all bread is used.

Sauté onion and celery in butter until tender. Place in a large mixing bowl; add crumbs and remaining ingredients, mixing well. Spoon into a well-greased 13- x 9- x 2-inch baking dish; bake at 325° for 40 to 45 minutes or until thoroughly heated. Yield: 12 to 15 servings. *Mrs. David R. Gallrein, Anchorage, Kentucky.*

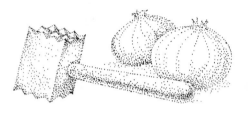

FRUITED CORNBREAD DRESSING

1 (12-ounce) box prunes, chopped
½ cup water
1 pound bulk pork sausage
½ cup butter or margarine
¼ cup chopped onion
2 cooking apples, peeled and chopped
¼ cup raisins
¼ cup molasses
2 (8-ounce) packages cornbread stuffing mix
1 cup water

Combine prunes and ½ cup water in a small saucepan. Bring to a boil; reduce heat and simmer 2 minutes, stirring constantly. Set aside.

Cook sausage in a skillet until lightly browned, stirring constantly. Remove sausage, and drain off drippings. Set sausage aside.

Melt butter in skillet; cook onion and apple just until tender. Combine all ingredients in a large mixing bowl, and mix well. Spoon into a well-greased 13- x 9- x 2-inch baking dish. Cover and bake at 300° for 45 minutes. Yield: 12 to 15 servings. *Kathryn Bibelhauser, Louisville, Kentucky.*

Serve A Soup
Or Stew

Here's a collection of tempting soups and stews just right for winter's chilly days. No matter what your preference, you'll find they all have one thing in common—that great homemade flavor.

If vegetable soup is your choice, try Hamburger Soup. It's filled with ground beef, vegetables, and noodles. And those who like meat stew will love this version of that Southern favorite, Brunswick stew.

Hamburger Soup, thick with meat, vegetables, and noodles, makes an inviting main dish.

HUNGARIAN STEW WITH NOODLES

½ cup vegetable oil
1 medium clove garlic
5 pounds lean beef for stewing, cut into
    1-inch cubes
4 medium onions, sliced
3 (6-ounce) cans tomato paste
2½ cups water
1 tablespoon paprika
2 teaspoons salt
1 teaspoon pepper
1 bay leaf
2 (8-ounce) packages medium egg noodles,
    cooked
2 tablespoons butter or margarine, melted
1 tablespoon minced fresh parsley
1 tablespoon grated lemon rind
½ teaspoon caraway seeds

Heat oil in a large Dutch oven; add garlic and cook 1 minute over medium-high heat. Discard garlic. Add beef and onion; cook until meat is browned, stirring occasionally. Stir in tomato paste, water, paprika, salt, pepper, and bay leaf; bring to a boil. Reduce heat; cover and cook over low heat 2 hours or until meat is tender; stir occasionally.

Toss noodles with butter and parsley. Top stew with lemon rind and caraway seeds; serve with egg noodles. Yield: 12 servings.   *Carolyn Brantley,*
Greenville, Mississippi.

Tip: Burned food can be removed from an enamel saucepan by using the following procedure: fill the pan with cold water containing 2 to 3 tablespoons salt, and let stand overnight. The next day, cover and bring water to a boil.

HAMBURGER SOUP

1 pound ground beef
1 medium onion, chopped
1 (16-ounce) can whole tomatoes,
    undrained
4 cups water
2 beef-flavored bouillon cubes
1 teaspoon salt
½ to 1 teaspoon pepper
1 bay leaf
¾ cup sliced celery
1 teaspoon Worcestershire sauce
1 (10-ounce) package frozen mixed
    vegetables
1 cup medium egg noodles, uncooked
½ teaspoon dried whole thyme

Cook ground beef and onion over medium heat until browned. Drain on paper towels; discard pan drippings. Add next 8 ingredients; bring to a boil. Cover and simmer 30 minutes. Add vegetables, noodles, and thyme. Bring to a boil; simmer, uncovered, about 20 minutes, stirring occasionally. Yield: 6 to 8 servings.   *Mildred Sherrer,*
Bay City, Texas.

Tip: Pouring a strong solution of salt and hot water down the sink will help eliminate odors and remove grease from drains.

BRUNSWICK STEW

1 (4½-pound) pork roast
1 (4½-pound) hen
3 (16-ounce) cans tomatoes, undrained and finely chopped
1 (8-ounce) can tomato sauce
3 large onions, finely chopped
2 small green peppers, finely chopped
¾ cup vinegar
¼ cup sugar
1 cup water
¼ cup all-purpose flour
1 tablespoon salt
½ teaspoon pepper
½ teaspoon ground turmeric
2 to 3 tablespoons hot sauce
1 (20-ounce) package frozen shoepeg corn

Place roast, fat side up, on rack in a roasting pan. Insert meat thermometer, being sure it does not touch bone or fat. Roast pork at 325° until thermometer reaches 170°. Cool. Trim and discard fat; cut pork into 2-inch pieces.

Place hen in a Dutch oven, and cover with water. Bring to a boil; cover and reduce heat. Simmer 2 hours or until tender. Remove hen from broth and cool. (Reserve broth for use in another recipe.) Bone hen, and cut meat into 2-inch pieces.

Grind pork and chicken coarsely in food processor or with meat grinder. Combine ground meat, tomatoes, tomato sauce, onion, green pepper, vinegar, and sugar in a large Dutch oven. Combine water and flour, stirring until flour is dissolved. Stir into meat mixture. Stir in salt, pepper, turmeric, and hot sauce. Cook over medium heat about 30 minutes, stirring occasionally. Add water, as needed, to reach desired consistency. Stir in corn, and cook an additional 10 minutes. Yield: 14 to 16 servings.

Note: Stew may be frozen. To serve, thaw and cook until thoroughly heated.
Roy Carlisle,
Columbus, Georgia.

CHICKEN NOODLE SOUP

1 (3½- to 4-pound) broiler-fryer
8 to 10 cups water
¼ teaspoon dried whole basil
1 tablespoon chopped fresh parsley
¼ teaspoon celery salt
⅛ teaspoon garlic salt
1 bay leaf
2 teaspoons salt
¼ teaspoon pepper
4 medium carrots, chopped
1 small onion, chopped
1 cup fine egg noodles

Combine first 9 ingredients in a large Dutch oven; cook 1½ hours or until chicken is tender. Remove chicken, and discard bay leaf. Let chicken cool. Remove meat from bones and dice meat; set aside.

Bring chicken broth to a boil; add carrots and onion. Simmer 30 minutes; add meat and noodles. Cook 15 minutes. Yield: 6 servings. *Mary Dishon,*
Stanford, Kentucky.

Steam A Pudding For The Holidays

Steamed puddings are those stately desserts that usually appear only during the holiday season. While they may all look alike, the flavors can be quite different, as these two recipes show.

Old-Fashioned Plum Pudding is a combination of suet, spices, currants, raisins, and several kinds of candied fruit. The recipe makes a generous five puddings, so plan to serve a large gathering, or give the extra puddings as a special holiday gift.

Steamed Mincemeat Pudding is an updated version of this traditional dessert. It lacks the suet, but features mincemeat, orange rind, and walnuts. A hard sauce laced with brandy is its sweet accompaniment.

STEAMED MINCEMEAT PUDDING

1 (9-ounce) package condensed mincemeat
1 cup orange juice
1 teaspoon grated orange rind
2 eggs
½ cup firmly packed dark brown sugar
1 tablespoon rum extract
½ cup fine, dry breadcrumbs
1 cup all-purpose flour
2 teaspoons baking powder
½ teaspoon salt
½ cup chopped walnuts
Brandied hard sauce (recipe follows)

Crumble mincemeat into a small saucepan; add orange juice and rind. Boil mincemeat mixture 2 minutes, stirring occasionally. Cool.

Beat eggs until lemon colored; add sugar, and beat until thick. Add rum extract, mixing well. Stir in mincemeat mixture and breadcrumbs.

Combine flour, baking powder, and salt; stir well. Add to mincemeat mixture, and mix well. Stir in walnuts.

Spoon mixture into a well-greased 1-quart pudding mold, and cover tightly with lid. (Or spoon mixture into a well-greased heatproof bowl, and cover with a double thickness of buttered aluminum foil; secure foil with string.)

Place mold on a shallow rack in a large deep kettle with enough boiling water to come halfway up mold. Cover kettle; steam pudding 1 hour in continuously boiling water (replace water as needed). Unmold and serve with brandied hard sauce. Store leftover pudding in refrigerator; reheat before serving. Yield: about 8 servings.

Brandied Hard Sauce:

½ cup butter or margarine, softened
2 cups powdered sugar, sifted
1 egg yolk, beaten
2 tablespoons brandy
½ teaspoon vanilla extract

Cream butter; gradually add sugar, beating until light and fluffy. Add remaining ingredients; mix well. Chill. Yield: about 2 cups. *Shirley Hodge,*
Delray Beach, Florida.

OLD-FASHIONED PLUM PUDDING

1½ pounds (13½ cups) breadcrumbs
1½ pounds finely chopped suet
3 cups sugar
1 quart milk
2 tablespoons baking powder
2 teaspoons ground cinnamon
1 teaspoon ground mace
1 teaspoon ground cloves
3⅓ cups currants
1 (15-ounce) package raisins
1 cup chopped candied citron
1 cup chopped candied lemon peel
1 cup chopped candied orange peel
1 cup halved candied cherries
2 cups all-purpose flour
Hard sauce (recipe follows)

Combine first 8 ingredients in a large mixing bowl; stir well.

Combine fruit and flour, stirring well. Add fruit mixture to breadcrumb mixture, and stir well. Spoon about 3¼ cups mixture into each of five greased 1-pound coffee cans or pudding molds. Cover cans with a double thickness of aluminum foil; secure foil with string. (Or tightly cover molds with lids.)

Place cans on a shallow rack in a large, deep kettle with enough boiling water to come halfway up cans. Cover kettle; steam puddings 3 to 4 hours in continuously boiling water (replace as needed). Unmold and serve with hard sauce. Store extra puddings in refrigerator; reheat before serving. Yield: about 40 servings.

Note: Depending on size of kettle and steaming utensils used, you may need to use more than one kettle, or repeat steaming process.

Hard Sauce:

1 cup firmly packed brown sugar
½ cup sugar
¼ cup cornstarch
¼ teaspoon salt
3 cups boiling water
½ cup butter or margarine
2 teaspoons vanilla extract
1 teaspoon ground nutmeg

Combine sugar, cornstarch, and salt in a saucepan; stir well. Add remaining ingredients. Cook over medium heat, stirring constantly, about 5 minutes or until thickened. Serve warm. Yield: 1 quart.
Mrs. Lowell R. Wilkins,
Rome, Georgia.

Pass The Dip And Crackers

A platter of bite-size vegetables, a basket of chips or crackers, a bowl or two of dip—and you're ready for a party.

If you're serving cold dips—like our creamy Dill Dip—try to make them a day ahead of time; the extra time will allow the flavors to blend and the taste to improve considerably.

But if you'd like to add warmth to your party, serve Chili Con Queso Supreme—it's a dip that's served hot and filled with green chiles.

CLAM DIP

1 (6½-ounce) can minced clams
1 (8-ounce) package cream cheese, softened
1 cup small-curd cottage cheese
½ cup mayonnaise
1 tablespoon Worcestershire sauce
½ teaspoon garlic powder
Salt to taste

Drain clams, reserving juice. Combine 1 to 2 tablespoons clam juice and cream cheese in container of electric blender; blend on medium speed until smooth. Add next 5 ingredients; process until smooth. Stir in clams. Serve dip with raw vegetables or crackers. Yield: about 1¾ cups.

Note: Additional clam juice may be added if dip is too thick after being in the refrigerator.
Mrs. James L. Marshall, Jr.,
Pulaski, Virginia.

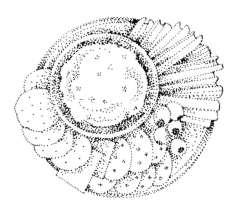

DILL DIP

1 (8-ounce) carton commercial sour cream
1 cup mayonnaise
1 teaspoon Beau Monde seasoning
3 tablespoons instant minced onion
3 tablespoons chopped parsley
1 tablespoon dried dillweed

Combine all ingredients, mixing well. Chill. Serve with fresh vegetables or potato chips. Yield: about 2 cups.
Mrs. H. A. Wagner,
Hendersonville, North Carolina.

DEVILED CHEESE DUNK

1 (5-ounce) jar pimiento cheese spread
1 (2¼-ounce) can deviled ham
½ cup mayonnaise or salad dressing
2 tablespoons minced parsley
1 tablespoon minced onion
4 drops hot sauce

Combine all ingredients; beat with electric mixer 5 minutes. Chill. Serve with crackers, potato chips, or fresh vegetables. Yield: about 1⅓ cups.
Mrs. W. J. Scherffius,
Mountain Home, Arkansas.

CHILE CON QUESO SUPREME

1 pound hot bulk pork sausage
2 pounds process American cheese, cut into 1-inch cubes
½ cup milk
1 (10-ounce) can tomatoes and green chiles, undrained and chopped

Place sausage in a skillet; cook over medium heat until done, stirring to break apart. Drain well.

Place cheese and milk in top of a double boiler; cook over medium heat until cheese is melted, stirring constantly. Stir in sausage and tomatoes and green chiles. Serve warm with tortilla chips. Yield: 5½ cups.
Lynda Gottschalk,
Winters, Texas.

FRESH FRUIT DIP

½ cup sugar
¼ cup cornstarch
½ teaspoon salt
2 eggs, beaten
1 cup pineapple juice
Grated rind and juice of 1 orange
Grated rind and juice of 1 lemon
2 (3-ounce) packages cream cheese, softened

Combine first 7 ingredients in top of a double boiler; cook over medium heat until smooth and thickened, stirring constantly. Remove from heat; cool.

Beat cream cheese with electric mixer until fluffy; add cooked mixture, beating until well blended. Chill. Serve with fresh apples or pears. Yield: about 2½ cups.
Cheryl Ann Jackson,
Live Oak, Florida.

Salad With Shrimp And More

When our test-kitchen staff tasted this very special Shrimp and Avocado Salad, the consensus was—delicious! The contrasting textures of firm fresh shrimp, creamy avocado, crunchy celery, and green pepper are united with lemon juice and basil, topped with a mayonnaise dressing, and given an attractive garnish of olives, eggs, and tomatoes.

Egg slices, ripe olives, and tomato garnish each serving of light, refreshing Shrimp and Avocado Salad.

A Quick Gazpacho From The Processor

A food processor saves time on just about every dish you prepare, according to Isabelle Stern of Birmingham. As co-owner of a popular gourmet kitchen shop, Isabelle is always looking for ways to save time on meal preparation.

"I've had a processor for years, and it really changes the way I cook at home," she explains. "I can prepare all sorts of things that I never had time for before. And since you can chop, slice, and mix all in the same bowl, it also saves time on cleanup chores."

The various blades are designed to perform different functions, but as Isabelle explains, each blade can do several things. For example, when preparing gazpacho, she uses the chopping blade to process the first vegetable mixture until it is soupy. Then she uses the same blade to coarsely chop additional vegetables. The difference is simply in the length of time the processor runs.

Here Isabelle shares a delicious food processor-adapted recipe for Gazpacho. Serve it as a first course at dinner, or for a refreshing, light lunch.

GAZPACHO

4 stalks celery, cut into 1-inch pieces
1 green pepper, quartered
1 medium cucumber, cut in half lengthwise
3 large tomatoes, peeled and quartered
1 small onion, quartered
1 tablespoon fresh parsley leaves
1 clove garlic, peeled
3 cups tomato juice
½ cup tarragon-flavored white wine vinegar
2 teaspoons salt
1 teaspoon pepper
1 teaspoon Worcestershire sauce
¼ to ½ teaspoon hot sauce

Position knife blade in dry processor bowl; place cover on top. With processor running, quickly drop half of celery, half of green pepper, half of cucumber, 8 tomato quarters, onion, parsley, and garlic through food chute. Process until finely chopped (stop processor and scrape down sides, if necessary). Remove mixture to a large bowl, and set aside.

Position knife blade in processor bowl. Add remaining celery, green pepper, cucumber, and tomato. Pulse 2 to 3

SHRIMP AND AVOCADO SALAD

3 cups water
¾ pound small shrimp
1 large avocado, cut into ½-inch cubes
1 tablespoon minced onion
¼ cup chopped celery
¼ cup chopped green pepper
½ teaspoon dried whole basil
¼ teaspoon salt
2 tablespoons lemon juice
¼ cup mayonnaise or salad dressing
¼ cup catsup
Dash of paprika
1 teaspoon lemon juice
Lettuce leaves
2 hard-cooked eggs, sliced
6 ripe olives, sliced
1 small tomato, quartered

Bring water to a boil; add shrimp, and return to a boil. Lower heat, and simmer 3 to 5 minutes. Drain well; rinse with cold water. Peel and devein shrimp.

Combine shrimp with next 4 ingredients; sprinkle with basil, salt, and lemon juice. Set aside.

Combine mayonnaise, catsup, paprika, and 1 teaspoon lemon juice; mix dressing well, and set aside.

Line 4 individual salad bowls with lettuce leaves, and fill each with shrimp mixture. Pour desired amount of dressing over top. Garnish with egg slices, olives, and tomatoes. Yield: 4 servings.

Clarissa Wells,
Lancaster, Ohio.

times or until vegetables are coarsely chopped; add to other vegetables.

Combine remaining ingredients, mixing well. Add juice mixture to vegetable mixture, stirring well. Cover and chill at least 3 hours. Yield: 8 servings.

Isabelle Stern,
Birmingham, Alabama.

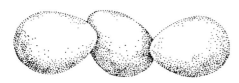

Eggs: The Microwave Method

Microwaved eggs are not only faster and easier than conventionally cooked eggs, they're creamier and fluffier. Another plus: there's no crusty pan to clean, and you don't have to use butter or oil to keep them from sticking.

Eggs are a delicate food and deserve delicate treatment. Unless eggs are scrambled or mixed with heartier ingredients, HIGH power should not be used. The egg yolk, which is higher in fat, cooks faster than the white. HIGH power will overcook the yolk before the white sets. All eggs should be removed from the microwave oven before they are completely set. Allow eggs to stand for 1 to 4 minutes to complete cooking.

To acquaint you with the advantages of microwaving eggs, we present a variety of recipes that range from a puffy omelet to Easy Eggs Benedict. Since wattage of microwave ovens varies, the cooking times will vary. A time range is given in our recipes to allow for the difference. To prevent overcooking, always check for doneness at the lower end of the range.

The following tips and techniques will ensure good results.

Scrambled eggs: Eggs scrambled in the microwave oven are fluffier than when conventionally cooked. It is not necessary to use butter or oil to prevent sticking; however, you can use it for added flavor, if desired. Scrambled eggs will cook first around the edges. Stir once or twice during the microwave cycle, breaking up set portions and pushing them to the center of the dish. After microwaving, let scrambled eggs stand 1 to 2 minutes to complete cooking; stir just before serving.

Poached eggs: Microwaved poached eggs are slipped into boiling water, much like conventionally poached eggs. The boiling water helps to set the white, without overcooking the yolk. Pierce egg yolks with a wooden pick before poaching; this prevents excess steam build-up, which will cause the yolks to burst. Let eggs stand 2 to 3 minutes before serving.

Puffy omelets: Microwaved puffy omelets (egg whites beaten and folded into yolks) rise higher and don't collapse as readily as when conventionally cooked. After about half the cooking time has elapsed, lift edges of omelet with a spatula so uncooked portions can spread evenly. Continue microwaving until the center is almost set. The center will complete cooking while you add the filling and transfer the omelet to a serving dish.

Hard-cooked eggs: Eggs cannot be hard-cooked in a microwave oven. Steam builds up inside the shell, causing the egg to burst from pressure. However, a product similar to hard-cooked eggs can be achieved by microwaving. Simply break eggs into individual custard cups or microwave-safe coffee cups; pierce each yolk with a wooden pick. Cover with heavy-duty plastic wrap, and microwave at MEDIUM (50% power) for ¾ to 1¼ minutes per egg (see recipe for Creamed Eggs in Patty Shells). While this product is not suitable for stuffing, it works well for creamed eggs, egg salad, or other dishes that use chopped eggs.

CREAMED EGGS IN PATTY SHELLS

4 eggs
2 slices bacon, coarsely chopped
¼ cup sliced fresh mushrooms
2 tablespoons all-purpose flour
¼ teaspoon salt
⅛ teaspoon pepper
1 cup milk
½ cup (2 ounces) shredded sharp Cheddar cheese
2 tablespoons chopped fresh parsley
4 baked patty shells
Paprika

Gently break 1 egg into a 6-ounce custard cup or microwave-safe coffee cup; repeat with remaining eggs. Pierce each yolk with a wooden pick. Cover each cup with heavy-duty plastic wrap; arrange cups in a circle on a microwave-safe platter. Microwave at MEDIUM for 3 to 5 minutes or until eggs are almost set, giving cups one half-turn.

Test eggs with a wooden pick (yolks should be just firm and whites should be almost set). Let eggs stand, covered, for 1 to 2 minutes to complete cooking. (If eggs are not desired degree of doneness after standing, cover and continue microwaving briefly.) Let eggs cool; cut into about ½-inch pieces.

Place bacon in a deep 1½-quart casserole; cover with waxed paper. Microwave at HIGH for 1½ minutes; add mushrooms, stirring well. Cover and microwave at HIGH for 2½ to 3½ minutes or until bacon is done. Remove bacon and mushrooms with a slotted spoon, reserving drippings in casserole. Set bacon and mushrooms aside.

Add flour, salt, and pepper to drippings; blend until smooth. Gradually stir in milk. Microwave at HIGH for 1½ minutes; stir well. Microwave at HIGH for 2 to 3 minutes, stirring at 1-minute intervals, until thickened and bubbly.

Add cheese, eggs, bacon, mushrooms, and parsley to sauce; stir until cheese melts. Microwave at MEDIUM for 1 minute. Spoon into patty shells; sprinkle with paprika. Yield: 2 to 4 servings.

BACON-AND-EGGS SCRAMBLE

4 slices bacon, diced
¼ cup sliced green onion
¼ cup sliced mushrooms
4 eggs
3 tablespoons milk
¼ teaspoon celery salt
⅛ teaspoon pepper

Place bacon in a 1-quart casserole. Microwave at HIGH for 2 minutes; add green onion and mushrooms, mixing well. Microwave at HIGH for 3 to 5 minutes or until bacon is almost done and onion is crisp-tender. Drain off drippings.

Combine eggs, milk, celery salt, and pepper in a small bowl; beat slightly. Add egg mixture to bacon mixture, mixing well. Microwave at HIGH for 1 minute. Break up set portions of egg with a fork, and push toward center of dish. Microwave at HIGH for 1 to 2 minutes or until eggs are almost set (eggs will be soft and moist), stirring once. Cover and let stand 1 to 2 minutes to complete cooking. Yield: 2 to 4 servings.

PUFFY SAUSAGE OMELET

¼ **pound bulk pork sausage**
2 **tablespoons chopped onion**
¼ **cup commercial sour cream**
3 **eggs, separated**
3 **tablespoons milk**
¼ **teaspoon salt**
¼ **teaspoon baking powder**
⅛ **teaspoon pepper**
1 **tablespoon butter or margarine**

Crumble sausage in a 1-quart casserole; add onion. Cover with waxed paper, and microwave at HIGH for 1½ to 3 minutes or until sausage is done; drain off drippings. Stir sour cream into sausage mixture; cover and set aside.

Beat egg whites (at room temperature) until stiff but not dry. Combine yolks, milk, salt, baking powder, and pepper; beat well. Gently fold egg whites into yolk mixture.

Place butter in a 9-inch pieplate. Microwave at HIGH for 30 to 45 seconds or until melted. Pour egg mixture into pieplate. Microwave at MEDIUM for 3 to 5 minutes or until omelet is partially set; lift edges with a spatula so uncooked portion spreads evenly. Microwave at MEDIUM for 2 to 4½ minutes or until center is almost set.

Spread sausage mixture over half of omelet. Loosen omelet with spatula, and fold in half. Gently slide the omelet onto a serving plate. Yield: 2 to 3 servings.

EASY EGGS BENEDICT

4 **(⅛-inch-thick) slices Canadian bacon**
Vinegar
4 **eggs**
2 **English muffins, split and toasted**
Hollandaise sauce (recipe follows)

Arrange Canadian bacon on a paper plate; cover plate with waxed paper, and set aside.

Place 2 tablespoons water in each of four 6-ounce custard cups; add ¼ teaspoon vinegar to each. Microwave at HIGH for 2 to 3 minutes or until water is boiling. Gently break 1 egg into each cup; lightly pierce each yolk with a wooden pick. Cover cups with heavy-duty plastic wrap, and arrange cups in a circle on a microwave-safe platter. Microwave at MEDIUM HIGH for 2 to 3 minutes or until almost all of white is opaque (egg will not be completely set). Let eggs stand 2 to 3 minutes.

Microwave Canadian bacon at HIGH for 1 to 1½ minutes or until hot. Place

1 slice Canadian bacon on each muffin half. Remove eggs from custard cups with a slotted spoon, and place 1 egg on each Canadian bacon slice. Top with hollandaise sauce. Serve immediately. Yield: 2 servings.

Hollandaise Sauce:

½ **cup butter or margarine**
3 **egg yolks**
1 **tablespoon plus 1½ teaspoons lemon juice**
¼ **teaspoon salt**
Dash of white pepper

Place butter in a 2-cup glass measure; microwave at HIGH for 45 seconds to 1 minute or until butter is melted (do not allow butter to boil).

Combine remaining ingredients in container of electric blender; blend until thick and lemon colored. With blender running, add melted butter in a slow steady stream; continue to process until thick. Yield: about ¾ cup.

Please Pass The Potatoes

Potatoes again? You'll hear no complaints when you serve Creamy Chive-Stuffed Potatoes. This version of twice-baked potatoes is enriched with butter, sour cream, chopped chives, and onion.

Onion also flavors our Fluffy Potato Casserole, a creamy blend of potatoes, cream cheese, and eggs topped with French-fried onion rings before baking.

CREAMY CHIVE-STUFFED POTATOES

8 **medium baking potatoes**
Vegetable oil
½ **cup butter or margarine, softened**
1 **(2-ounce) carton frozen chopped chives, thawed**
2 **tablespoons chopped onion**
1 **(16-ounce) carton commercial sour cream**
½ **teaspoon salt**
¼ **teaspoon pepper**
Paprika

Scrub potatoes thoroughly, and rub skins with oil; bake at 400° for 1 hour or until done.

Allow potatoes to cool to touch. Slice skin away from top of each potato. Carefully scoop out pulp, leaving shells intact; mash pulp.

Combine potato pulp, butter, chives, onion, sour cream, salt, and pepper; mix well. Stuff shells with potato mixture; sprinkle with paprika. Wrap in heavy-duty aluminum foil; bake potatoes at 400° for 10 minutes or until heated thoroughly. Yield: 8 servings.

Gloria Pedersen,
Brandon, Mississippi.

FLUFFY POTATO CASSEROLE

2 **cups mashed potatoes**
1 **(8-ounce) package cream cheese, softened**
1 **small onion, finely chopped**
2 **eggs, well beaten**
1 **tablespoon all-purpose flour**
¼ **teaspoon salt**
⅛ **teaspoon pepper**
1 **(3-ounce) can French-fried onion rings, crushed**

Combine first 7 ingredients; beat 2 to 3 minutes at medium speed of electric mixer. Pour into a greased 1½-quart casserole. Spread crushed onions evenly over top. Bake, uncovered, at 300° for 30 to 35 minutes. Yield: 4 servings.

Mrs. Farmer L. Burns,
New Orleans, Louisiana.

Irresistible Chocolate Treats

For those of us who love chocolate (and who doesn't), new recipes are always welcome. Peanut Butter-Chocolate Balls, chewy German Cream Cheese Brownies, and Blender-Quick Chocolate Mousse are three of the best chocolate treats we've tasted.

PEANUT BUTTER-CHOCOLATE BALLS

1½ cups graham cracker crumbs
1½ cups flaked coconut
1½ cups chopped nuts
1 (16-ounce) package powdered sugar
1 (12-ounce) jar crunchy peanut butter
1 teaspoon vanilla extract
1 cup butter or margarine, melted
½ bar paraffin
1 (6-ounce) package semisweet chocolate
  morsels

Combine first 7 ingredients, stirring well. Shape into 1-inch balls.

Melt paraffin in top of a double boiler; add semisweet morsels, and heat until melted, stirring constantly. Place several peanut butter balls in chocolate mixture; roll with spoon to coat evenly. Remove from mixture with spoon, and place on waxed paper to cool. Reheat chocolate if it thickens during dipping. Yield: about 9 dozen.

Note: Make these ahead of time, and freeze for later use. Remove from freezer 1 hour before serving.

Kitty Winchester,
Hamlet, North Carolina.

GERMAN CREAM CHEESE BROWNIES

1 (4-ounce) package sweet cooking
  chocolate
5 tablespoons butter or margarine,
  divided
1 (3-ounce) package cream cheese,
  softened
¼ cup sugar
3 eggs
1 tablespoon all-purpose flour
½ teaspoon vanilla extract
¾ cup sugar
½ cup all-purpose flour
½ teaspoon baking powder
¼ teaspoon salt
1 teaspoon vanilla extract
¼ teaspoon almond extract
½ cup chopped nuts

Melt chocolate and 3 tablespoons butter over low heat, stirring frequently; set aside to cool.

Soften remaining 2 tablespoons butter. Add cream cheese, creaming until light. Gradually add ¼ cup sugar, beating until fluffy. Stir in 1 egg, 1 tablespoon flour, and ½ teaspoon vanilla. Set aside.

Beat 2 eggs until lemon colored. Gradually add ¾ cup sugar, beating

until thick. Combine ½ cup flour, baking powder, and salt; add to egg mixture, mixing well. Stir in cooled chocolate, 1 teaspoon vanilla, almond extract, and nuts.

Pour half of chocolate batter into a greased 8-inch pan. Spread with cheese mixture; top with remaining chocolate batter. Cut through mixture in pan with a knife to create a marbled effect. Bake at 350° for 35 to 40 minutes. Cool; cut into 16 (2-inch) squares. Yield: 16 brownies.

Janet M. Filer,
Arlington, Virginia.

BLENDER-QUICK CHOCOLATE MOUSSE

4 eggs
1 (6-ounce) package semisweet chocolate
  morsels
¼ cup plus 1 tablespoon hot coffee
1 tablespoon vanilla extract
Whipped cream (optional)

Separate egg yolks and whites; bring whites to room temperature.

Place semisweet chocolate morsels in blender; blend until morsels are in small pieces. Add coffee, and blend until smooth. Add egg yolks and vanilla; blend 1 minute.

Beat egg whites until stiff; fold in chocolate mixture. Pour into a 1-quart casserole or soufflé dish. Chill several hours or until firm. Serve in individual dishes; top with whipped cream, if desired. Yield: 6 to 8 servings.

Mrs. R. S. Clements, Jr.,
Leeds, Alabama.

Make Your Own Beef Jerky

Early explorers packed their saddlebags with sun-dried beef jerky for their meat supply on long journeys. Today's backpackers, campers, and skiers can enjoy a modern version of jerky. Produced by a method that is similar to the old-fashioned sun-drying method, this jerky is oven dried for 10 hours.

Simply cut lean meat into long, thin strips about 1 inch wide. Sliced with the grain, it will be more tender. The result is a chewy, seasoned snack you can enjoy for your next outdoor excursion.

BEEF JERKY

1 (1- to 2-pound) flank steak
½ cup soy sauce
Garlic salt to taste
Lemon pepper to taste

Cut steak with the grain in long strips no more than ¼ inch thick. Combine meat and soy sauce; toss to coat evenly. Drain and discard soy sauce.

Sprinkle both sides of strips lightly with seasonings. Place strips in a single layer on an ungreased cookie sheet. Bake at 150° for 10 hours. (Do not allow temperature to go above 150°.) Yield: ¼ to ½ pound jerky.

Note: Partially freeze meat for easier slicing. Store jerky in airtight container.

Anne Ringer,
Warner Robins, Georgia.

Sweets With A Hint Of Cloves

The fragrance of cloves is a familiar scent emitting from a kitchen, especially when sweet foods are being made. Cloves add a spiciness to sweets that gives them a special flavor.

Try Molasses Sugar Cookies or Applesauce Cake, both spiced with ground cloves. Serve them with a warm cup of Apricot Spiced Punch, which uses whole cloves in the recipe.

APRICOT SPICED PUNCH

3 cups apricot nectar
3 cups apple cider
1 cup water
3 tablespoons sugar
3 tablespoons lemon juice
8 whole cloves
7 (4-inch) sticks cinnamon (optional)

Combine first 6 ingredients in a 3-quart saucepan; bring to a boil, stirring until sugar is dissolved. Remove from heat; let stand about 2 hours (flavor is improved if mixture stands). Reheat before serving. Serve with cinnamon sticks, if desired. Yield: about 7 cups.

Mrs. William S. Bell,
Chattanooga, Tennessee.

Tip: Keep staples—such as sugar, flour, rice, and spices—in tightly covered containers at room temperature.

APPLESAUCE CAKE

⅓ cup shortening
1⅓ cups sugar
1 egg
1⅔ cups all-purpose flour, divided
1 teaspoon soda
1 teaspoon salt
½ teaspoon ground cinnamon
¼ teaspoon ground cloves
¼ teaspoon ground allspice
⅓ cup water
1¼ cups applesauce
⅓ cup chopped pecans
⅔ cup raisins

Cream shortening; gradually add sugar, beating well. Add egg, stirring well.

Combine 1⅓ cups flour, soda, salt, cinnamon, cloves, and allspice; add to creamed mixture alternately with water, beginning and ending with flour mixture. Stir in applesauce.

Dredge pecans and raisins in remaining flour; stir to coat well. Fold into batter. Spoon batter into a greased and floured 9-inch square baking pan. Bake at 350° for 50 to 60 minutes or until done. Cool in pan before cutting into 3-inch squares. Yield: 9 servings.
Mrs. Hugh F. Mosher,
Huntsville, Alabama.

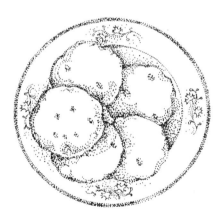

MOLASSES SUGAR COOKIES

¾ cup shortening
1 cup sugar
1 egg
¼ cup molasses
2 cups all-purpose flour
2 teaspoons soda
1 teaspoon ground cinnamon
½ teaspoon salt
½ teaspoon ground ginger
½ teaspoon ground cloves
Sugar

Cream shortening; gradually add 1 cup sugar, beating until light and fluffy. Add egg and molasses; mix well.

Combine flour, soda, cinnamon, salt, ginger, and cloves; mix well. Add about one-fourth of dry mixture at a time to creamed mixture, mixing until smooth after each addition. Chill 1 hour.

Roll dough into 1-inch balls, and roll in sugar. Place 2 inches apart on ungreased cookie sheets; bake at 375° for 10 minutes. (Tops will crack.) Yield: 4½ dozen.
Janet M. Filer,
Arlington, Virginia.

Mushrooms Add A Special Touch

When you want to add a special touch, think of mushrooms. Whether you slice a few over a simple green salad or turn them into a more elaborate dish, your family and friends will appreciate the flavor and texture mushrooms add.

Marinated mushrooms are always welcome as an appetizer, and they're a great make-ahead salad to accompany a special meal. Mushroom-Topped Muffin Stacks prove that mushrooms can make a sandwich that's out of the ordinary. Creamed mushrooms, another favorite, are served elegantly here in a ring of wild rice and chicken livers.

CREAMED MUSHROOMS IN WILD RICE RING

1 cup wild rice
1 cup chopped chicken livers
3 tablespoons butter or margarine, melted
Salt and pepper
½ cup chicken broth
1½ teaspoons cornstarch
Creamed Mushrooms

Cook wild rice according to directions on the package.

Sauté chicken livers in butter until browned. Sprinkle with salt and pepper. Add to rice, and mix well. Combine chicken broth and cornstarch, mixing until smooth. Add to rice mixture, stirring until thoroughly mixed.

Pack rice mixture into a greased 8-inch ring mold. Place ring mold in a shallow pan of water. Bake at 350° for 30 minutes. Allow to cool 10 minutes. Unmold and fill center with Creamed Mushrooms. Yield: 8 servings.

Creamed Mushrooms:

1 pound fresh mushrooms, sliced
2 tablespoons butter or margarine, melted
½ teaspoon salt
½ teaspoon chives
¼ teaspoon soy sauce
Dash of red pepper
3 tablespoons butter or margarine
3 tablespoons all-purpose flour
2 cups half-and-half
½ teaspoon salt
2 egg yolks

Place mushrooms in a 15- x 10- x 1-inch jellyroll pan; pour 2 tablespoons melted butter over mushrooms. Sprinkle with salt, chives, soy sauce, and red pepper. Broil 5 minutes, stirring mushrooms occasionally.

Melt 3 tablespoons butter in a heavy saucepan over low heat; add flour and cook 1 minute, stirring constantly. Gradually add half-and-half; cook over medium heat, stirring constantly, until thickened and bubbly. Stir in salt.

Beat egg yolks until thick and lemon colored. Gradually stir about one-fourth of cream mixture into yolks; add to remaining cream mixture, stirring constantly. Cook for 2 minutes over low heat. Stir in mushrooms. Yield: about 2½ cups.
Aileen Wright,
Nashville, Tennessee.

MARINATED MUSHROOMS

2 pounds fresh mushrooms
¼ cup lemon juice
½ cup cider vinegar
¼ cup water
2 tablespoons finely chopped onion
1 to 2 tablespoons minced garlic
1 tablespoon chopped fresh parsley
½ teaspoon salt
½ teaspoon sugar
⅛ teaspoon dried whole oregano
⅛ teaspoon pepper

Cover mushrooms with water in a large Dutch oven; add lemon juice, mixing well. Bring to a boil, and simmer 1 minute; drain.

Combine remaining ingredients; mix well. Pour over mushrooms, and toss lightly. Place mushrooms in a shallow container; cover and refrigerate 24 hours. Yield: 8 servings.
Diana Williams,
Greensboro, North Carolina.

Tip: Use a bulb baster to remove fat from broth, stew, or soup.

MUSHROOM-TOPPED MUFFIN STACKS

10 slices Canadian bacon
¼ cup butter or margarine, melted
½ cup chopped onion
1 pound fresh mushrooms, sliced
1½ cups commercial sour cream
⅓ cup milk
1 teaspoon paprika
1 teaspoon lemon juice
¼ teaspoon salt
⅛ teaspoon pepper
5 English muffins, split and toasted

Brown Canadian bacon in butter in a large skillet. Remove bacon and keep warm. Cook onion in drippings just until tender. Add mushrooms; cover and cook over low heat, stirring occasionally, until mushrooms are tender (about 5 minutes). Drain off drippings. Stir in the next 6 ingredients; heat thoroughly. Place one slice bacon on top of each muffin half; spoon mushroom sauce over top of each. Yield: 5 servings.   *Anne S. Reynolds,*
Raleigh, North Carolina.

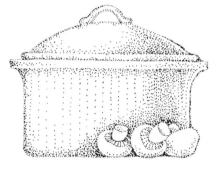

After The Feast, Special Leftovers

The holiday feast may be over, but many special meals are just beginning—thanks to leftover ham or turkey.

The turkey is diced for Southern Creamed Turkey, then simmered in a cream sauce and spooned over crusty cornbread—perfect for a brunch. Golden Turkey Casserole is a tempting one-dish dinner, with bits of turkey baked with rice and Parmesan cheese. And even when the leftovers seem to be getting slim, you probably still have enough for Turkey Soufflé. It's made with just a cup of finely chopped turkey and served with a dill-flavored sauce.

Leftover ham is equally versatile. We offer two ways to serve ham loaf: either baked with a brown sugar topping or unembellished and enjoyed with Creamy Mustard Sauce.

If the flavor of ham with Swiss cheese is one of your favorites, try our unique Zucchini-Ham-Cheese Pie instead of the usual sandwich. Of course, ham sandwiches are always good, and we have one that's exceptional: shredded ham tossed with walnuts, celery, and cranberry-orange relish to spread on slices of pumpernickel.

TURKEY SOUFFLE

3 tablespoons butter or margarine
3 tablespoons all-purpose flour
1 cup milk
¼ teaspoon paprika
½ teaspoon salt
Dash of pepper
1 teaspoon grated onion
1 cup finely chopped cooked turkey or chicken
1 tablespoon chopped fresh parsley
3 eggs, separated
Mushroom-Dill Sauce

Lightly grease bottom of a 1-quart soufflé dish. Cut a piece of aluminum foil long enough to circle the dish, allowing a 1-inch overlap; fold lengthwise into thirds. Wrap foil around dish so it extends 3 inches above rim; secure with string tied around dish.

Melt butter in a heavy saucepan over low heat; add flour, stirring until smooth. Cook 1 minute, stirring constantly. Gradually add milk; cook over medium heat, stirring constantly, until thickened and bubbly. Stir in paprika, salt, and pepper. Remove from heat; stir in onion, turkey, and parsley.

Beat egg yolks until thick and lemon colored; gradually stir in about one-fourth of hot turkey mixture. Combine with remaining hot mixture, stirring constantly.

Beat egg whites (at room temperature) until stiff but not dry; gently fold into turkey mixture. Spoon into prepared soufflé dish. Bake at 325° for 50 minutes or until golden brown. Remove collar. Serve with Mushroom-Dill Sauce. Yield: 6 servings.

Mushroom-Dill Sauce:

2 tablespoons butter or margarine
2 tablespoons chopped onion
2 tablespoons all-purpose flour
1¼ cups milk
¼ teaspoon dried dillweed
1 (3-ounce) can chopped mushrooms, undrained
¼ teaspoon salt
Dash of pepper

Melt butter in a heavy saucepan over low heat; add onion, and sauté until tender. Add flour and cook 1 minute, stirring constantly. Gradually add milk; cook over medium heat, stirring constantly, until thickened and bubbly. Stir in remaining ingredients. Yield: about 1½ cups.   *Sheila J. Heatwole,*
Virginia Beach, Virginia.

GOLDEN TURKEY CASSEROLE

1 chicken-flavored bouillon cube
1¼ cups boiling water
¼ cup butter or margarine
¼ cup chopped onion
¼ cup chopped green pepper
¼ cup all-purpose flour
1 teaspoon salt
¼ teaspoon pepper
3 cups diced cooked turkey
2 cups cooked rice
¼ cup chopped pimiento
2 tablespoons grated Parmesan cheese
¼ cup cornflake crumbs
1 tablespoon butter or margarine, melted

Dissolve bouillon cube in boiling water; set aside to cool. (1¼ cups turkey broth or chicken broth may be substituted for bouillon.)

Melt ¼ cup butter in a medium skillet. Add onion and green pepper; sauté until tender. Add flour, stirring until smooth; cook 1 minute, stirring constantly. Gradually add bouillon; cook over medium heat, stirring constantly, until thickened and bubbly. Stir in salt and pepper.

Combine turkey, rice, pimiento, Parmesan cheese, and sauce; mix well. Spoon into a greased 1½-quart casserole dish. Combine cornflake crumbs and 1 tablespoon melted butter, mixing well. Sprinkle on top of casserole. Bake, uncovered, at 350° for 30 minutes. Yield: 6 servings.

Mrs. Robert Bryce,
Fairport, New York.

Tip: When food boils over in the oven, sprinkle the burned surface with a little salt. This will stop smoke and odor from forming and make the spot easier to clean. Also, rubbing damp salt on dishes in which food has been baked will remove brown spots.

SOUTHERN CREAMED TURKEY

1 chicken-flavored bouillon cube
1 cup boiling water
⅓ cup butter or margarine
⅓ cup all-purpose flour
1½ cups milk
½ teaspoon garlic salt
½ teaspoon imitation butter-flavored salt
½ teaspoon salt
Dash of pepper
3 cups diced cooked turkey
1 (2-ounce) jar chopped pimiento, drained
Dash of paprika
2 tablespoons white wine or sherry
  (optional)
Cornbread (recipe follows)
Parsley sprigs (optional)

Dissolve bouillon cube in boiling water; set aside to cool (1 cup turkey or chicken broth may be substituted).

Melt butter in a heavy saucepan over low heat; add flour, stirring until smooth. Cook 1 minute, stirring constantly. Gradually stir in bouillon and milk; add garlic salt, butter-flavored salt, salt, pepper, and turkey. Cook over low heat, stirring constantly, 8 to 10 minutes or until thickened and bubbly. Stir in pimiento and paprika; add wine, if desired. Cook an additional 2 to 3 minutes.

Slice cornbread squares in half horizontally; open and spoon the creamed turkey over the top. Garnish with parsley sprigs, if desired. Yield: 8 to 10 servings.

Cornbread:

¾ cup all-purpose flour
½ cup cornmeal
1 tablespoon baking powder
2 tablespoons sugar
½ cup milk
1 egg
¼ cup melted butter or margarine

Combine dry ingredients. Combine milk, egg, and butter; add to dry ingredients, stirring just until moistened. Pour into a greased and floured 9-inch square cakepan. Bake at 425° for 20 to 25 minutes; then cut into squares. Yield: 8 to 10 servings.
Mrs. Malcolm Bowles,
Mableton, Georgia.

Tip: Avoid purchasing green-tinted potatoes. The term used for this condition is "light burn," which causes a bitter flavor. To keep potatoes from turning green once you have bought them, store in a cool, dark, dry place.

TANGY HAM SALAD SANDWICH

½ cup diced celery
⅓ cup chopped walnuts
⅓ cup mayonnaise
¼ cup cranberry-orange relish
1 tablespoon minced onion
1 teaspoon Worcestershire sauce
2 cups shredded cooked ham
10 slices pumpernickel bread

Combine first 7 ingredients; mix well. Spread ½ cup ham mixture on each of five bread slices. Top each with remaining slices of bread, and cut in half. Yield: 5 servings. *Kay Castleman,*
Nashville, Tennessee.

ZUCCHINI-HAM-CHEESE PIE

1 large onion, thinly sliced
2 small zucchini, thinly sliced
1 large clove garlic, crushed
⅓ cup olive or vegetable oil
2 cups slivered cooked ham
1¼ cups commercial sour cream
1 cup (4 ounces) shredded Swiss cheese
1 teaspoon dried dillweed
1 teaspoon salt
¼ teaspoon pepper
1 baked 10-inch pastry shell
2 tablespoons butter or margarine, melted
½ cup dry breadcrumbs
¼ cup grated Parmesan cheese

Sauté onion, zucchini, and garlic in hot oil about 5 minutes or until zucchini is crisp-tender. Remove from heat; stir in ham, sour cream, Swiss cheese, dillweed, salt, and pepper. Spoon into pastry shell.

Combine butter, breadcrumbs, and Parmesan cheese; mix well, and sprinkle in a 2-inch band around edge of pie. Bake at 350° for 35 minutes or until bubbly. Let stand 10 minutes before serving. Yield: 6 servings.
Connie Scopes,
Metairie, Louisiana.

HAM AND POTATO SALAD

4 cups diced cooked potatoes
1½ cups diced cooked ham
1 cup diced celery
⅓ cup sweet pickle relish or chopped
  sweet pickles
2 hard-cooked eggs, chopped
1 teaspoon celery seeds
½ teaspoon salt
Dash of white pepper
2 teaspoons prepared mustard
½ cup mayonnaise

Combine potatoes and ham, tossing well. Add celery, pickle relish, and eggs; toss gently. Sprinkle celery seeds, salt, and pepper over mixture. Combine mustard and mayonnaise, mixing well; add to potato mixture, stirring gently. Chill several hours for flavors to blend. Yield: 6 to 8 servings. *Eva G. Key,*
Isle of Palms, South Carolina.

HAM LOAF

2 pounds cooked lean ham, ground
1 pound lean ground beef
½ pound bulk pork sausage
1½ cups tomato juice
2 cups soft breadcrumbs
½ cup finely chopped celery
1 medium onion, minced
2 eggs, well beaten
1 teaspoon coarsely ground pepper
¼ cup plus 2 tablespoons firmly packed
  brown sugar
½ cup catsup
1 teaspoon dry mustard
½ teaspoon ground nutmeg
Creamy Mustard Sauce (optional)

Combine first 9 ingredients, mixing well. Spread evenly in a greased 2-quart shallow casserole.

Combine sugar, catsup, mustard, and nutmeg; mix well, and spread over meat mixture (see note). Set casserole in shallow pan of water, and bake at 350° for 1½ hours. Yield: 8 to 10 servings.

Note: The loaf may be baked without the brown sugar sauce, then served with Creamy Mustard Sauce.

Creamy Mustard Sauce:

1 cup mayonnaise
¼ cup prepared mustard
½ cup whipping cream, whipped

Combine mayonnaise and mustard; mix well. Fold into whipped cream. Yield: about 2 cups.
Katharyn B. Riley,
Kingsport, Tennessee.

Right: *Add warmth to your holiday cocktail buffet with Hot Spinach Dip (page 249), Sausage Stuffed Mushrooms (page 248), and Sausage Balls in Cheese Pastry (page 248). Fresh fruits and assorted cheeses provide an additional festive look.*

Page 274: *Nothing can match the sweet aroma and rich traditional goodness of these home-baked pies. Clockwise from top: Chocolate Meringue Pie (page 238), Cheery Cherry Tarts (page 238), Pineapple Pie (page 237), and Macadamia Pie (page 238).*

Tuna Stretches The Budget

The days when you could buy a can of tuna for a quarter are long gone, but tuna is still a good buy when you consider how it can be stretched. By adding a few inexpensive ingredients to a 7-ounce can of tuna, the result can be four French Toasted Tuna Sandwiches. The sandwiches are dipped in a batter similar to that for French toast.

Barbecued Tuna can be prepared with ingredients you probably have on hand. Serve it over rice, noodles, or split hamburger buns for a quick and easy main dish. And if you're looking for an unusual, elegant appetizer, serve Tuna Mousse or Tuna Mound.

FRENCH TOASTED TUNA SANDWICHES

1 (7-ounce) can tuna, drained and flaked
¼ cup finely chopped celery
¼ cup finely chopped onion
¼ cup sweet pickle relish
¼ cup mayonnaise or salad dressing
8 slices sandwich bread
2 eggs, beaten
½ cup milk
¼ cup butter or margarine, melted

Combine tuna, celery, onion, pickle relish, and mayonnaise; stir well. Spread 4 slices of bread with tuna mixture; top each with another slice of bread.

Combine eggs and milk; beat well. Dip sandwiches into egg mixture; sauté in butter over medium heat 4 minutes on each side or until golden brown. Serve immediately. Yield: 4 sandwiches.
Mrs. Harland J. Stone,
Ocala, Florida.

TUNA MOUSSE

1 envelope unflavored gelatin
½ cup cold water
2 (7-ounce) cans water-pack tuna, drained and flaked
2 cups mayonnaise
2 tablespoons grated onion
2 tablespoons lemon juice
½ teaspoon celery salt
Fresh ground pepper to taste
1 (4½-ounce) can small shrimp, drained (optional)

Soften gelatin in water in a small saucepan. Cook over medium heat, stirring constantly, until gelatin is completely dissolved (about 1 minute); set aside.

Place remaining ingredients, except shrimp, in container of electric blender. Process until well mixed. Gradually add gelatin mixture; process until smooth. Stir shrimp into tuna mixture, if desired. Pour tuna mixture into an oiled 5½-cup mold; chill until firm. Unmold mousse; serve with crackers. Yield: 5½ cups.
Julia Morton,
Linville, North Carolina.

CREAMY TUNA RING

1 envelope unflavored gelatin
¼ cup cold water
2 (7-ounce) cans tuna, drained and flaked
2 hard-cooked eggs, chopped
½ cup chopped pimiento-stuffed olives
½ cup chopped celery
1 (8-ounce) carton commercial sour cream
¾ cup mayonnaise or salad dressing
¼ cup lemon juice
2 tablespoons minced fresh parsley
1 tablespoon minced onion
½ teaspoon salt
Lettuce leaves
Tomato wedges (optional)
Cucumber slices (optional)

Soften gelatin in water in a small saucepan. Cook over medium heat, stirring constantly, until gelatin is completely dissolved (about 1 minute); set aside.

Combine tuna and next 9 ingredients; stir well. Add gelatin mixture to tuna mixture; stir well, and spoon into an oiled 5-cup ring mold. Chill until firm; unmold onto a lettuce-lined plate. Garnish with tomato wedges and cucumber slices, if desired. Yield: 6 servings.
Mrs. John F. Woods,
Memphis, Tennessee.

BARBECUED TUNA

½ cup chopped onion
1 tablespoon vegetable oil
½ cup chopped celery
½ cup chopped green pepper
1 cup catsup
1 cup water
2 tablespoons brown sugar
2 tablespoons vinegar
2 tablespoons Worcestershire sauce
1 tablespoon prepared mustard
½ teaspoon salt
½ teaspoon pepper
2 (7-ounce) cans tuna, drained
Hot cooked rice, noodles, or split hamburger buns

Sauté onion in oil in a large skillet until tender. Add next 10 ingredients; simmer 20 minutes.

Add tuna; simmer 10 minutes, stirring occasionally. Serve over hot rice, noodles, or split hamburger buns. Yield: 6 to 8 servings.
Sandra Russell,
Maitland, Florida.

TUNA-EGG CROQUETTES

1 (7-ounce) can tuna, drained and flaked
1 cup dry breadcrumbs, divided
¼ cup finely chopped onion
2 tablespoons parsley flakes
½ teaspoon salt
1 tablespoon plus 2 teaspoons Worcestershire sauce
1 egg, slightly beaten
3 hard-cooked eggs, finely chopped
½ cup all-purpose flour
2 eggs, beaten
Vegetable oil

Combine tuna, ½ cup breadcrumbs, onion, parsley flakes, salt, Worcestershire sauce, and 1 egg; mix well. Add hard-cooked eggs; stir gently.

Shape tuna mixture into balls or patties, using ⅓ cup for each croquette (mixture will be loose). Dredge each croquette in flour; then dip into beaten eggs, and coat each with remaining ½ cup breadcrumbs.

Heat ½ inch oil to 350°; fry croquettes until golden. Yield: 8 servings.
Eloise Haynes,
Greenville, Mississippi.

Tip: When you need just a few drops of onion juice for flavor, sprinkle a little salt on a slice of onion; scrape the salted surface with a knife or spoon to obtain the juice.

TUNA MOUND

1 cup butter or margarine, softened
1 (8-ounce) package cream cheese, softened
2 (7-ounce) cans tuna, drained and flaked
2 tablespoons chopped green onion
1 tablespoon lemon juice
¼ teaspoon dried whole tarragon, crushed
¼ teaspoon salt
Dash of pepper
Leaf lettuce
1 hard-cooked egg
¼ cup minced fresh parsley

Cream butter and cream cheese until fluffy. Add tuna, onion, lemon juice, tarragon, salt, and pepper; beat at medium speed of electric mixer until thoroughly mixed. Chill tuna mixture several hours.

Shape tuna mixture into a mound on a lettuce-lined serving plate. Press egg through a sieve. Garnish tuna mound with sieved egg and parsley. Serve with crackers or party rye bread. Yield: about 4 cups.

Margie Elmore,
Rockville, Maryland.

Show Off With Fantans

Here we share a recipe for those wonderful, buttered, pull-apart rolls often found in bakeries. The secret to their fanlike shape lies in how the dough is cut and placed in the muffin cups.

FRENCH FANTAN ROLLS

1 cup milk, scalded
½ cup shortening
½ cup sugar
1 teaspoon salt
2 packages dry yeast
¼ cup warm water (105° to 115°)
4 eggs, beaten
½ teaspoon imitation butter flavor
½ teaspoon lemon extract
About 6 cups all-purpose flour
¼ cup melted butter or margarine, divided

Combine milk, shortening, sugar, and salt; stir until shortening melts. Cool to 105° to 115°.

Dissolve yeast in warm water in a large mixing bowl. Stir in milk mixture, eggs, and flavorings. Gradually stir in flour to make a soft dough.

Turn dough out onto a floured surface, and knead until smooth and elastic (about 5 minutes). Place in a well-greased bowl, turning to grease top. Cover and let rise in a warm place (85°), free from drafts, 1 hour or until doubled in bulk.

Punch dough down, and divide in half. Turn dough out onto a lightly floured surface. Roll each half into a 12- x 6-inch rectangle. Brush 2 tablespoons butter over top of each. Cut each rectangle into 6 (1-inch) strips. Stack 6 strips of dough, butter side up, on top of one another. Cut each stack of dough into 12 pieces about 1 inch wide. Place pieces in greased muffin cups sideways (cut side down).

Cover and let rise in a warm place (85°), free from drafts, for 30 minutes. Bake at 425° for 10 to 12 minutes or until golden brown. Yield: 2 dozen.

Mrs. Robert Collins,
Fairfax, Missouri.

Fruit Warms Up To Winter

Fruit has a delicious way of adapting to all seasons. Winter brings a new crop of apples and citrus, along with meals that call for hot fruit side dishes and the special flavors of the season—mincemeat, coconut, nutmeg, pecans. It all adds up to a host of dishes just right for cool weather meals.

Mincemeat is spooned into apples in Baked Mincemeat-Filled Apples; then after baking in apple juice, they're savored hot with a rum-flavored topping. For fresh fruit, but on the lighter side, try a salad of oranges, pineapple, apple, and banana chilled in a honey-citrus dressing.

Canned fruit also comes into its own in the wintertime; try apricots, plums, and peach halves served hot in our Baked Fruit Compote.

HONEY FRUIT SALAD

1 (15¼-ounce) can pineapple chunks, undrained
2 medium oranges, peeled and sectioned
1 medium apple, peeled and diced
1 banana, peeled and sliced
½ cup chopped pecans
½ cup orange juice
1 tablespoon fresh lemon juice
¼ cup honey

Combine first 5 ingredients in a large bowl. Combine orange juice, lemon juice, and honey in a small bowl; mix well. Pour over fruit, tossing gently. Chill thoroughly. Yield: 4 to 6 servings.

Patsy Hull,
Montgomery, Alabama.

BAKED MINCEMEAT-FILLED APPLES

6 large baking apples
1 cup prepared mincemeat, divided
1½ cups apple juice
¼ cup frozen apple juice concentrate, thawed and undiluted
½ cup commercial sour cream
1 tablespoon dark rum
⅛ teaspoon ground nutmeg
½ cup sugar

Core apples to within ½ inch from bottom; peel top third of each. Place apples in a shallow baking dish. Stuff each with about 2 tablespoons mincemeat; pour 1½ cups apple juice over apples. Bake at 375° for 50 to 60 minutes or until tender, basting occasionally with apple juice.

Combine remaining mincemeat, apple juice concentrate, sour cream, rum, and nutmeg; mix well. Chill.

Remove apples from oven; sprinkle with sugar, and broil until golden brown. Just before serving, spoon about 2 tablespoons sour cream mixture over each apple. Yield: 6 servings.

Mary Kennon,
Rome, Georgia.

BAKED FRUIT COMPOTE

1 (16-ounce) can apricot halves, drained
1 (16-ounce) can whole purple plums, drained
1 (16-ounce) can peach halves, drained
3 or 4 thin orange slices, halved
½ cup orange juice
¼ cup firmly packed brown sugar
½ teaspoon grated lemon rind
2 tablespoons butter or margarine, melted
½ cup flaked coconut

Alternate rows of apricots, plums, and peaches in a 12- x 7½- x 1½-inch baking dish. Place half an orange slice between each peach.

Combine orange juice, brown sugar, and lemon rind; mix well, and pour over fruit. Spoon butter over plums; sprinkle coconut over all fruit. Bake at 425° for 15 to 20 minutes or until coconut is toasted. Yield: 8 to 10 servings.

Mrs. John Rucker,
Louisville, Kentucky.

December

Nothing will fill you with the holiday spirit more quickly than taking one glance at our giant Christmas cookies, the pride of the entire foods staff. We think you'll agree that Santa Claus with his billowy white beard is truly a charmer.

If December feasting finds you with too many guests and too little space, our buffet menu will allow you to serve a meal with minimum space and utensils. Our recipes also let you spend last-minute time with your guests rather than in the kitchen.

In the South, homemade candy is as much a part of Christmas as a decorated tree, and this chapter offers several kitchen-tested favorites. In fact, the whole test kitchen had a hand in pulling the taffy and thoroughly enjoyed it.

Animate The Season With Decorated Cookies

The increasing popularity of cake decorating as a hobby opens a whole new world of fun and creativity when you apply the basic decorating procedures to cookies. With our recipe and step-by-step directions you can create a cookie wonderland to use as Christmas decorations or to give as gifts.

Basic decorating techniques and holiday candies bring these cookies to life. Brightly wrapped packages are tied with ribbons of Royal Icing. Swirls of icing give a three-dimensional look to Santa's beard and fur-trimmed suit. Red-hot lips made of tiny cinnamon candies make Mrs. Claus seem so real you'll think she can talk. And a bright-red jellybean nose is sure to guide Rudolph and his sleigh full of candy on their Christmas journey. Assorted candies and decorator sprinkles are held in place with Royal Icing.

The gingerbread cookie recipe makes enough dough for all five figures. The decorating steps are for the Santa Claus cookie, but decorating suggestions are given for each of the other shapes. Patterns are on page 303 and photographs of cookies are on pages 292 and 293.

Although our decorating ideas are geared for adults, children could lend a helping hand. You'll need to plan lots of time for this project; even though the basic procedure is not difficult, it is time-consuming and tedious. But if your youngsters can resist eating these special cookies, they can be frozen and displayed again next year.

GINGERBREAD COOKIES

1¾ cups sugar
¾ cup honey
¼ cup butter or margarine
⅓ cup lemon juice
1 tablespoon finely grated lemon rind
6 cups all-purpose flour
¼ cup plus 2 tablespoons baking powder
⅛ teaspoon salt
1½ teaspoons ground ginger
1 teaspoon ground cinnamon
¼ teaspoon ground nutmeg
¼ teaspoon ground cloves
1 egg, well beaten
1 egg yolk, well beaten
Royal Icing
Assorted candies and decorator sprinkles

Combine sugar, honey, and butter in a 4-quart Dutch oven; bring to a boil, stirring constantly until sugar dissolves. Remove from heat; add lemon juice and lemon rind, mixing well. Let cool to room temperature.

Combine flour, baking powder, salt, and spices; stir well. Add 2 cups flour mixture, egg, and egg yolk to sugar mixture; mix well. Gradually add remaining flour mixture, mixing well. Shape dough into a ball; lightly knead until smooth.

Place three-fourths of dough on a greased and floured 16- x 12-inch cookie sheet. Roll dough to about ¼-inch thickness, covering entire cookie sheet. Arrange patterns for sleigh, elf, and Mrs. Claus on cookie sheet. Cut around patterns with the tip of a knife. Remove excess dough; combine with remaining dough, wrap in waxed paper, and refrigerate until needed.

Bake cookies at 325° for 30 minutes or until firm and golden brown. Remove from oven. Carefully slip a spatula under cookies to loosen; let cool 1 minute on cookie sheet. Transfer to wire rack to complete cooling. Repeat procedure with remaining dough, using patterns for Rudolph and Santa Claus. Decorate with Royal Icing, assorted candies, and decorator sprinkles. Yield: 5 large cookies.

Note: Store in cardboard box at room temperature or freeze in airtight container. Avoid making during humid weather because cookies tend to pick up moisture and become soft.

Royal Icing:

3 large egg whites
½ teaspoon cream of tartar
1 (16-ounce) package powdered sugar
Paste food coloring (red, yellow, black, brown, green, and purple)

Combine egg whites and cream of tartar in a large mixing bowl. Beat at high speed of electric mixer until frothy. Add half of powdered sugar, mixing well. Add remaining sugar, and beat 5 to 7 minutes at high speed or until mixture is stiff and holds a peak. Color small amounts of icing with paste food coloring as needed during decorating. Yield: about 2 cups.

Note: Icing dries very quickly; keep covered at all times with a damp cloth. Do not double this recipe. If additional icing is needed, make two batches.

Santa Claus Cookie

To enlarge each cookie pattern, make a grid of 1-inch squares or use graph paper marked off in 1-inch squares. Copy the design from the pattern (page 303) on the prepared grid, working square by square. Then trace the enlarged pattern onto thin paper. Cut out around the pattern, ¼ inch from the tracing line.

Step 1—Place paper pattern on top of cookie, and mark details of pattern by punching holes through paper with a large needle.

Step 2—Remove pattern, and connect dots on cookie by scratching lines onto cookie with a needle.

Step 3—Use parchment paper bag and metal decorator tip No. 3 (outline tip). Fill bag half full of Royal Icing. Pipe icing on top of lines you have just made to outline the figure and its inside details.

Step 4—Place a small amount of Royal Icing into separate bowls, and color with red, black, and yellow paste food coloring. Also mix small amounts of red and yellow paste coloring with white Royal Icing to get a flesh-tone color for face. Slowly add just enough water to flesh-tone icing, to some of white icing, and to half of black and red icing to make a good flowing consistency (hereafter called flow-in icing). Reserve undiluted, white, yellow, red, and black icing for piping details. Keep icing covered with plastic wrap to prevent it from drying out. If icing separates during decorating process, stir well before putting into parchment bags.

Fill parchment cones about half full of flow-in icing. Snip off small tip of cone and apply icing to cover areas between outline, beginning with black for shoes and belt, flesh for facial areas, red for suit and facial accents, then white for beard and fur trim. Spread icing into corners and hard-to-reach areas with a toothpick.

Work with one color at a time, allowing icing to dry before changing colors. Try to avoid using excess icing as it will spill over into another color area. If the flow-in icing is too watery, it will not dry properly and may run under outline into other color areas. If air bubbles form in icing, use a clean straight pin to remove them.

Step 5—To create a three-dimensional effect on Santa's beard, moustache, eyebrows, and fur trim on suit, use tip No. 3 to pipe swirls of undiluted white Royal Icing on top of white flow-in icing before it dries. Pipe details of eyes and eyelashes on top of white flow-in icing with undiluted black Royal Icing; use undiluted red for mouth. Pipe belt buckle on top of black flow-in icing with undiluted yellow Royal Icing. Allow decorated cookies to dry thoroughly before storing, wrapping for gifts, or using for holiday display.

Mrs. Claus Cookie

Follow procedure for transferring pattern, outlining, filling in with flow-in icing, and piping on swirls of icing for hair as given for Santa Claus cookie. Carefully distribute decorator sprinkles on top of flow-in icing before it dries. Pipe rickrack for dress trim at neck and cuffs with undiluted white Royal Icing, using tip No. 3. Pipe facial details and glasses as shown on page 292. Attach candy cane and cinnamon candy lips to cookie using undiluted Royal Icing.

Rudolph Cookie

Follow basic steps for Santa Claus cookie. Color small amounts of Royal Icing for brown antlers and pink ears; add water for flowing consistency. Pipe on collar with undiluted red Royal Icing using straight edge of tip No. 46. Make jingle bells by piping an "X" of undiluted black Royal Icing on top of yellow milk chocolate candies using tip No. 3. Attach jingle bells and red jellybean nose with Royal Icing.

Elf Cookie

Follow basic steps for Santa Claus cookie. Tint Royal Icing with paste food coloring to desired colors for packages; add water to make flowing consistency. Use assorted decorator sprinkles for package wrappings, distributing sprinkles on top of flow-in icing before it dries. Allow flow-in and sprinkles on one package to dry before decorating next package. For package ribbon and bows, use undiluted red Royal Icing and tip No. 46. Use Royal Icing to attach cinnamon candies for cheeks and toes of slippers.

Sleigh Cookie

Follow basic steps for Santa Claus cookie. Outline sleigh with undiluted red and yellow Royal Icing as shown in photograph, using parchment paper bag and metal decorator tip No. 14. Pipe rickrack next to red outline using tip No. 3 and undiluted white Royal Icing. Create a sleigh full of goodies with assorted candies and gum (small candy canes, jellybeans, small gum pieces, milk chocolate candies, cinnamon candies, and small individually wrapped peppermints and after-dinner mints). Attach candies to cookie sleigh with Royal Icing.

Bake A Tradition

Towering cakes, crusty breads, buttery cookies, and classic pies are as essential to the holiday celebration as a Christmas tree and mistletoe. For Southern families, it's time to bring out those treasured holiday recipes that have been handed down from generation to generation.

We've gathered a whole collection of favorite holiday recipes from our readers. Our foods staff is in total agreement that they are some of the most delicious we've ever published.

For many families, no celebration is complete without chocolate cake. Our version is particularly delicious—two sour cream-flavored layers spread with a rich fudge icing. Holiday Mincemeat Pie is equally appealing. The filling is laced with orange juice and chock full of raisins and pecans.

If you try the Crème de Menthe Cookies, you'd better go ahead and make two batches because they won't last long. Neither will the Yummy Sweet Rolls, not with that luscious cream cheese filling tucked inside the yeasty dough.

This is just a sampling, and we think you'll discover many other recipes that will become part of your family's holiday tradition from this season on.

CHOCOLATE FUDGE CAKE

½ cup butter, softened
1 (16-ounce) package brown sugar
3 eggs
3 (1-ounce) squares unsweetened chocolate, melted
2¼ cups sifted cake flour
2 teaspoons soda
½ teaspoon salt
1 cup commercial sour cream
1 cup hot water
1½ teaspoons vanilla extract
Frosting (recipe follows)

Cream butter; gradually add sugar, beating well. Add eggs, one at a time, beating well after each addition. Add chocolate, mixing well.

Combine flour, soda, and salt; gradually add to chocolate mixture alternately with sour cream, beating well after each addition. Add water, mixing well; stir in vanilla. (Batter will be thin.)

Pour batter evenly into 2 greased and floured 9-inch cakepans. Bake at 350° for 45 minutes or until cake tests done. Let cool in pans 10 minutes; remove from pans, and place on wire racks to complete cooling.

Spread frosting between layers and on top and sides of cake. Yield: one 9-inch layer cake.

Frosting:

4 (1-ounce) squares unsweetened chocolate
½ cup butter
1 (16-ounce) package powdered sugar, sifted
½ cup milk
2 teaspoons vanilla extract

Combine chocolate and butter; place over low heat until melted, stirring constantly. Combine sugar, milk, and vanilla in a medium mixing bowl; mix well. Set bowl in a large pan of ice water, and stir in chocolate mixture; then beat at high speed of portable mixer until spreading consistency (about 2 minutes). Yield: frosting for one 9-inch layer cake. *Sherre L. Harrington, Columbia, South Carolina.*

OLD-FASHIONED POUND CAKE

1 cup butter, softened
½ cup shortening
3 cups sugar
5 eggs
3 cups all-purpose flour
1 teaspoon baking powder
1 cup milk
1 teaspoon vanilla extract
1 teaspoon lemon extract

Cream butter and shortening; gradually add sugar, beating until light and fluffy. Add eggs, one at a time, beating well after each addition.

Combine flour and baking powder; add to creamed mixture alternately with milk, mixing well after each addition. Stir in vanilla and lemon flavorings.

Pour batter into a greased and floured 10-inch tube pan. Bake at 350° for 1 hour and 15 minutes or until cake tests done. Cool in pan 10 to 15 minutes; remove from pan, and cool completely. Yield: one 10-inch cake.
Mrs. W. H. Sellars, Spartanburg, South Carolina.

Tip: Prepare your favorite sheet cake. Cut enough servings for one meal, wrap, and freeze. If unfrosted, toppings or frosting can be varied. Instant dessert!

WHITE FRUITCAKE

1 (16-ounce) package candied cherries, finely chopped
1 (16-ounce) package candied pineapple, finely chopped
1 (4-ounce) package candied citron, finely chopped
1 (4-ounce) package candied lemon peel, finely chopped
1 (4-ounce) package candied orange peel, finely chopped
1 (15-ounce) package golden raisins
2 cups slivered almonds
4 cups chopped pecans
4 cups all-purpose flour, divided
2 cups butter, softened
2¼ cups sugar
1 dozen eggs
½ teaspoon ground nutmeg
½ teaspoon ground cloves
½ teaspoon ground ginger
2 teaspoons ground cinnamon
2 teaspoons baking powder
¾ teaspoon salt
1 (8-ounce) jar apple jelly
1 cup apple brandy or other brandy
1 tablespoon lemon juice
2 teaspoons vanilla extract
Candied pineapple rings
Candied cherries

Combine first 8 ingredients; dredge with 1 cup flour, stirring to coat well. Set aside.

Cream butter in a large mixing bowl; gradually add sugar, beating until light and fluffy. Add eggs, one at a time, beating well after each addition.

Combine 3 cups flour, spices, baking powder, and salt; add to creamed mixture alternately with jelly and brandy, mixing well after each addition. Stir in fruit mixture, lemon juice, and vanilla.

Spoon batter into 2 waxed paper-lined and greased 10-inch tube pans. Place a large pan of boiling water on lower oven rack. Bake cakes at 275° for 3 hours to 3 hours and 15 minutes or until they test done.

Cool cakes completely in pans. Remove from pans, and garnish with candied pineapple rings and candied cherries. Chill before serving. Yield: two 10-inch cakes.

Mrs. J. W. Riley, Jr.,
Kingsport, Tennessee.

Tip: Heat a knife blade in hot water; dry off quickly for ease in slicing fresh bread. A wet knife does a smooth job when cutting fresh cake.

HOLIDAY SAVARIN

1 package dry yeast
¼ cup warm water (105° to 115°)
2 tablespoons sugar
¼ teaspoon salt
2½ cups all-purpose flour, divided
3 eggs
6 tablespoons butter or margarine, softened
¼ cup finely chopped candied citron
Kirsch Syrup
Apricot Glaze
Whole blanched almonds, halved lengthwise and toasted
Candied cherries, halved
Candied citron
Chantilly Crème

Dissolve yeast in warm water in a large bowl; stir in sugar and salt. Add 2 cups flour, beating well with a heavy-duty electric mixer. Add eggs, one at a time, beating well after each addition. Beat dough 2 minutes, scraping the bowl often with a spatula. Add butter, 1 tablespoon at a time, beating well after each addition.

Combine remaining ½ cup flour and ¼ cup citron, stirring to coat citron; stir into dough (dough will be very stiff). Cover and let rise in a warm place (85°), free from drafts, 45 minutes or until doubled in bulk.

Stir dough down; spoon evenly into a well-buttered 6-cup ovenproof ring or tube mold. Cover and let rise in a warm place (85°), free from drafts, 20 to 30 minutes or until doubled in bulk. Bake at 375° for 25 to 35 minutes or until bread sounds hollow when tapped.

Invert bread on a cooling rack, and set in a large, shallow pan. Spoon Kirsch Syrup over hot bread, also using syrup that drips through rack; cool. Place bread on serving plate.

Brush some of Apricot Glaze over bread; arrange almonds, cherries, and citron on top. Brush remaining glaze over almonds and candied fruit. Spoon Chantilly Crème into center of bread. Yield: 8 to 10 servings.

Kirsch Syrup:

1¼ cups water
1 cup sugar
½ cup kirsch or other cherry-flavored brandy

Combine water and sugar; bring to a boil. Lower heat, and simmer 5 minutes. Cool 15 minutes; stir in kirsch. Set aside 2 tablespoons syrup for Apricot Glaze. Yield: about 2 cups.

Apricot Glaze:

½ cup apricot preserves
2 tablespoons Kirsch Syrup

Melt preserves over low heat; press through a sieve, discarding pulp. Stir in Kirsch Syrup. Yield: about ⅓ cup.

Chantilly Crème:

1 cup whipping cream
2 tablespoons powdered sugar
1 teaspoon vanilla extract

Whip cream until frothy. Gradually add sugar and vanilla, beating until stiff peaks form. Yield: about 2 cups.

Doris Amonette,
Tulsa, Oklahoma.

CHRISTMAS WREATH

2 packages dry yeast
2¼ cups warm water (105° to 115°), divided
¼ cup butter or margarine
¼ cup shortening
1 egg, slightly beaten
½ cup sugar
2 teaspoons salt
6½ to 7 cups all-purpose flour, divided
1 egg white
1 tablespoon water
Glaze (recipe follows)
Candied cherries
Toasted sliced almonds

Dissolve yeast in ½ cup warm water. Melt butter and shortening; stir in egg, sugar, salt, and remaining warm water. Combine yeast mixture and butter mixture, mixing well; gradually add 2 cups flour, mixing well. Beat at medium speed of electric mixer for 2 minutes. Gradually stir in enough of remaining flour to make a soft dough.

Turn dough out on a lightly floured surface, and let rest 10 minutes. Knead about 10 minutes or until smooth and elastic. Place in a greased bowl, turning once to grease top. Cover and let rise in a warm place (85°), free from drafts, until doubled in bulk.

Punch dough down, and divide in half; shape each into a ball. Divide 1 ball of dough into 3 equal portions, and shape each into an 18-inch rope. Firmly pinch ends of the 3 ropes together at one end to seal. Braid ropes together; firmly pinch ends together to seal.

Carefully transfer braid to a well-greased baking sheet; shape into a circle with a 5-inch diameter hole. Join ends of braid; firmly pinch ends to seal. Invert a well-greased 3½-inch custard cup in center of wreath. Repeat procedure with remaining dough.

Cover and let rise in a warm place (85°), free from drafts, until doubled.

Combine egg white and 1 tablespoon water, mixing well; gently brush over wreaths. Bake at 375° for 25 to 30 minutes or until golden brown. Carefully transfer to wire rack to cool.

Spread half of glaze over each wreath. Garnish each with candied cherries and almonds. Yield: 2 loaves.

Glaze:
2 cups powdered sugar, sifted
3 tablespoons milk
2 teaspoons vanilla extract

Combine all ingredients, mixing well. Yield: about 1 cup.
Susie Dent,
Saltillo, Mississippi.

FESTIVE CRESCENTS
1 package dry yeast
¼ cup warm water (105° to 115°)
1 cup butter or margarine
½ cup shortening
2 tablespoons sugar
2 teaspoons salt
3 egg yolks
1 (13-ounce) can evaporated milk, divided
5 cups all-purpose flour
½ cup sugar
2 teaspoons ground cinnamon
Filling (recipe follows)

Dissolve yeast in warm water; set aside. Melt butter and shortening; stir in 2 tablespoons sugar, salt, egg yolks, and ¼ cup evaporated milk. Add yeast mixture, mixing well. Add remaining evaporated milk alternately with flour, beating well after each addition. Shape dough into a ball (dough will be soft). Cover and chill 3 hours or overnight.

Combine ½ cup sugar and cinnamon; mix well. Sprinkle about 2 tablespoons sugar mixture on a large wooden board. Divide dough in half, and shape each into a ball. Place 1 ball of dough on surface sprinkled with sugar; roll dough into a 15-inch circle. Sprinkle one-third

of remaining sugar mixture over dough. Cut into 16 wedges. Place a heaping tablespoon of filling on each wedge; roll up, beginning at wide end. Place on greased baking sheet, point side down. Repeat procedure with remaining dough.

Let rise in a warm place (85°), free from drafts, for 30 minutes. Bake at 350° for 18 to 20 minutes or until lightly browned. Yield: about 2½ dozen.

Filling:
1 cup finely chopped walnuts
1 (6-ounce) package semisweet chocolate morsels
½ cup chopped maraschino cherries

Combine all ingredients, and mix well. Yield: about 2½ cups.
Alice McNamara,
Eucha, Oklahoma.

YUMMY SWEET ROLLS
1 cup commercial sour cream, scalded
½ cup melted butter or margarine
½ cup sugar
1 teaspoon salt
2 packages dry yeast
½ cup warm water (105° to 115°)
2 eggs, beaten
4 cups all-purpose flour
Filling (recipe follows)
Glaze (recipe follows)

Combine sour cream, butter, sugar, and salt; mix well. Let mixture cool to lukewarm.

Dissolve yeast in warm water in a large mixing bowl; stir in sour cream mixture, then eggs. Gradually stir in flour (dough will be soft). Cover tightly, and chill overnight.

Divide dough into 4 equal portions. Turn each portion out on a lightly floured surface, and knead 4 or 5 times. Roll each into a 12- x 8-inch rectangle. Spread one-fourth of filling over each rectangle, leaving a ½-inch margin around edges. Carefully roll up jellyroll fashion, beginning at long side. Firmly pinch edge and ends to seal.

Cut each roll into 1½-inch slices. Place slices, cut side down, 2 inches apart on greased baking sheets.

Cover and let rise in a warm place (85°), free from drafts, 1½ hours or until doubled in bulk. Bake at 375° for 12 minutes or until golden brown. Drizzle glaze over each roll. Yield: about 2½ dozen.

Filling:
2 (8-ounce) packages cream cheese, softened
¾ cup sugar
1 egg
2 teaspoons vanilla extract
½ teaspoon salt

Combine all ingredients. Process with food processor or electric mixer until well blended. Yield: about 2 cups.

Glaze:
2 cups powdered sugar, sifted
¼ cup milk
2 teaspoons vanilla extract

Combine all ingredients, mixing well. Yield: about 1 cup.
Mrs. S. M. Phillips,
Candler, North Carolina.

CRANBERRY-BANANA BREAD
2 cups fresh cranberries
1 cup sugar
1 cup water
⅓ cup shortening
⅔ cup sugar
2 eggs
1¾ cups all-purpose flour
2 teaspoons baking powder
½ teaspoon salt
¼ teaspoon baking soda
1 cup mashed banana
½ cup coarsely chopped walnuts

Combine cranberries, 1 cup sugar, and water; cook over medium heat about 5 minutes or until cranberries begin to pop. Drain and set aside.

Cream shortening; gradually add ⅔ cup sugar, beating until light and fluffy. Add eggs, one at a time, beating well after each. Combine dry ingredients; add to creamed mixture alternately with banana, mixing well after each addition. Fold in cranberries and walnuts.

Line a greased 9- x 5- x 3-inch loafpan with waxed paper; grease waxed paper. Spoon batter into pan. Bake at 350° for 60 to 65 minutes or until bread tests done. Cool 10 minutes in pan; remove from pan. Yield: 1 loaf.
Mrs. A. H. Foley,
Lumberton, Mississippi.

Tip: For an attractive pastry crust, brush the top with milk or slightly beaten egg white before baking. Sprinkle top with sugar for a special glaze.

APRICOT COOKIE ROLLS

½ cup flaked coconut
½ cup apricot preserves
¼ cup finely chopped walnuts
1 cup butter, softened
1 cup commercial sour cream
½ teaspoon salt
2 cups all-purpose flour
Powdered sugar (optional)

Combine coconut, preserves, and walnuts; mix well, and set aside.

Cream butter; add sour cream and salt, mixing well. Gradually stir in flour.

Divide dough into fourths; wrap in foil, and chill at least 4 hours. Roll 1 portion to ⅛-inch thickness on a well-floured cloth or board; keep remaining dough chilled until ready to roll. (Dough will be slightly soft.)

Cut dough into 2½-inch squares; spread each with ½ teaspoon coconut mixture. Starting with a corner, carefully roll each square; moisten opposite corner, and seal. Place on greased cookie sheets, seam side up; bake at 350° for 16 to 18 minutes or until tips are lightly browned. Repeat with remaining dough. Let cool; sprinkle lightly with powdered sugar, if desired. Yield: about 5 dozen.

Dolores J. Pritts,
Huntsville, Alabama.

BUTTER PECAN SHORTBREAD COOKIES

1 cup butter, softened
½ cup firmly packed brown sugar
2¼ cups all-purpose flour
½ cup finely chopped pecans
Decorator icing (recipe follows)

Cream butter; gradually add sugar, beating until light and fluffy. Gradually add flour, mixing well. Stir in pecans. Divide dough in half, and chill at least 1 hour.

Roll 1 portion of dough to ¼-inch thickness between sheets of waxed paper; keep remaining dough chilled until ready to use. Remove top sheet of waxed paper. Cut dough into desired shapes with a cookie cutter; remove excess dough. Place greased cookie sheet on top of cookies; invert and remove waxed paper.

Bake at 300° for 18 to 20 minutes or until lightly browned. Remove immediately to wire rack to cool. Repeat with remaining dough. Trim with decorator icing. Yield: about 4 dozen.

Decorator Icing:

¼ cup butter, softened
2 cups powdered sugar, sifted
2 tablespoons milk
½ teaspoon vanilla extract
Red or green food coloring (optional)

Cream butter; gradually add sugar, beating until well blended. Add milk and vanilla, mixing until smooth. Stir in food coloring, if desired. Yield: enough frosting for 4 dozen cookies.

Mrs. Hurley M. Barker,
Milton, North Carolina.

CREAM CHEESE COOKIES

1 cup butter or margarine, softened
1 (3-ounce) package cream cheese, softened
1 cup sugar
1 egg yolk
2½ cups all-purpose flour
1 teaspoon vanilla extract
Candied cherries or pecan halves

Cream butter and cream cheese; gradually add sugar, beating until light and fluffy. Add egg yolk, beating well. Add flour and vanilla; mix until blended. Chill dough at least 1 hour.

Shape dough into 1-inch balls, and place on greased cookie sheets. Gently press a candied cherry or pecan half into each cookie. Bake at 325° for 12 to 15 minutes. Yield: about 7 dozen.

Wilma Havens,
Huntsville, Alabama.

CREME DE MENTHE COOKIES

¾ cup butter, softened
½ cup sugar
1 egg
2 cups all-purpose flour
½ teaspoon salt
2 cups powdered sugar, sifted
3 to 4 tablespoons green crème de menthe
1 (6-ounce) package semisweet chocolate morsels, melted

Cream butter; gradually add sugar, beating until fluffy. Add egg, and mix until well blended. Add flour and salt, mixing well. Chill about 30 minutes.

Work with half of dough at a time; store remainder in refrigerator. Roll dough to ⅛-inch thickness on a sheet of waxed paper (dough will be soft). Cut dough with a 2-inch cookie cutter, and

remove excess dough. Place cookie sheet on top of cookies; invert and remove waxed paper.

Bake at 325° for 7 to 8 minutes; do not brown. Remove cookies to wire rack; let cool completely.

Combine powdered sugar and crème de menthe; beat until smooth. Spread mixture evenly on half of cookies; top with a second cookie. Frost top of each cookie with chocolate. If desired, place a rosette of crème de menthe mixture in center of each. Yield: about 2½ dozen.

Mrs. Victor J. Seine,
Austin, Texas.

APPLE-PECAN TARTS

½ cup butter or margarine, softened
1 cup sugar
3 eggs, slightly beaten
¼ teaspoon salt
¾ cup dark corn syrup
1 teaspoon vanilla extract
1½ cups peeled, finely chopped apple
1¼ cups coarsely chopped pecans
Pastry for a double-crust 9-inch pie
Pecan halves

Cream butter; gradually add sugar, beating until light and fluffy. Add eggs, salt, corn syrup, and vanilla; mix well, and stir in apple and chopped pecans. Set aside.

Roll dough to ⅛-inch thickness on a lightly floured surface. Line 12 tart pans with pastry; flute edges. Fill each with pecan mixture. Bake at 325° for 45 minutes or until done; cool. Garnish with pecan halves. Yield: 1 dozen.

Elizabeth Moore,
Huntsville, Alabama.

HOLIDAY MINCEMEAT PIE

Pastry for double-crust 9-inch pie
½ cup sugar
½ cup light corn syrup
½ teaspoon salt
¼ cup shortening
2 eggs, beaten
½ cup crumbled condensed mincemeat
1 cup chopped pecans
1 teaspoon vanilla extract
2 tablespoons orange juice
1 tablespoon lemon juice
½ cup seedless raisins

Roll half of pastry to ⅛-inch thickness on a lightly floured surface; fit into a 9-inch piepan.

Combine sugar, corn syrup, salt, and shortening in a small saucepan; bring to a boil, stirring occasionally. Remove from heat.

Combine remaining ingredients; gradually add warm syrup, stirring constantly. Spoon mixture into pastry shell.

Roll out remaining pastry to ⅛-inch thickness; cut into ¾-inch-wide strips, and arrange in lattice design over filling. Seal and flute edges.

Bake at 350° for 40 minutes or until golden brown. Cool before serving. Yield: one 9-inch pie.

Mrs. Tillman L. Bishop,
Pottsboro, Texas.

FLUFFY PUMPKIN PIE

1 (16-ounce) can pumpkin
1 cup milk
½ cup sugar
1 teaspoon ground cinnamon
½ teaspoon ground nutmeg
¼ teaspoon ground ginger
¼ teaspoon ground cloves
¼ teaspoon salt
1 tablespoon rum (optional)
3 eggs
1 unbaked deep-dish 9-inch pastry shell

Combine pumpkin, milk, sugar, spices, and salt; stir well. Add rum, if desired.

Separate 1 egg, and set white aside; combine yolk and remaining 2 eggs, beating well. Stir into pumpkin mixture.

Beat egg white (at room temperature) until stiff; fold into pumpkin mixture. Pour filling into pastry shell. Bake at 425° for 45 minutes or until pie is firm in center. (Crust may need to be covered with foil after about 30 minutes of baking to prevent overbrowning.) Cool before serving. Yield: one 9-inch pie.

Mary Boden,
Stuart, Florida.

CRANBERRY-RAISIN PIE

Pastry for double-crust 9-inch pie
2 cups peeled, sliced cooking apples
1 cup fresh cranberries
¼ cup raisins
1 cup sugar
¼ cup all-purpose flour
1 tablespoon margarine

Roll half of pastry to ⅛-inch thickness on a lightly floured surface; fit into a 9-inch pieplate.

Combine apples, cranberries, raisins, sugar, and flour; mix well. Spoon into pastry shell, and dot with margarine.

Roll remaining pastry to ⅛-inch thickness; cut into ½-inch-wide strips, and arrange in lattice design over filling. Seal and flute edges.

Bake at 400° for 50 to 55 minutes or until golden brown. Cool before serving. Yield: one 9-inch pie.

Mrs. Addis Vestal,
Lexington, Tennessee.

Entertain Buffet Style

If space in your dining room limits you to entertaining buffet style, here are some guidelines to make it easier on you and your guests, as well as a menu to try.

Choose finger foods and dishes that are served with only one large spoon or fork so that guests can serve themselves easily and quickly. Limit the menu to foods that require just a fork; wrap them in individual napkins and tie with ribbons for easy pick-up.

Serve hot foods from a chafing dish or warming tray to keep them at the right temperature and make them just as appealing when guests return to the buffet for seconds.

Our menu suits buffet service perfectly. Guests help themselves to easy-to-serve, bacon-wrapped meatballs. Mushrooms in Patty Shells provides two foods in one and eliminates the need to serve bread and butter. Tangy Marinated Broccoli and Sherried Fruit Casserole simplify last-minute preparation for the hostess because they're assembled the day before.

The dessert is effortless, too. Our Tropical Bars are buttery squares rich with coconut and pineapple.

Burgundy-Bacon Meatballs
Mushrooms in Patty Shells
Tangy Marinated Broccoli
Sherried Fruit Casserole
Tropical Bars
Wine

BURGUNDY-BACON MEATBALLS

24 slices bacon
1 pound ground beef
3 tablespoons finely chopped onion
½ cup Burgundy
1 cup soft breadcrumbs
1 egg, beaten
1 teaspoon salt
1 teaspoon dry mustard
½ teaspoon thyme
¼ teaspoon pepper
½ cup Burgundy
Mustard Sauce

Partially cook bacon until it is transparent; drain on paper towels, and set aside.

Combine the next 9 ingredients; mix well. Shape into 1-inch balls. Cut bacon slices in half crosswise; wrap bacon around each meatball and secure with a wooden pick.

Place meatballs on a jellyroll pan; bake at 375° for 20 to 25 minutes or until bacon is done and meatballs are brown. Drain on paper towels; transfer to a chafing dish containing ½ cup Burgundy. Serve with Mustard Sauce. Yield: 4 dozen.

Mustard Sauce:

½ cup Dijon mustard
½ cup mayonnaise
1 teaspoon Worcestershire sauce

Combine all ingredients in a small bowl; mix well. Yield: 1 cup.

Eleanor Brandt,
Arlington, Texas.

MUSHROOMS IN PATTY SHELLS

10 frozen patty shells
2 tablespoons butter or margarine
1 pound fresh mushrooms, sliced
1½ cups commercial sour cream
¾ cup grated Parmesan cheese
3 tablespoons dry sherry
Dash of garlic powder
Fresh parsley

Bake patty shells according to package directions.

Melt butter in a large skillet. Add mushrooms and sauté; drain. Stir in sour cream, cheese, sherry, and garlic powder; cook over low heat until thoroughly heated. Spoon into patty shells. Garnish with parsley, if desired. Serve immediately. Yield: 10 servings.

Sherry Phillips,
Knoxville, Tennessee.

Offer guests this colorful, easy-to-serve buffet: Mushrooms in Patty Shells, Tangy Marinated Broccoli, Sherried Fruit Casserole, Burgundy-Bacon Meatballs, and Tropical Bars.

TROPICAL BARS

¾ cup butter or margarine, melted
2 cups all-purpose flour
½ cup sifted powdered sugar
¼ cup all-purpose flour
2 cups sugar
1 teaspoon baking powder
4 eggs, well beaten
½ cup flaked coconut
1 (8-ounce) can crushed pineapple, drained
1 teaspoon grated lemon rind
Powdered sugar, sifted

Combine butter, 2 cups flour, and ½ cup powdered sugar; mix well, and press into a well-greased and floured 13- x 9- x 2-inch baking pan. Bake at 300° for 25 minutes.

Combine next 7 ingredients; mix well. Spread filling over first layer while still hot. Bake an additional 40 to 45 minutes or until firm. Sprinkle with powdered sugar. Cool, and cut into bars. Yield: about 2½ dozen.

Mrs. Paul Raper,
Burgaw, North Carolina.

Appetizers For Any Occasion

Greet your guests with a festive array of snacks and appetizers. In this selection of recipes, you'll find dips, spreads, and finger foods ranging from elegant to easy.

Prepare big batches of Southern Salted Pecans and Baked Caramel Good Stuff to have on hand for those drop-in neighbors. For dips, we offer a creamy avocado selection and subtly flavored Blue Cheese Dip.

If the occasion calls for something a little more special, offer festive Mushroom Canapés. Or, serve Ham and Pimiento Spread on party rye bread.

TANGY MARINATED BROCCOLI

3 bunches broccoli
1 cup cider vinegar
1 tablespoon sugar
1 tablespoon whole dried dillweed
1 teaspoon salt
1 teaspoon garlic salt
1 teaspoon pepper
1½ cups vegetable oil
Lemon slices (optional)

Trim off large leaves of broccoli. Remove stalks, separate into flowerets, and wash thoroughly. Drain and place in a large shallow container; set aside.

Combine next 7 ingredients, mixing well; pour over broccoli. Toss gently to coat; chill at least 24 hours, stirring several times. Garnish with lemon slices, if desired. Yield: 10 to 12 servings.

Diana Williams,
Greensboro, North Carolina.

Tip: Marshmallows can be cut easily with scissors dipped in hot water.

SHERRIED FRUIT CASSEROLE

1 (8-ounce) jar spiced apple rings, drained
1 (15¼-ounce) can sliced pineapple, drained
1 (16-ounce) can peach halves, drained
1 (16-ounce) can pear halves, drained
1 (16-ounce) can apricot halves, drained
½ cup butter or margarine
2 tablespoons all-purpose flour
½ cup firmly packed brown sugar
¾ to 1 cup sherry

Cut apple rings and pineapple slices in half. Arrange fruit in layers in a 2-quart casserole, and set aside.

Melt butter in a heavy saucepan over low heat; add flour and sugar, stirring until smooth (about 1 minute). Gradually add sherry; cook over medium heat, stirring constantly, until thickened. Pour over fruit; cover and chill 8 hours or overnight.

Let come to room temperature; bake at 350° for 25 minutes or until bubbly. Yield: 10 servings.   *Mrs. Bob Nester,*
Charleston, West Virginia.

BAKED CARAMEL GOOD STUFF

8 cups puffed wheat cereal
½ cup walnut pieces
½ cup pecan pieces
½ cup dry roasted peanuts
½ cup butter or margarine
1 cup firmly packed brown sugar
¼ cup light corn syrup
¼ teaspoon salt
¼ teaspoon soda
½ teaspoon vanilla extract

Combine first 4 ingredients in a large bowl. Set aside.

Melt butter in a medium saucepan; stir in brown sugar, corn syrup, and salt. Bring mixture to a boil, stirring constantly. Boil over medium heat 5 minutes, without stirring. Remove from heat; stir in soda and vanilla. Gradually pour hot syrup over cereal mixture, stirring well. Spoon mixture into a buttered 15- x 10- x 1-inch jellyroll pan. Bake at 300° for 15 minutes. Stir well, and bake an additional 15 minutes. Cool completely in pan. Break into pieces, and store in an air-tight container. Yield: about 10 cups. *Mrs. W. P. Chambers, Louisville, Kentucky.*

SOUTHERN SALTED PECANS

1 cup butter
4 cups pecan halves
1 tablespoon salt

Melt butter in a large skillet; add pecans and salt. Stir well to coat pecans; remove from heat. Place pecans in a 13- x 9- x 2-inch baking pan. Bake at 200° for 1 hour, stirring every 15 minutes. Drain on paper towels. Yield: 4 cups. *Mrs. F. D. Garrison, Hondo, Texas.*

BLUE CHEESE DIP

1 (8-ounce) package cream cheese, softened
½ cup commercial sour cream
½ cup (4 ounces) crumbled blue cheese
1 teaspoon lemon juice
½ teaspoon prepared horseradish
¼ cup grated carrot
¼ cup finely chopped green onion tops
2 tablespoons chopped pimiento
2 tablespoons chopped parsley
¼ cup cooked bacon pieces

Combine cream cheese, sour cream, and blue cheese in container of an electric blender or food processor; blend until smooth. Stir in remaining ingredients. Chill well. Serve with fresh vegetables. Yield: 2½ cups.

Susan Settlemyre, Raleigh, North Carolina.

Tip: Don't throw away asparagus stems. They are delicious sliced thin and stir-fried quickly in hot oil.

MUSHROOM CANAPES

½ pound fresh mushrooms
1 small onion, minced
2 tablespoons chopped fresh parsley
3 tablespoons melted butter or margarine
½ to ¾ cup breadcrumbs
Salt and pepper to taste

Wash mushrooms; pat dry. Remove stems and chop. Place caps in buttered baking dish.

Sauté stems, onion, and parsley in butter. Add breadcrumbs, salt, and pepper; stir well. Stuff caps with mixture; bake at 350° about 15 minutes. Yield: about 1½ dozen. *Mrs. Paul E. Kline, Palm Beach Gardens, Florida.*

HAM AND PIMIENTO SPREAD

1½ cups finely chopped cooked ham
1 (4-ounce) jar chopped pimiento, drained
½ cup chopped parsley
½ cup mayonnaise

Combine all ingredients in a medium bowl; stir well. Chill. Serve on party rye bread or crackers. Yield: about 3 cups.
Eleanor K. Brandt, Arlington, Texas.

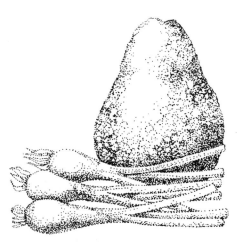

AVOCADO DIP

1 ripe avocado, peeled and mashed
2 (3-ounce) packages cream cheese, softened
2 tablespoons milk
1 tablespoon lemon juice
1 tablespoon grated onion
¼ teaspoon salt

Combine first 3 ingredients; beat until smooth. Add remaining ingredients, and blend well. Serve with fresh vegetables or crackers. Yield: about 1½ cups.
Katie Bender, Rickman, Tennessee.

Stretch The Meat With A Main-Dish Pie

Your family will never recognize yesterday's ham or turkey when it's baked in a savory meat pie. In fact, meat pies stretch any kind of meat—sausage, tuna, ground beef—into a satisfying one-dish dinner. To round out the menu, add a salad and dessert.

A regular pastry shell is used for Deep-Dish Pizza Pie. Make your own, or substitute a commercial one for speed and convenience. But for Tuna Pie With Cheese Roll Crust, take a few extra minutes to roll out the attractive cheese-pimiento pinwheels that grace the top of the pie.

For meat pies in the turnover fashion, try Vegetable-Beef Pies. Eat them right from the oven, or pack them for a fall picnic. They're great, either hot or cold.

TURKEY PIE

Pastry for double-crust 9-inch pie
1 medium onion, chopped
1 clove garlic, crushed
1 (4-ounce) can sliced mushrooms, drained (optional)
¼ cup butter or margarine, melted
2 tablespoons all-purpose flour
1½ cups milk
½ teaspoon salt
½ teaspoon pepper
¼ teaspoon dried thyme leaves
2 cups cubed cooked turkey
1 (10-ounce) package frozen peas and carrots, thawed

Roll half of pastry to ⅛-inch thickness, and fit into a 9-inch piepan.

Sauté onion, garlic, and mushrooms, if desired, in butter about 5 minutes or until tender; blend in flour. Cook 1 minute, stirring constantly. Gradually add milk; cook over medium heat, stirring constantly, until thickened and bubbly. Stir in salt, pepper, thyme, turkey, and vegetables; spoon into pastry shell.

Roll out remaining pastry to ⅛-inch thickness; carefully place over pie, leaving a 1-inch rim beyond edge of pan. Seal and flute edges; cut slits in top for steam to escape.

Bake at 375° for 35 minutes or until golden brown. Yield: 6 to 8 servings.
Elaine Gunter, Newport, Tennessee.

VEGETABLE-BEEF PIES

½ pound ground beef
1½ tablespoons all-purpose flour
1 teaspoon salt
1 teaspoon pepper
1 beef bouillon cube
¼ cup hot water
1 tablespoon chopped fresh parsley
1 cup finely diced potatoes
1 cup finely diced turnip roots
½ cup thinly sliced carrots
½ cup thinly sliced celery
5 piecrust sticks
Milk

Sauté ground beef in a large skillet until browned; drain off pan drippings. Add flour, salt, and pepper to meat; stir until blended. Dissolve bouillon cube in water, and add to meat mixture. Cook until thickened, stirring occasionally. Add parsley and vegetables; cover and cook about 7 minutes or until vegetables are crisp-tender.

Prepare piecrust sticks according to package directions. Divide dough into 4 equal portions. On a lightly floured surface, roll each portion into a 10-inch square; cut each square into four 5-inch squares.

Spoon about 2 tablespoons meat mixture on each pastry square; fold into a triangle, making sure edges are even. Using a fork dipped in flour, press edges together to seal.

Place pies on ungreased baking sheets. Lightly brush with milk, and cut slits in top for steam to escape. Bake at 350° for 25 to 30 minutes or until golden brown. Serve hot or cold. Yield: 16 servings.
Mrs. H. J. Sherrer,
Bay City, Texas.

HAM PIE WITH CHEESE CRUST

6 medium carrots, coarsely chopped
1 medium onion, coarsely chopped
4 medium potatoes, coarsely chopped
3 cups cubed cooked ham
½ teaspoon salt
¼ teaspoon pepper
1 (10¾-ounce) can cream of mushroom soup, undiluted
1 cup milk
½ cup frozen green peas, thawed
Cheese Crust

Combine carrots, onion, and a small amount of water in a large saucepan; cover and cook over medium heat about 10 minutes. Add potatoes, ham, salt, and pepper; cover and cook about 5 minutes or until potatoes are tender. Drain mixture, discarding liquid.

Combine ham-vegetable mixture, soup, milk, and peas; stir well. Spoon into a lightly greased 2½-quart casserole. Top with Cheese Crust; seal and flute edges. Cut slits in top for steam to escape. Bake at 350° for 35 minutes or until golden brown. Yield: 6 servings.

Cheese Crust:

2 cups all-purpose flour
1 teaspoon salt
⅔ cup plus 2 tablespoons shortening
½ cup (2 ounces) shredded sharp Cheddar cheese
4 to 6 tablespoons cold water

Combine flour and salt; cut in shortening and cheese until mixture resembles coarse meal. Sprinkle evenly with cold water, and stir with a fork until all dry ingredients are moistened. Shape into a ball; chill. On a lightly floured surface, roll pastry to fit top of casserole. Yield: pastry for one 2½-quart casserole.
Mrs. Harvey Kidd,
Hernando, Mississippi.

TUNA PIE WITH CHEESE ROLL CRUST

3 tablespoons butter or margarine
½ cup chopped green pepper
½ cup chopped onion
¼ cup plus 2 tablespoons all-purpose flour
½ teaspoon salt
3 cups milk
1 (12½-ounce) can tuna, drained and flaked
1 tablespoon lemon juice
Cheese Rolls

Melt butter in a large saucepan; add green pepper and onion, and sauté until tender. Blend in flour and salt; cook 1 minute, stirring constantly. Gradually add milk; cook over medium heat, stirring constantly, until thickened and bubbly. Stir in tuna and lemon juice.

Spoon tuna mixture into a lightly greased 1½-quart casserole; top with Cheese Rolls. Bake at 450° for 30 minutes or until rolls are browned. Yield: 8 servings.

Cheese Rolls:

1½ cups all-purpose flour
1 tablespoon baking powder
½ teaspoon salt
Dash of red pepper
3 tablespoons shortening
⅓ to ½ cup milk
¾ cup (3 ounces) shredded sharp Cheddar cheese
¼ cup chopped pimiento

Combine dry ingredients, and cut in shortening until mixture resembles coarse meal. Stir in enough milk to make a soft dough.

Turn dough out onto a lightly floured surface. Roll dough into a 12- x 8-inch rectangle, and sprinkle with cheese and pimiento. Starting at short end, roll up dough, jellyroll fashion. Cut into 1-inch-thick slices. Yield: 8 rolls.
Mrs. Harland Stone,
Ocala, Florida.

DEEP-DISH PIZZA LUNCHEON PIE

1 unbaked 9-inch pastry shell
1 pound bulk pork sausage
¾ cup chopped onion
4 eggs, slightly beaten
½ cup milk
½ teaspoon dried oregano leaves
⅛ teaspoon pepper
1 cup (4 ounces) shredded Cheddar cheese
1 (8-ounce) can pizza sauce or tomato sauce
3 slices Cheddar cheese, cut in half diagonally

Prick bottom and sides of pastry shell with a fork; bake at 425° for 6 to 8 minutes. Let cool on wire rack.

Combine sausage and onion, and cook until sausage is browned; drain well. Combine eggs, milk, and seasonings; beat lightly. Stir in sausage mixture and shredded cheese; spoon into pastry shell. Bake at 375° for 25 to 30 minutes or until set.

Spread pie with pizza sauce, and top with Cheddar slices. Bake an additional 5 to 8 minutes or until cheese triangles melt. Yield: 6 to 8 servings.
Mrs. Ronnie Wright,
Campbell, Missouri.

Pick A Sweet Potato Favorite

There's no denying Southerners are partial to sweet potatoes. The proof is in the number of ways this copper-colored vegetable is used. Here we've included some old-fashioned favorites, such as Sweet Potato Biscuits.

Sweet potatoes should never be refrigerated. The best temperature for storing is 65°, but never store them below 55°. If refrigerated, the potatoes will turn black, lose flavor, and rot.

SWEET POTATO BOATS

6 medium sweet potatoes
Vegetable oil
¼ cup molasses
¼ cup butter or margarine, melted
⅛ teaspoon ground nutmeg
¼ teaspoon ground cinnamon
¼ teaspoon salt
½ cup whipping cream

Wash potatoes well; rub with oil. Place on a baking sheet, and bake at 400° for 1 hour or until tender.

Cool potatoes to touch. Slice skin away from top of each potato. Carefully scoop out pulp, leaving shells intact. Combine pulp, molasses, butter, nutmeg, cinnamon, salt, and whipping cream. Beat with electric mixer until light and fluffy.

Spoon potato mixture into shells. Bake at 450° for 10 to 12 minutes or until thoroughly heated. Yield: 6 servings. *Mrs. Farmer L. Burns, New Orleans, Louisiana.*

SWEET POTATO BISCUITS

¾ cup cooked, mashed sweet potatoes
½ cup melted butter or margarine
2 tablespoons brown sugar
2 cups all-purpose flour
2 teaspoons baking powder
1 teaspoon salt
½ teaspoon soda
¾ cup buttermilk

Combine sweet potatoes, butter, and brown sugar; beat at medium speed of electric mixer until blended. Combine flour, baking powder, and salt; stir well. Stir soda into buttermilk until it is dissolved.

Combine all ingredients, stirring just until moistened. Turn dough out onto a floured surface, and knead lightly 6 to 8 times.

Roll dough to ½-inch thickness; cut with a 1½-inch biscuit cutter. Place on an ungreased baking sheet; bake at 400° for 18 to 20 minutes. Yield: about 2 dozen. *Mrs. F. Glenn Moore, Jr. Winchester, Tennessee.*

Tip: To prevent a soggy crust in custard pies, brush egg white on the uncooked pie shell; bake at 425° for 5 to 10 minutes. Add filling, and bake according to recipe directions.

SWEET POTATO BAKE

3 cups cooked, mashed sweet potatoes
½ teaspoon salt
1 egg
3 tablespoons butter or margarine, softened
3 tablespoons orange juice
½ cup crushed peanut brittle

Combine sweet potatoes, salt, egg, butter, and orange juice; beat until smooth. Spoon into a lightly greased 1½-quart casserole. Top with peanut brittle. Bake, uncovered, at 350° for 20 minutes. Yield: 4 to 6 servings.
Mrs. Thomas Lee Adams, Kingsport, Tennessee.

SWEET POTATO SURPRISE CAKE

1 cup vegetable oil
2 cups sugar
4 eggs, separated
¼ cup hot water
2½ cups sifted cake flour
1 tablespoon baking powder
¼ teaspoon salt
1 teaspoon ground cinnamon
1 teaspoon ground nutmeg
1½ cups grated uncooked sweet potatoes
1 cup chopped pecans or walnuts
1 teaspoon vanilla extract
Creamy Coconut Frosting
Pecan halves

Combine oil, sugar, egg yolks, and water; beat at medium speed of electric mixer just until combined. Combine dry ingredients, and add to oil mixture; mix just until moistened. Stir in sweet potatoes, pecans, and vanilla.

Beat egg whites until stiff but not dry; fold into batter. Spoon batter into 3 greased 9-inch cakepans; bake at 350° for 25 to 30 minutes or until cake tests done.

Immediately invert layers on wire cooling racks. Cool 5 minutes, and remove pans; cool completely. Spread Creamy Coconut Frosting between layers and on top and sides of cake. Garnish with pecan halves. Yield: one 9-inch layer cake.

Creamy Coconut Frosting:

1 (13-ounce) can evaporated milk
1 cup sugar
½ cup butter or margarine
3 egg yolks
1 teaspoon vanilla extract
1½ cups flaked coconut

Combine milk, sugar, butter, egg yolks, and vanilla in a heavy saucepan; cook over medium heat, stirring constantly, about 12 minutes or until thickened. (Mixture will be consistency of a pudding.) Remove from heat, and stir in coconut; beat until cool. Yield: frosting for one 9-inch layer cake.
Melba Martin, Bath Springs, Tennessee.

SWEET POTATO CHEESECAKE

1⅔ cups graham cracker crumbs
⅓ cup butter or margarine, melted
2 envelopes unflavored gelatin
½ cup cold water
3 eggs, separated
¾ cup sugar
½ teaspoon salt
⅓ cup milk
2 (8-ounce) packages cream cheese, softened
1¼ cups cooked, mashed sweet potatoes
1 cup whipping cream, whipped
2 teaspoons vanilla extract
1 teaspoon grated orange rind

Combine graham cracker crumbs and butter; mix well. Press mixture into bottom and 1½ inches up sides of a 9-inch springform pan; chill.

Soften gelatin in cold water in top of a double boiler. Add egg yolks, sugar, salt, and milk. Place over water; bring water to a boil. Reduce heat and cook, stirring constantly, until slightly thickened. Add cream cheese and sweet potatoes; beat until smooth.

Beat egg whites until stiff but not dry. Fold egg whites, whipped cream, vanilla, and orange rind into sweet potato mixture; spoon into prepared pan. Refrigerate until set. Remove sides of springform pan. Yield: 10 to 12 servings. *Kathleen D. Stone, Houston, Texas.*

Tip: Store spices away from any direct source of heat as the heat will destroy their flavor.

SWEET POTATO PONE PIE

1½ cups cooked, mashed sweet potatoes
⅔ cup firmly packed brown sugar
½ teaspoon salt
¼ teaspoon ground cinnamon
2 eggs, beaten
1 tablespoon lemon juice
1 cup milk
1 unbaked 9-inch pastry shell
Pecan halves (optional)

Combine first 7 ingredients; beat just until smooth.

Pour filling into pastry shell. Bake at 450° for 15 minutes; reduce heat to 325°, and bake an additional 30 minutes or until set. Garnish with pecan halves, if desired. Yield: one 9-inch pie.

Mrs. Harland J. Stone,
Ocala, Florida.

Cranberries For Color And Flavor

Early settlers concocted the first cranberry sauce, and also made ruby-red dye from cranberry pulp. Then as now, the cranberry was treasured for its bright color as well as its distinctive tart flavor.

Our readers have discovered that cranberry sauce can be more than just a side dish for turkey. Berry Barbecued Pork Roast sports a cranberry-barbecue basting sauce. Spoon any leftover sauce over individual meat slices.

For a warming and satisfying beverage on a chilly winter evening, serve Hot Cranberry Punch. It's colorful and spicy, guaranteed to take the chill away.

Firm cranberries with a high luster indicate freshness. Berries will stay fresh in the refrigerator for 7 to 10 days. Cranberries also freeze well in an airtight container for up to a year.

BERRY BARBECUED PORK ROAST

4 cups fresh cranberries
1 cup sugar
½ cup commercial barbecue sauce
½ cup orange juice
1 (4- to 6-pound) pork loin roast
Orange slices (optional)
Parsley (optional)

Wash and sort cranberries; drain well. Combine cranberries, sugar, barbecue sauce, and orange juice in a large saucepan, mixing well. Bring to a boil over medium heat, stirring constantly. Continue boiling without stirring, 5 minutes; set aside.

Place roast, fat side up, on rack in a roasting pan. Insert meat thermometer, being sure it does not touch bone or fat.

Roast pork at 325° until thermometer reaches 170°, basting often with cranberry sauce during the last 30 minutes of baking time. Let stand 10 to 15 minutes; serve with remaining sauce. If desired, garnish with orange slices and parsley. Yield: 8 to 12 servings.

Charlotte A. Pierce,
Greensburg, Kentucky.

CRANBERRY PORK CHOPS

6 (1-inch-thick) pork chops
Salt
All-purpose flour
Vegetable oil
2 cups fresh cranberries
1 cup sugar
1 cup water

Sprinkle pork chops with salt, and dredge in flour. Brown on both sides in small amount of hot oil; remove from skillet. Drain well and place in a 13- x 9- x 2-inch baking dish.

Wash and sort cranberries; drain well. Sprinkle cranberries over pork chops; sprinkle with sugar. Add water; cover and bake at 350° for 40 minutes. Remove cover, and bake an additional 30 minutes or until done. Yield: 6 servings.

Mrs. Victor J. Blume,
Waxahachie, Texas.

CRANBERRY-ORANGE NUT BREAD

1 cup whole wheat flour
1 cup all-purpose flour
1½ teaspoons baking powder
½ teaspoon soda
1 cup sugar
Boiling water
Juice of 1 orange
2 tablespoons butter or margarine
1 egg, well beaten
1 cup chopped cranberries
½ to 1 cup chopped walnuts

Combine flour, baking powder, soda, and sugar; set aside.

Add enough boiling water to orange juice to make ¾ cup liquid; add butter and stir until melted. Stir into dry ingredients. Add egg, mixing until smooth. Fold in cranberries and walnuts.

Spoon batter into a greased and floured 9- x 5- x 3-inch loafpan; bake at 350° for 50 to 55 minutes or until bread tests done. Yield: 1 loaf.

Heather Riggins,
Nashville, Tennessee.

HOT CRANBERRY PUNCH

4 cups fresh cranberries
2 quarts water
2 tablespoons grated orange rind
6 cinnamon sticks
12 whole cloves
1 quart orange juice
1 cup lemon juice
1½ cups sugar

Wash and sort cranberries; drain well.

Combine cranberries, water, orange rind, cinnamon sticks, and cloves in a large Dutch oven. Bring to a boil, reduce heat, and simmer 5 minutes or until cranberries pop. Strain mixture, discarding pulp, and stir in the remaining ingredients.

Place over medium heat, stirring constantly, until sugar is dissolved and mixture is thoroughly heated. Yield: about 3 quarts.

Ro Ann North,
Fort Smith, Arkansas.

CRANBERRY COBBLER ROLL

2 cups fresh cranberries
1¾ cups all-purpose flour
½ teaspoon salt
⅓ cup shortening
7 to 8 tablespoons cold water
1½ cups sugar, divided
½ cup butter or margarine
1 cup hot water
½ teaspoon vanilla extract

Wash and sort cranberries; drain well and set aside.

Combine flour and salt; cut in shortening with pastry blender until mixture resembles coarse meal. Sprinkle cold water evenly over surface; stir with a fork until all dry ingredients are moistened. Divide dough in half.

Roll half of dough into a 9-inch circle on a lightly floured surface. Place 1 cup cranberries on top; sprinkle with ½ cup sugar and dot with one-third of the butter. Roll up and press ends together to seal; place seam side down in a well-greased 12- x 8- x 2-inch baking dish.

Repeat with remaining dough and place beside first roll in baking dish. Slightly flatten each roll with hand. Sprinkle remaining ½ cup sugar over top and dot with remaining butter.

Bake at 325° for 45 minutes; combine hot water and vanilla, and pour in dish around edges of rolls. Bake an additional 15 minutes. Serve warm. Yield: 8 servings.
Mrs. R. S. Barnes,
Birmingham, Alabama.

Flavor Dessert With Coffee

Here's a dessert that not only looks different, but has an unusual and delightful taste. Strong cold coffee and ground almonds flavor a rich, buttery filling, which is then sandwiched between layers of ladyfingers. A whipped cream topping is spread over the dessert, and toasted almonds add the finishing touch to Mocha-Almond Dessert.

MOCHA-ALMOND DESSERT
1 cup unsalted butter, softened
½ cup sugar
5 egg yolks
¼ cup plus 3 tablespoons cold
   strong coffee
2 teaspoons vanilla extract
¼ cup plus 1 tablespoon toasted ground
   almonds
8 to 10 ladyfingers, split lengthwise
1 cup whipping cream, whipped
Sliced almonds, toasted

Cream butter; gradually add sugar, beating until light and fluffy and sugar is dissolved. Add egg yolks, one at a time, beating well after each addition.

Gradually add coffee to creamed mixture, beating well. Stir in vanilla and ground almonds.

Arrange ladyfingers around sides of a 1½-quart mold; spoon in half of creamed mixture. Top with a layer of ladyfingers, and add remaining creamed mixture. Top evenly with the remaining ladyfingers. Cover; chill 24 hours.

Unmold dessert onto a serving plate. Spread whipped cream evenly over dessert. Garnish with sliced almonds. Yield: 8 servings. *Florence Costello,*
Chattanooga, Tennessee.

Getting To The Heart Of A Coconut

According to our test kitchen staff, getting into a fresh coconut is easy. First you pierce the soft areas at the top of the coconut with a sharp instrument; drain off the milk. Then give the nut a few firm blows with a hammer until the shell cracks and falls off. Peel the meat and then grate or chop it by hand or in a food processor.

FRESH COCONUT CAKE
¾ cup shortening
2 cups sugar
½ cup milk
½ cup water
3 cups sifted cake flour
1 tablespoon baking powder
¾ teaspoon salt
½ teaspoon vanilla extract
½ teaspoon lemon extract
6 egg whites
Seven-Minute Frosting
Fruit-Nut Filling
1¾ cups shredded fresh coconut

Cream shortening; gradually add sugar, beating until light and fluffy.

Combine milk and water. Combine cake flour, baking powder, and salt, stirring well; add to creamed mixture alternately with milk mixture, beginning and ending with flour mixture. Stir in flavorings.

Beat egg whites (at room temperature) until stiff peaks form; fold into batter.

Line bottom of two greased 9-inch round cakepans with waxed paper. Pour batter into cakepans. Bake at 350° for 30 minutes. Cool in pans 10 minutes; remove from pans, and peel off paper. Cool completely.

Prepare Seven-Minute Frosting, reserving 2 cups for use in Fruit-Nut Filling; set remaining frosting aside.

Spread Fruit-Nut Filling between layers. Frost top and sides of cake with Seven-Minute Frosting. Sprinkle with coconut. Yield: one 9-inch layer cake.

Seven-Minute Frosting:
3 egg whites
½ cup water
Dash of salt
2¼ cups sugar
1 tablespoon light corn syrup
1 teaspoon vanilla extract

Combine egg whites (at room temperature), water, and salt in the top of a large double boiler; bring water to a boil. Beat egg white mixture until foamy. Reduce heat to low. Gradually add sugar and corn syrup, beating constantly with electric mixer on high speed for 7 minutes.

Pour mixture into a large mixing bowl. Add vanilla, and beat 8 to 10 minutes or until frosting is thick enough to spread. Yield: enough for one 9-inch layer cake.

Fruit-Nut Filling:
2 cups Seven-Minute Frosting
¼ cup chopped dates
¼ cup chopped candied cherries
¼ cup chopped candied pineapple
¼ cup chopped pecans
¼ cup shredded fresh coconut

Combine all ingredients; stir gently to blend. Yield: enough filling for one 9-inch layer cake. *Katharyn B. Riley,*
Kingsport, Tennessee.

FRESH COCONUT CREAM PIE
1 cup sugar
⅔ cup cornstarch
¼ teaspoon salt
1 quart milk
4 egg yolks
2 tablespoons butter
1½ teaspoons vanilla extract
1 cup finely chopped fresh coconut,
   divided
1 baked 9-inch pastry shell
½ cup whipping cream
1 teaspoon powdered sugar

Combine sugar, cornstarch, and salt in a heavy saucepan; stir in milk. Cook over medium heat, stirring constantly, until thickened and smooth.

Beat egg yolks until thick and lemon colored. Gradually stir about one-fourth of hot milk mixture into yolks; add to remaining hot milk mixture, stirring constantly. Cook 5 minutes, stirring constantly. Remove from heat; add butter and vanilla. Cool. Stir ⅔ cup coconut into cooled filling. Pour filling into pastry shell; chill overnight.

Beat whipping cream until foamy; gradually add powdered sugar, beating until soft peaks form. Spread over pie; sprinkle with remaining coconut. Yield: one 9-inch pie. *Joyce Magee,*
Stone Mountain, Georgia.

Hot Chocolate In Minutes

While the weather's nippy, it's the perfect time to try your hand at microwaving hot chocolate. Here are four delicious ways to take the chill off a winter day.

For hot chocolate that's party special, serve a liqueur-laced version like Flaming Brandied Chocolate or Café Colombian Royal.

Deluxe Hot Chocolate Mix can be stored in the refrigerator for up to two weeks. Then when you're ready for a quick cup, just stir in milk that's been heated in the microwave. You'll also want to try our Creole Hot Chocolate. It's spiced with cinnamon and nutmeg and served with a dollop of whipped cream.

Since wattage of microwave ovens varies, the cooking times will vary. We give a time range in our recipes to allow for the difference. To prevent overcooking, always check for doneness at the lower end of the range.

Hot chocolate can be heated in microwave-safe mugs, bowls, or casseroles. Be sure there is no metallic trim on the container. Here are some other tips.

—Fill containers only two-thirds full to prevent boilovers.

—When heating two mugs, arrange them about 2 inches apart in the center of the oven. When microwaving more than two mugs, arrange them in a circular pattern.

—To prevent a skin from forming on milk, cover with heavy-duty plastic wrap; also stop microwaving before the milk boils.

—Before flaming liqueurs, microwave at HIGH just until hot; ¼ cup will heat in about 30 seconds.

—Prevent breakage of glass mugs by placing a metal spoon in each before adding hot liquids.

—Stir hot chocolate thoroughly before serving to combine heated portions with unheated portions.

FLAMING BRANDIED CHOCOLATE

3 cups milk
½ cup chocolate syrup
¼ cup crème de cacao
¼ cup brandy
Vanilla ice cream

Combine milk and chocolate syrup in a deep 2½-quart casserole or bowl, mixing well. Cover with heavy-duty plastic wrap. Microwave at HIGH for 5½ to 6 minutes or until thoroughly heated. Stir in crème de cacao, and set aside.

Place brandy in a custard cup or small bowl. Microwave at HIGH for 30 to 45 seconds or until hot. Ignite brandy. When flame dies, stir brandy into chocolate mixture. Ladle chocolate into mugs, and top with a scoop of ice cream. Yield: 4 cups.

CREOLE HOT CHOCOLATE

3 (1-ounce) squares unsweetened chocolate, coarsely chopped
½ cup sugar
1 teaspoon ground cinnamon
¼ teaspoon ground nutmeg
1 cup water
4½ cups milk
Sweetened whipped cream
Ground cinnamon

Combine chocolate, sugar, 1 teaspoon cinnamon, nutmeg, and water in a deep 3-quart casserole or bowl. Microwave at HIGH for 5 to 6 minutes, stirring twice, or until chocolate melts. Gradually stir in milk. Cover with heavy-duty plastic wrap, and microwave at HIGH for 8 to 9 minutes or until thoroughly heated.

Beat hot chocolate with a rotary beater until foamy. Ladle into mugs; top with whipped cream, and sprinkle with cinnamon. Yield: 5½ cups.

CAFE COLOMBIAN ROYAL

½ cup whipping cream
1 tablespoon powdered sugar
2 (1-ounce) squares semisweet chocolate, coarsely chopped
2 tablespoons sugar
¾ teaspoon ground cinnamon
¼ teaspoon ground nutmeg
3 cups water
1 tablespoon instant coffee granules
2 cups milk
¼ cup Kahlúa or other coffee-flavored liqueur
½ teaspoon vanilla extract
Ground cinnamon

Beat whipping cream until foamy; gradually add powdered sugar, beating until soft peaks form. Place cream mixture in refrigerator.

Combine chocolate, 2 tablespoons sugar, ¾ teaspoon cinnamon, nutmeg, and water in a deep 3-quart casserole or bowl. Microwave at HIGH for 8 to 10 minutes, stirring twice, or until chocolate melts and water is boiling. Add coffee granules, stirring until dissolved. Gradually stir in milk, and cover with heavy-duty plastic wrap.

Microwave at HIGH for 2 to 4 minutes or until thoroughly heated. Stir in Kahlúa and vanilla. Pour into mugs; top with whipped cream, and sprinkle with cinnamon. Yield: 5½ cups.

DELUXE HOT CHOCOLATE MIX

1 (15-ounce) can sweetened condensed milk
1 (6-ounce) package semisweet chocolate morsels
1 teaspoon vanilla extract
1 cup whipping cream, whipped

Combine sweetened condensed milk and chocolate morsels in a medium bowl. Cover with heavy-duty plastic wrap; microwave at MEDIUM HIGH for 2 to 3 minutes, stirring twice, or until most of the chocolate morsels are soft. Stir until chocolate melts. Stir in vanilla, and let cool; fold in whipped cream. Cover and store in refrigerator for up to 2 weeks.

To serve, spoon about 3 tablespoons chocolate mixture into the desired number of mugs. Fill the mugs with hot milk, stirring until well blended. Yield: about 18 servings.

Note: To heat milk, pour into a microwave-safe bowl; cover with heavy-duty plastic wrap, and microwave at HIGH according to the following times: For 2 servings (1⅓ cups milk), 2½ to 3 minutes; 4 servings (2⅔ cups milk), 4½ to 5 minutes; 6 servings (4 cups milk), 5½ to 6 minutes; 12 servings (8 cups milk), 9 to 11 minutes.

Right: *Add elegance to your holiday table with one or more of these entrées. Clockwise: Royal Crown Roast of Pork (page 252), Roast Turkey with Oyster Stuffing (page 251), Standing Rib Roast (page 252), Holiday Duckling (page 251), and Country Ham in Apple Cider (page 251).*

Page 294: *A Southern Christmas wouldn't be complete without festive cakes such as these: Old-Fashioned Pound Cake (page 279), White Fruitcake (page 280), and Chocolate Fudge Cake (page 279).*

Basic decorating techniques, assorted candies, and decorator sprinkles bring these big gingerbread cookies to life. See page 278 for recipe and directions and page 303 for cookie patterns.

Desserts Should Be Special

Looking for a dessert to turn an average meal into something special? We think you'll agree with our taste panel that one of these flavorful treats is just what you need.

Our spectacular Brownie Pudding will quickly become a favorite in your home. Hidden beneath the brownie layer is a luscious chocolate sauce to spoon over each serving. We suggest topping each portion with whipped cream or ice cream for added flair.

LEMON CUSTARD IN MERINGUE CUPS

3 egg whites
½ teaspoon vinegar
¼ teaspoon vanilla extract
⅛ teaspoon salt
1 cup sugar
Lemon Custard

Combine egg whites (at room temperature), vinegar, vanilla, and salt; beat until frothy. Gradually add sugar, 1 tablespoon at a time, beating until stiff peaks form. Do not underbeat.

Spoon meringue into 6 equal portions on unglazed brown paper. Using back of spoon, shape meringue into circles about 4 inches in diameter; then shape each circle into a shell (sides should be about 1½ inches high).

Bake at 300° for 45 minutes. Cool meringues away from drafts. Spoon Lemon Custard into shells. Yield: 6 servings.

Lemon Custard:

1 cup sugar
¼ cup plus 1 tablespoon cornstarch
⅛ teaspoon salt
1½ cups boiling water
3 egg yolks
¼ cup lemon juice
2 tablespoons grated lemon rind

Combine sugar, cornstarch, and salt in a heavy saucepan; stir well. Add water, and cook over low heat, stirring constantly, until thickened.

Combine egg yolks, lemon juice, and rind; beat well. Gradually stir about one-fourth of hot mixture into yolks; add to remaining hot mixture, stirring constantly. Cook custard, stirring constantly, 10 minutes or until smooth and thickened. Chill. Yield: about 2½ cups.
Mrs. Paul Raper,
Burgaw, North Carolina.

ORANGE-APPLE CRISP

2¼ cups thinly sliced, peeled cooking apples
1 teaspoon ground cinnamon
½ teaspoon ground nutmeg
Juice of 1 orange
¾ cup all-purpose flour
1 cup firmly packed brown sugar
¼ cup butter or margarine, softened
1½ teaspoons grated orange rind
Whipped cream or ice cream (optional)

Place apples in a lightly greased 9-inch pieplate. Combine cinnamon and nutmeg; sprinkle over apples. Add enough water to orange juice to equal 1 cup; pour over apples.

Combine flour and sugar; cut butter into flour mixture with pastry blender until mixture resembles coarse meal. Add orange rind, mixing well. Sprinkle over apple mixture. Bake at 350° for 35 to 40 minutes. Spoon dessert into serving bowls; top with whipped cream or ice cream, if desired. Yield: 6 to 8 servings.
Joan B. Piercy,
Memphis, Tennessee.

ALMOND WHIPPING CREAM CAKE

1½ cups sifted cake flour
2 teaspoons baking powder
½ teaspoon salt
1 cup whipping cream
2 eggs
1 cup sugar
1 teaspoon vanilla extract
1 (3-ounce) package cream cheese, softened
1 cup sifted powdered sugar
½ teaspoon almond extract
1 cup slivered almonds, toasted

Combine flour, baking powder, and salt; set aside.

Beat whipping cream until peaks form; add eggs, and beat until smooth. Add sugar; beat until dissolved. Stir in vanilla; fold in dry ingredients. Pour into a greased and floured 8-inch square pan; bake at 375° for 25 to 30 minutes or until wooden pick inserted in center comes out clean. Cool.

Beat cream cheese until light; add powdered sugar, and beat until smooth. Add almond extract; blend well. Stir in almonds; spread frosting on cake. Yield: 9 servings.
Mrs. Beckwith D. Smith,
Jacksonville, Florida.

BROWNIE PUDDING

1 cup all-purpose flour
¾ cup sugar
¾ cup chopped pecans or walnuts
½ cup milk
¼ cup cocoa
2 tablespoons butter or margarine, melted
2 teaspoons baking powder
1 teaspoon vanilla extract
¼ teaspoon salt
1¾ cups hot water
¾ cup firmly packed brown sugar
2 tablespoons cocoa
Whipped cream or ice cream

Combine first 9 ingredients; stir well. Spread batter evenly in an ungreased 11- x 7- x 2-inch baking pan.

Combine hot water, brown sugar, and 2 tablespoons cocoa; stir well. Pour mixture over batter; bake at 350° for 35 minutes. Serve warm with whipped cream or ice cream. Yield: 6 servings.
Kathleen Branson,
Thomasville, North Carolina.

MINCEMEAT-PEACH PIE

1 (9-ounce) package dry mincemeat
½ cup water
1 (16-ounce) can peach pie filling
1 tablespoon grated orange rind, divided
Pastry for double-crust 9-inch pie
2 teaspoons half-and-half
1 tablespoon sugar

Combine mincemeat and water in a saucepan; bring to a boil, and boil 1 minute. Remove from heat; stir in pie filling and 2 teaspoons orange rind. Pour into a pastry-lined 9-inch pieplate; top with remaining pastry. Trim edges; then seal and flute. Cut slits in crust to allow steam to escape. Brush crust with half-and-half.

Combine remaining orange peel and sugar; sprinkle over pastry. Bake at 425° for 30 to 35 minutes or until browned. Yield: one 9-inch pie.
Mrs. Roland P. Guest, Jr.,
Jackson, Mississippi.

Tip: Most fruits are best stored in the refrigerator. Allow melons, avocados, and pears to ripen at room temperature; then refrigerate. Berries should be sorted to remove imperfect fruit before refrigerating; wash and hull just before serving.

SPICY BUTTERNUT SQUASH PIE

2 butternut squash
2 unbaked 8-inch pastry shells
3 eggs, slightly beaten
½ cup sugar
½ cup firmly packed light brown sugar
½ teaspoon ground cinnamon
½ teaspoon ground ginger
½ teaspoon ground nutmeg
3 tablespoons cornstarch
1 (13-ounce) can evaporated milk
Whipped cream (optional)

Peel squash; slice in half lengthwise, and remove seeds. Cut into slices; place in saucepan, and cover with water. Cover and cook 15 minutes or until tender; drain. Puree pulp in food processor, or mash thoroughly. Set aside 2 cups squash puree; store remainder in refrigerator for other uses for up to 5 days.

Prick bottom and sides of pastry shells with a fork; bake at 400° for 8 to 10 minutes.

Combine squash and remaining ingredients except whipped cream, mixing well. Sieve mixture; pour half into each pastry shell. Bake at 375° for 40 to 45 minutes or until set; cool. Serve with whipped cream, if desired. Yield: two 8-inch pies.   *Mrs. Guy C. Allen,*
Birmingham, Alabama.

Broil and serve Oysters à la Casino right in the shell for a delightful appetizer.

Oyster Favorites, With A Big Difference

What's different about oysters on the half shell and fried oysters? The answer can be found in Oysters à la Casino and Hangtown Fry.

For Oysters à la Casino, the oysters are broiled on the half shell with a topping of bacon, onion, green pepper, and a hint of Roquefort. Batter-fried oysters actually become the filling for a fluffy omelet in Hangtown Fry.

OYSTERS A LA CASINO

2 dozen unshucked oysters
4 slices bacon
¼ cup finely chopped onion
3 tablespoons finely chopped green pepper
2 teaspoons butter or margarine
2 teaspoons crumbled Roquefort cheese
1¼ teaspoons Worcestershire sauce

Wash and rinse oysters thoroughly in cold water. Shuck oysters, reserving deep half of shells; place oysters in colander to drain. Set aside.

Cut bacon slices in half lengthwise; cut each half into thirds crosswise. Set aside.

Place oysters in half shells; arrange on a rack in a broiling pan. Place a piece of bacon over each oyster. Combine onion and green pepper; spoon evenly over each oyster.

Melt butter in a small saucepan. Add cheese and Worcestershire sauce; cook over low heat until cheese is melted, stirring constantly. Spoon sauce over oysters. Broil 4 inches from heat 10 minutes. Yield: 24 appetizer servings.
Jan Gardner,
Warrenton, North Carolina.

FRIED OYSTER BUBBLES

1 (12-ounce) can fresh Select oysters, drained
2 eggs
¼ cup prepared horseradish
½ teaspoon salt
¼ teaspoon pepper
2 cups soft breadcrumbs
Vegetable oil

Dry oysters between paper towels.

Combine eggs, horseradish, salt, and pepper; mix well. Dredge oysters in breadcrumbs; dip in egg mixture, and coat with breadcrumbs.

Heat 1 inch of oil to 375°. Fry oysters in oil until golden brown; drain on paper towels. Yield: 4 servings.
Mrs. Parke LaGourgue Cory,
Neosho, Missouri.

COMPANY OYSTER STEW

1 pint oysters
Milk
¼ cup butter or margarine
2 medium onions, thinly sliced
1 stalk celery, sliced
1 clove garlic, quartered
1 carrot, thinly sliced
1 sprig of fresh parsley, chopped
⅛ teaspoon dried thyme leaves
2 cups milk
1 cup whipping cream
½ teaspoon salt
⅛ teaspoon pepper
⅛ teaspoon Worcestershire sauce
⅛ teaspoon hot sauce

Drain oysters, reserving liquid. Add milk, if necessary, to oyster liquid to measure 1 cup. Set aside.

Melt butter in a Dutch oven; add onion, celery, garlic, carrot, parsley, and thyme. Cover and cook over medium heat about 10 minutes or until onion is tender; stir occasionally.

To vegetable mixture, gradually add 2 cups milk, cream, and reserved oyster liquid, stirring constantly. Heat thoroughly (do not boil).

Add oysters to stew; simmer 5 to 8 minutes or until edges of oysters curl. Stir in remaining ingredients. Yield: about 9 cups. *Mrs. William B. Moore, Selma, Alabama.*

SCALLOPED OYSTERS WITH MACARONI

1 cup elbow macaroni
12 (2-inch-square) saltine crackers, broken in small pieces
1 pint oysters, drained
½ teaspoon salt
¼ teaspoon pepper
1 cup milk
¼ cup butter or margarine
¼ cup saltine cracker crumbs

Cook macaroni according to package directions.

Sprinkle half of broken crackers in a greased 1½-quart casserole; top with half of macaroni. Spoon half of oysters over macaroni; sprinkle with ¼ teaspoon salt and ⅛ teaspoon pepper. Repeat layers.

Pour milk over oyster mixture. Dot with butter and sprinkle cracker crumbs over top. Bake at 350° for 45 minutes or until browned. Yield: 4 servings. *Mrs. W. H. Colley, Jr., Donelson, Tennessee.*

HANGTOWN FRY

1 dozen oysters
2 tablespoons all-purpose flour
1 egg, beaten
¾ cup cracker crumbs
3 tablespoons butter or margarine
6 eggs
½ teaspoon salt
Freshly ground pepper to taste

Dredge oysters in flour; dip in beaten egg, and dredge in cracker crumbs. Melt butter in a 10-inch omelet pan or heavy skillet over medium heat; cook oysters in butter until golden brown, turning once.

Combine 6 eggs, salt, and pepper; beat well. Pour over oysters in skillet. As mixture starts to cook, gently lift edges of omelet with a fork, and tilt pan to allow the uncooked portion to run underneath; cook until set. Yield: 4 servings. *Maryanne Southard, Delmar, Delaware.*

Add Fruit To The Menu

Whether in a salad, main dish, or dessert, fruit will add sparkle to any menu, especially during the winter. For a salad course, serve fruit in Grapefruit Aspic. Our Aloha Chicken Salad, colorful with green grapes, mandarin oranges, and pineapple chunks, is excellent as an entrée for a light lunch. Should you prefer to hold the fruit until dessert, we recommend peppermint-accented Marinated Fruit Bowl—oranges and pineapple sweetened with honey.

MARINATED FRUIT BOWL

1 (20-ounce) can pineapple chunks
12 to 15 oranges, peeled, seeded, and sectioned
½ cup honey
1 to 2 drops peppermint extract

Drain pineapple, reserving juice. Combine pineapple and orange sections in a large bowl.

Combine pineapple juice, honey, and peppermint, stirring well; pour over fruit, tossing well. Cover and refrigerate several hours or overnight. Yield: 6 servings. *Mrs. Glenn Gunsallus, Albany, Georgia.*

ALOHA CHICKEN SALAD

4 cups chopped cooked chicken
2 cups diced celery
1 cup mayonnaise or salad dressing
1 (20-ounce) can pineapple chunks, drained
1 cup chopped pecans
2 (11-ounce) cans mandarin oranges, drained
1 pound seedless green grapes
Lettuce leaves (optional)

Combine all ingredients except lettuce leaves in a large bowl; toss until well mixed. Chill. Serve on lettuce leaves, if desired. Yield: 8 servings. *Billye Harris, Dallas, Texas.*

GRAPEFRUIT ASPIC

2 medium grapefruit
1 (3-ounce) package lemon-flavored gelatin
1 tablespoon sugar
¾ cup boiling water
1 tablespoon lemon juice
⅓ cup slivered almonds, toasted and chopped
Lettuce (optional)
Lemon slices (optional)
Mayonnaise (optional)

Peel and section grapefruit over a bowl, reserving juice. Add enough water to juice to make ¾ cup; set aside.

Dissolve gelatin and sugar in boiling water. Add grapefruit juice and lemon juice; chill until the consistency of unbeaten egg white. Fold in grapefruit sections and almonds. Spoon into a 4-cup mold; chill until firm.

Unmold on lettuce leaves, and garnish with lemon slices and a dollop of mayonnaise, if desired. Yield: 4 to 6 servings. *Florence L. Costello, Chattanooga, Tennessee.*

Tip: When packing fruit to be frozen, allow headspace between the food and closure because foods will expand as they freeze.

Frozen Vegetables Save Time

Although there's nothing quite like the flavor of garden-fresh vegetables, commercially frozen foods offer a good alternative when favorites are out of season. Often the prices are lower than their fresh or canned counterparts, and since frozen foods are already prepared and partially cooked, you'll rely on their speed and convenience in cooking.

Some recipes, such as Squash Pats, exclusively use frozen vegetables. Others like Zucchini-and-Corn Medley combine the frozen product with fresh food available year-round.

FRENCH QUARTER GREEN BEANS

3 (9-ounce) packages frozen French-style green beans
3 tablespoons butter or margarine
1 (10¾-ounce) can cream of mushroom soup, undiluted
1 (3-ounce) package cream cheese, softened
1 teaspoon dried onion flakes
1 (8-ounce) can water chestnuts, drained and sliced
¼ teaspoon garlic salt
¼ teaspoon pepper
1½ cups (6 ounces) shredded Cheddar cheese
1 (2½-ounce) package slivered almonds
Paprika

Cook green beans according to package directions; drain. Melt margarine in a Dutch oven; add soup and cream cheese. Cook over low heat, stirring constantly, until cream cheese is melted and mixture is smooth. Remove from heat; stir in green beans, onion flakes, water chestnuts, garlic salt, pepper, and Cheddar cheese.

Spoon mixture into a lightly greased 2-quart casserole. Top with almonds; sprinkle with paprika. Bake, uncovered, at 375° for 45 minutes. Yield: 8 servings.
Martha L. Taylor,
Greenville, South Carolina.

Tip: All strings can be easily removed from string beans after washing if they are plunged into boiling water for 5 minutes. Drain in colander, and string.

SWEET-AND-SOUR KALE

1 (10-ounce) package frozen chopped kale
½ cup sugar
½ cup vinegar
6 slices bacon, chopped
3 eggs, beaten

Cook kale according to package directions; drain well. Combine sugar and vinegar; stir well.

Fry bacon in a large skillet until crisp. Pour vinegar mixture and eggs over bacon. Cook over medium heat, stirring occasionally, until eggs are almost done. Stir in kale; cook until heated thoroughly and eggs are desired degree of doneness. Yield: 4 servings.
Mrs. William S. Wheatley,
Winchester, Virginia.

OKRA-TOMATO BAKE

½ pound bacon
1 medium onion, finely chopped
1 (10-ounce) package frozen cut okra, thawed
1 small green pepper, finely chopped
2 tablespoons instant rice
1 (16-ounce) can whole tomatoes, undrained
1 tablespoon sugar
Dash of garlic salt
¼ teaspoon salt
⅛ teaspoon pepper
1 tablespoon grated Parmesan cheese
¼ cup fine dry breadcrumbs
1 tablespoon butter or margarine, melted

Cook bacon in a large skillet until crisp; drain on paper towels, reserving bacon drippings in skillet. Crumble bacon, and set aside.

Cook onion and okra in reserved bacon drippings until lightly browned. Drain on paper towels; place in a lightly greased 1½-quart casserole. Add green pepper, rice, and crumbled bacon; mix well.

Combine tomatoes, sugar, garlic salt, salt, and pepper in container of electric blender; blend on low speed 1 to 2 minutes. Pour over mixture in casserole; top with Parmesan cheese. Combine breadcrumbs and butter; mix well. Sprinkle on top of casserole. Bake at 350° about 45 minutes. Yield: 6 servings.
Mrs. H. Mark Webber,
New Port Richey, Florida.

SQUASH PATS

1 (10-ounce) package frozen yellow squash
1 egg, beaten
¼ cup all-purpose flour
¼ cup cornmeal
2 teaspoons baking powder
½ teaspoon salt
1 medium onion, finely chopped
Vegetable oil

Cook squash according to package directions; drain well. Mash squash, and set aside.

Combine squash and egg; stir well. Combine flour, cornmeal, baking powder, and salt; stir well. Add squash mixture and onion; stir until blended.

Drop squash mixture by heaping tablespoonfuls into hot oil. Cook until golden brown; turn and flatten to about ½-inch thickness. Cook until golden brown, and drain well on paper towels. Yield: 15 patties.
Jean McCoy,
Pineville, North Carolina.

ZUCCHINI-AND-CORN MEDLEY

1 tablespoon bacon drippings
⅓ cup chopped onion
½ cup chopped green pepper
1 clove garlic, minced
1 (16-ounce) package frozen whole kernel corn, thawed
4 cups thinly sliced zucchini
1 teaspoon salt
¼ teaspoon pepper

Heat bacon drippings in a large skillet. Add remaining ingredients; cover and cook over medium heat 5 to 10 minutes or until zucchini is crisp-tender. Stir occasionally. Yield: 8 to 10 servings.
Pauline Miller,
Elk City, Oklahoma.

A Shortcut To Carrot Cake

With a food processor, Laurie Lussky of Louisville, Kentucky, can prepare her Fresh Coconut-Carrot Cake in only a fraction of the time it takes with conventional methods. She not only lets the processor do the work of shredding the carrots and fresh coconut, but also uses it to mix the batter. Even the frosting is prepared in the processor.

Benedictine Sandwich Spread is another of her old favorites that she's adapted to easy preparation in the food processor. It chops the onion and cucumber, then smoothly blends the vegetables with softened cream cheese.

Laurie likes to try new recipes, too, adapting many to the food processor. "Before I chop anything," she says, "I ask myself if this can be done in the food processor."

FRESH COCONUT-CARROT CAKE

1½ cups whole wheat flour
½ cup unbleached all-purpose flour
2 teaspoons baking powder
2 teaspoons soda
1 teaspoon salt
2 teaspoons ground cinnamon
2 teaspoons freshly grated nutmeg
3 tablespoons wheat germ (optional)
1¼ cups pecan pieces
5 to 6 medium carrots, peeled
1 medium coconut, shelled
2 cups firmly packed brown sugar
4 eggs
1½ cups vegetable oil
1 teaspoon vanilla extract
Cream Cheese Frosting
Carrot curls

Position knife blade in processor bowl. Combine first 7 ingredients in processor bowl; add wheat germ, if desired. Process 10 seconds. Remove flour mixture to a large mixing bowl. Add pecans to processor bowl; pulse 3 to 4 times or until pecans are chopped. Remove pecans, and set aside ¼ cup for garnishing.

Position shredding blade in processor bowl. Slice carrots into about 5-inch lengths. Fill food chute with carrot pieces, alternating thick and thin ends. Shred, using moderate pressure with food pusher. Reload food chute, and shred remaining carrot pieces. Remove carrots from bowl; set aside.

Peel brown husk from coconut, and cut meat into pieces to fit chute. Shred, using firm pressure with food pusher. Set aside ¼ cup coconut for garnishing. Add remaining coconut, 1 cup chopped pecans, and carrots to flour mixture; stir well.

Position plastic blade in dry processor bowl; add sugar and eggs. Process 10 seconds or until mixture is smooth. With processor running, pour oil and vanilla through food chute; process 10 seconds or until well combined. Add sugar mixture to flour mixture, mixing well.

Spoon batter into 3 well-greased and floured 9-inch cakepans. Bake at 350° for 35 minutes or until cake tests done. Let cool in pans 10 minutes; remove from pans, and place on wire rack to cool completely. Spread Cream Cheese Frosting between layers and on top and sides of cake. Garnish with ¼ cup chopped pecans, ¼ cup shredded coconut, and carrot curls. Chill. Yield: one 9-inch layer cake.

Cream Cheese Frosting:
1 (8-ounce) package cream cheese, softened
½ cup unsalted butter, softened
1 (16-ounce) package powdered sugar, sifted
1 teaspoon vanilla extract

Cut cream cheese and butter into about 1-inch pieces.

Position plastic blade in processor bowl; add cream cheese and butter. Process 8 to 10 seconds or until mixture is smooth. Add sugar and vanilla; cover and process 15 to 20 seconds or until well combined (scrape bowl once, if necessary). Yield: frosting for one 9-inch layer cake.

BENEDICTINE SANDWICH SPREAD

1 medium onion, peeled and cut into chunks
1 cucumber, peeled and cut into chunks
2 (8-ounce) packages cream cheese, softened
¼ teaspoon salt
3 drops green food coloring

Position knife blade in processor bowl; add onion and cucumber. Process 3 to 5 seconds. Stop processor, and scrape sides with a rubber spatula. Process 3 to 5 additional seconds or until vegetables are finely chopped. Remove vegetables, and drain well.

Position plastic blade in bowl. Cut cream cheese into about 1-inch pieces; place in processor bowl. Process 8 to 10 seconds or until mixture is smooth.

With processor running, add vegetables and salt through food chute; process 20 to 25 seconds or until well combined. Add food coloring; process about 5 seconds. Scrape sides; process about 5 seconds or until well combined.

Spoon mixture into a covered container, and thoroughly chill. Spread on pumpernickel bread and top with lettuce leaves, if desired. Yield: about 2½ cups.

Ladle Up A Golden Punch

When guests drop in for a holiday visit, serve them a cup of Golden Fruit Punch. Or for a holiday party, ladle this sparkling punch from a bowl. Add an ice ring to keep it chilled, and float fresh orange and lemon slices on top for a festive look.

GOLDEN FRUIT PUNCH

1 (12-ounce) can frozen orange juice concentrate, thawed and undiluted
1 (12-ounce) can frozen lemonade concentrate, thawed and undiluted
1 (46-ounce) can unsweetened pineapple juice
1 quart apricot nectar
2 cups unsweetened grapefruit juice
⅔ cup sugar
1 (33.8-ounce) bottle ginger ale, chilled
Orange slices (optional)
Lemon slices (optional)

Combine juices and sugar in a punch bowl, and stir until sugar dissolves; chill. To serve, add ginger ale and ice cubes or ring. Garnish with orange and lemon slices, if desired. Yield: about 4½ quarts.
Martha Rabon,
Stapleton, Alabama.

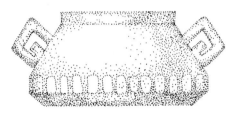

Quick Meals For Busy Days

Shopping, parties, and the general holiday bustle may leave you short on time and ideas for everyday family meals. To get you through those days, count on serving main dish casseroles.

Give yourself a break with that leftover Christmas ham; chop some and add it to our quick and easy Ham and Noodle Casserole. Or try our fancy-enough-for-company chicken casserole. Scallops are available and a welcome change at this time of year. Try them in Chip and Cheese Scallops; crushed potato chips give this casserole a crunchy finish.

ZESTY CABBAGE BEEF BAKE

1½ pounds ground beef
1 medium onion, chopped
1 small head cabbage, coarsely chopped
1 teaspoon garlic powder
⅛ teaspoon salt
⅛ teaspoon hot sauce
1 (15½-ounce) jar commercial spaghetti sauce
3 cups cooked rice
2 cups (8-ounces) shredded mozzarella cheese

Cook ground beef and onion in a skillet until beef is browned; drain off drippings, and set aside.

Place cabbage in boiling salted water to cover; return to a boil, and cook 8 minutes. Drain well, and set aside.

Stir garlic powder, salt, and hot sauce into spaghetti sauce; set aside.

Layer rice and beef mixture in a greased 13- x 9- x 2-inch baking dish. Sprinkle beef lightly with salt; place cabbage on top, and spread with spaghetti sauce. Sprinkle cheese over sauce; bake at 350° for 25 to 30 minutes. Yield: 12 to 15 servings.

Mrs. Robert A. Bailey,
Knoxville, Tennessee.

Chopped ham, noodles, and cheese combine for a quick and nutritious Ham and Noodle Casserole.

BAKED ZUCCHINI AND SAUSAGES

2 pounds medium zucchini
2 eggs, beaten
2 tablespoons water
1 cup soft breadcrumbs
6 tablespoons vegetable oil, divided
1½ pounds Italian sausage
¼ cup butter or margarine
½ cup chopped onion
¼ cup all-purpose flour
1 (14½-ounce) can chicken broth
½ cup half-and-half
½ cup grated Parmesan cheese

Wash zucchini and remove ends; cut diagonally into ½-inch slices. Combine eggs and water, mixing well. Dip zucchini slices in egg mixture; coat with breadcrumbs. Pour 2 tablespoons vegetable oil in a skillet; brown one-third of zucchini slices over low heat. Repeat with remaining vegetable oil and zucchini. Place zucchini along edges of a greased 13- x 9- x 2-inch baking dish.

Place sausage in a skillet; cook over low heat about 20 minutes or until done, turning often to brown evenly. Drain off excess grease. Place sausage in center of casserole.

Melt butter in a saucepan over medium heat; add onion, and sauté 1 minute. Stir in flour; remove from heat. Gradually add chicken broth, stirring constantly. Return to heat; cook until smooth and thickened, stirring constantly. Stir in half-and-half and cheese. Pour sauce over zucchini and sausage. Cover with foil. Bake at 375° for 30 minutes. Yield: 8 servings.

Grace Bravos,
Reisterstown, Maryland.

Tip: Wash most vegetables; trim any wilted parts or excess leaves before storing in crisper compartment of refrigerator. Keep potatoes and onions in a cool, dark place with plenty of air circulation to prevent sprouting.

HAM AND NOODLE CASSEROLE

1 (8-ounce) package egg noodles
1½ cups chopped cooked ham
1 cup (4 ounces) shredded sharp Cheddar cheese, divided
1 (10¾-ounce) can cream of chicken soup, undiluted
½ cup milk
2 tablespoons butter or margarine

Cook noodles according to package directions; drain. Place half of noodles in a buttered 2-quart casserole.

Combine ham and ¾ cup cheese; sprinkle half of ham mixture over noodles. Combine soup and milk, mixing well; pour half of soup mixture over ham mixture. Repeat layers. Sprinkle with remaining ¼ cup cheese; dot with butter. Bake at 375° for 30 minutes. Yield: 6 servings. *Shirley Thrasher,*
St. Petersburg, Florida.

COMPANY CHICKEN BAKE

1 (8-ounce) package egg noodles
2 (3-ounce) packages cream cheese, softened
1 cup cream-style cottage cheese
⅓ cup sliced pimiento-stuffed olives
⅓ cup chopped onion
⅓ cup chopped green pepper
¼ cup minced parsley
3 cups diced cooked chicken
1 (10¾-ounce) can cream of mushroom soup, undiluted
⅔ cup milk
½ teaspoon salt
½ teaspoon poultry seasoning
1½ cups soft breadcrumbs
3 tablespoons melted butter or margarine

Cook noodles according to package directions; drain. Place half of noodles in a buttered 12- x 8- x 2-inch baking dish.

Combine cream cheese and cottage cheese; beat 2 to 3 minutes with electric mixer. Stir in olives, onion, green pepper, and parsley. Spread half of cheese mixture over noodles.

Place half of chicken over cheese mixture. Combine soup, milk, salt, and poultry seasoning; place over medium heat, stirring occasionally, until warm. Spread half of soup mixture over chicken. Repeat layers.

Combine breadcrumbs and butter; spread evenly over casserole. Bake at 375° for 30 minutes. Yield: 8 to 10 servings.

Evelyn Weisman,
Kingsville, Texas.

CHICKEN ENCHILADAS

1 (2- to 2½-pound) broiler-fryer, cut up
1 teaspoon salt
1 sprig fresh parsley
1 teaspoon peppercorns
1 small onion, quartered
1 stalk celery, cut into pieces
1 tablespoon all-purpose flour
1 cup commercial sour cream
10 (6-inch) flour tortillas
1 medium onion, diced
2 cups (8 ounces) shredded Monterey Jack cheese, divided

Combine first 6 ingredients in a Dutch oven; cover with water, and cook chicken until tender. Remove chicken from broth. Strain broth, reserving 2 cups for sauce. Bone chicken, and cut meat into small pieces; set aside.

Gradually stir ¼ cup reserved broth into flour in a medium saucepan; stir until smooth. Add remaining 1¾ cups broth; cook over low heat, stirring constantly, until smooth and thickened. Remove from heat; add sour cream, stirring gently to blend. Set aside.

Wrap tortillas tightly in foil; bake at 350° for 15 minutes. Spoon about 1 tablespoon chopped chicken onto each tortilla; sprinkle with diced onion and about 1 tablespoon cheese. Roll tightly, and place in a 12- x 8- x 2-inch baking dish. Pour sour cream sauce over enchiladas; sprinkle with remaining cheese. Bake at 350° for 15 to 20 minutes or until bubbly. Yield: 5 servings.

Annette Ogden,
San Antonio, Texas.

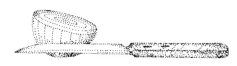

CHIP AND CHEESE SCALLOPS

1 pound scallops
1 tablespoon finely chopped onion
3 tablespoons butter or margarine, melted
3 tablespoons all-purpose flour
½ cup milk
⅛ teaspoon pepper
1 (4-ounce) can sliced mushrooms, drained
2 tablespoons grated Parmesan cheese
2 tablespoons chopped pimiento
1 tablespoon chopped fresh parsley
½ cup (2 ounces) shredded Cheddar cheese
1½ cups crushed potato chips

Rinse scallops. Place scallops in boiling water to cover; reduce heat, and simmer 2 minutes. Drain, reserving 1 cup cooking liquid.

Sauté onion in butter in a medium saucepan until tender. Add flour and cook 1 minute, stirring constantly. Combine reserved cooking liquid and milk; gradually add to flour mixture. Cook over medium heat, stirring constantly, until thickened and bubbly. Stir pepper into sauce.

Remove sauce from heat. Add scallops, mushrooms, Parmesan cheese, pimiento, and parsley; stir well. Spoon scallop mixture into a greased 1½-quart casserole. Bake at 350° for 10 minutes. Sprinkle Cheddar cheese over scallops, and top with potato chips. Bake an additional 10 minutes. Yield: 4 to 6 servings.

Lilly S. Bradley,
Salem, Virginia.

Indulge In Homemade Candy

Holidays mean that even dieters are apt to indulge in those forbidden sweets, and what could be more worthy of the indulgence than a batch of homemade candy. No one could resist melt-in-your-mouth Peanut Butter Fudge or chocolate-covered Butter Creams, crunchy coconut-filled Orange Peanut Brittle, or maybe a batch of good Old-Fashioned Taffy.

When it comes to making your own candy, especially fudge, taffy, or peanut brittle, be sure to follow cooking instructions exactly. To judge temperature, the cold-water test may be used in most cases, but for maximum success, our test kitchen recommends using a candy thermometer.

ALMOND BUTTER CRUNCH

1½ cups whole blanched almonds
2 tablespoons butter or margarine
½ teaspoon salt
¾ cup butter or margarine
1½ cups sugar
3 tablespoons water
1 tablespoon light corn syrup

Place almonds in a saucepan; add water to cover. Bring to a boil; reduce heat, and simmer 2 minutes. Drain well. Split almonds lengthwise with a paring knife.

Melt 2 tablespoons butter at 450° in a 15- x 10- x 1-inch jellyroll pan; add almonds and salt, stirring well. Bake 8 to 10 minutes, stirring occasionally. Spread almonds evenly in pan; set aside.

Melt ¾ cup butter in a heavy Dutch oven; stir in sugar, water, and corn syrup. Cook, without stirring, until mixture reaches soft crack stage (290°). Remove from heat, and pour in a thin stream over almonds. Cool and break into pieces. Yield: about 1 pound.

Tip: New cast-iron cookware should always be seasoned before using. Rub the interior of the utensil with oil or shortening, and place in a 250° or 300° oven for several hours. Wipe off oily film, and store. If scouring is necessary after using the utensil, re-season the surface immediately to prevent rusting.

PEANUT BUTTER FUDGE

2 cups sugar
½ cup half-and-half
¼ cup light corn syrup
¼ teaspoon salt
2 tablespoons butter
1 cup crunchy peanut butter
½ cup finely chopped roasted peanuts
1 teaspoon vanilla extract

Combine sugar, half-and-half, corn syrup, and salt in a small Dutch oven. Cook over low heat, stirring constantly, until sugar is dissolved.

Continue to cook, without stirring, just until mixture reaches soft ball stage (234°). Remove from heat, and add butter (do not stir). Cool mixture to lukewarm (110°). (It may be necessary to tilt pan to measure temperature.)

Add remaining ingredients; beat with a wooden spoon until fudge is thick and begins to lose its gloss (2 to 3 minutes).

Pour fudge into a buttered 8-inch square pan. Mark warm fudge into 1-inch squares. Cool, and cut. Yield: about 5 dozen squares. *Dorsella Utter, Columbia, Missouri.*

OLD-FASHIONED TAFFY

2½ cups sugar
½ cup water
¼ cup vinegar
⅛ teaspoon salt
1 tablespoon butter or margarine
1 teaspoon vanilla extract

Combine first 5 ingredients in a small Dutch oven; cook, without stirring, over medium heat just until mixture reaches soft crack stage (270°). Remove from heat. Stir in vanilla.

Pour candy onto a well-buttered 15- x 10- x 1-inch jellyroll pan or slab of marble. Let cool to touch; pull candy until light in color and difficult to pull. (Butter hands if candy is sticky.) Divide candy in half, and pull into a rope, 1 inch in diameter. Cut taffy into 1-inch pieces; wrap each piece individually in waxed paper. Yield: about 40 (1-inch) pieces. *Edna Peavy, Atlanta, Georgia.*

Tip: The weather is a big factor in candymaking. On a hot, humid day it is advisable to cook candy 2° higher than in cold, dry weather.

DATE LOAF CANDY

3 cups sugar
1 cup milk
1 (8-ounce) package dates, chopped
1 tablespoon butter
4 cups pecans or walnuts, chopped

Combine sugar, milk, and dates in a large saucepan; cook over medium heat, stirring constantly, just until mixture reaches soft ball stage (234°). Remove from heat; stir in butter and pecans.

Divide mixture in half. Place each half on a damp tea towel; shape each into a 10- x 2-inch log. Roll logs up in towels, and let cool at least 30 minutes. Unwrap and cut into slices. Yield: two 10-inch logs. *Judy Irwin, Mabank, Texas.*

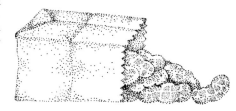

ORANGE PEANUT BRITTLE

1 cup sugar
1 cup raw peanuts
1 cup light corn syrup
2 tablespoons flaked coconut
1 tablespoon grated orange rind
1 teaspoon soda

Combine sugar, peanuts, and corn syrup in a heavy Dutch oven; cook over medium heat, stirring constantly, until mixture reaches soft crack stage (about 290°). Remove from heat. Stir in coconut and orange rind. Add soda, and stir well.

Spread mixture thinly onto a warm, buttered 15- x 10- x 1-inch jellyroll pan (work quickly). Let cool, and break into pieces. Yield: about 1 pound.
Larry A. Bonorato, Huntsville, Alabama.

BUTTERMILK CANDY

2 cups sugar
1 cup firmly packed brown sugar
1 teaspoon soda
1½ cups buttermilk
¼ cup butter
1 teaspoon vanilla extract
1 cup pecans or walnuts

Combine sugar, soda, and buttermilk in a heavy 3-quart saucepan; cook over medium heat, stirring constantly, just until mixture reaches soft ball stage (234°).

Add butter and vanilla; beat until slightly thickened. Stir in pecans. Spread mixture in a buttered 9-inch square pan. Cool and cut into 1½-inch squares. Yield: about 3 dozen squares.
Mrs. Ron Bain, Nashville, Tennessee.

BUTTER CREAMS

½ cup butter, softened
1 (1-pound) package powdered sugar, sifted
2 tablespoons milk
1 teaspoon vanilla extract
¼ teaspoon salt
4 (1-ounce) squares unsweetened chocolate
1 tablespoon melted paraffin

Cream butter; gradually add sugar, beating well. Stir in milk, vanilla, and salt. Chill mixture overnight or until firm. Shape into ¾-inch balls.

Combine chocolate and paraffin in top of a double boiler; place over hot water, stirring until chocolate is melted. Using 2 forks, quickly dip balls, one at a time, into chocolate mixture. Place on waxed paper; refrigerate until chocolate is firm. Yield: about 5 dozen.
Mrs. Robert L. Spence, Charlottesville, Virginia.

CHOCOLATE RUM BALLS

1 (6-ounce) package semisweet chocolate morsels
1 (7-ounce) jar marshmallow creme
1 tablespoon imitation rum extract
3 cups crisp rice cereal
½ cup shredded coconut
½ cup chopped pecans

Melt chocolate in the top of a double boiler; let stand until cool but not set.

Combine melted chocolate, marshmallow creme, and rum extract; stir well. Add cereal, coconut, and pecans, stirring gently to blend. Shape into 1-inch balls. Chill until firm. Yield: about 4½ dozen.

Note: Rum balls may be rolled in additional coconut or pecans, if desired.
Judy Irwin, Mabank, Texas.

Christmas Cookie Patterns

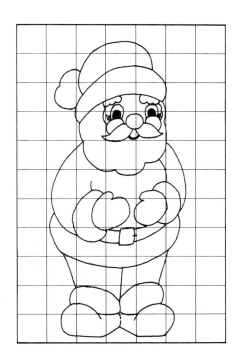

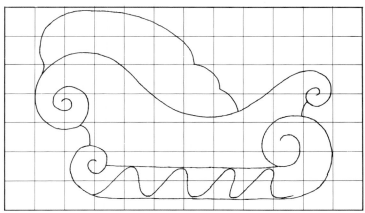

To enlarge each cookie pattern, make a grid of 1-inch squares or use graph paper marked off in 1-inch squares. Copy the design from the pattern on the prepared grid, working square by square. Then trace the enlarged pattern onto thin paper. Cut out around the pattern, ¼ inch from the tracing line.

Recipe for Gingerbread Cookies and step-by-step decorating directions begin on page 278.

Appendices

EQUIVALENT WEIGHTS AND MEASURES

Food	Weight or Count	Measure or Yield
Apples	1 pound (3 medium)	3 cups sliced
Bacon	8 slices cooked	½ cup crumbled
Bananas	1 pound (3 medium)	2½ cups sliced, or about 2 cups mashed
Bread	1 pound	12 to 16 slices
Bread	About 1½ slices	1 cup soft crumbs
Butter or margarine	1 pound	2 cups
Butter or margarine	¼ - pound stick	½ cup
Butter or margarine	Size of an egg	About ¼ cup
Cabbage	1 pound head	4½ cups shredded
Candied fruit or peels	½ pound	1¼ cups cut
Carrots	1 pound	3 cups shredded
Cheese, American or Cheddar	1 pound	About 4 cups shredded
cottage	1 pound	2 cups
cream	3 - ounce package	6 tablespoons
Chocolate morsels	6 - ounce package	1 cup
Cocoa	1 pound	4 cups
Coconut, flaked or shredded	1 pound	5 cups
Coffee	1 pound	80 tablespoons (40 cups perked)
Corn	2 medium ears	1 cup kernels
Cornmeal	1 pound	3 cups
Crab, in shell	1 pound	¾ to 1 cup flaked
Crackers		
chocolate wafers	19 wafers	1 cup crumbs
graham crackers	14 squares	1 cup fine crumbs
saltine crackers	28 crackers	1 cup finely crushed
vanilla wafers	22 wafers	1 cup finely crushed
Cream, whipping	1 cup (½ pint)	2 cups whipped
Dates, pitted	1 pound	3 cups chopped
Dates, pitted	8 - ounce package	1½ cups chopped
Eggs	5 large	1 cup
whites	8 to 11	1 cup
yolks	12 to 14	1 cup
Flour		
all-purpose	1 pound	3½ cups
cake	1 pound	4¾ to 5 cups sifted
whole wheat	1 pound	3½ cups unsifted
Green pepper	1 large	1 cup diced
Lemon	1 medium	2 to 3 tablespoons juice and 2 teaspoons grated rind
Lettuce	1 pound head	6¼ cups torn
Lime	1 medium	1½ to 2 tablespoons juice
Macaroni	4 ounces (1 cup)	2¼ cups cooked

Food	Weight or Count	Measure or Yield
Marshmallows	11 large	1 cup
	10 miniature	1 large marshmallow
Marshmallows, miniature	½ pound	4½ cups
Milk		
evaporated	5.33 - ounce can	⅔ cup
evaporated	13 - ounce can	1⅝ cups
sweetened condensed	14 - ounce can	1¼ cups
sweetened condensed	15 - ounce can	1⅓ cups
Mushrooms	3 cups raw (8 ounces)	1 cup sliced cooked
Nuts		
almonds	1 pound	1 to 1¾ cups nutmeats
	1 pound shelled	3½ cups nutmeats
peanuts	1 pound	2¼ cups nutmeats
	1 pound shelled	3 cups
pecans	1 pound	2¼ cups nutmeats
	1 pound shelled	4 cups
walnuts	1 pound	1⅔ cups nutmeats
	1 pound shelled	4 cups
Oats, quick-cooking	1 cup	1¾ cups cooked
Onion	1 medium	½ cup chopped
Orange	1 medium	⅓ cup juice and 2 tablespoons grated rind
Peaches	4 medium	2 cups sliced
Pears	4 medium	2 cups sliced
Potatoes, white	3 medium	2 cups cubed cooked or 1¾ cups mashed
sweet	3 medium	3 cups sliced
Raisins, seedless	1 pound	3 cups
Rice, long-grain	1 cup	3 to 4 cups cooked
pre-cooked	1 cup	2 cups cooked
Shrimp, raw in shell	1½ pounds	2 cups (¾ pound) cleaned, cooked
Spaghetti	7 ounces	About 4 cups cooked
Strawberries	1 quart	4 cups sliced
Sugar		
brown	1 pound	2¼ cups firmly packed
powdered	1 pound	3½ cups unsifted
granulated	1 pound	2 cups
Whipping cream	1 cup	2 cups whipped

CANNED FOOD GUIDE

Can Size	Number of Cups	Number of Servings	Foods
8-ounce	1 cup	2 servings	Fruits, Vegetables
10½- to 12-ounce (picnic)	1¼ cups	3 servings	Condensed Soups, Fruits and Vegetables, Meats and Fish, Specialties
12-ounce (vacuum)	1½ cups	3 to 4 servings	Vacuum-Packed Corn
14- to 16-ounce (No. 300)	1¾ cups	3 to 4 servings	Pork and Beans, Meat Products, Cranberry Sauce
16- to 17-ounce (No. 303)	2 cups	4 servings	Principal Size for Fruits and Vegetables, Some Meat Products
1 pound, 4 ounce (No. 2)	2½ cups	5 servings	Juices, Pineapple, Apple Slices
27- to 29-ounce (No. 2½)	3½ cups	7 servings	Fruits, Some Vegetables (Pumpkin, Sauerkraut, Greens, Tomatoes)
46-ounce (No. 3 cyl.)	5¾ cups	10 to 12 servings	Fruit and Vegetable Juices
6½-pound (No. 10)	12 to 13 cups	25 servings	Institutional Size for Fruits and Vegetables

EQUIVALENT MEASUREMENTS

Use standard measuring cups (both dry and liquid measure) and measuring spoons when measuring ingredients. All measurements given below are level.

3 teaspoons	1 tablespoon
4 tablespoons.................................	¼ cup
5⅓ tablespoons...............................	⅓ cup
8 tablespoons.................................	½ cup
16 tablespoons...............................	1 cup
2 tablespoons (liquid)	1 ounce
1 cup..	8 fluid ounces
2 cups	1 pint (16 fluid ounces)
4 cups	1 quart
4 quarts	1 gallon
⅛ cup...	2 tablespoons
⅓ cup...	5 tablespoons plus 1 teaspoon
⅔ cup...	10 tablespoons plus 2 teaspoons
¾ cup...	12 tablespoons
Few grains (or dash)	Less than ⅛ teaspoon
Pinch...	As much as can be taken between tip of finger and thumb

HANDY SUBSTITUTIONS

Even the best of cooks occasionally runs out of an ingredient she needs and is unable to stop what she is doing to go to the store. At times like those, sometimes another ingredient or combination of ingredients can be used. Here is a list of substitutions and equivalents that yield satisfactory results in most cases.

Ingredient Called For	Substitution
1 cup self-rising flour	1 cup all-purpose flour plus 1 teaspoon baking powder and ½ teaspoon salt
1 cup cake flour	1 cup sifted all-purpose flour minus 2 tablespoons
1 cup all-purpose flour	1 cup cake flour plus 2 tablespoons
1 teaspoon baking powder	½ teaspoon cream of tartar plus ¼ teaspoon soda
1 tablespoon cornstarch or arrowroot	2 tablespoons all-purpose flour
1 tablespoon tapioca	1½ tablespoons all-purpose flour
2 large eggs	3 small eggs
1 egg	2 egg yolks (for custard)
1 egg	2 egg yolks plus 1 tablespoon water (for cookies)
1 cup commercial sour cream	1 tablespoon lemon juice plus evaporated milk to equal 1 cup; or 3 tablespoons butter plus ⅞ cup sour milk
1 cup yogurt	1 cup buttermilk or sour milk
1 cup sour milk or buttermilk	1 tablespoon vinegar or lemon juice plus sweet milk to equal 1 cup
1 cup fresh milk	½ cup evaporated milk plus ½ cup water
1 cup fresh milk	3 to 5 tablespoons nonfat dry milk solids in 1 cup water
1 cup honey	1¼ cups sugar plus ¼ cup liquid
1 square (1 ounce) unsweetened chocolate	3 tablespoons cocoa plus 1 tablespoon butter or margarine
1 clove fresh garlic	1 teaspoon garlic salt or ⅛ teaspoon garlic powder
1 teaspoon onion powder	2 teaspoons minced onion
1 tablespoon fresh herbs	1 teaspoon dried herbs or ¼ teaspoon powdered herbs
¼ cup chopped fresh parsley	1 tablespoon dehydrated parsley
1 teaspoon dry mustard	1 tablespoon prepared mustard
1 pound fresh mushrooms	6 ounces canned mushrooms

METRIC MEASURES

Approximate Conversion to Metric Measures

When You Know . . .	Multiply by . . .	To Find . . .	Symbol
	Mass (weight)		
ounces	28	grams	g
pounds	0.45	kilograms	kg
	Volume		
teaspoons	5	milliliters	ml
tablespoons	15	milliliters	ml
fluid ounces	30	milliliters	ml
cups	0.24	liters	l
pints	0.47	liters	l
quarts	0.95	liters	l
gallons	3.8	liters	l

COOKING MEASURE EQUIVALENTS

Metric Cup	Volume (Liquid)	Liquid Solids (Butter)	Fine Powder (Flour)	Granular (Sugar)	Grain (Rice)
1	250 ml	200 g	140 g	190 g	150 g
¾	188 ml	150 g	105 g	143 g	113 g
⅔	167 ml	133 g	93 g	127 g	100 g
½	125 ml	100 g	70 g	95 g	75 g
⅓	83 ml	67 g	47 g	63 g	50 g
¼	63 ml	50 g	35 g	48 g	38 g
⅛	31 ml	25 g	18 g	24 g	19 g

APPROXIMATE TEMPERATURE CONVERSIONS—FAHRENHEIT TO CELSIUS

	Fahrenheit (°F)	Celsius (°C)
Freezer		
coldest area	-10°	-23°
overall	0°	-17°
Water		
freezes	32°	0°
simmers	115°	46°
scalds	130°	55°
boils (sea level)	212°	100°
Soft Ball	234° to 240°	112° to 115°
Firm Ball	242° to 248°	116° to 120°
Hard Ball	250° to 268°	121° to 131°
Slow Oven	275° to 300°	135° to 148°

	Fahrenheit (°F)	Celsius (°C)
Moderate Oven	350°	177°
Hot Oven	425° to 475°	218° to 246°
Deep Fat	375° to 400°	190° to 204°
Broil	550°	288°

To convert Fahrenheit to Celsius:
    subtract 32
    multiply by 5
    divide by 9

To convert Celsius to Fahrenheit:
    multiply by 9
    divide by 5
    add 32

TIMETABLE FOR ROASTING BEEF AND LAMB

Kind and Cut	Approximate Weight	Internal Temperature	Approximate Total Cooking Times at 325°F.
	pounds		hours
Beef			
Standing ribs* (10-inch ribs)	4	140°F. (rare)	1¾
		160°F. (medium)	2
		170°F. (well done)	2½
	6	140°F. (rare)	2
		160°F. (medium)	2½
		170°F. (well done)	3½
	8	140°F. (rare)	2½
		160°F. (medium)	3
		170°F. (well done)	4½
Rolled ribs	4	140°F. (rare)	2
		160°F. (medium)	2½
		170°F. (well done)	3
	6	140°F. (rare)	3
		160°F. (medium)	3¼
		170°F. (well done)	4
Rolled rump	5	140°F. (rare)	2¼
		160°F. (medium)	3
		170°F. (well done)	3¼
Sirloin tip	3	140°F. (rare)	1½
		160°F. (medium)	2
		170°F. (well done)	2¼
Lamb			
Leg	6 to 7	180°F. (well done)	3¾
Leg (half)	3 to 4	180°F. (well done)	2½ to 3
Cushion shoulder	5	180°F. (well done)	3
Rolled shoulder	3	180°F. (well done)	2½
	5	180°F. (well done)	3

*Standing ribs (8-inch ribs) allow 30 minutes longer.

TIMETABLE FOR ROASTING STUFFED CHILLED POULTRY

Kind of Poultry	Ready-To-Cook Weight	Approximate Amount of Stuffing	Approximate Total Roasting Times at 325°F.
	pounds	quarts	hours
Chicken			
Broilers or fryers	1½ to 2½	¼ to ½	1¼ to 2*
Roasters.............................	2½ to 4½	½ to 1¼	2 to 3½†
Capons and caponettes	4 to 8	1¼ to 1¾	3 to 5
Duck	3 to 5	½ to 1	2½ to 3
Goose	4 to 8	¾ to 1½	2¾ to 3½
	8 to 14	1½ to 2½	3½ to 5
Turkey			
Fryers or roasters (very young birds)	4 to 8	1 to 2	3 to 4½
Roasters (fully grown young birds)	6 to 12	1½ to 3	3½ to 5
	12 to 16	3 to 4	5 to 6
	16 to 20	4 to 5	6 to 7½
	20 to 24	5 to 6	7½ to 9
Halves, quarters, and half breasts	3½ to 5	1 to 1½	3 to 3½
	5 to 8	1½ to 2	3½ to 4
	8 to 12	2 to 3	4 to 5

*Or roast unstuffed at 400°F. for ¾ to 1½ hours
†Or roast unstuffed at 400°F. for 1½ to 2¾ hours

TIMETABLE FOR COOKING FISH AND SHELLFISH

Method of Cooking	Product	Market Form	Approximate Weight or Thickness	Cooking Temperature	Approximate Total Cooking Times
Baking	Fish	Dressed	3 to 4 lbs.	350°F.	40 to 60 min.
		Pan-dressed	½ to 1 lb.	350°F.	25 to 30 min.
		Steaks	½ to 1 in.	350°F.	25 to 35 min.
		Fillets		350°F.	25 to 35 min.
	Clams	Live		450°F.	15 min.
	Lobster	Live	¾ to 1 lb.	400°F.	15 to 20 min.
			1 to ½ lb.	400°F.	20 to 25 min.
	Oysters	Live		450°F.	15 min.
		Shucked		400°F.	10 min.
	Scallops	Shucked		350°F.	25 to 30 min.
	Shrimp	Headless		350°F.	20 to 25 min.
	Spiny lobster	Headless	4 oz.	450°F.	20 to 25 min.
	tails		8 oz.	450°F.	25 to 30 min.
Broiling	Fish	Pan-dressed	½ to 1 lb.		10 to 15 min.
		Steaks	½ to 1 in.		10 to 15 min.
		Fillets			10 to 15 min.
	Clams	Live			5 to 8 min.
	Lobster	Live	¾ to 1 lb.		10 to 12 min.
			1 to 1½ lbs.		12 to 15 min.
	Oysters	Live			5 min.
		Shucked			5 min.
	Scallops	Shucked			8 to 10 min.
	Shrimp	Headless			8 to 10 min.
	Spiny lobster	Headless	4 oz.		8 to 10 min.
	tails		8 oz.		10 to 12 min.

Method of Cooking	Product	Market Form	Approximate Weight or Thickness	Cooking Temperature	Approximate Total Cooking Times
Cooking in water	Fish	Pan-dressed	½ to 1 lb.	Simmer	10 min.
		Steaks	½ to 1 in.	Simmer	10 min.
		Fillets		Simmer	10 min.
	Crabs	Live		Simmer	15 min.
	Lobster	Live	¾ to 1 lb.	Simmer	10 to 15 min.
			1 to 1½ lbs.	Simmer	15 to 20 min.
	Scallops	Shucked		Simmer	4 to 5 min.
	Shrimp	Headless		Simmer	5 min.
	Spiny lobster	Headless	4 oz.	Simmer	10 min.
	tails		8 oz.	Simmer	15 min.
Deep-fat frying	Fish	Pan-dressed	½ to 1 lb.	375°F.	2 to 4 min.
		Steaks	½ to 1 in.	375°F.	2 to 4 min.
		Fillets		375°F.	1 to 4 min.
	Clams	Shucked		375°F.	2 to 3 min.
	Crabs	Soft-shell	¼ lb.	375°F.	3 to 4 min.
	Lobster	Live	¾ to 1 lb.	350°F.	3 to 4 min.
			1 to 1½ lbs.	350°F.	4 to 5 min.
	Oysters	Shucked		375°F.	2 min.
	Scallops	Shucked		350°F.	3 to 4 min.
	Shrimp	Headless		350°F.	2 to 3 min.
	Spiny lobster	Headless	4 oz.	350°F.	3 to 4 min.
	tails		8 oz.	350°F.	4 to 5 min.

TIMETABLE FOR ROASTING FRESH PORK

Cut	Approximate Weight	Internal Temperature	Approximate Cooking Times at 325°F.
	pounds		minutes per pound
Loin			
Center	3 to 5	170°F.	30 to 35
Half...	5 to 7	170°F.	35 to 40
End...	3 to 4	170°F.	40 to 45
Roll..	3 to 5	170°F.	35 to 40
Boneless top	2 to 4	170°F.	30 to 35
Crown..	4 to 6	170°F.	35 to 40
Picnic shoulder			
Bone-in..	5 to 8	170°F.	30 to 35
Rolled..	3 to 5	170°F.	35 to 40
Boston shoulder	4 to 6	170°F.	40 to 45
Leg (fresh ham)			
Whole (bone-in).....................................	12 to 16	170°F.	22 to 26
Whole (boneless)....................................	10 to 14	170°F.	24 to 28
Half (bone-in).......................................	5 to 8	170°F.	35 to 40
Tenderloin..	½ to 1	170°F.	45 to 60
Back ribs...		cooked well done	1½ to 2½ hours
Country-style ribs		cooked well done	1½ to 2½ hours
Spareribs...		cooked well done	1½ to 2½ hours
Pork Loaf..		cooked well done	1¾ hours

TIMETABLE FOR ROASTING SMOKED PORK

Cut	Approximate Weight	Internal Temperature	Approximate Cooking Times at 325°F.
	pounds		minutes per pound
Ham (cook-before-eating)			
Whole....................................	10 to 14	160°F.	18 to 20
Half......................................	5 to 7	160°F.	22 to 25
Shank portion..........................	3 to 4	160°F.	35 to 40
Butt portion............................	3 to 4	160°F.	35 to 40
Ham (fully cooked)			
Whole....................................	10 to 12	140°F.	15 to 18
Half......................................	5 to 7	140°F.	18 to 24
Loin......................................	3 to 5	160°F.	25 to 30
Picnic shoulder (cook-before-eating)..............	5 to 8	170°F.	30 to 35
Picnic shoulder (fully cooked).....................	5 to 8	140°F.	25 to 30
Shoulder roll (butt)................................	2 to 4	170°F.	35 to 40
Canadian-style bacon...............................	2 to 4	160°F.	35 to 40

VEGETABLE GUIDE

Selecting and Storing Vegetables

1. Buy fresh vegetables in season that are crisp, bright in color, and free from decay.

2. Compare prices of fresh versus frozen or canned vegetables. For example, if you are buying tomatoes for soup, you may find that canned ones would be the most economical. Some vegetables will remain fresh for a day or so after picking; others, like corn, start losing their flavor as soon as they are picked.

3. Buy only that amount of vegetables which can be stored properly. Although most vegetables should be washed and dried before storing, potatoes, onions, and garlic should never be washed. Do not soak fresh vegetables; too much moisture increases the possibility of spoilage and decay. Store immediately in vegetable crisper of refrigerator, or wrap in plastic wrap or plastic bags, and refrigerate. Immediate storage helps vegetables retain freshness and nutritional value. To prevent browning of leaves keep head lettuce intact without removing core or leaves until ready to use.

4. Put frozen vegetables into the freezer as soon as possible after purchase. Follow package directions about thawing before cooking. If frozen packages have been broken, rewrap in moistureproof paper or aluminum foil.

5. Store canned foods in a cool, dry place. Discard any cans that are puffed at ends—usually an indication of spoilage.

Amount to Buy	Servings per Pound or Unit	Amount to Buy	Servings per Pound or Unit
Artichokes	1	Green Pepper	½ to 1 whole per serving
Asparagus	3 or 4		
Beans, snap or green	4	Greens	4 or 5
Beets, diced, without tops	4	Mushrooms	4
Broccoli	3 or 4	Okra	4
Brussels Sprouts	4 to 6	Onions, cooked	3 or 4
Cabbage		Peas	¾ pound per serving
Cooked	3 or 4	Potatoes	2 or 3
Raw, diced or shredded	6 to 8	Rhubarb	4 or 5
Carrots		Rutabaga	2 or 3
Cooked	3 or 4	Spinach	
Raw, diced or shredded	5 or 6	Cooked	3
Cauliflower	3 or 4	Raw	6
Celery, raw	8 to 10	Squash, summer	3 or 4
Corn	1 to 2 ears	Squash, winter	2 or 3
Cucumber	1 regular for 2 to 3 servings	Sweet Potatoes	3
Dry Beans, Peas, or Lentils	10 or 11	Tomatoes	4 or 5
Eggplant	4	Turnip	4 or 5

Glossary

à la King—Food prepared in a creamy white sauce containing mushrooms and red and/or green peppers

à la Mode—Food served with ice cream

al Dente—The point in the cooking of pasta at which it is still fairly firm to the tooth; that is, very slightly undercooked

Aspic—A jellied meat juice or a liquid held together with gelatin

au Gratin—A food served crusted with breadcrumbs or shredded cheese

au Jus—Meat served in its own juice

Bake—To cook food in an oven by dry heat

Barbecue—To roast meat slowly over coals on a spit or framework, or in an oven, basting intermittently with a special sauce

Baste—To spoon pan liquid over meats while they are roasting to prevent surface from drying

Beat—To mix vigorously with a brisk motion with spoon, fork, egg beater, or electric mixer

Béchamel—White sauce of butter, flour, cream (not milk), and seasonings

Bisque—A thick, creamy soup usually of shellfish, but sometimes made of pureed vegetables

Blanch—To dip briefly into boiling water

Blend—To stir 2 or more ingredients together until well mixed

Blintz—A cooked crêpe stuffed with cheese or other filling

Boil—To cook food in boiling water or liquid that is mostly water (at 212°) in which bubbles constantly rise to the surface and burst

Boiling-water-bath canning method—Used for processing acid foods, such as fruits, tomatoes (with high-acid content), pickled vegetables, and sauerkraut. These acid foods are canned safely at boiling temperatures in a water-bath canner.

Borscht—Soup containing beets and other vegetables, usually with a meat stock base

Bouillabaisse—A highly seasoned fish soup or chowder containing two or more kinds of fish

Bouillon—Clear soup made by boiling meat in water

Bouquet Garni—Herbs tied in cheese-cloth which are cooked in a mixture and removed before serving

Bourguignon—Name applied to dishes containing Burgundy and often braised onions and mushrooms

Braise—To cook slowly with liquid or steam in a covered utensil. Less-tender cuts of meat may be browned slowly on all sides in a small amount of shortening, seasoned, and water added.

Bread, to—To coat with crumbs, usually in combination with egg or other binder

Broil—To cook by direct heat, either under the heat of a broiler, over hot coals, or between two hot surfaces

Broth—A thin soup, or a liquid in which meat, fish, or vegetables have been boiled

Capers—Buds from a Mediterranean plant, usually packed in brine and used as a condiment in dressings or sauces

Caramelize—To cook white sugar in a skillet over medium heat, stirring constantly, until sugar forms a golden-brown syrup

Casserole—An ovenproof baking dish, usually with a cover; also the food cooked in it

Charlotte—A molded dessert containing gelatin, usually formed in a glass dish or a pan that is lined with ladyfingers or pieces of cake

Chill—To cool by placing on ice or in a refrigerator

Chop—A cut of meat usually attached to a rib

Chop, to—To cut into pieces, usually with a sharp knife or kitchen shears

Clarified butter—Butter that has been melted and chilled. The solid is then lifted away from the liquid and discarded. Clarification heightens the smoke point of butter. Clarified butter will stay fresh in the refrigerator for at least 2 months.

Coat—To cover completely, as in "coat with flour"

Cocktail—An appetizer; either a beverage or a light, highly seasoned food, served before a meal

Compote—Mixed fruit, raw or cooked, usually served in "compote" dishes

Condiments—Seasonings that enhance the flavor of foods with which they are served

Consommé—Clear broth made from meat

Cool—To let food stand at room temperature until not warm to the touch

Court Bouillon—A highly seasoned broth made with water and meat, fish or vegetables, and seasonings

Cream, to—To blend together, as sugar and butter, until mixture takes on a smooth, cream-like texture

Cream, whipped—Cream that has been whipped until it is stiff

Crème de Cacao—Chocolate-flavored liqueur

Crème de Café—A coffee-flavored liqueur

Crêpes—Very thin pancakes

Croquette—Minced food, shaped like a ball, patty, cone, or log, bound with a heavy sauce, breaded and fried

Croutons—Cubes of bread, toasted or fried, served with soups, salads, or other foods

Cruller—A doughnut of twisted shape, very light in texture

Cube, to—To cut into cube-shaped pieces

Curaçao—Orange-flavored liqueur

Cut in, to—To incorporate by cutting or chopping motions, as in cutting shortening into flour for pastry

Demitasse—A small cup of coffee served after dinner

Devil, to—To prepare with hot seasoning or sauce

Dice—To cut into small cubes

Dissolve—To mix a dry substance with liquid until the dry substance becomes a part of the solution

Dot—To scatter small bits of butter over top of a food

Dredge—To coat with something, usually flour or sugar

Filé—Powder made of sassafras leaves used to season and thicken foods

Fillet—Boneless piece of meat or fish

Flambé—To flame, as in Crêpes Suzette or in some meat cookery, using alcohol as the burning agent; flame causes caramelization, enhancing flavor

Flan—In France, a filled pastry; in Spain, a custard

Florentine—A food containing, or placed upon, spinach

Flour, to—To coat with flour

Fold—To add a whipped ingredient, such as cream or egg white to another ingredient by gentle over and under movement

Frappé—A drink whipped with ice to make a thick, frosty consistency

Fricassee—A stew, usually of poultry or veal

Fritter—Vegetable or fruit dipped into, or combined with, batter and fried

Fry—To cook in hot shortening

Garnish—A decoration for a food or drink; for example, a sprig of parsley

Glaze (To make a shiny surface)—In meat preparation, a jelled broth applied to meat surface; in breads and pastries, a wash of egg or syrup; for doughnuts and cakes, a sugar preparation coating

Grate—To obtain small particles of food by rubbing on a grater or shredder

Grill—To broil under or over a source of direct heat, such as charcoal

Grits—Coarsely ground dried corn, served boiled, or boiled and then fried

Gumbo—Soup or stew made with okra

Herb—Aromatic plant used for seasoning and garnishing foods

Hollandaise—A sauce made of butter, egg, and lemon juice or vinegar

Hominy—Whole corn grains from which hull and germ are removed

Jardiniere—Vegetables in a savory sauce or soup

Julienne—Vegetables cut into long thin strips or a soup containing such vegetables

Kahlúa—A coffee-flavored liqueur

Kirsch—A cherry-flavored liqueur

Knead—To work a food (usually dough) with the hands, using a folding-back and pressing-forward motion

Marinade—A seasoned liquid in which food is soaked

Marinate, to—To soak food in a seasoned liquid

Meringue—A whole family of egg white-sugar preparations including pie topping, poached meringue used to top custard, crisp meringue dessert shells, and divinity candy

Mince—To chop into very fine pieces

Mornay—White sauce with egg, cream, and cheese added

Mousse—A molded dish based on meat or sweet whipped cream stiffened with egg white and/or gelatin (if mousse contains ice cream, it is called bombe)

Panbroil—To cook over direct heat in an uncovered skillet containing little or no shortening

Panfry—To cook in an uncovered skillet in shallow amount of shortening

Parboil—To partially cook in boiling water before final cooking

Pasta—A large family of flour paste products, such as spaghetti, macaroni, and noodles

Pâté (French for paste)—A paste made of liver or meat

Petit Four—A small cake, which has been frosted and decorated

Pilau or Pilaf—A dish of the Middle East consisting of rice and meat or vegetables in a seasoned stock

Poach—To cook in liquid held below the boiling point

Pot Liquor—The liquid in which vegetables have been boiled

Pot Roast—A larger cut of meat cooked with liquid added

Preheat—To turn on oven so that desired temperature will be reached before food is inserted for baking

Puree—A thick sauce or paste made by forcing cooked food through a sieve

Reduce—To boil down, evaporating liquid from a cooked dish

Remoulade—A rich mayonnaise-based sauce containing anchovy paste, capers, herbs, and mustard

Render—To melt fat away from surrounding meat

Rind—Outer shell or peel of melon or fruit

Roast, to—To cook in oven by dry heat (usually applied to meats)

Roux—A mixture of butter and flour used to thicken gravies and sauces; it may be white or brown, if mixture is browned before liquid is added

Sangría—A beverage based on dry red wine and flavored with various fruit juices or brandy; served cold

Sauté—To fry food lightly over fairly high heat in a small amount of fat in a shallow, open pan

Scald—(1) To heat milk just below the boiling point (2) To dip certain foods into boiling water before freezing them (also called blanching)

Scallop—A bivalve mollusk of which only the muscle hinge is eaten; also to bake a food in a sauce topped with crumbs

Score—To cut shallow gashes on surface of food, as in scoring fat on ham before glazing

Sear—To brown surface of meat over high heat to seal in juices

Set—Term used to describe gelatin when it has jelled enough to unmold

Shred—Break into thread-like or stringy pieces, usually by rubbing over the surface of a vegetable shredder

Simmer—To cook gently at a temperature below boiling point

Singe—To touch lightly with flame

Skewer—To fasten with wooden or metal pins or skewers

Sliver—A fine thin slice

Soak—To immerse in water for a period of time

Soufflé—A spongy hot dish, made from a sweet or savory mixture (often milk or cheese), lightened by stiffly beaten egg whites

Steam—To cook food with steam either in a pressure cooker, on a platform in a covered pan, or in a special steamer

Steam-pressure canning method—Used for processing low-acid foods, such as meats, fish, poultry, and most vegetables. A temperature higher than boiling is required to can these foods safely. The food is processed in a steam-pressure canner at 10 pounds' pressure (240°) to ensure that all spoilage microorganisms are destroyed.

Steep—To let food stand in not quite boiling water until flavor is extracted

Stew—A mixture of meat or fish and vegetables cooked by simmering in its own juices and liquid, such as water and/or wine

Stir—To mix with a steady, circular motion with a spoon, whisk, or beater

Stir-fry—To cook quickly in oil over high heat, using light tossing and stirring motions to preserve shape of food

Stock—The broth in which meat, poultry, fish, or vegetables has been cooked

Syrupy—Thickened to about the consistency of egg white

Toast, to—To brown by direct heat, as in a toaster or under broiler

Torte—A round cake, sometimes made with breadcrumbs instead of flour, which may contain dried fruits and nuts

Tortilla—A Mexican flat bread made of corn or wheat flour

Toss—To mix together with light tossing motions, in order not to bruise delicate food, such as salad greens

Triple Sec—Orange-flavored liqueur

Veal—Flesh of a milk-fed calf up to 14 weeks of age

Velouté—White sauce made of flour, butter, and a chicken or veal stock, instead of milk

Vinaigrette—A cold sauce of oil and vinegar flavored with parsley, finely chopped onions and other seasonings; served with cold meats or vegetables

Whip—To beat rapidly to increase air and increase volume

Wok—A round bowl-shaped metal cooking utensil of Chinese origin used for stir-frying and steaming (with rack inserted) of foods

Recipe Title Index

An alphabetical listing of every recipe by exact title

Month-by-Month Index

An alphabetical listing within the month of every food article and accompanying recipes

General Recipe Index

A listing of every recipe by food category and/or major ingredient

B

Bacon
Appetizers, Hot Bacon, 248
Bundles, Bean, 246
Eggs Scramble, Bacon-and-, 267
Mushrooms with Bacon, Stir-Fried, 123
Rice, Bacon Fried, 115
Roll-Ups, Chicken Liver
and Bacon, 200
Sandwiches, Open-Faced Cheesy
Bacon, 78
Soup, Bacon-Topped Cheese, 224
Tomatoes, Bacon-and-Egg-Stuffed, 162

Bananas
Bananas Foster for Two, 115
Bread, Cranberry-Banana, 281
Bread, Whole Wheat Banana, 88
Brownies, Chocolate-Banana, 160
Cake, Peanut Butter-Banana, 87
Coffee Cake, Banana-Sour Cream, 186
Crush, Banana, 88
Cupcakes, Banana-Cocoa, 130
Ice Cream, Banana Split, 176
Ice Cream, Straw-Ba-Nut, 177
Jam, Rosy Peach-Banana, 142
Muffins, Banana, 88
Pudding, Delicious Banana, 9
Slush, Banana-Orange, 48
Soup, Avocado-Banana-Yogurt, 78

Barbecue
Catfish, Barbecued, 157
Chuck Steak, Marinated Barbecued, 156
Dressing, Barbecue Salad, 74
Meat Loaf, Barbecued, 60
Pork, Barbecued, 72
Pork Roast, Berry Barbecued, 288
Ribs, Apple Barbecued, 111
Ribs, Barbecued, 111
Ribs, Smoky Barbecued, 111
Spareribs, Barbecued Country-Style, 73
Tuna, Barbecued, 275

Beans
Baked
Beefy Baked Beans, 136
Franks, Hawaiian Baked Beans
and, 136
Ham, Baked Beans with, 136
Medley, Baked Bean, 100
Quick Baked Beans, 136
Black Beans and Rice, 222
Creole Beans and Rice, 223
Dip, Prairie Fire Bean, 195
Green
au Gratin, Green Beans, 116
Bacon-Topped Green Beans, 123
Bundles, Bean, 246
Cheesy Green Beans, 157
Dilly Green Beans, 116
French Quarter Green Beans, 298
Pole Beans, Old-Fashioned, 100
Salad, Garden Medley, 122
Salad, Lettuce and Green Bean, 79
Sour Cream, Green Beans in, 116
Spanish Green Beans, 116
Lima
Casserole, Swiss Lima Bean, 191
Creole, Lima Beans, 191
Deluxe, Lima Beans, 26
Medley, Carrot-Lima-Squash, 123
Rancho Lima Beans, 191
Succotash, Easy, 165

Pinto
Chalupa, Bean, 223
Pie, Pinto Bean, 40
Red Beans and Rice, 58
Salad, Chilled Bean, 178
Soup, Bean, 25
Soup, Capitol Hill Bean, 222

Beef
Beef Elégante, 125
Bouilli, 58
Bourguignon, Royal Beef, 106
Chalupa, Bean, 223
Corned
Pie, Reuben Meat, 189
Salad, Corned Beef, 104
Salad, Vegetable-Corned Beef, 148
Sandwiches, Meal-in-One, 218
Sandwiches, Reuben, 201
Dip, Hot Cheesy Beef, 85
Jerky, Beef, 269
Kabobs, Marinated Steak, 184
Kabobs, Steak-and-Shrimp, 184
Kabobs, Teriyaki Beef, 207
Liver
Creamy Liver and Noodle
Dinner, 11
French-Style Liver, 10
Gravy, Liver and, 10
Kabobs, Liver, 185
Spanish-Style Liver, 11
Oriental, Beef and Cauliflower, 220
Pies, Carry-Along Beef, 224
Roasts
Beer-and-Onion Sauce, Roast in, 124
Chuck Roast, Marinated, 59
Pot Roast, Polynesian, 59
Pot Roast, Swedish, 59
Pot Roast with Spaghetti, 59
Pot Roast with Vegetables, 59
Rib Roast, Standing, 246
Rib Roast with Yorkshire Pudding,
Standing, 252
Salad, Roast Beef, 223
Sauerbraten, Quick, 139
Tenderloin, Marinated, 146
Sandwiches, Beef and Pork
Tenderloin, 175
Sandwich, Saucy Beef Pocket, 92
Steaks
Chuck Steak, Marinated
Barbecued, 156
Flank Steak, Grilled, 152
Round Steak, Parmesan, 106
Swiss Steak Cheese Skillet, 106
Swiss Steak, Deviled, 107
Stew, Oven Beef, 64
Stew with Noodles, Hungarian, 263
Stir-Fry Beef and Pea Pods, 19
Tamales, 195

Beef, Ground
Baked Bean Medley, 100
Baked Beans, Beefy, 136
Cabbage Beef Bake, Zesty, 300
Casserole, Firecracker Enchilada, 260
Casserole, Ground Beef and
Sausage, 260
Casserole, Italian, 81
Casserole, Seashell-Provolone, 189
Casserole, Taco, 33
Chili
Double-Meat Chili, 12
Hot Texas Chili, 222

Ranch Chili and Beans, 11
Roundup Chili, 12
Simple Chili, 11
Spicy Chili, Old-Fashioned, 11
Filet Mignon, Mock, 81
Filling, Beef, 81
Flips, Pea, 7
Foo Yong Patties, 223
Hamburgers
Burgundy Burgers, 156
Saucy Burgers, 93
Lasagna, Beefy, 81
Lasagna, Quick 'n Easy, 10
Meatballs
Burgundy-Bacon Meatballs, 283
Polynesian Meatballs, 207
Saucy Party Meatballs, 149
Swedish Meatballs, 80
Tamale Meatballs, 194
Zesty Meatballs, 250
Meat Loaf
Barbecued Meat Loaf, 60
Rolled Stuffed Meat Loaf, 80
Party Snacks, Beefy, 249
Peppers for Two, Stuffed, 84
Peppers, Mexican Green, 65
Picadillo (Spicy Beef Over Rice), 193
Pies, Vegetable-Beef, 286
Pizza, Best Ever Homemade, 233
Rancho Lima Beans, 191
Rollups, Beef-and-Cabbage, 63
Roulades, Beef, 80
Salad, Dude Ranch, 15
Sandwiches, Hearty Pocket, 93
Sausage Dinner, Beefy, 9
Soup, Hamburger, 263
Soup, Quick Beefy Vegetable, 25
Spaghetti with Pizzazz, 85
Spanish Steak, 80
Taco Casserole, 33
Taco Pie, Crescent, 80
Tacos, 196

Beets
Apples, Beets and, 137
Cake, Chocolate Beet, 40
Cauliflower, Chilled Beets and, 137
Creamy Beets, 136
Orange-Ginger Beets, 137
Pickled Beets, Easy, 137

Beverages
Alcoholic
Artillery Punch, Chatham, 121
Bloody Mary, 221
Bloody Marys, 51
Café Colombian Royal, 290
Café Diablo, 259
Café Royal, 259
Chocolate, Flaming Brandied, 290
Cider, Red Apple, 259
Eggnog, Creamy, 259
Eggnog, Thick and Creamy, 261
Gin Punch, 160
Health-Kick Punch, 174
King Alfonso, 259
Margaritas Supreme, Frozen, 160
Orange Blossom Flips, 51
Pineapple Punch, 128
Pink Coconut Frost, 128
Rum, Hot Buttered, 259
Rum Slush, Easy, 129
Sangría, Easy Citrus, 218
Sangría, Punchy, 160

Drop *(continued)*

Cream Cheese Cookies, 282
Oatmeal Cookies, Chocolate-, 105
Oatmeal Cookies, Easy, 105
Oatmeal Cookies,
  Old-Fashioned, 106
Oatmeal Cookies, Orange-Glazed, 60
Oatmeal Cookies, Peanutty, 106
Oatmeal-Spice Cookies, Giant, 105
Raisin Cookies, Alltime Favorite, 24
Rolled
Apricot Cookie Rolls, 282
Chocolate Cookies, Chewy, 208
Choco Surprise Cookies, 60
Crème de Menthe Cookies, 282
Currant Teacakes, 88
Fruit Cookies, Rolled, 15
Gingerbread Cookies, 278
Lemon Pecan Dainties, 208
Molasses Sugar Cookies, 270
Oatmeal-Coconut Cookies, 218
Oatmeal Cookies,
  Slice-and-Bake, 105
Oatmeal Nut Crispies, 208
Peanut Butter Cookies,
  Double, 209
Pecan Cookies, Easy, 208
Shortbread Cookies, Butter
  Pecan, 282

Corn
Casserole, Fresh Corn, 165
Casserole, Salami-Corn, 209
Chowder, Corn and Cheese, 228
Cornbread, Fresh, 165
Foiled Corn on the Cob, 165
Fritters, Golden Corn, 165
Mexican Corn, 157, 165
Microwaved Corn on the Cob, 122
Pudding, Corn-Cheese, 244
Pudding, Fresh Corn, 157, 165
Salad, Corn, 247
Salad, Garden Medley, 122
Sauté, Corn, 165
Scalloped Corn, 164
Soup, Corn, 56
Succotash, Easy, 165
Tomatoes with Corn, Baked, 161
Zucchini-and-Corn Medley, 298

Cornbreads
Carrot Cornbread, 89
Cornbread, 272
Cottage Cheese Cornbread, 90
Cracklin' Cornbread, Southern, 119
Dressing, Cornbread-Sage, 262
Dressing, Fruited Cornbread, 262
Flatbread, Mexican, 197
Fresh Cornbread, 165
Hush Puppies, Cracker, 99
Hush Puppies, Peppery, 221
Mexican Cornbread, 198
Muffins, Cornmeal, 90
Muffins, Four-Grain, 46
Sticks, Buttermilk Corn, 120
Ultimate Cornbread, 90

Cornish Hens
Apricot-Glazed Cornish Hens, 84
Brandy-Buttered Cornish Hens, 32
Elegant Cornish Hens, 227
Flambé, Cornish Hens, 227
Wild Rice Stuffing, Cornish
  Hens with, 64

Crab
Cakes, Crispy Fried Crab, 119
Casserole, Crab-Egg, 260
Casserole, Creamy Crab and Spinach, 3
Dip, Creamy Crab, 135
Flounder, Crab-Stuffed, 120
Meunière, Soft-Shell Crab, 57
Pie, Hot Seafood, 32
Puffs, Crab, 20
Salad, Crab-Stuffed Tomato, 148
Seafood Boil, Low Country, 119
Soup, Creamy Crab, 224
Soup, Elegant Crab, 188
Spread, Baked Crab, 86
Stone Crab Claws
  Sauce, Stone Crab Mustard, 3
  Sauce, Tangy Stone Crab, 3

Cranberries
Bread, Cranberry-Banana, 281
Bread, Cranberry-Orange Nut, 288
Chutney, Cranberry, 243
Cobbler Roll, Cranberry, 288
Dessert, Cranberry Apple, 253
Pie, Cranberry-Raisin, 283
Pork Chops, Cranberry, 288
Pork Roast, Berry Barbecued, 288
Punch, Hot Cranberry, 288
Punch, Hot Spiced, 250
Salad Ring, Cranberry, 247
Tarts, Cranberry-Cream Cheese, 154

Crêpes
Beef Roulades, 80
Chicken Crêpes, 39
Florentine, Crêpes, 190
Nutritious Brunch Crêpes, 44
Whole Wheat Crêpes, 44

Cucumbers
Chicken-Cucumber Mold, 175
Dressing, Cucumber, 74
Salad, Grapefruit-Cucumber, 100
Soup, Creamy Cucumber, 171
Sour Cream, Cucumbers in, 178
Spread, Cucumber, 31

Curry
Chicken Divan, Curried, 83
Dip, Curry, 84
Dressing, Curry, 242
Ham with Rice, Curried, 111
Lamb Curry with Rice, 83
Salad, Curried Apple-Raisin, 24
Salad, Curried Rice, 84
Salad, Curry Spinach, 242
Shrimp Curry, Sour Cream, 83

Custards
Baked Custard, 219
Crema, 175
Flan Almendra, 199
Lemon Custard in Meringue Cups, 295

D

Dates
Apricot-Stuffed Dates, 250
Bars, Date-Nut, 166
Bars, Date-Oat, 172
Cake, Date Nut, 5
Candy, Date Loaf, 302
Cookies, Rolled Fruit, 15
Loaf, Blue Ribbon Date-Walnut, 15
Pie, Date-Pecan, 15
Salad, Festive Fruit, 16
Stuffed Dates, Apricot-, 250

Desserts. *See also* specific types.
Amber Bombe, 255
Apple Delight, 109
Baked Alaska, Apple, 226
Baked Alaska, Brownie, 66
Bananas Foster for Two, 115
Buñuelos, 199
Cannoli, 58
Charlotte Russe, 71
Charlotte Russe, Fresh Lemon, 13
Cherry Dessert, Holiday, 255
Chocolate-Mint Cups, 71
Coffee Mallow, 109
Cranberry Apple Dessert, 253
Crema, 175
Custard, Baked, 219
Daiquiri Soufflé, Elegant, 69
Flan Almendra, 199
Fruit Compote, Baked, 276
Lemon Custard in Meringue Cups, 295
Mincemeat-Filled Apples, Baked, 276
Mint Patty Alaska, 219
Mocha-Almond Dessert, 289
Mousse, Blender-Quick Chocolate, 269
Mousse, Crème de Menthe, 109
Mousse, Peach Macaroon, 153
Orange-Apple Crisp, 295
Orange Cream Dessert, 254
Orange Elegance, Baked, 13
Parfaits, Chilled Orange, 219
Parfaits, Crunchy Peanut Butter, 6
Parfaits, Lime, 153
Parfaits, Mocha-Mallow, 219
Peanut-Chocolate Dessert, 86
Peppermint Bavarian, 153
Peppermint Wafer Dessert, 7
Pineapple Dessert Soufflé, 153
Raspberry Sauce Dessert, 147
Roulage, Chocolate-Mocha, 216
Sopaipillas, 197
Tarts, Grasshopper, 220
Tipsy Pudding, Parson's, 156
Trifle, Savannah, 121
Vacherin Moka, 55

Dips. *See* Appetizers.
Dressings. *See* Stuffings.
Duck
Holiday Duckling, 251
Dumplings
Green Peas and Dumplings, 102
Peach Dumplings, 143

E

Eggnog
Creamy Eggnog, 259
Pie, Eggnog, 254
Thick and Creamy Eggnog, 261
Eggplant
Bake, Eggplant, 82
Casserole, Easy Eggplant, 202
Casserole, Super Eggplant, 202
Grilled Eggplant, 202
Italian-Style Eggplant and Zucchini, 26
Ratatouille, Quick-and-Easy, 212
Sausage-Eggplant Main Dish, 211
Stuffed Eggplant, 158
Stuffed Eggplant, Ham-, 162
Stuffed Eggplant, Rolled, 63
Eggs
Benedict, Easy Eggs, 268
Bunwiches, 92

Eggs (continued)

Casserole, Crab-Egg, 260
Casserole, Squash and Egg, 146
Creamed Eggs in Patty Shells, 267
Croquettes, Tuna-Egg, 275
Foo Yong, Egg, 19
Foo Yong Patties, 223
Omelets
    George's Omelets, 68
    Ham and Cheese Omelet, 123
    Sausage Omelet, Puffy, 268
    Swiss Oven Omelet, 189
Rice, Egg Fried, 19
Salad, Tossed Shrimp-Egg, 4
Sandwiches, Eggsclusive, 130
Scrambled
    Bacon-and-Eggs Scramble, 267
    Casserole, Scrambled Egg, 51
    Cottage-Scrambled Eggs, 49
    Sonora, Eggs, 196
    Wild Rice, Scrambled Eggs with, 42
Stuffed
    Deviled Eggs, Best, 159
    Deviled Eggs, Nippy, 217
    Pecan-Stuffed Eggs, 78
    Stuffed Eggs, 155
Tacos, Breakfast, 43
Tomatoes, Bacon-and-Egg-Stuffed, 162

F

Fish. *See also* Seafood.
Amandine, Fillet of Fish, 54
Amandine, Orange Lake, 99
Catfish, Barbecued, 157
Catfish, Golden Fried, 99
Catfish Meunière, 57
Ceviche (Marinated Raw Fish), 194
Chowder, Tasty Fish, 188
Flounder, Crab-Stuffed, 120
Flounder in Wine Sauce, Fillet of, 179
Haddock, Baked, 179
Halibut, Chinese-Style Fried, 179
Herbed Fish and Potato Bake, 34
Herring Dip, Yogurt, 232
Huachinango a la Veracruzana
    (Veracruz-Style Red Snapper), 193
Lemon-Coated Fillets, 53
Mackerel Creole, 126
Poached Fish in Creamy Swiss Sauce, 53
Snapper Rome, Fillet of, 57
Sweet-and-Sour Fish, 54
Trout Delmonico, 57
Trout in Wine Sauce, 180
Frankfurters
Baked Beans and Franks, Hawaiian, 136
Cabbage Skillet, Frankfurter-, 166
Crusty Franks, 166
Hash Browns, Franks and, 166
Skillet Dinner, Frankfurter, 166
Spanish Frankfurters, 166
Frog Legs
Crispy Frog Legs, 99
Frostings, Fillings, and Toppings
Butter Frosting, 129
Butter Pecan Frosting, 229
Chantilly Crème, 280
Chocolate Frosting, 171
Chocolate Nut Frosting, 140
Coconut Frosting, Creamy, 287
Cream Cheese Frosting, 140, 253, 299

Cream Cheese Frosting, Deluxe, 120
Cream Cheese Frosting, Fluffy, 245
Date Filling, 15
Fruit-Nut Filling, 289
Heavenly Frosting, 140
Honey-Walnut Filling, 21
Lemon Filling, Creamy, 70
Mocha Filling, 55
Orange Buttercream Frosting, 70
Orange Glaze, 257
Orange Glaze, Nutty, 45
Orange Topping, Whipped, 254
Peanut Frosting, Creamy, 87
Pineapple Filling, 140
Ricotta Filling, 58
Royal Icing, 278
Rum Cream Topping, 255
Seven-Minute Frosting, 289
Spinach-Mushroom Filling, 215
Strawberry Glaze, 35
Fruit. *See also* specific types of
    fruit or dish.
Brandied Fruit, Hot, 48
Canning
    Berries (except Strawberries), 128
    Peaches, 128
Casserole, Sherried Fruit, 284
Cheesecake, Fruit-Glazed, 24
Compote, Baked Fruit, 276
Delight, Winter Fruit, 243
Dip, Fresh Fruit, 265
Dressing, Fruited Cornbread, 262
Filling, Fruit-Nut, 289
Marinated Fruit Bowl, 297
Picks, Fruit on, 159
Punch, Golden Fruit, 299
Rhapsody, Fruit, 158
Salad, Easy Fruit, 221
Salad, Favorite Summer, 158
Salad, Winter Fruit, 248
Sherried Fruit Mélange, 158
Vanilla Fruit Cup, 183

G

Grapefruit
Aspic, Grapefruit, 297
Delight, Winter Fruit, 243
Dressing, Grapefruit French, 101
Drink, Three-Fruit, 50
Marmalade, Combination Citrus, 50
Salad, Grapefruit Combo, 50
Salad, Grapefruit-Cucumber, 100
Sherried Broiled Grapefruit, 50
Supreme, Grapefruit, 50
Gravies. *See* Sauces.
Greens
Kale, Sweet-and-Sour, 298
Turnip Greens and Ham Hock,
    Southern, 119
Grits
Cheese Grits, Baked, 49, 99
Cheese Grits, Garlic, 47
Scrambled Grits, 48
Shrimp Stew and Grits, 118
Soufflé, Grits, 30

H

Ham
Asparagus Dinner, Ham-, 10
Baked Beans with Ham, 136

Biscuits, Ham-Filled Angel, 159
Casserole, Ham and Noodle, 300
Cauliflower, Main-Dish, 83
Country Ham in Apple Cider, 251
Curried Ham with Rice, 111
Kabobs, Honey Ham, 156
Loaf, Ham, 272
Loaf, Spicy Ham, 110
Omelet, Ham and Cheese, 123
Patties, Pineapple-Ham, 110
Peppers, Ham-Stuffed Green, 65
Pie with Cheese Crust, Ham, 286
Pie, Zucchini-Ham-Cheese, 272
Plum Ham, 110
Potato Salad, Ham and, 272
Quiche, Ham, 110
Raisin Ham, 124
Rice, Savannah Red, 119
Salad Boats, 93
Sandwiches, Meal-in-One, 218
Sandwiches, Virginia Ham, 155
Sandwich, Tangy Ham Salad, 272
Spread, Ham and Pimiento, 285
Strata, Ham and Broccoli, 261
Stuffed Eggplant, Ham-, 162
Turnip Greens and Ham Hock,
    Southern, 119
Waffles, Ham, 44

I

Ice Creams and Sherbets
Amber Bombe, 255
Baked Alaska, Apple, 226
Baked Alaska, Brownie, 66
Banana Split Ice Cream, 176
Butter Pecan Ice Cream, 176
Cake, Praline Ice Cream, 84
Chocolate Ice Cream, 176
Delight, Ice Cream, 69
Lemon Ice Cream Pie, 70
Mint Patty Alaska, 219
Peach Ice Cream, Deluxe, 176
Peppermint Ice Cream, 176
Raspberry Ice Cream, 176
Straw-Ba-Nut Ice Cream, 177
Strawberry Ice Cream, 177
Sundaes, Mauna Loa, 126
Tarts, Lemon Ice Cream, 152
Vanilla Ice Cream, 176

J

Jams and Jellies
Apricot Jam, Golden, 31
Citrus Marmalade, 101
Citrus Marmalade,
    Combination, 50
Peach-Banana Jam, Rosy, 142
Pear Butter, Spiced, 218

K

Kabobs
Beef Kabobs, Teriyaki, 207
Ham Kabobs, Honey, 156
Lamb Kabobs, Savory, 184
Liver Kabobs, 185
Shrimp Kabobs, 150, 184
Steak-and-Shrimp Kabobs, 184
Steak Kabobs, Marinated, 184

Desserts *(continued)*

Cookies, Orange-Glazed Oatmeal, 60
Cream Dessert, Orange, 254
Crisp, Orange-Apple, 295
Parfaits, Chilled Orange, 219
Pears, Orange Poached, 218
Pie, Orange Ambrosia, 237
Shortcake, Fresh Orange, 100
Tarts, Frozen Orange, 154
Dressing, Orange-Coconut, 158
Frosting, Orange Buttercream, 70
Glaze, Nutty Orange, 45
Glaze, Orange, 257
Peanut Brittle, Orange, 302
Porc à l'Orange, 242
Salad, Orange-Carrot, 89
Salad, Orange Walnut, 246
Sauce, Broccoli with Orange, 243
Sauce, Chicken in Orange-Almond, 13
Syrup, Orange, 228
Topping, Whipped Orange, 254

Oysters
Brochette, Oysters, 56
Casino, Oysters à la, 296
Fried Oyster Bubbles, 296
Hangtown Fry, 297
Rockefeller, Southern Oysters, 212
St. Jacques, Oysters, 103
Sandwich, Oyster Submarine, 92
Scalloped Oysters with Macaroni, 297
Stew, Company Oyster, 297
Stew, Oyster, 221
Stuffing, Roast Turkey with Oyster, 251

P

Pancakes
Oatmeal Pancakes, 44
Potato Pancakes, Moist, 36
Pumpkin Pancakes, 228

Pastas. *See also* specific types.
Fettuccine Alfredo, 236
Pesto, 242
Seashell-Provolone Casserole, 189
Straw and Hay Pasta, 211

Peaches
Cake, Peaches and Cream, 142
Cobbler, Peachy Blueberry, 143
Dip, Creole Peach, 142
Dumplings, Peach, 143
Ice Cream, Deluxe Peach, 176
Jam, Rosy Peach-Banana, 142
Mousse, Peach Macaroon, 153
Pie, Mincemeat-Peach, 295
Salad, Georgia Peach, 142
Salad, Pickled Peach, 104
Spiced Peaches, Brandy, 142

Peanut Butter
Balls, Chocolate-Peanut Butter, 87
Balls, Peanut Butter-Chocolate, 269
Bars, Peanut Butter-and-Fudge, 172
Cake, Peanut Butter-Banana, 87
Cookies, Choco Surprise, 60
Cookies, Double Peanut Butter, 209
Frosting, Creamy Peanut, 87
Fudge, Peanut Butter, 302
Muffins, Peanut Butter, 86
Parfaits, Crunchy Peanut Butter, 6

Peanuts
Bars, Chewy Peanut, 172
Brittle, Orange Peanut, 302

Brittle, Peanut, 87
Cookies, Peanutty Oatmeal, 106
Dessert, Peanut-Chocolate, 86
Frosting, Creamy Peanut, 87
Salad, Peanut-Apple, 5

Pears
Bread, Pear, 218
Butter, Spiced Pear, 218
Pie, Deep-Dish Pear, 219
Poached Pears, Orange, 218
Salad, Festive Fruit, 16

Peas
Black-Eyed
Flips, Pea, 7
Hopping Good Peas, 7
Hopping John, 7
Salad, Black-Eyed Pea, 112
Green
Casserole, Asparagus and Peas, 152
Cauliflower and Peas with Curried
Almonds, 82
Country-Style Peas, 101
Dumplings, Green Peas and, 102
Mushrooms, Green Peas with, 101
Onions, Buttered Peas with, 242
Salad, Creamy Pea, 111
Scallions, Peas and, 101
Sherry, Peas with, 102
Pods, Stir-Fry Beef and Pea, 19

Pecans
Ball, Deviled Pecan, 258
Cake, Butter Pecan, 229
Cookies, Butter Pecan Shortbread, 282
Cookies, Easy Pecan, 208
Crispies, Oatmeal Nut, 208
Dainties, Lemon Pecan, 208
Dressing, Pecan-Sage, 262
Eggs, Pecan-Stuffed, 78
Frosting, Butter Pecan, 229
Frosting, Chocolate Nut, 140
Ice Cream, Butter Pecan, 176
Ice Cream Cake, Praline, 84
Ice Cream, Straw-Ba-Nut, 177
Muffins, Pecan, 16
Pie, Chocolate Pecan, 237
Pie, Date-Pecan, 15
Pie, Pecan, 57
Pralines, Creamy, 198
Salted Pecans, Southern, 285
Spiced Pecans, 31
Stuffing, Pecan, 32
Tarts, Apple-Pecan, 282

Peppers, Green
Chicken Peppers, Devilish, 65
Ham-Stuffed Green Peppers, 65
Macaroni-and-Cheese-Stuffed Peppers, 65
Mexican Green Peppers, 65
Rice-Stuffed Peppers, 65
Stuffed Peppers for Two, 84
Stuffed Peppers, Shrimp-, 162

Pickles. *See also* Relishes.
Beets, Easy Pickled, 137
Chutney, Cranberry, 243
Chutney, Rosy, 120

Pies and Pastries
Angel Pie, 238
Blueberry Cream Pie, Fresh, 144
Blueberry Kuchen, 143
Cannoli, 58
Chocolate-Amaretto Mousse Pie, 180
Chocolate-Cream Cheese Pie, 69
Chocolate Meringue Pie, 238

Chocolate Pecan Pie, 237
Chocolate Pie, Frozen, 154
Cobblers
Blackberry Cobbler, Deep-Dish, 186
Blueberry Cobbler, Fresh, 144
Cranberry Cobbler Roll, 288
Peachy Blueberry Cobbler, 143
Coconut Cloud, 70
Coconut Cream Pie, 238
Coconut Cream Pie, Fresh, 289
Cranberry-Raisin Pie, 283
Cream Cheese Pastries, 250
Date-Pecan Pie, 15
Dream Pie, 90
Eggnog Pie, 254
Foldovers, Preserve-Filled, 7
French Silk Pie, 247
Fruitcake Pie, 237
Fruit Pie, Japanese, 238
Ice Cream Delight, 69
Lemon-Apple Pie, Tart, 100
Lemon Ice Cream Pie, 70
Macadamia Pie, 238
Main Dish
Beef Pies, Carry-Along, 224
Ham Pie with Cheese Crust, 286
Mushrooms in Patty Shells, 283
Pea Flips, 7
Pineapple-Chicken Salad Pie, 138
Reuben Meat Pie, 189
Seafood Pie, Hot, 32
Tuna Pie with Cheese Roll
Crust, 286
Turkey Pie, 285
Vegetable-Beef Pies, 286
Zucchini-Ham-Cheese Pie, 272
Mincemeat-Cheese Pie, 253
Mincemeat-Peach Pie, 295
Mincemeat Pie, Holiday, 282
Mocha Meringue Pie, 242
Mud Pie, Tipsy, 255
Orange Ambrosia Pie, 237
Orange Shortcake, Fresh, 100
Pastries and Crusts
Cheddar Cheese Pastry, 219
Cheese Crust, 286
Chocolate Cups, 207
Flaky Pastry, 224
Pizza Crust, 233
Quiche Pastry, 107
Shortcake Pastry, 100
Triple-Crust Pastry, 186
Pear Pie, Deep-Dish, 219
Pecan Pie, 57
Pineapple Pie, 237
Pinto Bean Pie, 40
Pistachio Pie, 56
Puddin' Pies, President Tyler's, 43
Pumpkin Pie, Fluffy, 283
Pumpkin Praline Pie, 244
Sour Cream Pie, Tropical, 6
Squash Pie, Butternut, 40
Squash Pie, Spaghetti, 186
Squash Pie, Spicy Butternut, 296
Strawberry Yogurt Pie, 232
Sweet Potato Pone Pie, 288
Tarts
Apple-Pecan Tarts, 282
Cherry Tarts, Cheery, 238
Cranberry-Cream Cheese Tarts, 154
Grasshopper Tarts, 220
Ice Cream Tarts, Lemon, 152

A WELCOME AID FOR BUSY HOMEMAKERS

Protect your favorite recipes from spills and splatters.

Get a clear view of your entire recipe behind a protective shield with this durable, acrylic cookbook stand. Your book sits firmly at an easy-to-read angle, open to your working recipe, safe from sticky fingers, mixing splatters and accidental spills. After cooking, the stand can be wiped clean with a damp sponge. A generous 16¾″ wide by 12″ high, this stand can accommodate most cookbooks.

Price and availability are subject to change without notice.

Send your order with a check or money order for $12.95 to: